HANDGU '94

Edited By

JACK LEWIS

DBI BOOKS, INC.

About Our Covers

Big can be beautiful, and the Desert Eagle 50 AE pistol shown on our front cover demonstrates that fact quite well. Imported by Magnum Research, Inc., the Desert Eagle pistol is available in 357 Magnum, 41 Magnum, 44 Magnum, 50 AE and 50 Magnum.

Our 50 AE subject gun is impressive in all respects. The overall length of the pistol is 10.5 inches, height 5.9 inches, and the gun weighs 72.4 ounces—that's 4.5 pounds! The 6-inch barrel uses polygonal rifling, has a bore diameter of .495-inch, and an integral scope base.

The Desert Eagle is a gas-operated pistol that uses a rotating bolt for positive lock-up. The slide-mounted safety-catch is ambidextrous and locks the firing pin in addition to disconnecting the trigger bar from the sear.

Believe it or not, the Desert Eagle's recoil and muzzle flip are quite mild, and accuracy is said to be excellent.

Our cover gun is finished in polished hard chrome, but many other optional finishes are available. Standard offering is black oxide.

Our back cover shows a trio of other Magnum Research offings, all intended for the serious shooter.

On the left is the Baby Eagle in 9mm Parabellum with sixteen-shot magazine. This trim autoloader is also available in 41 AE (eleven-shot) and 40 S&W (ten-shot) calibers.

Of all-steel construction, this neat double-action pistol has extra-long slide rails for improved accuracy, combat-style trigger guard, ambidextrous thumb safety, decocker, and polygonal rifling. It has a 4.72-inch barrel, overall length of 8.14 inches and weighs 38 ounces. The gun is available in blue, matte hard chrome (shown) or brushed chrome. Conversion kits (barrel, magazine, springs) are available to convert the gun from 9mm to 41 AE or 41 AE to 9mm.

In the center is the new Mountain Eagle Target Edition pistol in 22 Long Rifle. This new gun has an 8-inch barrel, two-stage target trigger, jeweled bolt and fully adjustable sights with three interchangeable colored blades. Like the original Mountain Eagle, the new Target Edition is small, lightweight and very comfortable to shoot. It boasts state-of-the-art polymer and steel construction to hold up to a lifetime of shooting. The gun is shown with the Aimpoint 3000 red-dot sight.

On the right is the Magnum Research Lone Eagle single-shot pistol, chambered for 7mm BR Remington. Interchangeable 14-inch barreled actions quickly and easily convert the pistol to shoot the following fourteen calibers: 22 Hornet, 223 Remington, 22-250 Remington, 243 Winchester, 7mm-08 Remington, 7mm BR Remington, 308 Winchester, 30-30 Winchester, 30-06, 35 Remington, 357 Maximum, 358 Winchester, 44 Magnum, 444 Marlin.

The Lone Eagle's unique rotary breech and grip placement make it manageable for even novices to shoot with minimal felt recoil. The hand-filling stock is made of tough GE Lexan that will stand up to the toughest hunting conditions. The Lone Eagle is shown with a Leupold M8 2x EER scope, in addition to the fully adjustable open sights.

All in all, that's quite a pack of pistols from this innovative company, any of which you'd be proud to own and shoot.

Photos by John Hanusin.

Produced by

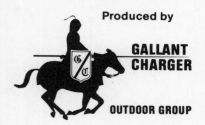

GALLANT CHARGER

OUTDOOR GROUP

EDITORIAL DIRECTOR
Jack Lewis

ART DIRECTOR
Brad Wood

PRODUCTION DIRECTOR
Sonya Kaiser

PRODUCTION COORDINATOR
Nadine Symons

DBI BOOKS, INC.

PRESIDENT
Charles T. Hartigan

VICE PRESIDENT & PUBLISHER
Sheldon L. Factor

VICE PRESIDENT — SALES
John G. Strauss

TREASURER
Frank R. Serpone

ISBN 0-87349-143-2   Library Of Congress Catalog Card Number 88-72115

CONTENTS

SECTION ONE:

HANDGUNS

TODAY

POLICE PISTOL UPDATE

By Tony Lesce

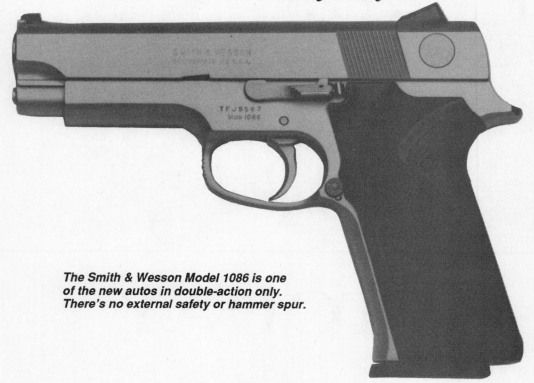

The Smith & Wesson Model 1086 is one of the new autos in double-action only. There's no external safety or hammer spur.

Official Acceptance Of The Auto Is Moving Faster Than The Ability To Train Officers!

The compact SIG/Sauer P225 (top) is a short-barreled, eight-shot version of the double-column P226 (bottom). The P225, with a round chambered, holds nine-rounds while the P226 holds 16.

THERE'S BEEN a clear trend toward auto pistols by American police during the 1980s, and this is continuing into the '90s as more agencies are making the change from revolvers. It's safe to say that, by the end of the century, almost all American police officers will be using auto pistols.

The transition has been overdue, and is now taking place swiftly as American police officers realize that armed offenders take advantage of every technical improvement, unhampered by policy directives because they use the latest firearm they can buy or steal. By contrast, a police firearms instructor must write a proposal for new equipment and forward it to his command staff, then wait for a committee to study the proposal and bring in a recommendation. Finally, the chief must approve the proposal and plan for it in the following year's budget.

Police firearms instructors know their officers vary in skill and size, and they must plan around these diversities. They also know street conditions are not the same as those found in practical pistol matches, and that competent firearm handling when the target is shooting back is far removed from sterile match conditions.

New York City's annual Firearms Discharge Reports are the most authoritative sources for information regarding what actually happens in gunfights, because the nation's largest city has the largest municipal police agency and the greatest number of shooting incidents and gunfights of any jurisdiction. According to the 1991 report, New York police officers hit their targets with 28 percent of their shots, counting all shooting incidents. These included shooting pit bulls (70 shots fired), protecting one's partner (40 shots fired), resisting a "snatch" by a perpetrator and miscellaneous incidents

The hit rate by officers in gunfights, however, dropped to 15 percent. Perpetrators hit was even worse: slightly over 14

SIG/Sauer offers an optional 20 round, extra-capacity magazine for the highly respected P226.

percent. This shows the difference between hit potential in nominal shooting incidents and accuracy when there's hot lead coming from the target.

Better marksmanship is an obvious need, and several studies have shown that the hit rate improves when officers use auto pistols. For example, at this writing, most New York

This third-generation 9mm Smith & Wesson Model 5906 pistol is outfitted with Novak sights, 14-round double-column magazine.

officers still use .38 Special revolvers, but a small number have made the transition to autos. During 1990, New York officers using Glock 19 autos attained a 47 percent hit rate overall in shooting incidents, and 38 percent in gunfights. An important reason is that a shorter, lighter trigger pull disturbs the handgun's alignment less.

The New York City Police Department's studies showed that officers don't even use the sights in most shootouts, because of close range, urgency and poor light. Thus, tritium sights are not standard issue. Practical pistol match gurus insist on watching the front sight closely, but this works best on the range, not on the street. Over 71 percent of shooting incidents in the New York report took place at seven yards or less, and point-shooting is the dominant form of directing shots.

Marksmanship in poor light is even more important, because 58 percent of New York's shooting incidents took place in poor light or darkness. With wide-spread recognition that many police-felon shootouts take place in poor light, there's been a prolonged effort to develop a practical and robust low-cost night sighting system.

After several false starts, including several "flashlight shooting stances" developed by people who named them after themselves, consensus has settled on tritium self-illuminated night sights. A flashlight draws fire, and reflections from nearby walls can illuminate the shooter. Tritium sights produce dim light dots visible only to someone behind the sights, and do not disclose the officer's position.

Following these needs, handgun manufacturers have followed several definite themes in producing pistols suitable for police service.

Officers feel more comfortable with more rounds in the magazine. One reason is because few police officers are expert shots, and as we've seen, rounds fired in combat most often miss. Even those who score "expert" on the range during qualification find their marksmanship impaired when the adrenalin starts pumping. An expert shot accustomed to precise sight alignment on a well-lit range loses his advantage when both sights and target are less visible.

Another reason is that some lawbreakers are using high-capacity autos and officers want parity. The killing of New Jersey State Trooper Philip Lamonaco in 1981 by a suspect armed with a double-nine precipitated the agency's change from revolvers. The New Jersey State Police tested several auto pistols and decided on the Heckler & Koch P7 M8, modified with a thumb-operated magazine release. The original P7 had a butt-heel release.

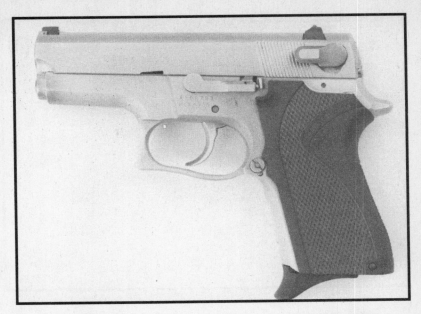

This S&W M6906 has a shorter (3 1/2-inch) barrel than the M5906 and a 12-round double-column magazine to fit in the chopped grip.

Yet, another reason is officers sometimes face multiple assailants. Having a double-column auto provides an advantage over the six-shot revolver. Trooper Lamonaco was found with his revolver empty, apparently having been struck by eight shots before he could reload. Investigators found 13 9mm cases on the scene.

The need to reload during a gunfight is not common in the field, although reloading drills are part of police firearms training and qualification courses. The New York report cites only two instances in which an officer had to reload his handgun during an incident. This is quite significant statistically, because of the large number of incidents reported.

Many widely accepted police autos have double-column magazines. The SIG P226 and Glock 17 are typical, holding 15 and 17 rounds respectively, plus one up the spout. A +2 optional floor plate increases the Glock's magazine capacity by two rounds. Glock's .45 ACP model, the Glock 21, also has a double-column magazine, as does its 10mm version, which holds 15 rounds.

Even the larger-caliber autos have followed the trend toward more ammunition capacity. The Glock 22, chambered for the .40 S&W, holds 15 rounds. Other double-column .40 S&W autos are the Beretta Model 96 and the S&W Model 4006.

Extra-capacity magazines are available for double-column autos. SIG's extra-length magazine holds 20 rounds, Glock's 32 and Smith & Wesson has a 20-round magazine for its 5900 series. These extra-long magazines protrude from the grip frame and are not for everyday use, but for situations requiring more ammunition capacity.

Safety has been a prime concern of police firearms instructors and administrators because of the danger of injury and liability. An accidental discharge can lead to a megabucks lawsuit.

Revolvers have internal safeties, but once cocked, they can discharge if dropped or carelessly handled. Inspector Paul Weston, formerly of the New York City Police Department, pointed out that some officers didn't know how to uncock a revolver safely. One officer solved the problem by firing it into a toilet bowl.

Older single-action autos suffered severe safety problems, an important reason for American police officers not rushing to adopt them. The Model 1911, for example, sometimes would fire during loading, when the slide dropped. Uncocking the Model 1911 was just as delicate an operation as uncocking a revolver. Worst of all, it was necessary to put the manual safety to "off" to operate the slide and load a round into the chamber. The grip safety wasn't of much help, because just holding the pistol deactivated it. John Browning omitted it

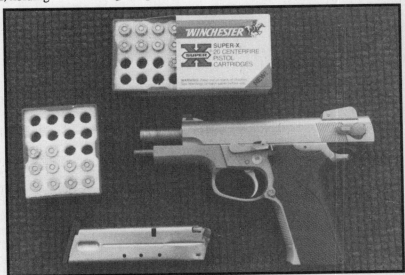

To handle the .40 S&W cartridge, Smith & Wesson introduced the Model 4006. Its external dimensions are similar to the 5900 series.

Beretta's model for the .40 S&W is the 96. It holds 10 rounds in a double-column magazine.

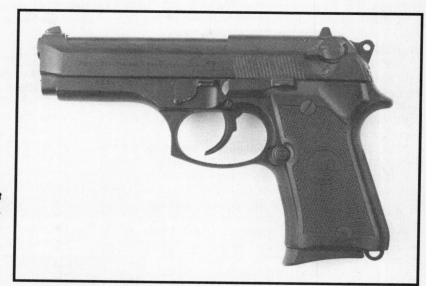

The cut-down Beretta 92 compact holds 13 rounds of 9mm instead of the standard 15.

from his last design, the P-35 High-Power double-nine, and none of the recent major designs incorporate grip safeties.

The slide-mounted Walther-type decocking safety was an improvement, because it allowed loading the pistol with the safety "on," and it uncocked the hammer safely. The design included a rotating firing-pin block to prevent discharge even if the pistol was dropped. The Heckler & Koch squeeze-cockers are safe, unless the shooter squeezes the front grip strap to cock the action. If he drops the pistol or even relaxes his grip, the pistol uncocks and becomes safe.

The trigger-linked firing pin block was another step forward, and this is now a standard design feature. A spring-loaded sliding block prevents the firing pin from moving forward unless the shooter pulls the trigger. The trigger bar moves a lever that pushes the firing pin block up out of the way to allow firing. This happens only at the end of the trigger's travel, and the firing pin is safe up to that point.

Manual safeties appear to be on the way out, because some autos — such as the SIGs — have decockers. Others, such as the Glock, have no external safeties or decockers at all.

Some feel there's a need for an external safety to impede a suspect who "snatches" an officer's firearm. This is questionable without figures to show how many suspects took officers' firearms from the holster, where the safety normally would be on, versus the number who took them from officers' hands, with the safety off.

In any event, having an external safety adds an extra step to bringing the handgun into action. This relates to various "snatch-resistant" holsters, with extra catches and impediments to removal of the handgun. Special safety holsters are slower on the draw, and manufacturer's instructions stress the need for extensive practice in drawing the firearm.

The trend is also away from magazine safeties. Of the major manufacturers, only Smith & Wesson still provides this feature. The main argument against the magazine safety is that it makes the handgun inoperable during a tactical reload, when the officer changes the magazine before his handgun is completely empty. Having a round in the chamber to handle an unexpected occurrence is always reassuring, especially in the stress of a shootout, when reloading takes several seconds.

This is the Glock 17 which holds a standard 17-round magazine. A 33-round magazine is available only for law enforcement purposes.

The second gun, back-up gun and off-duty gun are not necessarily the service firearm. Few service guns are suitable for off-duty carry in the view of many officers, and a back-up gun in an ankle holster is unlikely to be a twin to the one that hangs on the belt. The second gun, sometimes carried in the briefcase or under the seat cushion, can be the same as the service auto, because compactness is not vital.

Common experience shows that different handguns require different handling habits. S&W revolver cylinder latches open forward and Colt's pull back. S&W autos have slide safeties, while SIGs have no external safeties. Trigger pulls are different, and even actuating systems vary, as in the squeeze-cocking Heckler & Koch P7 line.

It's counter-productive to carry a back-up that operates differently from the duty pistol, because making the transition in the urgency of a gunfight can get the officer killed. A compact Model 60 Chief revolver may look cute, but it doesn't use the same ammunition as an auto. Magazines do not fit

Field-stripping the Glock shows its simplicity. The slide and barrel resemble the SIG's lock-up system.

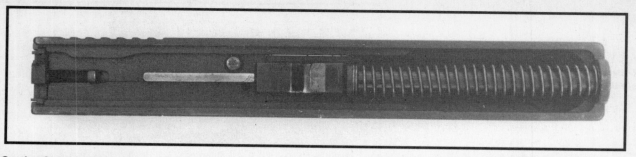

On the Glock's slide, the small round plunger located just behind the chamber is the firing pin block.

This is the original Heckler & Koch squeeze-cocker. It holds eight rounds and has a butt/heel magazine release.

revolvers, and speedloaders don't fit autos. Glock magazines don't fit Smiths, and Smith & Wesson magazines don't fit Glocks.

This is why there's been a trend toward making compact models of duty autos. If the service weapon jams, runs out of ammunition or is lost, the officer draws his back-up without having to remember different operating features. Some compacts, such as the S&W 6906, accept magazines from larger Smith autos.

The 9mm Beretta Model 92 SB-F comes in two versions — standard with a 4.9-inch barrel and 15 rounds in the magazine — and compact, with a 4.3-inch barrel and 13 rounds. Beretta's new Model 96, chambered for the .40 S&W, has the same barrel length as the Model 92, but there's room for only 10 of the fatter rounds in its double-column magazine.

The Glock 17 was followed by the chopped Glock 19, with a shorter barrel and holding fewer rounds. Glock followed the same practice with the Glock Models 22 and 23, externally the same dimensions as the 17 and 19, but chambered for the .40 S&W. The Glock 23 magazine holds 13 rounds, two fewer than the Glock 22.

The net result has been that a typical uniformed officer, formerly equipped with a revolver and two speedloaders, had an ammunition supply of 18 rounds, but with one of the new 9mm autos, the officer has that many in the handgun. Adding two extra magazines, the officer carries as many as 58 rounds on his belt, depending on pistol model and caliber.

One reason the New Jersey State Police adopted the Heckler & Koch pistol is its compactness. This allows one firearm to serve both as a service auto and off-duty weapon.

In the urgency of a gunfight, complications are unwelcome, because they can be life-threatening. A second's delay during a match can cost the shooter points; during a real-life affray, the delay can cost him his life.

The double-action revolver has long been a favorite, because bringing it into action requires only drawing, sighting or pointing and pulling the trigger. The shooter has the choice of cocking the hammer for long-range shots where a lighter trigger pull is helpful.

Manual safeties found on early auto pistols were merely complications in gunfights. Over two decades ago, when some police agencies began authorizing autos, many officers didn't use manual safeties, instead depending on the double-action mode to keep the auto safe. This brought up liability problems, because an accidental discharge might be traced to "negligence" in not using the factory-designed safety. This led to the new concept of internal safeties, such as a cam to lock the firing mechanism until the trigger is fully to the rear. The Glocks require only pulling the trigger to go off safe and fire.

Another step toward simplicity was simplifying the trigger pull. The shift from a double-action first shot to a single-action for follow-up shots bothered some shooters, even some experts. There have been several approaches to solving this problem.

The H&K P7 M13 holds 13 rounds in a double-column magazine. The magazine release is behind the trigger.

Modifying the hardware is the most common approach. The Heckler & Koch pistols have squeeze-cocking single-action-only triggers. The Glock models fire from half-cock, in what Glock labels the "Safe Action." The latest hardware modification is the double-action-only auto. These models do not have external safeties or decockers, and provide a consistent, albeit long and heavy, trigger pull.

Auto pistols are more sensitive than revolvers to the type of ammunition used. Revolvers will fire anything from squib loads to magnums, because operation is by actuating both cylinder and hammer manually. Self-loaders need ammunition with a sufficient recoil impulse to work the slide.

Revolvers carry their rounds in the cylinder chambers, while autos feed them individually after each shot. Some types of bullets have contours that don't feed well. Burrs and dents in the magazine lips also cause failures to feed. This is why autos require more care in selecting duty ammo and maintenance of the pistol and its magazines.

Given the trend toward hiring minority and female officers, there's a greater need for elegantly designed handguns that these officers can hold and shoot. It's difficult to combine high ammunition capacity with a short trigger reach, which is why some agencies allow officers with small hands to carry a single-column version of the standard double-column auto. The SIG Sauer P225, for example, is easier for officers with small hands than the bulkier and heavier P226.

Good ergonomics has been apparent in the new generation of Smith & Wesson autos. The Model 1006, for example, chambered for the 10mm Auto cartridge, is heavy for a small shooter, but even a shooter with a small hand can reach the trigger. Relief cuts in the frame behind the trigger help the shooter with short fingers.

Aftermarket suppliers also contribute to ergonomics. The Glock 21, chambered for the .45 ACP, has a large grip, given the fat .45 rounds. Robar Inc., of Phoenix, Arizona, uses a metallic compound to fill in the hollow in the backstrap, then machines it down to a smaller configuration.

From time to time, there have been enhanced calibers proposed for police use to replace the standard .38 Special. A common choice is the .357 magnum, but controlled tests against the .38 Special by both the New York and New Jersey State Police showed that officers firing the magnum round had fewer hits. These tests involved male officers only, except for one female in the New Jersey test. The single female officer firing scored 258 with the .38 Special, dropping to 137 with magnum rounds. It would be interesting to see the results of new tests using only female officers.

Summing up the opinions of many commentators, the ideal law enforcement handgun should have the power of a .44 magnum, recoil of a .22, the size and weight of a Walther PPK —and cost as much as a Raven MP-25. No such ideal handgun exists, so the choice is between many real-world compromises.

Medium calibers, such as the .38 Special and 9mm Luger, have fared best in police service. This is because they have adequate power, yet are mild enough for many non-expert shots to use adequately during training and qualification. Importantly, the handguns made for them are adaptable to medium and small hands. However, there have been occasional doubts cast about the adequacy of medium service loads.

On March 11, 1986, a bloody shootout took place in Miami between eight FBI agents and two felons, one of whom used a Ruger Mini-14 with devastating effect on the lawmen. Both suspects died in the affray, but only after killing two FBI agents and wounding five.

One of the FBI's conclusions regarding this shootout was that the Winchester 9mm Silvertip did not have adequate penetration. Consequently, the FBI Firearms Training Unit set out to develop a new round. The result was an odd configuration of the 10mm Auto cartridge, loaded down to medium velocity with a 180-grain bullet. The FBI's tests showed this round would, according to its own testing procedure, theoretically provide a "success rate" of between 92.5 percent and 95 percent. By comparison, two existing rounds in use had a rate of 90 percent. The highest-rated 9mm round scored 82.5 percent.

H&K's P7 M10 is designed for the .40 S&W. This auto is more bulky than the M13, yet holds only 10 rounds.

The compact Raven .25 ACP is a reliable hide-out gun. With six rounds, it's adequate for last-ditch defense.

Taking the FBI's figures at face value, and ignoring that the .45 ACP rounds were fired from three different model autos and the 10mm rounds from two, it's still hard to understand why the FBI decided to go ahead with the new round, when existing .45 ACP cartridges worked just as well and were less bulky. At the time, the 10mm appeared to be the wave of the future to uncritical observers. This soon faded, however.

A sidelight was that FBI tests showed that the Norma full-power 170-grain JHP scored 100 percent, as did the 158-grain JHP Federal Hydra-Shok .357 magnum. These perfect scores were academic, as the FBI was not going to standardize on a revolver cartridge, and the full-house Norma's recoil appeared too powerful for general use.

Despite the new theories of "stopping power," based mainly on laboratory work with gelatin blocks that have the same density as pig muscle, there's still no hard consensus on exactly what makes a bullet more effective and which calibers are the best for street use. In short, the experts disagree.

If we take the new "penetration" theory of disabling power seriously, there's only one choice: full-metal jacket bullets, already in production for decades. However, almost nobody seems to be willing to take it this far, and the vast majority of law enforcement ammunition uses a jacketed hollow-point design.

The FBI's downloaded 10mm Auto, which received a lot of publicity when it arrived on the scene, is now a dead issue. This is just as well, because autos chambered for it are extra-large, heavy and unsuitable for general use. The new .40 S&W round combines similar ballistics with a shorter case, giving an overall length about the same as a 9mm cartridge. To many, this is the ideal solution, because it allows using a larger, more powerful cartridge in a medium frame pistol that officers of small stature can handle. The net effect is that the .40 S&W knocked the bottom out of the market for the 10mm.

Bullet effectiveness is an emotional issue, as well as a scientific and operational one, and there are many "true believers." The politically correct bullet for the .40 S&W is the 180-grain JHP fired at about 980 fps. But manufacturers are hedging their bets and producing 155-grain high-velocity JHP loads. Winchester, Federal and Hornady offer 155-grain loads that exceed 1100 fps.

Another trend has been refinement of bullet design for enhanced terminal ballistics. Early JHP bullets sometimes did not expand for several reasons. Velocity was too low, or the front cavity filled up with clothing, stopping the hydraulic effect that opened up the nose.

Another problem was separation of jacket and core, reducing penetration. Several new bullet designs have appeared, such as the Winchester Black Talon, Hornady XTP and PMC-Eldorado Starfire. The Winchester uses a reverse-taper jacket — thicker at the front — to lock the core into the jacket to avoid fragmenting.

Winchester and Hornady score the jacket noses to enhance mushrooming effect. The PMC Starfire has internal flutes in the cavity. The Federal Hydra-Shok uses a central post in the cavity to redirect incoming material laterally, forcibly opening the cavity. The net effect is a bullet that opens more reliably over a greater range of impact velocities.

During the last two decades, the old practice of simply providing new equipment to officers has given way to planned introduction, accompanied by training of all officers in its use. This came about because of several court decisions, such as Peplow vs. Margate, mandating that police agencies are responsible for ensuring their officers know how to use equipment properly, supported by documentation of training courses.

Although certain private firearms instructors claim their students become expert shots after attending their expensive courses, police firearms instructors don't have this luxury. Their students range from really competent firearms handlers to those who never have fired a shot before. Police instructors can't provide the individualized instruction offered by private shooting schools. With limited time, firearms instructors must ensure that students reach a certain level of competence, then document it with a "qualification" course in which shooters must have a passing score.

This becomes more difficult when students must unlearn their revolver-handling habits and adapt to the new autos requiring radically different techniques. Some have little interest in firearms, and attend the course only because the job requires it. Although these minimal-interest students can pass, they're not going to maintain their skills as well as shooting enthusiasts who practice on their own time and often buy their own ammunition.

Some shooters have trouble getting used to the double-action first shot and the single-action pull of subsequent shots.

An important part of transition training is practice in clearing malfunctions. Although, with a top-quality pistol and carefully chosen ammunition, failures are rare, it builds confidence to know the jam-clearing drill.

Police handguns of innovative design have appeared during the last two decades. The Heckler & Koch squeeze-cocker was radical in its firing mechanism and action. Instead of using a locked breech, the new pistol has a hole to bleed gas from the barrel into a recoil-retarding cylinder, where it pushes against a piston attached to the slide. This retards slide operation until pressure in the barrel drops with the bullet's exit. Heckler & Koch pistols also have fluted chambers, allowing propellant gas to break the fired case free and aid extraction.

The Glock design has fewer moving parts than most others, and this contributes to its reliability. Takedown is especially simple. Instead of using a rotating lever, the pistol has a spring-loaded catch which the shooter pulls to disengage the slide. When the slide goes back onto the frame rails, it rides over the catch, automatically locking in place.

The most innovative designs are European, not American. This is significant, because police officers are at least as patriotic as any other citizen, but many chose foreign handguns on the basis of design and quality.

There are now several tritium night sight systems, some factory installed, and others produced as aftermarket replacements. Some, such as the Armson Trijicon and SIG Betalight, use standard three-dot sight pictures. Others, such as the P-T sights produced by Innovative Weaponry, Inc., use new concepts, such as contrasting green and yellow dots, or a dot front sight and horizontal bar rear sight.

We can depend on continuing refinement of both hardware and training methods based on changing tactical doctrines. At the moment, the new .40 S&W appears to be gaining ground because of its greater power, but the continuing influx of officers of small stature ensures the 9mm never will drop out of police service.

Many innovations have come about recently, but some have not gained wide acceptance. Heckler & Koch pistols are more expensive than most competitors, which resulted in their not gaining full acceptance. The FBI 10mm Auto flared briefly, the died. The Double-Action-Only auto is still relatively new, and only time will tell whether this concept becomes popular. Police firearms training will intensify, both to avoid liability and because police firearms instructors understand that skill is more important than hardware. The most advanced bullet design from a high-tech auto pistol doesn't do any good unless it hits the target in a vital spot. The only way to promote this is to train officers enough to enable them to hit their targets.

IS THE .40S&W INACCURATE?

By Chris Christian

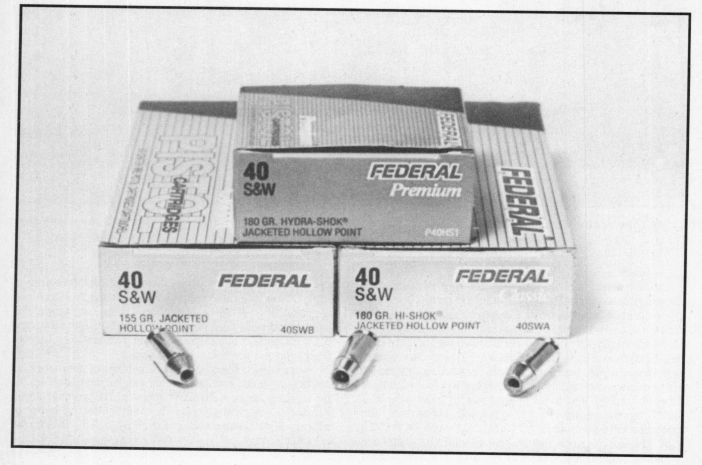

The Author Feels The Answer Is A Qualified Yes... And No!

SOME CARTRIDGES prove their mettle in combat, but the .40 S&W literally was born of battle.

April 11, 1986, will come to rank ultimately as one of the more important days in the history of the development of law enforcement equipment and tactics. On that day — in what now is commonly called the FBI Miami Shootout — nine FBI agents attempted to arrest two dangerous murderers. The criminals did not submit peacefully.

When the shootout was over, both criminals were dead. So were two of the agents, along with five wounded.

The lessons learned in that tragedy prompted a series of comprehensive studies. In fact, the Miami episode may well be the most studied gunfight in the annals of law enforcement history.

One of the conclusions drawn was that the Winchester 115-grain 9mm Silvertip used by the FBI agents was not the best choice under those circumstances. The FBI immediately embarked on a lengthy series of tests to determine what might be a better choice.

"All other things aside," says one FBI spokeperson, "Miami was an ammunition failure. Agent Dove delivered a perfect shot on the assailant who was responsible for the casualties among the agents, before any of those casualties occurred. The bullet failed to penetrate sufficiently to stop him quickly. It didn't have to happen, and we're determined it won't happen again."

Bullet penetration, rather than the previously accepted theory of a large temporary wound cavity, became one of the primary concerns.

Existing cartridges and bullet types were examined carefully in shooting tests using 10 percent ballistic gelatin. Then, obstacles — including car window glass, various densities of clothing, wallboard and plywood — were placed in front of the gelatin. This might well be one of the most comprehensive

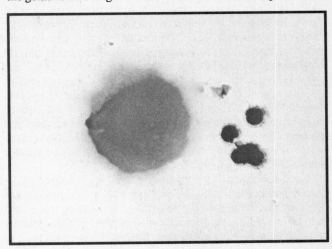

Left, Federal's three .40 S&W loads showed consistent accuracy and velocity levels during author's extensive tests. Above, the best performer for the day was Blazer's PHP JHP with a typical .75-inch group from a 25-yard bench rest. The .40 S&W Contender (below) from T/C's custom shop removed mechanical variables for the accuracy tests.

and objective tests of handgun performance ever done.

When the tests were completed, it was determined that the 10mm Auto was the most efficient cartridge of those tested. Unfortunately, its recoil and muzzle blast were deemed too severe for a defensive handgun.

Equalling the 10mm was the .357 magnum. It, too, was plagued by what was deemed excessive recoil, and since the FBI was wedded to semi-autos anyway, it was dismissed.

The next most effective load was the 185-grain .45 ACP JHP. Strictly as an experiment, 10mm ammunition was loaded down to 950 fps to duplicate .45 ACP performance. To everyone's surprise this "10mm Lite" almost equalled the effectiveness of the full-charged load, without the muzzle blast and recoil. The FBI decided that .40/180JHP/950 fps was the way to go.

There were, however, some drawbacks to that approach. For starters, such a combo required a 10mm round that, in turn, requires a large-frame semi-auto handgun to contain the power of the cartridge. There also was some question as to the wisdom of reducing the load on the 10mm round from a nominal 1,200 fps to 950 fps.

Such down-loading does leave a lot of space in the case in which powder can shift around, possibly producing erratic ignition, not to mention the possibility of reducing functional reliability. Neither is particularly desirable in a firearm on which you may have to bet your life!

Lights went on at Smith & Wesson and Winchester, and a simple question was asked: If you're only going to use part of the cartridge's capability, do you need to use the whole cartridge and does it have to be in a large-frame gun?"

The answer seemed to be, no!

Even before the first lot of S&W 10mms went to the FBI, there was a whole new cartridge on the scene — the .40 S&W.

Created by reducing the overall length of the 10mm, it matched the "10mm Lite" ballistics (.40/180JHP/950 fps) and did so in a round compact enough to fit easily into existing mid-size high-capacity 9mm framed guns.

It may well have been the first round in history ever created to fit the criteria of comprehensive test data relating to the performance of law enforcement handgun rounds.

It also was a publicist's dream, and before long, virtually every gunmaker with an existing full-size 9mm in his line began chambering those guns for the .40 S&W. Ammo makers, too, were swept up onto the wave. In fact, within less than two years of its introduction, there were as many factory loads available for the new .40 S&W as for the venerable .45 ACP.

It was then that the first few vague mutterings about "the emporer's clothes" began to be heard.

It started quietly, mostly among gun writers, when alone with other gun writers. Someone would ask, "What kind of groups are you getting with the .40 S&W? I don't seem to be able... ."

To put it bluntly, the vast majority of the new .40 S&W semi-

The highest velocity recorded during author's test was produced by Hornady's 155-grain JHP. It sizzled out at 1340 fps.

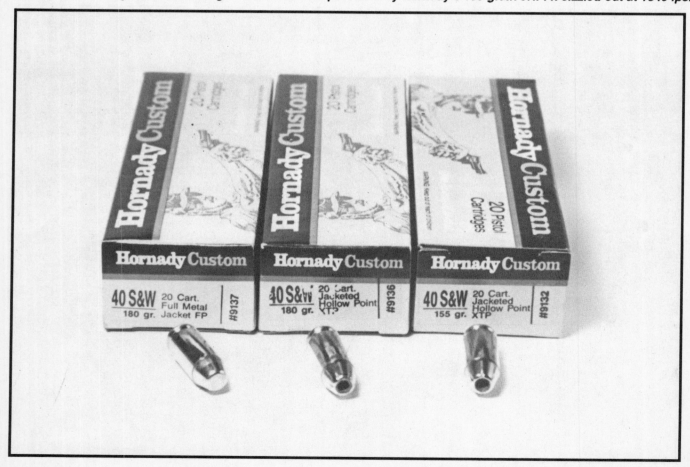

autos were not producing accuracy. Indeed, accuracy levels of the new guns seemed to fall far short of expectations. Some gun testers opined that any group in the 2.25-inch range was considered excellent, with larger groups often the rule. Some of the guns shot so poorly that a number of early "tests" in various handgun publications didn't even print group sizes!

Then someone started playing the Blame Game.

"It's the twist rate in the barrels," said one. "No," opined another, "it's the factory ammunition." Others blamed the guns, design of the cartridge — or both!

One writer went so far as to venture the opinion that we "might have a problem cartridge here."

It is obvious that, from the standpoint of the level of accuracy one should expect from a well-made, service-grade semi-auto, the .40 S&W gun and load combinations then available were falling far short of expectations, but I had a hard time swallowing the blame-the-ammo theory.

My first experience with the .40 S&W was a revolver, the now-discontinued Smith & Wesson Model 610. This was a sturdy N-frame model made back in the days when S&W was cranking out new styles just about as fast as politicos currently break their campaign promises.

Chambered for the 10mm, and using half moon clips, it could fire the .40 S&W in the same manner that a .357 can fire .38 Special rounds. And fire them it did!

I tested one of the first 610s out, and with the then available .40 S&W fodder, it performed quite well. A look through my record books showed its tightest groups were about 1.80 inches, while few factory rounds spread wider than 2.30. Overall average was about 2.10.

As my U.S. Navy instructors were fond of saying, "Remember those figures, because you will see them again!"

I consider that level of accuracy to qualify as "good" for a revolver; not "excellent" or "average," but falling right in between. If the factory ammunition was inherently inaccurate, or if the design of the cartridge was such, the Smith & Wesson 610 failed to show it.

Unfortunately, when it came to test vehicles of the non-

TABLE 1
.40 S&W ACCURACY TEST

Test Gun: Thompson/Center Contender, 10-inch bull barrel with 2.5x-7x T/C Recoil Proof Scope

Test results are the average of five five-shot groups at 25 yards. Center to center measurements.

LOAD	GROUP SIZE
Federal 140 SWA 180-gr. Hi-Shok JHP	1.12 in.
Federal P40HS1 180-gr. Hydra-Shok JHP	1.25 in.
Federal 40SWB 155-gr. JHP	1.21 in.
CCI Blazer #3591 180-gr. TMJ	1.25 in.
CCI Blazer #3590 180-gr. FMJ FP	1.25 in.
Hornady Custom #9137 180-gr. FMJ FP	1.25 in.
Hornady Custom #9132 155-gr. XTP JHP	1.40 in.
Hornady Custom #9136 180-gr. XTP JHP	1.30 in.

The .40 S&W (center) has ballistics nearly identical to the .45 ACP (right) while offering magazine capacity approaching the 9mm (left).

TABLE 2
.40 S&W VELOCITY TEST

Test Gun: Thompson/Center Contender, 10-inch bull barrel.

Test results are from five-shot groups using Oehler 35P with start screen 10 feet from muzzle.

LOAD	MAX FPS	MIN FPS	AVERAGE	ES
Hornady #9132	1371	1320	1340	51
Hornady #9137	1104	1023	1068	81
Hornady #9136	1164	1121	1142	43
CCI Blazer #3590	1112	980	1080	132
CCI Blazer #3591	1183	1086	1155	97
Federal 40SWB	1280	1233	1262	47
Federal 40SWA	1088	1001	1063	87
Federal P40HS1	1165	1120	1134	45

ES = maximum velocity spread between five shots.

semi-auto handgun type, that was pretty much all there was, and even that no longer is available.

Was it the ammo? There was one way to find out. I called the custom shop at Thompson/Center Arms, (P.O. Box 5002, Farmington Rd., Rochester, NH 03867) and asked them to chamber a 10-inch bull barrel for the .40 S&W. As one terminally afflicted with "Contenderitis," I long ago discovered that they generally will give us about as much accuracy as any cartridge has to give.

If the problem truly lay with the factory ammunition or the inherent design of the cartridge, the Contender would show it.

Once the barrel arrived, it was cleaned and adorned with a Thompson/Center 2.5x-7x Recoil Proof scope. Tests were conducted on my backyard range from a sturdy benchrest at 25 yards. The scope was used at 7x to minimize aiming errors.

I did not have a full range of fresh factory ammo on hand, but what I had was a good representative sample. The test rounds were: Federal's 40SWA 180-grain JHP, the P40HS1 180-grain JHP Hydra-Shok and their 155- grain 40SWB JHP. Hornady ammo consisted of the #9137 180-grain FMJ FP, the #9132 155-grain XTP JHP and the #9136 180-grain XTP JHP. From CCI, I had two of their Blazer rounds, the #3591 180-grain TMJ and the #3590 180-grain PHP JHP.

Prior to accuracy testing, all rounds were run over my Oehler 35P, and it would seem the .40 S&W can produce some interesting velocities from a 10-inch barrel, as Table 2 will show. As for accuracy, Table 1 illustrates what this barrel was capable of producing.

Compared to what many are achieving from currently available semi-auto handguns, the accuracy levels are excellent. But comparing the accuracy of a Contender to a semi-

auto is like comparing Cindy Crawford to Rosanne Arnold. It's not quite fair.

A better comparison is to match the .40 S&W to other popular rounds when fired from the same test gun. That wasn't hard to do.

Among my collection of Contender barrels are those in .357, .45 ACP and .44 magnum. All have been tested extensively — using the same 2.5x-7x T/C scope — with a number of factory rounds. Results are recorded in my notebooks.

If the .40 S&W is inherently inaccurate, then it should be reflected when compared to large numbers of factory rounds fired from the other barrels under identical conditions. It would seem the .40 S&W isn't too bad!

In the .357 barrel — including .38 Special loads — the smallest groups recorded were 0.50-inch. The largest, 1.25-inch. The .45 ACP just about mirrored those results, being just a few thousands of an inch larger on both ends. The .44 magnum — including .44 Special loads — produced a 0.65-inch group on the small side and 1.356-inch group on the large side.

At the worst, the .40 S&W was no more than 0.25-inch less accurate than the five well-established rounds when fired from the same type of test vehicle, under the same conditions. That's one-quarter-inch difference at 25 yards!

Interestingly, I find that, when the same .38/.357 and .44 Spec/.44 magnum loads are fired from revolvers — specifically a S&W 586 and a S&W Model 29 Classic Hunter — the group sizes of the individual loads increase by a factor of 2x to 2.25x. A load that does 1.25 in the Contender will do somewhere around 2.5 in the revolvers.

Go back to the figures for the groups fired from the S&W

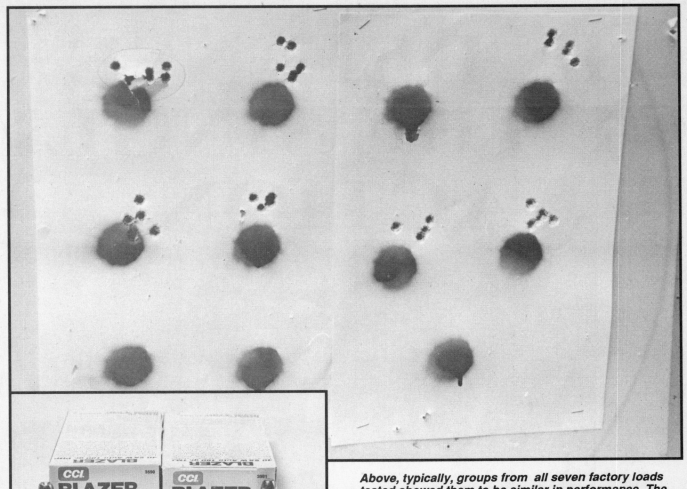

Above, typically, groups from all seven factory loads tested showed them to be similar in performance. The Blazer 180-grain PHP JHP (left) yielded the best groups.

Model 610 and you'll see that relationship holds pretty true. It looks to me like the factory .40 S&W loads show no more appreciable difference in their accuracy levels than do other popular mid- to large-bore loads. If the .40 S&W isn't delivering, I don't think I'd blame the ammo.

It may be that the original premise that a .40 caliber round can be stuffed into existing 9mm-size handguns was wrong.

Consider this: The .40 S&W operates at pressures that are rather high for a semi-auto handgun cartridge fired from many existing locking systems. SAAMI specs list it at 37,400 psi. That is greater than those for the 9x19. Research has shown that those pressures also peak quickly. While other cartridges build their pressure as the bullet moves down the barrel, this one seems to "get it all at once." That can lead to premature unlocking of the slide in some guns.

The early Tanfoglio guns clearly exhibited both a "wipe" mark on the primer indicating the slide/barrel group was unlocking even before the firing pin had retracted, and definite vertical stringing of groups. Guns using a Browning-type lock-up system also exhibit the same condition. Not all guns, do, however.

The HK P7M10 uses a gas-retarding system to delay the unlocking until the bullet has left the barrel. Numerous accuracy tests with this gun show group sizes ranging from 1.20 to 3.5 inches, with averages of about 2.5 inches. That's the accuracy I would expect from a service-grade, semi-auto handgun with any cartridge.

The Smith & Wesson Performance Shop has produced some guns that will group between .90 and 2.20 inches. They, however, are using a heavy slide and frame combo.

It would seem that, despite earlier predictions, the .40 S&W may not be able to achieve its best accuracy in 9mm-size guns. It is obvious that something needs to be done to slow down the slide velocity and attendant premature unlocking. That may well require a heavier gun.

In that respect, the answer to the question, "Is the .40 S&W inaccurate?" could be a qualified, "yes, it is in some guns."

In answer to the question, "Is the cartridge itself inherently inaccurate?" there is a different answer. "No."

I find no fault with the ammunition itself. In fact, it seems to be quite good stuff, and once gunmakers learn how to wrap the right gun around it, we'll have a self-defense cartridge that should be as good as any.

After all, it was born of combat.

★ IN DEFENSE ★ OF THE SINGLE ★ ACTION ★

By J. Burke

*Even in .22 rimfire (top), this single-action displays Colt's famous, classic lines .
Ruger's flat-top single-action (bottom) was the first .44 mag available to consumers.*

IT WAS 3:30 in the morning; eighteen miles out of Beeville, Texas. I was wearing stovepipe bullhide boots, my BVDs and a worn-out Stetson that draws flies in the daylight.

My old four-cell flashlight was tucked under one arm as I tugged on a cotton string that disappeared into the depths of a cement stock tank. I quickly retrieved a cool can of *Big Red* soda, and returned to my old field table and a stately mesquite tree which held a hissing gas lantern.

Not long before, something moving slightly faster than the pack of coyotes on its heels streaked past my decades old canvas tent. Getting more sleep was impossible; worse, it was much too early for a breakfast fire.

I grabbed a handful of current gun magazines from the wooden ammunition crate I use as a chuckbox. Satisfied no rattlesnake had meandered within my small circle of light, I let Sadie, the Wonder Lab, exit our tent and join me for some cold Spam and leathery tortillas.

As I settled in for a couple hours of pleasurable reading, I couldn't help noticing each of those leading gun magazines featured a high-capacity sem-automatic pistol on its cover. By the mellow glow of the lantern, I tried to remember how many times a single-action revolver had graced the cover of a major gun magazine in recent years. There were notable exceptions...but not many.

Although I own my share of double-action revolvers and autoloaders, I use a single-action wheelgun for most of my handgunning chores. The design, in my opinion, has seen

The Ancient Wheel Gun Still Meets This Texan's Varied Needs!

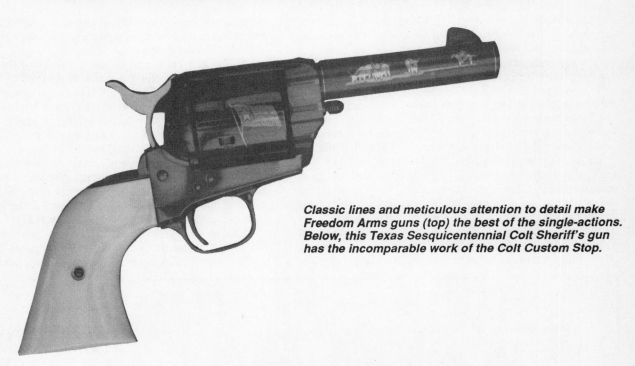

Classic lines and meticulous attention to detail make Freedom Arms guns (top) the best of the single-actions. Below, this Texas Sesquicentennial Colt Sheriff's gun has the incomparable work of the Colt Custom Stop.

only two truly monumental improvements in more than 150 years of continuous use.

The first single-action revolver milestone was the upgrade from percussion ignition to self-contained metallic cartridges. The second history-making event was Ruger's introduction of their New Model series in 1973, finally creating a single-action safe to handle and carry fully loaded.

As I mused over all the high-tech autoloading hardware showcased in my mobile gun library, I decided to take a look at whether my preference for the old single-action was based on practicality or a general reluctance to accept the Twentieth Century.

I'd start by examining what uses I have for a handgun.

Next, I'd list the critical features necessary to accomplish my handgun tasks. And finally, I'd know if the concept originated by a boy-sailor in 1830-31 really meets my beltgun needs, or if the single-action should be relegated to back room museum display cases.

Like most handgun enthusiasts, I'm neither a member of the law enforcement community nor on active military duty. In addition, I no longer am a regular participant in organized competitive shooting, but few are the days over the past three-and-a-half decades during which I have not fired or at least handled a handgun. More often than not, that handgun has been a single-action. Still, maybe I was missing something.

As a boy, my interest in handguns was purely pleasurable,

The special cased Colt Sheriff's Model, commemorating the birth of Texas, is a supreme investment opportunity.

but as an adult, my single most important reason for owning a handgun is for convenient personal and home defense within legal limitations.

That may not be a popular public statement in liberal quarters these days, but it's a fact. Much like a fire extinguisher, a defensive handgun quietly serves me every day, a critical piece of equipment that must be properly maintained and secured but which may prove indispensable in an emergency. With that sober reality out of the way, my remaining handgun uses are decidedly recreational.

The handgunning times I like best are when I'm leisurely enjoying the freedom of a working ranch or other large chunk of real estate, like when I'm wandering along the Devil's River near the beautiful West Texas town of Sonora. Legendary Texas Ranger Captain John Coffee "Jack" Hayes surely had his reasons for giving the river its scandalous name early in the history of Texas, but it is heavenly territory to me!

On rare occasion I may not fire a shot all day. If I do, I'll be engaging "targets of opportunity." Perhaps a distant dirt clod, an unsuspecting varmint or even an empty bean can discarded months before by a *mojado* hoping to improve life for his family far to the south.

My main motivation on these rambling excursions is solitude and a chance to look for shed deer horns, fancy rocks or anything man made and as old as possible. The privilege of

wearing a good handgun afield, just as my father and grandfather and his father before him did, makes my rural wanderings all the more pleasant.

As far as I know, the name of this fun-filled shooting pastime comes from the sound of a .22 rimfire slug striking an empty tin can. While plinking, I'm likely to burn up a substantial quantity of ammunition. Given a safe backstop and the willingness to clean up punctured metal or plastic containers after a shooting session, plinking provides excellent practice under nearly actual field conditions.

A target range session is where my handgun practice becomes precise. Whatever my primary use for a specific handgun, I like to know where a bullet exiting its barrel will strike at specific distances, and how well I can group both factory ammunition and my favorite handloads.

Like an ever-growing number of handgun enthusiasts, I like to do a portion of my hunting with a handgun. Time spent trailin' around, plinking and at the target range, all help ready

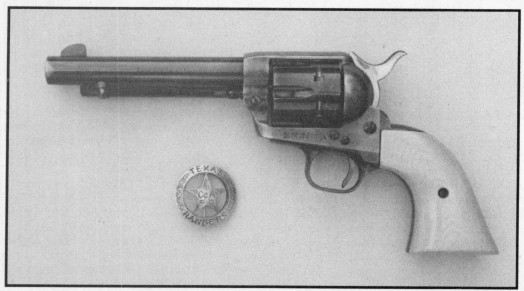

Model "P" Colts with a Texas Ranger badge are a top collector item.

The New Model Ruger (top) allows all six chambers to be filled. A Colt (bottom) and any "old model" or flat-top Ruger needs an empty chamber under the hammer.

me for this challenging sport. Without a hundred hours or so of preparation for every hour actively handgun hunting, the odds of keeping my freezer full would be pretty low.

I became a youthful handgun collector when I scraped enough cash together to own more than one belt gun. My first "collection" consisted of a surplus Model 1917 Smith & Wesson double-action revolver in .45 ACP (with halfmoon clips) plus a well worn Colt #3 derringer in .41 rimfire.

Ever since, buying, selling, trading or just researching classic handguns has provided me with a major source of enjoyment. But, like any youngster, I made my share of mistakes and sometimes ended up "buying high and selling low," as I gained experience with every type and caliber of handgun I could lay my hands on.

More than anything else — more now than ever before — I absolutely, positively demand a handgun that can be stored safely, handled, carried and worn in a loaded condition. Avoiding an accidental discharge is all-important.

So how does the single-action stack up? Like any other quality firearm, just fine, given a thorough understanding of each manufacturer's products and adherence to the basic rules of safe firearms handling.

Colonel Colt's single-action products should be filled with only five cartridges, not six. The hammer must rest on the sixth empty chamber. The same goes for Bill Ruger's now classic "Old Model" single-actions—those produced before the modifications of 1973. For the uninitiated, that's every Ruger single-action on which screw heads are visible on one side of the cylinder frame. Be sure to check both sides.

New Model Ruger single-actions feature a patented vertical transfer bar which makes the revolver capable of firing a cartridge only when the hammer is in the full-cock position. When the hammer is down and the trigger is in its forward position, the transfer bar is below a notch in the hammer's profile, keeping it from coming in contact with the firing pin.

Given proper gun handling procedures and an unaltered

Author's flat-top Ruger .44 magnum has been a faithful performer for more than three decades.

The original Colt Bisleys (right) once were not well received. Today, they are highly prized by collectors. Below, this commemorative Colt Sheriff's model is as accurate as it is beautiful.

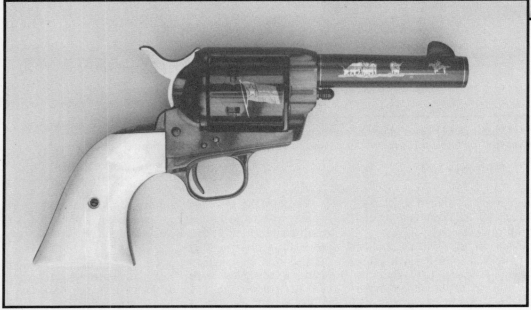

firearm, a New Model Ruger is safe to carry with all six chambers loaded, but I know a number of highly experienced single-action men who prefer a "belt-and-suspenders" approach and load only five shells, even on these improved sixguns!

Freedom Arms' custom quality products feature a hammer safety bar which is positioned between the hammer and receiver to keep the hammer from striking the firing pin. This is when any of their revolvers, in calibers from .22 rimfire to the thunderous .454 Casull, are in the " hammer safety" mode. Even so, the manufacturer recommends loading one shell less than full capacity in their five-shot stainless steel masterpieces.

Incidentally, the only single-action revolver accidents I have personal knowledge of over all these years were the result of unsafe gun handling techniques coupled with the quick-draw craze which took hold in the latter half of the 1950s. The reintroduction of Colt's Single Action Army revolver and the advent of television westerns produced thousands of inexperienced, would-be Old West "gunfighters." Unfortunately, some of those greenhorns found their fledgling Hollywood hobby more dangerous than playing catch with live rattlesnakes!

My handguns must work when called upon. I need a system I can count on to fire a cartridge when I need or simply want to.

Of all the single-actions I have owned or used regularly, only two ever failed to pass my reliability test. The score might

have been significantly different had I been involved in the gun-torturing practice of fanning, which went hand-in-hand with quick-draw theatrics.

The first of my single-actions to fail was the old Colt derringer mentioned earlier. Metal fatigue and general neglect, coupled with my incessant attempt to fire the mouldy Nineteenth Century shells that came with the little pistol, caused the mainspring to break.

About two years ago, I had the opportunity to buy an early second generation Colt SAA at a great price in what seemed to be excellent condition. However, one look at the burred screws it was sporting indicated unseen trouble. In spite of this, I bought the handsome Colt.

Using light loads, I fired my new possession three times without trouble. With the fourth shot, the bolt dropped below its proper position in the frame and I had a free-wheeling .45 Colt cylinder.

Fearing the worst, I rushed my bargain to pistolsmith Jim Stroh of Atlanta. A $5 spring restored my prize to as new mechanical condition. Stroh also returned the burred screws to factory-new for a modest fee.

Inexpensive replacement parts quickly restored both of these ailing Colts to perfect health. In my experience, the rugged simplicity of the single-action makes it the most reliable of handguns.

I treat all my handguns the same, from the least expensive to the most valuable. That's the kind of respect they deserve.

This Freedom Arms Deputy U.S. Marshal in .454 Casull has a three-inch bull barrel.

But there are those times, mostly while hunting, when a handgun is likely to take some unexpected knocks. A handgun that can't stand up to a bit of adversity is likely to ruin an otherwise fine outing—if not cost you more dearly in a serious situation. The single-action's solid frame provides a rigid base for its barrel, cylinder and cylinder pin. It possesses a minimal number of moving parts, and is not sensitive to minor variations in ammunition. There is no part routinely removed from the single-action which would turn it into a single-shot firearm or make it totally incapable of firing a cartridge.

Other than mashing the sights, there is little damage you can do to a single-action. Excessively heavy loads have been known to dislodge the odd cylinder pin, but Freedom Arms has even solved this unlikely problem by adding a retaining screw that passes vertically through the front of the cylinder pin and into shallow threads near the base of the barrel.

The single-action is the sporting handgun most likely to remain usable even under adverse conditions.

I want to hit what I'm shooting at, and in the hands of a competent shooter, the single-action revolver is capable of delivering startling accuracy.

The great Elmer Keith was proving the single-action's accuracy, especially at long range, more than a half a century ago. Like many handgunners my age, his classic long out-of-print book *Sixguns* contained then-unconventional thinking that modern silhouette shooters confirm on a regular basis.

It is only in the competition-grade .22 rimfire category that I am unable to fire a single-action revolver with equal or better results than with any other style of handgun. But the recent introduction of Freedom Arms' Model 252 Silhouette and Varmint Class single-actions in that caliber may allow me to claim a "clean sweep" for the old single-action in the accuracy department.

This may seem a strange requirement for someone who does his deer and turkey hunting with a single-shot rifle, but I expect a limited number of follow-up shots from my handguns. For defensive purposes, this is a must; for my other shooting activities, it is a convenience.

Following the manufacturer's strictest instructions, a Freedom Arms single-action gives me three follow-up shots after the first one. Colts, as well as "Old Model" Rugers, give me a fourth.

My New Model Rugers provide five more immediately useable shots after touching-off the first one. If I need more firepower than that, I'm in combat and remiss for not bringing along a Texas Ranger or a battalion of the 101st Airborne!

I need calibers from diminutive to awesome. Single-action revolvers are available in a full range of calibers from .22 rimfire through the .454 Casull in production guns. The fine array of custom pistolsmiths working today will build you a single-action in smaller or larger calibers as well as in various wildcat and obsolete chamberings.

Some handgun tasks are best tackled with short barrels; other activities require the advantages of a longer sighting radius plus the extra energy and velocity which can be achieved through lengthier barrels. My Freedom Arms Deputy U.S. Marshal Model in .454 Casull is equipped with a three-inch bull barrel. First generation Colt Single Action Army revolvers were produced with barrels as long as 18 inches; Colt's Custom Shop will make you one today. Virtually every practical barrel length between these two extremes also is available currently in a single-action revolver.

I most appreciate the looks of case-hardening and bluing on a handgun. But for using purposes, I prefer stainless steel construction. Both of these alternatives are available in the single-action as well as virtually every form of plating or other enhancement you can apply to a firearm

Fixed sights are all I require for some applications, but long-range shooting is tackled best with adjustable sights. I have even come to appreciate the advantages of mounting a scope on a handgun used strictly for hunting.

Bill Ruger was the first modern manufacturer to take the single-action seriously as a sporting firearm. Except for the nifty little Bearcat, Ruger .22 single-actions always have been equipped with at least semi-adjustable sights. Centerfire Rugers have had fully adjustable sighting equipment from the first specimen to leave the original "Red Barn" manufacturing facility.

To meet the sophisticated field demands of their savvy clientele, Freedom Arms offers the greatest variety of single-action sighting options. Colt's Custom Shop will entertain building one of their legendary Single Action Army revolvers to your personal needs and tastes, but the cost is not exactly minimal!

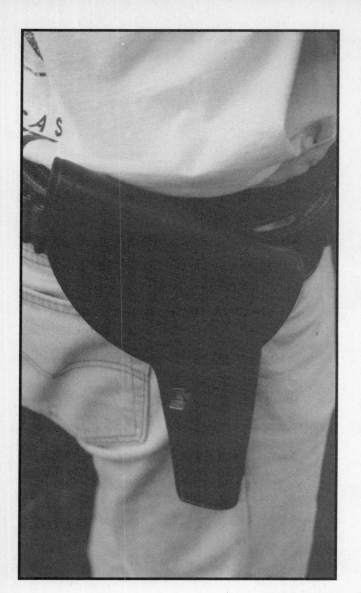

To become proficient at handgunning— and to stay that way — requires considerable practice, but my budget always is limited and I need a source of cheap ammunition. If reloading is involved, I want to keep it as trouble-free as possible.

The .22 rimfire and CCI's centerfire Blazer ammunition cover the "inexpensive" category. Rimmed, straight-wall centerfire cartridges produce the easiest brass to reload. Again, the trusty single-action revolver easily meets my requirements.

I want handguns that are either collectible when I acquire them or will be soon thereafter. To qualify in this category, other handgun aficionados must lust for my treasures.

An excellent way to confirm the current value of virtually any firearm is by consulting two excellent volumes from DBI Books. One is Jack Lewis' *The Gun Digest Book of Modern Gun Values;* the other, *Flayderman's Guide to Antique American Firearms.*

To zero-in further on the market in your area, walk the handgun in question down the aisles of a major gun show. If you're clutching a Colt, flat-top or "three-screw" Ruger or a Freedom Arms product, you won't get past the first row of tables without generating serious interest By the time you hit your stride and round the third row, you'll be causing a quiet riot!

Any high quality firearm can be expected to increase in value. But old, limited edition and commemorative single-actions are sure-fire investment opportunities.

By the time I finished listing what uses I have for my handguns and whether or not the single-action provides all the

Even durable single-action revolvers deserve the care of a full-flap holster when venturing into rough terrain.

Author's immaculate Freedom Arms Deputy U.S. Marshal SA in .454 Casull is carried in a tough Freedom leather holster of equivalent quality.

Above, Colt Peacemakers in .45 Colt (top) and .22 Long Rifle are great choices for just trailin' around. Right, this stainless Ruger Blackhawk in .357 magnum downed a West Texas turkey just in time for Christmas.

features required, the sun was two hours above the horizon. Sadie, my canine companion, was anxious to see if she could outrun a few of the local jackrabbits in the one hundred-yard dash.

I strapped on my Bianchi gunbelt containing a full compliment of cartridges. The matching Model #1L holster was filled with one of my favorite handguns, a stainless Ruger Super Blackhawk. I had reviewed my long-standing choice of the single-action revolver for my handgunning needs. The old "thumb buster," as my friend, Senior Texas Ranger Captain (Ret.) Clint T. Peoples, still calls the single-action, had passed with flying colors!

As Sadie and I moved down a century-old cattle trail, I knew I wouldn't encounter an enemy bunker requiring fifteen-plus shots of suppressive fire as quickly as I could pull the trigger. I also was confident I wouldn't be interrupting a drug deal and need to display even a fraction of the legendary double-action revolver skills possessed by Bill Jordan of U.S. Border Patrol fame.

But, in addition to all the practical reasons why the simple, often maligned single-action revolver is the right handgun for me, there's more.

Sam Colt's company and The Republic of Texas were born in the same year. The former played a significant role in the settling of the latter, and their histories are forever entwined. The single-action revolver was highly prized by both the North and the South in The War Between The States. The single-action was used by opposing forces in a desperate 1876 Indian battle which put a damper on America's centennial

celebration and doomed the free life of this continent's original settlers.

Trying to list the famous and infamous individuals who carried a single-action revolver from the Indian War-era until the Wild West was wild no more would be a formidable task. And a young Army lieutenant, who carved two notches in the ivory grip of his plated and engraved Model P Colt in 1916, was still wearing that Single Action Army revolver as he became one of the most memorable American generals of World War II—George Patton!

Every single-action I have ever held, from the oldest black powder Colt through the latest Freedom Arms offering, reminds me of that handgun's place in history as well as its continuing usefulness. No other firearm provides me with as much satisfaction.

THE MINIEST MAGNUM

— Chris Christian

The Diminutive .22 Winchester Rimfire Magnum Is More Than Adequate In A Host Of Roles!

I'M NOT a big fan of crows at any time, and I take an especially dim view of them at dawn, when they greet the new day in a raucous manner 50 yards behind my trailer. I guess I'm not much of a morning person.

This crow had been playing that game for the last few days, and he'd finally worn out his welcome.

Easing out of bed with as much grace as I'm capable of mustering BC — before coffee — I managed to locate a camo

jacket, face mask and gloves. The last thing I grabbed before heading out the door was one of my 10-inch Contenders.

It wasn't hard to pinpoint the crow's location with the racket he was making, but his exact position was a bit more complicated. After several minutes of peeking carefully around the backside of the trailer, I had him spotted in the top of a big pine about 100 yards away.

I don't advocate tossing bullets skyward, but behind the

Author fired the three-shot groups (right) from 100 yards. The .22 magnum has become popular for NRA Hunter Pistol competition (below).

crow stretched several miles of what some Florida real estate agents refer to as "a prime lowland investment opportunity." The rest of us call it swamp. It was a perfectly safe shot.

The gun was sighted dead on at 100 yards and would hold groups of just over an inch. Turning the T/C scope to 6x, I let my breathing settle down and began a slow trigger press.

At the crack of the gun, the crow tumbled out of the tree to reaffirm my faith in the .22 Winchester rimfire magnum.

Introduced about 1959, the concept behind the .22 WRM was simple: increase the power of the .22 LR round — in effect, bridging the gap between it and some of the lower-powered .22 centerfire rounds like the Hornet — yet keep the convenience and relatively low cost of a rimfire.

Being only 9 years old, I was not seriously impacted at the time. As I grew into adolescence and began roaming the then sparsely populated hill country of northern California, I began to appreciate the round's merits.

Paper route money had provided a .22 LR rifle and enough ammo to terrorize the local jackrabbit population. This, it must be understood, was the the pre-1968 GCA days when the government didn't really give a hoot if a kid had a .22 rifle, as long he didn't get wild with it. The local dairy ranchers know every jack I took out meant more food for their stock, and once they decided I knew the difference between a Holstein and a bunny, I had hunting grounds aplenty and even the gift of an occasional box of ammo.

It didn't take me long to realize the .22 LR's shortcomings. Any jackrabbit over 80 yards away was relatively safe, and even those hit at extended range often managed to wander a considerable distance before I was able to apply the coup de gras.

I needed more power, but a centerfire was out of the question. Even if I could have afforded the ammo Mom never would have gone for it. I'd used up a year's worth of pleading just to get the rimfire!

About that time, I discovered the .22 magnum, and by toting a few more papers, I was able to trade up to one. It looked enough like my previous .22 that Mom never knew the difference (although I suspect I'll be hearing about that, if she ever reads this).

While she didn't see any change, I certainly did! The difference was significant. Before any jackrabbit could start planing his immediate future, he had to be at least 140 yards away. Even then, his continued longevity was no sure bet.

That happy state of affairs continued for a couple more years, until I woke up one day and found myself wearing a U.S. Navy uniform, which would be my standard garb for the next decade. Jackrabbits and .22 magnums were forgotten as more pressing matters arose.

By the time I found myself in a position to wander around the woods again, I was in Florida. There were no jackrabbits, and reloading enough rounds to keep my collection of centerfire guns fed took up all of my shooting time.

If it hadn't been for a sudden plaque of crows, I might never have rediscovered what a dandy little cartridge the .22 magnum truly is.

I live on a little 10-acre chunk of ground in north-central Florida. Bordering the east side is a rather significant swamp, while the south and west sides have a few small homesteads scattered within 200 to 500 yards of my place.

Since my work for firearms publications requires I do a fair amount of test shooting, there is a 150-yard range on the property. I do have some neighbors, but a gentleman's agreement has been worked out. Rimfires are fine any time, but the big boomers I restrict to the mid-day hours during the week, allowing nearby residents to enjoy the solitude of mornings, evenings and weekends.

The only problem was the crows. They started flocking around the cracked corn I was putting out to feed the doves, quail and squirrels, eating it faster than I could buy it. They'd also taken a liking to the place, and I think I've made my feelings on early morning serenades quite explicit.

I had a 7mm TCU Contender that would reach out and "touch" a crow at 200 meters, but I knew the noise level was a bit more than the neighbors would bear cheerfully at dawn. So, too, would any .22 centerfire. And, I didn't have one, nor did I have any interest in setting up to reload yet another round.

I tried sorting the critters out with a Marlin Model 60 .22 LR rifle and simply relearned the lessons of 25 years ago: 75 yards was about as far as I could hit them, and the crows figured that out quickly.

If you've ever tried to slip to within 75 yards of a crow that doesn't want you within 75 yards of him, you can appreciate my problem.

It was an awkward situation, and might have remained so if I hadn't seen first-hand what a 10-inch-barreled Contender chambered for the almost-forgotten .22 magnum would do. That lesson came one day when I was waxed thoroughly in the Class A arena of NRA Hunter Pistol by a fellow who was popping the centerfire targets with a .22 magnum Contender.

I wound up in second place in that match, and I would rather not say by how many targets he took first. Suffice to say it was a waxing.

A brief chat at the end of the match, a target at 100 meters and few three-round groups fired showed me the round I'd grown up with — and forgotten in my rush to load the "biggest and best" — might just be what I required.

Even from an impromptu benchrest, this shooter was getting three-shot groups that cracked the one-inch mark. There was enough power to topple a 20-pound steel ram!

It didn't take long to add a .22 WRM barrel to my Contender system, and when I checked out available fodder, I found a pleasant surprise.

During my jackrabbit busting days, if you wanted a .22 magnum load you had two choices: a 40-grain JHP and a 40-grain solid. Today, the situation has changed.

The venerable 40-grain loads still are available, and as loaded by Federal, Winchester and CCI, they offer more performance than one has a right to expect from a rimfire.

Two newer offerings, however, provide added versatility and performance. Capitalizing on their success with the .22 LR Stinger, CCI recently introduced the 30-grain .22 magnum Mini-Mag +V. From the 10-inch Contender, it sizzles across the Oehler screens at an average of 2,051 feet per second — over 300 fps faster than the 40-grain loads! This bullet is quite frangible, and what it does to a crow is impressive.

Although it is the least accurate round, in my gun, it still has minute-of-crow accuracy. It has become my favorite for potting backyard pests, since it generally goes to pieces when it hits something, thus reducing the chance of a ricochet.

I would not recommend it for larger critters such as bobcats, raccoons and other varmints. I have doubts as to whether it will offer reliable penetration. In that situation, the 40-grain JHP is a better choice. Better yet is the second new .22 magnum offering.

The rising popularity of NRA Hunter Pistol silhouette competition prompted Federal Cartridge Company to introduce a 50-grain JHP. In the rimfire silhouette game, the targets are smaller and lighter than for conventional silhouette. To avoid ripping up the targets, only straight-walled cases are allowed, and it is becoming quite popular for shooters to use the .22 magnum.

The 50-grain load was developed to provide a bit more power on 100-meter rams, and the bullet does this job quite well. It also offers a flatter trajectory than most of the other authorized cartridges, resulting in fewer sight changes during the match.

It's also turned out to be an astonishingly effective game load. Although it doesn't equal the other rounds on paper, the heavier bullet offers increased penetration and excellent expansion.

I've taken a number of bobcats and raccoons with it at ranges up to 130 yards. Its field performance has been good enough that I've retired the 7mm TCU I used to use on turkeys with reduced handloads, and shifted completely over to the .22 mag and the 50-grain JHPs. Not having to begin each spring turkey season with a reloading and sight-in session is most convenient!

In fact, convenience pretty much describes the .22 magnum. Prior to its acquisition, I had to do some creative reloading with two other centerfire rounds to do the same job.

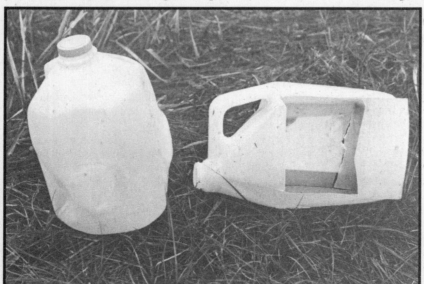

I don't mind reloading, but if I can avoid it I consider that a plus. The 10-inch Contender, with the appropriate factory load, now takes care of virtually all my varmint hunting, backyard pest control, had increased my scores in one of my favorite handgun matches and puts my two wild turkey limit in the freezer each spring. That's a lot of versatility from one 10-inch barrel!

Even in shorter barrels the little magnum still can be a sterling performer. Actually, it becomes an ideal cartridge for one popular breed of handgun, the trail gun or kit guns.

The water-filled plastic jug (right) literally exploded when hit with a 40-grain .22 magnum hollowpoint. The jug on the left took a 40-grain .22 LR hollowpoint.

When fired from a barrel of three or four inches, the .22 magnum will deliver essentially the same ballistics as will a .22 LR fired from a 16-inch-barreled rifle, and it will do it with a better bullet. It also will do it more reliably.

Due to its design and construction, the .22 WRM—at least, in my experience—is much less susceptible to contamination from oil, water, solvents or even the lube used on inexpensive grades of .22 LR fodder.

Misfires with the cheaper grades of the latter are not uncommon, but with the .22 WRM, they are exceedingly rare. In fact, I've never experienced one.

A glance at chart #2 will show the chronographed velocities achieved in a four-inch-barreled Smith & Wesson Model 651. Note the energy figures produced. That leads us to another area of the .22 WRM round that is seldom discussed: its potential value for self-defense. It's a lot better choice than many might assume. Actually, it's superior to several cartridges commonly used for that purpose.

Savvy pistoleros won't pay much attention to that revelation, and I don't blame them. Those who understand handguns and self-defense are going to be toting some far more serious hardware than a rimfire. Although it's worth noting that, when it comes to deep concealment back-up guns, there's a lot of real pros with one of the little North American Arms .22 mag derringers, or if you're lucky enough to find one, one of the old High Standard .22 mags.

Knowledgeable handgunners likely will have something more substantial than the .22 mag, at least as a primary gun. But, there is a large group of gunowners—about 20 million at last count—who might seriously benefit from the little magnum. It's a natural for the "one-gun owner."

These folks — and they come from all walks of life — don't have much interest in firearms from a sporting point of view. They own a gun strictly for self-defense. If smart, they may do a little practicing every now and then, but by and large, they don't. They buy a small handgun, load it, tuck it into a drawer — and hope they never have to use it.

For this group of gun owners, a short-barreled .22 magnum revolver might be one of their most effective choices.

A revolver is inherently more reliable than a semi-auto under conditions of long-term storage. You load one up, tuck it into a nightstand drawer. Five years later, you can pull it out, point it at the target and the chances are excellent all rounds will fire.

Semi-autos can have springs go weak, lubricants dissipate or gum up — and we have to remember whether there is a round in the chamber or the safety is on.

Even if the semi-auto does function, some of the more popular nightstand guns won't match the power of the .22 mag. The .25 ACP tosses a 50-grain FMJ bullet at about 760 fps; good for 65 foot-pounds of energy. Those small autos

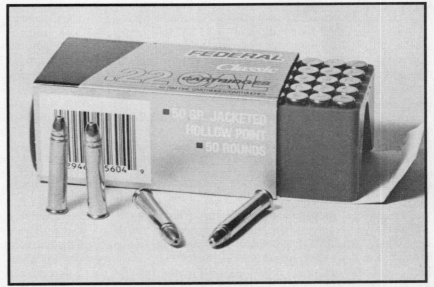

The 50-grain Federal load is one of author's favorites, both for silhouette competition and hunting. Its heavier slug assures adequate penetration.

CHART #1

LOAD	VELOCITY	ENERGY	ACCURACY
Federal 50-gr. JHP	1,354 fps	202 fpe	1.3-inch
Federal 40-gr. FMJ	1,630 fps	236 fpe	1.1-inch
Win. 40-gr. JHP	1,694 fps	256 fpe	1.3-inch
Win. 40-gr. FMJ	1,675 fps	250 fpe	1.1-inch
CCI 40-gr. JHP	1,687 fps	254 fpe	1.0-inch
CCI 40-gr. FMJ	1,705 fps	259 fpe	.75-inch
CCI 30-gr. Mini Mag +V	2,051 fps	280 fpe	1.8-inch

Test gun: 10-inch Contender with T/C 2x-7x scope and mounts.
All velocities recorded 10 feet from the muzzle with Oehler 35P Chronograph.

Accuracy figures are average of five three-round groups from 100-yard benchrest.

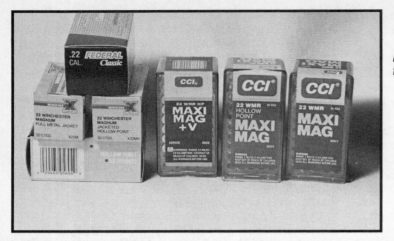

Readily available .22 fodder has bullet weights from 20 to 50 grains with hollowpoints and FMJs.

chambered for the .22 LR produce similar results, with even less reliability. The .32 ACP will throw a 71-grain FMJ at 900 fps for 129 fpe. Expansion is non-existent, however, and a 40-grain .22 mag JHP at 1,250 fps is going to be a better choice.

In a semi-auto, you have to move up to the .380 ACP before you better the .22 magnum, and that round offers more recoil than many novice shooters can handle. In comparison, the magnum rimfire produces more muzzle blast and flash, but recoil is virtually nil. The .380 suffers the ills of the semi-auto under long term storage.

In revolvers, the mag round easily beats the .22 LR, and will offer more penetration and expansion than any .32 S&W factory load. You have to move up to the .32 H&R magnum or the .38 Special before you improve on .22 magnum ballistics. Also, snubbies in those two calibers are not as easy to hit with as is a .22 magnum revolver.

Such guns are readily available. Taurus offers the eight-shot Model 941 in three or four-inch barrel, blue or stainless steel, with adjustable sights. Smith & Wesson has the Model 651, a slick little six-shot number in stainless steel, with a four-inch barrel and adjustable sights, as well as the full-size stainless Model 648 with a six-inch barrel and adjustable sights. A bit larger than required, it's a finely-crafted handgun nonetheless.

Load up a Taurus eight-shot 941, possibly with a staggered loading alternating the 50-grain Federal JHP with the 40-grain

CCI solid, and you've got a personal protection arm. Not difficult to control, it will outperform any .22 LR, .25 ACP, .32 ACP (with the possible exception of the Winchester Silvertip round) and any .32 S&W Long in factory loadings. Ammo also is significantly less expensive, which hopefully might encourage an occasional bit of much-needed practice.

Back in 1972, I was badge #16 with the Armed Forces Police Detachment at the Subic Bay Naval Station, Republic of the Philipines. My beat was Olongapo City, right outside the main gate, and probably one of the "liveliest" military police beats in the world at the time. All shipping traffic to and from Vietnam passed through.

It was lively enough that the AFPs routinely kept two clean, pressed uniforms in their locker at the station. The chances of making it through a 12-hour shift without our original garb being sullied by mud, blood and beer weren't much good, and we did favor a crisp appearance.

One night, I was riding the Investigative Unit — a two-man car with one AFP and an Olongapo City policeman. Our function was to investigate incidents involving Americans and Philipine Nationals (PNs), but as often happens in law enforcement work, we handled whatever came up.

Late in the shift, a young Philipino woman ran up to Rolli's side of the van and told him there had been a shooting. She directed us to one of the little stilt huts along the river bank.

A young male PN had taken two in the chest and was quite dead. One round had exited without much indication of

This trim 10-inch Contender and Uncle Mike's holster make a fine field platform for the smallest magnum.

The 50-grain Federal load has accuracy and power for 125-yard shots on game the size of bobcats or turkeys.

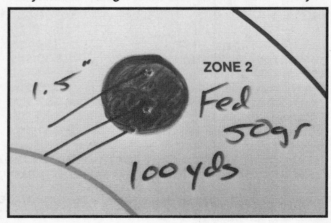

This .22 J-frame, six-shot Smith & Wesson Model 651 with its four-inch barrel makes an excellent trail gun.

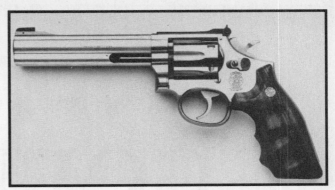

Wheelgunners can get the .22 magnum in the handsome Smith & Wesson Model 648. It's powerful and accurate.

CHART #2

.22 magnum performance from four-inch S&W Model 651

LOAD	VELOCITY/fps	ENERGY/fpe
Federal 40-gr. FMJ	1,120	111
Federal 50-gr. JHP	1,040	120
Win. 40-gr. JHP & FMJ	1,200	127
CCI 40-gr. JHP & FMJ	1,250	139
CCI 30-gr. +V	1,500	150

All velocities taken 10 feet from the muzzle with Oehler 35P Chronograph. Energy figures computed from tables in Speer #11 reloading manual.

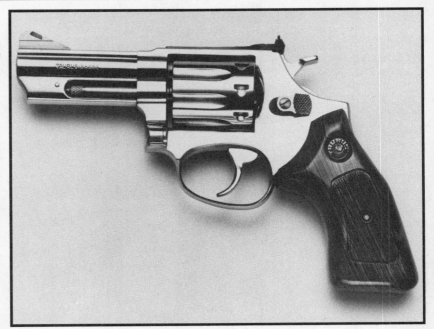

Taurus' eight-shot Model 941 is usually overlooked as a self-defense gun. It will outperform a number of other cartridges.

expansion, and the second appeared to be lodged in the spinal column. Both rounds appeared to have passed through the heart.

A couple of beat cops already had the shooter, and the gun, and I was somewhat surprised to find the gun was a Ruger Single Six Convertible stuffed with 40-grain Winchester .22 magnum solids.

Two years later, while stationed as a smallarms marksmanship instructor at Florida's Jacksonville Naval Air Station, I got another look at the .22 magnum.

I was moonlighting as a special deputy with the Jacksonville Sheriff's Department, assigned to provide one-on-one guard functions with whatever prisoners were brought into University Hospital.

My charge one night was a young member of the local gene pool who had chosen burglary as a career. He apparently wasn't too good at it, because in addition to a growing arrest record, he seemed to have miscalculated his latest target and run into an irate homeowner who popped him in the upper arm with a .22 magnum hollow-point. The doctors weren't certain he'd regain full use of the arm. A pity.

Two incidents don't make an ironclad case for the .22 magnum in a self-defense role, but they impressed me! As overlooked as it often is, our miniest magnum can be an exceedingly useful cartridge in an astonishingly wide range of roles.

GUNFIGHTER COUNTRY

The National Tactical Invitational Is Where The Real Gunslingers Show Their Stuff

By Frank James

Photos by Waldo Lydecker

HAS IPSC — formally, the International Practical Shooting Confederation — gone too far with scoped guns and open front holsters? Many obviously think so. The U.S. Practical Shooting Association has even put new emphasis on a recently introduced "limited" class featuring non-compensated, iron sighted pistols. But are race pistols the only thing wrong with today's sanctioned practical pistol shooting?

Gunfighting is a subject too indiscreet to discuss in some circles and some feel it really isn't germane to the average

Skip Gochenour, an investigator and one of the tournament organizers, briefs shooters on the few rules of the National Tactical Invitational.

citizen. But wasn't IPSC created in the first place to foster further developments in the art and science of firearms self-defense?

Plainly great advancements have been made and the scope-sighted, compensated, ultra-high capacity pistols in the hands of the IPSC Master Class shooters clearly demonstrate the gains made, in terms of both speed and accuracy, but how do the lessons learned in IPSC apply to today's streets?

Equally important, has the training for today's law enforcement officers kept pace with the lessons learned on these same dark streets?

The National Tactical Invitational is a new pistol match that tries to test and challenge each competitor in a different manner than the usual IPSC match. It is a contest designed to test tactics — street tactics.

That was the motivating logic behind the second National Tactical Invitational pistol match held in June, 1992, near Harrisburg, Pennsylvania.

The National Tactical Invitational came from the thoughts and labor of three people; Skip Gochenour, Chuck Davis and

Walt Rauch. All have carried, or are carrying a gun on a daily basis, either as police officers, government agents or criminal investigators. None of them felt satisfied with the commonly encountered firearms training in terms of real life threats, or the techniques stressed in today's different handgun competitions.

The problem is that much of today's competition places an emphasis on equipment, and not on the reasoning, or the individual's reaction to completely unknown or unpredictable situations. Even the judgment of the shooter in many contests is never called into question. He usually is told what to do, then graded on how quickly he does it and the degree of accuracy he exercised with his shooting while doing it.

In other words, IPSC shooting often gives lip service to the concept of solving a problem while equipped with a gun. However, real-life, lethal-force encounters don't provide the shooter with a scenario walk-through prior to the encounter, or even allow the competitor advance knowledge of what the various engagement distances will be. More importantly, the number of adversaries, what they are shooting and where they

Dick Thomas competed in the event despite being on crutches. Instead of moving to each position, he engaged all the targets from the start position.

are located aren't known either.

Make no mistake, IPSC has been a great benefit to the shooting sports and firearms training, both in terms of improved equipment and improved shooting techniques, but Davis, Rauch, and Gochenour wanted to explore self-defense firearms and tactics further than what had been done previously, at the same time, heading off in a new direction. The National Tactical Invitation match is that new direction.

One of Skip Davis' pet peeves is that most police officers only do what they are told to do. They are not taught how to *react*. "For example," he explains, "We don't *do* on demand. We do our drills on direction!"

Using this observation as a guide, it was obvious to these three men that new and unusual targets were needed to avoid foreseeable responses. Skip Gochenour went to Dave Powley, a member of the S.I.G.H.T.S. gun club near West Shore, Pennsylvania, and described what he wanted in a reactive metal target. (S.I.G.H.T.S. was also the host pistol range for the National Tactical Invitation match.)

The "Skipper" target was the result. This steel target is every bit as innovative as the Pepper Popper and certainly more unpredictable. In terms of common self-defense sidearms and calibers, it takes, at the minimum, two well-placed hits to neutralize this target. For instance, it was not uncommon for competitors using 9x19mm Glocks or Brownings to hit the target as many as five times before it would fall. Yet, two well-placed hits with a .45 auto usually would drop the steel plate from its perch atop the post — but not always.

Was this real world training? Many veterans think so, because few live targets react the same every time. That's one of the reasons there is so much controversy over the subject of handgun stopping power. Few living things can be predicted to react like a mathematical formula. Training and competition should be unpredictable.

The advantage gained with the Skipper target from a training point of view is the shooter no longer can shoot one or two fast shots and move to the next target. He must respond to the reaction of the target, and this is not something he can anticipate quickly.

Tournament rules stipulate the shooter must make sure he has neutralized the target before engaging the next series of targets. In this sense, the Skipper target places greater premium on observation and follow-through.

But the American Tactical Shooting Association is concerned with more than just creating new steel targets. The match in 1992 consisted of six stages. Some of them didn't

After hitting the mover, this shooter neutralized the two near skippers, reloaded and moved to the next position.

Penalty points are given for not using cover properly and not protecting the chest. The shooter (above) stays low and uses cover as he engages the moving target.

The window station (below) featured ten poppers, five on the right, five on the left. To add to the challenge, this competitor is holding the window open with head.

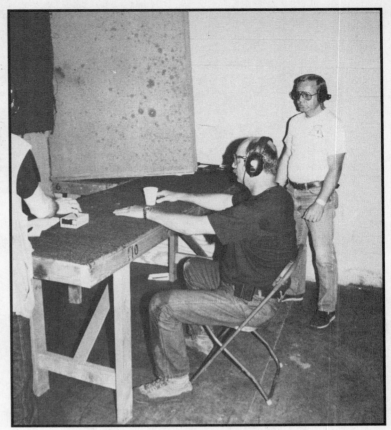

Ken Hackathorn awaits the start signal in the "This is a hold-up" restaurant scenario. Unarmed, the competitor, with his back to the dining area, must search for a gun before engaging the targets.

even involve firearms or, more correctly, conventional firearms. Others took the unarmed contestant into simulated real-world situations that required the individual to find a firearm and engage all the bad guys, and they were not all out in open view.

All of this was more reality oriented than common IPSC shooting, and the biggest single reason for this reality influence was that everything was conducted as a surprise course of fire. There was no advance intelligence, no walk-throughs and no stage briefing.

Going into each stage cold, the individual didn't know how many "shoot" targets there were to be engaged, how many "no-shoot" targets there were to protect — or the target locations. Additionally, all targets wore clothing and had "cartoon" faces. Shoot targets invariably displayed a weapon of some sort, whether it was a picture of a firearm, an edged weapon or some sort of blunt instrument.

It goes almost without saying that for this system to work, only ladies and gentlemen, in the finest definition of the terms, could compete, because to give a fellow competitor advance knowledge of the details on an upcoming course of fire would be more than beyond the rules of chivalry. It would be cheating. It would instill a false sense of confidence that in an identical situation in the real world could cost the officer or his partner dearly.

But it is the surprise course of fire that validates the the American Tactical Shooting Association's claim to reality-based competition. It brings to the surface the mistakes individuals under stress in a lethal force situation commonly perpetrate.

For instance, if the shooter is not pre-programmed to the

The hotel room station begins with the shooter seated and his gun and spare magazine somewhere on the bed.

At the hotel room station, the shooter must carry reloads. This shooter holds a spare magazine.

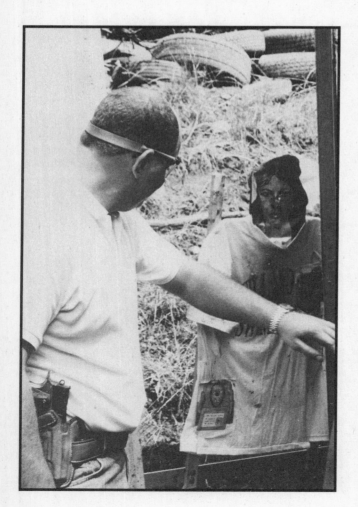

This competitor opened this closet door, saw the muzzle of a double-barreled shotgun and mistakenly shot a cop.

course of fire during a pre-match walk-through, many competitors develop tunnel vision and auditory exclusion — just like in real world gun-fights. They walk past bad guys. They fail to open doors — even small closet doors — to inspect what is on the other side, and if they see a target holding a gun, they shoot it — only to discover the cartoon target is holding a badge in the other hand.

We know all of these things occur in the real world, usually as a result of a sad series of events where good people get hurt.

The first stage of the 1992 match was the "standards" and a little exercise called "windows." The standards were nothing more than three shooting positions, a mover-target and five skipper targets. The exercise was simple: shoot the mover twice, then engage two skippers from the first position. Reload and move to the second position, engaged the mover again and two more skippers. Reload, if needed, and move to the last position where you again engage the mover and the last skipper.

Penalties were given if the shooter exposed the major portion of what would be his own A-zone, while engaging the target or during reloading, so the shooter had to use cover, which, at the second position, was not as high as the average person's knees. The mover always started whenever the shooter reached the shooting position, so the prudent shooter reloaded before leaving the previous shooting position.

Throughout this match, penalties were given for leaving behind essential equipment such as partially loaded magazines or just live rounds of ammunition. Range officer Hersh Gooden had a keen eye for these details.

All reloads had to be tactical reloads, where the shooter had to save his partially spent magazine before reloading. We were told in the only briefing prior to the match that penalties would be assessed if the shooter even allowed a magazine to hit the dirt. Only a few competitors used revolvers, but these shooters were permitted to drop their speedloaders after reloading.

"Windows" was a simple exercise in which the shooter started behind a wall of hard cover. He had to open a window and hold it open while engaging five pepper popper targets on the right, then five on the left. Some of the contestants used their heads on this one, in every respect, and full definition of the phrase. Some questioned real world practicality of the technique, but whatever worked was the rule.

In the "night moves" segment the contestant was disarmed and brought backward into a curtained restaurant scenario. After being seated, he was told there were four bad guys and a hidden gun somewhere behind him. He had three minutes to find the gun and engage the bad guys.

The gun was a five-shot snub nose .38 Special and it was lying on one of the tables. Three of the bad guys were in plain view, but the fourth was hidden in what could be described best as a bathroom stall off the dining room. Many contestants — myself included — failed to investigate the limits of the room and therefore did not find the bathroom-style stalls or the hidden bad guy.

"Room service" was a stage meant to duplicate the average hotel room. Unfortunately, a heavy thundershower the night before had turned this stage into a muddy quagmire that resembled something out of a World War I trench in Flanders. Even with this difficulty (you just imagined you were in a hotel with *really* poor housekeeping), the stage was realistic to the extent the contestant was confronted with a number of unknowns.

People failed to clear closets, because they walked past the door, and when they did open the closet door, they shot both the bad guy and the policeman inside. They didn't shoot bad guy targets laying on the ground in adjoining rooms because they assumed they were shooting-range trash.

Of course, the really interesting part to the whole scenario was the fact the contestant was supposed to be clothed only in a towel.

I carried the pistol and one spare magazine, but since we were not supposed to be wearing clothes — let alone any spare

Using modified Smith & Wessons that fire a laser beam, contestants learn the difficulty of finding and removing the bad guy before being found.

While awaiting their turn, competitors don't discuss a stage with a shooter who hasn't competed.

mag carriers—I shot everything one-handed, while others put the spare magazine in their mouths and shot two-handed. At the start, the thought of doing the same thing briefly came to mind, but I declined on the basis that I might have to shout a verbal command as part of the exercise and wanted to be able enunciate any instructions clearly.

"How do I get out of here?" was an event involving a simulated warehouse where the contestant was admitted, then forced to exit the back of the warehouse as it was being burglarized. It was the contestant's job to survive, but he couldn't shoot the workers still left inside.

This scenario had a "slickster" target that many objected to, as well as its possible real world implications. As the contestant exited the rear door, a trigger on the door would activate a target immediately to the shooter's right that would virtually make it appear out of thin air. Some felt this was improbable, while the match organizers emphasized that many who have worked fugitive squads experienced exactly that phenomenon of fugitives seemingly appearing out of nowhere.

Early in this stage was a wall with a counter opening and two "no-shoot" targets. I passed them by without inspection, because no weapons were shown, but then neither were their hands visible and that was my mistake, because behind these two was a pepper popper that activated other targets down range. I should have come close enough to visually inspect where the hands of the target were, and to see if they were being held hostage by an unseen gunman. This was exactly what the scenario called for. I learned on that one.

One of the best scenarios didn't involve conventional firearms at all. It was also a widow-maker, because only 10 contestants out of a field of 75 contestants successfully completed this course of fire.

It was a laser-tag game with modified Smith & Wesson Model 64 stainless steel revolvers. Each contestant wore a receiver vest as did the bad guy, while the fun-house was filled with innocent bystanders. The objective was to hunt the bad guy down and get him to surrender or to shoot him before he shot you.

Match winner Gary Wistrand probably said it best, after successfully engaging his adversary: "That proved 27 years of law enforcement training wasn't for nothing. I learned that if you only show a little bit of the gun barrel and one eye, he can't shoot you, but you can shoot him."

He also credited many years of barricade shooting as his opponent came out shooting high from behind cover. Wistrand went low barricade, waited, and shot him when he came out again at high barricade. Good training pays off.

The last stage involved a simulated car and was called "Sunday drive." The scenario was similar to what many of us witnessed on the evening news during the '92 Los Angeles riots when criminals overtook a truck, dragged the driver out and beat him to near death. All of this was in the view of a news helicopter hovering overhead.

The car, for reasons that plague every match organizer, turned out at the last minute to be a motorless vehicle made from scrap iron and black pipe, but the targets were superb. The remote control, computer-guided, turning targets provided each shooter with a fast sequence of different events. It was enough to confuse the hell out of anyone. But every veteran of a gunfight I ever have interviewed agreed his gunfight was mass confusion.

All of these surprise courses of fire took each contestant one more step in a different direction. Don't get me wrong, I'm a USPSA member and I believe in IPSC, but I'm also

Recreating a scene from the L.A. Riots, shooters had to leave the vehicle before engaging targets.

The heavy latex shroud over the pepper popper targets enabled all competitors to shoot the falling steel targets at close range. The far targets are computer controlled.

open-minded enough to realize that, as shooters, contestants, and trainers, we should be able to push the envelope a little farther away from the emphasis on gadgets and more toward individual reaction.

The surprise course-of-fire pistol match is a difficult match to organize and orchestrate, but it also neutralizes the issues of gun capacity, sights and the type of holster, because a high-capacity pistol offers little advantage if you walk past unseen targets.

This match forced each competitor to confront his mistakes and analyze what he personally did wrong on a reactive course of fire.

The organizers are onto something extremely positive, and are right when they say we don't do what the situation demands, but what we are instructed to do. Often this is for no other reason than simple muscle training.

One of the goals is to increase the speed of our thinking and thereby our reaction and response times to unpredictable scenarios.

Hopefully, the American Tactical Shooting Association will grow and hold more surprise courses of fire with these unpredictable targets. Everyone will learn more about this craft, about himself and about tactics.

That's the reason it can be described as a Gunfighter's Tournament.

For further information contact: American Tactical Shooting Association, c/o Walt Rauch, P.O. Box 510, Lafayette Hill, PA 19444.

WHAT IS A RACE GUN?

By Chris Christian

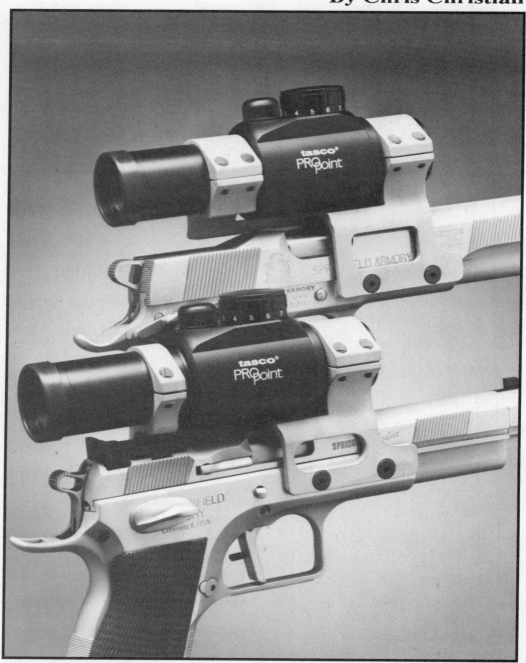

Race gun at top is strictly optically sighted. Gun at bottom allows shooter to quickly remove scope and shoot iron sights. The shooter can decide which system serves his needs best.

These State-Of-The-Art Blasters Are More Than Just Custom Handguns!

IF THERE is a single identifying characteristic associated with the growing sport of action pistol shooting, it is the Race Gun — that sleek, highly refined, hand-built creation that seemingly sports every conceivable bell and whistle — and some that seem totally inconceivable!

For most shooters, such handguns bear little in common with those we own and use. In fact, some of the more futuristic examples of the breed would look more natural in the hands of Luke Skywalker than those of their present owners.

Yet, for those who derive their income from competitive handgun shooting, there is an excellent reason for their existence.

"What we call a race gun," explains Mike Plaxco, "is nothing more than a state-of-the-art competition package that is designed to take every advantage allowed a competitor."

Plaxco does know a few things about "competitive advantages."

As one of the country's — make that the world's — top action shooters, he has won just about every title worth winning — some more than once. Currently, he "races" guns full-time as a member of Team Smith & Wesson, and teaches others to do the same at his own shooting school, the Plaxco Academy (21621 Roland Cut-Off, Roland, AR 72135).

For Plaxco, a race gun is more than just an exotic toy. It is a working tool; a precise one.

"A race gun is basically like a blueprinted automobile engine," he continues. "What you are doing is paying the gunsmith to hand-fit each part for maximum reliability and accuracy."

One reason hand-fitting is required is tolerance stack. Mass-

World class shooter Mike Plaxco depends upon state-of-the-art tools as a member of Team Smith & Wesson. But he is quick to point out that just having a batch of accessories on a handgun does not make it a first class race gun.

produced parts all exist within a certain tolerance range. That's the only way mass production will work. Unfortunately, if four or five interrelated parts that must fit and function together all happen to fall to one side of the tolerance range, they may not function, even though they are "within spec."

"If your slide," Plaxco explains, "has .005-inch tolerance, your frame has .005-inch tolerance and your barrel has .015-inch — and if all of those tolerances just happen to be on the extreme left of their range — you may have to take the rear sight all the way to the right, then find the gun shoots still to the left. That's how you can get a lemon gun — or car — right from the factory."

While all the top-ranked shooters work hard to enjoy the fruits of their labors, one fruit they try to avoid is the lemon!

"The primary concern for a race gun," states Plaxco, "is reliability. It must be 100 percent and the gun must shoot dirty, as well as clean. If you can't run the gun past 2,000 rounds without cleaning it, something is wrong."

With reliability assured, it is time to start adding the features that will aid a competitor. And, not every exotic accessory may be an aid.

"One thing people have to be careful with regarding race guns," explains Plaxco, "is the natural tendency to make a change or add a component in the hope that it helps. Any change must be one that gains you some advantage, or it becomes a disadvantage. Some of the more exotic things being done to race guns today actually compromise reliability and longevity, and that really isn't a gain."

According to Plaxco, a perfect example of that is the ubiquitous extended slide release.

"A lot of shooters have these, and most of the savvy ones are taking them off. Some of these are heavy enough to slide-lock the gun before the magazine is empty, and some aftermarket parts are suspect as to quality. And, they are not needed anyway.

"We have found that — for a right-handed shooter — when you reload the magazine, your left thumb is right there, so it is no problem to learn to depress the factory slide release with it. Learning proper technique then allows you to remove a part that is not needed, and can only contribute to a lack of reliability. That is the essence of a real race gun."

Here's how Plaxco would set up a semi-auto race gun:

Bevelled mag well: Developed in the days of the .45 ACP (with a straight magazine) bevelling the well and adding a funnel allowed shooters to get the magazine into the gun quicker. It is debatable if that feature is needed on the double-stacked magazine guns in common use today. There's already a pretty big funnel in the frame itself.

Magazine pad: "Contrary to some opinions," Plaxco notes, "these do not provide protection for the magazine when dropped from the gun onto the ground. In fact, the added weight makes the mag hit the ground harder and increases risk of damage. Their purpose is to let the shooter seat the magazine positively by extending the base beyond flush with the gun butt."

Raised beavertail grip safety: This is an advantage,

Race guns that work for men shooters may not be the best bet for a smaller woman like S&W shooter Judy Woolley.

Rob Leatham runs the Master's Action Event with a lightweight, Minor caliber race gun. However, this gun would be totally inappropriate for an IPSC competition.

Above, compensators are a key to reducing recoil. Note ejected case above Allan Fulford's sight. Yet, action is cycled and the gun is back on target. Below, IPSC guns must be heavier to handle thousands of rounds.

since it can bring your hand in closer alignment with the bore and thus reduce muzzle rise. But, some shooters with large hands cannot shoot one, because the slide hits the web of his hand.

"Simply adding race gun features to your gun is counter-productive if the gun doesn't fit," Plaxco states.

In that case, the shooter would be better off with a standard beavertail safety, since that race gun feature is an aid to consistent shooting grip and comfort.

Ambidextrous safety: An asset in any competition that requires weak hand shooting; it's not a factor in those that don't.

Oversized or extended magazine release: "Some of these," Plaxco claims, "are so large that they can interfere with your shooting grip and even cause you to dump the magazine in the middle of a string accidentally." While Plaxco does use one, it is not overly large. He feels this part should be fitted to the shooter.

Squared trigger guard: In years past, a shooting grip that put one or more fingers on the trigger guard was popular with some shooters and the squared trigger guard became the mark of the race gun. Today, most shooters have discovered, and most instructors teach, that better control is achieved with the off-hand wrapped around the grip, making the squared (or hooked) trigger guard about as useful as those proverbial "female glands on a male hog."

Mud flap: One of the stranger automotive terms associated with race guns, this is a shield (frame-mounted or integral with the thumb safety itself) that prevents the thumb from contracting the slide during cycling. If that occurs with light minor caliber loads, it can cause a jam.

Oversized thumb safety: Many shooters find that resting the thumb of the master hand on the thumb safety provides a more comfortable grip and precludes the possibility of the thumb accidentally knocking the safety on during recoil. An aid, it's the reason for the existence of the mud flap.

Fitting the gun: Just as an experienced shotgunner will want his gun fit to his body, so will the race gunner want his pistol fit to his hand. This is done by selecting the length of the trigger (up to and including one that is adjustable for length of pull), the height and width of the beavertail, a flat or arched mainspring housing (if a Colt Government Model) or modifications to the backstrap on the Tanfoglio guns (including the P9, TZ, Witness, et al) and even the width of the grips.

Combined with the other controls, this should produce a handgun that becomes a part of the shooter's hand. Checkering or stippling the front and back straps is another possible aid that should be done for function rather than appearance. Plaxco, in fact, deliberately dulls the diamond points on his checkering, because it is more comfortable.

Once the gun is comfortable, functional, reliable and hand-fitted for accuracy, the matters of compensator and sight

This Tanfoglio race gun features a heavy duty scope mount that secures scope fore and aft of the adjustment turrets.

system need to be addressed.

"The compensator," explains Plaxco, "is an important part of the high-tech competition gun, because it affords a reduction in muzzle rise and allows the shooter to deliver accurate multiple shots quickly."

But, not all compensators are created equal.

"A common misconception," Plaxco continues, "is that a compensator works due to jet propulsion of gases escaping upward out of the ports to drive the muzzle down. Not so. The reason an effective comp works is due to the flat area on the front plate of the compensator. When the gases escaping the barrel hit that flat area, instead of keeping the gun from going up, this impact actually pushes the gun forward. The more flat surface available at the front of the compensator, the more effective the compensator will be."

Also, the smaller the diameter of the exit hole, the more effective the comp. Plaxco feels that the best compromise is .008-.010-inch overbore diameter, but the exit hole must be perfectly centered with the bore.

"Ideally," he states, "you want to use all of the gases around the bullet and have none of the gases follow the bullet out of the comp. Any gas that follows the bullet out is lost in terms of redirection to reduce muzzle rise and actually contributes to it. In effect, it works against the comp. In multi-chambered comps, the first chamber usually will catch most of the gas and

the second should get the rest. Beyond two chambers, I question whether there is any true advantage in regard to utilizing the gas.

"The heavier comp," Plaxco adds, "can be a disadvantage, because the extra weight on the muzzle end can make it harder to stop and start the gun on multiple targets and it can cause more wear on the muzzle/slide/bushing fit and put more pressure on the hood and lugs. That will make the gun shoot loose more quickly."

Another factor is that the more gas there is to work with, the greater the degree of effectiveness from a well designed comp. That is one reason the majority of contemporary race guns are chambered for such high-pressure rounds as the .38 Super, 9x21 and .356 TSW. The amount of gas produced by the venerable .45 ACP will not produce the same degree of reduction in muzzle rise, and adds to the problem with a heavier bullet that also increases recoil.

Yet, any of the above calibers can make the Major power factor easily. Not surprisingly, the top shooters pick the ones offering the greatest advantage.

Sighting systems: In years past, the venerable Bo-Mar iron sight was the first choice of most competitors. In terms of trouble-free operation, they still are a popular choice, especially at the club level. In the rarified atmosphere of top level competition, however, that is not the case.

Custom accessories from European American Armory show the wide range of components available for their race guns.

"If you look at those people who are winning in competition," says Plaxco, "the number using iron sights is a small percentage and it will become less. For a shooter who has mastered the fundamentals, shifting to optics will increase his speed and accuracy once he learns how to use them." And, it seems, if one can keep them functioning.

"Optics haven't caught up with race gun technology yet," Plaxco admits. "I'm speaking of the electronic red dot sights that are the best choice for IPSC-style matches.

"Right now, we have $3,000 to $5,000 race guns mounting $250 optics. There doesn't seem to be the demand for the scope makers to gear up to build a high-end optical unit. Yet, the gun is no better than its optics."

Part of that problem stems from the sheer number of rounds race gunners fire. That can be 100,000 a year!

There also is a significant difference in the recoil harmonics generated by a handgun, as opposed to rifle or shotgun. Optics that might live happily for years on a long gun can have a short lifespan in IPSC-style handgun competition.

One way to help enhance the reliability of optics is through "scope doctoring."

"We call this 'hotrodding a scope'," Plaxco explains. "Basically, the scope is gone through completely and all internal wiring joints are hard-soldered, then coated with a sealing compound. As the gun recoils, the wires flex slightly each time, and as we all know, if you flex a wire too much it will break. Sometimes, the actual sight adjustments themselves are beefed up. The whole point is to try to bullet-proof the scope for durability."

Some scope makers are attempting to address that problem. Gilmore Sports Concepts' (5949 S. Garnett, Tulsa, OK 74146) Red Leader line of red dot sights features a number of "hotrodding" steps in the manufacturing process.

Another way to help keep optics in action is with the proper scope mount. A number of mounts on the market only secure the scope at one point — normally ahead of the adjustment turrets — and scopes thus mounted seem to have a significantly higher malfunction rate than scopes secured with two

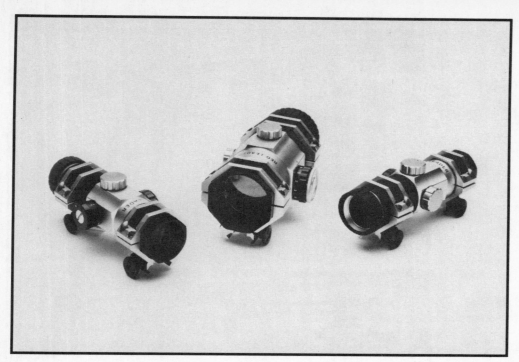

Breakage is a problem for sights. These Gilmore Red Leader models are beefed up for serious competition.

This no frills auto is a race gun if it provides the competitor with every advantage allowed for the match he is shooting.

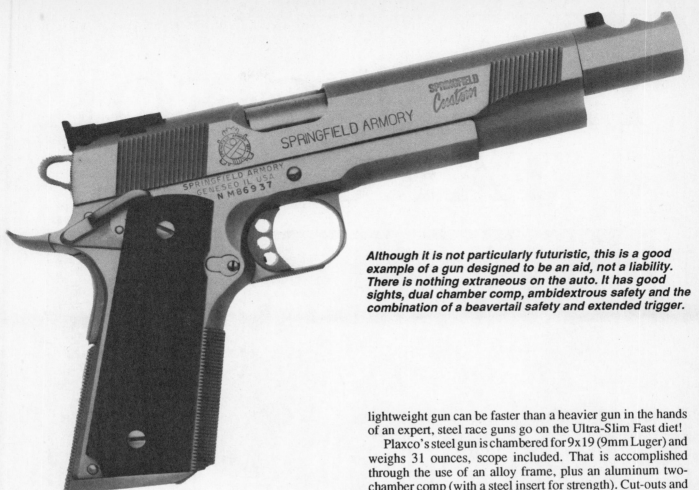

Although it is not particularly futuristic, this is a good example of a gun designed to be an aid, not a liability. There is nothing extraneous on the auto. It has good sights, dual chamber comp, ambidextrous safety and the combination of a beavertail safety and extended trigger.

rings — fore and aft of the turret.

Still, optics will experience a larger number of malfunctions than will iron sights. "Most of the serious competitors keep a working inventory of 10 to 20 scopes," says Plaxco. "It's the price we pay for the advantage optical sights give us."

The most important factor to consider in a race gun is exactly what kind of race you'll be running! "A race gun," Plaxco states, "is built to maximize all of the legal opportunities available to a competitor for that particular match. Because of that, a race gun for one match may not be a race gun for another match."

Plaxco cites his own "working battery" of S&W Performance Shop race guns as an example. "In a Steel Challenge-type match," he explains, "speed is an advantage. And, we use light loads. The one I use drives a 9mm 115-grain bullet at about 950 fps."

As a point of comparison, a factory 9mm 115-grain load will clock at about 1150 fps.

"The reason for the light load," he continues, "is that they are allowed, they reduce recoil and by keeping the bullet at subsonic velocities, we can hear it hit the plates (which do not fall in this type of match) much more easily than with a load that produces a crack when it breaks the sound barrier. The load offers an advantage, and we build the gun around it."

Given the fact that the light load is used, and that a lightweight gun can be faster than a heavier gun in the hands of an expert, steel race guns go on the Ultra-Slim Fast diet!

Plaxco's steel gun is chambered for 9x19 (9mm Luger) and weighs 31 ounces, scope included. That is accomplished through the use of an alloy frame, plus an aluminum two-chamber comp (with a steel insert for strength). Cut-outs and flutes on the slide trim more ounces, as does the titanium scope mount. Metal also is relieved in non-stress areas to further reduce weight. Some common race gun features are also missing.

"Reloading in the Steel Challenge is not a factor," he notes, "so I don't need a larger mag well. You don't shoot weak hand, so the ambidextrous safety goes. Ditto an oversize magazine release."

When Plaxco shifts to a Major caliber IPSC gun, so do the requirements for a race gun.

"The Major loads used in IPSC would beat that steel gun to death," he continues, "so we use a different race gun."

Chambered for the high intensity .356 TSW (a 9x21-1/2) this gun tips the scales at 46 ounces with its steel frame and comp, ambidextrous safety (weak hand shooting required) funnelled mag well (got to reload fast in IPSC), not to mention heavier scope mounts, oversized magazine release and a general beefing up for long term durability with Major caliber loads.

"The two matches are different in the rules and requirements," Plaxco notes. "So are the race guns we use."

The same also would apply to a Bianchi-type match, a bowling pin match or the Action Event at the Masters…or any other match.

"In the old days," Plaxco grins, "we tried to use one basic race gun for everything. Nowadays, that won't work."

Which makes today's race gun only as good as the race you are running!

TESTING FOR TARGETS

By Chris Christian

Author checks groups fired with the Vindicator and Model 586. He was impressed with their accuracy.

MORE THAN a few shooters will tell you revolvers are passe as target arms. Nothing, however, could be further from the truth. Revolvers remain quite popular and, in some cases, are more effective than semi-autos.

This is certainly true in the case of metallic silhouette competition. Magnum revolvers have the power and the accuracy to drop 200-meter rams. Few semi-autos do. You'll also find a lot of wheelguns on the line in NRA action-style matches. The prestigious Bianchi Cup is literally dominated by double-action revolvers and there's a good reason for it.

In this game, speed is important — but accuracy is final. Even top shooters, whose careers were built with comped semi-autos, have found the long, smooth double-action revolver trigger pull affords them greater trigger control under

stress — and hence better scores — than does the lighter SA auto trigger.

That may sound contradictory, but, when guys like Mike Enos and Rob Leatham shift to double-action revolvers for the Bianchi Cup, you can bet there's something to it! That's one reason why revolvers are also extremely popular at bowling pin matches.

Where revolvers really come into there own, however, is at the grassroots level — local club matches. Again, there's an excellent reason for it.

Foremost may well be economy. A top-quality revolver can be purchased for notably less than a standard "service-grade" auto pistol. Out of the box, the revolver will offer a significant edge in accuracy and may require nothing more than a trigger job and a new set of grips to be competition

The E.A.A Vindicator is Compared To The Proven Smith & Wesson Model 586

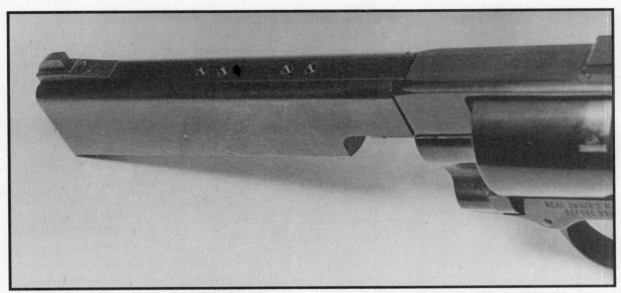

The barrel shroud on the E.A.A. Vindicator is drilled and tapped for Weaver bases. Attaching a scope or LED sight is a snap. The bottom of the shroud is drilled and tapped for E.A.A. accessory barrel weights.

ready. Semi-autos generally need some serious tuning.

Should one desire further customization, bolt-on accessories are much easier to install on a revolver and less expensive. Wheelguns are also much easier on cartridge cases, which gets you more reloads per shell. They are not nearly as finicky concerning fodder as are the self-feeders.

No, wheelguns have not gone the way of the passenger pigeon!

Which may be the reason European American Armory (P.O.Box 3498, Bright Station, Hialeah, FL 33013) decided the time was right to introduce a double-action revolver designed and intended strictly for competitive use.

The EAA Vindicator is a six-shot double-action revolver available in .22 LR, .38 Special and .357 magnum. Offered only in a six-inch barrel length, EAA makes no bones about the gun's intended use. Printed in bold capital letters in the instruction manual is the following: *Please understand this gun is designed for the serious competition shooter and is not designed as a carry gun or home defense gun. EAA offers other products that meet the requirements of home defense or carry gun."*

When you state your intentions that clearly, you invite comparison, and what better way to evaluate the new Vindicator than to compare it directly with a revolver that already has proved itself a winner in top-level competition — the Smith & Wesson model 586.

For those few shooters who may not be familiar with the

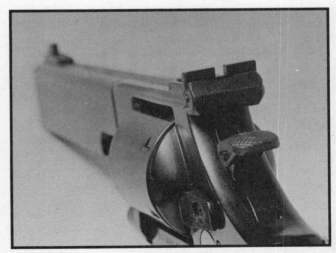

The Vindicator's rear sight is adjustable for windage and elevation. Author preferred it to the S&W sight.

S&W 586, it was introduced some years back as a slightly beefed-up version of the company's famous Model 19. That gun, a K-frame model, had enjoyed long popularity with competitors, lawmen and sportsman. It was discovered, however, that continued use of full-house .357 magnum loads shortened the life of this medium-frame gun.

Smith & Wesson's solution was to beef up the frame, thus

The E.A.A. Vindicator (top) and Smith &Wesson Model 586 are similar in size, weight and balance.

creating the new L-frame, while keeping the handling qualities that had made the K-frame guns so desirable. The intention was to produce a mid-size service revolver capable of digesting a steady diet of full-house .357 loads. They did that, but possibly through some sort of Grand Cosmic Intervention, they also created an uncannily accurate and smooth target-grade revolver. Indeed, it wasn't more than a couple of years after its introduction that Californian John Pride took one — literally — out of the box, added a few bolt-on accessories and won the Bianchi Cup!

Since then, the gun has earned an enviable reputation among wheelgun aficionados. The Model 586 in my own personal battery has proved itself to be one of the most accurate mass-produced double-action revolvers I have ever fired!

How good is the new Vindicator? Here's how it compared directly against my 586, (a straight stock gun with no after-factory work), in the key points:

Durability is impossible to measure accurately in the limited number of rounds (about 150) fired from each gun during the course of the tests. But some opinions — and that's all they can be called — can be ventured based upon common sense and observation.

The S&W is designed for continued use with 46,000 CUP .357 magnum loads. The .38 Special Vindicator model supplied by EAA for testing is intended to handle loads in the 18,900 CUP class. Forcing cone, bolt hand and cylinder of the S&W are noticeably beefier than those on the Vindicator. Both guns are constructed of strong, modern steels with quality springs and should last a long time with appropriate loads.

Durability: Smith & Wesson, on a hunch.

The beefy forcing cone on the Model 586 (above) is intended for full-house .357 magnum loads.

The Vindicator's forcing cone (below) is more lightly constructed than the Model 586 and is only intended for target level .38 Special loads.

Bullets used for test loads were (from left) Speer 148-grain BBWC, Speer 158-grain swaged SWC, NBC cast 180-grain FP and the Federal 38A factory round. They delivered fine accuracy in both guns.

Reliability: The S&W 586 used in this test already had digested several thousand rounds and was well broken in. The Vindicator, fresh from the factory, did develop a glitch the first time I put it through sustained rapid fire. The cylinder tightened up on the ejector rod bushing causing the trigger pull to increase.

Removing that assembly, cleaning and lubing it stopped the problem. I should have done that before the test and can't really blame the gun for it.

I did notice, however, that the cylinder/ejector rod/bushing assembly is fitted rather tightly. The cylinder chambers are also "tighter" than those on the Smith. A fired case from the Smith cannot be inserted in any of them.

Tolerance that tight, combined with normal powder and lead fouling have the potential to create reliability problems if one neglects proper cleaning. My Smith 586 has never bobbled.

Reliability: A nod to the Smith, on another hunch.

Double-Action Trigger: S&W revolvers are legendary for their fine double-action pulls. Even if they are poor from the factory, virtually any semi-competent gunsmith can slick them up. The good smiths can make them incredible. On my Brownell's trigger-pull gauge, the factory pull on my Smith measured 9.75 pounds, with the distinctive S&W hesitation many revolver shooters, including this one, prefer at the end of the pull.

The Vindicator trigger measured 13.5 pounds, with the same S&W hesitation. In reading the instruction manual, I discovered the trigger pull is adjustable. Removing the grips gives access to an adjustment screw located on the left side of the frame just behind the trigger guard.

I followed the instructions to lighten it. It "felt" somewhat lighter, but only showed a one-pound decrease on the scale. It didn't compare to the 586.

DA trigger pull: Clear winner, S&W.

SA trigger pull: The Smith measured 3.5 pounds. The Vindicator measured 2.9 pounds and was just as crisp. The Vindicator also featured an adjustable trigger stop with a separate locking set-screw. It's a better single-action trigger.

SA trigger: Clear winner, Vindicator.

Sights: My 586 features the standard black S&W K-frame rear sight and their clever four-position front sight. This allows you to change the elevation of the front sight to four adjustable, pre-set positions simply by rotation of a wheel on the sight to bring the desired position to bear. It's handy, allowing me to sight the gun in for four different loads and dial that load in without changing the rear sight setting. I love it!

The Vindicator features a standard Patridge front sight retained with a single Allen-head screw, and an excellent rear sight that presents a Bo-Mar-like solid sight picture.

Both rear sights are fully adjustable for windage and elevation, but the sight picture on the Vindicator, because of the sharper rear sight, was more positive than the Smith.

Unfortunately, there was not enough downward elevation adjustment in the Vindicator rear sight to center the groups at point of aim. The best I could get was about 3.5 inches above point of aim at 25 yards. A call to EAA revealed that they do not, at this time, have higher front sights — which is what the gun needed for this shooter. Still, it would be a simple matter for a good smith to build it up.

For me, the ideal set up would be the S&W four-position front sight with the EAA rear. But, since I'm comparing factory guns, I'd have to say the Vindicator offered a sharper sight picture.

Sights: Advantage, Vindicator — with a possible trip to a gunsmith.

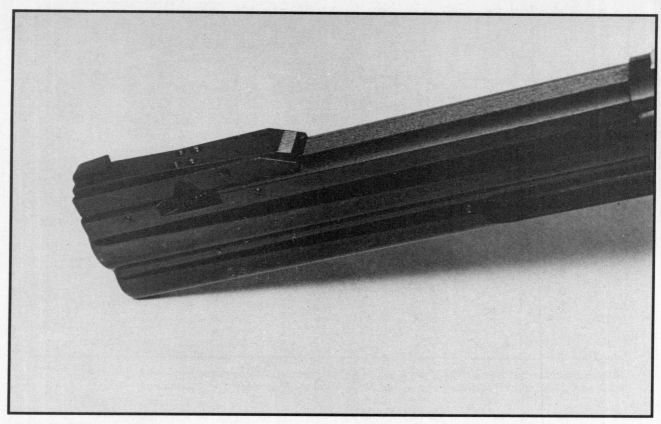

Author has a lot of admiration for the Smith & Wesson four position front sight. The gun can be zeroed for four different loads (or ranges) and switched from one to another without adjusting the rear sight.

Grips: The S&W featured their standard target grips. Most shooters replace them as a matter of course, and there are plenty of good aftermarket grips for this gun.

The Vindicator has an abbreviated stud-type frame and used Hogue-style slip-on grips. Smooth, with well-designed finger grooves, they were more comfortable and offer better control. No aftermarket grips exist that I know of. But, if a shooter found these uncomfortable, the stud-type frame gives a custom grip maker much wider latitude in fitting custom grips than does the full square butt frame of the Smith.

Grips: Slight advantage, Vindicator.

Accessories: Obtaining bolt-on parts for the S&W — scope mounts, grips, different trigger, hammer and sight configurations — is easy. The gun's been around long enough that such items are readily available, The Vindicator is too new for that, so they thoughtfully include much of what you might want with the gun.

As the test model came from EAA, the top of the detachable barrel shroud is drilled and tapped with four threaded holes that look like they'd mate up prefectly with Weaver bases. The Smith doesn't have that.

The bottom of the barrel shroud has three large holes drilled and tapped for the installation of barrel weights that should be available from EAA by the time you read this. I've already mentioned the Vindicator's adjustable trigger stop.

Some shooters like wide triggers, some like narrow triggers. My S&W features a smooth, narrow trigger. The Vindi-

cator has a narrow, slightly grooved trigger. But, a detachable trigger shoe — with countersunk screw holes — comes with the latter gun. So does a hammer shoe that slips over the narrow hammer via a set screw and retaining roll pin. You can buy these accessories for the Smith. They come with the vindicator.

Accessories: Clear winner, Vindicator.

Load versatility: The S&W is chambered for .357 magnum and will handle all .38 Special loads. The Vindicator is intended for standard, not Plus P, .38 "minor" caliber loads. That would seem to give the nod to the Smith, but maybe not.

A look at Table #1 shows that the velocities of the loads tested were up to 40 feet per second lower in the Smith. This is due to the longer magnum chamber and is common when firing .38 Special loads through a .357.

What it means is simple: To achieve the same velocities as the Vindicator, the Smith would require somewhere between .3 and .5 additional grains of powder per load. More cost, more recoil.

If you are only using Minor caliber (120 to 125 Power Factor) loads, the Vindicator is a better bet. If you may need to make Major (170 to 175 PF) or may want more punch for a bowling pin match, the Smith is the choice.

Load versatility: You pick!

Accuracy: Accuracy testing was conducted from a sand-bagged rest on my 25-yard backyard range. All firing was

The trigger adjustment screw on the E.A.A. Vindicator does lighten the trigger pull, but it does not compare with the trigger adjustment features on Smith & Wesson Model 586.

Table #1		
	S&W 586	**EAA Vindicator**
Load:	**Accuracy/Velocity/Power Factor**	**Accuracy/Velocity/Power Factor**
Federal 38A	1.45/768/113.6	1.53/785/116
Load #1	1.51/790/124.8	1.47/829/130.9
Load #2	1.54/841/124.4	1.46/871/128.9
Load #3	1.41/793/134	1.44/805/136

All velocities measured with an Oehler 35P chronograph with start screen set 12 feet from muzzle. All group measurements are center to center.

done single-action, using the standard iron sights. Six groups of six rounds each — a full cylinder — were fired with each load and gun. The largest and smallest groups were tossed out and the remaining four were averaged for center-to-center measurement.

Fodder used consisted of the Federal .38 Special Match Wadcutter (#38A), which has proved itself as a consistently accurate round. I also included three of my match reloads: (#1) The Speer 158-grain swaged SWC over 3.9 grains of Winchester 231; (#2) the Speer 148-grain bevel-based swaged wadcutter ahead of 3.6 grains of 231; (#3) the National Bullet Company's 180-grain cast FP (actually weighs 169 grains) with 3.6 grains of 231.

No attempt was made to tailor "match grade" loads. I grabbed a two-pound coffee can of mixed .38 brass and did not sort by headstamp, trim to uniform length or use cases with a limited number of firings. Whatever came out of the can was fitted with a Federal #100 primer and the bullet seated with a medium roll crimp.

Quite frankly, I expected this to be a cakewalk for the S&W. My experience has been that it is an exceptionally accurate mass-produced revolver. I still consider it that. But, a glance at Table #1 will show the Vindicator to be every bit its equal.

Accuracy: Not a nickel's worth of difference!

Author tested both revolvers at 25 yards, using a rest and standard factory sights. The six-shot group (left) was fired with the Vindicator and Federal .38A. It was typical of the performance of both guns.

Editor's Note: At the time this article was written, the subject handgun was being marketed as the Vindicator. However, European American Arms found that Pachmayer, Ltd. sells a unit with the same name. As a result, the E.A.A. Vindicator is no more. The same gun now is marketed as the E.A.A. "Windicator."

Shootability: You can measure each individual aspect of a firearm, but I don't feel that is a valid indicator of how the unit will preform. A gun is the sum of its parts and they must work smoothly together.

My method of determining how well that occurs is pretty straightforward. With a DA revolver, I load the cylinder and lay out 12 to 18 rounds of extra ammo. In this case, I discovered my HKS S&W K-frame speedloaders worked with both guns, so I loaded two. Putting up a six-inch bullseye at 25 yards, I ran the 18 rounds through the gun double-action just as quickly as I could get the sights on target — about six to eight seconds per cylinder — and get the gun reloaded. If the resulting 18-round group is six inches or less, I feel the gun is pretty "shootable".

The Smith produced a group measuring 5.5 inches horizontally by 4.3 inches vertically. The Vindicator's effort was a circular affair measuring 4.8 inches.

The Smith felt "easier" to shoot, but the Vindicator shot a group that would have scored better. I attribute that to the sights and grips. Had I been using the Herrett grips I normally shoot on the Smith and a better rear sight, I think the Smith — by virtue of its better DA trigger — probably would have won. But, we're comparing factory gun to factory gun.

Shootability: Slight edge to Vindicator.

It would seem the new Vindicator stacks up quite well against the Smith! Both guns share similar size and balance. The S&W weighs 47 ounces, while the EAA offering tips the scales at 44.

The S&W 586 has been discountinued in the configuration I tested, but the stainless steel version — the 686 — is available at a suggested list price of $494. The Vindicator is close at $474.95.

It would appear shooters looking for a competition-grade revolver wouldn't go wrong with either.

SECTION TWO:
NEW HANDGUN TESTS

HANDGUNS
94

E.A.A.'S WITNESS

By Roger Combs

Witness Long Slide pistol, chambered in .45 ACP, is manufactured in Italy by Tanfoglio and is being imported by European American Armory. Witness is available in 9mm, .41 AE, .40 S&W as well as .45 ACP.

IT SEEMS a simple concept: Shoot, hit and knock standard bowling pins off a table. They must fall to the floor or ground to be scored. Almost any centerfire handgun and ammunition may be used; the shooting distance is not that great. The shooter with the quickest, most accurate handgun, firing ammunition with sufficient knock-down power should win. In some matches, mini-pins are shot with .22 rimfire guns. But knocking bowling pins off a table is not that simple.

There are several variables that the competitor is not able to control. That makes bowling pin shoots so much fun and such a challenge. The pins seem to have minds of their own,

and they refuse to cooperate with the shooter. Where they are hit by a bullet, the order in which they are struck and what they do after being hit determines the kind of score the shooter will get. A shooter may be the fastest and the most accurate, but still not have the best score in this type of competition matches.

Bowling pin matches may be shot with either autoloading pistols or revolvers. In most club shoots, auto pistols are the most popular.

Depending upon the rules of the local range, the shooters may or may not be allowed to reload during a round of pin shooting. There may be only five bowling pins on the table

Speed, Accuracy, Power Are Required To Knock Bowling Pins Off The Table.
This Auto Helps!

and the pistol may have 13 or 14 rounds in the magazine — but that may not be enough to knock all the pins off the table. It is not that unusual to see a shooter empty two complete magazines during his run and still have pins on the table.

Bowling pin targets are not limited to five pins lined up on a table. There may be three, six, nine or more pins. Some matches have three or five pins on one level, plus two more pins two feet higher on shelves above the table. Which do you shoot first? Leave the two shelf pins for last so they do not fall down to knock a pin over, but leave it lying on the table? Shoot the first shelf pin and fire fast enough to get the lower table pins out of the way before they can be struck? Shoot in a U pattern? Bowling pin shooting is a simple game, but there is more to it than simply fast, accurate shooting. Considerable luck is involved.

Why bowling pins in the first place? For the answer to that, we have to go back a couple of decades to Michigan and the digs of Richard Davis, president of the company that manufactures Second Chance body armor. About 20 years ago, Davis recalls, he and several other shooters were lamenting all the rules and restrictions governing most competition shooting. It was becoming too complicated. Watching for tiny holes in paper was boring; there should be more action to please shooters and spectators. The targets should fall down when hit, they concluded.

At first, Davis and cohorts tried standing up stiff, laminated body armor. When shot, most of the armor would fall over. However, even when using old sets or manufacturer seconds, body armor targets could get rather expensive. And not everybody had access to such targets.

Through his contacts with Michigan's Walled Lake Police Department, Richard Davis located a supply of used bowling pins and decided to try them as targets. The first competition was fired from 18 feet, then stretched to 25 feet. At that

Staggered-column magazine will hold 10 rounds of .45 ACP ammunition. The EAA Witness auto may be carried in cocked-and-locked mode, with a round in the chamber. Finish is matte blue and chrome.

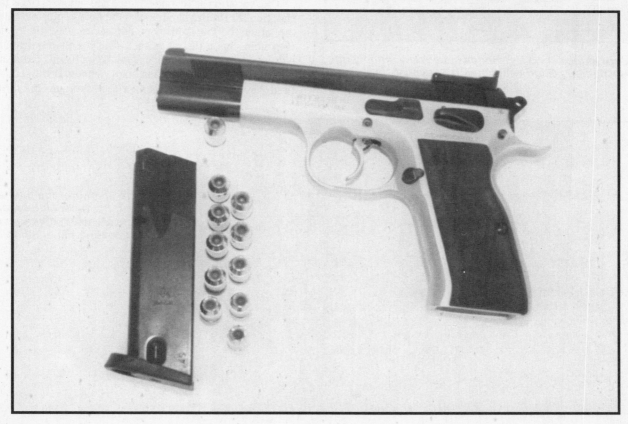

distance, the profile of a bowling pin represents the kill zone of an average human at 25 yards. And bowling pins are universally available at nominal cost.

It was determined early on that the competition would not be out of a holster; there would be no fast-draw and no possibility of an early discharge injuring a shooter. The shooter lines up at a railing with the handgun resting on it

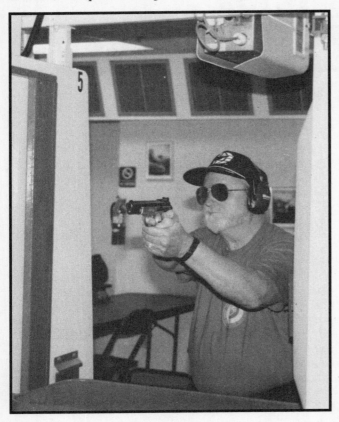

Modern indoor shooting ranges have sound and flying-brass baffles. Good ventilation is essential.

while awaiting the signal. Davis prefers to use the report of a blank round to start the Second Chance Shoot each June in Central Lake, Michigan, but any sound — even a voice command — is satisfactory for local club and range shoots.

Some club managers have tried putting nine pins on the table for the shooters who have large-capacity 9mm pistols. However, it would seem the extra number of rounds is no advantage over the seven or eight-round magazines in a standard Model 1911 .45 ACP pistol, because of the lighter loads of most 9mm ammunition.

The sport has evolved into knocking down five pins with five shots from guns of any caliber. Variations on that pattern are limited only by imagination and money, however. Within the basic concept, one may conjure up all sorts of mutations for bowling pin shoots. Richard Davis has come up with at least 10 variations for his Second Chance Shoot, including several team categories.

Davis breaks down the competition into two types of guns and two types of shooters. Shooters are divided into either Ordinary Standard Shooter (OSS) or Master Blaster (MB). An OSS may be male or female, novice or veteran. Once the shooter has established credentials by finishing at the top of an individual or team event, he or she becomes known as Master Blaster. From then on, whenever the MB shooter competes at the Second Chance, it must be against the higher level of competition. There are not that many Master Blasters, even after nearly 20 years of competition.

The designations refer only to the Second Chance Shoot in Michigan and are not related to any other state or local matches. Some leagues and local shoots establish other competition classifications and/or age groups. Other than the safety restrictions and the bowling pin targets, rules and regulations are held to a minimum.

One variation at Second Chance and other shoots is that of shooting .22 rimfire handguns at the pins, requiring only that the targets be knocked over, not necessarily off the table. Depending upon the range facilities, events requiring shotguns or rifles at longer ranges may be included. Team events may be two or three persons, men, women or mixed. Arms fired may be revolvers, pistols, rifles, shotguns or combina-

This is the line-up of bowling pins as the shooter sees it. For most club or range meets five pins are used, although there is no rule designating the number.

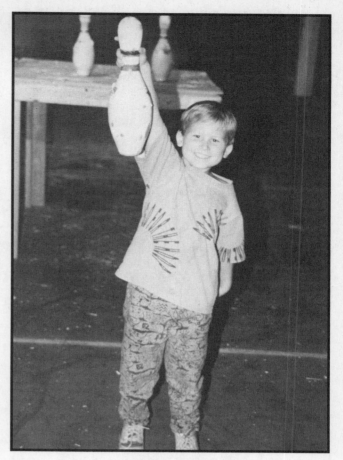

After several rounds, bowling pins bear the scars of hits. At distance of about seven yards, bowling pin presents approximately same target area as human at 25 yards. Hits should be centered to be effective. Seven-year-old Tyler Combs, above, helps re-set pin knocked downed by his father.

tions of any of the above.

Ranges are not restricted to 25 feet. If the competition takes place outdoors, some events may be shot at 90 or 100 yards, but using falling steel plates rather than bowling pins as targets.

The Second Chance shoot defines a stock gun as follows: A semi-auto handgun with a barrel of no more than five inches, and weighing no more than 44 ounces with an empty magazine. Revolvers are limited to barrels of up to 8 3/8 inches and a total unloaded weight of 48 ounces. Barrels may be Mag-na-ported, but extended sights, optical sights, laser beams, extended muzzle brakes and weighted magazines are prohibited. Shooters cannot wear weighted wrist straps, gloves and the like.

A pin gun is described as any gun customized specifically for shooting bowling pins. Handguns in this category can have any barrel length, but the total weight is to be no more than 64 ounces empty. No optical sights or laser beams are allowed, and the shooter is not allowed to add weights to hands or wrists. Pin guns may be either semi-autos or revolvers. Modifications are limited only by imagination and budget.

The novice bowling pin shooter probably will start with whatever handgun he — or she — already has in the cabinet. There is some advantage to having a heavier handgun of at least .38 Special caliber, if a revolver, and at least 9mm if using a pistol. If there is a choice, move up to .357 magnum or .44 magnum in a revolver. Double-action is preferred, but some bowling pin shooters favor .44 magnum single-action revolvers. But there can be no more than one miss for five pins, as reloading is a bit tedious.

Some shooters prefer the large-capacity 9mm pistols. They will not worry so much about missing the pins; they shoot more rounds, faster. Not all competitors agree with that philosophy, but if a 9mm pistol is available, it is a good way to start. Hit in the right place, the pin will fly off the table just as it would if hit with a more powerful round.

Probably the most popular caliber used by most bowling pin shooters is the .45 ACP. It has power, is commonly available from suppliers and a variety of ammunition loads is no problem. There also will be plenty of pistols chambered for the .38 Super, too. Speed, accuracy and power play equal parts when attempting to knock common bowling pins off a table.

Top shooters will clear five pins from a table in less than five seconds; the champions in far less time. A good time for most beginners might be anything under 10 seconds, with four rounds of six or seven seconds each a probable win at a local club shoot. A quick recovery and fast target alignment are essential to quick times. Many beginners will waste a full second in acquiring the target, then lining up the sights for the first shot.

Plenty of practice is essential to overcome this habit. Most pin shoots start with the gun in hand, resting on the bench or on the rail in front of the shooter.

At home, using an empty gun, it is beneficial to practice faster first shot timing again and again. Begin with the movements slow and deliberate, then pick up speed as the muscles and eyes become accustomed to the activity. Concentrate on sight alignment each time the gun comes up to eye level.

The handgun must fit the shooter's hand and be comfortable to shoot. It should be easy to reload for matches, too. An autoloading pistol in .45 ACP is recommended for the beginning bowling pin shooter. The .45 has plenty of knock-down power and a wide variety of factory ammunition is available if the shooter is not yet into reloading.

European American Armory is a relatively new importer of quality firearms, mostly Italian and German. The Italian-made Witness Sport Long Slide pistol is turned out in 9mm, .41 AE, .40 S&W and .45 ACP. In 9mm, the magazine will hold 19 rounds; in .45, it is possible to load 10 rounds in the magazine, plus one in the chamber.

These pistols are made by Tanfoglio, the action based on the CZ system. The trigger, designed to be fired single- or double-action, is tuned at the factory. With the dozens of

EAA Witness Long Slide pistol features an adjustable rear Supersight. As indicated, a counter-clockwise turn of screw on top will move the sight a click upward.

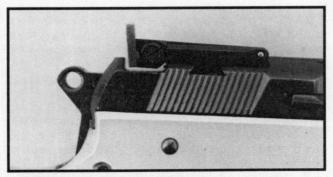

A clockwise turn of the windage screw, above, moves the sight and the bullet strike to the left. Vertical grooves in rear of slide facilitate moving slide to rear.

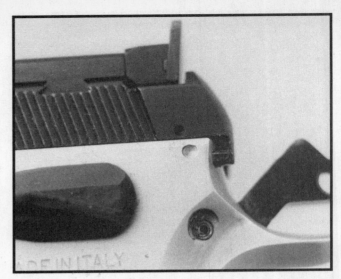

Marks on the rear of the slide and on the frame must be aligned for take-down. Hammer is cocked to pull back slightly, held in place as slide stop is removed.

accessories and options available through EAA, the Witness may be converted to a full-house competition gun using factory parts. Several barrel lengths, finish options and compensated or non-compensated barrels are available in the Witness line.

The weight advantages of the long slide and 4-3/4-inch barrel also help provide an increase in sight radius and decrease in recoil and muzzle flip. The long slide version includes an extended safety lever on the left side and a sighting system called Supersight.

The rear sight is adjustable for windage and elevation, using a small screwdriver. For an elevation change, turning the screw on top of the rear sight in a clockwise direction will lower the sight and the impact of the bullet. The windage adjustment screw is positioned on the right side of the Supersight. A clockwise turn will move the strike of the bullet to the left.

Weight of the pistol is about 38 ounces, unloaded. The shorter barreled version of the Witness will be a couple of ounces lighter. The gun's frame is made of stainless nickel steel, while the slide, hammer, safety lever, slide release, magazine release, and front and rear sights all carry a dark blue matte finish. The wood grip panels on the test gun are of deeply checkered wood. Numerous other options also are available for the Tanfoglio Witness. It is an attractive package.

The slide has serrations on each side, front and rear, typical of many modern, custom competition handguns. Other serrations are found on the magazine release button, on the rounded hammer spur, on top of the safety lever and slide release, and on the front and back of the grip frame. All these touches help control the pistol during loading, sighting and shooting.

The trigger guard is rounded at the front with no serrations on the outside. The curved trigger is also smooth, which many shooters of bowling pins prefer. The magazine well is beveled at the mouth to facilitate faster magazine loading. The 10-round magazine is tapered slightly at the top to feed out one round at a time while the lower portion widens to accommodate the rounds.

The frame design is such that in most shooters' hands, the

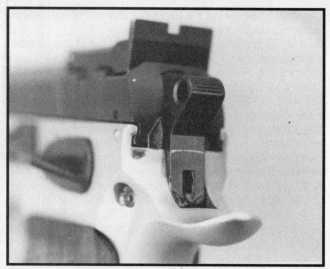

Hammer is rounded, serrated for easier cocking to shoot single-action first shot. Shooter's hand is well protected by long beavertail sweep at the rear of the pistol's frame.

Mechanical safety lever, above, is pushed into firing position, revealing red dot on left side of frame. Lever is rotated upward for Safe mode, below. Safety lever, slide stop lever are in same positions as on Model 1911.

grip feels only slightly wider than that of a typical Model 1911 Government Model. GM frames are all of same size. The magazine release is on the left side, just behind the trigger guard in roughly the same location as with the M1911. When pressed, the magazine slips out smoothly and quickly to make way for a loaded holder.

The standard magazine flares at the bottom to the sides and front so the entire well is enclosed when a magazine is inserted. The standard bumper has a concave surface on the bottom. Competition bumpers are available from EAA in a choice of brass or aluminum, in a variety of identifying colors.

Adding bumpers to a magazine for competition shooting is simple. They are slipped over the bottom of the magazine and held in place by a spring-loaded pin. Press the pin in and slide the unwanted bumper free, replacing it with the new one and allowing the pin to snap back into locking position.

The slide release and safety lever are on the left side of the Witness' frame. They, too, are in the same approximate location as with the more familiar M1911 pistol. The Safe position is when the safety lever is up. Rotating the lever downward reveals a red warning dot and places the pistol in the Fire mode.

The rear of the Witness frame has a slight hand swell for a comfortable grip. The frame sweeps back in a beavertail shape, positioning the hand high up on the pistol. Hammer and slide cannot touch any part of the shooting hand as the action cycles.

The pistol has enough mass, especially with a fully loaded magazine inside, to absorb most of the firing recoil. It does not exhibit some of the torque to the left and upward that some .45 ACP pistols do. Re-acquiring the target for shots after the first one can be relatively rapid, an essential for successful bowling pin shooting. The Supersight offers a sharp, clean notch in the rear and blade in the front, easy to align.

The test pistol, when first shot, exhibited a rather rough double-action trigger action. There seemed to be a grinding feel as the trigger was pulled back. A call to the importer's headquarters in Florida confirmed the problem. The CZ design is susceptible to a build-up of dirt and oil in the action,

and the pistol should be carefully cleaned after each firing. One suggestion is to apply extra-thin cleaning oil to the action with the gun field-stripped, then leave the frame assembly upside-down on a rag or towel for at least a half hour while the grunge runs out. Adequate lubrication after cleaning also is essential.

Field-stripping the pistol is quick and easy, requiring no tools. As always, the first step is to insure the gun is unloaded. Remove the magazine, pull the slide to the rear, look into and feel the chamber to make sure it is empty.

Pull the hammer all the way back to cock the gun. There are two take-down marks on the left side of the slide and frame behind the safety lever. Pulling the slide to the rear less than a quarter-inch will line up the two marks. The two marks in alignment, the take-down lever/slide stop is pushed from the right side to get it started, then the part is pulled free from the left side. The operation takes some juggling and dexterity. Three hands make it easy.

The barrel and slide assembly now are pushed forward on their rails and off the frame. With the slide and barrel assembly held upside-down, compress the recoil spring to remove the spring and its guide. Use care here, as the spring and guide can fly off if not held securely. With barrel and slide separated, the pistol is disassembled. Any further work should be done only by a qualified gunsmith.

Thus disassembled, the pistol may be cleaned and oiled. As mentioned, use plenty of solvent down in the action and turn it upside down on a rag to let the residue and dirt drain out while cleaning the barrel and other parts. Once clean, leave a light coat of oil on all moving parts for the next shooting session. Reassembly is reverse of take-down and is even easier.

The first shot with the EAA Witness may be either single- or double-action. With a round in the chamber, the hammer may be cocked and the safety locked for a single-action trigger pull. Or a round may be in the chamber and the hammer left down for a double-action first shot. For bowling pin or other

target shooting, most gunners probably will prefer single-action for the first round.

The Tanfoglio-made Witness is somewhat ammunition-critical. The test crew ran through several hundred rounds at the range, utilizing a supply of several brands and loads of factory ammunition. All the fully jacketed, round-nose loads fed well, but for bowling pins, a hollow-point bullet seems more efficient. Loads of up to 230 grains were tested, but results seemed better with 185-grain loads. Two particular loads functioned without any hitch and knocked the pins off the table when they were hit. These were the Federal 185-grain jacketed hollow-point and the Pro Load 185-grain jacketed hollow-point. PMC/Eldorado also produces a 185-grain hollow-point load that performs well in the Witness.

The least successful loads were the semi-wadcutters. For some reason, the pistol did not want to accept most of the loads we tested with that type of bullet.

As with most double-action triggers, this one has a rather long pull in that mode. Single-action pulling, however, is light and crisp. The shooter of CZ-type actions must keep in mind that the trigger must return forward before the action will recycle for another shot. Those used to an M1911-type action will have to get used to letting off the trigger somewhat more

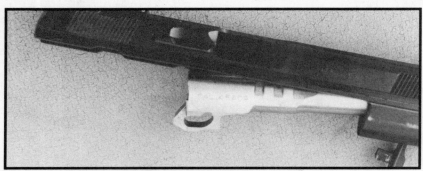

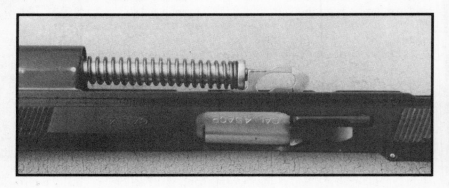

Field-stripping the Witness is simple and straight-forward. The slide and barrel assembly is placed upside-down and the recoil spring and guide, below, are carefully removed. Finally, the barrel is slipped out and upward from the slide, as at left.

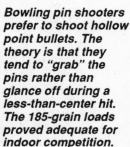

Bowling pin shooters prefer to shoot hollow point bullets. The theory is that they tend to "grab" the pins rather than glance off during a less-than-center hit. The 185-grain loads proved adequate for indoor competition.

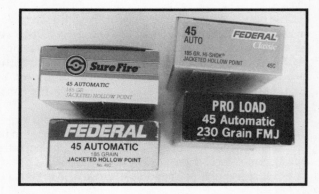

Calibers:	9mm, .41 AE, .40 S&W, .45 ACP
Barrel:	4 3/4 inches
Length overall:	8 1/3 inches
Weight unloaded:	38 ounces
Finish:	Blue and chrome
Magazine capacity:	9mm, 19 rounds; .40 S&W, 14 rounds; .41 AE, 13 rounds; .45 ACP 10 rounds
Sights:	Adjustable for windage and elevation
Safety:	Internal firing pin block, frame-mounted sear block
Importer:	European American Armory, P.O. Box 3498 Bright Station, Hialeah, FL 33013

Field-stripped, the Witness pistol breaks down into six main components. Long Slide model has 4 3/4-inch stainless steel barrel.

than they are accustomed to doing.

Some shooters complained that there is too much over-travel in the trigger action after the hammer drops. This problem can lengthen competition times in a fast-action sport such as bowling pins. The problem can be solved with the addition of a trigger-stop. Tanfoglio makes and EAA imports just such a trigger for the Witness. EAA offers other competition accessories for the Witness line, including scope sight mounts, sights, extended magazine releases, special frames, sights, extended and ambidextrous safeties, compensators and ported barrels, hammers and grips.

Incidentally, EAA is supporting handgun competition fi-nancially. An awards program offers several thousand dollars in prizes to shooters at specified North American matches. There are several ways to participate. The eligible matches include — but are not restricted to — such events as the Steel Challenge, USPSA Nationals, the Ernie Hill Desert Classic, Canadian Nationals and several others. Details of eligibility and registration requirements are available from EAA.

The Second Chance and other bowling pin tournaments may not be among those listed for cash awards from EAA, but they are a fun and excellent way of getting experience at this kind of shooting. The Tanfoglio Witness Long Slide is a pistol with which to get started.

TAURUS PT 101

By Tom Ferguson

The author took an immediate liking to the Taurus PT 101, attracted by the automatic's polished finish.

IN THE few years since it was introduced in 1990, the .40 Smith & Wesson has become one of our major defense and law enforcement calibers. Pistols chambered for this centerfire are typically double-action types with a large magazine capacity. Accuracy is good, reliability is excellent and most of all, recoil is light. Never intended to compete with the longer 10mm Auto or .45 ACP, the .40 S&W was designed as an improvement over the 9mm Parabellum for defensive use. Although the street verdict isn't yet in, the .40 S&W appears to be just that.

Taurus handguns are manufactured in Brazil, and have become well established in the United States over the last couple of decades. Both revolvers and autoloaders are offered,

including a Beretta look-alike in 9mm Parabellum, the PT 99. This always has been a sturdy, reliable and accurate handgun offered at an economical price. Finishes range from blued steel to nickel plate and now, stainless steel. As Taurus officials gained insight to the U.S. market, workmanship and appearance improved steadily until today, the Taurus has to be ranked right along with the top domestic gunmakers.

The latest Taurus is a good example. Dubbed the PT 101, the pistol is chambered for the popular .40 S&W cartridge. Big, bright and beautiful is the only way to describe it. The frame is of alloy, polished to a brightness that resembles nickel.

The barrel and open-topped slide are of stainless steel, also

This Entry In The .40 S&W Sweepstakes Does Itself Proud!

The PT 101 field-strips easily. Note the locking lug that is loosely fitted into a dovetail on the barrel.

polished bright. The grip plates are of Brazilian walnut, a dense, well-colored brown wood, with the gold Taurus logo in the center. The result is one of the most handsome pistols ever to leave the Taurus plant — and one of the most handsome made anywhere.

Instead of crude stamping, the slide markings are laser engraved, offering a clean, precise appearance. The lettering is large enough to read, but small enough to be tasteful. On the left of the slide is the round Taurus logo and *Taurus Int. Mfg. Inc.* On the right it says, *PT 101 AFS, Cal. .40 S&W*. Running a fingertip over the lettering shows it's really cut into the metal by the laser. Tom Conrad of Taurus tells me it should be just as durable and resist holster wear as well as the more common stamping.

The magazine holds 11 .40 S&W cartridges, making this a 12-shot pistol with one up the spout. The magazine has stout construction and three observation holes along the back side, numbered 4, 7 and 11, for accounting purposes. This model carries a fully adjustable rear sight, made of blackened steel

for greater visibility. The windage screw isn't marked, but the elevation screw has an arrow showing which way to turn for elevation. The front sight is a blade — integral with the slide — with a small red dot in the center. For some unknown reason, the oddly shaped hammer is made of black steel, not stainless, but provides a pleasant contrast.

Over the years, the controls of the Taurus and other double-action pistols have varied functionally. On the PT 101, the safety mechanism combines all the desirable features into one neat unit. The frame-mounted safety lever works in standard M1911 style. Pushed up, it locks the slide regardless of hammer position. Thumbed down to a horizontal position, it puts the pistol in the firing mode and exposes a red warning dot.

When depressed further, the lever drops the hammer and returns the gun to a safe condition. This is a one-hand operation, useful when the magazine and chamber are still loaded. The trigger is re-set in the double-action position.

On the test gun, the double-action pull was some 10

pounds, but smooth and free of backlash. Single-action pull runs five pounds, but feels lighter and is managed easily. The safety is ambidextrous and, due to the construction, allows the gun to be carried cocked-and-locked, if that seems desirable.

The original ballistics of the .40 S&W practically duplicate the subsonic 10mm FBI load. Both use a 180-grain JHP bullet at a listed velocity of the 950 to 980 feet per second. In turn, such ballistics have a lot in common with the century-old .38-40 Winchester. This old black powder number used a 180-grain flat-point bullet advertised at a nominal 950 fps, but seldom achieved in the various revolvers chambered for it.

Although widely used in the waning days of the Old West, the .38-40 did not build an outstanding reputation as a manstopper in the way of the .45 Colt. Actual street results indicate that neither have the 10mm subsonic or the .40 S&W, nor are they likely to do so. This is entirely the result of loading the .40 S&W and 10mm subsonic below published velocities, much like the older .38-40 was done in decades past. Smokeless .38-40 loads were reduced gradually to pathetic velocities ranging from 630 to 720 fps. Mild to shoot, and easy on aging revolvers, they didn't offer much stopping power.

The initial popularity of the .40 S&W owed much to the fact it was dimensioned to fit into 9mm-size autoloaders. The then-new round also had mild recoil, but there was something else.

When Smith & Wesson officials announced their new cartridge, the Las Vegas hotel room was filled with gunwriters, publishers, dealers and professional gun persons of vast collective knowledge. To the last individual, they recognized the .40 S&W, although a bit shy of bullet weight, was closely similar to the Remington .41 magnum police load of 1964. This revolver round failed in the market place, but the .410-inch diameter, 210-grain SWC, at a true 950 fps, was a proven manstopper.

An eternal gripe is that factories tend to publish optimistic velocities. What the shooter's chronograph reads all too often is below that of published ballistic tables. At times, this is due to factors beyond the maker's control, such as barrel length, action type and bore dimensions. As an example, it was just such excessive tolerances which gnawed so mightily at the .38-40's reputation and eventually killed it.

On the other hand, suppose a manufacturer, during later shakedown trials, develops a powder/bullet combination which is slightly off in velocity, but gives better overall performance? We can hardly blame them for offering the load with better virtues. Something like that may be happening to the .40 S&W.

During a recent chronograph session, the various 180-grain JHPs I fired didn't give the almost-1000 feet per second I expected. Instead, they registered an average of 861 fps to a slightly higher 920 feet per second. So who can say they won't be good street cartridges anyway? Can a fight be won more certainly with an additional 70 or 80 feet per second? I think so, and I also think that although the velocity difference is small, there is a point of diminishing returns. I'd rather have 990 fps than 920 fps.

As a matter of fact, I'd prefer more velocity than that. Fortunately, for shooters who feel the same, the .40 S&W loads carrying the lighter, 155-grain JHP came along shortly after the 180-grain load. These vary widely in velocity, but are always much faster than the original cartridge.

Barrel length of the Taurus PT 101 is five inches — among the longest of .40 caliber pistols. Thus, the velocities chronographed are about as much as one can expect from the loads tested. Five shots from an original box of Winchester 180-grain JHPs clocked 873, 909, 899, 909 and 887 feet per second. The average was 896 with an extreme spread of 30 fps. This is not nearly 1000 feet per second; it doesn't even come within a hundred feet per second of that figure. Recoil was mild in the Taurus, however, and the three-inch group was acceptable combat accuracy.

Winchester's newest ammo is the Black Talon, using a

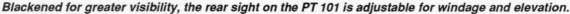

Blackened for greater visibility, the rear sight on the PT 101 is adjustable for windage and elevation.

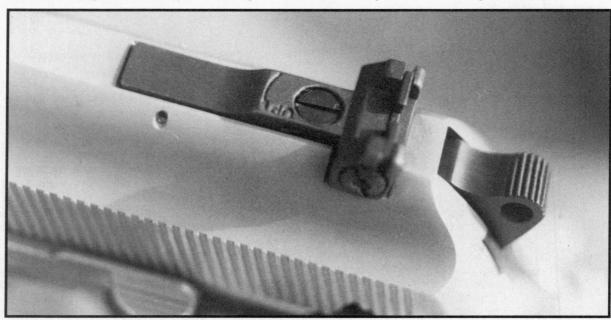

The PT 101's ambidextrous safety lever (right and below) also serves as a decocking lever. When it is positioned up, the auto is on safe. Moved to the horizontal mark, the gun is ready to fire. Thumbed down, the lever drops the hammer into safe mode.

bullet designed for maximum penetration and expansion. Ideally, the bullet expands on impact and turns itself into a good imitation of a runaway buzzsaw to create terrific tissue damage. Five of them went 893, 909, 910, 921 and 920 feet per second, respectively. They averaged 911 feet per second, not the advertised 990 fps. Group size at 25 yards was slightly better, measuring 2 1/2 inches. Throughout the tests there was an occasional flyer, which I discounted, because it appeared with all brands of ammo and could have been shooter error.

Federal's Hydra-Shok 180-grain JHP offered the best accuracy in the Taurus PT 101. They were also the most uniform. The Oehler chronograph said 863, 861, 865, 855 and 863 fps; an average of 861 feet per second. This is an extreme spread of only 10 feet per second, which, combined with a fine bullet, turned in a centered group measuring only an inch and a half.

Switching over to Federal's Classic 155-grain JHP was like changing from the .38 Special to a .357 magnum. The recoil increase was pronounced, and, in fact, directly comparable to the .357. The conventional-looking Classics went 1206, 1221, 1206, 1214, then 1204 fps for an average velocity of 1211. These proved fully as accurate as the 180-grain Hydra-Shoks, with a similar 1 1/2-inch group.

There were two failures to feed. However, the only malfunctions encountered with the PT 101 during test firing. In both instances, the rounds released early from the magazine lips, jamming the cartridge mouth against the upper edge of the chamber. The gun was easy to clear, but when fired, both rounds moved the point of impact a full five inches from the other bullet holes. This is an indication that each cartridge must be uniformly chambered to maintain the same point of impact.

When it comes to the 155-grain .40 loads, there's great variation in velocities among major brands. Moreover, there is practically no way for the average shooter to find out how each performs, unless he reads a gun article which happens to list the velocity of his favorite load or owns an ammo company catalog.

At one time in history, ammo makers printed the nominal velocity on the box, but this hasn't been done in years. Too many shooters found it differed from what they got in their firearm and objected. Today, the makers figure zero information is somehow better than a ballpark figure that might cause complaint.

At first, the wide variation in velocity among 155-grain .40 S&W loads seems a disadvantage and an undesirable situation. Actually, it contributes greatly to the versatility of this cartridge. Winchester offers an excellent 155-grain, flatnosed, truncated cone FMJ with mild recoil and good accuracy. This would be a good choice in police jurisdictions where hollow-points aren't permitted — or for deepest penetration in almost any medium.

In a defense scenario the likelihood is it would work as well as anything. Fired over the chronograph screens at a 25-yard ringed target, it produced a three-inch group. The rounds clocked 1099, 1116, 1083, 1095 and 1095 for an average 1097 fps. Compare this with the 1211 fps produced by the Federal

Author found the Taurus PT 101 an accurate paper-puncher, clustering groups that would be meaningful in combat.

Classics! Recoil is on a level with .38 Special +P cartridges.

Black Hills 155-grain JHP offered the highest velocity readings for the day. The big Taurus blew them through the screens at 1283, 1257, 1277, 1296 and 1273. This is moving right along for a diminutive round like the .40 S&W, and it averaged 1277 fps. Group size was a good, combat-ready 2 1/2 inches.

The .40 S&W isn't thought of normally as a field cartridge; it's main purpose is defense. However, given this high velocity and flat trajectory, it could take whatever game for which the .38 Super is thought proper, and then some. Younger shooters may not realize it, but there once was — and may still be — a clique of outdoorsy shooters who believed the .38 Super M1911 Colt was the best field cartridge available in autoloaders. Now, with Black Hills 155-grain ammo, the .40 S&W will top the older round.

Given the wide selection of ammo types and differing velocities available in .40 S&W, I favor a pistol with adjustable sights. The PT 101 has them, and can be made to print where you look.

Field-stripping couldn't be easier. Merely punch in the takedown button from the right side, flip down the takedown lever on the left and the slide/barrel assembly will run forward off the frame. The recoil spring and guide can be removed as a unit, then the barrel can be removed by pulling it out from the

rear. Use caution when removing the barrel, for the locking lug is fitted into a loose dovetail and may slide out. Monkeying with the double-action mechanism in the frame isn't recommended, and may require special tools.

Though I haven't seen the term used in a long time, the Taurus PT 101 falls into what once was called the category of "service/utility" firearms. That means it would be equally at home in a police officer's holster or that of an outdoorsman. It needs only the proper selection of ammo for the envisioned task.

Summing up, the PT 101 is practically corrosion proof, is field-stripped easily for cleaning and has all the needed safety features. There's even a lanyard loop at the rear of the butt, as useful to an outdoor person as a soldier or cop. The former often use a lanyard to keep the pistol from being jerked out of the holster while negotiating heavy brush or to prevent it's loss in water.

Concealment? At M1911 size, you're not likely to forget you are carrying the PT 101. Thanks to a lack of conformity in modern clothing, however, concealing even a big gun depends entirely on what you wear. Under a coat is no problem, and an outside-the-pants shirt will do if chosen carefully.

Whatever use the prospective buyer has in mind for it, the reliability, accuracy and cosmetic excellence make the PT 101 a top choice in .40 S&W caliber autos.

THE CZ-75 COMPACT

By Tom Ferguson

This Cut-Down 9mm Shows Excellent Handling & Accuracy Qualities

SINCE BLACK powder days, the major problem in designing concealable defense guns has been power — actually, the lack of it. Until recent times, the smaller autos in .25, .32 and .380 ACP were about the best technology could come up with.

One way to achieve more power is to take a service-type pistol of proven effectiveness, then trim it down a bit to make it more concealable and more portable. An early example, dating back to 1949, is the Colt Commander. Made with an alloy frame, the Commander version was a shortened and

While there are a lot of concealable rigs available, author prefers a simple means of carry, like this belt slide holster.

lighter contender for a new service pistol.

At the time, there were so many M1911s in government arsenals that the Commander had to rely on civilian sales — and the public likes it. No compact is truly as easy to pack as pistols of lesser caliber, but heavier bores are infinitely more comforting if the owner anticipates real need.

One pistol that meets that standard is the new compact version of the well-known CZ-75 9mm. When introduced, the CZ-75 was hailed as the best double-action service pistol of its type, and still holds onto most of that reputation. Now considered slightly obsolescent in some quarters due to the lack of a decocker or hammer drop, it remains a well-made, large-capacity double action auto of great reliability and accuracy.

There's a tendency on the part of experts to regard the decocking lever as mere frippery, while much of the public distrusts them. My own opinion is that the decocker device is a must on police weapons, but on a personal defense gun such as the trim compact CZ-75, it's a matter of small importance. The manual that accompanies the CZ Compact gives safe instruction on lowering the hammer by hand.

This compact 9mm is a chunky little rascal with traditional appearance and substantial heft. It has a deep-blued finish over well-polished metal and checkered walnut grips. It feels good in the hand, with a curved, comfortable backstrap and all corners rounded. One renowned pistolsmith once said a defense gun should feel like a well-used bar of soap and the CZ-75 Compact does. The magazine floor plate is curved to provide a rest for the little finger, adding to the comfort factor.

Controls consist of a manual safety lever mounted on the left side of the frame and the slide release in the usual place. Both are flattened and rounded in a way that makes snagging unlikely.

When the hammer is cocked, the safety lever moves up to cover a red warning dot, indicating the gun is in its safe mode. Pushed down, the weapon is ready to shoot. Cocked-and-locked fans will no doubt carry it in this mode. On the other hand, the hammer may be lowered on a loaded chamber and the safety ignored, thanks to internal safety designs.

The latter would be my preferred method of carry, but as in most things, I'm not a fanatic. I've even carried the Colt M1911

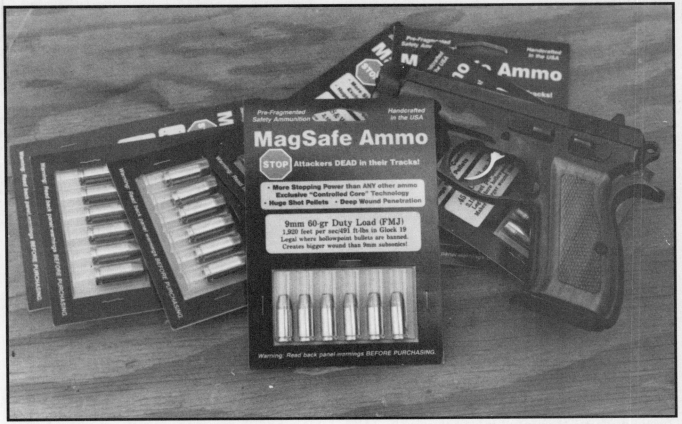

The author likes the pure stopping power of Mag-Safe ammunition. The 9mm FMJ bullets will push beyond 1500 fps.

.45 auto with the hammer down on a loaded chamber, although now it's regarded as unsafe in some quarters. I'd like to see an attorney prove that in a fair court of law, with an undoctored gun. The point may be moot, since most guns today are updated with firing pin locks as in the '80 Series Colts.

The slide rides inside the frame as on the bigger CZ-75 version and carries a slightly elevated striated rib. The sights are fixed combat style, with two white dots on the rear and a white vertical bar on the ramped front. This allows high visibility, even if tritium sights are better. I'm starting to believe all defense guns should be equipped with these glow-in-the-dark sights.

The extractor is wide, flat and positive in action. Trigger and barrel are left in the white, which contrasts nicely with the blued expanses. The trigger guard is oval, but flattened and grooved in front, perhaps in the hope Magic Johnson or someone with similar hand size will find it useful. Reach to the trigger is three inches, about right for an adult male, but perhaps a stretch for small-statured persons. The trigger pull is smooth and light in both double and single action, with none of the grittiness sometimes found in close copies of the CZ-75. It is, in fact, a darned good trigger. The main fault of DA triggers in general is overtravel, which can disturb the sights before the gun fires. The CZ-75 Compact has none.

Charging the chamber of the Compact is slightly more difficult because the slide is inside the frame. The rear has slanted grooves, of course, but they are less easy to grasp than on many pistols. I prefer to cock the hammer to lessen resistance when putting one up the spout.

Supposed advantage of an inside-the-frame slide is longer bearing surface on the rails, which contributes to greater accuracy. The famed SIG P-210 was made so, and has an enviable reputation. Before computer controlled machinery came along, I don't think it mattered. Now that machining is computer controlled and utterly precise, I tend to think the claim to better accuracy is true.

Certainly I was surprised at the accuracy of the compact in the shooting tests. It consistently delivered two-inch groups offhand at 20 yards with a variety of ammo. The usual service pistol or revolver does no better than three-inch groups at the same distance, so this is quite an improvement in accuracy, and especially good for a defense gun.

Mischievously, I'm always tempted to load high-capacity pistols with several bullet configurations to see if I can make them stutter. There was a time not so long ago when no European pistol would digest anything but FMJ round-nose bullets, but no longer. They seemed to have learned their lesson, and realize American shooters have access to many different types of expanding bullets. Now the pistols are throated, relieved and eager to eat anything that comes along.

The CZ-75 Compact is a 13+1 auto, so I first loaded four rounds of 124-grain Federal Match 9mm ammo with flat noses. On top, I put in four 115-grain Silvertips, then five Black Hills 124-grain JHPs. In a rather casual Weaver stance,

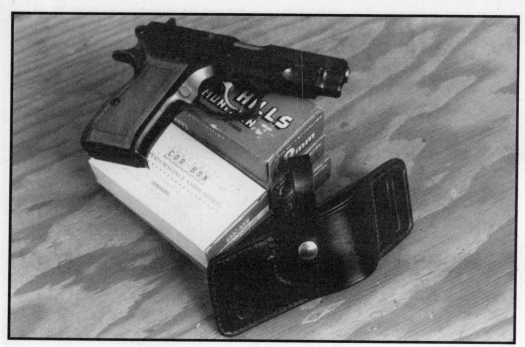

The Action Arms CZ-75, a stack of 9mm ammunition and the no-nonsense slide holster make a respectable defensive combination.

I fired on a reduced silhouette target placed at 20 yards. Previously I believed most European pistols in 9mm were sighted in with the 115-grain bullets, but the heavier 124-grain Black Hills loads made a well-centered two-inch group to the point of aim.

The CZ-75 Compact likes this load. The Winchester Silvertips were equally accurate, but printed some two inches low. I can live with that, given the expansiveness of the human torso. The flat-tipped Federals made confetti of the group shot with Black Hills ammo of similar weight. The upshot was that I had 13 rounds in a group that would have done any service pistol proud. My only regret was that, at the time, I had no 9mm subsonics on hand to try for point of impact.

There were no malfunctions resulting from this mixed-bag of defense ammo, and that left me with an impression of reliability. This was strengthened as the shooting went on; through some six boxes of 9mm ammo there was not a single failure of any kind.

I believe all true defense shooting is close and quick, and long-range sniping is unlikely. My usual routine is to toss out some kind of action target — usually empty plastic bottles of gallon size — then shoot at them hurriedly and instinctively. With the CZ-75 Compact, I began with the 124-grain Black Hills stuff at seven yards, the hammer down on an empty chamber. The smooth double auto trigger pull helped in gaining a first-round hit, and I could move the bottles with almost unerring predictability.

Unlike some shooters of aging yore, I couldn't pick just part of the gallon jug to hit, but I moved most of them. I'm well aware that such sloppy generosity won't win any medals, but it will settle a lot of truculent hash. Since defense shooting is all about the latter, I'm content with any pistol which reliably stays on such small targets, and never seek to improve or criticize the accuracy.

The barrel length of the CZ-75 Compact measures 3 3/4

inches. No accuracy, but some velocity will be lost from that delivered by longer barrels. Fortunately, the 9mm cartridge is one that does well in abbreviated tubes. When ignited, it gets to work real fast and loses only a small percentage of its original vehemence.

Velocity and bullet design are critical to the 9mm cartridge. In my opinion, it's best to have the highest possible velocity, coupled with the fastest expanding of bullets. Lest I be thought paranoid, I'll say that I more or less grew up with pistol bullets which were cosmetically attractive, but offered little expansion in real life.

There are some cartridges with the powder capacity to drive a glass marble fast enough to expand, but the 9mm is not one of them. Without expanding bullets, the 9mm is pretty hopeless on human opponents. Any bullet design that shatters in any test medium is just about right. In spite of learned opinion, I'm not convinced that great or even modest penetration is needed for defense use. Human beings are upright creatures with a vast, exposed vital area at which to shoot. Unlike all-fours animals, they require no shooting through heavy shoulder bones. A two- or three-inch-deep wound is likely to prove fatal from front or rear — and quickly at that. If it doesn't, that's what the other rounds in the gun are for — to try, again!

Pondering 9mm ballistics can drive the compact-shooter bananas, but there's really not much of a problem. I'd simply choose the load that gives the highest velocity in longer guns, confident it also will give the highest velocity in short ones. As a basic rule of thumb, it ain't bad.

For many years my favorite 9mm load was the Winchester 95-grain JSP, delivering about 1250 feet per second in standard barrel lengths. This was a light-recoiling, viciously expanding bullet that was just what I wanted. Today, I'd be more likely to load the excellent CorBon 115-grain JHP at 1350 fps in the compact CZ-75 9mm. At the least, I'd feel good

The Action Arms CZ-75 Compact received high marks from the author for reliability, handling and its 14-round carry.

with the Remington 115-grain +P at 1250 fps. The closer a 9mm bullet comes to exploding on contact, the better I like it.

We call it defense shooting, but in reality, firing a pistol at another is a distinctly hostile act. The 9mm load with the most animosity has to be the Mag-Safe Plus-P load. Bullet weights vary with intended use, but all are light and extremely fast. A typical example is the 9mm Police Load, which utilizes a 68-grain frangible, birdshot-loaded bullet at 1850 fps. The Mag-Safe hits, it explodes, making a large cavity. Still hurtling forward, the birdshot and jacket fragments drive deep, making a "rathole" wound much like that created by a shaped charge used in heavy ordnance to penetrate armor.

Mag-Safe owner Joe Zambone has video tapes to show some 12-13 inches of penetration in gelatin, if that impresses anyone. Frankly, I rather like the huge entrance wound. Where frangible or expanding bullets are banned by law (can you imagine being restricted when your life is at stake?) Mag-Safe offers FMJ bullets of light weight driven to high velocities above 1500 fps. It's like being hit by a meteorite from outer space, one supposes.

Thanks to an unusually good grip, the CZ-75 Compact comes to hand quickly from belt or holster. The feel rivals the older Browning Hi-Power, and it points just as well. There's no use pretending, however, that it is especially easy to carry. In spite of the trimming, the compact is still rather heavy and it doesn't conceal well in anything short of an inside-the-pants

rig. Thin persons can wear these in reasonable comfort; thick persons cannot. My personal choice of a holster would be a thin belt slide; more concealable than any pouch style holster and just as secure. Coat pockets? Forget it, the compact will sag you over.

I confess that wearing a concealed handgun always has been a bother to me, and virtually none of the tricky, high-dollar concealment rigs seem to work. Anyway, I resent the necessity, and if a need is anticipated, would just as soon stick the thing in my waistband and cover it with a coat or jacket. If the need proves real, I'd rather have the CZ-75 Compact 9mm than any .25 or .32 auto — and nearly any .380 pistol. I'd make an exception for the Walther PP, which is an exceptional defense pistol.

Some autos have a tendency to throw the first hand-chambered round wide of the main group, usually a couple of inches. The CZ-75 Compact test gun was accompanied by a computer (what else?) diagram showing this characteristic, but in defense use, I doubt that it matters. At any rate, I was unable to demonstrate this on target paper, and all my groups were together with no fliers.

Summing up, I found the compact 9mm had 100 percent reliability, excellent handling virtues — and it carries a total of 14 rounds. I think of it as a more concealable fighting pistol and not a true hideout. I'd be satisfied carrying it anywhere and feel the only possible improvement would be glowing tritium sights.

T/C's .375 WINCHESTER HUNTER

By Chris Christian

A handloaded Hornady 270-grain RN dropped this hefty hog in his tracks with a broadside shoulder shot.

This Blue-Collar Handcannon Is One Of The Most Versatile Hunting Rigs Available

Above, .375/Contender combination offers hunters the versatility of a flat-shooting handgun for open country or a heavy bullet for thick cover. Simply switching rounds would allow author (right) to handle this hog.

THE PIG was huge. Even a quick glimpse at 80 yards was enough to convince me this was one of the biggest wild hogs I'd ever seen in Florida.

Normally, that would be enough to cause me to turn my attention elsewhere. I long ago gave up hunting teeth, preferring to pack the freezer with tender, wild pork. A boar hog that size was going to be one of the rankest, toughest critters around, and it's a brave man who can even stay in the kitchen while one is being cooked, let alone eat it!

But I had seen something else that prompted me to give this hog another look — a bobbed tail. For those of you not familiar with porcine physiology, that usually means only one thing — at some distant point in the pig's past he was captured and, to put it in somewhat delicate terms, had certain male organs surgically removed in a non-surgical environment.

The purpose of said surgery is to cause him to lose interest in the ladies and devote his energy to eating and growing fat, instead of fighting with other boar hogs. What results is a "barr hog," some of the finest eating walking around on four feet.

For convenient identification, the tail is bobbed at the same time the other parts are bobbed, allowing the "surgeon " to pick his pig out quickly at a distance.

This is common practice in Florida's ranch country, and since wild hogs are no respecters of fences and property lines, these pigs tend to wander considerably. The determining factor as to whom actually owns the hog is whose property he happens to be on at the moment. Since I had this landowner's permission to pop any pig that passed, he was my hog.

The only problem was I'd better collect quickly. Not only was the late afternoon sun beginning to dance along the tree line, but the pig was working his way slowly toward one of the thickest ti-ti swamps in the state. Even a solid heart/lung shot would give him time to get into the tangle, and with several inches of water on the ground, tracking would be impossible. If I wanted to guarantee this pig making it to the freezer, he had to drop virtually in his tracks.

Mindful of that, I eased open my Thompson/Center Contender and removed the chambered round, replacing it with one of Hornady's big 270-grain round-nose soft-points.

It took only a minute or so to work my way to within 70 yards of the pig, find an impromptu rest alongside a convenient tree and line up for a broadside shot on the muscular shoulders. The muzzle flash lit up the swamp, but when vision returned, the hog was down for the count.

The thumb-size slug had blown through both shoulders before whistling off into the woods and the pig probably was dead before he hit the ground!

Knowing that my partner, Mike, had heard the shot and would have the swamp buggy along shortly, I took a moment to admire the hog and to reflect on the fact that whomever had decided to chamber the venerable Contender for the .375 Winchester cartridge had come up with a mighty fine combination.

Introduced in 1978, the .375 Winchester is a good example of a breed of cartridges that refuses to die. Mated with a beefed-up version of the Winchester Model 94 known as the Big Bore 94, the quick handling carbine answered the need for a large-caliber, moderate-velocity round for heavy cover hunting.

As currently loaded by Winchester, factory fodder is available in 200- and 250-grain jacketed soft-points. From the 20-inch barrel of the Big Bore 94, the former cruises along at approximately 2,300 feet per second, while the latter follows behind at about 2,000 fps. Given proper bullet placement, either of those rounds is capable of clean kills at any range under 200 yards on just about anything that walks in North America, except, possibly, the big bears.

Even then, if faced with a belligerent bruin, I can think of a lot of other rifle cartridges I would rather not have in my hands than a Big Bore 94 stuffed with 250-grain loads. Despite its pedestrian nature, those are the kind of ballistics that just seem to "get the job done."

When Thompson/Center announced the .375 would be the only new cartridge introduction into its Contender line for the 1991-1992 season, the reaction was sort of ho-hum. It wasn't a round many handgunners had much experience with, and I think a lot of them failed to realize the potential this round had as a big game cartridge.

As is often the case when rounds originally designed for carbine-length barrels are placed in single-shot pistol barrels, in the 14-inch Contender barrel, the factory 200-grain load zips across my Oehler 35P chronograph at a respectable 1,960 feet per second and produces 1,706 foot-pounds of energy. By the time the slug reaches 150 yards, it's still packing more energy than the .44 magnum produces at the muzzle!

The 250-grain load clocks in at 1,685, good for 1,578 fpe, and enough bullet weight to pretty much assure penetration to the vitals on just about any North American game.

While those ballistics can be duplicated and even exceeded by a few other cartridges chambered in the Contender, this is the first time they have been offered in an off-the-rack factory barrel that feeds on store-bought ammo.

For handgun hunters who are not reloaders and lack the inclination to join that fraternity, this is of no small significance.

When sighted in 2.5 inches high at 100 yards, the 200-grain load will be dead-on at somewhere around 150 yards and not drop eight inches below the line of sight at 200. At the longer range, it still is packing almost 800 foot-pounds of energy, and to my way of thinking, that makes it a legitimate 200-yard deer round.

If larger game is on the menu, the 250-grain load arrives at 100 yards with more energy than the 300-grain .44 magnum loads produce at the muzzle.

That's a lot of versatility from a one-gun/two-load combo, and I can't think of another non-wildcat that offers it.

For those who reload, performance can even be improved. Although the .375 has a slight body taper, it is essentially a straight-walled case and loads with a standard three-die set readily available from RCBS and probably others, as well. Unprimed brass is available from Winchester and requires nothing more than a quick pass through the belling die before loading.

Bullet selection in .375 caliber is not overly extensive, but certainly adequate. Sierra offers a 200-grain flat-point JSP (#2900) designed expressly for the .375 Winchester. Hornady's offer is a 220-grain flat-point JSP of their Interlock design, which is intended to expand reliably in the working range of

The flat-shooting .375 gives deer hunters the ability to drive a bullet to the vitals from virtually any angle.

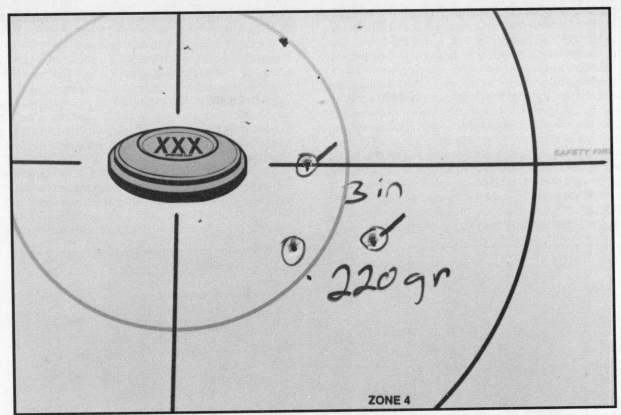

The benchrest group from author's 14-inch Contender Hunter shows more than adequate accuracy for big game. In fact, author's favorite 220-grain Hornady handload will usually group a bit tighter than shown.

the .375 Winchester — 1,600 to 2,200 fps.

There are a number of powders suitable for the .375 Winchester, but a look through the available loading data indicates Hercules Reloder 7 probably is the best choice. This is the only powder I have used with this round, and I have found no reason to regret that decision.

With either bullet, 38.0 grains of R-7 (recommended maximum charge for the Hornady 220 FP in their fourth edition manual) will bring velocities of slightly over 2,000 fps from the 14-inch Contender barrel. The Sierra bullet crimps nicely in the canalure, but the heavier Hornady slug must be seated out a bit farther. This is a matter of no consequence in the single-shot Contender.

Ballistically, both rounds slightly edge the factory round, but not by enough of a margin to make much difference in the field. My experience has been that the Sierra bullet is a bit "softer" than the Hornady slug and offers a slight increase in expansion on thin-skinned, deer-size game, while the Hornady seems to have the edge in penetration.

The Hornady is the one that sees the most use in my .375s and its performance has been eminently satisfactory. I would not hesitate to use this load on elk-size game.

In the accuracy department, both reloads — at least, in my guns — will outperform the factory load. I have yet to be able to achieve much better than a 3.5-inch average (from a 100-yard benched three-shot group) with store-bought ammo, but consistently average three shots in the two to 2.5-inch range with the reloads. That's not earthshaking, but fairly good for a straight-walled case and more than adequate for big game.

Duplicating the heavier factory load took a bit more time, since I was unable to find any load data on the subject.

For this, I selected the two Hornady offerings in the 270-grain weight. The #3710 SP has proved to be a sterling performer in the .375 JDJ, and the #3714 RN, theoretically, should offer a slight increase in expansion over the spire-point at the reduced velocities achievable in the .375 Winchester.

Sticking with Reloder 7, I began at 30.0 grains and slowly worked up to 34.0 grains. At that charge weight, the RN crimped nicely in the canalure and zipped across the 35P screen at 1,710 fps, good for 1,752 fpe!

The spire-point, due to its longer shank, required seating out well beyond the canalure, but functioned perfectly. Its velocity and energy equalled that of the RN. Pressure signs were perfectly normal. Indeed, the cases literally fell out of the gun.

The spire-point was the clear accuracy winner, delivering the tightest group I have yet fired with the .375 Winchester — a neat three shot cluster going 1.5 inches. On average, however, it fell into the two to 2.5-inch realm.

The round-nose was somewhat of a disappointment on the range. Averages of 3.5 inches were the best I was able to get. However, I had to remind myself that when I feed one of these big slugs into the chamber I'm not potting ground hogs. This is a big bullet for big critters and its field performance has been outstanding.

Although there are a few other bullets available in .375, including an interesting-looking, 235-grain spire-point from Speer and a number of 300-grain projectiles, I have not found the need to go beyond the 220- and 270-grain Hornady slugs for field use. I believe that two-load approach will handle just abut any critter I'm likely to take on with a handgun.

One factor which pleased me immensely was the relationship of impact points of the two different weight bullets. The heavier slugs print two inches above the 220-grain load. Since I keep that sighted in two inches high at 100 yards, the heavier bullets are only four inches above point of aim, allowing me to interchange loads in the field without re-sighting and with only a minor adjustment in point of aim. I can live cheerfully with that kind of versatility!

Another interesting possibility concerns the use of cast lead bullets. Straight-walled cases normally show a surprising affinity for reduced cast bullet loads, and I doubt the .375 Winchester would be any different. There are a number of moulds available — plus some commercially cast slugs — that probably could be cobbled up into some fine loads for the silhouette competitor or those desiring some lighter practice loads.

If there is a drawback to the Contender .375 Winchester, it is the law — more specifically, Newton's Third Law, which states, "For every action there is an equal and opposite reaction." Obviously, when one starts propelling 270-grain slugs at 1,700 fps, the individual doing the propelling will notice the event in short order! Recoil from the 14-inch Contender is rather vigorous. But, while no one is likely to repeal Newton's Third Law, Thompson/Center did find a way to amend it.

My initial experience with the .375 Winchester was with the plain 14-inch barrel. And, while not as bad as some modern handcannons, it did get my attention. Even with 200-grain loads, muzzle rise was in the neighborhood of 50 to 60 degrees. The 270-grainers would get the muzzle even more

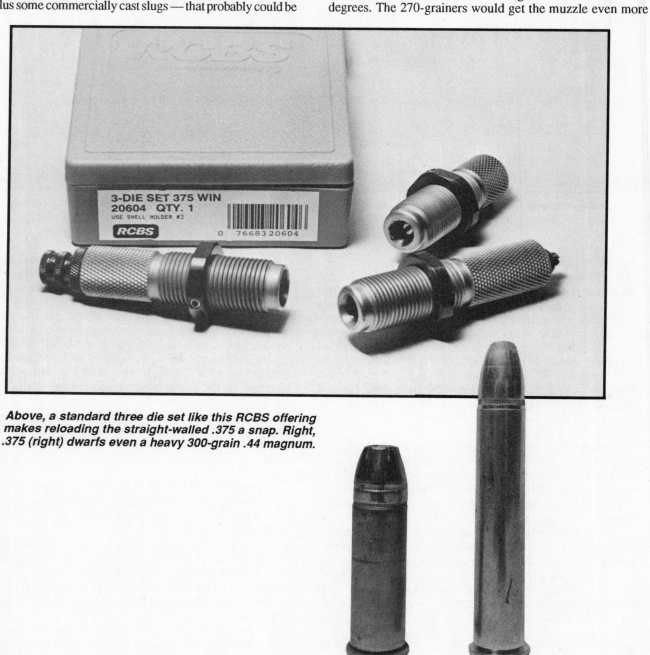

Above, a standard three die set like this RCBS offering makes reloading the straight-walled .375 a snap. Right, .375 (right) dwarfs even a heavy 300-grain .44 magnum.

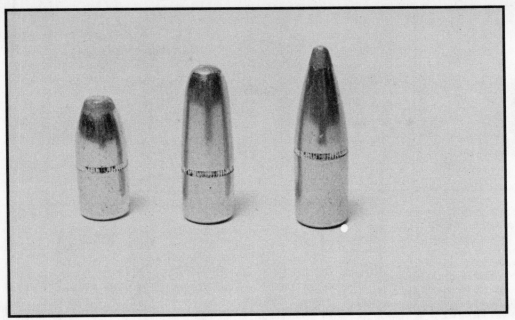

Three of author's favorite projectiles for the .375 are (from left) Hornady's stocky 220-grain FP and Hornady's fast 270-grain offerings in round nose and spire point.

The Winchester 200-grain soft point shoots flat enough to make the .375 Contender a real 200-yard deer round.

vertical than that! This was accompanied by a rather sharp snap. Even with the Pachmyr grips I favor, that would start to take some skin off the web of my shooting hand after 25 or so rounds.

The recoil was enough that I took to wearing a leather glove in the field in order not to leave any skin on the rough bark of whatever tree I decided to use as a field rest!

I had pretty much resigned myself to that sort of pain — until I had the opportunity to test fire the Hunter barrel, with its integral Muzzle Tamer recoil arrestor. If the plain barrel was a tiger, this was an entirely different breed of cat — a pussycat!

The Hunter barrel measured the same 14 inches, but the last 1.5 inches is taken up with the Muzzle Tamer. I can only conclude this is one of the few products I've had the opportu-

nity to test that actually lives up to its name.

With the Muzzle Tamer, recoil in all loads was reduced to a 20- to 25-degree muzzle rise. And while there was still noticeable rearward thrust, the sharp snap was moderated to a firm "push." The difference in felt recoil between the two barrels — using identical loads — was comparable to the difference I would experience in firing my S&W .44 magnum Classic Hunter with 240-grain loads, and then shifting to my S&W Model 586 with 158-grain .357 magnum loads. It's that significant!

Don't get me wrong. There is still some recoil. But, it's not any more severe than ny S&W .44 mag. That's certainly controllable, and since I'm getting as much power at 150 yards as the .44 delivers at the muzzle, with better accuracy, I will live with it cheerfully.

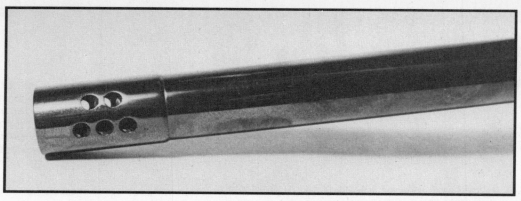

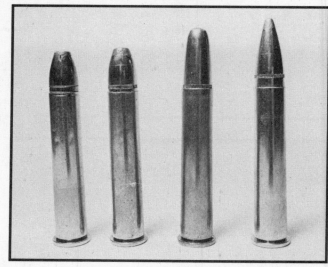

Above, the Muzzle Tamer on author's Hunter Contender offers a significant reduction in recoil over the plain 14-inch barrel. Right, from left are the 200-grain Winchester factory load, the 220-grain Hornady FP, the 270-grain Hornady RN and the 270-grain Hornady spire point. The mix of light and heavy slugs makes the .375 a versatile hunting handgun.

That reduction in recoil also will spell longer life and less trouble with scopes and mounts — two major problem areas on hard-kicking handguns — and that was enough for me to trade off the plain 14-inch barrel and concentrate on the Hunter barrel.

There is a slight velocity loss of about 80 feet per second. The 220-grain load now clocks about 1,920 fps, while the 270-grain loads are reduced to 1,640. That doesn't change trajectory or killing power enough to even consider, except possibly for those shooters who would prefer to pick nits than shoot game.

So how does the new .375 Contender fit into the overall handgun hunting picture? Quite nicely, thank you.

In the Contender line, it fills a noticeable niche between the .35 Remington and .45-70. The former, with a 14-inch barrel, will propel the 180-grain Hornady Single Shot Pistol bullet at about 2,100 fps, producing 1,764 fpe. The 200-grain Sierra .375 virtually duplicates that velocity, energy and trajectory. Moving to heavier slugs, the .35 Remington will drive a 200-grain soft-nose at about 1,850 fps. Compared to the .375's 1,920 fps from the shorter Hunter barrel with the 220-grain Hornady, there is no practical difference. For deer-size game, a hunter is well-equipped with either.

Moving into heavier bullets, however, eliminates the .35 Remington. There simply isn't enough powder capacity to drive a .358 caliber, 250-grain slug much beyond 1,500 fps and that comes off a serious second best to the velocity the .375 can generate with the 270-grain pill, even from the shorter barrel.

The .45-70 will exceed the .375 Winchester. Hornady's 300-grain hollow-point, handloaded to 1,800 fps, shoots almost as flat as does the .375 Winchester's 200- and 220-grain loads out to 200 yards. The heavier 350-grain flat-point will produce about 500 fpe more power for heavy-cover hunting. This, however, comes at the expense of a rather unwieldly 16-inch barrel, recoil that borders on the extreme and it requires handloading.

In factory rounds, the .45-70 has the edge only in the heavier bullets at closer ranges.

If one is looking for a good compromise between the flat shooting capabilities of the .35 Remington and the bone-crushing power of the .45-70, the .375 Winchester fits the bill. If one considers only factory-available ammo, the .375 wins hands down!

How does the .375 Winchester stack up to the .375 JDJ, arguably the finest, and most versatile, big-game handgun cartridge ever created? In identical 14-inch barrels, the JDJ round drives the same bullets 200 to 300 fps faster. That's all.

Whether that difference is enough to warrant the added expense of a custom barrel, increased recoil and the inconvenience of dealing with a wildcat round that requires multiple loading steps, including fire forming cases, is something the shooter will have to decide for himself.

I find the whole approach to the .375 Contender decidedly appealing — buy your barrel over the counter, slap it on your existing Contender frame, and grab a box of store-bought ammo. It's certainly a blue-collar approach to high-tech handgun hunting that equips one well for just about any critter on the continent.

EMF'S U.S. CAVALRY SINGLE-ACTION

By Gary Paul Johnson

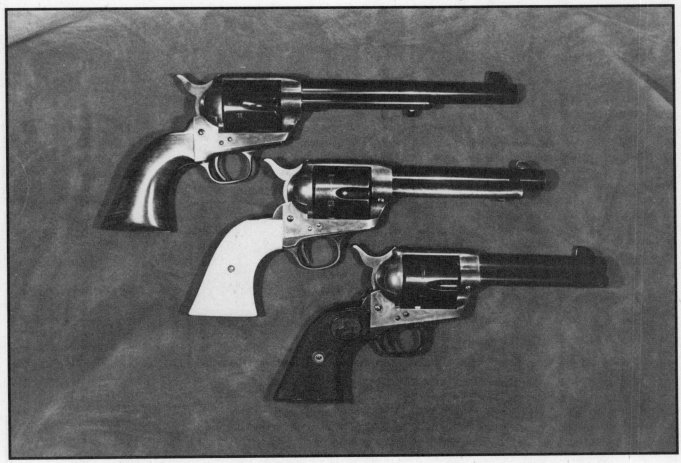

NO STRANGER to the Single Action Army revolver, Boyd Davis developed the famous Great Western revolver in the mid-1950s and sold it through his Early and Modern Firearms Company. That gun was patterned after the Colt single-action, and today is a sought-after collector's item in itself.

Some years later, Mr. Davis moved Early and Modern Firearms (EMF), to Santa Ana, California, and designed a "new" single-action revolver to be a close copy of the original Colt. He also began to offer other models built to his own demanding specifications. His goal was to create and make available the finest Old West reproduction firearms in the world. It looks as if he may have done just that.

One of Davis' prime considerations was to market reproductions of original Colt and Remington revolvers which were as exact as possible in every detail. The arms producer he chose to make these antique-style handguns was the famous arsenal of Italy's Armi San Marco.

For years, Boyd Davis worked closely with the Italians, supplying tooling and materials to get every aspect of his guns as close as possible to the originals. In 1991, he established EMF's Hartford program and applied it to his reproduction of the Colt single-action revolver.

The Hartford project can be thought of as a product improvement program. Through it, Davis sought to make his single-actions better than they had every been. He explained to me how difficult it was getting a close copy of the original Colt single-action revolver we commonly call the "first generation" model.

One of the guns EMF chose as the flagship of its new family was a copy of what we know as the Marshal Colt, or the model adopted by the U.S. Cavalry in 1873. This famous revolver had a number of aspects unique to it, such as its one-piece walnut grip with its military acceptance cartouche, plus its U.S. and special military acceptance marking.

Early on, I put in my order for one of these guns, but EMF held off until early in 1993, when Davis finally was satisfied that he had ironed out the wrinkles before offering the finest U.S. Cavalry revolver reproduction the world had ever seen. After seeing the new Hartford U.S. Cavalry Model, I can't argue.

The original 7 1/2-inch barreled revolver carried by the U.S. Cavalry served as the model handgun of the West. Many hundreds of these U.S.-marked Colts go on to see wide use on the frontier, but today original U.S.-marked Marshal Colts are almost priceless.

EMF's Hartford U.S. Cavalry reproduction is a beautiful handgun. Its 7 1/2-inch barrel and other steel parts are finished

Detail on the EMF SAA is superb. Note the excellent fit of the loading gate, grip and radiused front of the chambers.

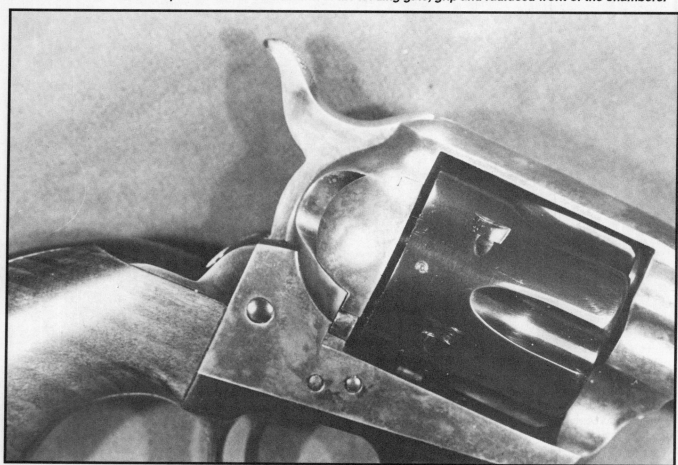

Specifications:

EMF U.S. Cavalry Hartford Model.
Caliber: .45 Colt
Velocity: 900 fps.
Operation: Single action revolver.
Number Of Shots: 6
Barrel Length: 7 1/2 inches.
Overall Length: 12 7/8 inches.
Weight: 38 ounces.
Safety: Hammer notch
  (gun shipped in non-firing mode).
Finish: Blue with case colors.
Stock: One-piece hardwood.
Sights: (front) Fixed blade.
  (rear) Fixed "U" notch.
Features: Original-type U.S.
  Cavalry markings.

On the frame of the EMF Hartford are original patent dates of the Model P and the classic U.S. markings.

The forged hammer and frame on the EMF Hartford are fully color case hardened.

in a rich, lustrous, deep blue, while its frame, hammer and loading gate carry a rich color case-hardened finish like the originals.

The Cavalry model features the original style of bullseye ejector head, base pin retention screw and front-radiused cylinder. The frame bears the initials "U.S." stamped on the left side, in the same place as the Colt Single Action Army guns of more than a century ago, and the cylinder bears inspector's marks as found on the old guns. The one-piece, hardwood stock bears a copy of an original inspector's cartouche stamp.

While some other current reproductions use a newly-designed hammer safety system, EMF's revolvers do not. They are 100 percent original in this respect. What is more, their parts will even fit the original Colts.

Especially important is the shape of the grip and the small radiuses and contours which are significantly different in most single-action reproduction revolvers offered today. I have thoroughly and closely examined the Hartford U.S. Cavalry model next to my original 1909 and 1968 "second generation" Colt Single Action Army revolvers, plus an original U.S. Cavalry-issue Colt. The shape and other aspects of the EMF gun are as close to the real McCoy as I've seen.

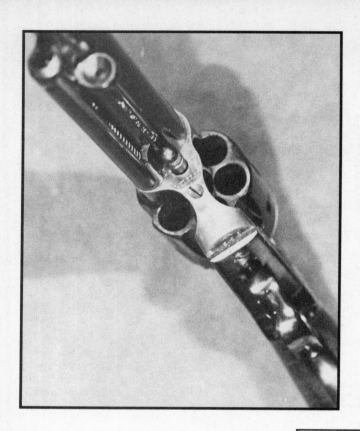

Above, the one-piece stock of the EMF U.S. Cavalry bears an original style cartouche. Dimensions of the handsome grip are identical to those of the original Colt.

Left, the Hartford U.S. Cavalry model uses the black powder-type frame with a screw to retain cylinder pin.

Accuracy Chart

Five Five-Shot Groups Hand-Held From 50 Feet

Cartridge	Velocity	Small Group	Large Group	Average
Black Hills 230-grain RNL	838 fps	1.69"	2.26"	1.93"
Black Hills 200-grain JHP	904 fps	3.5"	4.22"	3.88"
Remington 250-grain RNL	824 fps	1.81"	2.44"	2.19"
Four Corners 255-grain SWC	907 fps	1.78"	2.56"	2.26"

Unlike other makers of reproduction guns, Armi San Marco does not cast its parts, but makes them from true forgings just like the originals. Being made of the most modern steel, however, the Hartford U.S. Model is built far better than the original Marshal Colts and will handle full-power loads. It is especially suitable for reenactments, collecting, displays or anything else for which one would want a SAA.

Prior to shooting the EMF Hartford U.S. Model, I treated the bore and all internal parts with Tetra-Gun Care lubricants. I have found this lubricant treatment truly makes my guns work easier, and gives them somewhat of a trigger job to boot. Applying Tetra to the bore not only eliminates leading and other fouling in my guns, but seems to increase accuracy and velocity, as the maker claims. It also goes farther in fighting rust.

Over the years, I've owned a number of Colt SAAs with 7 1/2-inch barrels, and the EMF gun handled and shot exactly like them. I also found it to be at least as accurate as any Colt I've ever shot, and it shoots close to point of aim.

As I began my first live-fire test, I loaded one round of Black Hills .45 LC 230-grain RNL into a chamber, skipped the next one, and loaded four more. Then, when I cocked the hammer, the empty chamber came up under it, and I let the hammer down safely with no primer beneath it. I was using our club's indoor 50-foot range, so the groups shot are slightly better than one might expect at 25 yards.

I cocked the hammer, brought the gun up onto the target and squeezed the trigger. The long barrel provided excellent stability, as I felt the trigger start to break, and the front sight simply hung there at six o'clock. When the hammer fell, the

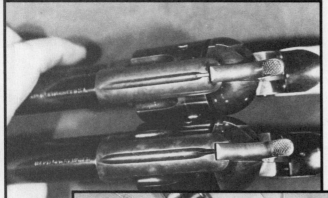

new-old gun barked, and raised in my hand. I put it down and looked at the target, but I couldn't make out a hit. I hoped it was in the black.

In touching off the remaining four shots, I began to see that the hits were indeed in the area at which I was aiming, and they looked good. I then switched to a rest, and shot five test groups with this load. Most groups measured well under two inches, superb for an out-of-the-box SAA revolver of this type. My like-new second generation Colt 4 3/4-inch .45 Colt revolver certainly will not shoot this well.

Next, I shot some Four Corners .45 Colt ammunition, and found it to produce average groups of about two inches at the same distance. Remington's 250-grain RNL load was about the same, but when I tried Black Hills' 200-grain JHP, I found that this gun seems to prefer lead bullets as accuracy fell off to 3.5 to four inches at 50 feet. All empty casings either fell out of their chambers on their own, or did so with a slight nudge from the ejector rod, and there were no malfunctions whatever.

EMF wisely specified that the Hartford Model's modern nomenclature be marked on the bottom of the barrel next to the ejector housing. Small print indicates that the gun is made in Italy. Other than a couple of other small proof marks, the gun gives the impression of being an original. Atop the barrel is stamped, HARTFORD, CT. MODEL. The last three digits of the gun's serial number are stamped on all major parts.

Other than its markings, I can find surprisingly few dis-

crepancies between the Hartford Model and an original Colt. Yes, the one-piece stock is made of hardwood rather than walnut, and its grain runs horizontally rather than vertically, as in the original. Also, the trigger guard is more squared on the bottom rather than being rounded as on early Colts. Finally, the back of the flutes in the cylinder are radiused as those found on later Colts rather than rounded as on the early first generation guns. Still, the Hartford Model is much closer to the originals than the so-called "third generation" Colt SAAs we have seen during the past decade.

Overall, I must give the EMF a grade of 95 percent, while similar guns rate a grade of 92 percent by my standards. The Hartford U.S. family also includes a 5 1/2-inch barrel Artillery Model, and a 3 3/4-inch "civilian" version.

To compliment the new EMF Hartford U.S. Cavalry revolver, I ordered two holsters from Trailrider Products, P.O. Box 2284, Littleton, CO 80161. This outfit makes a variety of authentic 19th Century-style Western and military leather gear. Included are a reproduction U.S. Cavalry rig and a copy of a rare U.S. Cavalry holster, the Miller-Fachet.

EMF's Hartford U.S. Cavalry single-action is of extremely high quality and closely follows the original Model P patterns because of the hard work and dedication of Boyd Davis in bringing us the best reproductions possible. His company offers a full line of quality historic reproduction rifles and handguns. For more information, contact EMF Co., Inc., 1900 Warner Ave., Suit 1-D, Santa Ana, CA 92705.

AMT POCKET-POWER BACK UPS

By Chris Christian

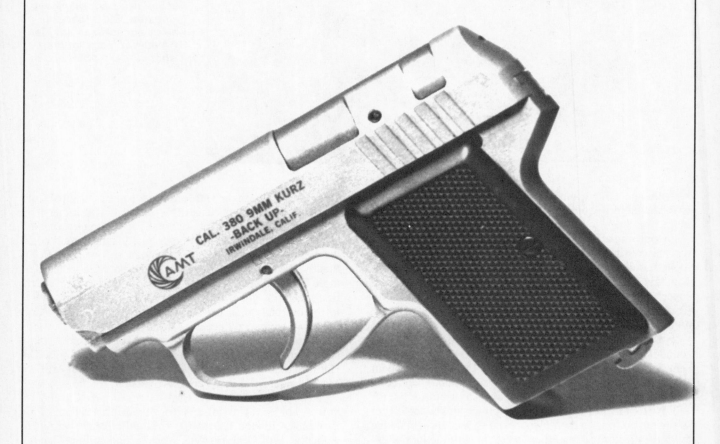

This Pint-Size Pair Of .380s Pack A Lot Of Punch In A Small Package

THERE WAS a time when the term "pocket pistol" was in wide usage. In essence, it was a generic term used to describe any number of compact handguns, either semi-auto or revolver, that could be conveniently tucked into a pocket for daily carry.

There was wide latitude where use of the term was used. The late J.H. Fitzgerald of Colt fame, for example, carried a pair of pistols for pocket use, but they were chopped down Colt New Service revolvers in .45 caliber. However, the designation generally described small-frame handguns chambered for equally small rounds, like the .22 LR, .25 ACP, .32 ACP, .32 S&W Long and .38 S&W. In fairly recent times, that list was expanded to include the .380 ACP and the .38 Special.

Purpose of such handguns was straightforward: be small enough to be carried on a daily basis, at the same time offering a measure of close-range personal protection. In that respect, they were truly "defensive" arms.

Given their relative lack of power and a rather casual regard for accuracy, they were hardly the tool of choice for anyone seeking a confrontation. Yet they were compact and, as Bill Jordan once observed, "They would outreach a switchblade."

Today, we seldom hear of the "pocket pistol." The guns still are here, of course. If anything, need for such firearms is even greater now than at any point in this country's history. But, due to numerous changes in both men's and women's fashions, there are precious few handguns that now can fit into a pocket!

Those that still meet that requirement generally are chambered for nothing more potent than the .25 ACP, which has been characterized as a "nice gun to carry if you don't want to carry a gun."

There still remains a need for a classic pocket pistol chambered for a cartridge powerful enough to perform its intended task, should such an unfortunate situation ever arise.

That's why a pair of new AMT Back Up handguns should prove highly popular among those who feel they do have a legitimate right to protect themselves from society's more violent misfits.

Called the DAO Backup and the Back Up II, both are dimensionally identical. Crafted from stainless steel alloys — a decided advantage for any handgun that will be carried a lot — they have an unloaded weight of a scant 18 ounces. Length is 5.0 inches, with a height of 3.5 inches. At the thickest portion — the grip panels — width is just 11/16-inch. The grips are of a black carbon fiber composite with impressed checkering to provide a non-slip gripping surface.

Either will slip easily into a Levi pocket. In fact, they are little larger than virtually any .25 ACP, yet these back-ups are chambered for the .380 ACP, which most experts agree is the minimum power level for a cartridge intended for self-defense. In actual street usage, the .380 ACP has proved to be about as effective as the .38 Special fired from a two-inch barrel.

Magazine capacity is five rounds. Additional magazines are available from AMT (6226 Santos Diaz St., Irwindale, CA 91702), and come in two styles: One offers a finger rest extension on the floorplate that some people find offers a better grip; the other has a flat bottom that provides maximum concealability. Magazines are interchangeable between both guns.

The magazines feature a provision for take-down and cleaning, a "witness" hole at round number four and a red plastic follower. They appear sturdy and well-made and, during 400-plus test rounds from both guns, there was not a hint of trouble from any of the three different magazines rotated between them.

Although the guns are virtually identical in dimensions, in operation, they are quite different. This provides the individual with the choice of two methods of operation.

The DAO Back Up (double-action-only) could be described accurately as a "stainless steel Seecamp in .380 ACP." Those familiar with the Seecamp custom guns — along with their price and the lengthy wait to get one — should recognize that for what it is worth!

Two different magazines are available for the Back Up pistol. Both performed flawlessly during author's test.

This action operates with a spring-loaded inertia firing pin and only can be fired/discharged by deliberately pulling the lengthy double-action trigger. When the trigger is pulled, the hammer — shielded in a cut-out within the slide and frame — rides back to the release point, then comes forward to strike the firing pin. As the slide cycles to feed a fresh round, the hammer rides back with it, then moves forward to stop at a point short of contact with the firing pin. You cannot thumb-cock this hammer. You only can discharge the gun with the double-action trigger.

The owner's manual states the trigger pull is about eight pounds. My Brownell's/Chatillon Trigger Pull Gauge (as well as a trigger finger educated through many years of DA revolver work) told me it was about 16 pounds. That's a pretty stiff pull, although I suspect it could be lightened easily. One would have to be brain-dead to have an accidental discharge with this gun. Aiding in the safety arena is a small window at the rear of the chamber that shows whether a round is chambered. There are no other safeties, levers or controls on this gun. It is trim and pocket-ready.

This is the type of gun that can be carried in deep concealment, grabbed with either hand and put into action with nothing more than the trigger finger. Given its size, operating characteristics and power, it may well be one of the best law enforcement back-up guns available.

The manual specifically recommends against carrying the gun with a round in the chamber, but given the design, I suspect that was written by a liability lawyer, not an engineer. I don't recommend ignoring safety warnings in the owner's

The DAO Back Up isn't much larger than a .25 ACP pocket pistol, yet it is chambered for the more potent .380 ACP.

manual, but I personally would carry it with one in the chamber and five in the magazine.

One feature of the DAO I did not like was the sights; more specifically, the lack of them. The sighting system on this gun is nothing more than a channel milled into the top of the slide, running full length from muzzle to rear. I can understand the need for a "snag-freed profile" on this type of gun, but I feel this is going overboard.

It is possible the designers figured that since this was a close range, point-and-shoot pistol anyway and, with the long DA pull, accuracy would be limited, sights were not required.

I disagree. Any type of front sight would provide a useful reference point similar to the front bead on a shotgun. The DAO model has more than enough potential accuracy to benefit from better sights; AMT should consider adding them.

The Back Up II is a totally different breed of cat. This is a classic single-action, internal striker-fired semi-auto. Once a round is chambered, the striker is cocked and two manual safeties come into operation. The first is a frame-mounted, left-side, sliding safety button. Up is for Safe; down for Fire, with a visible red dot at the Fire position. A grip safety (a la the Colt Government Model) must be depressed by hand pressure to allow the pistol to fire.

Normally, I don't care for grip safeties on full-size semi-autos, because you can take an effective shooting grip and not depress them. On a miniscule little pistol like this one, however, you have to take the type of grip that will depress it. Being a striker-fired action, the dual safeties make sense. It is

a good feature on this type of gun.

With both safeties in the fire position, a short, single-action pull of about nine pounds lights it off. That may sound like a heavy trigger pull and, with a full-size gun, it would be. However, on a small self-defense gun like this one, I would not want a pull any lighter than six or seven pounds. Little guns, light triggers and stress situations can make for unpleasant accidents!

Even with the nine-pound trigger, this gun displayed some surprising accuracy. Part of that was undoubtably because this model has some usable sights.

A small front post and an equally miserly fixed rear notch adorn the gun. While they are no more prone to snagging than the channel sights on the DAO model, they did make a significant difference when it came to target time.

There are some operating features common to both guns: Both styles are designed to feed rounds into the chamber from the magazine only. Single loading rounds can cause a malfunction. Should one desire to carry the gun with a round in the chamber, the procedure is to insert a magazine loaded with five rounds, retract the slide and let it fly forward forcefully to chamber a round, then remove the magazine, replace the round and re-insert the magazine.

Neither handgun has a magazine safety and each will fire with — or without — the magazine inserted, if there is a round in the chamber. The DAO model has a chamber-loaded window, but the Backup II has no such indicator. You have to think; always good advice around any firearm!

The magazine catches on both guns are located on the heel of the butt, in the manner of many European pistols. This is an excellent feature on any pocket pistol, since a frame-mounted, push-button magazine release can be depressed in pocket carry and disengage the magazine without your being aware of it.

Neither gun will lock the slide back when it is empty. Other than the sights on the DAO model, this was the only other feature on the guns I did not like.

As one who has used smallarms, including handguns, in combat, I can assure you it is a rare individual indeed who can count the number of rounds he has fired under stress conditions. A positive means of knowing when the gun has to be recharged is important!

When either of these guns runs dry, the slide goes right back forward on an empty chamber. What you get is a hollow "click" when you pull the trigger, and that — at the wrong time — can go beyond embarrassment. It could be fatal.

Correcting that deficiency would require some serious re-engineering, perhaps, but it should be done.

Still, I was impressed with both guns. That feeling only increased when I got to the range.

A defensive handgun that will not feed and fire the best available factory ammunition is, at best, a placebo: You might feel prepared, but you really are not. In this respect, reliability of both guns was good! In fact, it was better than that.

On hand for these tests was a wide variety of fresh factory ammo. Those rounds included: From Federal Cartridge Co., the 90-grain Hydra-Shok JHP (P380HS1); 90-grain Hi-Shok

Author tested both guns offhand at 20 yards and found the pint-sized AMT Back Up II a surprising performer.

JHP (380BP); and the 95-grain FMJRN (380AP). Hornady was represented by the 90-grain XTP JHP (#9010) and the 100-grain FMJRN (#9015). The classic Winchester Silvertip 85-grain JHP and their 95-grain FMJ (X380AP) were their representatives, while CCI's excellent Blazer rounds — 88-grain JHP (#3504) and the 95-grain (TMJ #3505) also were on hand. From PMC/El Dorado came their 90-grain FMJ (380A) and the 90-grain JHP (380B). That list includes six hollow-point rounds in varying shapes, and five hardball loads.

Each of the above rounds was fired 10 times over the screens of my Oehler 35P, using the Back Up II. The DAO model was not chronographed, because I was unwilling to risk

Chronograph tests showed surprising velocities from factory .380 ammo and the small auto with its 2 1/2-inch barrel.

TABLE 1

Velocities are the average of 10 rounds fired over Oehler 35P chronograph with start screen 20 feet from the muzzle of the AMT Back Up II.

LOAD	VELOCITY/FPS	ENERGY/FPE
Federal 90-gr. Hydra-Shok JHP (P380HS1)	922	168
Federal 90-gr. Hi-Shok JHP (380BP)	851	144
Federal 95-gr. FMJ (380AP)	880	163
CCI Blazer 95-gr. TMJ (#3505)	802	134
CCI Blazer 88-gr. JHP (#3504)	820	131
Winchester Silvertip 85-gr. JHP (X380ASHP)	850	136
Winchester 95-gr. FMJ (X380AP)	826	145
Hornady 100-gr. FMJ (#9015)	778	134
Hornady 90-gr. XTP JHP (#9010)	875	153
PMC/El Dorado 90-gr. FMJ (380A)	840	140
PMC/El Dorado 90-gr. JHP (380B)	853	144

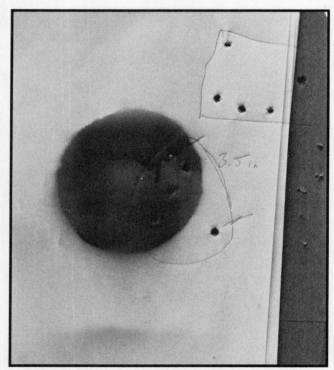

Using the Back Up II, author fired the five-shot group (upper right) from 20 yards. After correcting the amount of front sight used, author built the 3 1/2-inch group.

my Skyscreens on a gun with no sights and a 16-pound trigger!

Both barrels are identical. They come off the same assembly line, and should produce almost identical results. A look at Table 1 will show the velocities and muzzle energies produced from the DAO 2.5-inch barrel.

Reliability testing was fairly straightforward. I made certain four full magazines — 20 rounds — of each load went through both guns during the course of plinking and paper-target popping. That works out to 220 rounds per gun. Prior to the shooting, both guns were cleaned and lubricated with Tetra-Gun SLC. They received no further attention until the tests were completed.

The DAO version simply was amazing! During the entire 220+ rounds there was precisely *one* malfunction, and that was probably my fault. Late in the tests, when the gun was getting rather grungy, I inserted a magazine of PMC ball ammo and half-heartedly pulled the slide back and released it. The round failed to seat fully, and I had to tap the rear of the slide with the palm of my hand to put the slide into battery.

That was it! I never have seen any other pocket pistol digest so many rounds, in such a wide variety of configurations, without numerous malfunctions!

The Back Up II didn't fare as well. During chronographing, it refused to feed the Federal Hydra-Shok and Federal Hi-Shok. Surprisingly, it suffered several feeding malfunctions with the Federal ball ammo, as well. They were all identical: The round would be halfway into the chamber and tipped

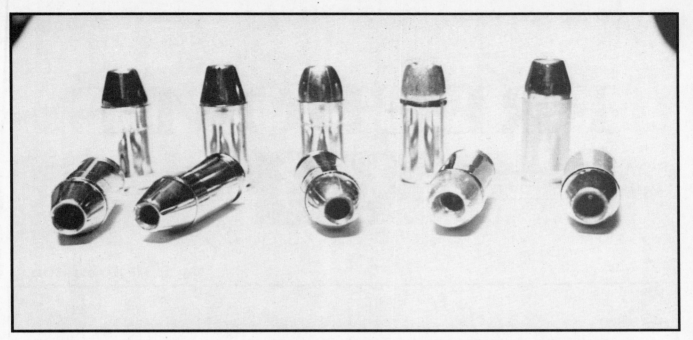

From left: Federal's Hydra-Shok, Hornady's XTP, Federal's Hi-Shok, Winchester's Silvertips and CCI's Blazer.

upward toward the top of the chamber. That's not good, but the cure is simple.

The Back Up models do not feature a feed ramp that is integral with the barrel. Instead — as with the Colt Government Model — the barrel and frame come together to form the ramp. On the Back Up II, there was a slight burr at the juncture of frame and barrel. Quick inspection showed it was stripping copper jacket material. There was a definite copper smear on the ramp.

Apparently, that burr was enough to tip some rounds upward and cause a feeding failure. It would take me less than 20 minutes to strip the gun and smooth the ramp with a Dremel polishing tip and some jeweler's rouge. A competent gunsmith could do it in 10 minutes. That would cure the problem, and it is something I do on every semi-auto in my personal battery as a routine matter.

With that done, I have no doubt the Back Up II would be just as reliable as the DAO. Even with the burred feed ramp, it still gobbled up every other round without problems.

The ejection pattern on both guns was positive: three to five feet upward and two to four feet to the shooter's right and slightly forward. You won't duck brass with these.

Were I going to define the term "oxymoron," "pocket-pistol accuracy" would do the job! Little guns, heavy trigger pulls and short, crude sights won't get you to the winner's circle at Camp Perry. After the AMT session, however, I had to revise my opinion, partially.

Just for the heck of it, I stapled up an 11x17 piece of white copy paper at 20 yards and spray-painted a six-inch bull in the middle. That size copy paper is slightly smaller than the average male torso and I figured if I could keep half of the rounds on it at 20 yards I'd be doing good.

From a firm Weaver hold, the first group from the Back Up II went into four inches! It was high and slightly right. After I corrected the amount of front sight in the sight picture, the next five rounds clustered around the right side of the bull and measured 3.5 inches. The Back Up II continued to do that with every round tested: Load five, take a steady hold, squeeze 'em off carefully from 20 yards and you got three- to four-inch groups in the center of the target.

Backing off to 50 yards, I fired five rounds, using the Weaver stance and five from a kneeling position. Three were center hits, one was one-half-inch off the paper high and right (a shoulder shot) and two more were an inch low, but centered (belt-level hits guaranteed to ruin any miscreant's day). That's six torso hits out of 10 rounds at 50 yards with a .380 you can stuff in your front Levi pocket!

The DAO Back Up couldn't match that. But after I figured out how to get the channel sight aligned with just a hint of the bottom showing at the muzzle, I was able to keep five rounds in six- to eight-inch groups centered on the 11x17 target at 20 yards.

Give the gun a set of sights and lighten the trigger a bit, and I suspect I would have been able to keep everything centered in four- to six-inch groups. That's more than adequate for this gun's intended use.

I was impressed with both guns, especially with the fact that the two different action types give shooters a choice. For a deep-cover back-up gun that may have to be grabbed with either hand and put into close-range action from an awkward position, the DAO would be a perfect choice. However, it should be noted that some people — the elderly or small-framed females — may not have the hand strength to operate the long DA pull. In that case, the Back Up II would be a better choice.

It would be hard to go wrong with either, however. And I've already decided that when the package of test guns goes back to AMT there only will be one in the box — and a check for the other.

I just haven't decided which one I'm going to keep yet!

FREEDOM'S
353

By Phil Johnston

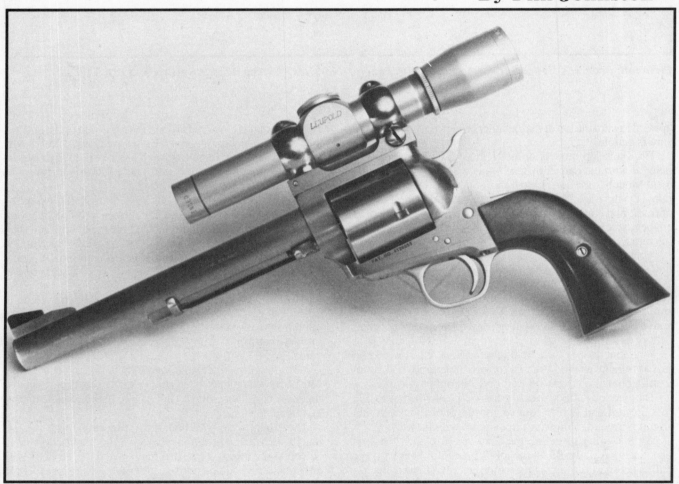

The Freedom Arms 353 is a .454 with smaller holes. The author found the new offering to be a fine hunting firearm.

The temperature was in the high teens, with just enough of a North Dakota breeze to make it perfectly clear where a whitetail would not show up. I was 16 feet up in an aluminum stand quite appropriately called the White Tail Hunter, produced by Lakeshore Products, Incorporated (855 W. Chicago Rd., Quincy, MI 49082).

While the North Dakota season lasted three more days, my time was about out because of a planned late season pheasant hunt. This was to be my last morning in the White Tail Hunter. Half an hour earlier, I let another typical young buck go after having him "dead to rights" at 30 yards or so. This was just one of a dozen or so I'd had the reticle on in nearly two weeks of

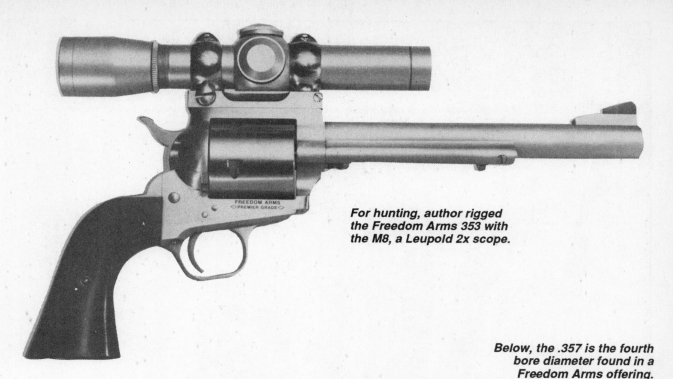

For hunting, author rigged the Freedom Arms 353 with the M8, a Leupold 2x scope.

Below, the .357 is the fourth bore diameter found in a Freedom Arms offering.

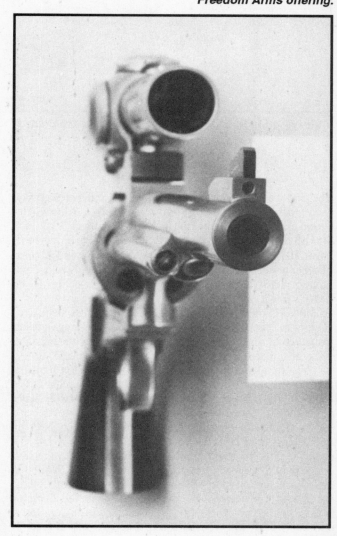

hunting on my farm. I'd rattled-in young bucks, had grunted in a couple of forks and had seen a magnificent five-pointer at long range, for just a minute or so, that would go near 20 inches. When you see a buck like that, even though he was beyond the reach of my .357 magnum, you don't take lesser bucks until the last minute.

As I continued to admire the muted sunrise and six to eight inches of snow in "my" woods, the slightly crusted snow gave away the approach of five whitetails. They were completely oblivious to my presence, and two does passed directly under my secure position. The buck with the does was not the big five-pointer, but he was a nice four-by-four and this was, after all, the last morning. I cocked the Freedom Arms 353 again, but this time I knew I'd squeeze off a shot. The buck stopped about 30 yards out, as I settled the reticle of the Leupold M8 2x scope behind his shoulder. The crack of the 357 broke the silence and I knew the shot was good. The buck moved about five yards, and I launched a second 180-grain slug in his direction before he slumped in his final resting place. The '92 deer season was over.

Rarely do I recommend a .357 magnum for hunting white-tail deer, although I've used that caliber on fox, coyote, antelope and deer with reasonably good results. Still, the .357 magnum is the smallest revolver that should go in the field when the quest is for antelope and/or deer. In fact, when the stable includes revolvers that shoot as well as a .357, and are chambered for the .44 magnum or .45 Colt, or better still, the .454 Casull, a .357 rarely is considered. At least that was the case until Freedom Arms began cutting .357 diameter holes in the cylinders and barrels of their newest gun, the 353.

The Freedom Arms single-action five-shooter is no new-comer in the world of handgun hunting. The big .454 got its start almost 40 years ago, when Dick Casull began rebuilding Colt single actions to handle a .45 Colt case stuffed with triplex powder charges behind 230-grain and heavier bullets.

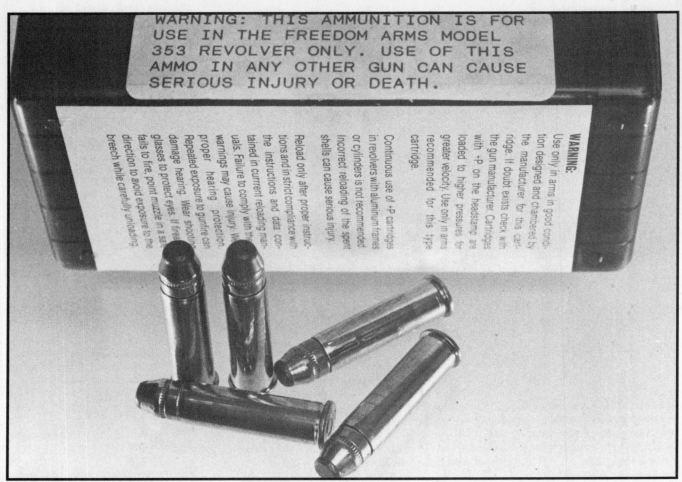

The following text appears within the image (ammunition box warnings):

WARNING: THIS AMMUNITION IS FOR USE IN THE FREEDOM ARMS MODEL 353 REVOLVER ONLY. USE OF THIS AMMO IN ANY OTHER GUN CAN CAUSE SERIOUS INJURY OR DEATH.

WARNING: Use only in arms in good condition designed and chambered by the manufacturer for this cartridge. If doubt exists check with the gun manufacturer. Cartridges loaded with +P on the headstamp are loaded to higher pressures for greater velocity. Use only in arms recommended for this type cartridge.

Continuous use of +P cartridges in revolvers with aluminum frames or cylinders is not recommended. Incorrect reloading of the spent shells can cause serious injury.

Reload only after proper instructions and in strict compliance with the instructions and data contained in current reloading manuals. Failure to comply with these warnings may cause injury. Wear proper hearing protection. Repeated exposure to gunfire can damage hearing. Wear shooting glasses to protect eyes. If firearm fails to fire, point muzzle in a safe direction to avoid exposure to the breech while carefully unloading.

This 180-grain special load from Cor-Bon is designated "...for use in the Freedom Arms Model 353 revolver only."

The .454 was born in factory form in 1983, and it comes as no secret that I've been in love with the Freedom Arms single-action ever since. I've successfully used a vintage 7 1/2-inch .454 all over the place to bust critters like Alaskan brown bear, a fine Dall sheep, several good mule deer bucks and a bunch of other animals as well. I'm but one of the gang of handgun hunters who find the Freedom Arms single-action to be today's finest hunting gun. Period.

Since its inception, the big 17-4 PH stainless steel five-shooter has been chambered for the .45 Colt, .44 magnum and even the .22 rimfires in the case of the tack-driving 252. The latest chambering is for the oldest magnum, the .357.

I've often said that I typically find the .357 too light for heavy work, and too heavy for light work — at least in the field. While hundreds of hunters exist who probably have made "perfect" shots on whitetail deer, bear or whatever, with successful results, the case is that there are better calibers for the real world of hunting. Although the Freedom Arms 353 still is a .357 magnum, adding the chambering to the line added another hunter's gun to the arsenal, as well. While I'd not use the 353 on bear, elk or moose, I do now firmly plunk the 353 (not just any .357, though) into whitetail domain. Loaded with state-of-the-art heavy handloads or Cor-Bon's excellent "FOR 353 ONLY" loads, the 353 is one of today's great hunting guns.

The 353 shares everything with the other calibers in the Freedom Arms lineup, except the size of the holes. The big single action sample was shipped with Freedom's standard ramp front sight and rear blade that is adjustable for windage and elevation. The Premier grade sample displayed all the quality typically present in Freedom Arms offerings, immediately. It carried the brushed finish with laminated rosewood grips. It took me about 10 minutes to pull the Leupold M8 2x scope off my Premier grade .44 magnum and switch it to the 353. While I still love open sights for much of what I do, when hunting anything seriously or wringing out such a tack-driver, to be fair to the firearm manufacturer and the ammo companies, considering these "vintage" eyes, a scope gets the nod.

The 353 features a barrel that carries cut rifling with six lands and grooves that make one right-hand turn in 14 inches of bullet travel. This contrasts with a twist of 1-18 3/4-inch more common in other .357s. Obviously, the FA 353 is designed with heavy projectiles in mind. The barrel is rifled by Ed Harris and is mirror smooth. Freedom Arms also has been messing with an electronic/chemical wash rifling system in the rimfire 252, and I expected to find such a barrel on the newest 353. Such is not the case. I visited the Freedom Arms factory in September, and asked sales manager Randy Smith

The soft-point bullet of the Cor-Bon cartridge has two cannelures, the lower one is used for the special 353.

why the 353 didn't feature the "electronically rifled" barrel. Put simply, Freedom Arms was ready to roll with the 353 and the outfit that does the electronic wash rifling wasn't. It probably doesn't matter, anyhow. Still, the barrel of a 252 is a sight to behold, and the electronic/chemical wash process leaves a mirror-bright bore that adds slightly to velocity while providing exceptional accuracy. In addition, while leading isn't a problem in a rimfire, such isn't always the case when working with high velocities and cast bullets in a centerfire. Freedom Arms acknowledges that the electronically rifled barrels tend to lead far less than a typical cut barrel. Be that as it may, the sample 353 carried a barrel that was rifled more conventionally. They may switch at any time, however.

Single actions typically feature less-than-perfect triggers, with a heavy and longish hammer fall. While little can be done with the hammer fall on a big hunting gun like the Freedom Arms single action, the trigger on the sample is nearly of target quality. This one breaks like ice at 3 1/2 pounds, and if I had ordered it, it would have been ordered this way. My other FA guns also break like ice, so this came as no surprise.

The 353 is no small package — naturally, since it's simply a .454 with smaller holes. The gun weighs seven ounces more than the .454, hitting the scales at 59 ounces, unloaded, with open adjustable sights. As one would expect, this heavy-weight tames the recoil of the entire spectrum of .357 ammo with ease. This is one of the most pleasant hunting guns you'll ever shoot.

Typically, the range work confirmed that Freedom Arms still builds one accurate revolver. While the slow twist barrel tended to prefer the heaviest bullets, the gun turned in a few five-shot, 50-yard groups that went under three inches with lightweights like Federal's 110-grain JHPs. Still, the 353 came to life as the bullet weight went up — silhouette shooters take note. While sub-three-inch groups were the norm with light bullets, sub-two-inch groups became commonplace as bullets surpassed 145 grains in weight. In fact, Black Hills

Ammunition's excellent 158-grain JHPs left the 7 1/2-inch barrel averaging 1240 fps or so, and slipped into two groups that measured .75-inch and 1.25-inch, center-to-center. The load would do okay for picture book shots on whitetails out to 40-50 yards, but the 353 is capable of so much more.

The nearby chart tells a lot of what I learned, but we've got to note a few worthy mentions. Remington's 180-grain JHP is a warm .357 load that launches an excellent bullet at 1300 fps and the 353 will keep them under two inches at 50 yards. I managed to run 10 of them into 4 3/4 inches at *100 yards*, striking only one to two inches below that 50-yard zero. If one is restricted to a more normal .357, and doesn't handload, this Remington ammo is the clear-cut winner as a hunting round. Period.

Still, I wanted to see what the big, heavy, .454-framed 353 would do. I decided to cook up some 353 *only* handloads, and then come up with a hunting load designed again for only the 353. Hornady's silhouette bullet is dubbed the JTC-SIL and weighs 180 grains. When loaded over 18.0 grains of WW 296 the bullet leaves the 7 1/2-inch 353 barrel doing 1560 fps or so, and 10 of them slipped into two groups that measured 1 3/8-inch and 1 1/2-inch, center-to-center, at 50 yards. While not a hunting bullet, this load should be a place for silhouette shooters to start.

I also got a chance to work with a semi-factory load that should get the nod from any 353 owners who don't handload but want to hunt medium-weight, thin-skinned game, up to and including the deer family. Peter Pi, owner and manager of Cor-Bon (Box 10126, Detroit, MI 48210), has been building high-performance bullets and ammunition for quite some time. I've used his bullets on the likes of Dall sheep out of my pet .454, and wanted to wring out some of his ultra-hot 180-grain JSP ammo in the 353.

Up front, as Cor-Bon makes it perfectly clear, this ammo is loaded *only for the 353*. It features a 180-grain jacketed soft-point bullet that carries a cannelure in two locations, one for

AMMUNITION	VELOCITY/ES/SD	5-SHOT GROUP	COMMENTS
Black Hills Ammunition **158-grain JHP**	**1,236/103/43 fps** **1,239/79/31 fps**	3/4" 1 1/4"	
CCI Blazer **125-grain JHP**	**1,572/102/37 fps** **1,523/73/29 fps**	2 13/16" 2 5/16"	
Federal **110-grain JHP**	**1,527/30/16 fps** **1,540/42/22 fps**	2 15/16" 4 1/2"	
Federal **180-grain JHP**	**1,121/63/25 fps** **1,139/49/19 fps**	2 1/2" 2 1/8"	
Remington **125-grain Med. Vel.**	**1,287/116/43 fps** **1,282/53/22 fps**	4 5/8" 4 3/4"	
Remington **180-grain JHP**	**1,297/18/06 fps** **1,300/45/17 fps**	1 7/8" 2"	**Top factory load for hunting** **med. game with "standard"** **.357 magnum**
Winchester **125-grain JHP**	**1,669/43/18 fps** **1,658/65/19 fps**	3" 2 3/8"	
Winchester **145-grain** **Silvertip HP**	**1,498/62/23 fps** **1,470/66/29 fps**	2 1/2" 4 5/8"	**Called flyer opened** **otherwise good group of 1 1/4"**
Winchester **158-grain JHP**	**1,405/45/16 fps** **1,395/37/15 fps**	3 1/8" 2"	
Cor-Bon 180-grain JSP **For Freedom Arms 353** ONLY	**1,558/37/14 fps** **1,580/33/11 fps**	2 1/4" 2 5/8"	**Less Than 4" @ 100 yds** **Top hunting load for 353 ONLY**
Hornady 158 XTP HP **18.0 Winchester 296** **Remington 71/2 primers**	**1,460/63/25 fps** **1,453/90/33 fps**	2" 2 1/4"	
Speer 160-grain HJ SWC HP **18.0 Winchester 296** **Remington 7 1/2 primers**	**1,550/62/29 fps** **1,571/24/09 fps**	3 9/16" 2 5/8"	
Speer 180-grain FMJ **18.0 Winchester 296** **Remington 7 1/2 primers**	**1,445/80/35 fps** **1,430/120/52 fps**	2 3/16" 1 1/2"	
Hornady 190-grain JTC-SIL **18.0 Winchester 296** **Remington 7 1/2 primers**	**1,498/44/17 fps** **1,490/34/12 fps**	1 3/8" 1 1/2"	
Magma 157-grain cast BB SWC **sized .3575" lubed with Rooster** **18.0 Winchester Red 296** **Remington 7 1/2 primers**	**1,644/55/22 fps** **1,622/28/11 fps**	8" 14 7/8"	**Group opened while group** **was shot. Leading badly.**
Magma 157.5-grain cast BB SWC **sized .3575" lubed with Rooster** **19.0 Winchester Red 296** **Remington 7 1/2 primers**	**1,684/31/12 fps** **1,693/63/26 fps**	11 3/8" 10.0"	
Magma 157.5-grain cast BB SWC **sized .3575" lubed with** **Rooster Red** **20.0 Winchester 296** **Remington 7 1/2 primers**	**1,752/39/17 fps** **1,751/76/31 fps**	14 1/2" 6 5/8"	**Cleaned before last cast group.**

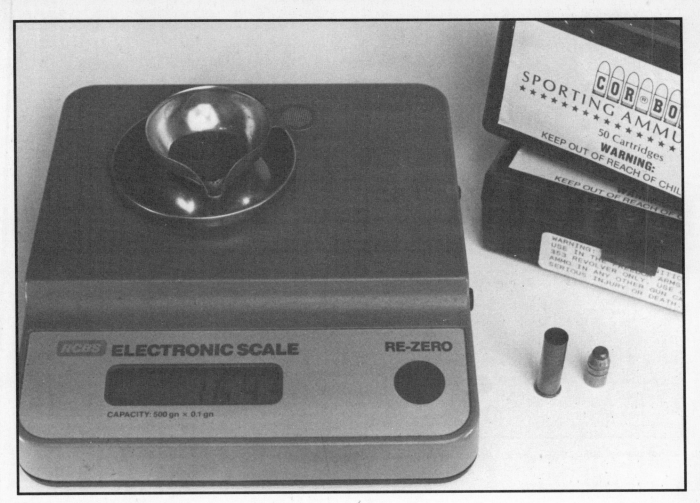

Above, Cor-Bon's "for 353 only" ammunition is loaded with 16.4 to 16.5 grains of what looks like Accurate #9.

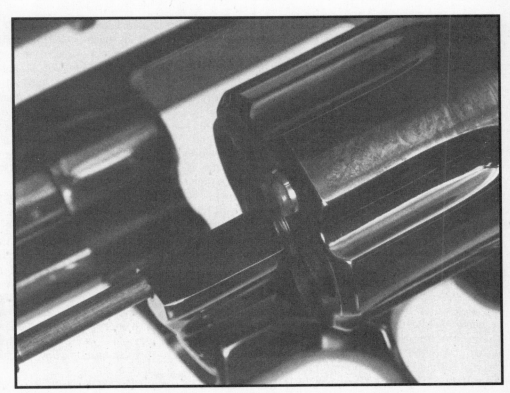

Right, the special Cor-Bon ammunition should never be loaded into anything other than a Freedom Arms 353. It is too long for a Python.

Author carries all of his Freedom Arms revolvers in a slightly modified shoulder holster from Michaels of Oregon.

long seating and use in the 353 and one for more typical seating and use in "other" .357s. I hated to do it, but pulled one of the great looking 180-grain bullets and dumped the ball powder into the pan of my RCBS electronic scale. The scale indicated a charge weight of 16.4-16.5 grains, and the powder looks an awful lot like Accurate's #9 — a powder that is gaining a wide reputation as a replacement for 296. In fact, Freedom Arms is using #9 in their factory .454 loads now, as well. The Cor-Bon ammo also appears to have a Remington 7 1/2 "rifle" primer seated in the factory-fresh Winchester cases. Deer season was at hand, so I quickly sighted the 353 in at 100 yards with five Cor-Bon loads and slipped down-range to check the 100-yard group after accounting for two 50-yard groups of 2 1/4 inches and 2 5/8 inches. The 100-yard group was on the money after zeroing one inch high at 50, and the five Cor-Bons slipped into a group just under four inches, center-to-center. That's a hunting load, with excellent accuracy to boot. One must remember that this was done with a 2x scope — not the power necessary for benchrest groups at 100 yards, by the way.

I also wanted to cook up a handload that would duplicate, or nearly duplicate the Cor-Bon 180s. Hornady has been gaining a great reputation with their XTP bullet line, and three boxes of a brand new 180-grain XTP hollow-point design arrived in time for deer hunting, but too late for extensive range testing. The new XTP HP weighs 180 grains and carries a dual cannelure for long or normal seating. I grabbed a few clean, once-fired Winchester cases and a fresh supply of Accurate #9 powder, a few Remington 7 1/2 primers, and gathered everything around my Dillon RL 550. I set the powder measure to throw 16.5 grains of #9, and loaded five rounds to run out the door and check for extraction and signs of pressure. The five cases extracted normally, but the primers indicated that this was about as far as I wanted to go. They were quite flat, with just a tad of cratering. Still, the gun operated normally, and the rig shot the 180-grain Hornady XTPs right where the Cor-Bon ammo went. Next, I just had to find a buck.

The first round that caught the whitetail buck went through both lungs and exited on the far side. I was unable to recover the Cor-Bon bullet. I typically keep shooting until I run out of ammo, or the critter is down, and anticipated that I'd get more than one shot. I stuffed the five-shot cylinder of the FA 353 with one Cor-Bon factory load, and four of my hot, 353-only XTP loads. After the first shot, the buck moved slightly closer, and I launched an XTP his way. This bullet hit a rib on entry, went through the top of the heart and ended up lodged just under the skin on the far shoulder. The recovered bullet expanded well, and weighs 170.2 grains — retaining 95 percent of its starting weight. The two shots were within an inch or so.

During the last few weeks, we've been dining on venison

For his "For 353 Only" handloads, author used Hornady 180-grain XTP HPs over 16.5 grains of Accurate #9 and Remington 7 1/2 primers. The recovered bullet (right), taken from a whitetail buck, retained 95 percent of its weight.

and I've been doing a lot of thinking about the .357 cartridge, as well as the Freedom Arms 353. Have I changed my thinking? Not really. A normal .357 magnum is marginal at best in the real hunting world. While the Remington 180-grain load takes a typical .357 as far as it can, such a load should be reserved for picture book shots at a calm, stationary deer at no more than 50 to 60 yards, in my book. Such a load is not a brush-bucking, bone-crushing 100-yard load. If other than this picture book shot is the case, I'd feel far better equipped with a .44 magnum or better still, the .454.

What about the 353, loaded to its full potential? Yep, the 353 so loaded ends up flat in the middle of the old .357 Maximum's territory, and the Maxi is (or is it was?) a whitetail round, pure and simple. A 180-grain bullet at 1500 to 1600 fps generates just shy of 1000 foot-pounds of muzzle energy (80 fpe more than a typical .41 magnum loaded with 210-grain bullets), and a well designed .357 bullet at this velocity should penetrate like a freight train. That 180-grain Cor-Bon may still be going, for all I know. The 353, when loaded with 180s at 1600 fps, can be zeroed one to two inches high at 50, and it'll be right on the mark at 100 yards. Although I've not chronographed the XTP handload, I'm going to guess that 16.5 grains of Accurate #9 and Remington

7 1/2 primers launch the Hornady 180s at 1600 fps or so.

The new 353 Premier Grade gun with adjustable sights carries a suggested 1993 retail price of $1,385 and the Field grade goes for $1,115. To be sure, that's a lot of change. If I was looking for but one perfect hunting gun, to take me from called coyote through deer, moose, elk and maybe even a bear or two, I'd take the .454, hands down. Still, if I wanted the quality offered by Freedom Arms, with less recoil and noise, and knowing full well that the gun would be used on nothing bigger than a deer, any species, the 353 just might be a logical choice.

The 48 folks currently employed by Freedom Arms are still turning out the finest revolver in the world. Period. The 353 is a winner, and a great addition to the line. I sincerely hope that Bob Baker forgets that this 353 is where it is. Surprise, surprise — I will probably set my stands in about the same spot on the farm next year, and I'll probably hunt for that big five-by-five with a .357 magnum wheelgun. Not just any .357, though. It'll be this 353, stuffed, most likely, with one Cor-Bon load (to go first), and four Hornady XTPS. After all, why mess with success? Finally, with 353-only loads, there is a perfect .357 magnum for deer hunting. The cartridge just got a whole lot better, and handgunners got a whole lot luckier with the introduction of the 353.

THE .45/.410 THUNDER FIVE

By Tom Ferguson

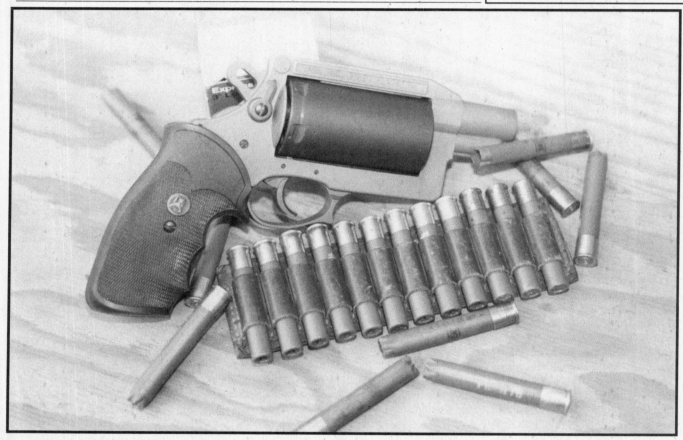

The Thunder Five revolver is a unique firearm. The huge handgun is capable of handling .45 Colt and .410 shotshells.

This Combo Revolver Has Great Potential For Law Enforcement And Home Defense

The revolver's extractor stroke is short, barely freeing the cases from the chambers. They must be pulled out manually.

MOST SAVVY Americans keep a firearm of some type for home defense, and a large percentage of those are handguns. The usual gunowner already has been through the home protection scenario in his mind, and concludes that a rifle or shotgun, despite folding stocks and short barrels, is simply too unwieldy for indoor use. It would be nice to have the enhanced hit probability of the shotgun, and the first-round lethality, but by Federal law, fighting shotguns must have 18-inch barrels and be 26 inches in overall length.

There's no set rule for manufacturers, but most build "riot" shotguns with 20-inch barrels, even longer than required by law. It's a situation that guarantees difficulty in bringing the gun's muzzle on target, and there is a danger of having the shotgun wrested away during a close encounter with a home intruder.

On the other hand, there is another option. How about a large, capable and utterly reliable revolver with the ability to chamber both a powerful handgun cartridge and an equally powerful shotshell? None of the virtues of the handgun's pointability or retention capability would be sacrificed, but the hitting potential of the shotgun would be there when it's needed most.

The option exists in the Thunder Five, a massive revolver chambered for .410 shotshells and the .45 Colt cartridge.

The well-named Thunder Five is distributed by C.L. Reedy and Associates, Inc. of Melbourne, Florida. It weighs 48 ounces; a full three pounds to soak up the recoil of three-inch .410 shells or heavy .45 Colt loads. Other than the long, unfluted cylinder, it looks like an ordinary double-action revolver with a five-shot capability. Looks are deceiving however, and this is one revolver with some unusual features.

The frame of the Thunder Five is a casting, and a clean, well-done casting at that. According to Chuck Reedy, it requires no machining after it drops from the mold. To obtain a finely finished frame in this manner speaks well of the design, but even more unusual, it includes the two-inch barrel as well, complete with rifling! Although the rifling is the standard one turn in sixteen inches for the .45 Colt, it appears nearly straight due to the short barrel. The fixed sights of the Thunder Five are regulated to hit point of aim at thirty feet with the standard 255-grain .45 Colt bullets. Both front and rear sights are protected by metal ears which are part of the frame itself.

Fans of detective and spy novels will be delighted to learn the Thunder Five revolver is provided with the manual safety they've read of so often. It's located on the left side of the frame, and consists of a lever which operates vertically in a 180-degree arc. When the lever is turned up, a red warning dot is exposed, indicating the gun can be fired. Turned downward,

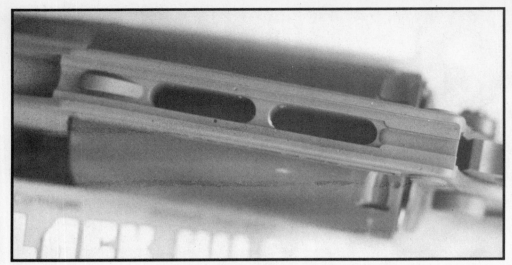

The Thunder Five's frame has elongated openings to lighten the revolver's weight.

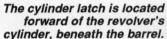

The cylinder latch is located forward of the revolver's cylinder, beneath the barrel.

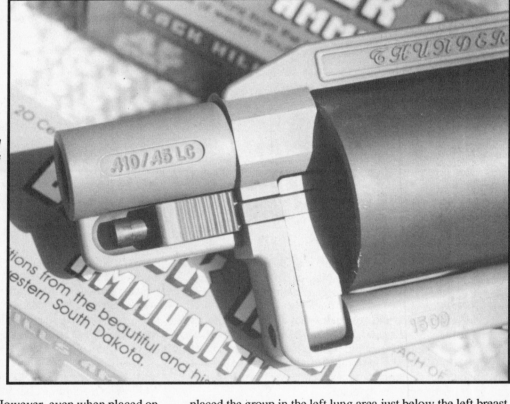

it places the revolver on safe. However, even when placed on safe, the action can be snapped once, after which the action is locked from further movement. The firing pin is locked by the safety lever immediately, so the snap does no harm. As with any safety, however, the shooter should keep the muzzle pointed in a safe direction, and refrain from snapping it that one time.

The Thunder Five safety is efficient and completely reliable. The way to a happy and uneventful life, however, is in not tempting mechanical devices.

The firing test began at seven yards, using some fairly ancient Peters .45 Colt cartridges from the 1960s. The target was a reduced size silhouette measuring only 10 by 14 inches. The 250-grain bullets made a 3-1/2-inch group in the upper left shoulder of the target. On a full-size silhouette, this would have

placed the group in the left lung area just below the left breast. Considering the difficulties encountered by firing a .45 Colt bullet from a 410 shotgun chamber, this is good accuracy. Apparently the "straight" rifling provides enough twist to keep the bullets flying point-on, and gives them decent accuracy.

Subsequent groups from Black Hills 255-grain .45 Colt printed slightly better groups of around three inches, but also were a bit above the point of aim. Only later did I learn from Chuck Reedy that the sights are regulated for 30 feet, not the 21-foot distance I chose. At whatever distance, this solid, heavy and traditional .45 slug would be my choice. The two-inch barrel most likely won't build enough steam to open (expand) a JHP bullet. True, the flat-tipped .45s in solid persuasion don't start out fast either, but then momentum keeps them plowing ahead to give the penetration for which

The manual safety lever moves in a 180 degree arc. In the up (fire) position, a red dot and "F" are visible.

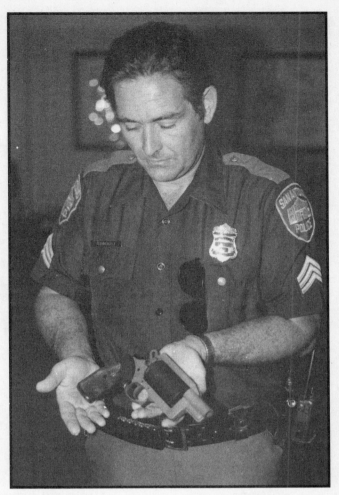

After inspecting the gun, San Antonio Police Sergeant Jim Prendergast declared it suited for law enforcement.

the .45 Colt is famous. It's a heavy, bad-news thump for any antagonist.

The other side of the coin is that the short barrel offers .410 shotshell performance out of all proportion to its length. The Thunder Five will chamber and fire 2 1/2 or three-inch .410 loads, and the big revolver really shows its teeth with the latter. Oddly enough, recoil is not bad, dampened by the three pounds of steel in the Thunder Five. The gun has Pachmayr combat grips installed, and these tend to reduce felt kick as well.

Muzzle whip is reduced to a minimum, and fast, repeat shots are possible with the heaviest of shot loads. The shotshells used in the test were Remington three-inch loads with #6 shot. At seven yards, the cloud of pellets completely covered up the reduced silhouette target, which was holed from top to bottom. After making this "pattern," the hurtling pellets completely penetrated the quarter-inch plywood target backing. Ouch! This proves the 410 shotload is possessed of enough malicious impetuosity to make it a serious defense proposition. The two-inch snout of the Thunder Five places no undue handicap on velocity.

About a decade ago, Winchester began producing .410-bore buckshot loads carrying three pellets of 000 (.36 caliber) buck. This was partially in response to the marketing of a twin-barreled derringer by American Derringer of Waco, Texas. The derringer is popular, so now we have the right load for it. Some of this Winchester ammo was on hand, so it was given a try in the Thunder Five.

On the same reduced silhouette target, one 000 ball would hit close to where the sights looked, but the other two invariably landed 12 to 14 inches away. When fired from a Thompson/Contender .45/.410 with a 10-inch barrel, the performance is identical. This is not a bad derringer load at short range, but the hits are too widespread and the pellets are too few to inspire confidence.

A better load for the Thunder Five can be constructed by using Speer .350-inch diameter round balls intended for muzzleloading arms. Beginning with Remington three-inch .410 factory loads, open the crimp and pour out the shot, leaving the plastic shot sleeve in place. Five of the .350-inch balls weigh exactly the same, and no pressure problems will result. The balls can be inserted and pressed down into the shot sleeve with the blunt end of a dowel or even a pencil.

Be certain the balls are pressed home fully, leaving no air space over the powder charge. There will be a tiny gap near the mouth of the case, since the column of round balls is slightly shorter than the original charge. One can dribble a few loose birdshot pellets on top of the last ball to close the gap and make an even deadlier load. Press the star crimp back in place with a Lee star crimper, and the load is finished. If it seems desirable for complete waterproofing, a few drops of candle wax will seal the crimp

These homemade buckshot loads perform with excellence in the Thunder Five. At the same seven-yard distance, the balls make a tight pattern of some four to five inches, spreading little. This would make a far more lethal entry wound than the three widely spaced .36 caliber hits from the Winchester derringer cartridges. Moreover, the Speer balls strike practically to the same point of aim as the .45 Colt bullets. Now that the Thunder Five has appeared, is it too much to ask for a

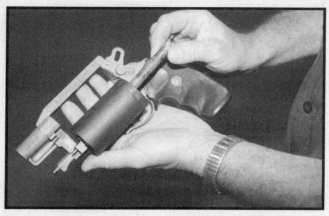
Loading .410 shotshells in the Thunder Five is simple.

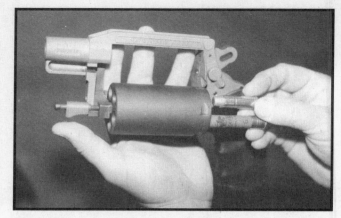
With .45 Colt and .410 shotshell, this is no ordinary gun.

SPECIFICATIONS

Caliber:	**.45 Colt or .410-bore shotshells**
Action:	**Single- or double-action**
Capacity:	**Five shots**
Length:	**Nine inches, overall**
Weight:	**48 ounces**
Barrel Length:	**Two inches**
Safties:	**Internal draw bar safety, ambidextrous hammer blocking safety lever.**
Finish:	**Durable phosphate finish**
Features:	**Fixed combat sights; hammer, trigger and trigger guard, Pachmayr grips, plastic carrying case**
Accessories:	**Nylon or leather hip holsters, ambidextrous shoulder holster, illuminated dot sight, sleeve inserts for 9mm, .38/.357 .380 cartridges, interchangeable cylinder assembly in .45-70 caliber.**
Suggested Retail Price:	**$499**
Distributor:	**C.L. Reedy & Associates, Inc, 2485 Grassere Dr., Melbourne, FL 32904**

factory load carrying the five-ball payload?

Having established the point of impact on paper, the Thunder Five was given a workout in double-action instinctive shooting. Initially, the double-action pull was rough and heavy, even binding at times. Chuck Reedy explained this was probably due to the phosphate finish of the trigger, tiny particles wearing away to give a gritty, tough pull. He suggested light lubrication to wash away these small particles. As the gun wore in however, this proved unnecessary. With use, the DA pull smoothed out wonderfully and the binding disappeared.

Reloading with .410 shells laden with three-quarters of an ounce of #6 shot, I declared war on gallon plastic milk jugs at 20 feet, literally firing from the hip.

I found it relatively simple to bounce the jugs — with many pellet holes — as often as I liked. From observing the pellet strikes around the jug on the dusty ground, it appeared the Thunder Five consistently tosses a birdshot pattern approximately three feet long and two feet wide, in a large, oval-shaped shot storm. Multiple hits were recorded quickly, which proves a point. The Thunder Five, aside from home protection duty,

The massive cylinder of the Thunder Five will hold five .45 Colt rounds or .410 shotshell. It's simple and handy.

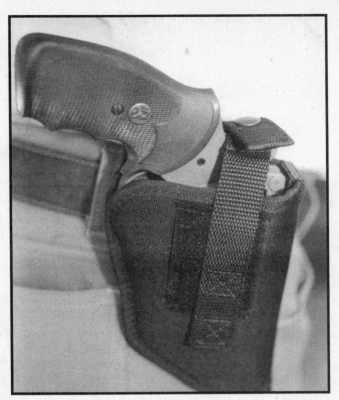

Surprisingly, the Thunder Five is a compact package when holstered. The manufacturer of the revolver also offers nylon and leather holsters and nylon shoulder rig.

would be an ideal entry weapon for police SWAT teams.

In a phone conversation with Reedy, it was learned the Thunder Five was indeed designed from the ground up to provide law enforcement with just such a weapon. It's far more compact than any shoulder shotgun and, in fact, can be carried on the hip in holsters of leather or nylon which are available from the company. The handgun has the same double-action capability so familiar to many police officers and is more reliable than any stiff, complex auto or pump gun.

Power? There is plenty on hand. With .45 Colt loads, the Thunder Five is a superb heavy revolver. In .410 bore, we have shot sizes ranging from #4 birdshot through #9, with slugs and Winchester buckshot to boot. Any or all can be alternated in the cylinder for greater versatility. If we're lucky, some major manufacturer may pick up and produce the five-ball buckshot load described earlier.

From a law enforcement point of view, the Thunder Five is an opportunity too good to pass up. At close range, the .45 Colt loads or .410 shot column would pack a lethal punch. Across a room, the lighter shot such as #6 would freckle an opponent so severely he wouldn't be able to return fire or retain his weapon. At the same time, the sleet of birdshot probably would inflict only a non-lethal wound! This is law enforcement combat at its best: to dominate and end a confrontation

without taking a life needlessly. SWAT personnel take notice!

During test firing, we found little to criticize on the Thunder Five. Despite the fact that the .45 Colt bullets make a 1-3/4-inch jump to the barrel from the long chambers, close-range accuracy was about equal to that of the average service revolver. Few of them will shoot tighter than three inches on paper.

Then there is the manual safety. Easy to operate, it is placed where the cylinder latch is on ordinary revolvers. From necessity, the latch is positioned on the ejector rod where it enters the barrel shroud up front. Opening the Thunder Five's cylinder takes some getting used to, but the drill is learned quickly.

The extractor stroke is unusually short, moving just a quarter-inch. This lifts the fired case from the chamber, where it may be flicked out with a fingernail. All the cases — both .45 Colt and .410 shotshells — extracted easily and gave no problems by sticking; and the extractor star doesn't ride over the rims. In short, our test Thunder Five gave perfect functioning and exceptionally versatile, reliable shooting.

Later, there will be an interchangeable cylinder in .45-70 caliber, as well as chamber inserts to accommodate .380/9mm and .38/.357 magnum cartridges. As mentioned, several types of holsters are available, as well as an illuminated red dot sight which is becoming popular.

The Thunder five is an incredibly versatile package and has a great future in law enforcement, as well as in home defense.

PARA-ORDNANCE P12.45 COMPACT

By Tom Ferguson

WHO'S OLD enough to remember the first "Bobcat" .45 auto from the late 1960s? If vague memory serves, the so-called Bobcat pistols were GI .45 autos cut down in the gun shop at Lackland AFB, Texas. The trim little .45s were intended to replace the .38 Special snubnose revolvers carried by Air Force police investigators in plainclothes.

Since the Lackland Air Force facility is a manufacturer capable of building guns from scratch, whittling down the .45 auto wasn't much of a task. Or was it? Years later, I met a gunsmith who worked on the project, and he confessed they were never able to get the guns to function reliably. Thus, the idea sort of faded away — at least with regard to the Air Force. The few Bobcats that were produced inspired copies by many other gunsmiths however, and at least one commercial attempt — the Detonics .45 auto.

Here's A Short .45 ACP Auto That Cures The Author's Dislike For The Breed!

The Para-Ordnance P12.45 Compact with its shortened grip and slide (right) is compared to the standard M1911 pistol.

It's not an easy thing to cut down the old M1911 Government Model and get complete reliability. Still later, another pistolsmith I respect told me that even in the Colt Commander the recoil impulses are different — "not like the Government Model," he said. The art of building good functioning into a small .45 auto is more recent than many think, in my opinion. But that's another story.

If you remember what the Air Force Bobcat looked like, then the new P12.45 Compact from Para-Ordnance looks just like that in profile. It's a M1911 with the slide and butt shortened, but the P12.45 has some improvements. It has a Commander-style hammer instead of a trimmed-back spur, and the grip is enlarged to take an 11-round magazine. With one in the pipe, that makes a P12.45. That means four shots more capacity than the old Bobcat or its copies. It's more firepower for the .45 auto, in keeping with the modern trend.

Frankly, I never liked the Bobcat or any other short-barreled .45 ACP. The grip is just short enough to be too short, and it doesn't feel right. The barrel length makes me feel even worse for ballistics reasons.

The standard .45 ACP load utilizes a 230-grain FMJ bullet at 800 fps, give or take a few feet per seconds. This velocity is from the five-inch barrel of the big Government Model, and is pretty marginal to my way of thinking. It can hardly stand to be reduced by firing in shorter tubes lest the legendary punch of the cartridge be compromised. As for the hotter 185-grain JHPs, these are meant to expand (hopefully) from five-inch barrels also, not runty 3 1/2-inch ones. In my view, the regular five-inch pipe is none too long for the .45 ACP. This is a prejudice I've had for years.

But I'll have to get over that, I suppose. The short .45s produce something like 730 fps with the 230-grain hardball

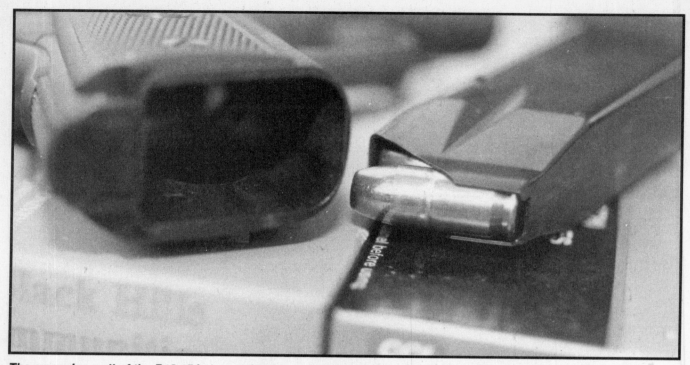

The magazine well of the P12.45 is larger than those on M1911 because of the double-column, 11-round magazines.

and perhaps 850 fps with the 185-grain JHPs. The British .455 Webley auto cartridge earned a pretty good reputation in World War II as a short-range manstopper, with a 225-grain FMJ bullet traveling at only 700 fps.

Going back to black powder days, the Colt Army Model 1860 .44 emptied a lot of saddles with closely similar ballistics. High velocity is fine when you can get it, but up close it may not be the total answer. Logic tells me to concede that the short .45s are lethal weapons, indeed.

It happened that I test-fired the P12.45 on the same outing with a modern 9mm pistol I like a lot.

The 9mm performed magnificently, spitting out 115-grain JHPs at speeds up to 1300 fps in Plus-P loadings. The fast bullet left neatly cut holes in the silhouette paper — small, neat, round holes. They were little holes that made little groups.

The P12.45 left ragged holes; big ones at that. The bullets were 200-grain SWCs from Black Hills, loaded to IPSC specs, for about 850 fps. They made it through the paper okay, but tore and ripped it grudgingly. The thought occurred that such bullets would be found by a coroner just under the skin on an opponent's back, after letting in a lot of air and daylight. For an analogy between the 9mm and the .45, think of a rapier thrust as opposed to a broadsword stroke. Either one could get you, but the broadsword is more awesome and dreadful in the fullest sense of the word.

While shooting the P12.45, I noticed a strange but pleasant difference from other miniature .45s I've fired. The enlarged grip gives a better feel over that of the thinner-handled, single-column pistols. Recoil is softened due to more surface area, no doubt, but the bigger grip shifts the gun so it points more naturally. True, the handle is so short it nearly leaves the last

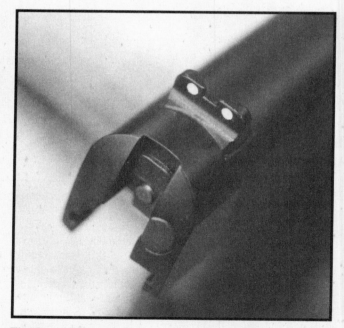

The Para-Ordnance P12.45 compact features high profile fixed combat sights with the customary three white dots.

finger dangling. In recompense however, the magazine floor plate is a thick, tapered slab of black synthetic which accommodates the little finger nicely. Those like me who dislike shooting other small .45s will find the P12.45 more comfortable.

Some years back, Para-Ordnance introduced their alloy

The front sight on the P12.45 has the standard white dot.

frame to the market. The intent was that a shooter could buy the frame, install the top works from his .45 auto, and have a high-capacity, 14-shot .45 automatic. When this was done, the completed gun weighed no more than the standard M1911 Government Model — about 40 ounces. Later, the company began producing steel frames, then complete guns. I have a custom Para-Ordnance .45 built on a steel frame by pistolsmith Ace Hindman, of Kerrville, Texas. I haven't weighed it, but in truth the steel frame seems but little heavier than the alloy job and is no burden. I'm told alloy frames stand up well, but for my purposes, steel is just fine.

The P12.45 compact is the smaller version of the bigger 14-shot pistol, and it has the steel frame. For a compact, an alloy frame makes more sense to me, but the gun is so satisfactory my complaint lacks enthusiasm. The frame is finished in a fine black matte — sort of an uptown Parkerizing.

The slide has a modern black coating I've seen before, but can't recall the exact nomenclature. It's similar to, but better than black enamel, and won't flake or rub off. The ejection port is opened up to let the fired cases out. The sights are high profile fixed, with the familiar three white dots for fast acquisition. The short trigger is black synthetic and so are the grip plates, impressed with the Para-Ordnance logo. There is a functioning grip safety, and the tang is the curved anti-bite style. This pistol won't nip you. The mainspring housing is grooved and flat, which it must be on a small pistol. The controls are strictly M1911, in the usual places, and the safety clicks positively on and off. Mushy, clickless safeties on M1911 pistols are a sore point with me. They can and will wipe off without notice when carried in concealment next to the skin.

The recoil spring guide is black synthetic, perhaps to aid the dual recoil springs in cushioning recoil. The barrel is swelled at the muzzle to engage the bushing tightly, and the recoil spring plug is secured by a tongue-and-groove system.

In disassembling the gun, the instruction manual follows

While the barrel is belled, the Para-Ordnance system retains the bushing and plug like the standard M1911.

the usual M1911 method except a screwdriver is recommended to push the plug inward and turn the locking lug out of its notch. Frankly, it's just as easy to pull the slide back to the disassembly notch and push the slide stop out. When this is done the slide and barrel assembly can be pulled forward off the frame.

While thus meddling with the P12.45, I realized none of the parts stuck or were hard to remove, although the fittings were close. This was strange, for I handle new pistols frequently, and good quality ones at that. Most of them show some reluctance to come apart and I'm used to that fact of life. Gradually it dawned on me that the P12.45 was displaying unusually good workmanship; far better than I expected. It is, in fact, a good pistol, well made of excellent materials.

The P12.45 comes in an attractive black plastic case with two magazines. Two spare magazines — this is really unusual, and why most manufacturers are so stingy with magazines is beyond me. Even a well-made magazine is a cheap part; yet many otherwise quality pistols are shipped with just one, or at most, a grudging spare.

Pistol shooters know you can never have too many magazines, but gun makers think you won't need any, or maybe just one. Perhaps they can't decide if they are in the pistol business or the magazine-selling business. I'd rather pay for extra magazines up front than go whining around for spares.

The good news is that the P12.45 comes with two extra 11-shot magazines. The bad news is, you can only get nine or 10 cartridges into them. There's no doubt in my mind they'll hold 11 shots, but putting them all in is tough. While range testing the gun, I'd load the magazines to capacity, and thought I was shooting 11 shots, but I wasn't. I'd recommend loading all three magazines to capacity, and leaving them that way. In six months or a year, the springs will weaken enough that the full

The Para-Ordnance P12.45 fits nicely into standard M1911 holsters like this open model from Pro-Line.

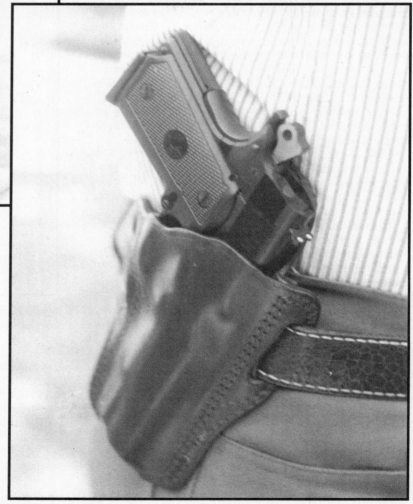

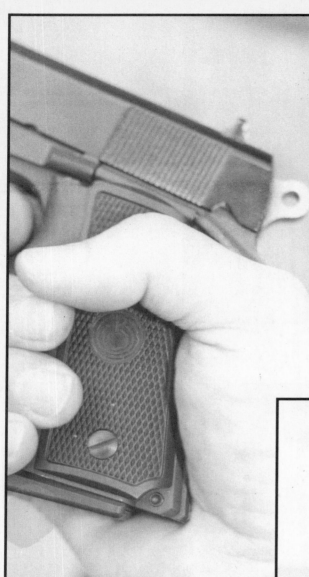

The P12.45 compact, with its double-column magazine, fills the hand (above). The extended magazine provides a rest for the little finger.

Disassembled, the Para-Ordnance reveals its compact features. Note the short barrel bushing and belled barrel muzzle.

11 shots can be loaded. No, it won't hurt them.

Additional good news is that while firing nine or 10 shots from the 11-round magazines, the well-made P12.45 exhibited no malfunctions. Apparently it needs no "breaking-in" period or waste of good ammo. This is a gun you can load and go with, right out of the box. My shooting was done with the mentioned Black Hills 200-grain. SWC IPSC ammo, and Winchester 185-grain Silvertips. I fired from a Weaver stance at 20 yards to get the big, ragged holes.

In fact, they were so ragged I suspected keyholing, and walked down to examine the silhouette; no such thing. The bullets were spinning true, but heavy mass at low velocity made the entrance wounds tattered. It will do that on flesh, also. I was impressed. In a defense gun of this type, meant for meanness, it would not have hurt my feelings if the bullets were indeed keyholing. Imagine a .45 caliber slug going sideways through an adversary. It is terribly lethal.

Groups? The group size ran about four to five inches. I can shoot better than this with an accurized gun, but not much better with an ordinary service or defense gun. If you think that kind of shooting won't win a lot of gunfights, get a ruler and place it horizontally between your breasts. When you can shoot such groups in daylight or dark, excited or calm, drunk or sober, then you will be a pretty tough cookie.

I like the P12.45, and showed it to Sean Walsh, a detective with the San Antonio police department. Walsh is a M1911 fan, and knows which end the bullet comes out of on any other gun. He liked the P12.45, too, but suggested the mainspring housing be rounded for greater comfort.

If this was done, the P12.45 would feel like the old M1903 Colt pocket automatic in .32 or .380 caliber.

After experiencing the P12.45's shooting and handling qualities, I seem to have lost all my prejudice against short .45 autos. That's funny, since I haven't changed my mind about anything since 1955. If you get a chance to shoot one, maybe it will happen to you.

MAGNUM RESEARCH'S
MOUNTAIN EAGLE

By Steve Comus

I T IS CALLED the Mountain Eagle, and the name aptly describes one of the most logical applications of this .22 long rifle, semi-auto pistol. The Mountain Eagle is the newest addition to the line of firearms marketed by Magnum Research — the company that made the legendary Desert Eagle line of pistols a reality.

Although the rimfire Mountain Eagle has some similarities in appearance to the time-honored centerfire Desert Eagle models (like the triangular outside barrel contour), it is totally different in other ways — like in the weight department.

Desert Eagle pistols are big, brawny and heavy. They hold up forever, and can handle really powerful ammo. The Mountain Eagle, however, is among the lightest of the .22 rimfire semi-autos. But any weight differential is more than compensated for in the handling and performance of the amazingly handy Mountain Eagle design.

The Mountain Eagle has an ingeniously inspired use of both polymer, aluminum alloy and steel, resulting in a full-size, serious handgun that weighs just 21 ounces unloaded. That is totally exciting data for outdoorsmen who tackle what

This Full-Size .22 Pistol Has The Right Stuff

The safety (right) on the Mountain Eagle is unique. As shown, the pistol is ready to fire. Just to the front of the safety is the slide release button. The magazine release is on the forward portion of the grip, behind the trigger.

Here, the slide is locked to the rear. The target quality rear sights are adjustable for windage and elevation.

The solid steel bolt reflects the exceptional quality of workmanship on all of the Mountain Eagle's metal parts.

the elements and terrain can dish out when they are camping, hiking or hunting. Both the pistol and a good supply of ammo can be carried in a backpack without adding much weight.

Because most of the pistol is made of polymer, the rig is extremely weather and climate resistant. In fact, Magnum Research may not be promoting one particular potential use for the pistol — a use in which the Mountain Eagle would shine brightly. The Mountain Eagle might be considered as one of the finest "survival" handguns of all time. It would be a worthwhile investment, even if the handgun were to be purchased, sighted-in and then put in with the survival gear for long term storage.

The only sad part about such a squirreling away is that the owner would be missing out on the magnum levels of enjoyment the pistol is ready to provide on a regular basis. This is the kind of pistol that seems okay at first, but then becomes more and more interesting and more and more fun as it is shot time after time after time.

The Mountain Eagle may be what many shooters would term a "plastic pistol," and it has the initial feel of synthetic. However, it is when the shooting begins that the appreciation for the overall design and construction kicks into high gear. This is a serious handgun.

The Mountain Eagle is full-size in every respect. That means it fills the hand for a controlled hold when shooting. And the balance is such that it sits with neutral balance in the hand (neither muzzle nor butt-heavy).

The grip area of the pistol features a series of moulded-in horizontal striations front and back, with an integral checkering pattern and eagle logo on both sides. The finish, coupled with the ergonomically designed handle, contributes to non-slip handling, even with cold and wet hands. Horizontal striations also are integral with the concave front of the trigger guard — this designed to aid in two-handed shooting. During the test sessions, the two-handed grip worked extremely well, and accounted for the better groups obtained.

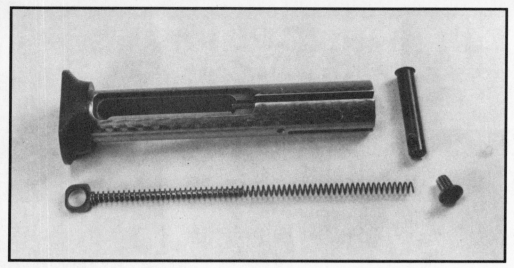

Disassembled, at top left, is the bolt's main body. Below it is the recoil spring and guide. To the right is the bolt stop pin (top) and the takedown screw (bottom) .

The action of the Mountain Eagle is based upon a steel bolt assembly inside a tubular aluminum alloy receiver. It is, to the front of the receiver, that the barrel group is attached. The reason it is called a barrel group is that major components include a thin, rifled steel barrel sleeve inside the polymer outer barrel shell. An interchangeable front sight post is pinned to the top of the polymer-covered barrel. For the shooting sessions, the author opted for a bright blaze orange front sight (different colors are available). It was a choice that comes highly recommended, because it makes target acquisition and sight alignment quick and easy.

The test model sported a 6 1/2-inch barrel and wore a fully adjustable rear sight. Both front and rear sights ride somewhat high on the Mountain Eagle. This also proved to be handy when shooting. With the high, large profile sights, target acquisition was enhanced, and it was effortless to keep the sights on target, even when moving targets were encountered. The receiver top is drilled and tapped for scope sight mounting. However, for most purposes, the standard sights are sufficient.

Controls on the Mountain Eagle are traditional in their operation and location. For example, the magazine release button is located on the left side of the grip frame just aft of the trigger, a la Model 1911 Colt. The pistol comes standard with a 15-round magazine (plus one round in the chamber for a total capacity of 16 shots). A 20-round magazine also is available.

The magazine itself is intriguing. It is made of polycarbonate and borders between translucence and clear. That means it is easy to determine visually how many rounds are in the magazine. Its design also is high tech. It is of the double-stack-column configuration on the bottom, narrowing to an in-line

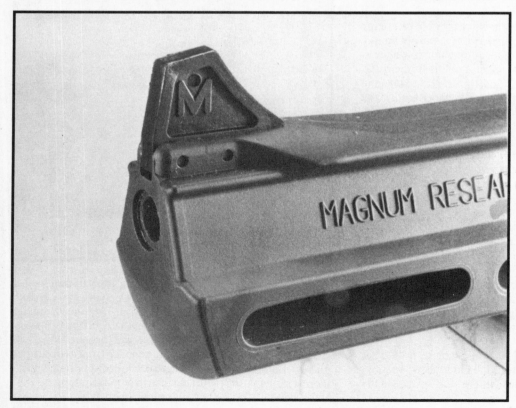

The front sight post comes in orange, white and black.

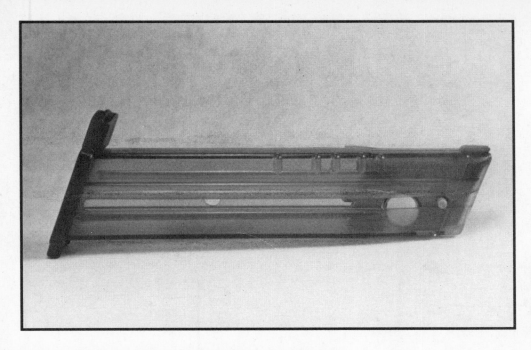

Left, the magazine for the Mountain Eagle is made of tough plastic. Below, the ribs on the front of the grip and trigger guard greatly enhance performance.

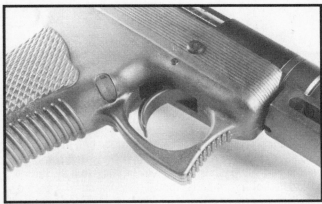

single-column configuration on top where the cartridges feed into the gun. This means it feeds as well as a single-column magazine, but has the added capacity of a double-column magazine. Cleaning the inside of the magazine is easy.

To clean the inside of the magazine, there is a vertical slot in the left side which allows access. This slot is there primarily to allow an extension of the follower to move up and down with finger pressure to aid in loading. However, it also serves as a lengthwise window for cleaning. There also are two round holes in the right side of the magazine, which not only allow access there, but also allow the insertion of a punch to hold the follower down at two different levels to help in the cleaning process, as well. The base of the magazine slides on and off, allowing even more access to the inside.

The internal design of the Mountain Eagle magazine is also intriguing, because it does not feature a spring that pushes the follower upward as do most traditional magazines. Rather, it has a coiled flat spring which is similar to that in a clock. One end of the spring is attached to the inside wall of the magazine at the top, and the coil itself is inside the plastic follower assembly. As the follower assembly is pushed down by successive cartridges, the spring uncoils, exerting upward pressure on the ammunition and feeding it out the top.

There is one note of caution here, however. Shooters must avoid using certain types of aerosol cleaners — those that contain 1.1.1 Tri-choroethylene (tric). Examples are Gunk Out or Crud-Cutter. These chemicals react with the plastic in the magazine and can harm it. For cleaning, it is better to use isopropyl alcohol or more standard gun solvents/lubricants like WD-40 or Hoppes No. 9.

Other controls on the Mountain Eagle also are simple, and in the traditional places. To open the action, pull backward on the actuator handle, which also serves as a cap on the rear of the bolt. It has flared areas on both sides to make it easier to pull. If an empty magazine is in place when the bolt is pulled to the rear, the slide will remain locked back, as it does after the last shot has been fired.

To release the bolt and allow it to spring forward, push downward on the round bolt release button which is located on the left side of the frame, about an inch above the magazine release button. On the test pistol, the button was noticeably hard to push at first, but following a lengthy range session, the system had settled into an easy operating mode.

To the rear of the bolt release button is the manual safety. It features ribs that form a positive contact with the thumb or finger when it is operated. When the safety lever is to the rear, the pistol is on "safe," and when the lever is pushed forward (actually, it goes forward and slightly down in an arc), the pistol is in the "fire" mode. When the pistol is off "safe," there is a small red dot visible at the rear of the slot in the frame where the lever travels forward and backward.

Operation of the safety is a double-motion proposition. When it is rearward and on "safe," it clicks upward into a small notch in the frame. To take it off safe, it is necessary to push the lever down and forward simultaneously. This feature precludes the safety from being bumped out of position inadvertently.

A closer look at the safety features reveals that they are comprehensive. For example, when the safety is engaged manually, a conventional disconnect/bar blocks the sear, the sear is disconnected, the trigger is blocked and the hammer is blocked. There are also automatic safety features built into the

The size, design and texture of the grips all contribute to the high quality of the gun.

pistol. The disconnect bar is actuated by the bolt on its backward travel from the front of the breech face, effectively preventing out of battery fire; and the pistol cannot be cocked while the safety is in the "safe" mode.

Disassembly of the Mountain Eagle for routine cleaning and maintenance is relatively simple and straight-forward. Starting with the bolt in the closed position on an empty chamber, remove the rear takedown screw which is located at the back of the grip frame. Use a 1/8-inch hex wrench to remove the screw. Once the screw is out, lift up on the bolt/barrel/receiver assembly and remove the entire assembly from the grip sub assembly.

Next, remove the bolt stop pin which is located at the rear of the receiver, just behind the rear sight. The bolt stop pin lifts upward and out and can be removed with fingers (no tools needed). Note, however, that the recoil spring and guide rod, which are at the top of the bolt, may spring loose upon removal, so care is needed to avert problems like losing a part, or hitting one's self in the face. There is really no major problem here, but since anything that can happen probably will sometime somewhere, it is prudent to take appropriate caution.

To remove the recoil spring and guide, lift upward and rearward until they come out of the bolt. This is as far as the pistol needs to be disassembled for routine maintenance and cleaning.

Although reassembly is essentially the reverse procedure, there are a couple of tips that can help it go slicker and quicker. First, insert the guide rod into the recoil spring and insert both of them into the slot in the top of the bolt. The yoke of the guide rod needs to be flush with the top of the slot. Next, insert the bolt into the receiver and then insert the bolt stop pin through the receiver. Here is where it is advisable to pay particularly

close attention to the threaded hole in the bottom of the bolt stop pin. It is drilled at an angle, and it is necessary for the hole to be angled downward toward the rear of the bolt when it is inserted. Also, when inserting the bolt stop pin, it is necessary to push the actuator handle at the rear of the bolt inward so the hole through the receiver is aligned properly. It is a good idea once the bolt stop pin is all the way in place that the threaded hole in the bottom remains pointed rearward and downward so it will be in proper alignment when the takedown screw is inserted after the bolt assembly is re-installed into the top of the grip assembly.

To put the two major groups together, align the recoil lug at the front of the receiver group with the front of the grip and rotate the receiver downward onto the top of the grip as the bolt stop in is guided into the grip hole at the rear of the grip. This can require a bit of jiggling to align all of the parts, but there is no need to force anything. The two assemblies do rotate back together without force. Then, make certain that the bolt stop pin is still aligned properly and insert the takedown screw. Do not over tighten the screw when replacing it. The pistol is now reassembled and ready for action.

The real fun comes in the shooting of the Mountain Eagle. Noticeable right from the beginning is the feather-like feel of the pistol. Because it has a neutral weight distribution, it feels even lighter in the hand than it actually is. This means that shooting the Mountain Eagle is as easy as pointing a finger at the target and pulling the trigger.

Speaking of the trigger, the trigger pull on the Mountain Eagle actually is quite nice, but the test model needed a little break-in period before the trigger came up to its long term potential. The pull is best described as slightly gritty with a slightly noticeable amount of travel. However, after firing a couple dozen rounds through the pistol, the grittiness began to

The one-piece main frame allows the .22 pistol to be full-sized, yet lightweight.

disappear and the overall pull smoothed out. Following a couple hundred rounds, the trigger became noticeably smoother and more consistent, with a nice pull of 3 1/2 pounds. This helped in the overall performance of the pistol.

Like most firearms, the test pistol exhibited preferences for some kinds of ammunition over others. This characteristic tends to be a factor of individual firearms, and can vary significantly from one firearm to another, even within a model line. Hence, it is a good idea to try a number of different loadings through any firearm to help determine which one or ones it likes best.

The Mountain Eagle is a a .22 long rifle proposition. That means that .22 shorts or longs will not work properly in it, and .22 rimfire magnum cartridges are too big.

In all, six different loadings were tried in the test pistol. Performance ranged from outstanding to miserable. The pistol showed a decided preference for Remington's Thunderbolt loading, producing a 3/4-inch group off the bench at 25 yards (with open sights). That was the smallest group achieved in the workout, and credible by any standards. Yet, the same pistol hated Remington's Viper loading, throwing bullets all over the target in a random "pattern" rather than a group.

Showing a similar lack of manufacturer preference, the test pistol decided it didn't like PMC's Zapper load, but loved PMC's Sidewinder 50s load. The Zapper loads would not function the action, and the group at 25 yards with that load was a mediocre 1 3/4-inches. However, with the PMC Sidewinder 50s loading, the best group measured exactly one inch, which was strung left to right, meaning part of the size of the group easily could have involved a degree of pilot error.

CCI's SGB loading produced unimpressive two-inch groups, while Winchester's Super-X loading came through with 2 1/4-inch groups. Interestingly, another Mountain Eagle which was shot more informally shot the Super-X loads best. So, it definitely is a matter of individual firearm preference when it comes to what loads work best.

Interestingly, out of the six different loadings used, two produced superior performance out of the test pistol. Either could be considered as "best bet" for that particular pistol in normal use. More extensive testing of other loadings might divulge other ammo that the pistol would handle well— and that is something that shooters should do with their personal firearms: try as wide a variety of loadings as possible, and then stock up with whatever ammo works best.

The Mountain Eagle is the kind of handgun that one learns to like and appreciate more and more as it is shot again and again. It may be somewhat non-traditional in materials and looks, but it is a serious handgun in action.

Judging from the way the pistol is designed and built, it likely would hold up for a lifetime of shooting, since the metal parts are substantial where they need to be, and finished off well. The "plastic" parts of the pistol are rigid enough to do their jobs, yet afford a weight level that could not be achieved with heavier materials.

Of the several logical uses of the Mountain Eagle, plinking and informal target work probably rank highest for most shooters. But this is more than just a plinking gun. It also has a more serious side.

As was mentioned earlier, the Mountain Eagle is perhaps one of the best "survival" handguns ever produced. And, it would make a nearly perfect camp pistol.

Or, it is ideal for its promoted purposes — as a handgun for hikers and backpackers who want to have a firearm with them, but who do not want or need anything heavy anchoring them in their endeavors.

Finally, the Mountain Eagle is a totally credible small game hunting handgun. For edible game like squirrels and rabbits, it is a most logical choice.

Overall, the Mountain Eagle is an impressive entry into the handgun market. Also, it is a representative of a whole new generation of firearms, making use of advanced technology in construction and design. Yes, it is a most valid choice for anyone who wants a pistol that shoots well, carries easily and doesn't need a lot of maintenance.

ROSSI'S MODEL 720 BRAWLER

By Russ Thurman

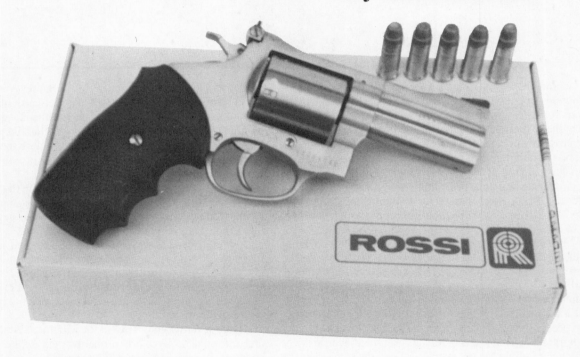

This Three-Inch .44 Special Is Built Tough For No-Nonsense Action!

WHEN ROSSI'S .44 Special with its three-inch barrel arrived for a test drive, I knew the new offering from Interarms had found a place in my modest collection of short-barrelled revolvers.

Such firearms always have had such an appeal. As a kid watching black and white television, I never grasped why so many of my buddies were fascinated by the shootin' iron packed by Wyatt Earp. Each week, Hugh O'Brien would drag his Butline Special out of his low-slung holster to dispatch a whole herd of outlaws. It always seemed a bit unfair, what with the lengthy Butline barrel reaching halfway down the town's dusty street. Most of the bad guys had powder burns on their sweat-stained shirts. After each week's show, the toy department at the Rexall drug store would be invaded by more

Rossi's .44 Special, with its three-inch barrel, has a handsome stainless steel finish, contrasted by black rubber grips.

The new .44 Special has a deep one-piece rib, barrel and shroud as illustrated.

converts looking to own their own toy Butline revolvers.

Youngsters weren't the only ones infected. Shortly after the TV series began, Old Man Mathews obtained a huge revolver that looked much like the Butline Wyatt hauled around town. He and a bunch of his friends would shoot the firearm at a fence post behind the overly greasy and rundown Mobility Repair Shop. Old Man Mathews owned the place. He called it that because in addition to fixing pickup trucks, cars and tractors, he also shod horses. He had little respect for the animals because of what they did in his shop's entryway while he was fitting them with shoes, but most of us thought what the horses did added a lot to the shop's decor and we secretly cheered when such an event occurred.

Nope, I just didn't take to long-barrel shootin' irons. Short-barreled revolvers seemed to have so much more character.

My best buddy, Beans, had actually fired a Model 1917 Smith & Wesson .45 ACP that had a shortened barrel. The '17's hammer and trigger guard also had been reworked. The spur had been removed and the guard shortened. A ramp sight had been added to the front of the stubby barrel and the stocks switched to hard-rubber grips.

With a 3-1/2-inch barrel, the revolver had a menacing look. Just lying on a table, it looked like it wanted to jump up and slap you across the face. The work had been done by Beans' brother, Walter, who had returned from World War II with a cigar box full of medals and a dashing scar over his right eye. There's little doubt that my awe of Walter made owning a chopped revolver like his an overwhelming goal in my young life.

Since those days too long ago, there has been a steady parade of double-action revolvers, sporting short barrels, that have passed through my small arsenal. Like Walter, I also had

The three-inch barrel on the .44 Special is built tough.

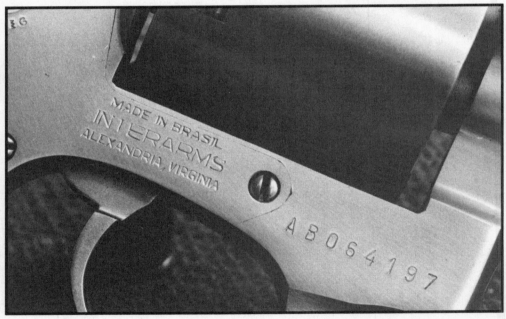

Made in Brazil, the Rossi is imported by Interarms.

a few long-barrel revolvers chopped down to the 3-1/2- to four-inch mark, but none of them grew in favor and eventually were traded off—except one. Mostly, I took to manufacturer's models that had the character-enhancing short barrel.

A Charter Arms Bulldog was one of my favorites. It packed five rounds of .44 Special into a cylinder that look nearly as long as the three-inch barrel. I picked it up on a trade from a gent who wanted an old .30-30 I had. The Bulldog's original walnut grips were badly marred and the square-notched rear sight had undergone some amateur surgery, but it still captured my heart.

A Smith & Wesson Chiefs Special Model 60 was another star in my short-barreled hall of fame. Its two-inch barrel looked like an afterthought, but it was a great shooter. One S&W I never owned but wanted badly was a Model 40

Centennial. Hammerless with a two-inch barrel and a grip safety, it shouted distinction and also a hefty price.

So, when I open the Interarms box containing the Brazilian-made Rossi Model 720, I knew I had a strong candidate for my gun safe. The stainless steel Rossi has a finger-grooved rubber grip, an adjustable rear sight, a non-fluted cylinder with bolt cuts between its five chambers and a contoured, deeply grooved top strap.

The initial check-up revealed the following data: it weighs just a half-ounce below two pounds, with a barrel diameter of .659-inch. The three-inch barrel is contoured from the muzzle to the frame and .113-inch thick. From top to bottom, the barrel measures 1-3/8 inches. This includes the underlug and ramp. The underlug measures .5-inch with the grooved top/ramp adding .506-inch. At the frame, the barrel measures 1-3/16 inches.

To reduce glare, the front sight ramp on the new Rossi .44 Special is serrated. The sight features a red insert.

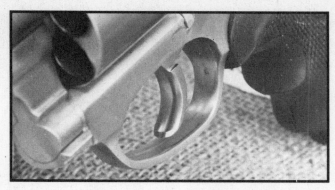

The rounded trigger on the .44 Special is comfortable, allowing superb control, aided by finger-grooved grips.

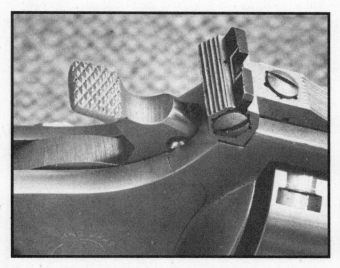

The hammer on the Rossi .44 Special is square with deep cross-hatched serrations. The sight is adjustable.

For positive action, bolt cuts are carved deep between chambers. From grip to muzzle, the Rossi is built solid.

The deeply checkered hammer spur is .402-inch in width and .330-inch deep. The sights are black with the front blade featuring a red insert and the adjustable rear sporting a white outline.

While a real looker, I was anxious to find out how well the new offering from Rossi would perform in comparison to a few veterans from my personal arsenal.

I first selected a Charter Arms Bulldog Pug. It took the place of my Charter Arms Bulldog which now resides with an Alaskan hunting guide. The Pug is every bit what its name suggests. The 2-1/2-inch barrel makes it look like a street brawler with a chip on his shoulder. Like its big brother, the Bulldog, the Pug carries five rounds of .44 Special. It has a blue finish, neoprene stocks and fixed sights. With an overall length of 7-1/4 inches, it weighs 19 ounces. The trigger is a bit wide, the way I prefer, with a single-action pull of 4-1/2 pounds. Double-action is managed with a pull just shy of 14 pounds.

While the hammer on the Pug is only a bit bobbed, practice is needed to safely cock the revolver for single-action fire. Not to be left to assumption, such practice should be done with an empty cylinder. When an inexperienced hand is trying to cock a bobbed hammer, I seek safety. Too often, the shooter still has a finger on the trigger while pulling the hammer back! Remember: finger off, hammer back.

Next in this all-star evaluation was a Terminator that's been worked over by Jovino. With a 2-3/4-inch barrel, it will take six .44 magnums. The blue finish has been replaced by electroless-nickel, the rear sight is adjustable and it tips the scales at 41 ounces. The trigger has a snappy 40 ounces of pull

While the Rossi .44 Special is small compared to hefty revolvers, its performance speaks with great authority.

Short-barrelled revolvers long have been a favorite of the author. The new Rossi proved to be a good shooter.

in single-action and 10-1/2 pounds in double-action.

Remember Walter's chopped Model 1917 .45 ACP? The one veteran I've kept from my earlier days of seeking short-barreled revolvers is a like S&W Model 1917 that has a barrel cut to 3-3/16 inches. The odd length was necessary to preserve the Smith & Wesson name that is stamped on the right side of the barrel. It has a mini-vent rib, fixed sights and Pachmayr stocks.

The hammer has been bobbed to near excess. However, I still can cock it with a special technique I've used for a number of years. I place my first thumb joint on the modest spur and pull back while rotating my thumb forward until I've got a piece of the hammer's face. This gives me a sure grip and I never worry about the hammer getting away from me.

The 1917 has a single-action trigger pull of 3-1/2 pounds plus a smidgen, and a double-action pull that creeps near 14 pounds.

An early morning session at the range provided some interesting data as I ran the new .44 Special Rossi up against my three all-stars.

The pint-sized Charter Bulldog Pug seemed almost cocky as it whipped out 10 Winchester 200-grain Silvertips. They raced through the screens of an Oehler Model 35P at an average 711 feet-per-second.

The new Rossi was next. With a barrel half an inch longer than that of the Pug, it tossed the 200-grain .44 Special Silvertips downrange at an average of 736 fps. The Rossi is heavier than the Pug by three-quarters of a pound, making it easier to handle the stout .44 Special round. But the Pug is not to be discounted. Charter Arms built a lot of backbone into the lightweight revolver and it has devoured hundreds of rounds without fail.

The stubby Model 1917 then stepped to the line. Ten shots of 185-grain Winchester Silvertips listed an average speed of 856 fps. These Silvertips were 15 grains lighter than the .44 Specials and they clocked 145 fps faster than the Pug and 120 fps faster than the Rossi.

The most impressive speedster through the Rossi was Remington's 200-grain lead bullets. Ten rounds were marked by the Oehler screens at an average 829 fps.

To gain an appreciation for .44 magnum performance that can be obtained from a short-barreled revolver, I pumped 10 rounds of 210-grain Silvertips through the Terminator. Even with its 2-3/4-inch barrel, it tipped the Oehler meter at an average 1131 fps. The Winchester catalog reports a speed of 1250 fps from a test gun that sported a four-inch barrel. The Terminator only lost 119 fps, despite having a barrel 1-1/4 inches shorter than the test gun.

This adds to the substantial body of evidence that short-barreled revolvers can and do get the job done as carry guns. Too often, short-barreled firearms are discarded not for their merit, but because of the Wyatt Earp Syndrome: If it's longer, it's better. Not so.

When it comes to the diameter of a barrel, I long have favored .429 and .451/.454 bores. Honestly, is there anything the larger .44 and .45 caliber can't do better than the .355 or

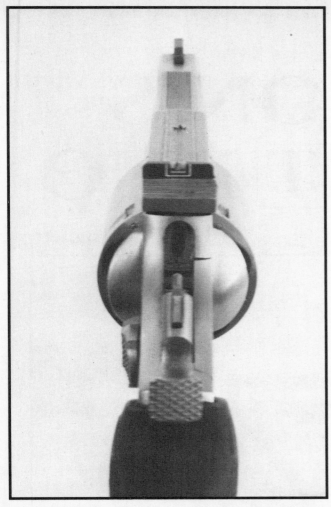

The rear sight has a white outline, making it easy to fix a solid sight picture with the red insert on the front sight.

The chopped revolvers from the author's arsenal include (from top): Charter Arms .44 Special, Rossi .44 Special, Terminator .44 magnum and S&W M1917 .45 ACP.

.357? I don't think so, but when it comes down to a life and death situation, I figure nothing should be picked over the big boys.

The new Rossi fills all these requirements and more. It has a sturdy build, providing a certain confidence for the shooter. It just feels good when gripped in a firing position. And, it's built to be fired and fired often. The bolt cuts between the chambers mark it as a serious firearm, one that's sure to establish a firm, reliable reputation.

At first glance, the adjustable sights on the Rossi seem to be an unnecessary feature. Are they really needed for the up-close and personal operation for which it was designed? No, but what about distances out to 25 yards? At the range, I easily managed some braggable groups that averaged .953-inch for four five-shot efforts.

Why am I sold on this new Rossi? It has all the characteristics of a time-tested, dependable firearm. Primarily, as a revolver, it is as basic as you can get in a modern-day handgun. Shooters understand the basics and when in doubt they return to them, even over many of today's automatics.

I have a number of autos that see action on occasion. There's a 9mm, a 10mm and a M1911 .45 ACP. All of them have been under the gunsmith's knife, receiving extensive surgery. The .45 probably has seen daylight more than the other two. Carried behind my right hip, it's comfortable enough to be forgotten until needed.

Most of the work, though, goes to the Terminator and the customized M1917. However, it took a passel of money to get them into proper shooting shape. For a sizeable amount less, in dollars and work, you can own the new Rossi .44 Special. This five-shot, stainless steel revolver with its three-inch barrel is a brawler.

WESSON'S NEWEST DUO

by Hal Swiggett

The Stainless .38 Special Snubby & .357 Magnum Fixed-Barrel Compliment Each Other

A LOT of water has flowed under the bridge since Dan Wesson introduced his interchangeable barrel revolvers a quarter of a century back. Dan died November 24, 1978. His company fell on hard times — then harder times in strange hands.

Three or so years ago, control of the company was returned to the Wesson family. Seth and Carol Wesson, son and daughter-in-law of the founder, have it on solid footing with updated tooling and several new products.

Proof is the issuing of an all-new two-inch, .38 Special +P, five-shot revolver that tips the scale at only 22-1/2 ounces. So sturdy is its construction that it is being considered for the .357 magnum cartridge. It is typical Wesson in that its barrel is interchangeable.

The other half of this newly introduced duo is a fixed barrel six-inch .357 magnum. It weighs 45-1/2 ounces with its full length, heavy, integral shroud. It holds six shots, of course.

Trigger pull of the little one is 3-1/2 pounds single-action and 13 pounds when pulling it through. The six-incher lets go at 38 ounces and double-action at 11 pounds.

The little +P .38 is relatively tiny, measuring only 4-1/2 inches in height by 6-3/4 inches in length. Pocket-size for sure!

This revolver has been fired extensively with a mixture of six different loads, five factory and my personal (and a lot of others') handload. Factory ammunition included 158-grain lead semi-wadcutter and 125-grain semi-jacketed hollow-point +P, both from Remington. Winchester's contribution included the Super Match 148-grain lead mid-range round and the 95-grain Silvertip hollow-point. The Norma 148-grain lead wadcutter filled out my factory lineup.

My handload consisted of Speer's 148-grain bevel base

The new Wesson .38 Special +P handled a variety of ammunition brands with ease during author's analysis.

Author used these six loads for testing the new six-inch Wesson .357 Magnum. It proved an excellent shooter.

The barrel for the .357 is also available in two- and four-inch lengths, both in stainless or satin blue finish.

wadcutter over 4.5 grains of Bullseye set off with CCI's 500 primer. This, by the way, is the handload I recommend for home protection. Flat-fronted bullets across a bedroom hit with a whole bunch of authority. They do not have to produce ozone-burning velocity to make themselves known.

If suggesting a factory load from those on my shelf, it would be either Winchester's 95-grain Silvertip HP or Remington's 125-grain +P SJHP for personal protection duty.

This little Wesson .38+P two-incher is round-butted and wears a pebble-like surfaced black rubber grip. Very comfortable to say the least. Wesson's full-size, heavy-barreled six-inch .357 magnum wears a grip of the same surface and material but of combat configuration. Its rear sight is adjustable with a red insert up front. This insert is interchangeable, as with all Wesson adjustable sight revolvers, so any of their colors could be used.

This .357 magnum six-shot, has a cylinder designed so cartridge heads are flush with the outside length; viewed from

the gun's side, cartridges cannot be seen.

The little .38+P is conventional in that cartridge rims rest on the cylinder face so they are visible with the revolver closed and ready for duty. This gun also has fixed sights

My ammunition shelf produced eight .357 magnum factory loads: From Federal were the 110-grain JHP, 158-grain lead SWC, 180-grain Hi-Shok JHP Classic and the 158-grain JHP Hydra-Shok. A pair of Remington loads — 125-grain SJHP and 140-grain SJHP — also were available. Loads from Winchester and Norma respectively were the 145-grain Silvertip HP and a 158-grain full metal-jacket SWC. In all, 370 rounds were fired at one sitting without a hitch in any git-along.

I don't happen to be a .357 magnum fan. On the other hand, my feeling is that this caliber is far better than most being touted for law enforcement use at the moment. It is — and always will be — bullets hitting their target that counts, not how many were sent that direction.

Were I to lean toward the .357 magnum for varmints or

These are the adjustable rear sights on the full-sized .357 Magnum. It is also available with fixed sights.

It is easy to determine which of the revolvers has the fixed barrel. The .357 is on the left, the .38 to the right.

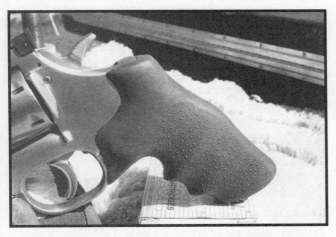

The revolver's' grips are black rubber with pebble grain. The grips with finger grooves are on the .357 Magnum.

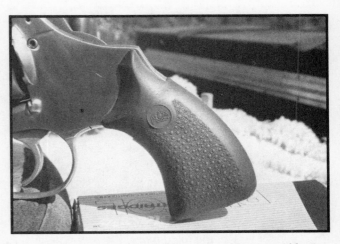

The .38+P wears a black rubber grip with a round butt.

small to medium game — meaning whitetail deer up to 150 pounds — this fixed-barrel Wesson with its beautiful trigger and stuffed with Federal's 180-grain Hi-Shok loads would handle such duty with aplomb. I had no problem hitting rather small targets of opportunity — meaning rocks and clods — on the 50-yard berm. Add 10 or 15 yards to this, and any whitetail's heart/lung area would be a cinch for the practiced shooter.

Twenty-five yard targets were no contest for the accuracy of this particular revolver. The range I use provides shooting at both 25 and 50 yards from the same bench. It is a huge layout, offering handgun, rifle, plinking, skeet, trap, Crazy Quail, country doubles and archery.

My targets, by the way, are not conventional. Typing paper of 8-1/2x11 inches with a three-quarter-inch coral Avery dot in the center serves me well. Why coral? It would be nice if I could provide a better reason, but the stationery dealer I first visited for the item had only this color in the size I wanted. It's easy to see, so I've stuck with it. They come 1,000 to the package.

Initially, the late Dan offered 2-1/2, four or six-inch interchangeable barrels, blued only, and with fixed or adjustable sights. It was in 1971, I believe, that his recessed barrel nut was introduced. Calibers and chamberings offered then were the .357 magnum and .38 Special, both with interchangeable barrels and one-piece grips.

Introduced later, Pistol Pacs were marketed in a padded case. Included were the revolver and usually three barrels of varying lengths, along with a tool for changing them and an extra grip. That Dan Wesson was innovative is without question.

Just looking at his revolver design proves that point. Who else offers a swingout cylinder with the release latch *in front*?

Wesson Firearms' current catalog lists 12 chamberings, in 29 models, ranging from .22 Long Rifle through the .445 Super Mag and .45 Colt. Included are stainless steel, bright blue and satin blue finishes. Barrel lengths run from 2-1/2 inches through 10 inches, all interchangeable for like calibers.

A big plus with Wesson revolvers is that each frame has been designed and produced as a magnum rather than a traditional design upgraded to handle magnum loads. In fact Dan often was accused of "over-engineering" and readily pled guilty to that accusation.

His cylinder latch, for instance — up front, next to the

The small Wesson packs five rounds of .38 Special +P.

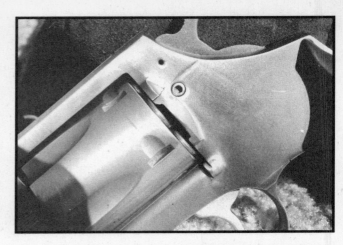
The heads of the .38 Specials can be seen even when the lightweight revolver's cylinder is locked and ready.

The cylinder wall of the fixed-barrel Wesson provides added protection for the six rounds of .357 Magnum.

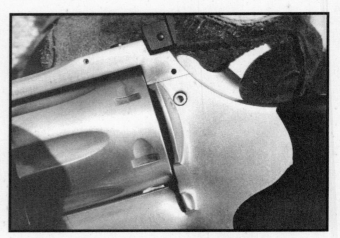
Once the cylinder of the new Wesson .357 Magnum is locked into position, the six cartridges can not be seen.

With the .357, author was able to hit small targets at the 50-yard mark. Targets at the 25-yard line were no contest for this Wesson.

In 1991, Seth accepted the posthumous induction of his father into the American Handgunner Hall of Fame.

Dan Wesson founded the company that bears his name.

barrel — ensures positive alignment between the cylinder and barrel. It also keeps the latch out of the way of the shooter's thumb while firing. It also eliminates the possibility of accidentally opening the cylinder during recoil.

This cylinder/crane assembly locks shut to the frame with its latch in the crane itself, not at the rear of the cylinder and, at the front of the ejector rod or at the rear of the cylinder alone. Rear lockup is equally strong; a spring-tensioned ball bearing in the frame snaps into a perfectly machined recess in the center of the solid extractor.

Wesson's interchangeable barrel/shroud allows barrels to be changed in less than a minute once the procedure is learned.

Wesson revolvers are noted for their short, fast double-action. The mainspring is a coil spring rather than the traditional fragile flat spring. This company's products also have fewer parts than other revolvers. These parts are designed for strength and simplicity in assembly and function. Initial assembly requires little fitting, and repairs, if necessary, are made easily.

All Wesson barrels are produced from heat-treated steel using cut rifling. Because of the unique frame design, Wesson revolvers can accommodate almost any shape or grip design a shooter might dream up. The ability to accept one-piece grips makes this possible.

Accuracy of Wesson revolvers has been established and documented in metallic silhouette competition almost to the point of being legendary.

That Dan Wesson was a perfectionist is reflected in the little two-inch .38 Special+P under discussion. Weighing less than a pound and a half, it has every ingredient of the biggest, longest-barreled, compensated .445 Super Mag ever turned out. It lives up to the standards Dan Wesson set for revolvers bearing his name. The same goes for the six-inch fixed barrel stainless steel .357 magnum described earlier.

The late Elgin Gates — sometimes described as the father of modern silhouette shooting and head of the International Handgun Metallic Silhouette Association for a long time — once said of Dan Wesson, "He was one of the great men of the firearms industry and of his time; one of those individuals who made things happen. He kept the handgun world honest, because he built the best guns that brains and material could turn out. Because of that, the others dared not to do less."

The Outstanding American Handgunner Awards Foundation saw fit to honor Dan Wesson's dedication to handgunning by inducting him into the American Handgunner Hall of Fame during their annual awards banquet in San Antonio in 1991. I had the honor of making that posthumous presentation to his son Seth.

Dan Wesson's dedication to constant improvement placed him in that Hall of Fame. That the company bearing his name is alive and well in the hands of the fifth generation of the Wesson family is assured. Seth and Carol Wesson will see to that.

SMITH & WESSON'S MODEL 915

By Terry Murbach

This 9mm Auto Is Third Generation And Shows It!

Author liked the M915's business-like appearance. The steel slide and aluminum alloy frame have a matte black finish.

JUST BETWEEN you, me and the target stand over there, I will bet that if we plied the head honcho at Smith & Wesson with a choice liqueur, we would get him to admit that S&W's third generation autoloading pistols have outsold their wildest expectations.

Up until the third generation guns were introduced, S&W's reputation was that of a fine revolver manufacturer who made good autoloading pistols — if you lucked out and got one that really worked. This reputation was no altogether undeserved, though the public possibly gave it more credence than it deserved. The S&W first and second generation guns worked as well as any of their contemporary competition, in my opinion.

Still, the perceived faults of the S&W second generation 9mm pistols (M439, 539, 639, 559, et al) spurred S&W's research and development of the current third generation pistols.

I have fired S&W third generation pistols in 9mm, .40 S&W, 10mm Auto and .45 ACP. To the best of my recollection, I have never had a malfunction, stoppage or jam in a third generation pistol, if I was using the *correct* magazines. This latter point is important, because some of S&W's .45 ACP magazines for the M645 and M745 did not do their job for sour apples, and they kept right on mucking up the works when used in a third generation M4506, M4516 or M4586. The last two incarnations of S&W's .45 ACP magazines have worked

perfectly in all my S&W .45s, including the M645 and M745. Trials and tribulations with those two .45s at times were so frustrating I darn near tossed them into the Maumee River — and all of it was magazine-related. (Don't ever lose sight of the fact that 98 percent of all autoloading pistol problems are magazine related. Magazines are the heart, soul and guts of any autloading pistol from any manufacturer.)

Thankfully, none of the S&W 9mm, .40 or 10mm pistols seemed to have suffered through the same teething problems, and none of these guns ever have malfunctioned for me. I have shot them until they were so unbelievably filthy dirty I could peel the crud off with my thumbnail. The guns just kept chugging along. If there is one accolade deserved by S&W's third generation pistols, it is that they work!

While the S&W third generation 9mm pistols have sold exceedingly well, they were priced at the top end of such things. The lower priced imported 9mm pistols pretty well had the bottom end of the pricing structure all to themselves until Bill Ruger got his P85-P89 9mm pistols up and flying straight. Now there is a third player among the low-priced 9mm pistols, the Smith & Wesson Model 915.

When I received a new M915, I was struck by two things immediately: what a business-like pistol. It looks just like my S&W M5904. I received the M5904 in 1989, and it is a rather early version of that system of pistols. It is a pre-Novak rear sight version, and that makes it quite comparable to the new

The new M915 is a no-frills version of the M5904 (left).

The M915 (left) is similar to the M5904 (right). The magazine for the M915 has holes to show exactly how many rounds it is holding.

M915, as this gun has an identical non-Novak style rear sight. Let me emphasize strongly at the outset that the M915 is not a "cheapened" version, per se, of the M5904 pistols. Rather, it is a less expensive version that drops or changes some basic M5904 features, but does not change the basic structure or integrity of the original M5904. At the same time, the M915 has a couple of features that are improvements over the original M5904. In essence, the M915 is a no-frills M5904.

The M915's exterior finish is a matte black on both the steel side and aluminum alloy frame. This means the finish was applied over a less highly polished metal surface, and that saves lots of money.

Although built alike, the rear sight on the M915 (left) is unadorned, while the M5904 rear sight has two dots.

SHOOTING STATISTICS FOR THE S&W M915 VS. M5904

	M915		M5904	
	VELOCITY+Sd	GROUP	VELOCITY+Sd	GROUP
Black Hills 115 gr. JHP	1133-28	3.44"	1164-10	2.34"
Black Hills 124 gr. JHP	1122-16	3.77"	1123-12	3.12"
Black Hills 147 gr. JHP	923-15	3.65"	942-15	3.44"
Blazer 124 gr. TMJ	1106-10	5.66"	1117-11	5.37"
Aggregate averages	1071-17	4.13"	1086-12	3.56"

All groups were fired at 25 yards and simultaneously chronographed on an Oehler M35P system. Groups are averages of two 10-shot strings.

At the same time, both the frame and slide are matched nearly perfectly in color and texture; quite a feat of skill in metal finishing. Furthermore, the machine cuts on the M5904's frame from trigger guard forward have been eliminated on the M915. This definitely makes for a stronger frame on the latter. Also, the M915's frame has a nice looking, rounded trigger guard instead of that weird triple-curved, square-front guard on the M5904. The original M5904s were issued with the arched grip frame.

The M915s have the straight-back grips with which I became quite enamored on the S&W M4006 .40 S&W pistol. The new stocks on the M915 are of higher quality than those on the older M5904. The new ones are darker in color and more cleanly moulded with a sharper feeling and looking checkering pattern.

Their straight-backed configuration fits my hand more "tightly," for lack of a better description, than the arched housing. I find this most puzzling, as the straight-backed grip style is nearly identical in shape and size to the old S&W M59s of yesteryear, and that gun felt like a 2x4 and pointed like a canned ham for me. I do love the feel of the new straight-

backed third generation pistols.

The M915 is furnished with one stainless steel magazine. Smith & Wesson is in the process of switching to stainless magazines on all their autoloading pistols, with the blued ones being phased out as they are used up. It sounds like a stellar idea to me.

The M915 also drops the ambidextrous hammer drop safety that is included on nearly the entire line-up of third generation pistols. The single safety is for a right-handed person, which is all well and good…except I am not one! In addition, the lever on the M915's safety is notably thinner than that on the original M5904, but still appears to be operated as easily as the old-style, thicker lever. It seems to me that S&W dropped the ball a bit in designing the third generation safety by not making the operating pedal easily detachable on the left side as well as the right, so we owners could put it where we needed it!

The new M915 9mm has one other feature that rather startled me once I realized what I was feeling and seeing. The double-action stroke on the M915 is distinctly and noticeably shorter than that on the older M5904 pistol.

The M915 performed without flaw during the author's range test using Black Hills 115-grain JHP ammunition.

Long a fan of the M5904 (left hand), author enjoyed shooting the new M915.

The latter gun has a smoother stroke, but that is because I shot the bejabbers out of it previously. Both guns have that crisp DA stroke that seemingly goes "dead" when it releases the hammer, and the sights never waver. Nowhere have I seen nor heard just when S&W shortened the DA trigger stroke.

My shootout between the new M915 and the M5904 consisted of shooting hundreds of rounds of Black Hills 115-grain jacketed hollow-points 124-grain JHPs and 147-grain JHPs through them for function tests. There were no stoppages during the entire test program, and both guns put all of the loads quite near point-of-aim, shooting two-handed offhand at 50 feet.

Rapid-fire tests were controlled easily, though the square-butt grip frame was easier for me to control.

The M915's accuracy statistics were definitely below that delivered by its older brother, the M5904. Please keep in mind, though, that the M5904 had three years of usage and thousands of rounds fired through it. It is thoroughly broken-in, and the M915 started at point zero. Generally speaking, it takes at least 1,000 rounds of ammunition to thoroughly break-in an autoloading pistol. The more and harder you shoot them, the better they get.

You can take this to the bank: the new, less expensive third generation M915 9mm upholds the Smith & Wesson tradition in fine style. It is a good autoloading 9mm Parabellum and, at suggested retail, it is $170 less than its fancier brother, and competitively priced with the myriad of 9mm imported pistols.

SECTION THREE:

RECENT HANDGUNS

UPDATED

HANDGUNS 94

BROWNING'S MICRO BUCK

By Steve Dick

Author used a Browning Micro Buck Mark Standard with four-inch barrel to take a grouse (opposite page).

This .22 Rimfire Brings New Fun To Casual Plinking

WHILE SCANNING the current addition of our Washington State game laws pamphlet, I found the definition of what firearms were legal for taking grouse had been changed. For many years, it was accepted custom to harvest grouse with whatever firearm the hunter had with him. As a result, I have killed as many birds with centerfire rifles and pistols as I have with a shotgun. The new rules decree that only shotguns and .22 rimfire firearms are legal before and after deer and elk season. During those two big game seasons, we still are free to use whatever arm we choose.

A large percentage of my own small-game hunting is incidental to other outdoor activities such as hiking, backpacking, picking mushrooms and huckleberries, and gener-

ally working around the woods. Because of this, I tend to favor a compact handgun for any and all edible targets of opportunity. After trying a wide variety of .22 LR handguns and loads, I eventually concluded that this round was only adequate when used in a handgun capable of delivering surgical accuracy. In most cases, this required a heavy, target handgun that usually was less than ideal for trail use. While I would have preferred to continue using either the .32 magnum or .38 Special as my woods carry gun, I no longer had that option. A second look at the .22 LR handguns available seemed to be in order.

My ideal .22 LR trail gun would need to be a semi-auto, have a good set of adjustable sights, be compact and provide a high level of accuracy. I prefer semi-autos over revolvers due to the fact they are usually more accurate and are easier to load and unload. This quality is important if you spend a lot of time getting in and out of pickups and are legally required to carry the gun unloaded while in the vehicle.

Adjustable sights are essential, if the shooter is going to take full advantage of the wide range of .22 LR ammo available today. Compact is self-explanatory in a trail gun. Accurate means capable of shooting groups of no larger than 1 1/2 inches at 50 feet.

It was at about this time I noticed Browning had introduced a new version of their made-in-the USA Buck Mark .22 pistol. This one is called the Micro Buck Mark.

From its beginnings as a basic, economy-model plinker in 1985, the Buck Mark line has evolved into a series of specialized target and hunting pistols. The Micro differs from the other models by having been cut back to a stiff four-inch bull barrel. Along with making the Micro more compact, the shorter barrel reduces the weight of the pistol to 32 ounces. At present, the Browning is available in three models: the Micro Standard with black rubber grips, the Micro Buck Mark Plus with laminated wood grips and the Micro Standard Nickel with a protective nickel finish.

Browning is now using what they call the "Pro Target Sight" on both the Micro and the standard-size Buck Mark. To increase the accuracy of sight adjustments, the windage and elevation screws offer 16 clicks per revolution instead of the more common 12. The large surface of both screws also is intended to provide longer wear, a more positive feel of movement and a louder click when adjusted.

If you have ever tried to adjust your sights without taking your hearing protection off, you will appreciate these last changes instantly. Suggested retail on the Standard Buck Mark Micro is $244.95, making it one of the more competitive priced handguns in its class.

Though it obviously has considerable potential as a trail gun, what originally caught my eye about the Micro was that several distributors listed it as "ambidextrous." Being a southpaw, I knew true ambidextrous .22 autos were few and far between. Just to make sure, I called a Browning distributor and was told, "Yes, the safety on the Micro is ambidextrous."

This sounded like an outstanding idea to me, so I quickly ordered a standard model Micro with black grips. Unfortunately, when the pistol arrived, I found the safety still was in the common right-hand thumb position of the left side of the gun. The only obvious ambidextrous feature about the Micro

was that the grips work equally well in either hand. Given the fact I normally carry a .22 auto with the chamber empty, it actually wasn't that big of a handicap. Still, it would have been nice had it been ambidextrous.

Sighting in the Micro, I found the short, bull barrel gave the pistol a rock-steady, centered-over-the-hand balance I found conducive to good shooting. Once the gun was printing the standard high-velocity solids close to point of aim, I dug out a wide cross-section of .22 LR ammo types from my cache.

Using an Outer's Pistol Perch rest, I proceeded to fire five-round groups with each type. On a few occasions, when I felt there might have been shooter error involved, I repeated groups. The Micro proved easily capable of putting everything I tried in to my 1 1/2-inch minimum at 50 feet.

Back when I was shooting IHMSA .22 silhouette on a regular basis, one shooter I knew swore by Federal's promotional brand Lightning high-velocity long rifle solids. The Micro seemed to like Lightnings equally well, grouping five rounds just under an inch. CCI's standard velocity Mini-Group turned in a three-quarter-inch cluster and their high velocity .22 LR HP produced an outstanding five-eighths-inch group.

I recently read an article by a known handgun expert wherein he discussed how he went about measuring his hand-rested semi-auto pistol groups. He automatically threw out the first round chambered, because its point of impact was different than those cycled from the magazine by the gun. He then refused to count at least two more rounds as being shooter error. In the end, only the three closest holes were considered in judging the true accuracy potential of the gun in question. While I don't necessarily agree with this system, practically every brand of ammo I tried in the Micro would give a sub-one-inch, 50-foot group.

Running the same cross-section of .22 ammo over my Oehler 35P chronograph was equally interesting. Most of the standard high-speed solids turned in around 970 feet per second with only the forementioned Federal Lightning (1026 fps) and Remington HV (1040 fps) clocking more than 1000 feet per second.

Interestingly enough, with the exception of Eley Club, the standard velocity loads averaged 982 fps. My guess is that the high-velocity loads require longer barrels in order to reach their full potential. The standard velocity loads had the added advantage of slightly less muzzle blast. Those shooting solids probably would be well advised to find which load works best in their own handguns without consideration of its high- or standard-velocity rating.

The CCI Mini Mag hollow-points for which my Micro had shown a preference crossed the screens at a reasonable 1036 feet per second. From past experience, I don't expect much expansion at this velocity, but its excellent accuracy should make up for that. CCI Stinger was the pure velocity champ at 1229 fps, with Remington's Yellow Jacket at 1142 fps, the CCI Mini Mag +V scoring 1110 fps and the Remington Viper traveling at 1142 fps.

Eley Club was the slowest load at 873 fps, though for some reason, the box of Remington HV hollow-points I tried only produced an av average of 888 feet per second. I would guess this was one of those stray lots of ammo that sometimes slip by. The Remington long rifle HP always has produced good results for me in the past.

In the process of sighting-in the Micro, testing for accuracy, chronographing, shooting a little informal silhouette and general plinking, I fired several hundred rounds with only a single malfunction. That one problem was with the flat-point Winchester Super Silhouette round failing to feed, something I've had happen with a number of firearms. The only cleaning the Micro received was a few quick wipes of the breech area and a Break-Free-soaked rag over the slide and rails.

Because I intended to carry the Micro as a trail gun, I required a holster that would not interfere with my pack. Looking over what was available, I settled on El Paso

The author packs the Browning Micro Buck in a copy of the military shoulder holster designed for .45 auto.

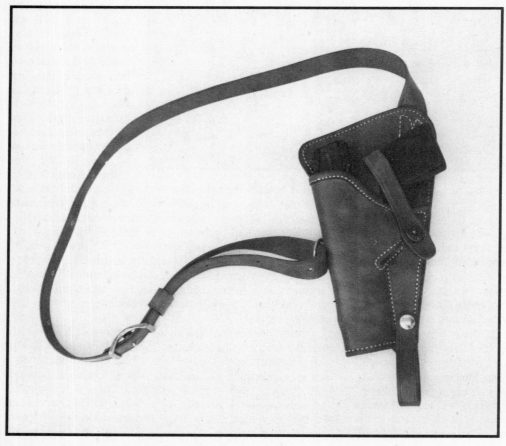

Handsome and sturdy, this M1942 shoulder rig is from El Paso Saddlery, Box 27194, El Paso, TX 79926.

Saddlery's M1942, a reproduction of the classic military "tanker" shoulder holster. Considering the fact that the Micro was a new model and that I needed a left-handed holster, I thought I had better call them first before ordering. As in the past, El Paso's answer was, "No problem. We can turn out a custom version in around 30 days."

While waiting for the M1942, I tried the Micro in a Michael's of Oregon nylon holster originally bought for a four-inch-barrel revolver. With a little adjustment of the keeper strap, the Micro fit just fine.

As tradition, my wife and I make an early September trip to the high country to pick wild huckleberries. Given the fact huckleberries are one of the blue grouse's favorite foods, I usually can expect to pick up a few birds in the same areas. This year's berry crop was a near total failure but I still managed to bag one blue with the Micro. That made the trip a success for me.

With the exception of a left-handed safety, there still is little I can think of to improve the Browning Micro for trail use. It's compact, extremely accurate, reliable and reasonably priced. I expect mine to be providing many more grouse and snowshoe rabbits for our table in the coming years.

For more information on the Micro, contact Browning, Rt. 1, Morgan, UT 84050.

BROWNING MICRO BUCK MARK .22 LR
MEASURED OVER AN OEHLER 35P AT 10 FEET

.22 LONG RIFLE	VELOCITY (FPS)
CCI Hollow Point Mini Mag	1036
CCI Solid Mini Mag	972
CCI Stinger	1229
CCI Mini Mag +V	1110
CCI Mini Group	978
Winchester Super Silhouette	980
Winchester .22 Standard Velcity	967
Winchester Extra Power	962
Federal .22 Silhouette	947
Federal .22 High Power	975
Federal Champion Standard Velocity	991
Federal Lightning	1026
Federal Pistol Match	994
Remington HV Hollow-Point	888
Remington HV Solid	1040
Remington Viper	1091
Remington Yellow Jacket	1142
Eley Club Standard Velocity	873

The Buck Mark Micro fired outstanding groups with practically every brand of ammunition the author tried.

THE MITCHELL P.08

By J.B. Wood

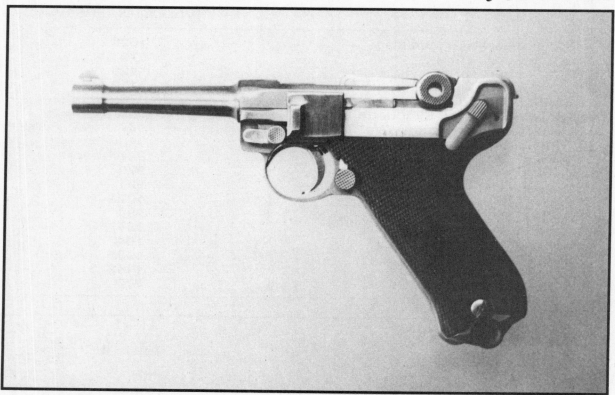

This Clone Is Produced
Right Here In The USA!

MY FIRST reaction, when I heard about this pistol, was disbelief. They're going to make the legendary Luger, here in the United States, in stainless steel? Right. If they do manage to do it, I figured, it would (A) cost a fortune, and (B) probably wouldn't work. An alternate scenario was that it would be like the original cosmetically, but would be entirely different mechanically.

Well, I was wrong on all counts. The magic of investment casting and CNC machining has kept the cost reasonable. Except for one or two small differences, the original design was followed faithfully. And, most importantly of all, it *works*. Over the past few weeks, I have been trying out a regular production pistol — not a tool-room prototype — and it is perfect in every way.

At this point, let's backtrack a bit and clear up a touchy detail: In the first paragraph, I used the name "Luger" — perfectly proper, as it is the name of the original designer of the gun.

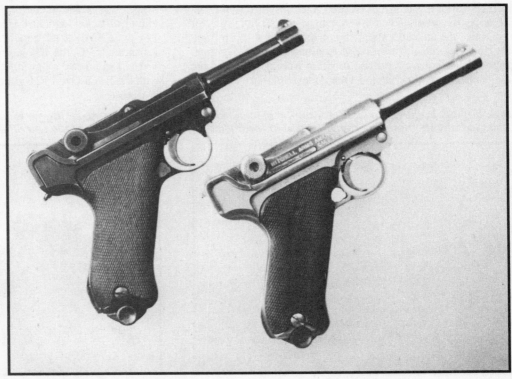

The Mitchell Arms Luger is a faithful remake of the famous German firearm.

However, as a trademark name for a pistol of this configuration, the name is owned by Stoeger Industries. It has been registered by the firm since the days when they were the sole U.S. commercial importers of the gun. So you and I can call any pistol of this design a Luger — but Mitchell Arms can't.

Down the years, the gun has had several designations. "Parabellum" is one. In countries where it has been an official military sidearm, it has been known by the year of its adoption, "P.08" in Germany, as used by the army. "Modell 04" in the German navy. The Swiss used it first, as the Ordonnanz Modell 1900. Among collectors and shooters in America, it has always been the Luger.

Those of us who like to shoot these fine pistols have watched with alarm as prices for matching-number guns have climbed to awesome levels. Even my quite ordinary DWM 1923 Commercial Luger is now almost too valuable to shoot. Many shooters have searched for guns with mismatched numbers, with no collector interest and more reasonable prices. Now that the Mitchell version is here, they need not search.

The new pistol is a handsome gun, with clean lines and nicely cut edges that match the look of the German originals. When I first received the Mitchell pistol, I took it apart to see whether there were any mechanical differences. For comparison, I used my original DWM Commercial Luger.

The trigger lever housing of the Mitchell pistol is changed

The author's original DWM 1923 Commercial Luger (left) is compared to the Mitchell Arms version.

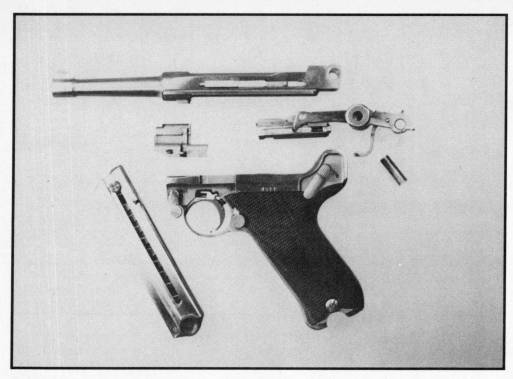

Field-stripped, the Mitchell Luger reveals many parts that are stronger than those featured on original Lugers.

slightly on the inside. It is heavier at the bottom, with a straight, full-length pin for the lever. In the frame, the takedown lever has a self-contained ball and spring for positioning, rather than the old round-wire torsion type.

Inside the frame at the rear, the arms of the recoil spring lever are shorter and thicker for added strength. On the barrel extension, the little "shelf" above the sear is missing. It served no real mechanical purpose, and leaving it off greatly simplified the casting and machining of the extension. Until I started the takedown and comparison, I didn't notice it wasn't there.

The rest of it was just as Georg Luger designed it in 1898. Some parts would even interchange; the firing pins, for example. As an experiment, I put the Mitchell barrel and toggle assembly on my DWM original, using the original trigger lever housing. Fit and function were perfect, and the magazines also interchanged. Of course, I didn't try to fire the

combination, as the headspace and other factors might not have been right.

So, mechanically and cosmetically, it's a Luger. But, how does it shoot? At the range, I fired it from a casual rest at 50 feet, trying several different loads. In the first full magazine, there was a glitch on the second round, but it never happened again, through more than 50 rounds. Obviously, a case of "new gun syndrome" or a weak load.

The best five-shot group was with the Winchester 115-grain Silvertip hollow-point, measuring 1 1/4 inches, all in the black. Also well-centered in the black was the Hansen 123-grain full-jacket load, at 1 1/2 inches. Next was the Magtech 124-grain FMJ, at 1 5/8 inches, all in the black. The Federal 124-grain SWC, the 124-grain CCI Blazer and the old Super Vel 112-grain JSP all grouped into 1 3/4 inches. Best group with the RWS-Geco 123-grain FMJ was two inches, and the

Like original Lugers, the extractor on the Mitchell 9mm rises to indicate there is a round loaded in the chamber.

The modernized trigger lever housing on the Mitchell (right) is one of the few differences from the original.

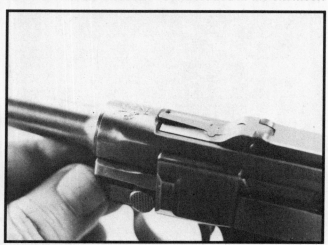

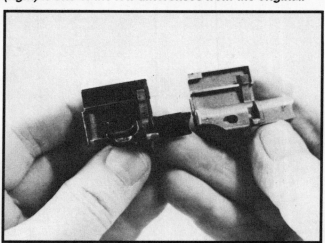

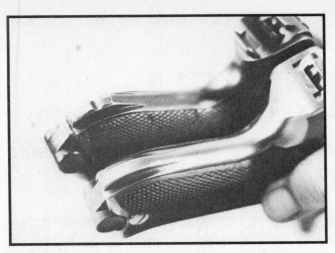

The Mitchell Luger (bottom) features a stock lug just like the original but it doesn't have the attachment cuts.

Like the original, the Mitchell is safe when the lever is back (above) and ready to fire when forward (below).

Federal 115-grain JHP 2 3/8 inches.

Well, I was impressed. Not only was it accurate, but the autoloader had run all of these loads without a malfunction. After that second-shot jam, it just kept shooting, all through the afternoon. The trigger pull of my pistol is excellent, with the usual amount of slack, then a firm four-pound let-off.

The sights are of classic pattern — an inverted-V front blade and a V-notch at the rear. The front sight is dovetail-mounted, with lateral adjustment possible by drifting. The rear sight notch is integral with the toggle link. The grip angle has, of course, that beautiful Luger slant that settles into your hand and makes the gun part of your arm.

There is no stock-attachment cut, but the maker has wisely left the lug projection at lower rear, where it helps the "feel" of the grip. I once owned and shot an Erfurt Luger that was made without the stock lug, and it never felt right.

The takedown for cleaning is exactly the same as an old original. You remove the magazine, move the barrel and toggle assembly slightly to the rear, then turn the takedown lever down. The trigger lever housing then is taken off, and the top assembly is moved forward off the frame. Pushing out the

main cross-pin at the rear allows the toggle assembly to be taken out.

Reassembly has only one important thing to remember: The recoil spring stirrup must drop into the frame in front of the arms of the recoil spring lever, just as in an old original. The easiest way to do it is to hold the gun upside down until the stirrup link is in the proper location, then turn it over.

As noted earlier, workmanship of the Mitchell pistol is excellent. A nice touch is the U.S. eagle seal on the chamber, neatly executed and reminiscent of the Lugers that were imported into this country in the old days for commercial sale.

Are there any points I could criticize? Well, just two small ones, and both are cosmetic. I would vote for polishing the safety lever, because its matte finish allows a faint casting line to show. And, I wish they had put the serial number somewhere else — the upper back of the frame, perhaps, leaving the left side above the grip plain.

Otherwise, it is simply beautiful. And, it works and is accurate. In future times, Don Mitchell should be remembered as the man who brought back this fine pistol, in stainless steel and at a reasonable price. With all of that, it is a remarkable engineering achievement.

The right side of the modern Luger has Mitchell's stamp.

TAURUS' MODEL 85CH

By Roger Combs

The stainless steel Taurus Model 85CH — concealed hammer — revolver presents a compact, smooth, integrated appearance.

THE TAURUS five-shot revolver is made for light loads and small hands. It is designed to be a pocket or purse defense handgun and meets this design criteria quite well. The little lightweight Model 85CH features a two-inch barrel and smooth, rounded hardwood grips. The model tested is of all stainless steel construction. A blue version is also available. The Taurus .38 Special revolver, with its concealed hammer, will fire double-action only.

The revolver's stainless steel components are highly polished and present a pleasing, modern, streamlined appearance. Everything fits together well. The gun is apparently put together by skilled hands in Brazil, then imported by Taurus

International in Florida. There are no ill-fitting parts and no rough, unfinished edges or surfaces to mar the appearance of the revolver. It looks as if it means business, and it does. Its business is protecting and defending its owner.

The smooth hardwood — one presumes Brazilian walnut — grips are in split halves. The wood is dark with pleasing grain patterns. The two halves fit together well and are held to the frame by a single screw about two-thirds of the way down the grip. A steel pin fits into holes near the bottom of the frame and wood halves to help keep them from unnecessary movement while in place. Brass Taurus identifying shields are embedded on each side of the grip panels, near the top. The

Five Shots, Concealed Hammer, Two-Inch Barrel And Light Weight Make This .38 Special Just Right For Defense

The Taurus is made in Brazil with care and craftsmanship worthy of any area. The logo is stamped into the frame, right side, just above the wood grip. Spelling of Brazil varies with location.

back strap of the frame is exposed at the rear of the grip as the wood projects slightly less than a half-inch below the metal. The grip is smoothly rounded at the bottom.

Moving upward, on the right side of the frame, is a stamped Taurus trademark logo. Just above the trigger are the identifying marks of the importer, *Taurus Int. Mfg. Miami, FL USA.* Forward of that is the serial number and "MADE IN BRAZIL." On the right side of the short barrel is the caliber, .38 Special. The left side of the barrel has the stamped legend, *TAURUS BRAZIL.*

The visible stainless steel is highly polished, except for the cylinder release button and the front end of the ejection rod. They are metal-checkered for non-slip operation. The top of the barrel and frame are dull matte-finished to reduce reflections and glare in the eyes of the shooter. The rear-facing surface of the long front sight blade is deeply grooved to further reduce light reflections. Sight blade measures 1-3/16 inches long. The rear sight is simply an open groove cut along the top and rear of the frame.

On the left side, the cylinder release latch button has a concave surface to help the thumb push it forward to open the cylinder. When the cylinder is open, the trigger cannot be pulled. The five-hole cylinder measures 1-1/2 inches long. With it open, a single push on the ejection rod removes all five rounds, fired or not. The five-pointed extraction star grabs each shell casing without slippage or hesitation.

Close examination of the open cylinder reveals the rear tip of the spring-loaded extraction rod in the center of the star. When the cylinder release latch is pressed forward, it bears upon the rod, running all the way through to push on the locking latch under the barrel, inside its lower ejector shroud. The latch is held in the shroud by a spring-loaded stainless steel pin, visible from the front of the gun beneath the muzzle.

When the hardwood grips are removed, three side plate holding screws are visible on the right side. A portion of the lowest, middle screw and all the rearmost screws are covered by the right side of the grip when it is in place. The wise shooter will check each of these screws for tightness from time to time, especially after a shooting session. Screws in those locations have been known to loosen with a lot of shooting. But use care and use only the correct screwdriver blade size so as not to bugger the screw slots. The same may be said for the single screw that holds the two grip sides on the frame.

With the hardwood grip sides removed, the simple working of the main spring is visible.

The back of the hammer, trigger and inside and outside of the trigger guard are polished smooth. The external surfaces of the revolver are contoured nicely, with no snags or sharp edges to catch on clothing, purse or holster, to hinder a fast draw. The overall appearance is simple, clean and professional.

The muzzle of the two-inch barrel extends one-eighth-inch forward of the ejector shroud on the bottom and the solid rib and front sight ramp on top. The concave curve shape of the shroud front is repeated at the front of the frame and the trigger guard.

When the trigger is activated, the fluted cylinder rotates in a counter-clockwise direction, when viewed from the shooter's perspective. The double-action trigger pull was measured at 13-1/3 pounds — not exactly a lightweight. Some women might complain that the force required to shoot the revolver is a bit too much for their strength. But the combination of the amount of trigger pull required and the double-action-only operation are designed-in safety measures. So is the concealed hammer. There is little possibility of snagging the hammer on anything as the firearm is being replaced or holstered, causing an unintended discharge. Firing the gun requires a planned, deliberate action by the shooter.

The smooth wood and rounded grip of the Model 85CH are meant for a small hand. Larger hands will find that the little finger may drop below the butt or all fingers may be a bit cramped for room on the forward portion beneath the trigger guard. The left side of the grip panel stock is relieved to accept the shooter's

The five-round cylinder swings open to the left side of the revolver. Note the smooth, hand-fitting contour of the rear of the frame and wood grip.

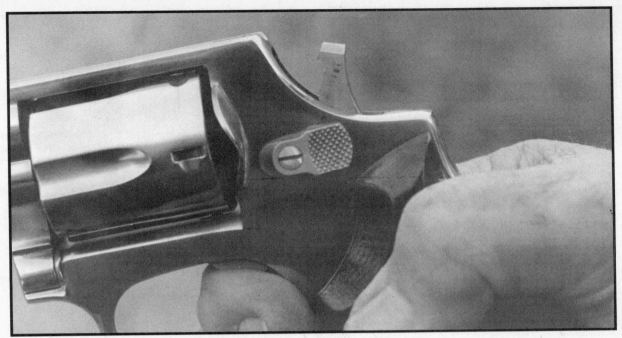

With careful double-action trigger control, the hammer action may be observed. Cylinder release slide is machine-checkered for non-slip operation. Cylinder opens by pushing release forward in normal manner.

Taurus revolver seems made for woman's hands. Control is easy with familiar two-handed grip.

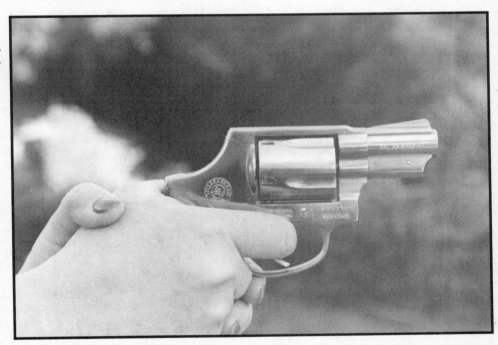

right thumb as the gun is fired. Ideally, the right-handed shooter's right thumb should bend downward at the joint, fitting into the concave recess in the grip. The tips of the trigger finger and the thumb will meet as the gun is fired, adding some extra confidence and control for the shooter.

With practice, the trigger and hammer action can be controlled by an experienced shooter, allowing the hammer to ride back and stop just short of the drop. Trigger control is important to many shooters for maximum handgun accuracy. Practicing this hesitation trigger technique is a good way to strengthen and train the muscles used to grip the revolver and pull the trigger. There will be less inadvertent hand movement as the hammer drops, improving accuracy. Trigger action is smooth through its movement. There is no grinding or rubbing evident to the shooter. The test crew experienced no accuracy-robbing roughness during testing. When the hammer falls, that is the end of the trigger pull. There is no noticeable over-travel.

A handgun such as the Taurus M85CH is certainly not a highly accurate, long-range target firearm. It is intended for close-in defensive fire, probably from a concealed carry. It is also an ideal household defense gun, provided it is locked away safely from the reach of children or strangers inside the house. It is brought into action quickly when needed, and there

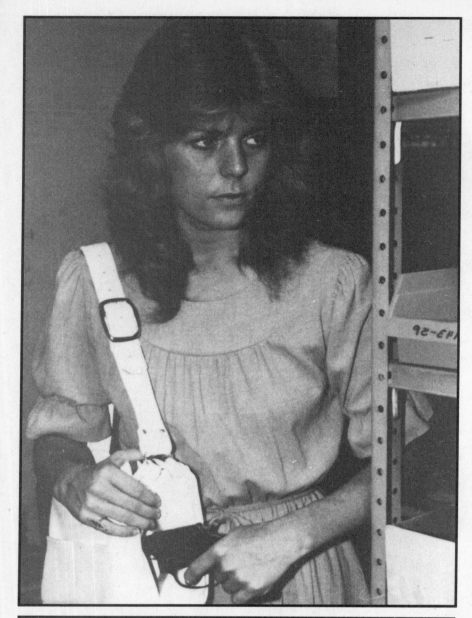

Company called Feminine Protection produces several models of purses with built-in, concealed holster. The five-round, stainless steel revolver would be ideal for undercover work.

TAURUS MODEL 85CH REVOLVER

Caliber:	.38 Special
Capacity:	5 rounds
Barrel:	2 inches
Weight:	21 ounces
Grip:	Brazilian walnut
Sights:	Front ramp; rear square notch
Country of origin:	Brazil
Suggested Retail:	Blue, $237; stainless, $297
Importer:	Taurus Interntional,16175 NW 49Ave., Miami, FL 33014

empty brass ejected without any apparent problems. None of the shooters achieved what might be termed tight target groups, but all rounds were kept in the "kill zone" on paper targets from ten yards or less range.

It was soon apparent that heavy bullet weights and powerful loads, including most Plus-P ammunition, were inappropriate for this revolver. The gun points naturally and is fast to get into action, but powerful loads tend to cause too much movement and loss of control by the shooter. The gun seems more easily controlled by women with small hands, shooting lighter loads.

Heavier, high-velocity loads in the Plus-P range with slugs traveling out the muzzle in excess of 900 feet per second (fps) caused the gun to bounce around in the shooter's hand too much. That movement made an accurate second or third rapid shot more difficult. For shooters with larger, perhaps stronger, hands, the problem was no less. The extra bullet velocity and hitting power are not worth the loss of control.

No damage will be done to the revolver from using higher

is little that might go wrong with the tough, well-made revolver design.

Several loadings of .38 Special ammunition were run through the revolver during testing. All rounds fired, and

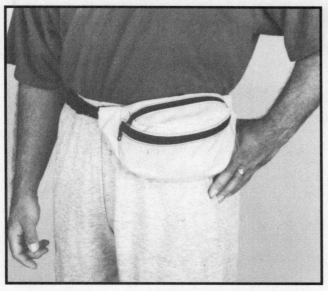
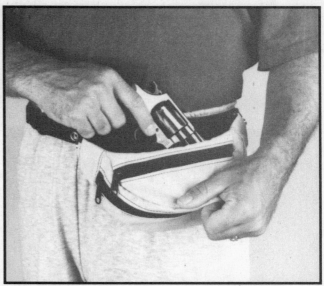

So-called fanny packs have become popular for recreation and casual wear. This model from Michaels of Oregon has concealed holster pouch inside the visible zippered pocket. Pouches are available in several bright colors and black.

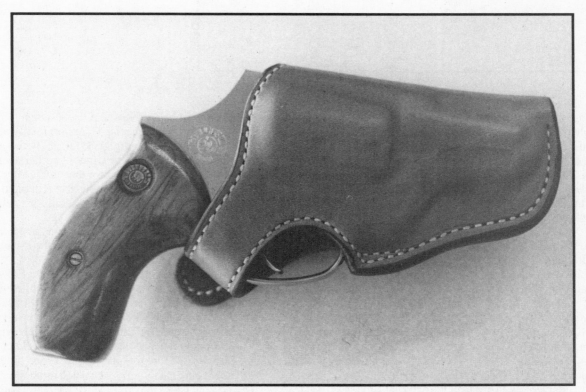

Bianchi Model 55L Lightning holster is just right for the Taurus revolver. Leather holster is shown in plain tan, for left- or right-hand carry. Revolver is retained by snap-open strap behind trigger guard.

velocity, heavier bullet loads. The Taurus is rugged enough to withstand the pounding from the more powerful factory-loaded ammunition, but the milder loads are adequate for home defense use and are easier to control.

Bullets of 110, 125 or 158 grains are considered to be about right for home and personal defense ammunition. They are easily available from most commercial civilian retailers at reasonable prices. The new Taurus owner needs to experiment with several loads from various manufacturers to discover which one or two his or her particular revolver prefers. No two handguns will perform exactly alike shooting the same ammunition.

The type of bullet selected to feed the gun is a matter for further consideration, too. Strictly for defense, most shooters

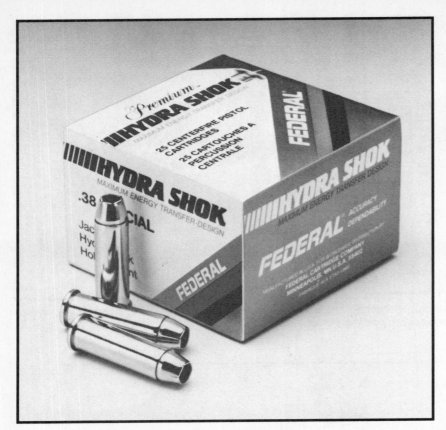

Combination of Taurus Model 85CH and Federal Hydra-Shok hollow-point is potent self-protection package. Hydra-Shok is a Plus-P load, requiring firm grip on firearm.

will probably opt for some sort of hollow-point bullet. Some may wish to shoot a lead semi-wadcutter round.

The revolver tested here seemed to prefer two factory loads, although everything the test crew tried was well digested. The Federal Hi-Power 158-grain lead semi-wadcutter and the Winchester Super-X 158-grain lead semi-wadcutter loads turned in the most gratifying accuracy combined with the most pleasant behavior for the shooter. The Winchester Super-X is listed at a measured muzzle velocity of 755 feet per second (fps) and the Federal Hi-Power shows the same speed.

Professionals, who may find use for the Taurus Model 85CH as a concealed primary or backup handgun, will find the Federal Premium Hydra-Shok ammunition equally accurate through the gun. The 129-grain Hydra-Shok hollow-point is a high-velocity Plus-P load, however, and some of the test crew noticed a tendency for the grip to slip in the hand if he or she did not maintain total concentration while firing.

The Hydra-Shok load is intended as a self-defense load, generating 945 fps at the muzzle through Federal's test barrel. That is considerably faster than the two standard loads tested, but accuracy suffered little at close range. The Hydra-Shok ammunition is a bit more expensive for the civilian buyer and is not a round for casual plinking or target work..

Carrying a revolver with a concealed hammer safely presents some special problems. The test crew tried the Taurus in a couple of concealment holsters designed to accept small revolvers with standard hammers. The revolver easily slipped out, even with the safety strap fastened. Tightening down the strap would not retain the gun. It would not be safe to carry this type of revolver in a holster that relies on a retention strap to hold in the handgun.

Under some circumstances, one might consider carrying the gun in a jacket pocket or purse. Bianchi International makes a holster for a concealed hammer revolver, called the Model 55L. It is a leather high-ride holster with a safety strap that snaps over the rear of the trigger guard, rather than over the hammer. It is designed to allow the middle finger to pop the safety strap snap open when a firing grip is applied to the gun. The trigger guard is covered and the holster is closed at the muzzle.

Other than that, some inside-the-pants concealment holsters have no top safety strap, relying on the trousers belt and holster design to help keep the gun in place.

For women, a company called Feminine Protection produces a series of handbags with a built-in, hidden gun compartment sandwiched between two outer pockets. A hook-and-loop fastener holds the handgun in place, ready for a quick draw when needed. The Taurus is ideal for this type of carry.

Several manufacturers, including Bianchi, Galco, KG Products, Michaels of Oregon and Triple K are producing belt pouches or fanny packs with special holsters concealed inside. These popular packs may be made of leather or padded nylon, in black or in a variety of colors. They offer quick, ready access to a concealed firearm, revolver or autoloading pistol. They are most appropriate with casual and vacation wear when a holster, jacket or purse is not easily worn.

All states and many counties and municipalities have their own rules and regulations regarding citizen-carried, loaded firearms. In most places, a license or permit is required. No matter the law, the decision to carry a loaded weapon is serious, carrying complicated moral and legal consequences. Where legal and/or morally required for defense, the Taurus Model 85CH revolver is made for the task.

BERETTA'S TIP-BARREL SEMI-AUTO

— **Jim Fender**

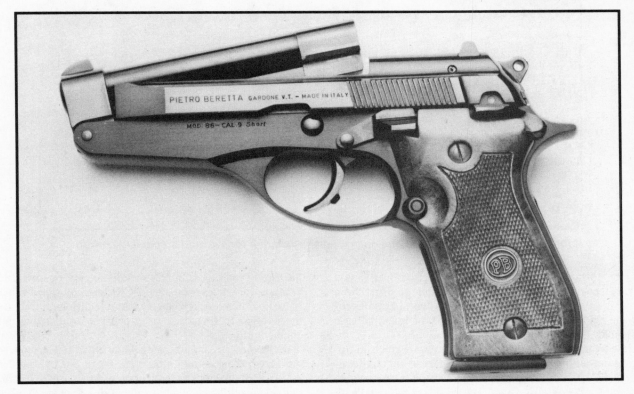

The author believes the tip-up barrel feature of the Beretta 86 (above) and the 21A are particularly well suited for the elderly and physically handicapped person who wants a home-defense firearm.

COMPETITION IS a wonderful thing. Manufacturers will tell you they like competition, but if most could continue to sell products which they have been making at a profit for years without worrying about competition, they would do so. Competition is change, and despite protestations to the contrary, manufacturers prefer the status quo over change anytime. Better the devil you know than the devil you don't know.

Had American automobile manufacturers been left to their own choices, the American public would still be driving around in late 1950s-style, gas-thirsty Ford and Chrysler cars with fancy tailfins, lots of chrome trim, AM radios only — and no seat belts or other safety devices.

The same is true for handguns for home-defense use. Without competition, our home-defense handguns would still be something on the order of two-shot derringers chambered for the .41 Short black powder cartridge. Competition forces manufacturers to be innovative in design to look for ways to improve their products, make them easier to use, or to adapt them to an entire class of people who weren't being served by the existing products. In the firearms business— as in any other manufacturing enterprise — to rest upon past successes

The Author Feels These Are Ideal Home-Defense Handguns For Senior Citizens

Handling the Beretta 86, author has gained an appreciation for the auto's special features.

is a sure formula for being left behind by the competition actively seeking ways to distinguish their products from competitors' wares. Yeah, manufacturers don't like competition — but it's great for us consumers of home-defense handguns.

Case in point: the relatively new Beretta Model 86 tip-barrel semi-automatic pistol in .380 Auto, the big brother of the Model 21A in .22 LR or .25 Auto which has been available for some years now. Big yawn, The market is saturated with .380 semi-automatics. What does the Beretta Model 86 have that sets it apart from its competitors? Radar-laid sighting systems? Mininuclear 90-grain warheads guaranteed to end hostilities with one shot? A flashing neon sign which announces to the world that the possessor of a Beretta Model 86 is one tough dude? No. Just sensible product improvements, such as the just mentioned tip-up barrel. Wait a minute. A tip-up barrel? On a .380 Auto?

Sure. And here's why. The United States is currently in the throes of a crime wave beyond anything we could have conjured up in our worst nightmares even 10 years ago. The causes of this crime wave are many, and far beyond the scope of this article to catalog. One of the major causes, though, is the insatiable demand for drugs such as "coke" or "crack." The number of American homes which have been burglarized in

the past 10 years by criminals seeking money, or such articles as silverware, television sets, VCRs and any other valuable household items which can be sold (usually for a fraction of their value) to finance their expensive drug habits defies enumeration.

In the process, innumerable American citizens have been terrorized, maimed and murdered. Since our overburdened police departments can't guarantee any particular citizen individualized 24-hour-a-day protection — nor are they under any legal mandate to do so — is it any wonder that more and more Americans are purchasing pistols for home defense?

And just who are the people purchasing home-defense firearms? Who among our population are at greatest risk of robbery, because they are the easiest targets since they are regarded as the most defenseless? Just what types of homeowner or apartment dweller do these scumbags seek out as their easiest marks? The elderly, people with physical handicaps and those who never have owned a firearm before, that's who.

Ironically, the people most in need of home protection firearms generally are the people least able to manipulate modern handguns such as a semi-automatic pistol. That means there is a sizeable segment of American society without access to home defense firearms suitable to their needs. Economists

Author likes the double-action mode of the Beretta Model 86.

This group was pumped-out rapidly in double-action with the Beretta 86 from 15-yards.

and market researchers call such a population a "market niche." All too often manufacturers develop a new product, then attempt to develop a market for the new product. Really smart manufacturers — those looking for a leg up on competitors — look for market niches, then design products to satisfy an identified need.

The Beretta Model 21A semi-automatic pistol in .22 LR and .25 Auto, with its distinctive tip-up barrel (the tip-up barrel feature actually goes back to the early part of this century when several pistols, most notably the Austrian Steyr 1909, incorporated this design) has been available for some years now. Actually, I believe at one time the .25 Auto version was called the Model 20, but now both the .22 LR and the .25 Auto are designated the Model 21. In 1991, after some six years of intensive development, Beretta introduced the .380 Auto Model 86 with its tip-up barrel. I must admit that when I initially came across the Model 86 in early 1991, I saw absolutely no reason for it. What did the Model 86 do that the Models 84 or 85 couldn't do just as well? And years ago I had

dismissed the Model 21A as little more than a toy. It took the combined efforts of Beretta's sales staff, director of marketing and Beretta's outside marketing research firm to persuade me to look twice at these semi-automatics. They did, and I'm glad.

I have a cousin of whom I'm quite fond (though we've been feuding good naturedly since we were teenagers, and I'd never admit it to her) and for the past several years I've been concerned about her increasingly evident Parkinson's disease. Thank goodness, modern medical science has come up with medications which have arrested the progress of this disease which affects the muscles and causes almost constant trembling of the hands. Consequently, my cousin has lost strength in her hands to the point that she experiences difficulty in shutting off the water tap properly at the kitchen sink.

Now, my cousin is no stranger to firearms. Years ago, she really enjoyed going out to the range with me and firing handguns. Her father had bought her several rifles and shotguns. I taught her to handle a pistol. She knows how to shoot and how to handle firearms safely. She also lives in a Mary-

Model 21A Spare Parts List

1	Barrel front mount pin	18	Magazine release
2*	Barrel assembly	19	Magazine release button
3	Hammer spring guide assembly	20	Magazine release spring
4	Trigger	21	Trigger spring
5	Trigger guard	22	Barrel release spring
6*	Slide	23	Firing pin
7	Grip screws	24	Firing pin spring
8	Barrel release	25	Sear
9	Recoil bar	26	Sear pin
10	Ejector	27	Hammer
11	Ejector pin	28	Hammer pin
12	Safety plunger	29	Trigger pin
13	Safety spring	30	Firing pin retaining pin
14	Safety	31	Trigger bar
15	Sear spring	32	Trigger bar spring
16	Recoil spring cover	33	Recoil spring plunger
17	Recoil spring		* Factroy Fitting Required

The Beretta Model 21A seems to disappear into author's hands (left) but the little .22 is still a performer, holding a group (below), at 15 yards, that would stop an intruder.

land suburb of Washington, D.C., an hour's driving time from our nation's capitol. This city also enjoys the dubious distinction of being the most crime-ridden city in our nation.

When my cousin arrived recently in New Hampshire for an extended visit, I gave her access to all my handguns and asked for her honest opinion as to the one she found the easiest to use. She liked several revolvers. She did not like a .45 Colt Government Model. Or a Glock. Or a Beretta 92. Even though the progress of the disease has been arrested, Parkinson's has left her without sufficient strength in her hands to manipulate the slides of these semi-automatics to chamber a round. Several years ago she could. Today she cannot. It was a sobering lesson for both of us.

She had liked shooting some of my semi-automatic pistols five or six years ago, and she still likes the type. She was enthusiastic about both Berettas. Sadly, she had difficulty in loading the magazines of either semi-automatic pistol, but these chores I gladly did for her. However, after only a few minutes' instruction she was quickly inserting loaded magazines into both the Model 21A and the Model 86, tipping up the barrels, inserting a loaded cartridge and locking the barrels into battery.

She could, with great effort, manipulate the slides of both pistols if the hammers were cocked, but she could not do so with the hammers forward. My cousin felt comfortable with both Berettas, and even though it required both hands to unlock the barrel, tip it up, insert a cartridge and lock it back in battery. She actually preferred the Model 86 to the Model 21A.

She liked the greater weight of the Model 86, and the size of the cartridge; she also liked the ambidextrous safety with larger control surfaces on the Model 86 than the small safety on the left side of the Model 21A. She also shot the Model 86 more accurately than the Model 21A.

Due to the impending visit of Hurricane Bob to New England, we were able to spend only an hour shooting at my range before we had to scurry for shelter. While she won't win any awards for group size, my cousin was able to keep two magazines of eight rounds each well within the torso of a standard man-size silhouette target.

Following the hurricane's departure, I returned to my range with close friends Richard and Shaw Wong, both avid firearms enthusiasts. While both much prefer 9mm and .45 ACP semi-automatics to the .22 LR and .380 Auto calibers, they graciously assisted by shooting and handling the two Beretta tip-barrel semi-automatics. Neither would trade their Beretta 92s, Colt Government Models or Sigarms P220s for the Model 21A or the Model 86.

Nevertheless, Richard and Shaw Wong were impressed with the functioning of the two pistols and quickly perceived the obvious safety advantages of the tip-up barrels. Both brothers shot the Model 86 alongside my own Beretta Model 85BB. They were able to shoot slightly smaller eight-round groups, firing double action on the standard silhouette targets from a distance of 15 yards, with the Model 86 than they were with the Model 85BB. When we were discussing why this was so, Shaw Wong said the slightly greater heft of the Model 86 helped him to get back on target slightly faster. The Model 86 does weigh approximately three ounces more than the Model 85BB.

Richard Wong felt the fact that the Model 86's barrel was held rigidly at the muzzle by the hinge pin arrangement provided slightly more inherent accuracy.

Both the Model 21A and the Model 86 won plaudits from both Wong brothers, because the pistols' blow-back features eliminated the extractors entirely and provided greater sim-

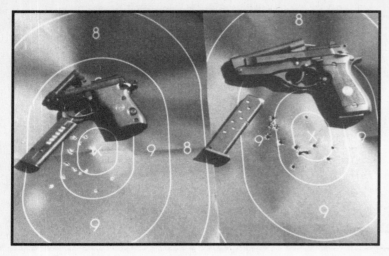

Left, the Beretta Model 21A .22 rimfire (left) and the Beretta Model 86 .380 Auto performed well during author's rapid-fire test at 15 yards. Below, Richard Wong compares the Model 86 tip-barrel (top) with the Beretta Model 85BB.

plicity. We were shooting Winchester 85-grain Silvertips, perhaps the best .380 Auto ammunition available over-the-counter today. So, malfunctions due to ammunition were not expected and, of course, did not occur.

I regretted having fired away a year or so ago some 1,000 rounds of really grungy Egyptian-made .380 auto military ball with a slightly thicker-than-standard extractor rim. I had experienced several malfunctions with that ammo when the extractor of my Model 85BB had been unable to snap over the extractor rim. This problem would not have been a factor with the Model 86 and its blow-back design.

This brings up the question of how the round in the chamber is ejected if the shooter doesn't wish to fire it? Easy enough. Just unlatch the barrel on either the 21A or the 86, cup the hand which is not holding the pistol behind the receiver and elevate the muzzle. The loaded cartridge will fall into your palm. Now, this might not work if a homeowner were to store a well lubricated 21A or 86 in a place where a lot of dust, sand or lint could accumulate. It's possible that over a period of time sufficient dust, sand or lint could penetrate into the chamber via the barrel for a loaded cartridge to seize slightly in the chamber.

Of course, firing the pistol would eject the empty case, though I would counsel that the 21A, 86, or any handgun maintained for home defense be inspected and cleaned periodically, and fresh ammunition substituted on at least a three-year inspection cycle. Running a brush into the chamber every six months or so and ensuring that the round kept ready for insertion in the barrel was clean and oil-free would negate any possible problems of this nature.

There is no pistol similar to the Beretta Model 21A on the market today, but the Model 86 does share some features with the Model 85. The eight-round magazines are interchangeable, as are the grip panels. I did supplement the Model 86's magazines with my Model 85 magazines to keep my cousin and the Wong brothers shooting without interruption. And I did switch one grip panel from the Model 86 to my Model 85 to confirm they were interchangeable.

I didn't attempt to interchange anything else, though I'm sure there are a number of parts such as the hammer, ambidextrous safety levers, and triggers which are interchangeable. Such commonality of parts between two major models of .380 autos should keep down the costs of manufacture and thus the ultimate cost to the consumer.

Both the Beretta 21A and the Model 86 are well-made handguns which anyone can select for home defense without apologizing for their choices. Both pistols have a particular safety advantage which no other semi-automatic pistols offer to an elderly person or a person afflicted with a physical handicap which affects strength or agility. A pistol with a loaded magazine and one extra round can be kept handy. If the need to resort to the use of the pistol ever arises, the magazine can quickly be inserted, the barrel tipped up, a cartridge inserted and the barrel locked into battery. Anyone looking for reliable and effective home-defense handguns can trust either Beretta tip-barrel to handle such a role with aplomb.

If you know an elderly or physically handicapped person who wants to arm himself or herself for home protection, you might be saving a life if you recommend either of these two Berettas to that person.

RUGER'S
SP101 .32 H&R
MAGNUM

By *Steven Dick*

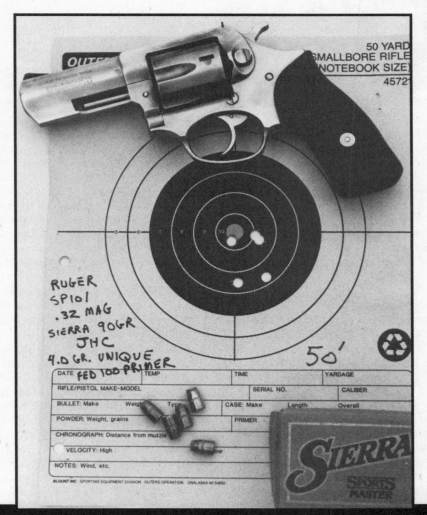

RUGER
SP101
.32 MAG
SIERRA 90GR
JHC
4.0 GR. UNIQUE
FED 100 PRIMER

50'

This Revolver Has Great Potential
As A Field Gun!

The author considers the Ruger SP101 .32 mag suited for target shooting, small-game hunting and defense.

FROM ITS beginnings in 1989 as the first of the small-frame, +P-rated .38 Specials, Ruger's SP101 family of revolvers has been growing by leaps and bounds. The stainless .38 Special was joined in 1990 by a .22LR in 2-1/4- and four-inch barrel lengths. Then 1991 saw the introduction of .357 magnum, 9x19mm and .32 magnum versions with a choice of 2-1/4- or 3-1/16-inch barrels.

In keeping with current handgun design trends, the stainless Ruger SP101 .32 magnum utilizes a full-length barrel lug to protect the ejector rod and add recoil dampening mass to the front of the revolver.

The .32 magnum version comes in a choice of 2-1/4- or 3-1/16-inch barrels. Both barrel lengths feature a white-outlined, windage-adjustable rear sight and a black ramp up front. The grips are one piece of Monsanto Santoprene synthetic rubber with high impact Xenoy resin inserts. Like all Ruger revolvers, the SP101 can be field-stripped into basic components for ease of maintenance. My 3-1/16-inch-barrel version tipped the scale at 29 ounces.

For reasons I fail to understand, the .32 magnum has not caught on with handgunners in any great numbers. This is unfortunate, as the round is a highly versatile chambering for a number of uses. It makes a far better handgun cartridge for small game than either the .22 long rifle or .22 magnum. Big-game hunters should find it ideal for finishing shots on downed quarry. A pound of Unique powder seems to last forever when recharging this small case and reloading brings ammo cost down to about the same level as the rimfire .22 magnum. Including Federal's excellent wadcutter round, .32 S&W long ammo, can be used for small pests and target practice.

As a trail gun the .32 magnum provides a relatively powerful round in a compact, lightweight package. For those concerned with self-defense, this cartridge falls into the same effective range as the .380 Auto and standard velocity .38 Special. The .32 magnum makes an excellent compromise round for one who intends to use his/her handgun mostly for small game, target and trail, but still would like to own a reasonably effective handgun for self-defense.

From 50 feet, rested on an Outer's Pistol Perch, the SP101 planted Federal's 85-grain jacketed hollow-point in a tight 1-1/16-inch group. The only problem with this performance was the fact the group fell three inches below point of aim.

When I tried Federal's 95-grain lead flat-point, I found the groups shifted up an inch and a half but remained below point of aim. Like many other .32 magnums I've used, the SP101 didn't seem to care for plain lead bullets, turning in groups in the 2-1/2-inch range. Remington's 98-grain round nose .32 S&W Long printed in roughly the same area as the magnum lead bullet, but the groups shrank back down to 1-1/4-inch.

I also tried my favorite handload of Hornady's 85-grain JHP over 4.2 grains of Unique only to find it, too, landed low.

Though either factory load probably would strike close enough to point of aim for self-defense work, I prefer something a bit more precise for small-game hunting. Of course, none of this would have been a problem had an adjustable rear sight been added to this version of the SP101.

When I mentioned my experience with the SP101 .32 magnum to fellow gunwriter Chuck Karwan, he suggested handloading heavier weight bullets. Checking my reloading catalogs, I found Sierra offered a .312-inch diameter 90-grain JHP and Speer a 100 JHP.

In the early days of the .32 magnum — before reloading component makers got around to adding reliable data to their manuals — a number of gun publications ran seat-of-the-pants articles on loading the round. Most of these early evaluators

Accuracy can be maintained with the easy-to-handle SP101, even when shooting the magnum one-handed.

The relatively heavy barrel of the Ruger SP101 (above) soaks up recoil. Author (left) considers the magnum an excellent small-game harvester for the outdoorsman.

seemed to favor medium- to slow-burning powders, and the results were often rather impressive. Whether the loads actually were in an acceptable pressure range or not remains questionable.

Current data in the standard reloading manuals seems to lean toward using the faster burning powders in the .32 magnum. After trying several propellents, I've pretty much settled on the old tried and true Unique as the most versatile fuel for this round. I've had little trouble matching factory velocities with all of the bullets currently offered.

The 90-grain Sierra JHP in front of 4.2 grains of Unique *(Sierra Handgun Reloading Manual No. 3)* still shot lower than point of aim. By cutting the charge to 4.0 grains, I was able to raise the group into the black with a six o'clock hold. Groups shot at 50 feet ran a respectable 1-1/6 inches when fired from the Outers Pistol Perch. Working up and down from Speer's No. 11 reloading manual, I soon found a charge of 4.6 grains of Unique put their 100-grain JHP right on the same point of aim.

Once I had acceptable handloads, I set up my Oehler 35P chronograph to compare velocities. Federal's factory 85-

Firing factory ammo, the sights of this SP101 proved to be right on for windage but a bit low in elevation.

grain JHP and 95-grain lead flat-point turned in an average of 1003 fps and 859 fps respectively from the Ruger. Remington's .32 S&W Long 98-grain lead round-nose registered a rather ho-hum 646 fps. On the other hand, Federal's 98-grain lead wadcutter target round averaged 703 fps.

Anyone forced to carry a .32 S&W Long handgun would be well advised to consider this target round over any of the round-nose versions. While neither sets the world on fire powerwise, the target bullet cuts a clean, full-caliber hole.

The aforementioned 4.2 grains of Unique behind the 85-grain Hornady delivered 1022 fps. The Sierra 90-grain JHP in front of 4.0 grains of Unique averaged 948 fps. As a comparison, I fired this last load through a 5-1/2-inch barreled Ruger Single Six for an average velocity of 1060 fps.

Moving up to the 100-grain Speer JHP, with 4.6 grains of Unique powder, it produced an average of 1031 in the SP101. Out of the longer barreled Single Six, the Speer bullet clocked an impressive 1137 fps. Using my computer program, I found this last load was producing 236 foot-pounds of energy from the 3-1/16-inch tube and 287 fpe from the 5-1/2-inch. While my original intent was only to equal factory .32 magnum loads, the Speer bullet was delivering performance more in the +P .38 Special range.

Over the last six months or so, I've carried the SP101 .32 magnum on a daily basis around the ranch or when hiking and hunting. During that time, the little revolver brought down several grouse and put an insurance shot into the head of a blacktail deer. Some question the use of the .32 magnum JHP bullet on edible game. My own experience is if velocities are kept down around 1000 feet per second, the bullet seldom expands enough to damage much meat. For finishing shots on larger game, I favor Federal's flat-point lead bullet.

At first, I thought the 29-ounce weight of the handgun might be a bit too heavy for a trail gun. Carrying the gun in my much-used El Paso Saddlery Tortilla holster, I soon forgot the revolver was on my belt.

Ruger's double-action triggers are well known for their smoothness and this SP101 is no exception. The single-action pull is probably adequate for a defensive handgun, but I think it could stand to be a little lighter for trail gun use. Because of the relatively heavy frame and barrel, the recoil of the .32 magnum SP101 is mild enough for even the most sensitive shooters.

All in all, I was highly pleased with the SP101, but if possible I would like to change a couple of things. First, I feel the revolver really needs adjustable sights if it is to see much use as a trail gun. Second, I think Ruger should consider offering the .32 magnum with a four-inch barrel as the maker has done with the .22 caliber SP101. Given the fact neither of these chamberings actually need the heavy barrel lug, a lighter version might add to the model's popularity with hikers and outdoorsmen.

SECTION FOUR:

AMMUNITION

& RELOADING

HANDLOADING THE .25 ACP

With New Tools And Materials, This Is An Easy, Simple Chore!

By J. Charles

NEAR THE turn of the century, John M. Browning developed a small centerfire pistol cartridge which was to be utilized in a compact and concealable pistol. Shortly thereafter, his efforts were introduced as the Browning Model 1905 pistol and the .25 ACP cartridge. The .25 cartridge was not especially powerful. However, it was quite suitable for use in a small, straight blow-back, self-loading pistol. Such vest pocket pistols became quite popular and remain so even today.

The .25 ACP achieves the ballistic performance equivalent to the rimfire .22 LR when fired in barrels of equal length. Having made that statement, it might seem as though the .25 should have become obsolete long ago. After all, the .22 LR is much cheaper to shoot and small pocket pistols are readily available in this chambering. The .25 ACP's chief asset is that it generally demonstrates much greater functional reliability than the .22 LR. This is due more to the .22 LR's length and rim rather than the design of the firearms chambered for this cartridge. The .25 has the centerfire primer and the essentially rimless case design that produces reliability in a well-made pocket pistol.

The benefits derived from reloading the .25 ACP are much the same as for other cartridges, with economic savings topping the list. However, in practice, there are some important differences and limitations of which to be aware. The .25 ACP is a puny case, and as such, it can present handling difficulties during the reloading process. Locating and recovering the spent brass from the ground can be a real chore. Also, there is only a limited selection of projectiles available for reloading use. In addition, there are only a few powders available that are readily suited for use in the .25 ACP.

Nearly all manufacturers of reloading equipment feature die sets for reloading the .25 ACP. In my own case, I chose Lee Precision's die for its features and low price. Lee's die set includes a shell holder which can save much grief since the .25 ACP is not a size common to other case heads. If purchasing another brand of dies, be sure to get a suitable shell holder at that time, or you probably will have to make another trip in search of one.

One's choice of projectiles in reloading the .25 is rather limited. It seems most component manufacturers basically offer only a round-nose full-metal-jacketed slug of 50 grains in weight. Perhaps this is best. The .25 ACP lacks the velocity and energy to provide both useful expansion and penetration reliably. The RNFMJ slug provides good penetration for the energy levels the .25 ACP generates. It also provides the high degree of feeding reliability necessary for the defensive purposes for which many .25 ACP pistols are employed.

Being a bullet caster changes little in the way of projectile choice. Most available moulds parallel the offerings of the major component manufacturers: a round-nose slug of approximately 50 grains. Home-cast slugs do have some advantages. They are obviously cheaper. They can be more accurate and just as reliable. More interestingly, they can be driven to higher velocities for a given powder charge weight.

For the purpose of this reloading project, I chose the Speer 50-grain RNFMJ for testing. If you prefer another brand, go to it. I would guess the results would be similar, remembering always to start with reduced powder charges when working up loads.

Since I cast bullets, I also decided to test some home-poured wheel-weight slugs from Lyman's #252435 mould. The mould was capable of producing well-formed slugs. Although I had purchased a lubrisizer die for the .25, I decided to use Lee's liquid alox lube.

To provide the greatest ballistic uniformity in the .25 ACP, it is best to weigh each charge instead of measuring.

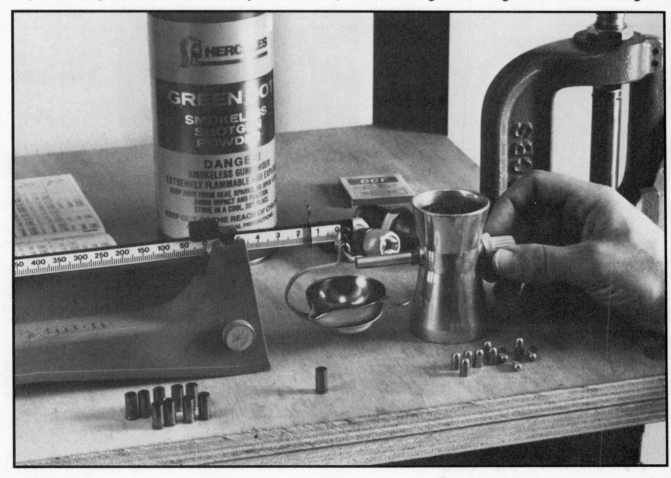

.25 ACP DATA

Test firearm: Beretta 950 BS C.O.L. .905"

Bullet	Powder	Maximum Charge	Velocity fps.
Federal	factory		797
Speer 50 gr. FMJ	700X	1.0	712
	WSL	1.1	780
	Green Dot	1.4	785
	Unique	1.6	731
	800X	1.8	739
	HS6	1.9	737
52 gr. LRN	700X	1.0	749
	WSL	1.1	832
	Green Dot	1.4	834
	Unique	1.6	790
	800X	1.8	824
	HS6	1.9	828

WARNING: *None of this data has been pressure tested. All loads are estimated as maximum or near maximum. Although these loads were safe in the test firearm, they may be unsafe in other firearms. This may be due to the firearm's condition or the reloading techniques employed in assembling the reloads. The author assumes no responsibility for the use of the data presented. All data should be reduced 15% for starting loads, and then the spent cases should be carefully examined for high-pressure signs before increasing charge weights.*

Useful projectile selection is rather limited for the .25 ACP. For testing, the author selected Speer's 50-grain RNFMJ (above). At right, handling .25 ACP projectiles during reloading is a bit tricky.

Results were quite good with virtually no leading and fine accuracy. This approach seems to work well if the cast bullet doesn't require sizing. It also is quick and neat to use. Besides, it is a pain to handle the tiny pills in and out of a lubrisizer.

In selecting powders, I chose a wide range of burn rates to learn what would prove optimum for the singular bullet weight. I was using a measure to dispense charges and almost immediately ran into problems with extreme velocity spreads of as much as 250 feet per second.

After pondering the situation, I weighed a series of metered charges and found the variation to run as much as 0.2 grain from the lightest to the heaviest charge. Ordinarily, this degree of accuracy in metered charges is satisfactory for handgun rounds and certainly sufficient for rifle loads. However, when utilizing charges of something just over one grain, it's obvious we are talking about a 20% variation in charge weights!

The worst culprits in this regard were the coarse flake powders such as Green Dot, Unique and 800-X. If you are

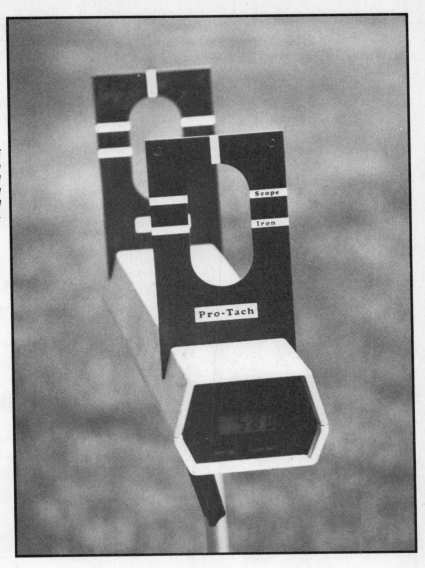

The author's starting charge for the .25 ACP test produced velocities that were quite anemic. By carefully controlling the powder weight and using 52-grain bullets, the author was able to obtain velocities that exceeded factory loads.

obsessed with one of these, take heed. I found that, if one is willing to weigh each charge carefully, one could obtain charge weights that were consistent within the error tolerance of the scale. More uniform ballistic results were achieved at the cost of a great deal of time.

Ball powders are the answer if you insist on metering charges as I do. I found it helped to always use the knocker when the meter lever was in the fill position to more uniformly pack the cavity. The WSL and HS-6 were a joy to use when metering charges. Not surprisingly, 700-X, a fine grain flake powder, gave fairly good results in measure use.

A Beretta Model 950BS was used for testing purposes. It represents a readily available firearm of quality at a moderate price. During the tests, there were no function failures of any kind involving either my test handloads or factory-loaded rounds.

A quick review of the accompanying handload data table will show that I was unable to find a satisfactory load with the 50-grain FMJ pill that would match the velocity of factory loads. However, it was relatively easy to exceed factory ballistics with several powders and the 52-grain lead round nose bullet. This demonstrates the advantage of lower bore

friction possessed by lead bullets. It should be noted that there appeared to be no significant difference in pressures or velocities achieved between bullets lubed with Lee's liquid alox and bullets lubed conventionally in a lubrisizer with 50/50 alox-beeswax lubricant. All loads shown in the handload data table utilized Lee's liquid alox. This practice can be recommended as long as the cast bullets do not require sizing in order to be properly seated into cartridges that will chamber readily in the particular firearm of interest.

During tests of the loading data presented, no formal accuracy tests were performed. Five-shot groups for all loads were fired at three-by-five-inch note cards at 30 feet. All loads were able to group within the confines of these cards, which indicates satisfactory accuracy for the defensive roles these loads may be expected to perform. Loads utilizing 700-X and WSL did seem to group noticeably better in the test firearm.

Constant practice is necessary for high proficiency with a firearm and is doubly advised for any firearm contemplated for defensive use. Reloading the .25 ACP permits a great deal of practice to be performed economically. I am confident you will find reloading the .25 ACP worth the extra challenges it presents.

MAGIC
BULLETS?

By Jim Shults

The destructive power of special bullets is evident in this test. A French .357 Arcane round disintegrates a two-litter bottle and a one-gallon jug, both filled with water. The bottle was blown in half and the jug was torn into many pieces.

Special Rounds
Are Available For
Police And Anti-Terrorist Use!

The search continues for the most powerful, yet safe, cartridge and the perfect firearm to launch it.

FOR OVER 40 years, there has been a search for the "magic bullet." This bullet would stop an armed adversary instantly. When hit, he'd drop like a rock. If you missed, the bullet would become harmless in another few feet. Yet, this perfect round would have an effective range of nearly 1,000 yards and accuracy of well under one-inch groups at 100 yards. Able to shot through most solid substances, it would expend all of its energy inside an opponent with no exit hole. This bullet, if you missed, would self-destruct on any light object so as not to penetrate a wall and hurt the innocents behind it. That bullet still does not exist. Does that surprise you?

Over recent years, however, there have been some interesting developments in pistol ammunition for self-defense and counter-terrorism. Before you rush out to buy the various types of ammunition we will discuss here, let me say most of it is not available to the average shooter; much of it was — and is — highly restricted; and some of it is out of production.

Since most of this ammunition is not just tough to obtain, but is impossible for the average gunowner or even police agencies to obtain, we can go into some detail as to actual effect against living tissue and both soft and hard body armor. To placate the law enforcement officers who may be wearing soft body armor and who do not want bullets out there which defeat their armor, let me offer assurance that these rounds are not available or are so rare that no bad guy will be able to lay hands on them. Besides, thanks to the anti-gun lobby, the knowledge of armor-piercing bullets was made public. Lastly,

if a criminal is captured with a gun loaded with armor-piercing ammunition, he has a whole new set of legal problems.

For what it is worth, if I had a choice, I would much rather be shot with an armor-piercing bullet than a soft-point, because with most conventional AP bullets, the wound channel is usually quite small compared to a conventional expansion-type bullet. There are exceptions, of course, that we will deal with later.

In the last couple of years, the FBI and a couple of super-duper "experts" have done some gee-whiz work and have announced that, if the projectile does not penetrate all the way through a person (FBI specification of 12 inches) and therefore reaches the deepest imbedded vital organs, it is not adequate. These guys have been using ballistic gelatin for their tests, as well as feedback regarding wounds from military and police records.

Bullets that might penetrate five to seven inches into a man's body to make a wound channel two inches in diameter with an ending wound cavity of four inches, yet does not hit a vital organ because it is not a deep penetrator, would be considered a failure by these experts!

For the most part, those who make such special ammunition are in the business of attempting to stop the bad guy. They are not after the perfect heart shot, which then will allow bleeding, and after 10 seconds when the bad guy's brain oxygen starves, he will pass out. In a gunfight, that is just too long a wait, especially if in close quarters.

If Joe Citizen is attacked by some guy out to do him harm,

Winchester introduced this metal piercing cartridge more than 40 years ago. It featured a 140-grain lead core, thick copper jacketed bullet that produced high velocities in .38 Specials and .357 magnums.

a shot from a Glaser round, as an example, might strike the baddie in the arm. This could result in near amputation of the arm, but the bullet would penetrate no further. If such a shot halts the guy's actions, that is good enough for me. I am not an executioner or in the law enforcement business; just a citizen trying to get out of a bad situation that I did not start.

Much of the ammunition discussed here is expensive, up to $4 or more per round. In addition, much of it is, to quote master firearms trainer John Farnam, "situation specific." This means it will work under certain circumstances and conditions, but not under others.

For example, a regular lead/copper bullet is a pretty dumb projectile. True, it does a decent all-round job. It will put a hole in the bad guy, though it may not stop him; it will reach out a distance (sometimes good, except when you miss); it will go through hard objects — and can over-penetrate, hurting innocents — but in the long haul, it does a good, average, all-round job.

A specialized round may blow hell out of the bad guy, stopping him instantly, but if he is behind a thin metal trash can, he may be safe (depending on the type of magic bullet you are using). This is the difference between a situation specific and regular round. However, if you mix them up in your pistol — and if things work out right or you have your gunfight scenario under your control — the case is much different.

Let me expand on this. If you have a house protection gun and you plan to use it, inside your house only, a low-penetration, highly violent round is, in my mind, definitely the best way to go. If you keep a car gun and you plan to use it only from inside your car if attacked, again the case can be made for a fairly violent bullet with low penetration, provided you don't get hijacked and have to fire through your window glass to get away. A cop for example, has a whole variety of situations in which he might need penetration through walls, car bodies or whatever, yet have decent stopping power. For such, he has to stay with fairly dumb, but all-round adequate performance ammunition. Life is full of compromises!

Federal Cartridge Company produces a line of fine ammunition. Their latest self-defense round carries the Hydra-Shok bullet. This is not an original idea by Federal. Actually, this round was originated by another firm aptly called Hydra-Shok; Federal purchased their design. The original bullet was an all-lead full wadcutter design, with the tip of the bullet less than one-tenth-inch from the mouth of the case. The hollow-point and expansion post were recessed deeply into the bullet.

The Federal modification has a conventionally exposed full-size bullet, with a lead core and soft copper jacket. The hollow-point has a long lead post in the center of the bullet. The theory goes that, as flesh begins to fill the hollow-point, said flesh is forced to the outside of the hollow-point by the expansion post acting in the manner of a snowplow. This all helps to force the round to expand more quickly. In the high-velocity 9mm 124-grain and .357 rounds, it really works. Their 240-grain .44 magnum is something to see in action, incidentally.

According to various after-action reviews drawn from actual gunfights, it appears this is a truly effective design. There have been shootings wherein the bad guy took a hit from a 9mm Hydra-Shok round and did, indeed, drop like that proverbial rock. Conversely, there was a recent shootout in which the baddie took a bunch of hits from the slower, subsonic 147-grain 9mm before he was persuaded to stop what he was doing.

It is important for the reader to realize in his evaluation of any type of ammunition that, just as with big-game animals, different people become incapacitated or die at different speeds; that's all there is to it. The key to success in any defensive shooting is the same as in any type of hunting: bullet placement where it counts — and lots of it.

Federal's Hydra-Shok is available in a variety of bullet weights and in several calibers. The most unique (not best) to me is their 147-grain 9mm. This round was the first of the major manufacturers' subsonic 9mms. Subsonic rounds typically are intended for firearms using silencers or suppressors, so the ballistic crack of the bullet breaking the sound barrier is absent. However, the advisability of taking a 9mm round known for high velocity and excellent penetration, then slowing it down and making it heavier for better penetration seems a little counter-productive. Oh well, it's the latest fad, and the ammunition companies do follow trends. Federal made a jillion of these for the FBI and others.

As self-defense rounds, my general recommendations with most lead or copper standard-design or traditional-looking and acting bullets are 115 to 125 grains in 9mm, 125 to 150 grains in .38 or .357, 150 to 160 grains in .40, and 210 to 230 grains in .45 ACP. This all assumes the lighter bullet weights are compensated for with higher velocities.

The newest of the rounds on the commercial market is Winchester's Supreme Black Talon round. Not enough people have been shot with this round at this time to give me any real-world feeling for it.

One "expert" declares it the greatest thing around, but he has no basis for that statement other than the projected capabilities, some gelatin tests and several big-game animals. Another writer stated it is the most "innovative and radical steps in his 25 years in the business." This kind of statement tells me he has not seen or shot the types of ammunition you will read about in the balance of this chapter.

The Black Talon SXT (Supreme Expansion Talon), at first glance, is a fairly conventional looking hollow-point round. The bullet is a normal lead-core, copper-clad combination. Instead of leaving the bullet copper colored, the factory has treated the copper so it is black. When examined more closely, one will see that the tip of the bullet has deep serrations to assist in peeling back the jacket for expansion. The main design feature of this round is that the walls of the copper jacket actually enter and go down into the hollow-point cavity. All the way down, the jacket is serrated.

The idea behind this design is that the tip will not blow apart, sometimes leaving only the base to penetrate as the bullet enters flesh. This round is designed to penetrate to FBI specifications, and peel back in a more controlled manner to the precise place where the petals of peeled lead and jacket meet the main body of the bullet near the base of the hollow-point area.

Due to the slower velocities and slower expansion rate, this round screws, due to the rifling spin, into soft targets causing more trauma. It is felt that this spin also will be present through flesh and that this action acts like firing a fan into the target.

Endorsed by the deep penetration advocates, the Talon SXT is available in 9mm, 40 S&W and 10mm as of this writing. With bullet weights in the high end, all of these rounds travel at a pretty slow subsonic 990 feet per second. In my opinion, the Talon 230-grain .45 ACP would be the best of the bunch at 900 fps. Due to the timed release of this bullet's expansion, it would appear there will be no hot loads, since performance is tied directly into the low velocity.

However, there will be .357 and .44 magnum loads coming out soon and Winchester is nearly finished with research on a .38 Special and .380 Auto round. It can be expected these rounds will have bullets near or at the high end of weights and slower velocities to enable the bullet to work the way Winchester research indicates works best.

The Talon will be the successor to the Silvertip, which will continue in production for now. In tests we conducted, firing the Silvertip .45 ACP into meat made a disappointing three-quarter-inch through and through hole. It was not especially impressive compared to a high-velocity round, but the .45 isn't any race horse, either. The Talon .45 exhibited the kind of penetration it is suppose to accomplish. We noted the meat, when hit, did not move much, which indicates a lower shock level.

The Black Talon from Winchester has bettered the successful Silvertip.

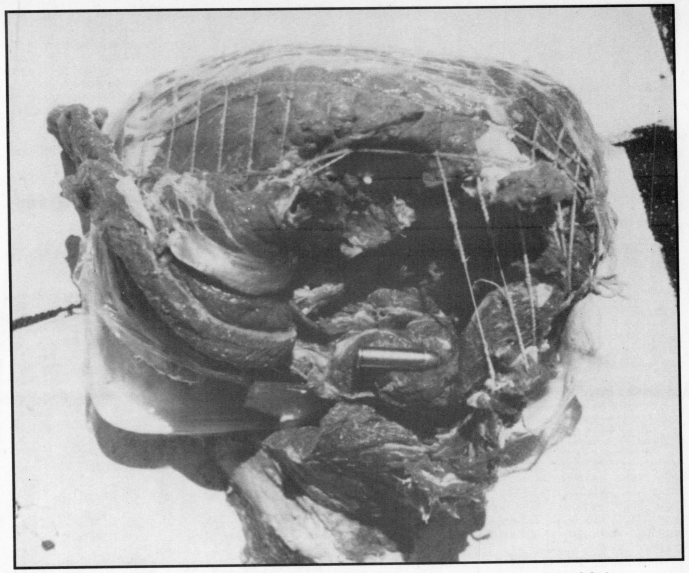

Glaser's .38 Special blew a destructive five-inch cavity into this eight-pound roast. There was no exit hole.

The bullet exhibited good expansion, and created a one-inch wound channel with the beginning of a 1 1/2-inch wound cavity. The channel was indeed torn up, and true to form, passed right through a six-inch-thick roast. The Talon looks like a pretty good all-purpose round at this early stage in its production, especially for hunting in the larger calibers.

Without doubt, the most effective purely anti-personnel round the average guy still is able to purchase in stores is the Glaser Safety Slug. A thin copper bullet cup is filled with number 12 lead shot and the end is sealed. When fired, the shot-loaded slug stays intact, until it strikes a soft object. The thin copper jacket is ruptured by the force against the lead shot and the whole thing ruptures quickly. The resulting explosively fragmented force is something to see, as the round literally explodes in its target and all energy is expended quickly in the target.

When fired through wood or a similar substance, the bullet will stay intact. The walls of the thin copper cup cannot fly apart, because the wood holds it together just as does the chamber of your gun. Ricochets or missed shots turn into relatively harmless dust upon hitting a hard object such as a car window or a sidewalk.

This round has been around for more than 15 years. Originally, this bullet was a copper cup filled with number 12 lead shot and liquid teflon, then capped with a teflon and glass epoxy cap poured over the short, shot-filled cup. This was basically a three-quarter-copper jacket for a lead bullet, leaving only the tip extending from the shell case. When tested originally by the government, this round in 9mm was found to deliver more energy into ballistic gelatin than a conventional .44 magnum.

The next evolution of this round was to eliminate the liquid teflon and to use a much longer copper carrier for the lead shot and to put a flat plastic lid on the end of the bullet to seal in the contents. The latest version features a small plastic ball crimped in place at the bullet's tip to hold the shot charge

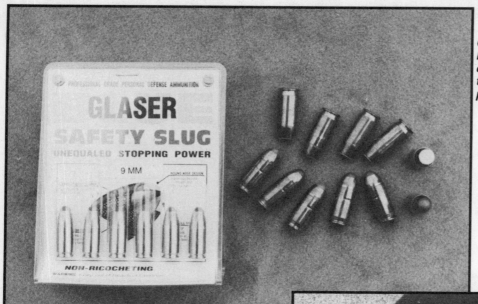

Glaser now uses a rounded bullet nose (bottom row) to ensure positive feeding for their super potent line of pre-fragmented cartridges

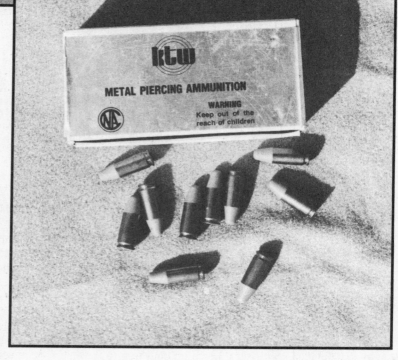

KTW's green teflon 9mm ammunition was developed for police officers only and the sales were extremely restricted. However, it was taken out of production because of inaccurate, negative reporting by the media.

intact. This ball end allows for the round to be fired in semi-automatic pistols with little or no feed problem.

When fired into an eight-pound beef chuck roast, the wound channel from a 9mm round measured two inches on average at point of entry. After five inches of penetration, the wound channel was four or more inches in diameter. There was no exit hole through the six-inch beef roast. Lack of deep penetration by this round is its only drawback, but when you figure the first six inches of a wound channel in living tissue will create a tissue-destroying cavity of four inches or larger, who needs great penetration? Though the bullet can be defeated by thin metal or even glass, Glaser states a hit from their .357 is the equivalent of a point-blank hit from a 12-gauge shotgun.

Glaser ammunition is available in a variety of calibers ranging from the .25 ACP through the .44 magnum. There are even 5.56mm and .30 caliber rifle rounds available. The 80-grain 9mm round travels at a pretty quick 1,650 fps velocity. The .357 has velocity of 1,800 fps and the new .40 S&W, with a 105-grain bullet, travels at 1,500 fps at the muzzle. The older, flat-tip Glaser was offered in a special police round which had another 200 feet of velocity to provide some penetration for soft armor. This round was distinguished by a black end seal and is no longer available.

The company is soon to come out with what is termed the Glaser Silver line. This round will be distinguished from the regular Glaser by having a gray plastic ball capping the end rather than the standard blue ball. The difference is that the Silver will utilize larger number 6 lead shot instead of the standard number 12. This will make available approximately 30 to 50 percent more penetration prior to total expansion of the bullet. This newer round is a reluctant concession by the company to the deep penetration gurus. Bullet weight and velocities will be the same as with the blue tip round.

In my opinion, the Glaser is a super-effective, low-recoil anti-personnel round and reports on animals hit by it talk of hamberger-type impacts. That I believe, judging by our own meat tests. The Glaser is a fine, low-penetration, sure-to-stop-a-fight round for home defense. They are sold in packages of

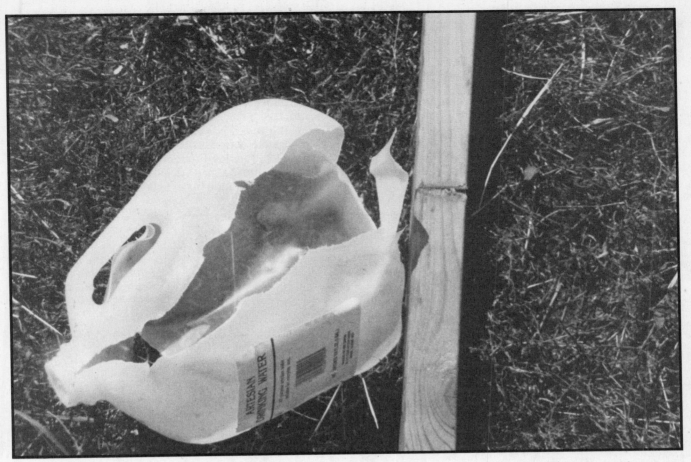

Illustrating its power, a Glaser round passed cleanly through a wooden 2x4 to destroy a plastic jug filled with water .

six or more and average $3 per round. Not cheap, but neither is your life!

In 1967, the KTW metal-piercing round was developed by Dr. Paul Kopsich, police officer Daniel Turcus, and a coroner's investigator, Don Ward. The original round carried a sharply pointed teflon-coated, 200-grain tungsten carbide bullet which was seated in a copper cup to engage the rifling. This round would not only crack an engine block, but would whizz right through engine block walls when fired from a .357 magnum. Its hard-hitting penetration in metal was phenomenal.

The round eventually evolved into the now familiar KTW round with its high-velocity, truncated-cone flat-tipped bullet made of a bronze alloy and covered with green teflon. The bronze alloy bullet will not begin to penetrate metal as did the original design.

The teflon on the original tungsten bullet provided some lubrication when under the pressure of passing through steel or metal — it mutated to a sort of liquid lubricant state. However, the later round which became popularized by the media idiots as the "cop killer bullet" (it never did) maintained the teflon as purely a sales gimmick.

The later variety with its 112-grain bullet in .357 magnum hummed along at 2,000 feet per second. When coupled with the somewhat pointed shape, it would sail through Kevlar armor as if it were not there. In testing years ago, I fired both

9mm and .357 magnum KTWs through over 40 layers of Kevlar. This round exhibits exceptional penetration through most solids and great tissue damage on meat targets.

Due to the KTW round's high velocity, even though it did not expand in soft media, its wound channel is a nasty two to three inches in meat, and its penetration is spectacular to say the least.

All of the KTW rounds are now collector items, especially the tungsten round. Sage International, the firm that last owned the KTW brand, stopped production in 1987 due to the adverse publicity of the "cop killer" lie propagated by the media. These rounds were available in 9mm, .38 Special and .357 magnum.

Talk about light bullets and lots of power, how about 2,800 feet per second from a .357 magnum? This screaming velocity was achieved by a round from France called the THV. Of all ammunition we tested in .357 and 9mm, this round was the most deadly.

The THV .357 magnum bullet is a super-light 45 grains. That's correct: *45 grains*! Constructed of a copper alloy, the interior of the bullet is hollow from the base right up to the tip. It needs to be, to take the huge powder charge which not only fills the case, but the hollow portion of the bullet, also.

The exterior shape of the wadcutter-type bullet is a tiny point which tapers up quickly to the .357 diameter, resulting in a shape much like that of a snowplow. When propelled through meat or almost any soft substance, the high velocity makes the bullet act like a snowplow going 2,500 miles per hour!

The effect of this bullet is absolutely awesome. The entrance hole into meat is three inches or more, and the wound channel is four inches with extended damage of nearly six inches around the final wound cavity! This round penetrated over eight inches of meat, blowing it to bits, exited the other side and was not recovered. Hydrostatic destruction on living tissue would be impossible to imagine.

Due to the bullet's light weight and wind grabbing shape, at 100 meters the velocity is under 650 feet per second making

it somewhat safer if it misses its intended close range target. Wood, light metal, soft armor, et cetera, have little effect on this round. It just keeps on trucking. Kevlar penetration was well over the 50 layers I recently had to test against.

This round was available in 2,650 fps .45 ACP, 2,500 fps .38 Special, 2,650 fps 9mm and 2,650 fps 7.65 (.32 auto). Of all of the rounds we have ever tested against such soft targets as meat, this French-made round appears the most deadly. This cartridge is used in the .357 magnums and 9mms of the French counter-terrorism team, GIGN. You will not find this little baby in your local sporting goods store.

Another super bad news round from France is the Archane. This round uses a pure copper bullet of relatively light weight

The size of the firearm is not the deciding factor in stopping power. Even this Beretta 86 can pack a punch.

This type of accuracy, when matched with a powerful bullet, means destruction.

due to its shape. A .357 round is about 80 grains in weight. This bullet has a sharp cone shape and features a deep crimp groove. The Archane was much ballyhooed about a dozen years ago when the French tried to get it into mass retail distribution in the United States as a high performance hunting round, as well as competition to the KTW as a police cartridge. It is available in several calibers from .380 to .44 magnum and even the .45 ACP.

Loaded to velocities nearing 2,200 feet per second for the .357 and 2,400 for the 9mm, this is a truly potent round second only to the THV for all-round nastiness. As with the THV, the Archane's sharp-pointed tip and sharp-ramped profile make it highly destructive in meat, with wound channels three inches in diameter and damage to nearly six inches in diameter for a final wound cavity, with penetration of well over eight inches.

Back in the late 1970s, when it was introduced in the United States, some gun magazines found the Archane .38 Special created cavities nearly 10 inches in diameter in clay tests where a standard .38 only went one inch in diameter. While interesting, clay tests have little to do with real life, but they do yield an apples to apples comparison

The German-made Action-Geschoss round has a plastic nose which, when fired, is blown free to expose a large cavity hollow-point bullet.

An Action-Geschoss .357 magnum blew a 2 1/2-inch hole through this roast. Ruler traces the bullet's path.

The 9mm Quick Defense cartridges features a thin copper cap over a large cavity hollow point to aid in feeding into semi-automatics.

against like rounds with different loads, et cetera. This cartridge never reached wide retail distribution to my knowledge in the U.S. due probably to its unsocial nature, high price of $2 per round in 1980 and, especially, is lack of availability.

The power of this round may be shown in this way. The standard .45 ACP copper-clad ball round, fired at Kevlar armor, did not penetrate even one layer of a 22-layer test panel at point-blank range due to its blunt shape and low velocity. The .45 ACP Archane went through 50 layers of Kevlar at 15 yards. Several years ago, I had access to a goodly amount of Kevlar, and I stacked up enough to make a panel 90 layers thick. Keep in mind that a 22-layer vest will stop a conventional .44 magnum round in less than 12 layers.

At 15 yards, the .357 Archane passed through all 90 layers, a one-half-inch wood backing, exited the other side and was not recovered.

This round is no longer available in the United States. It is expensive to make, since the bullets are machined individually on a lathe. I have not seen it available anywhere and I suspect the company may not be in the business of producing this round in production quantity any more, if even that amount. I would rate the Archane as the most efficient and deadly all-round pistol cartridge ever.

Geco of Germany produced a round they called the Action-Geschoss. The shape of the bullet is conventional, the unique feature being it has a large hollow-point exposed on the tip of the bullet. This hollow-point quickly tapers to a small one millimeter hole which passes through the entire bullet to the powder charge.

The bullet carries a plastic plug which results in a rounded tip. This plastic tip has a long tail which extends for some distance into the hollow-point. This rounded tip allows the round to feed smoothly in any type of pistol.

Once the firearm is discharged, the explosive force of the

National's line of cartridges includes a special metal piercing round (left) and tracer ammunition (right).

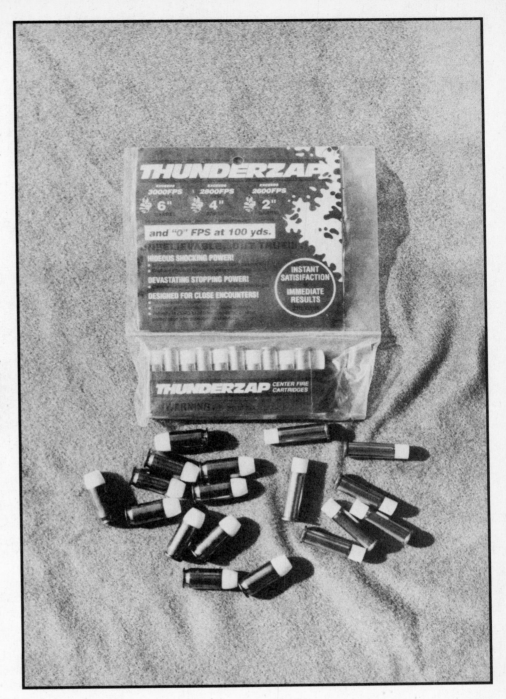

One of the newest types of specialized bullets is Second Chance's Thunder Zap. The super light cartridge offers extremely high velocities and great destructive force.

powder burning forces the plug out of the bullet, as the bullet passes through the barrel. Upon exiting the muzzle, the bullet's large hollow-point is fully exposed. The bullet, constructed of a copper alloy, offers typical deep 9mm penetration and excellent expansion in meat, typical of most hollow-points with high velocities.

Another round from Germany was the Quick Defense round. As with the Geco bullet, a large-diameter hollow-point is exposed to the air. Actually, the QD bullet's hollow-point is quite large and deep. This bullet has a thin copper cap over the end of the hollow-point to allow smooth feeding in auto pistols. When this round strikes its target, the frail cap simply is crushed out of the way.

This bullet's large hollow-point has a column of material

similar in design to Federal's Hydra-Shok bullet to aid in spreading the hydrostatic effect to assist in expansion of the bullet. Production of this bullet was at least threes years prior to Federal's acquiring the Hydra-Shok round from its inventor. In 9mm, this bullet weighs in at 86 grains.

Performance in 9mm exhibited a normal-size entry hole, but the wound cavity in meat was impressive. This relatively conventional bullet created a final cavity of nearly four inches. Penetration was typical 9mm. The Quick Defense has been available in several calibers, including .357 magnum.

American Ballistics produces a round with a bullet of soft copper alloy. Their TC-HXC bullet has a black teflon finish to reduce barrel friction. This round features a fully exposed large hollow-point. The bullet has knurling around the outside

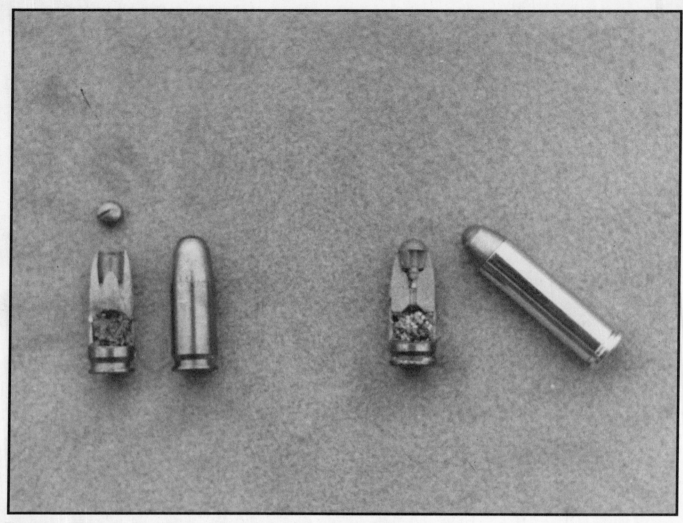

These 9mm cutaways are (left) the Quick Defense round and the Action-Geschoss next to the company's .357 round. Both 9mm cartridges have large, potent hollow-point bullets with plugs to facilitate feeding. They are destructive.

to provide a better gas seal where the rifling engages it. Loaded to traditional velocities for the respective caliber, these hollow-points resulted in excellent expansion in meat with the .357 magnum getting wounds of three inches.

This same company also produces a restricted availability metal-piercing round. This round's mild steel bullet is teflon-coated and also has knurling around the outside. Rockwell hardness is 35C. (Most firearm steel runs in the 32C to 36C Rockwell range). In 9mm, this round will penetrate a one-quarter-inch mild steel plate with ease. The company also produces 5.56 and 7.62mm metal-piercing rounds, as well as subsonic 9mm.

National Cartridge Company has a line of unique ammunition worthy of discussion. I am pretty sure it was National's high explosive .22 rimfire ammunition that was used in the attack on President Reagan. Fortunately, the rounds did not detonate — even the one hitting Brady in the skull. National produces exploders in several calibers, including .357 and .45 ACP. These simply are large hollow-points with a small powder charge that is capped off with a primer.

The idea is for the primer to detonate the powder charge and cause further damage. I have found these types of cartridges exhibit poor reliability in detonation except when something exceedingly hard is struck. Hitting a human rib for example, may not always detonate the charge, but hitting steel or thick wood, et cetera, will set off the charge much of the time. The charge doesn't blow the bullet up, it just blows out the primer, with additional flash and contamination doing minor secondary damage.

National produces a line of Black Steel metal-piercing rounds. Against mild steel, these rounds perform well. I like this line of tracer ammunition best. These rounds show where you are hitting, but more importantly, can be great as signal rounds for rescue, et cetera, for the guy in the field. This ammunition, like the other specialized types, is not cheap. They are in the $2 per round range.

Silent Partner Body Armor produces truly unique ammunition. Called the +P Multiplex, this round fires three lead projectiles in .38 and .357 magnum, and a two-projectile cartridge is available in 9mm. The concept behind this round is logical. Most police officers are shot with their own guns. If your pistol is loaded with ammunition which can penetrate body armor, you are a dead cop if the bad guy gets your gun. The Multiplex will not penetrate body armor, and therefore is

safe for police to carry in their pistols. That, at least, is the theory.

The Multiplex is a fine round of ammunition. Most doctors will tell you that creating trauma and bleeding are what quickly convince someone to stop doing what they were doing to you. If there is enough bleeding, the brain will starve for oxygen and that is the end of the gunfight. Multiplex accomplishes this without high armor-piercing velocities.

The lead projectile for the .38 Special and .357 magnum is a conventional 110-grain hollow-point backed up with two 70-grain lead slugs. When fired at close range, this cluster of lead weighing some 250 grains creates a significant wound channel. However, at, say, a 15-yard distance, the .38 opens up to a three-shot pattern of two to three inches; that's three holes for one shot. The .357 will group a little tighter due to its velocity.

Accuracy yields four-inch groups for the main bullet at 20 yards. Velocity of the .38 is 800 fps and for the .357, 1,065. Yes, this is slow, but expansion is good. The main bullet expands to about .50 caliber and the followers spread to .40. Again, the idea is to get more hits and create bleeding holes into the target, and yet not penetrate soft armor. At about $25 for 10 rounds, this ammo is not cheap, but what is your life worth?

Second Chance is the undisputed king of soft body armor. They invented soft body armor and the owner, Richard Davis, wearing such armor, has tested it against .38s and .357 magnums hundreds of times. He literally stands behind his product.

Davis has developed a high-velocity round which does not penetrate body armor. Called the Thunder Zap, this cartridge is available in .45 ACP and .38 Special. Work is under way toward developing a version for the .40 S&W. The round is not available in .357, since its 3,400 feet per second velocity — that's right, 3,400 fps — would go through body armor.

Richard Davis' thinking is the same as Silent Partners in regard to cops being shot with their own guns. There are no plans for a 9mm since the cartridge case is too restricted in capacity for the round to reach the necessary high velocity to do its work. With the .38 Special at 2,850 fps and the .45 at 2,550 fps, you get the idea.

How can such high velocities be achieved with light bullets? The .38 bullet weighs 32 grains and the .45 size goes a scant 48 grains. I noted that this round also utilizes a compressed powder charge to increase its speed. This round is fairly safe at only 80 yards since it sheds velocity so quickly that, according to Second Chance, it has zero velocity at 100 yards. Effective incapacitation range is under 30 yards, Davis reports.

The bullet is made up of a high-impact white nylon plastic with a huge hollow-point cavity and moulded-in gas check grooves. This round has low penetration against semi-hard objects such as the typical house wall. It will go through two layers of plaster board but upon exiting the second layer, only fragments emerge.

The idea of this round is high trauma and low penetration. The desired result is an instant end to the gunfight. In one gunfight, the bad guy took a hit in a shoulder from a government agent's handgun, and bits of his shoulder meat were found splattered on the wall behind him. The fight stopped immediately.

Obviously, this cartridge makes an excellent entry round for drug busts and for home defense due to low wall penetration coupled to high aggression stoppage. It has a huge fire ball, however. These rounds cost about $10 for ten rounds from the maker.

A PRESSING MATTER

By Dean A. Grennell

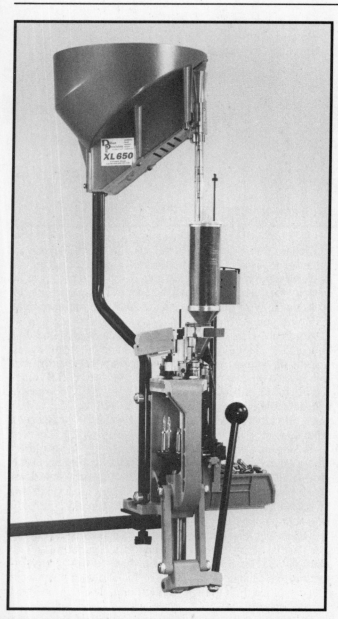

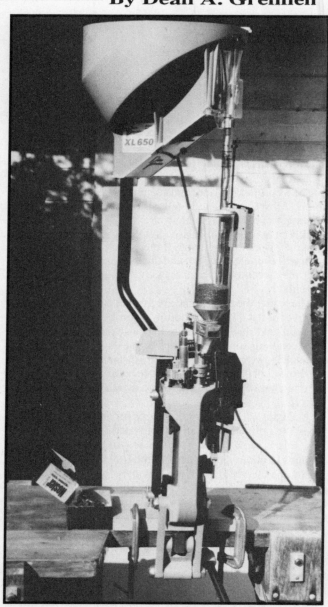

With the handle of the XL 650 up, the ram is positioned at the bottom of its downstroke. By pressing the handle forward, the primer will seat in the case at the #2 station.

With the handle fully down, the ram is at the top of its upstroke and the various dies are doing their jobs. The shell plate advances during the handle's downstroke.

Dillon's XL 650 Progressive Model Does It All!

DILLON PRECISION Products, Inc., 7442 East Butherus Drive, Scottsdale, AZ 85260, manufactures and direct-markets progressive reloading presses, along with a broad assortment of other shooter-related items. If you want a single-station press, they'll sell you an RCBS Rock Chucker for $84, less dies.

The current Dillon press line consists of the Square Deal B, the RL 550B, the RL 1050 and — most recently added — the XL 650. The Square Deal B is strictly for typical handgun ammunition and, set up to load .45 ACP, the current price is $208.95, with caliber change kits ranging from $52 to $114.45; it is manually advanced. Its production rate is about 300 rounds per hour.

The Dillon Model RL 550B is also manually advanced and capable of reloading over 120 different handgun and rifle cartridges. The basic press is $294 and, set up to load .45 ACP, it's $333.95, with caliber change kits from $65.45 to $131.40; caliber change kits do not include primer systems. Typical

WARNING: Read manual before operating

XL 650

Scottsdale, Arizona
Call Toll Free (800) 421-7632

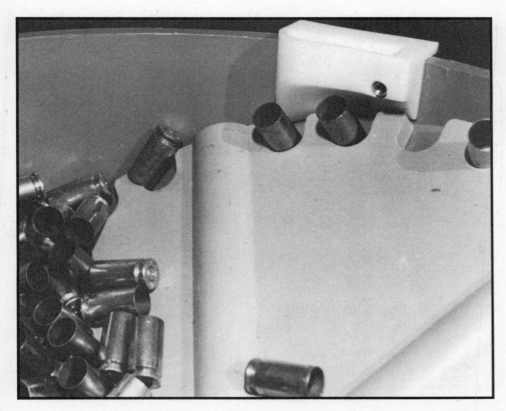

Above, you'd better believe you need to carefully read the instructions before you try to operate this baby! Dillon's toll-free number means advice is available. Left, looking from the top, it is fascinating to watch the automatic case feeder.

A case is being fed into the #1 spot in the five-station shell plate. A fresh primer is in #2 station. The shell plate moves clockwise. The brass pins can be removed if you want to pull a case.

production rate for the RL 550B is 500 rounds per hour. Like all the Dillon progressive presses, it has a buzzer that sounds when the supply of primers runs low in the feed tube.

The RL 1050 is the firm's top of the line machine, at $1049.95, set up to load .45 ACP or $1010.95 for the basic press. It includes a swager to remove military primer crimps and handles all the common handgun calibers plus .223 and 7.62x39mm. Production rate is quoted at 1000 rounds per hour and it comes with automatic case feed as a standard feature.

The XL 650 press was introduced to fill the gap between the RL 550B and the RL 1050. Price of the basic machine is $394.95, less dies. The optional automatic case feeder is $134.95, the optional powder check system is $49.95, and the

XL 650 can load virtually any popular rifle or handgun caliber, using standard 7/8x14 reloading dies. The XL 650 has five stations and is rated to produce about 800 rounds per hour.

The optional powder charge check die can be installed in the third station and will sound an alarm if the powder charge is abnormally high or low. When a proper charge of powder is present, the point of the contact pin centers itself in the groove of the grooved sleeve. Some adjustment may be required and, once it is made, a small lock nut can be tightened to secure the setting.

The test machine came with the automatic electric case feeder and the unit was set up for the .40 S&W cartridge, with the option to load the 10mm Auto or 10mm Magnum by means of changing the primer feed system from small to large

The three-position switch controls the automatic case feeder. A tiny microswitch (arrow) shuts off the feeder when the feed tube is full.

HIGH
OFF
LOW

The pointed pin at the top right corner of the powder sensor will sound the alarm if the powder level is too low or high. As the powder measure is activated, the sensor pivots over to put the point into the V-groove in the adjustable probe bar that examines the level of powder in the charged case.

diameter. The case feeder is a remarkable device, with all the bugs fully eradicated. You'd think it might feed an occasional case into the tube with the rim uppermost, but it never does. When the feed tube is full, the uppermost case depresses a small switch lever to turn off the feeder.

Some amount of assembly and adjustment is required in order to get the XL 650 operating properly. The machine is accompanied by a 26-page instruction booklet. Back in the early Sixties, I spent a few years writing operating manuals and instruction booklets as my primary job and I tend to view most such publications with a rather jaundiced eye, feeling I could have done the job better, myself. That is definitely not true of the Dillon XL 650 manual! It is written in a clear, easy-to-understand style and illustrated with some really excellent photographs and, had I produced it myself, I'd tend to feel insufferably smug about it.

Primers are fed from a vertical tube holding up to 100 primers and is enclosed by a sturdy steel tube. Any time you have a quantity of primers in contact with each other, there is a possibility of mass detonation and the steel tube is intended to protect the operator if that happens. The manual urges the use of eye protection and ear protection, as well.

Among the useful shooting gear offered by Dillon are the Dillon/Peltor Tactical 7-S High-Tech Stereo Hearing Protectors, currently selling for $134.95 a set, or $124.95 if you buy five or more. These are powered by a 9-volt battery and there

Here, we're at the top of the ram upstroke. The slide of the powder measure is fully extended and the powder sensor is pivoted forward.

is a switch/rheostat to turn them on and adjust the volume. You can also tune them to feed more input to one ear or the other. I have severe hearing loss and wear hearing aids in both ears. I can wear the hearing aids and the Dillon/Peltor ear protectors and hear more clearly and distinctly than with the hearing aids alone. In fact, the Dillon/Peltors are dandy for watching television although my wife thinks it looks rather ludicrous.

The point toward which I've been tacking amid all this discussion is that an ordinary pair of earmuff hearing protectors probably will prevent you from hearing the little buzzer alarms that go off when your powder charge is too big or too small, as well as the one that sounds when you're running low on primers. With the Dillon/Peltor units, you can hear the alarms and still be protected in case of possible loud noises such as a tube of primers detonating. The Dillon/Peltors suppress harmful noise from gunfire, meanwhile permitting you to hear range commands, conversation and the like even better than if you weren't wearing them.

As a preliminary to setting up the XL 650, I made a mounting board from a piece of white oak lumber a full one inch in thickness, counterbored from the underside for clearance of the bolt heads and washers. The XL 650 uses four 1/4-20 mounting bolts. In most instances, you'd just bolt it to the reloading bench but I prefer to attach it to a given sturdy surface by means of a pair of C-clamps. The portable shooting bench I've been using since late in 1978 works quite well for the purpose, as does my driveway work bench whose upper surface is 42 inches above the ground.

The mentioned dimension happens to be the distance from the upper edge of my belt to the ground and I determined a long time ago that it's the ideal height for a stand-up workbench. In operating the Dillon progressive presses, the primers are seated by pushing the operating handle forward at the conclusion of the up-stroke. If the bench is not solidly braced, you can reach around behind with your free hand to steady it when seating the primer. The machine is designed for operating the lever with your right hand and the system is not reversible.

Once the system is set up and going, you operate with full strokes, to the limit of ram travel. Avoid partial strokes, as that can cause damage to the primer feeding system. On the handle down-stroke, the case in station one is deprimed and full-length resized and the spent primers are deposited in a neat little catch-box for later disposal. If there is a primed case in station two, it will receive a charge of powder. If no case is present, no powder is dispensed. The powder charge at station three is checked and verified by the optional powder check system, if that's installed.

On the ram down-stroke, the shell plate is automatically advanced by one-fifth turn and, as noted, the primer is seated in the case at station two by pressing the operating handle forward. When in normal operation, this is when you position a bullet in the mouth of the case in station four, to be seated on the next ram up-stroke.

My shooting buddy Larry Packard helped me set up the XL 650 and we adjusted the powder measure to drop a charge of 8.8 grains of Accurate Arms No. 5 powder to drive the 135-grain Nosler JHP bullet. We set the cartridge overall length (COL) at 1.115 inches, the dimension Nosler recommends for that bullet in the .40 S&W case.

Both Accurate Arms and Nosler specify 9.0 grains of Accurate Arms No. 5 powder as the maximum charge for the 135-grain Nosler JHP bullet. Accurate Arms rates the maximum load at 1192 feet per second (fps) for 426 foot-pounds of energy, or 1192/426 as such data is often quoted. Nosler's data quotes it as 1117/374 and does not specify the length of their test barrel.

I guess I must've been pulling the triggers extra-hard or something, because the ballistics for the loads made up on the XL 650 were considerably brisker than either source suggests. Fired from a Ruger Model P91, the five-shot average was 1364/558. In a .40 S&W Browning Hi-Power, it averaged 1384/574 and, in a Colt Delta Elite fitted with a custom five-inch barrel from Bar-Sto Precision (Box 1838, Twentynine Palms, CA 92277) it went from a low of 1408 to a high of 1425 for a five-shot average of 1416/601, with a major power factor (MPF) at a thumping 191.16! Both the Ruger P91 and the converted Colt grouped the load to well under two inches in center-spread at a distance of 25 yards off the sandbagged benchrest.

I am by no means your typical reloader. In normal routine, I rarely make up more than five or ten rounds of a given load for testing and reporting. That makes progressive reloading presses of no more than limited value to me, handy though they may be to competitive shooters with a hot need for hundreds and hundreds of rounds of practice ammunition. In the example at hand, however, I'm willing to view things through a different knothole in the board fence. That's to say I can see benefits in producing lots of loads for it. The Bar-Sto/Colt is one of the sweetest-shooting pistols I've encountered in a goodly while and it's entirely possible I may never switch parts to make it handle the 10mm Auto round again. I have one load with which it delivers 25-yard groups under one inch in center-spread off the bench. That's with Nosler's 170-grain JHP bullet ahead of 10.0 grains of Accurate Arms No. 7 powder.

Be duly advised the load was developed before there was any published data for the .40 S&W. The current Accurate Arms booklet lists 9.7 grains of their No. 7 as the maximum load for the 170-grain jacketed bullets, at 1052/418, for a MPF of 178.84. My renegade reload does a trifle better than that and manifests no obvious signs of excessive pressures in my gun. Nonetheless, for obvious reasons, I cannot and do not recommend the load for use by others.

In the Dillon XL 650 press, cases are kept in position in the shell plate by small brass pins, which can be lifted out to remove the case for individual attention. That enables you to weigh the powder charge dropped into the case at station two or three.

The powder measure slide on the Dillon progressive presses is stoplessly adjustable by turning the small six-sided bolt head, clockwise to increase the charge weight and counterclockwise to decrease it. I've found it helpful to letter little plus and minus signs on the appropriate sides as an aid to memory.

Incidentally, Dillon has a new electronic powder scale they call the D-Terminator and it's a lulu. Maximum capacity is 1500 grains; nearly 3.5 ounces and it retails for $219.95, including both a 9-volt battery and an AC adapter.

Dillon publishes a sort of catalog/gunzine called The Blue Press and you can get on the mailing list for it by writing to the address given earlier or calling their toll-free number, 1-800-223-4570 or 1-602-948-8009. There's no charge and it offers interesting reading on shooter-related topics, as well as keeping you up to date on new items they offer.

SECTION FIVE:
HANDGUN ACCESSORIES

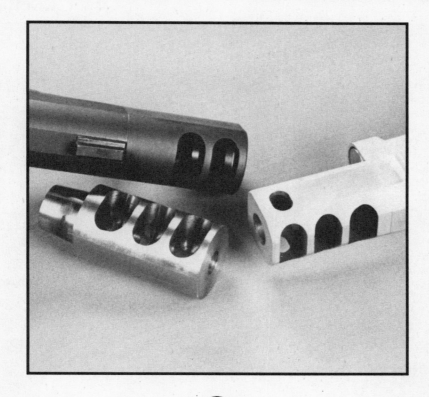

&
ACCOUTREMENTS

IS LEATHER BETTER?

By Charlie Smith

After more than three decades, Don Hume continues to oversee the production of his products.

Holstermaker Don Hume Feels It Is And Bases His Attitude On Behind-The-Gun Experience.

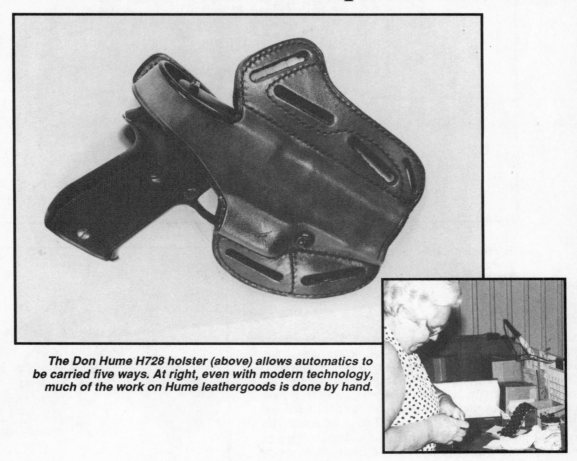

The Don Hume H728 holster (above) allows automatics to be carried five ways. At right, even with modern technology, much of the work on Hume leathergoods is done by hand.

It was January of '69, and I had just been sworn into for my first police job — deputy sheriff in Greene County, Arkansas. A local police officer sold me a Sam Brown rig pretty cheap, and it was certainly worth it. The flimsy floral design belt sagged like a swayback plowhorse, and the equally cheap holster flopped every time I moved.

It was the kind of rig that gets police officers killed. State Trooper John Purcell, my mentor, told me to get a rig from Don Hume out in Oklahoma. "His stuff is the best," John assured me. I did and it was. Over 20 years later, many cops are still convinced that Don Hume makes the best police leather anywhere.

Hume was reared in the hills of eastern Oklahoma, but following his Navy duty he settled in California and began what he assumed would be a career in law enforcement. While in the Navy, Hume began working with leather. Later, as a deputy sheriff with the San Diego County Sheriff's Department, he began crafting police holsters for the extra income.

The spark that flamed into the Don Hume Holster Company was born in a squad car one night. Hume recalls complaining to his partner about always being broke. He said it really bothered him that many of the prisoners they transported were better off than the officers. His partner suggested he turn his holstermaking hobby into a business.

From that small beginning in a single-car garage in California, it was a long way to a 20,000 square foot building on 10 acres in Miami, Oklahoma. When I asked Hume if he designed the holsters he built in those early days, he replied honestly, "No, I just copied what others had already done, but I was determined to make them better."

That is how he began making the famous Jordan Holster, which, by the way, was the first Hume holster that I bought. Inspector Jordan was stationed at Chula Vista, California, near Hume's patrol beat. Hume approached Jordan with the request to make a copy of Jordan's holster. His answer was, "You can use my name and design as long as you make a quality holster."

With the old S.D. Myers Saddle Company long out of the business, Don Hume Leathergoods is the only place to get a true Jordan holster. And Mr. Jordan still drops by occasionally to inspect the quality of the work.

Hume shares the fact that a lot has changed about the

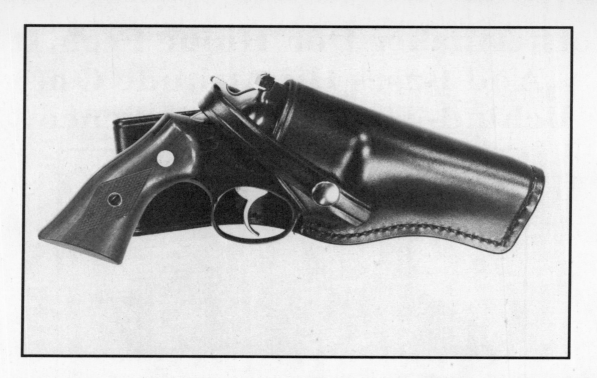

The above holster has belt and firearm tension screws. At right, this holster holds the revolver securely against the hip with the grip forward.

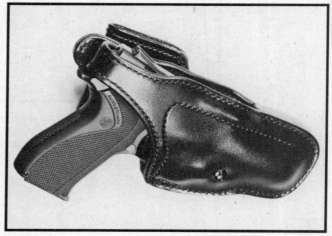

holster business in the last 40 years. In my mind, two things make Hume's company unique among holster companies. Look at his current catalog and you note that his market is clearly defined. Hume makes working holsters for working policemen. Certainly, he is not the only holstermaker to have a solid police background. John Bianchi, Tex Shoemaker and Bill Rogers come to mind. But most holster manufacturers try to be all things to all shooters. Hume is like the chicken commercial. He does one thing, and he does it right. (Actually he also makes other leather products such as tack for horses, but that is a secret, so don't tell).

Hume doesn't just rely on his own expertise when it comes to police leather. Nope, things have changed since the days when every police officer either wore a Jordan Border Patrol or a Threeperson-style holster. Today the emphasis is on new and better security holsters. Hume works closely with police firearms people throughout the country and uses their input and expertise to perfect his products.

Hume is not tied to his Miami, Oklahoma, office. On one road trip, he traveled out in the country to visit the range of a rural police department in the Midwest. When he introduced himself to the range officer, the lieutenant refused to believe he was *the* Don Hume until a catalog with a photo was produced to prove his identity.

When Hume first started making holsters, most of his sales were to officers who carried wheelguns. "You only had to make about three sizes of holsters in about three barrel lengths, and you could cover most of your business. No one foresaw the day when the semi-auto would come on so strong."

But the police switch to autos has been somewhat of a nightmare for holstermakers. Semi-automatic handguns are,

for the most part, not interchangeable in size and shape like the majority of revolvers. Every make and model requires a holster designed especially for it. And let a manufacturer make a slight change — the shape of the trigger guard, for example — and the holsters in inventory will no longer work and a new holster must be designed.

Hume's company uses real guns to build and fit all their holsters. On more than one occasion, a prototype has been received, a holster designed for it and a product run made, only to find out the gunmaker incorporated a change into his final version. That leaves the company with an inventory of holsters that will not work.

Hume and I share much the same philosophy about security holsters. There is such a thing as being too concerned with security. True, the holster has to retain the gun. But the only way to make a holster totally snatch-proof is to make one from which it is impossible to draw the gun, even for the officer. It is my observation — not Hume's — that many chiefs have such a fixation on weapon retention that they have lost sight of this fundamental fact. What is needed in a good police

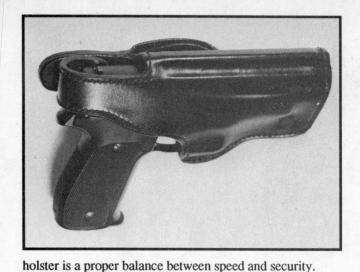

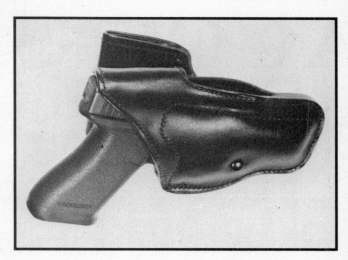

The H738-SH (left) will hold a variety of automatics in varying lengths. The H740-SH Lynx (below) features the Don Hume low-profile thumb-break safety strap.

holster is a proper balance between speed and security.

I got to try several of Hume's security holsters during my visit. But my pick for the best uniform police holster in the world is what they catalog as the "Tiger." It is a perfect example of that critical balance that I mentioned.

There is a second thing that marks Don Hume Leathergoods. That is leather. You will not find any nylon or plastic holsters in his catalog. And Hume sincerely intends for it to stay that way. "Leather is better" has become a company motto.

There is even a rumor that at a recent S.H.O.T. Show Hume and his people greeted the competition with a hardy slap on the back, leaving behind an "I Love Leather" sticker. Understand that this is strictly a rumor.

I see a place for synthetic holsters and belts in certain police applications — and even more in civilian handgunning. But there are just some things that are ordained from on high and that includes walnut gunstocks and leather holsters and belts.

I got a better feel for Don Hume during my tour of the plant rather than during our interview. When a fellow goes out of his way to go back and turn off a light which he left on, when he is on a first name basis with the assembly line workers in a rather large and complex plant, when he walks away from the interview to show a new worker a safer way of feeding a belt through a tooling machine — that's when I begin to get a feel for who Don Hume really is.

During my tour of the manufacturing operation, two things really got my attention. First, the amount of hand work that goes into every piece of leather — every worker was proud and took time to show me his or her job. And second, the large number of pieces that go into the second bins as not good enough for retail sales. I examined several seconds and could not find the flaw that caused them to be rejected until Hume would point it out to me.

While Hume still sells directly to individuals through his catalog sales, he is moving more into direct dealer sales. And he has an innovative, aggressive telemarketing program.

In his catalog are color photos of the ladies who make up his telemarketing staff. Few police officers are going to hang-up on these gals when they call, I can promise you that. Those ladies could talk me into buying a holster for a .410 shotgun!

"There was a day," Hume said, "when I used to dream of having 10 employees." Now with many times that number of employees, he has just turned 60 and isn't ready to slow down or hang it up just yet.

At lunch, Hume talked about his farm, his grandkids, and

The H723 is Hume's small-of-the-back holster. Easy to draw from, it's primarily designed for undercover work.

the earth-sheltered home he is going to build. He and his wife were getting ready to leave the next day for a Caribbean cruise, and I could see by the look my wife gave me that I was going to hear about Caribbean cruises during the drive back to Fort Smith.

Hume is a son of Oklahoma who worked hard and made it. I owe him a lot because on more than one occasion his holsters helped keep me alive. My law enforcement days are behind me now, but if I was starting all over I'd probably carry a Glock .45 instead of a Colt .357. But for my leather, make mine a Don Hume. His stuff is still the best!

DROP-IN ACCURACY FOR THE .45 ACP

By John Ross

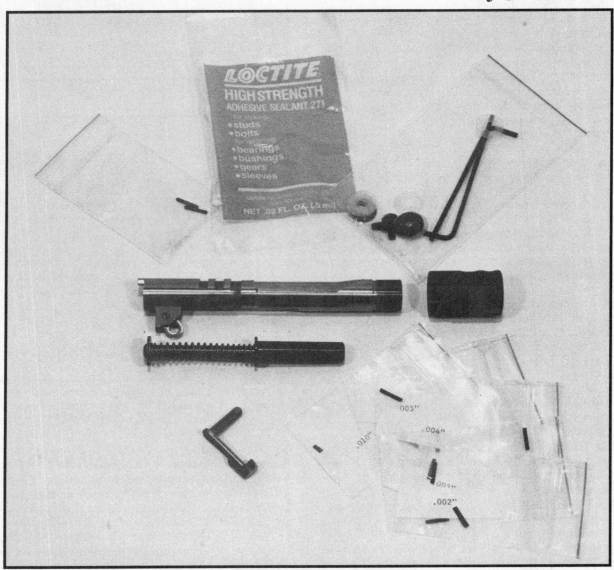

Surrounding the barrel, compensator and recoil system of the .45 are (clockwise) Loctite adhesive sealant, hex wrenches and spare buffer parts, shims, slide stop and rollers from Quadra-Comp II kit.

The Centaur System Shrunk This Shooter's Groups By More Than Half!

☆ ☆ ☆ ☆ ☆ ☆ ☆

The barrel and compensator treads are quickly cleaned with a degreaser like Birchwood Casey's Gun Scrubber.

A small amount of all-purpose grease lubes the roller and holds it in the trough of the slide stop.

IT WAS time I faced the facts. Accuracy from my aged Gold Cup ranged from awful to horrible. Sure, there were times when I was able to plunk five rounds in a couple inches at 25 yards, but on other occasions, groups from the semi-auto could barely be covered by a saucer.

Figuring my handloads were at fault, I tried lots of different fodder. No improvement. A red-dot sight, with two different mounts, failed to better performance significantly. I changed benchresting technique. Still no improvement.

Was an accuracy job by Clarke or Wilson in the offing? The money simply wasn't there to have the pistol precision-tuned.

For years, various magazines have carried the ad of Centaur Systems, Inc., for their drop-in Quadra-Lok bull-barrel kits. I'd dismissed their claims out of hand. Everybody knows match-winning accuracy doesn't come from a do-it-yourself kit.

That may be true. But after ordering and fitting a Quadra-Comp II system to my Gold Cup, groups with Winchester's

Supermatch 185-grain SWC ammo shrank from six inches to two inches-plus! And these are 10-shot groups. That's reasonable performance.

The Quadra-Comp II kit contains a bull barrel, a double-ported compensator threaded to fit the end of the barrel, a Wolff recoil spring system, and an adjustable slide stop.

The key to top accuracy in a 1911 Colt-style semi-auto is the play in the barrel as the pistol cycles. Is the barrel immobile when the slide is forward and the action cocked? When the gun fires, does the action unlock and the barrel drop the same way each time?

Sounds simple, but obviously it isn't. Too many moving parts and too many wear surfaces must be fitted. That's what keeps Messrs. Wilson and Clarke and a host of other masters at tuning the .45 auto in business.

You won't get that kind of accuracy from a Quadra-Comp II or their non-compensator-equipped Quadra-Lok II kit. What you will get is a handgun capable of two inches or less

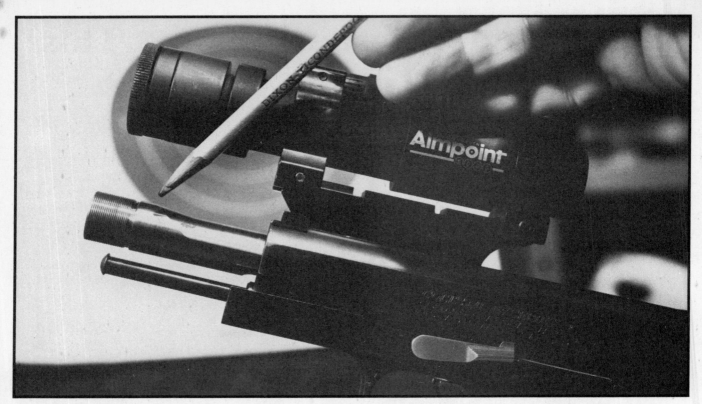

The oversized bull barrel is machined to fill the opening in the slide that is normally occupied by the barrel bushing.

The bull barrel is built 25 percent heavier than the National Match type.

at 25 yards — good enough to chew out the 10-ring.

Everyone knows one of the keys to 1911-style pistol accuracy is a tight lock-up between the barrel and slide. Normally, this is achieved with hand-fitting the bushing at the muzzle and the lug, link and slide stop under the breech.

The Quadra-Comp system features an "adjustable" slide stop made of stainless steel. It works like this: A trough, .570-inch long and .075-inch deep, is milled in the top of the slide stop pin. A hardened steel roller, .077-inch in diameter, fits in the trough. Under the roller, one builds a stack of steel shims which raises the roller until lock-up is tight.

As the height of the shim stack increases, it forces the roller to bear against the top of the bottom hole in the link, pushing the barrel up until its lugs are fully engaged in the slide and

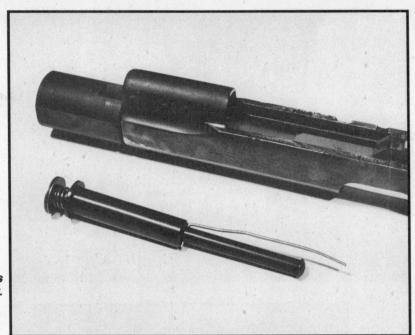

Wolff's captive recoil system enhances a gun's accuracy. It also makes field-stripping easier.

With shim stack of correct thickness, the slide should hang up about .08-inch from closing. With a firm push, it should go all the way home.

there is no play. The bottom hole in the system's link is oversize and should not be used with any other slide-stop.

You can feel when the height of the shim-roller stack is right. Barrel and slide — sans recoil system — are fitted to the frame and the slide stop with shims and roller are inserted. As you push the slide forward, about .08-inch before it reaches the end of its travel, you should encounter firm hesitation, as the barrel cams up into position.

With a strong push, you should be able to move the slide to the locked position. And it will take an equally hard tug to open the action. As long as you can manually open and close the action, it's okay. Lubricate the roller with wheel-bearing grease.

The adjustable slide stop locks up the rear of the barrel. The front, just aft of the muzzle, is machined .697-inch in diameter to just clear the front of the slide. There is no bushing to fit.

Centaur's concept is that the gap in the slide between the cut-out for the bushing and the recoil spring plunger provides a "V" trough. Camming up the rear of the barrel forces the muzzle down hard into the trough, so that when the slide is fully forward, the barrel does not move.

Centaur's system is available with either a five-inch or a 5.6-inch barrel threaded for a dual-port compensator. The barrel is of stainless steel heat-treated to 40 Rockwell, with six grooves, 16:1 to the left as per SAAMI specs. I chose the compensator to add weight (2.5 ounces) and reduce muzzle

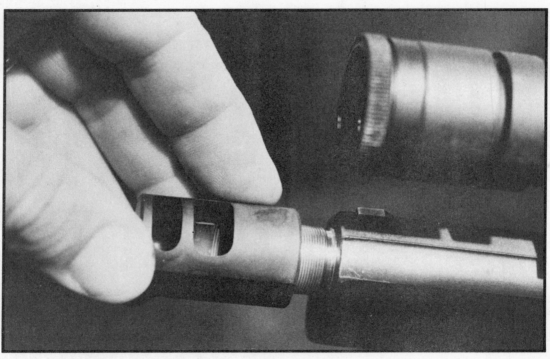

Two bands of Loctite #271 (left) are used to freeze the compensator to the barrel. The compensator is screwed onto the barrel (below) until it contacts the full-foward of the slide. It is then backed off.

jump. A vial of Loctite #271 is provided to freeze the compensator on the threaded muzzle.

Completing the package is a captive recoil system by Wolff. A plastic buffer is sandwiched between steel disks to absorb recoil of the slide. A full-length rod ensures that the recoil spring will not buckle in compression and affect accuracy. A plunger, called a recoil cap, rides over the spring, keeping it captive.

A hex-head screw holds the recoil cap on the rod. By removing the screw with the Allen wrench provided in the kit, one can change recoil springs and replace buffers as needed. The Quadra-Comp II model for the Colt Gold Cup came with a 15-pound spring. For flawless ejection with light target loads, I replaced the medium spring with a 10-pound one.

Installation of the Quadra-Comp system is easy and takes less than an hour, plus overnight for the Loctite to set up. First,

clean the barrel and compensator of all packing grease. Then field-strip your pistol in the normal manner.

Put the new barrel in the slide without the recoil system and begin the trial-and-error process of building the shim stack under the roller in the slide stop until you get it right. When the shim stack is high enough, you'll feel firm hesitation over that last .08-inch of slide travel.

My worn Colt required a stack of .020-inch thick before lock-up was perfect. If your shim stack is too thick, the slide will not close all the way. Once I'd determined the correct shim thickness, I daubed a little grease on the roller and set the slide stop aside.

I next compressed the recoil spring by pushing down on the cap and inserting a bent paper clip through a hole in the recoil rod, as per directions. After laying the barrel in the slide, I slid the compressed recoil system in place, fitted the slide to the

Gunsmith Les Kraft alters the feed ramp on the new barrel. It took 15 minutes to reduce ramp's angle. This greatly enhanced feeding.

frame, and inserted the slide stop, being careful not to drop the roller or shims. Pulling back on the slide allowed the paper clip to drop free, and the pistol was assembled.

Fitting the compensator was equally easy. Make two fine bands of Loctite on the barrel's threads. With the slide fully forward, screw the compensator down to the point where it contacts the slide. Now back it off to where the dual ports are vertical and the sides are perfectly parallel with the flats on the slide. Let it sit overnight for the Loctite to harden.

I could barely wait to get to the range to test the re-barreled Gold Cup and, in my haste, I forgot to check feeding of the pistol with dummy ammo.

Perhaps because my Gold Cup was used when I bought it and the feed ramp on the frame had been modified, I could not get any ammo — hardball, jacketed SWCs or handloads — to feed from magazines. The nose of the bullets would slam into the ramp and stop.

Polishing the ramp at the range failed to solve the problem, but 15 minutes work with needle files and a round finishing stone lessened the angle of the ramp slightly. I polished it to a mirror finish with my Dremel Tool and a felt buffer filled with jeweler's rouge. Now it feeds slick as a whistle with a wide variety of ammo.

I'm pleased with the Quadra-Comp II system. The Gold Cup shoots better now than it ever has for me. Cost of the unit, post-paid from Centaur Systems (1602 Foothill Road, Kalispell, MT 59901) is $224.95.

You can save $50 or so by ordering the Quadra-Lock II kit, which is virtually identical to the one I used, except there's no compensator. In addition to .45 ACP, kits are available in 10mm, .40 S&W, .38 Special and 9mm.

All kits contain great instructions, the barrel with link and pin installed, an adjustable slide stop, two rollers and extra shims, the Wolff recoil system, extra buffers and washers, two recoil rod screws, two hex wrenches, and the vial of Loctite #271 (in the compensator kit only).

SECTION SIX:

USIN' TIPS FOR

HANDGUNNERS

INSTINCT SHOOTING

By Jim Dickson

A Touch Of Zen, Coupled With A Lot Of Practice — And These Instructions — Can Change Your Shooting Style!

INSTINCT OR point shooting is both practical and useful. This system is fully as accurate as shooting with sights, and works just as well in the dark, where you can't see sights, as it does in the daylight.

The late Ed McGivern used instinct shooting to set his fantastic records, for he held guns below his line of sight. The late Lucky McDaniel would shoot BBs out of the air or make a five-gallon can dance at 500 yards with a rifle fired offhand by instinct shooting. This was the method employed by Wild Bill Hickok, John Westley Hardin and the rest of the top gunfighters of the Old West. It is the way pistols have always been intended to be fired from the time of the first horse pistols.

Indeed, the rudimentary sights found on most early 20th Century pistols were not intended to be used for anything except helping the shooter get started at pointing accurately. The manufacturers of the day knew that most pistol fights were quick, close and often in the dark, so they didn't bother with big sights that could snag in pockets.

Once a man mastered instinct shooting, he is quicker, more accurate and able to shoot 24 hours a day. The man dependent on sights needs enough light to see them. A shadowy figure 100 to 200 yards away in the dark is safe from a pistol shooter who must use sights he can't see, but the figure can be hit by a good instinct shooter.

The same is true of shooting in total darkness. The good instinct shooter can guide his bullets unerringly to any sound he hears. The man who uses sights can't even see his gun. Under these conditions he is virtually disarmed.

The instinct shooter moves with decisively greater speed than the man who must use sights. While the sight user is bringing the pistol up to his line of sight and assuming the proper stance his instructors have trained him to employ, the instinct shooter already has fired and hit his target, for he has only to point and squeeze the trigger, regardless of position or line of sight.

The methods for teaching this system were developed by the late great Lucky McDaniel. He was the first successful teacher of instinct shooting, and the originator of the Army's Vietnam-era quick-kill instinct shooting program. McDaniel lived just outside of Fort Benning, Georgia, and taught the troops as his contribution to the fight in Vietnam. Later, the Army began using his former students as instructors.

Without question, Lucky McDaniel was the greatest hand-and-eye coordination teacher who ever lived. He could perform any trick shot ever made and usually teach a student who never had fired a gun to accomplish the same shot in 15 minutes or less! His ability to transfer his skills to his students was uncanny. McDaniel made his living by teaching instinct shooting. In all, he personally taught approximately 100,000

Tossing targets into the air can be done with either hand. Most people can throw left-handed while shooting right-handed (above). If you have to toss targets with your right hand (below), hold the gun ready in your left hand, ready for a transfer to your right hand after the throw.

The classic duelist stance positions the shooter and gun in the best alignment while awaiting a thrown target.

people across the U.S. In what follows, I'll attempt to pass on what I learned from him.

He taught me, and I am passing on what I learned from him. The key to proper instinct shooting is what the Japanese call Zen. The shooter withdraws into the primitive part of the brain. Thoughts are allowed to pass by like a flock of birds, while the shooter's mind is like a pool of still water that perfectly reflects whatever passes by. Once the thinking part of the brain is made subservient to the older, reflexive, instinctive part of the brain, you will be able to react naturally and correctly. This takes practice, and martial arts study is the best place to master all phases of it.

Remember, don't think about it. Just do it. Babe Ruth could never have hit a ball if he thought about it and aimed for it. You have to keep your eye on the ball and just hit it. The same applies to instinct shooting. If you start thinking and aiming you miss. When you extend your finger to touch something, you don't aim, you just do it. Well, the principle is the same for instinct shooting.

Once you quit thinking about the distance between you and your target, you can hit it as easily at 100 or 200 yards as you can when you can touch the muzzle to it. Just keep both your eyes locked on the target, point and pull the trigger.

This brings us to the method of teaching instinct shooting at a target on the same level as you are. Stand like an old-time duelist with only your side pointed at the target. This also presents the smallest target to your opponent in a duel or a gunfight. Your feet should be spread naturally and facing the same direction as the body which is 90 degrees from the target.

Ignore the gun sights completely and stretch out the arm fully toward the target, keeping your wrist straight. Begin firing at a range of a few inches to a few feet so that the shots easily hit the center. Now step back each time you fire. If your group starts spreading, quit thinking about aiming. Don't move back so rapidly that you can't control your group size.

You soon will find that you have backed away as far as you had room to back, and yet you still are hitting the center of the target.

Don't rush this process. Rushing requires thinking, which detracts from simply doing. This method is fast and efficient. It works equally well with automatics or revolvers.

Speaking of revolvers, you will find that you can shoot double-action as easily as single-action with instinct shooting. When shooting single-action, turn the gun on its side to cock it or the cocking motion will disrupt the pointing of the gun by bobbing the barrel up and down. Swing the barrel to the right if you are right-handed.

To practice on targets on the ground at rabbit height, put some bottle caps or spent .22 cases on the ground about six to 12 inches apart, no more than about 15 to 20 feet from you.

Extend your arm full length, your body positioned sideways

Here's the proper extension to take a target from the sky.

in the manner of a duelist. Keep both eyes open and put your chin against your shoulder. Keep your wrist straight. Make all corrections at the shoulder. If you bend the wrist to point, you will miss high if you move the wrist up, miss low if you hold it down. Make no movement at the wrist or elbow.

Now lock your eyes on the bottom of the target, forgetting all else. Point and fire without looking at the gun. If you miss, move to another target at random. Do not try the first target twice in a row, for you will just miss in the same place. You should be able to hit quickly and easily. If you start hitting high or low, you are bending your wrist up or down.

To learn to shoot in total darkness, start in daylight, but you must be blindfolded. With your eyes lowered, have a friend take a tin can with a rock or two in it so it will rattle and throw it across the ground. Point at the sound and fire. You soon will be on target.

This technique can be used to teach the blind to shoot. Some years ago, there was a totally blind squirrel hunter who used a .22 rifle to get his bag limit on a regular basis. People couldn't believe it even when they saw it. He simply fired at the sound of the squirrel. Anyone who has done much squirrel hunting will know the high level of accuracy this demands.

The simple fact is that virtually anyone can get this good with practice. This is an easy technique to teach, because there is no tendency to try to aim or watch your arm to see whether it is pointing correctly when you are blindfolded.

Fast draw and instinct shooting are an American tradition dating back to the Old West. It is learned easily, but for safety's sake always practice with an unloaded gun. I don't know where people get the idea that the Old West gunfighters practiced with loaded guns. They didn't. The greatest gunfighter of them all, John Wesley Hardin, drew complaints from those who knew him because they said his constant drawing and snapping his empty guns was driving them crazy! The only time you fast draw a loaded gun is when you are in a gunfight!

To learn to make a fast draw, have a friend stand close and hold a small, empty cereal box or some similar item in front of you, then drop it. As it falls, you draw and shove the barrel of your handgun under it so it hits your barrel. You will find that this is the quickest, most instinctive fast draw learning method. I know it sounds foolish, but it works the best of all the training methods I've come across.

Remember, never insert the trigger finger in the trigger guard until the handgun clears the holster and the muzzle is coming to bear on the target. Follow this advice and you won't have a gimpy leg from shooting yourself. This applies doubly for a real gunfight. You'd look pretty foolish shooting yourself in a real shootout.

Hitting aerial targets is easy with instinct shooting. Clay

The proper hip-shooting form has the elbow placed inside the hollow of the hipbone with the gun level.

In the hip-shooting position, the entire body is locked in place. To shift the gun's aim, the entire body is rotated.

When shooting at a ground target, the form is that of a duelist. The eyes are locked on the base of the target.

targets are traditional for aerial shooting and among the best on which to learn the technique.

After you have gotten the hang of it, you can move on to shooting airborne charcoal briquets, then washers, pennies and finally, even BBs. Remember that the size of the target and the distance are not important. If you can see it and it is within the range of the cartridge, you can hit it. The eye will fix the target and direct the hand to it — if you just let it. Don't try to think about it or aim it. This is a much more precise aiming system than any sight you can put on a gun.

To learn how to hit an aerial target, first get a friend to throw them for you. The targets should be thrown in the same manner and direction each time. Assume the classic duelist position with the pistol pointed upward, the shooting arm bent. Concentrate on the top edge of the claybird going up and away from you in the direction you face. Now reach out and touch that spot as though there was no distance separating you.

To learn to score from the hip, throw a can or a clay pigeon on the ground 15 feet away. Face the target fully. The feet should be spread comfortably and the knees slightly bent. Lock the elbow of the shooting arm inside the hipbone, then look at the base of the target and forget the gun is there. Pull the trigger and you may score a hit. Don't be discouraged if your first couple of shots are off. Keep your eyes locked on the target, and you soon will hit it.

For multiple targets, remember to pivot the whole body in the manner of a gun turret, instead of moving the arm. Bend the knee to change elevation, not the arm.

When you have a can rolling and bouncing, make no corrections for the moving target or the increasing range. Keep your eye on the target and your eyes should do all the corrections without any conscious effort on your part. Conscious effort, thinking, analyzing and checking are the ways you miss in this game.

Ed McGivern was not the only handgun wizard who could shoot a tight group while fanning a handgun. You can learn to do it — if you don't mind ruining the lockwork on your single-action. Hard cocking and fanning will destroy it. Unless you are giving exhibitions for which they pay you enough for a new set of working parts for your gun on a regular basis, I advise you to just read this, not practice it.

I don't tear up my single-actions by fanning them, and I hope you won't ruin yours with this showman's trick. Still, there may be some out there who are paid showmen who need to know, so here it is:

Using the same stance as that for hip shooting, hold the trigger back and bring the palm of the left hand down on the hammer to fire the gun. Do this slowly at first, for you are rocking the gun with this movement. Keep your eyes glued to the target and you gradually can increase speed, until you can empty the gun in less than a second.

However, if you really feel fanning is the way to go, I recommend you forget the six-shooter and carry a single-barrel shotgun!

The so-called slip hammer gun is seen rarely today. It is a cut-down single-action with the barrel bobbed and the trigger removed for hideout use. It is not fanned, but the hammer is cocked and allowed to fall. To use this with sights requires a different technique than with regular guns, as you are working the thumb as the piece fires.

This is not a problem when shooting instinctively. There is a rocking motion, but it is not as severe as when fanning.

Here's the classic instinct shooting position when the target is on the same level as the shooter. The arm, elbow and wrist are straight. All movement is at the shoulder. The eyes are on the target, not on the gun.

However, you may have a less secure grip. Just go slowly at first, and you should have no trouble hitting and developing good speed.

Successful instinct shooting is a mental discipline involving trained reflexive action without thought. You cannot learn it, then go back to it a year later and pick up where you left off. You must train constantly so that everything is automatic.

The use of a BB pistol in the beginning is recommended, as you usually can see the BB in flight and tell where you are missing. This is particularly handy with aerial targets. The BB pistol also can be used indoors with a hanging curtain or heavy material such as denim for a backstop. Always wear shooting glasses to protect against a BB bouncing back in the eye, and clear the area of children and pets while shooting. These BBs do bounce. The BB gun in both pistol and rifle form is the classic instinct training weapon. In fact, the U.S. Army used Daisy airguns to train sharp shooters in the Vietnam era.

Occasionally, a student has a problem with his dominant eye. Simply put, the dominant eye is the one whose perception of a finger held at arm's length is not changed by the closing of the other eye. The non-dominant eye will cause the position of the finger to seem to move when the dominant eye is closed. Most right-handed people have a right dominant eye. If the left eye is dominant, they need to shoot left-handed. The reverse is true for a left-handed person with a dominant right eye.

Many people are latently ambidextrous. These people, like the truly ambidextrous, can fire two guns at once effectively. Wild Bill Hickok, John Wesley Hardin and many other famous gunfighters used two guns. There were tactical situations then — as there are today — in which only a gun in each hand will suffice. Firing at two men who were positioned in opposite directions. Wild Bill Hickok triggered both guns simultaneously — and killed both opponents. This is not as hard as it sounds. After you have been doing this type of shooting for a time, you should look at the target, turn your head and fire, hitting it. Japanese archers have done this little trick for centuries. The primitive brain knows exactly where the target is, and is trained now to hit it. It is as simple as that.

However, this is a serious mind and body discipline that requires constant practice to maintain. It will enable you to make successful shots that you can make no other way, but it demands perseverance and dedication.

TREE-HIGH CHALLENGE

By Mark Hampton

Midwestern Gray Squirrels Delight In Frustrating Handgun Hunters

THE ALARM clock broke the early morning silence. I stumbled out of bed, making my way to the coffee pot, my body in desperate need of a caffeine boost. After putting on my Mossy Oak camo gear, I made sure I had my gun, ammo and binoculars ready. Two hunting companions pounded on the door. My brother, Ronnie, and a shooting friend, John Summers, were making sure I wasn't getting too much sleep.

The discussion, over a cup of steaming coffee, turned to scopes — variable or fixed-power — what brand of ammunition shoots best and whether or not camo clothing is really necessary. Then discussion time was over, and it was time to hit the woods. The three of us were about to embark upon our regular Saturday morning squirrel hunt.

Here in my neck of the woods in Missouri, squirrel season lasts from somewhere around May 25, depending on which date Memorial Day falls, until December 31. Over half of the year can be spent out in the woods chasing these bushytail mammals.

Both grays and fox squirrels inhabit our woods, but gray squirrels can be most challenging. These nervous, little critters never seem to stay in one spot for long and prefer living around hardwoods with a good source of acorns handy.

Fox squirrels — sometimes called reds — like more open areas. Being diurnal creatures, early morning hunts usually find quite a bit of feeding activity taking place. At least that's what we were hoping to find on this particular morning.

Squirrels can be taken with scatterguns, but if a challenge is sought, a .22 rimfire is the only way to go. Let's go one step beyond. If you really want a challenge, hit the woods with a handgun. You may not take home your limit every time, but I'm not spending all my time in the woods just to see how many squirrels I can harvest in

the first place. It is a real challenge. Seldom have I ever taken my limit — six here in Missouri — but when that does happen, I feel just as thrilled as if I had taken a big buck.

We arrived in our hunting area just as the sun began to shed light in the woods. We split up and went in three different directions, two of us armed with handguns. My brother

While glassing for movement, this hunter keeps his Contender safe in a sturdy Michaels of Oregon holster.

This Freedom Arms .22 proved to be extremely accurate and an excellent choice for taking squirrels.

insisted on carrying a rifle.

Sneaking down an old road, I made sure my Thompson/Center Contender was armed with a high-velocity 40-grain Winchester round, and the scope setting on T/C's 2.5-7x model was on 3x.

It wasn't long before I heard the barking and chattering of two squirrels fussing between themselves. Slowly I eased my way toward the ruckus, trying not to make any noise in the leaves.

Finally, I was in a position to see one of the little grays sitting on a limb. We stared at each other briefly. With no gun rest available, I tried an offhand shot, but the crosshairs were off the squirrel's head more than they were on. The squirrel ran up the tree and found another limb. By now he was trying to see what I was, and why I was disturbing his early morning ritual.

Sneaking over to the nearest tree, I found a rest and tried once again to steady the crosshairs. I squeezed the trigger ever so slowly. This time the squirrel's luck came to an end.

Sneaking around the woods during the next few hours yielded more opportunities, while enjoying the early morning magic that appeals to many of us. I even managed to take two grays from offhand. It was a good morning's hunt, as the wind didn't come up until 10 or so. By then, we had met back at the truck. I had taken four grays and the others had eight between them.

It was great just being out in the woods, and the limited success we experienced just added icing to the cake. As we argued over whose turn it was to skin the squirrels, we were already making plans for our next hunt.

Scouting for hot spots is basically an observation of move-ments to and from the best acorn mast. If you live in an area where corn fields can be found next to standing timber, this would be an ideal spot to watch for movement.

In my area, the hickory nuts and white oak acorns provide a great food source for both fox and gray squirrels. Watch for cuttings, nut and hull litterings, under these type of trees, and you normally can determine where the most activity is occurring. Obviously, tracks in the mud or snow are an indication you're in good territory as are leaf nests in the crowns of hardwood trees.

Arriving at these locations early in the morning should put the hunter in the middle of action. Normally I scout and hunt at the same time. Fresh cuttings on the ground indicate squirrels are feeding in the area; a good place to sit for awhile and watch for activity. Some squirrel hunters like to park their tails in an area such as this and simply wait and watch, making the most of their patience. Others prefer to sneak around the woods, constantly moving about. Both methods have their advantages. I like to move slowly through the woods, listening for the distinct barking or simply watching the trees and limbs for movement. Once I know a squirrel is in a particular tree, I become something of a ninja stalker, invisibly inching my way forward. At least, I like to think of it in this manner.

Hunting squirrels with a .22 rimfire is tough. Make that a .22 handgun of some description, and you've got yourself a real challenge. One of the first things to consider is your target. A squirrel's head is smaller than a tennis ball, but it's not fluorescent green, and, most of the time, it doesn't stay in one place for long.

Whatever handgun you use must be capable of decent accuracy, or you're wasting time and effort. My favorite rig

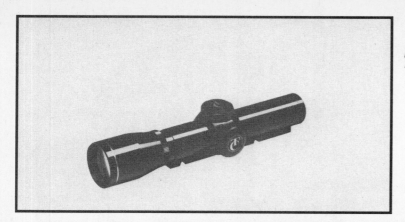

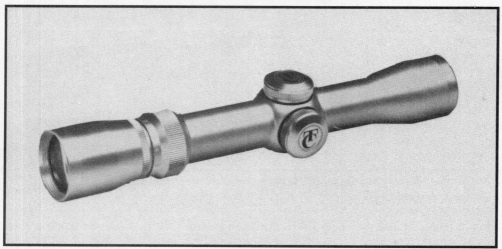

Thompson/Center has a number of recoil-proof pistol scopes that are ideal for squirrel hunting. At left is a 2.5x pistol scope with standard reticle.

This recoil-proof 2.5-7x scope from T/C Thompson features a lighted reticle.

for squirrel hunting is a 14-inch Contender. Topped with a scope, it's deadly accurate with Winchester or PMC ammunition. Since I do a considerable amount of hunting with a T/C, using the gun as much as possible, all year long, gives me an edge when big-game season rolls around. I am still using the same gun — only the caliber has changed.

Chasing squirrels gives me the chance to spend a lot of time in the woods doing what I enjoy the most — handgun hunting. Using a single-shot handgun such as the Contender is not a handicap as many people may believe. Accuracy is far more important than firepower.

There are several other quality .22 handguns floating around, all perfectly capable of delivering the necessary accuracy. The Anschutz Exemplar is a super-accurate bolt-action rig with a two-stage adjustable trigger. The trigger comes from the factory set at 9.85 ounces, so make sure the crosshairs are exactly where you want them before squeezing the trigger.

The left-hand bolt allows smooth operation so the hunter can load the gun with the right hand. The gun I was testing last summer was mounted with a 7x Burris and was unbelievably accurate with CCI ammo.

For the hunter who likes to move around the woods, this gun may be a little heavy. For those hunters who prefer to sit in one spot and watch den trees or feeding areas, the Exemplar may be just the ticket. I must have a rest of some kind before shooting this handgun, and prefer a rest no matter what handgun is used.

Autoloading pistol fans can enjoy their favorite handgun

while chasing bushytails, too. Ruger's Mark II models with a 10-shot clip is a fine choice. I prefer those with longer barrels mounted with good scopes for my time in the woods. The Smith & Wesson Model 41 is an excellent gun with accuracy and a superb trigger. Recently, I shot a lightweight S&W 622, and it is a pure joy to carry around all day. It is fairly accurate and, for those who prefer autoloaders, makes a fine companion. The Bernardelli Model 100 target pistol is another excellent choice and one I enjoy shooting.

Regardless what type or model handgun you choose, remember it must be able to hit a smallish target from 30 to 40 steps, with boring consistency. The vast majority of squirrels I've shot fall somewhere in the 25- to 45-yard area.

Once you decide on the perfect handgun for your needs, a quality scope will bring out the accuracy potential. Not that I have anything against squirrel hunting with open sights. It's down-right tough, but can be accomplished with young eyes. Early mornings, late evenings, and cloudy days can make things extremely difficult with iron sights. A scope aids the hunter in precise bullet placement, and when you're shooting at a target not much bigger than the size of a half-dollar, any little advantage is welcome. Several good scopes are available, both fixed-power or variable models, depending on preference.

Currently, my .22 squirrel gun is wearing a T/C 2.5-7x, although most of the time when I am hunting, the power is set on 3x or 4x. I also have had considerable experience with Bausch & Lomb scopes, both 2x and 4x models, and they always have given satisfactory performance. Burris makes a

The American Eagle .22 Long Rifle ammo (above) has a 40-grain lead bullet. At left, this hunter uses a tree for added gun support.

ton of handgun scopes, one, I am sure, will fit most every situation. I have been testing their 3-9x variable, and I really enjoy the clarity and compact size of these optics. The new Simmons 2.5-7x is another good choice for hunters who desire a variable scope. I mounted a new Simmons scope on an SSK .45-70 barrel with no problems. It should offer years of trouble-free service on a .22 rimfire.

After the hunter decides what handgun and scope will suit his needs best, choosing ammunition becomes the next choice. At first glance, this may appear an easy task. There are a lot of different types and brands of .22 rimfire ammunition available, a mind-boggling selection indeed.

The hunter needs to purchase several different brands and prepare to spend some time and effort on the range. When I begin the day with a new gun or scope, searching for the brand of ammunition a particular gun favors, I first sight-in at 25 yards. This process calls for the use of sandbags on a good, solid bench, though the hood of my Bronco works in a pinch.

After this, I back off to 50 yards and begin shooting 10-shot groups with each brand of ammo. You will be surprised, if you

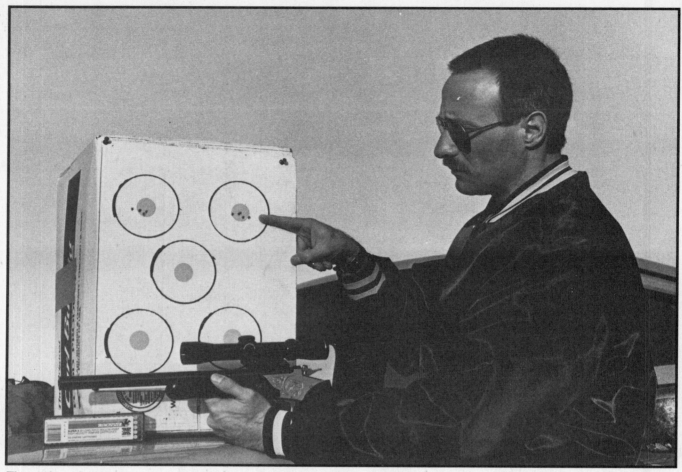

The author checks the accuracy of his scoped T/C Contender and Winchester ammo before an early morning hunt.

haven't done this before, at the drastic difference in group sizes from a dozen different brands. It doesn't take many 10-shot groups from 50 yards to determine what ammunition your barrel likes and dislikes. Every gun and barrel will be different, some more drastic than others, and even ammunition can vary with different lots and temperatures.

All of this may sound trivial, but remember, a squirrel's head is not very large, and there is a lot of space around the target, not much inside. My T/C barrel likes Winchester and PMC ammo, and that's all I feed through the 14-inch tube. Another barrel, stuck on another frame, may digest another brand of ammo more accurately. It just takes some shooting time to see, but that's why squirrel hunting is so enjoyable in the first place. It gives the hunter more time for hunting pleasure and the extra hours of shooting is time well spent.

Your gun and ammo may shoot differently in summer, too, as opposed to what happens in December. I just finished an afternoon squirrel hunt here in Missouri and, before heading to the woods, had to adjust the scope setting even though the same ammo was shot in the earlier months.

Incidentally, December is an ideal time to hunt squirrels. The woods are more open than earlier in the year and you can see much better. So can the squirrels. There is also less hunting pressure, and that's a big plus.

Here in my area, squirrels are active throughout the winter unless it's exceptionally cold. During late December, I nor-

mally hunt in the afternoon, the warmest time of day.

Tactics that were successful in the spring or summer won't necessarily work in winter. Your methods must be flexible. These late-season hunts will add a whole new dimension to your hunting endeavor. There is something about hunting in the snow that I just can't get enough of.

My hunting comrades and I have spent time, more than once, arguing whether or not camouflage clothing is necessary. If I am not wearing Mossy Oak or Treebark camo, at least, I am in olive drab rags of some kind. I just feel better sneaking through the woods. However, during deer season when Missouri hunters are required to wear fluorescent orange, squirrels seem to come from miles just to annoy me. I still can't make myself enter squirrel territory wearing deer hunting apparel, and I truly believe most hunters will benefit from wearing camo or dark colored clothing.

Before and after big-game season, squirrel hunting helps me get through the dull moments that haunt most sportsmen sometime during the year. And it sure beats sitting in the house watching television. Big-game seasons may not last all year, but there is still a challenge awaiting the aggressive sportsman. Just the thought of fried squirrel mixed with a platter of biscuits and gravy gives me the incentive to brave the elements. Regardless of the season, squirrel hunting with a .22 handgun is a major challenge.

Give it a try and find out for yourself.

SECTION SEVEN:
CUSTOM HANDGUNS

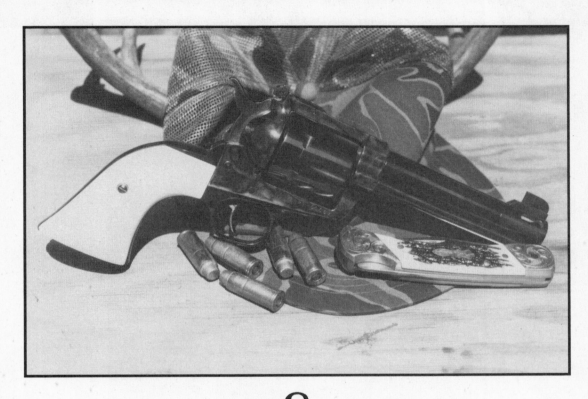

& GUNSMITHING

HANDGUNS
94

KING OF THE GUNWORKS

By *J.M. Ramos*

This beautiful Officer's ACP pistol features many custom accessories by King's Gun Works, including a comp barrel.

SOUTHERN CALIFORNIA has been the home base of some of the most talented and, perhaps, the earliest pioneers of custom pistolsmith masters in the likes of Frank Pachmayr and Armand Swenson. Joining their ranks is Arnold "Al" Capone, the founder of a successful company called King's Gun Works, Inc., located at 1837 W. Glenoaks Boulevard, Glendale, CA 91201.

Established in 1949, King's Gun Works has grown to become what may be the country's most innovative producer of custom accessories for the Colt 1911 pistol. During his first 20 years of operation, Capone was quite content to repair and customize an assortment of firearms for a large number of clients. However, by the late 1960s, Capone realized there was a good market for production-grade custom accessories for the 1911 pistol. This was generated by the ever-increasing demand among big-bore handgun shooters and law enforcement officers who carry the 1911 in their duties.

Shortened versions of the 1911 came into vogue and

This California Gunsmithing Enterprise Specializes In Upgrading The Model 1911

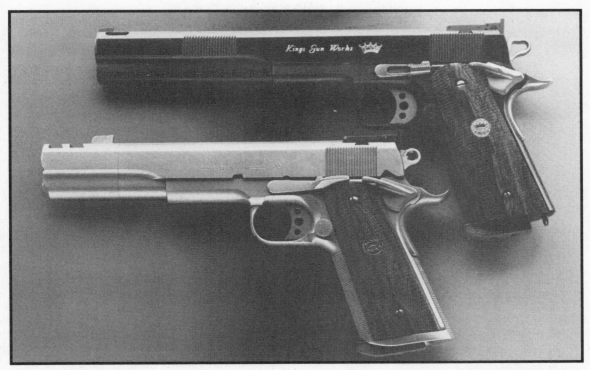

These full-house custom race guns were created for the serious competitor by King's Gun Works.

became a favorite carry gun, along with chopped 9mm double-action autos for off-duty cops and bodyguards. The trend also is well accepted in civilian circles for personal protection and home defense.

On the other hand, long slide models also became hot items among bullseye shooters as well as among handgun hunters. Unfortunately, in those early times both the chopped and long slide versions were only possible through the services of an experienced gunsmith who specialized in this type of modification.

Along with this line of options, masters of the craft began experimenting with extended and ambidextrous safeties, checkering of front and back of grip, installation of low-mount combat sights, ribs on top of the slide, bobbed or lightened hammers, triggers with stop screws, full length recoil spring guides, et al. To have such options built into a gun, the customer must send in the pistol to the gunsmith who will then spend weeks — or months — adding the custom touches. Such beautification usually is limited to those who can handle the expense involved in having one of these parade guns. On the positive side, these lovely irons shoot as well as they look — provided they are put together by somebody who knows what he is doing.

King's Gun Works has been producing fine accessories for the 1911 long before others started. Capone's early effort toward affordable pistol accessories started some 20 years ago and has inspired much of the vast array of custom replacement parts available today in the mail order market.

The 1980s proved to be the era of the super-hi-tech comp guns. High speed shooting has become the leading target event these days and the sport seems destined for greater popularity in the 1990s. Custom-grade accessories for these specialized shooting machines play an important role. As the masters of the range demand even more from their tools, their input from these shooting matches will become a basis for the future trend of competition guns, as well as for the gadgetries that will be incorporated. In creating their product line, King's Gun Works keeps a constant eye on such highly contested handgun sports. From such observation, they have learned how to put together accessories that provide the much needed edge to the shooter's gun. These competition-proven ideas are clearly evident on products that are refined further as new concepts are perfected.

King's production accessories consist of cast and fully machined components. Materials include both blued and

Author's personal carry gun features King's shortened recoil compensator, extended slide stop, match trigger, extended thumb safety, oversize magazine button and combat grips with King's medallion.

stainless steel to match finish or materials of individual guns. These components are available as "drop-in" units or highly specialized parts requiring individual fitting to the gun's frame or slide. Some of the more popular items in King's product line are a superlative extended slide stop, extended safety (also available in ambi-style), a drop-in-type grip safety for the Colt Commander, blued trigger for the Gold Cup, black trigger for the Commander, a recoil compensator for Government and Commander models (45 ACP), full-length recoil spring guide for Commander (also available for most other Colt models), an oversize magazine catch button that requires drilling and tapping of the magazine catch to install, and a beautiful cocobolo extended combat grip with King's own medallion. Their new polymer speed grip has a built-in thumb guard and bevelled bottom for speed reloading.

King's Gun Works has their own line of custom magazines, along with rubber base pads in assorted colors. The custom magazines are available in most popular calibers for the Model 1911 pistol. They come with a combination of "round follower" and a removable floor plate or with the traditional welded base and flat follower. The latter is more compatible for use with their colored rubber base pads. These magazines are available in blued or stainless steel.

Careful examination of King's magazines shows excellent workmanship and design, inside and out. They glide smoothly when inserted or ejected from the pistol's grip.

King's recoil compensator is an economical alternative to a full-house compensator device costing $250 to $300, with a matching barrel. Some of the more expensive items are "drop-in" types, while others will require fitting. King's Gun Works'

recoil compensator retails for around $40. This stainless steel device is machined from one piece of 416 bar stock, then heat treated to RC 30-35 hardness. It has the same dimensions as their National Match barrel bushing and will require only minor fitting to install. This is necessary so the individual pistol will benefit from tight fitting of barrel muzzle and gas seal for improved accuracy during firing.

Since this device simply replaces the regular barrel bushing, it does not require any alteration to the gun itself. While the basic size of the recoil compensator device matches perfectly with the Gold Cup or Government model, I found it too long for my personal taste when mated to the Commander. As a carry or off-duty gun, it will require a shorter compensator.

King's drop-in grip safety is available for both the Government and Commander models. This gadget is for those who do not want their guns altered and can alternate the sets of parts as they wish. The wide tang of the grip safety absorbs most of the recoil and reduces muzzle flip during firing. These drop-in units, however, do not have the maximum effect of the more involved hi-ride beavertail types that must be fitted to the pistol, requiring some removal of frame metal.

King's extended slide stop and extended safety devices also caught my curiosity and interest. These are superbly designed components that make operation of the gun faster and more convenient. These parts are made extra long purposely and can be shortened to suit individual tastes.

In my own full-size Gold Cup, I retained the full-length levers. In my Commander that is designed for carry, an oversize safety is not too practical, as the accidental release of

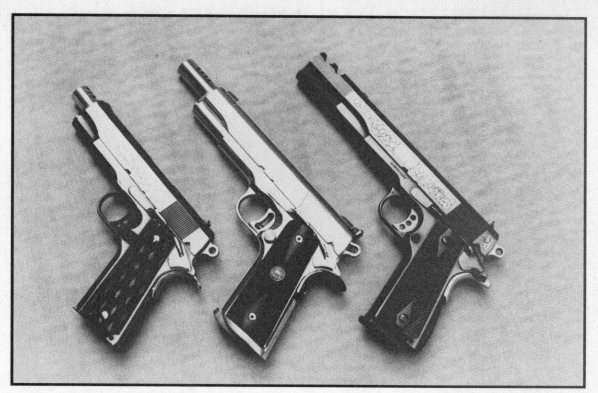

Author's trio of do-it-yourself custom 1911s feature an assortment of King's accessories. The gun on the left has a modified (shortened) recoil compensator, the center pistol carries a full-size recoil compensator while the gun on the right has a full profile compensator built from King's blank kit. Below, King's Speed Grip is moulded from polymer. It has a magazine chute for speed loading.

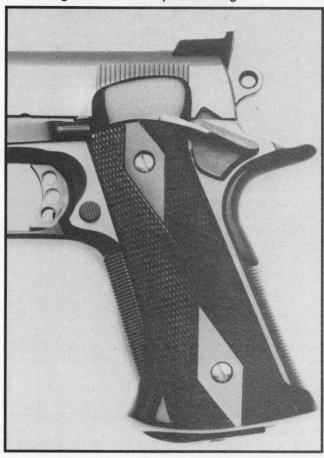

the safety could occur during holstering. For this reason, the safety lever was shortened with just enough length retained for convenient operation and width enough for fast manipulation.

On the original Colt safety design — except on the early 1911 pattern — the rear part of the raised portion of the lever is quite bothersome when the lever is operated. I removed this area on the King's safety and recut the straight serrations to criss-cross checkering using a metal checkering file. This improved the feel and aesthetics of the already sophisticated King's accessories.

Added for my personal use is raised checkering on the forward portion of the slide stop. When using a two-hand hold, I rest my non-shooting thumb on top of the rear portion of the slide stop. I thought it a good idea to checker this area so the thumb will stay put and not slip down during rapid firing.

After fitting all the necessary components, I headed for the range with a visiting friend from Holland, Tony Veldkemp, and his 12-year-old nephew, Peter Lindsay. Veldkemp is a reservist with the Dutch airborne regiment and experienced with many types of military hardware, while Peter had been shooting .22 rifles for eight months, but never had fired a handgun. Showing both the newly upgraded Commander and Gold Cup, they were impressed, especially Veldkemp who never liked the 1911 until he saw this one. He favors the double-action high-capacity 9mm handguns like those made by Walther and SIG.

Although he commented favorably on the look of both pistols, the Dutch shooter was quite leery regarding recoil of the .45 ACP compared to the milder 9mm Luger cartridge. I

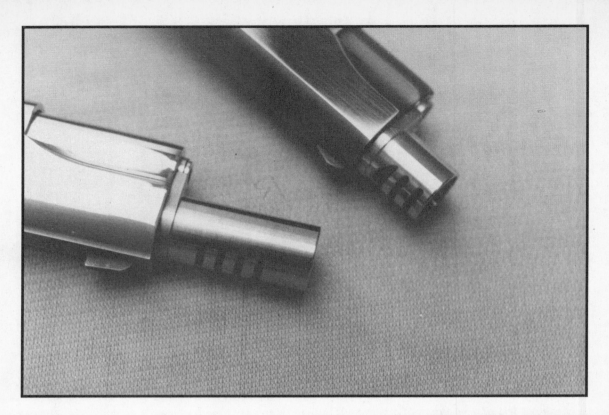

Above, the author's Commander pistol has a modified (shortened) recoil compensator (top) and the Gold Cup (bottom) features King's full-size recoil compensator.

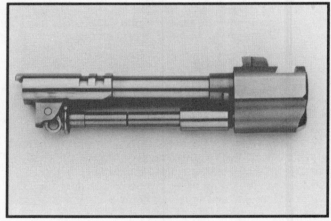

King's full-profile comp kit is complete with single shot in short version. Normally it is available in blank form so the gunsmith can tailor his personal comp design.

felt the compensator should do the job. This was not a full-house compensator system, but it offered good reduction in recoil and muzzle flip. I had brought 500 rounds of mixed Remington and Federal 230-grain full metal jacket and semi-wadcutter ammunition; no reloads. To be tested were four King's Gun Works magazines; two with rounded follower, the other two with the conventional flat follower. As a control, the original Colt factory magazine was used.

The first 10 minutes was spent to familiarize Veldkemp and Lindsay with the handling and safety precautions of the 1911, then all the magazines were loaded by myself and Veldkemp, while Lindsay was setting up targets starting at 15 meters. As the test progressed, the targets were set at 25 meters and on to 50 and 100 yards, with myself and Veldkemp shooting the Gold Cup. Before the new King's recoil compensator device was installed, my Gold Cup averaged five- to six-inch groups at 50 yards, while the Commander's best group at 25 yards was a three-inch spread in normal slow aimed fire.

While the Gold Cup normally can achieve phenomenal groupings out of the box, mine certainly had not. There had been a loose muzzle fitting and play of the receiver and slide mating despite the fact that it was quite new. Colt called this one of the "Ultimate" models with its bright stainless steel finish.

My blued Commander was also new. This one, as with most production grade guns had a loosely fitted frame and slide. Naturally, one cannot expect target accuracy when things are not perfectly put together. Would the precisely fitted King recoil compensator devices improve performance of these guns?

At 25 meters, the Gold Cup easily printed a 1-1/2-inch group. My best group at 50 yards was under three inches, versus the original five to six inches prior to the installation of the King's Gun Works part. At 100 yards, I was able to place five out of seven on the black but this could be improved by setting the sight properly for this range.

Veldkemp was not far behind, but he may have done better

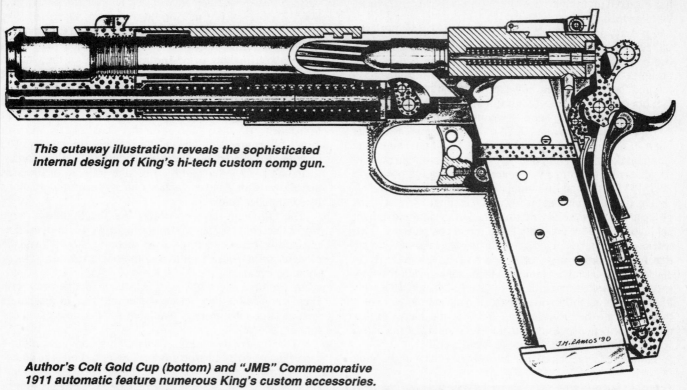

This cutaway illustration reveals the sophisticated internal design of King's hi-tech custom comp gun.

Author's Colt Gold Cup (bottom) and "JMB" Commemorative 1911 automatic feature numerous King's custom accessories.

had he spent more time shooting the big .45 over his favorite 9mm pistols.

Lindsay, on the other hand, was enthusiastic about trying these workhorses. Amazingly, this 12-year-old lad was able to fire both of the pistols comfortably, averaging a three-inch group at 25 meters after firing only two dozen rounds. He favored the Commander, however, for taste and its balance. He shot over 100 rounds of hot full metal jacket loads in this gun. He wanted more, but we ran out of ammo.

Lindsay fired my 9mm CZ-75 for comparison. The way he put it, if he could own a handgun now, he would choose the Commander fully equipped with King's components and forget the 9mm. From a youngster who fired a full power .45 ACP 1911 pistol the first time, his comment says a lot.

The results from that test were interesting. I sent my best group at 50 yards to King's Gun Works to show improvement achieved with their precisely fitted recoil compensator. Two weeks after that, I received a custom link from Arnold Capone that further shrank my groups and will cut down on flyers caused by the barrel not returning to the same position (a flaw in the barrel link design in the 1911 pistol). This special King's #3 link has a slightly wider distance between the two holes than does the factory part and it raises the barrel farther upward for better lock-up and slower dropping of the barrel which assists accuracy during rearward recoil.

I immediately replaced the factory barrel link with the King

part and made arrangements to test the gun at the Sightline Sport Shooting Club in Gormley, Ontario. Don Hinchley proposed testing of the upgraded Gold Cup and Commander be done by club members Dennis Nuutinen and Doug Youngson. Hinchley is the former president of the Ontario Handgun Association and is now president of both the Shooting Federation of Canada and Ontario Counsellors of Shooters. Sightline Sport Shooting Club — the largest, newest and most modern shooting facility in the province of Ontario — was founded by Hinchley, Dave Simms, Dave Harris and Bill Arnot, all members of the law enforcement community. The club is also shared by the province's local police forces, including SWAT units, in their regular training of firearms and allows testing and evaluation of newly acquired weapons by local police forces.

The following day, we headed for the Sightline range where Don Hinchley showed us the huge, well-laid-out shooting facility featuring a 20-position shooting range with all the modern gizmos necessary to accommodate various types of shooting events.

In addition, the club has a spacious lounge area with fireplace, satellite disk, video center and bar. In a separate area, a large classroom is available for the new members' training course.

At the front of the building, is the club's store/gunsmithing center managed by Charlie Taylor. Taylor's shop is an autho-

Arnold Capone (above, left) is president and founder of King's Gun Works. The author (above) examines some of the many custom accessories available from King's. Don Hinchley (left), president of the Shooting Federation of Canada, shot this group with a newly upgraded Gold Cup. Before installing King's parts, the pistol's best group was four inches at 15 meters.

Twelve-year-old Peter Lindsay fires author's Combat Commander with King's shortened recoil comp. With +P Federal FMJs, he was able to hit jugs at 15 meters, though he'd never fired a handgun before.

Author fired this group at 50 yards with his Gold Cup after King's upgrading accessories were installed.

rized Smith & Wesson Performance Center. This gunsmith underwent extensive training at the factory Smith & Wesson Performance Center and specializes primarily in Smith & Wesson products. I was impressed with the newly built shooting facility which had over 700 members in its first six months of operation.

For evaluation of the newly upgraded pistols featuring King's accessories, I felt it fitting to get the opinion of the experts who come to this place almost every day to shoot all types of handguns. Due to the poor weather conditions that day, there were few members around, so I had Don Hinchley do the first shooting of the two pistols.

When the pistols were laid out for him to check prior to actual shooting, Hinchley commented very favorably on their elegance. I bought 250 rounds of Eagle 230-grain full-metal jacket ammo from the club's store and that was used in the test.

Again, the four King's magazines were used. In the previous test two weeks earlier at another range — using various types of ammunition — there had been only two malfunctions with the semi-wadcutters. The two Colt magazines that came with the guns had suffered six malfunctions out of 100 rounds of semi-wadcutters. The King's magazines never experienced any malfunctions with full-metal-jacket ammo.

Don Hinchley chose to fire the Gold Cup first. It now was equipped with the King's new #3 link supplied by Arnold Capone. The target was set at 20 meters. His first five shots included three holes in the middle of the 10 ring, one in the nine and one in the eight. On his second group, all were in the 10 ring, measuring under one-inch. Impressive, indeed!

As for the felt recoil, Hinchley noted only a mild rating despite the hot-loaded FMJ ammunition. After shooting the full-size Gold Cup, he fired the Commander. He commented on the nice balance and good looks of the carry gun and how well it sits in the palm.

The best group he shot was not as phenomenal as the Gold Cup, but he still managed to keep the shots within the 10 and nine rings in three try-outs. He also noted that there was more recoil with the Commander, but the balance and feel of the smaller gun remained the same without noticeable flip.

Basically, the comments from the various shooters who have alternated shooting the two pistols are almost the same. The Gold Cup is definitely more controllable and accurate. However, most of the shooters who had the chance to fire them both picked up the Commander first. Aesthetically, the Commander seems to get the attention. However, the end result seems to favor the full-size Gold Cup.

In addition to their excellent performance in actual shooting, the shooters also admired the gadgetry used in the guns, as well as the quality and reliability of the magazines. If I'd had a pocketful of King's accessories that day on the range, I could have sold them all. Many observers expressed interest in the recoil compensator, especially the one modified for the Commander model. Arnold Capone will have to take a close look at producing a carry comp version of their famous recoil compensator device in the near future.

King's Gun Works entered the competitive custom pistolsmithing industry about 10 years ago — just as the popularity of IPSC-class pistols reached its accelerated stage.

King's now offers an extensive line of gunsmithing services, ranging from highly functional ultra-compact carry guns to the super high-tech competition guns. I found quality and workmanship of these highly customized pistols outstanding in every respect. Each of King's specially created custom pistols is crafted individually, assuring high standards of precision and workmanship that has made the company name a leader in the field of both accessory and custom pistolsmithing innovations.

King's Gun Works has proved itself not only the undisputed pioneer in the field of 1911 pistol accessory innovations, but they continue to lead the way in the development and production of more exciting and sophisticated bolt-on accessories for tomorrow's top shooter's.

A MATTER OF CUSTOM

By Jim Dickson

The Personal Handguns Of Inventor/Designer Max Atchisson Set A New Record For Originality

At left is the Standard AMT Back-Up. At right is Atchisson's contoured and lightened .380 Back-up. Despite being three ounces lighter, it is more pleasant to shoot because of its rounded contours.

THE FIREARMS designs of Max Atchisson are noted for originality and clearly thought out concepts. He has introduced more innovations than most designers, and his personal handguns reflect this. Each is carefully adapted to suit a particular need of its owner.

Atchisson wants it made clear that he doesn't do conversions, custom work or small limited-production runs. Handguns discussed here are simply his own pistols for his personal use. Some are for carrying, others for target work. In the 1950s and 1960s, Max Atchisson was an NRA Registered Target Shooter in the three-gun matches — .22 rimfire, centerfire and .45. He shot masters scores at the Los Angeles police range. After reaching his personal best, he was able to increase his scores by improving his equipment.

One pistol Atchisson uses is a highly modified AMT .380

AMT's standard .380 9mm Back Up weighs 18 ounces. The factory five-round magazine has a finger loop .

This is the AMT Back Up after Atchisson's treatment. It weighs 15 ounces and the magazine holds six rounds.

Back Up pistol. Originally an 18-ounce gun, it now weighs 15 ounces, and all the sharp angles are gone. This makes for less felt recoil despite the lighter weight, just as a rounded solid recoil pad is more comfortable than one with those sharp corners.

Most of the weight reduction came from the slide, where a long section was removed from the top just aft of the front sight. This not only lightened the gun, but greatly facilitated ejection by providing more exit space for the ejected case. The safety is cut at an angle and provided with ridges to give a positive contact surface when moving it from safe to fire position. The result is much more reliable and fast to handle than was the factory peg-shaped safety button.

The Back Up grip has a series of straight serrations for the thumb and index finger to grasp, because Atchisson carries the gun in his patented Shirt Tail Holster, which carries the gun grip upward inside his waistband. This unique holster design is a fast-to-use and extraordinarily concealable system for carrying small pistols. The sides of the pistol magazine are cut out. The bottom finger loop on the magazine was removed, and the bottom of the magazine follower ground. The bottom of the slide was rounded for the top cartridge. The magazine now holds six rounds instead of five. The guide spring rod is drilled hollow, and inside the grip there are a series of weight-reducing holes.

Atchisson felt both the altered and unaltered guns in this AMT design had insufficient hammer spring pressure for reliable firing. A hammer booster spring was added to both guns which stopped the problem.

Atchisson's personal .25 Bauer was cut from 10 ounces to 7 1/2 ounces. The trigger was skeletonized and a hole drilled through the frame. The rear end of the slide was made triangular, the magazine hollowed out, holes drilled under the grip.

The designer's Smith & Wesson Model 52 target model had its magazine altered for increased capacity so that it could be used in combat matches. Originally equipped with a five-round magazine, the magazine follower was altered and lowered by silver-soldering a piece of spring steel to it. This raised the magazine feed lips so they hit the bottom of the slide. The top of the feed lips then were stoned to relieve contact.

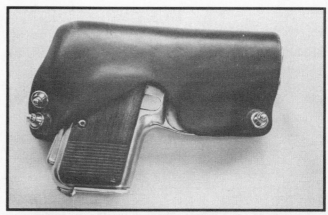

Tucked inside the waistband, the altered gun is carried upside down in Atchisson's patented Shirt Tail Holster.

This .25 Bauer was lightened by removing excess metal.

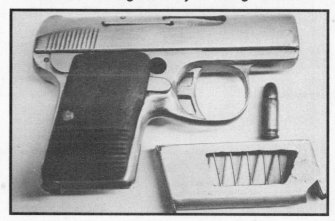

High Standard's Model G .380 pistol (right) received extensive modification by Atchisson, including the addition of a heavy compensated target barrel.

Above is the Luger without Atchisson conversion unit. At left, the .22 barrel insert has been installed and the .22 magazine sits inside the standard 9mm magazine.

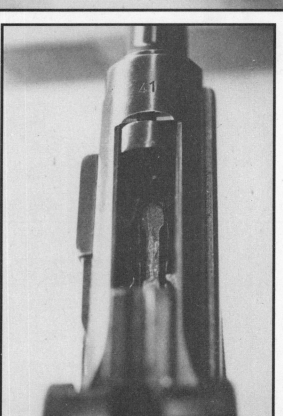

The magazine now holds eight rounds, plus one in the chamber. To get eight rounds into the magazine, Max Atchisson has altered the .38 Special cartridge fired in this gun to semi-rimmed. Called the .38 Special ARR (Atchisson Reduced Rim), the .440 rim diameter of the .38 Special is reduced to .409-.410-inch. In order to keep the brass from getting mixed up with regular .38 Specials, the designer paints the back of the cases black.

Atchisson's personal Model G .380 High Standard pistol was modified for centerfire matches. The barrel was turned down and a tube put on it along with target sights and a compensator.

A .22 conversion can be installed on any .45 Colt ACP easily. However, the original 1930 blow-back Colt Ace lacked sufficient power to operate the slide. The Ace even had to have a weak hammer spring for proper functioning. A roller was used to reduce hammer friction, and the design required a frame without an ejector.

Max Atchisson milled a place in a .22 Ace slide for the ejector and cut out the top of the slide as is done with a Beretta

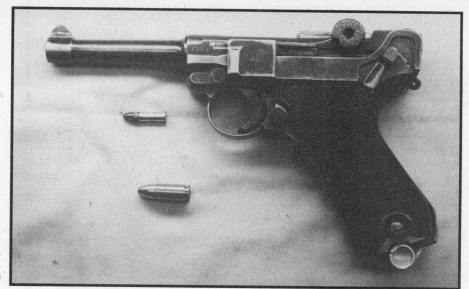

This is the 9mm Luger with Atchisson's .22 conversion unit.

The .38 S&W Wadcutter (left) was modified to the semi-rimmed ARR for the converted M52.

pistol to lighten it. He made his own front sight, a flat inclined plane, and mounted a S&W M52 target rear sight with the edges rounded so they wouldn't snag in a holster. This is his favorite outdoor carry gun. It is also extraordinarily accurate. When I fired it, the little gun put all of its bullets in one ragged hole.

This gun is a true blow-back, unlike guns made with floating chambers. Some folks claim the floating chamber jump gives recoil similar to that of the .45, but others feel it's more like a cracked baseball bat. One thing is sure. This is one of the easiest guns with which to shoot a tight group. This is one of the designer's favorite pistols. His gun uses Service Ace magazines. The pistol was given a baked-on molybdenum disulphide finish six years before this became a standard practice. This is a true conversion that will fit any gun!

The .32 S&W Long conversion for the M41 S&W comes next. Atchisson bought the .22 infinitive M41 originally in 1958 for competition shooting. About 1961 or 1962, Smith & Wesson came out with a bull barrel for the gun and this owner bought one. He promptly fired 10 rounds at 50 yards and got a score of 99 on slow fire. This sold him on the M41 bull barrel.

Atchisson had the original model with the long barrel and came up with the idea of converting it to .32 for use in centerfire matches. He bought two extra magazines and an extra slide.

To convert rimfire to centerfire, he closed the front part of the firing pin hole with a threaded plug. The plug was ground flush with the bolt face and staked. A new centerfire firing pin

The converted Smith & Wesson M52 Target Pistol is shown below with Atchisson's customized magazine.

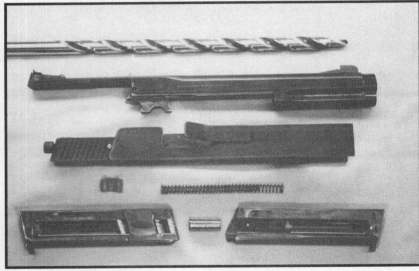

The .45 Colt that was transformed into a .22 by Atchisson. At left is the .32 S&W long conversion kit for the M41 S&W with the special bit used to bore the original .22 barrel prior to relining.

hole was drilled from the face of the bolt, upward at an angle to intersect with the original .22 firing pin hole.

The firing pin was altered by bending it in an arc shape to follow the center-firing pin hole. A rangekeeper fired the pistol and later told the Smith & Wesson rep about it. The sales rep knew there was no room for a centerfire firing pin, and declared such a conversion was impossible. The rangemaster replied, "But Atchisson has it! I fired the gun!"

Atchisson had silver-soldered one-eighth-inch steel plates to each side of the slide to give it the necessary weight. Finding the retaining pin inadequate, he installed a larger-diameter, high-carbon steel crosspin. The magazine, of course, was highly modified. The center was cut out and the lips cut away to fit the .32.

The recoil spring guide rod was removed, but Atchisson used the S&W operating spring, adding an additional spring on a smaller-diameter guide rod. This spring is wound in the opposite direction from the first, as all nested springs should be.

A nylon buffer was added to prevent the heavy slide from battering the gun's frame. An extension was added to the ejector so the .32 brass would eject properly. A deflector was added over the ejection port so the empty cases were dropped closeby for convenient recovery.

For the barrel, the designer — in this case, redesigner — bought a seven-sixteenths-inch, one-foot-long drill and had the end cut for a half-inch to .216, so it would follow the lands of the original .22 barrel when the barrel was drilled through.

The barrel was lined with a section of Russian Mosin Nagant barrel. The front sight mount was modified to make a flange that would fit the compensator mounting hole of the

At left is the M41 Smith & Wesson .22 Target Pistol. Atchisson rebuilt the auto into a .32 for use in centerfire competition. Below left is the M41, converted to a .32.

M41 barrel. The Russian barrel just happened to be the correct diameter for the .32.

To mount the .32 conversion unit, Atchisson put the operating springs together and positioned them in their hole. Lining up the end with the slide, he installed the slide.

"Drop the buffer in with the radius to the front and the flat part against the frame. Cock the slide and bring the barrel down and lock it," Atchisson says. "That's all there is to it."

Max Atchisson was shooting a Colt Python in centerfire matches when he noticed the hammer was touching his thumb. This sometimes resulted in the gun shooting two distinct horizontal groups. Grinding the hammer spur away so it cleared his thumb solved that problem.

To speed up the action, desirable for accuracy, the whole back end of the hammer was cut away. This speeded the action so much that snap caps were required for dry-fire practice to prevent broken firing pins. His target scores improved dramatically, however.

The double-action feature was removed to cut down on parts weight, since the gun was being used single-action only. This also helped speed up the gun. The front sight was cut square for a better sight picture.

The inventive shooter also has made a .22 conversion for a Luger pistol which fires from an open bolt and has a magazine that inserts inside the standard P-08 magazine. There are some details he was reluctant to see in print, so I will not discuss this gun at length.

Collectively, the guns covered offer an idea of the originality and practicality of Max Atchisson's inventions. He is proof that true inventors are born, not made. Inventing is a compulsion for the truly gifted inventor. With 23 patents, Max Atchisson is not only gifted, but productive, as well.

Atchisson is known for his .22 conversion kits for the M16 and his full-automatic shotgun designs. He specializes in recoil-cancellated designs in his combat weapons, so they are controllable in full-auto fire. Controllability is a factor that is receiving less and less attention in most new designs, as engineers slap a three-shot burst device on the gun and forget about it. A three-shot burst device can get you killed in combat when you are trying to hose down the enemy with full-auto fire!

Atchisson is a combat veteran having served in Korea as a machine gunner on a Browning M1919A4. He also was a machine gun instructor for the Marine Corps.

Prior to becoming a gun designer, he was a gauge designer. This is not uncommon. Hiram Maxim, John Pederson, John C. Garand, Bill Ruger and Eugene Stoner all were gauge designers before beginning gun design work.

Max Atchisson's designs are practical and well thought out. When he invents a full-auto shotgun for a soldier walking point, he knows from his own experience what walking point entails. The gun will be reliable and recoil cancelling for controllability. Basically, the shotgun will work.

Among the annals of gun designers Max Atchisson has proved to be among the most competent and well-rounded. More will be heard of him in the future.

Atchisson, the master gun innovator, outfitted the Colt Gold Cup (below) with a weight to reduce muzzle rise.

To boost the accuracy of the Python target revolver (below), Atchisson cut away the back of the hammer.

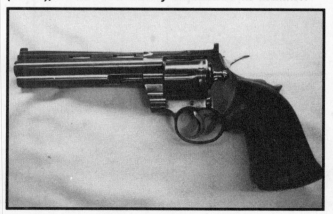

BOWEN CLASSIC ARMS .500 MAGNUM

By Hal Swiggett

This .50 Caliber Prototype Started A Trend!

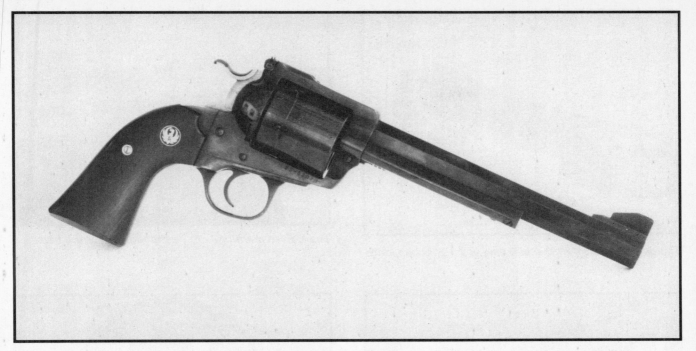

The .500 magnum is built on Ruger's Bisley New Model Super Blackhawk. The barrel is 7 1/2 inches long. Below, the first .500 magnum created by Bowen still has the original .44 magnum stamp. Bowen now removes these markings.

IF BIG is better, Hamilton Bowen's .500 Magnum Bisley five-shot single-action is the best. It is built on Bill Ruger's Bisley Model .44 magnum Super Blackhawk, and it feeds on 425-grain hard-cast .50-caliber bullets. These are encouraged to exit the 7 1/2-inch barrel via the thrust of 27.5 grains of H110 set off with large rifle primers from Winchester. Velocity is 1300+ feet per second.

Cases are hand-made from .348 Winchester brass cut to 1.4 inches in length, then worked into revolver status. I can't describe the process in detail, because there are a lot of things I can't/don't/won't do. Making cartridge brass is near top of that list.

The load, 27.5 grains of H110, is Hamilton's. Primers by Winchester are my addition. I've used them in hundreds, more like thousands, of rifle and handgun loads for many years and found no reason to change.

Initially, my bullets for this .500 magnum came from a source that has since dried up. They were listed as the 420-grain SWC (semi-wadcutter). They shot well. My limited supply of 150 disappeared rather soon. A letter ordering more brought forth no response. A special delivery letter provided identical results.

About that time, I met Roger Barnes (BRP, Inc., 1210 Alexander Road, Colorado Springs, CO 80909). I've been shooting his 425-grain SWC ever since and they look to be from the same mould as those first bullets. I also use a lot of

Barnes' .451-inch 305-grain bullets. These do a super job in both .45 Colt and .454 Casull. Actually, more are used in the .454, though a couple of my .45 Colt SAs see frequent use.

Since building this first .500 magnum, Bowen has upgraded its workmanship in that several changes have been made. It's still the same gun, but appearance-wise there are differences. Though not encouraged (in fact, just the opposite — it is discouraged) there is a .500 Maximum. It's the same five-gun as my .500 magnum but with a stretched case. The .500 Maximum case is 1.6 inches in length, using .348 Winchester brass. Only a couple have been made. Recoil, according to Hamilton, is horrendous.

His favorite of the moment is Bowen Classic Arms .50 Special. It still uses .348 Winchester brass, but it's cut to .44 Special length and loaded in like manner. Velocity is 800-1000 fps. Bowen describes it as quite mild to shoot. It, too, is a five-shot and built on the Ruger Redhawk action.

Most popular in his catalog is the .475. It can be built on either action — Redhawk or Blackhawk — and its base brass is conventional, traditional, age-old .45-70. It's a five-shot, as are the others.

Back to the subject of the moment — my prototype .500 magnum: those 425-grain bullets run right at 1350 fps. Earlier my mention of velocity was 1300+/-. For a reason. No two guns are going to produce identical results. Barrel length is the

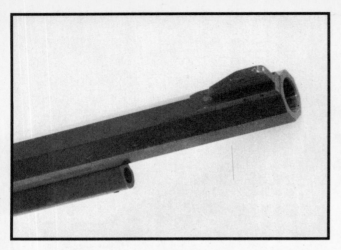

The octagon barrel of the .500 mag is 7 1/2 inches long.

The Bowen markings are on the left side of the barrel.

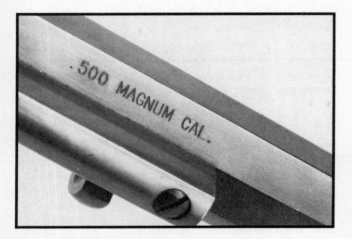

On the right side of the barrel is the caliber designation.

The .500 magnums are made from .348 Winchester brass.

predominant factor, but not the only factor. My point in bringing this up — please, read this carefully — is that this particular gun is producing, at 1350 fps with its 425-grain bullet, exactly the same velocity as Remington's factory-loaded 240-grain lead gas check .44 magnum. For this cartridge, Remington's current catalog lists 1350 fps, yet my bullet is 185 grains heavier!

The .500 magnum — the one here on my desk as this is written — weighs 49 ounces on my postal scale. Ruger's current catalog lists both their Super Blackhawk .44 magnum in blue or stainless at approximately 48 ounces.

Bowen Classic Arms starts with an over-the-counter Ruger revolver. Both the barrel and cylinder become history immediately upon arrival.

An octagonal barrel is installed. Mine measures .79-inch across the flats as it comes out of the frame and tapers to .73-inch at the muzzle.

The left side flat reads: BOWEN CLASSIC ARMS CORP. The other side is .500 MAGNUM CAL. All letters are the same in size.

Cylinder wall thickness is .072-inch in the thinnest area. Bolt cuts are almost centered between chambers. There are no flutes on the cylinder which is reamed and chambered in Bowen's shop. The cylinder pin, as might be expected, is held in place via a set screw. This ensures it will be around a while.

The grip is Ruger all the way, requiring no change whatever. The same goes for the rear sight. Up front, there is a 1.380-inch base set flush with the muzzle. Pinned to it is the sight blade of .120-inch width. This is grooved so as to be totally lacking in reflection.

Initially, the front sight was a problem for me. It wasn't of the correct height for me, at least. A brief trip back to BCA solved the problem. With the rear sight screwed down tight it prints my load dead on at 25 yards and again at 100 yards.

Trigger pull breaks, with no discernible movement, at 38 ounces. It's as clean as breaking glass.

Admittedly, .500 magnum single-actions aren't for everyone. Also admittedly, I'm long-known for wanting and shooting the biggest I can get my hands on. I have been guilty of shooting jackrabbits with this behemoth, along with a few cottontails. Head shots at the 10 to 20 yards usually necessary are a cinch and, truthfully, there is little head to pull off after such a shot.

Over the years, several exotics and whitetail deer have

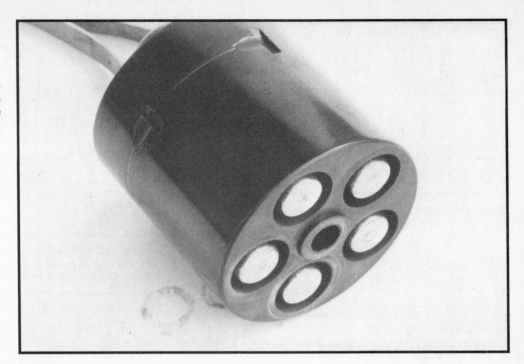

The large .500 magnum chambers are filled to the fullest when stuffed with 425-grain semi-wadcutters.

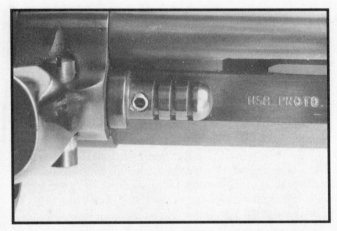

To be certain the cylinder pin stays in place during the firing of the .500, Bowen locks it in with a set screw.

One of the author's 320-grain .44 magnum handloads (left) is overshadowed by a 425-grain .500 magnum.

fallen to those 425-grain semi-wadcutters. In spite of its recoil, my .500 magnum truly is a fun gun to shoot.

About the man who built it: Hamilton Bowen is the founder of Bowen Classic Arms Corporation, a small company located in the hills of East Tennessee. After completing undergraduate studies in history and English he moved on to the gunsmithing school at Trinidad State Junior College in Trinidad, Colorado. Completing this course sent him back to Tennessee where he opened his own operation.

Bowen's principal stock in trade is caliber conversion barrel and cylinder work, basically on Ruger handguns. He is quick to point out that there is nothing wrong with Ruger handguns. Just the opposite, they are the only revolvers built to handle what he does to them. This does not mean his cartridges develop more pressure, because they do not, but the larger diameter and considerably more weight of bullets used

definitely develop more recoil. That he uses Ruger revolvers is a compliment to the product turned out by Bill Ruger.

Bowen makes conversion cylinders for five- or six-shot and from .22 through .50 on both single- and double-action revolvers. Barrels for single-actions can be supplied with integral scope bases and in octagonal or ovate-ribbed contour. L-frame-style barrels with grooved ribs and integral front sight bases — with or without integral scope mounting — can be fabricated for double-action revolvers. Along with general

Though the bullet design is slightly different, shown for comparison is a .44 magnum (left) and a .500 magnum.

Above, author's magnum has these special markings, designating it as the first of Bowen's .500 magnums. Below, the author is proud of his number one Bowen.

action tuning, accurizing, hand-finishing and detailing of single actions is a specialty.

Bowen Classic Arms also provides a full complement of services for Ruger .22 autos. This includes trigger work, rebarreling and sights.

A visit to the BCA shop reveals the usual lathe, and milling machine, along with many other tools and tooling. Absent is buffing equipment. There is none. Metal finishing is done by hand.

For those seeking additional custom work, BCA offers — among several others — .22 rimfire conversions for the Ruger Security-Six, plus Damascus barrels compatible with most single-action revolvers.

One full-out custom job was just completed for me. Hamilton Bowen took a five-inch Model 610 stainless steel Smith & Wesson double-action and turned it into the sweetest .38-40 you've ever seen. Showing it to another top gun writer recently brought forth the comment, "Man, I do believe you have something here!" I do too.

Other Bowen Classic Arms conversions that have passed through my hands have been another Ruger single-action .50 and a double-action .50. Both were five-shots, and both performed exactly as Bowen told me they would. Neither kicked like the one that lives here with me. On the other hand, one didn't have to ask whether they went off, either. But what else can you expect from .50 caliber 425-grain bullets? Something has to give — and it won't be BCAs converted revolver.

Incidentally, Hamilton Bowen is president of the American Pistolsmith Guild, which has put together a fine little 32-page, 5-1/2x8-1/2, booklet titled *Pistol & Revolver Safety Handbook*. It is thorough on all aspects of handling pistols and revolvers. Included are dry-firing procedures for both centerfire and rimfire handguns. Exploded views and parts lists for Ruger semi-automatic, Colt Model 1911A1, Smith & Wesson revolvers, plus the S&W Combat Masterpiece, Browning Hi-Power Model 35, Colt Single Action Army and Ruger Single-Six revolver are also included. The price, including shipping and handling, is $3.50. Send check or money order to: American Pistolsmith Guild, 26 Novak Dr., Stafford, VA 22554.

Two-and-a-half months from now, as this is put together, I will be in South Africa on my sixth safari. All of these outings

were with handguns except that first. I was told I had to include a rifle in my battery for that initial safari. I did. It took one trophy, one of the better ever taken. It is high up in the record book, right near the top. And it could have been taken with any of my handguns.

For the first time my .500 magnum is making the flight to Johannesburg. I'm not at all sure why it hasn't been there before, but to date my handguns have all been scoped. This time two will be. But, the .500 magnum is going along for the ride and just might see some action. That it will handle whatever it is asked to do is without doubt. And without a scope.

A brochure is available for $3 from Bowen Classic Arms Corp., P.O. Box 67, Louisville, TN 37777. It will give you all the details of work that can be done by BCA. A footnote: nothing comes out of BCA in a hurry so don't — make that *do not* — get impatient. BCAs work is the finest, and nothing is done in a hurry.

Back to the stamping on those flats of my .500 magnum's octagonal barrel: The bottom flat, right in front of the frame, in letters about half the size of those on both sides, reads: HSB PROTO..500M. Since it was number one I asked Hamilton to put it on there someplace. With his name. That's as close as I could get. HSB (Hamilton S. Bowen) PROTO (first) .500M (.500 magnum).

Now you know why I am so high on this particular Bowen Classic Arms .500 magnum. It all started with the one on my desk!

SECTION EIGHT:

A TOUCH OF

NOSTALGIA

REVIEWING A VETERAN

By Jim Dickson

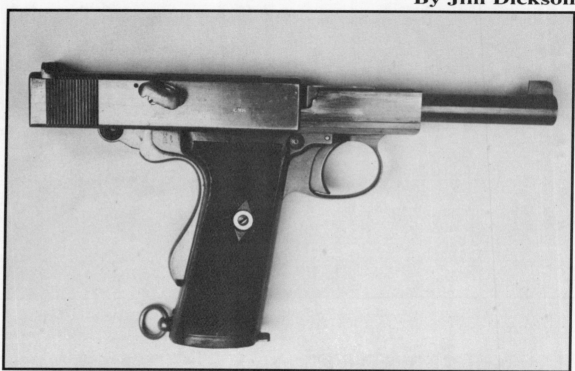

Here's the Webley & Scott Self-Loading Pistol with slide withdrawn and barrel down in the frame.

WHAT WOULD you think if someone told you of a standard military automatic in .45 caliber that has less recoil and muzzle jump than a .22 automatic? Add the fact that it has a recoil spring that will not lose strength from being compressed, and needs no replacement because of loss of tension due to age. Further, this mainspring is less prone to breakage than other types.

Most people's first reaction is that such a gun is impossible and could never be. Well, truth is that this handgun has been around since before WWI. I am speaking of the .455 Webley & Scott Self-Loading Pistol.

Designed by W. J. Whiting, F.T. Murry and J. Carter, the Webley auto is the only fully successful recoil-cancelling

pistol design of which I am aware. Unlocking the mechanism converts the upward jump of the barrel into a downward unlocking movement, effectively cancelling muzzle jump and recoil. There is no finer pistol for rapid-fire shooting than this jewel. There is virtually no perceptible movement of the muzzle when firing. Only the noise and slide movement let one know the shot is off. The gun is instantly ready for a second shot and the sight picture is barely disturbed by the movement of the slide.

The trigger pull has no creep and is as perfect as any ever made. After all, these same workmen also made the Best Quality doubles for which England is so famous. This perfect trigger pull aids in rapid fire, enabling the gun to be emptied

The Webley .455 Is A Collector Item Today, But It Was The Best Of Its Day!

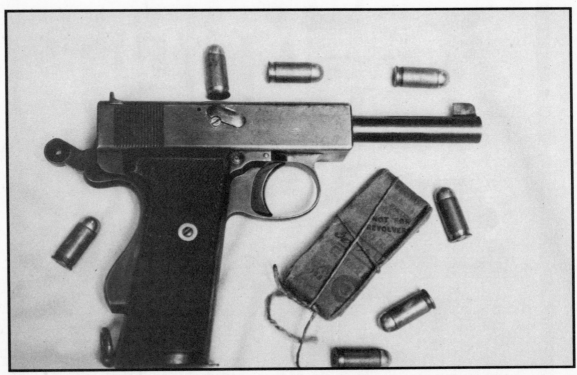

This is a WW I Navy issue Webley with its original ammo. The pistol is shown cocked. The grip safety is the only safety on this model and it proves adequate. It was made in December 1914.

as though fully automatic. But there is no fully automatic pistol that can put as many hits on target as fast as the rapid, aimed shots from the Webley.

The pistol has a boxy, angular appearance that looks clumsy, but proves quite practical. When the arm is extended full length with the wrist straight, the pistol is found to be pointing accurately at the target.

The wide, shallow V rear sight and blade front are unusually large for a pistol of its era, circa 1906. These help facilitate a quick sight picture, for the British soldier of that time was not likely to be a proficient instinct shooter. Still, this gun is perfectly at home with rapid-fire instinct shooting.

To my knowledge, this handgun's lack of muzzle jump and recoil never has been acknowledged in print, so it is unlikely many American shooters have ever spent any time with the funny-looking foreign gun, particularly since both the gun and the ammo for it always have been less than common.

The right grip of the Webley encases a powerful V-spring

that serves as the recoil spring. The advantages of such a leaf spring over a coil spring are significant. The leaf spring can stay compressed indefinitely without losing strength, as the coil spring will. Unlike the coil spring, the leaf spring can flex indefinitely without losing strength. A properly made and polished leaf spring is much less likely to break than a coil spring.

The only objection to the V-spring was that, if the right grip was broken, the spring would bite your hand as it flexed. In practice, though, there were few broken grips — if any. It's one thing to chip a hard rubber grip, but quite another to break it away completely. I can find no record of this ever occurring in combat. Had it posed a genuine problem, a steel plate could have been added to the right side grip under the hard rubber, but no request for such a reinforcement was made.

Functioning of the pistol is as precise and workmanlike as you would expect of a gun of such exquisite pre-WWI quality. Grasping the pistol depresses the grip safety, which makes the

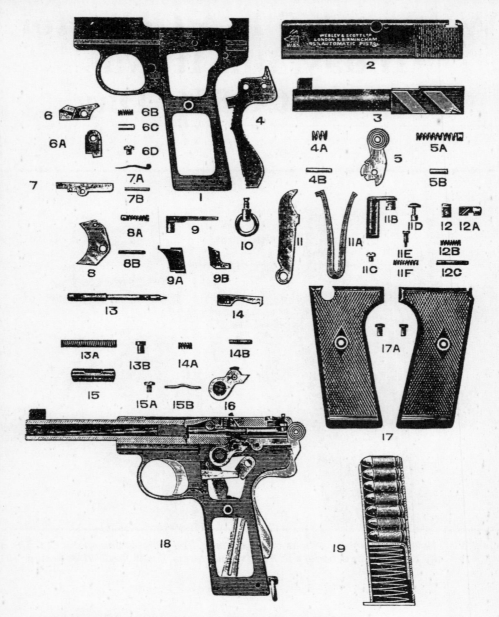

DESCRIPTION OF COMPONENT PARTS.

1   Body
2   Breech
3   Barrel
4   Safe
4a Safe Spring
4b Safe Axis
5   Hammer
5a Hammer Spring
5b Hammer Axis
6   Sear
6a Sear Tail
6b Sear Spring
6c Sear Axis
6d Sear Screw
7   Holding open Lever
7a Holding open Lever Spring
7b Holding open Lever Axis
8   Trigger

8a Trigger Spring & Plungers
8b Trigger Axis
9   Trigger Auxiliary Lever
9a Trigger Auxiliary Lever
        Cover Plate
9b Trigger Auxiliary Lever
        Tripping Lever
10 Swivel
11 Recoil Lever
11a Recoil Spring
11b Recoil Lever Bar & Breech
        Stop
11c Breech Stop Screw
11d Recoil Lever Stop
11e Recoil Lever Stop Screw
11f Recoil Lever Stop Spring
12 Magazine Bolt
12a Magazine Bolt Thumbpiece

12b Magazine Bolt Spring
12c Magazine Bolt Retaining
        Pin
13 Striker
13a Striker Spring
13b Striker Retaining Piece
14 Extractor
14a Extractor Spring
14b Extractor Axis
15 Back Sight
15a Back Sight Screw
15b Back Sight Spring
16 Breech Releasing Lever
17 Stock
17a Stock Screws
18 Section of Pistol
19 Magazine

sear lever touch the trigger lever. When the trigger is pressed, the trigger lever engages the sear lever to rotate the sear out of engagement with the hammer, which now falls against the firing pin, firing the weapon.

The barrel and slide are locked at the moment of firing by a locking shoulder on top of the barrel that engages the slide. As the barrel and slide recoil to the rear, the barrel moves down two diagonal grooves on each side of the barrel, unlocking the barrel from the slide and neatly canceling upward flip of the barrel with a downward unlocking motion. This also transmits the remaining recoil into the almost 90-degree angle of the frame's grip, where it is absorbed unnoticed, and straight into the arm of the shooter without any tendency to bounce the gun about.

The barrel strikes its receiver stop and the slide continues rearward, enabling the top-mounted extractor to draw the cartridge from the chamber wherein the ejector sends it on its way. The powerful V recoil spring is attached to a slide bar. It won't take being pushed around any farther, so it snaps everything smartly back into place.

The .455 SL cartridge was designed to provide maximum stopping power. The blunt 224-grain full-metal-jacket bullet travels at 710 feet per second.

The system has a positive disconnector by which the barrel forces the trigger lever away from the sear lever when the barrel is unlocked, thus preventing firing. The barrel must be fully locked in battery for the gun to fire.

The gun's magazine of heavy 20-gauge steel is noteworthy for its strong feed lips. Its two catch positions make the Webley the only automatic capable of being used as a single-shot pistol with the magazine held in reserve for emergencies. While this may sound stupid to today's theorists and practical shooters, the fact remains that there are times when it not only

is eminently practical, it can offer a life-saving advantage. In Korea, the Chinese communist soldiers often waited until they heard the *ping* of the M1 Garand's clip being ejected to attack. A miscreant counting how many shots have been fired by the Webley pistoleer would be in for a shocking surprise if he tried to rush the pistol holder.

One simply presses the magazine catch in the grip and rams the magazine all the way in to begin rapid firing. This double-position magazine catch business is a serious feature for one who knows how and when to use it. Men who have used a pistol extensively in close-quarters combat often consider time spent reloading under fire among life's hairiest moments.

When using the pistol with the magazine disconnected, by locking it in the first catch notch, the slide remains open after each shot. The cartridge is loaded singly in the barrel and the slide release lever depressed, sending the slide home.

True to its revolver heritage, the Webley firm did not add any safety other than a grip safety. Corporate feeling was that manual safeties could get someone killed before they were flipped off. The Webley automatic was every bit as safe as the Webley revolver to carry and use, they contended, and that was that. Webley even recommended the gun be carried cocked.

The Webley auto has few parts and these are notably massive and strong. Reliability is better than that of the Webley revolver and better than that of many of today's 9mm automatics.

The .455 SL cartridge fires a 224-grain full-metal-jacket bullet at 710 feet per second. The bullet is quite blunt, like the .600 Nitro Express, to give maximum impact transmission for stopping power. It was developed from the 1901 Webley-Fosberry revolver cartridge. The semi-rimmed case allows proper functioning in a magazine repeater, yet the cartridge can be fired in the standard Webley revolver in an emergency, though the reverse is not possible due to the full rim on the revolver cartridge. This one-way interchangeability went a long way toward placating logisticians' concerns over a new cartridge.

The cartridge and the gun provided acceptable accuracy out to 200 yards, so the Royal Horse Artillery bought these pistols with a shoulder stock and special sights adjustable to 200 yards.

Like the Mauser and Luger pistols, the stocked Webley was a success, except for the excessive muzzle blast common to all stocked pistols. A five-inch barrel is loud when that close to your ears, regardless of caliber. Ear protection in that era was neglected, so the problem helped bring an end to the handy pistol carbines used by so many nations.

Had they bothered to fit Maxim silencers of that era to the various stocked pistols, the users would have been much happier. Unfortunately, however, the intimidating value of a loud muzzle blast on both men and horses was greatly valued

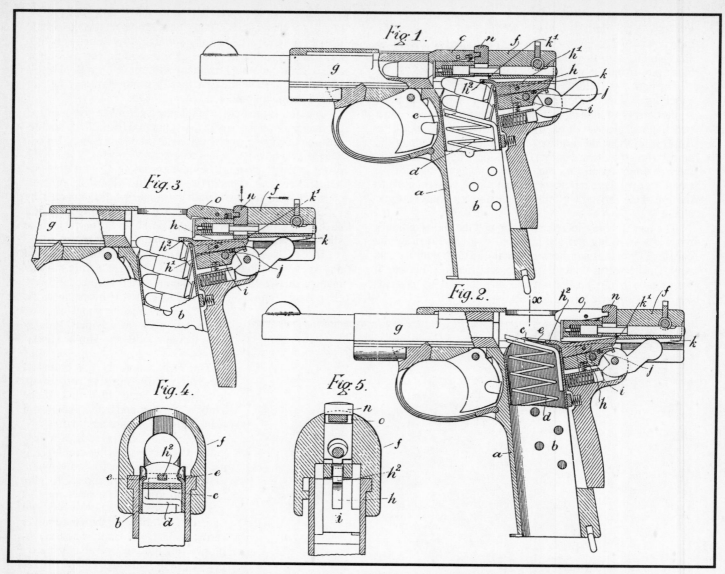

The design of the .455 Webley & Scott is simple. Its boxy appearance seems clumsy, but the gun is reliable.

by military theorists of the day. The U.S. Army's famed Pedersen devices which converted a M1903 Springfield into a semi-auto of about .32 ACP power, ultimately were ordered destroyed in 1931, after the Army failed to find a use for them.

History of this pistol begins in 1898, when the first crude design for the Mars auto pistol was submitted to Webley by an English inventor, one Hugh Gabbett-Fairfax. T.W. Webley saw the wave of the future in the automatic and backed the design for the powerful Mars pistol. Unfortunately, it was not successful.

Undaunted, T.W. Webley encouraged the head of his pistol design staff, William John Whiting, to develop automatic pistols. Whiting had been brought up since his youth by Henry Webley and was considered the most experienced and finest handgun designer in the British Isles.

In 1903, the first Webley .455 auto prototypes were made. This gun fired the standard .455 fully rimmed revolver cartridge. The early mechanism was totally different from that of

the final model. It utilized a conventional coil spring mounted beneath the barrel.

The locking system was composed of two catch arms that were unlocked by the rearward one-eighth-inch travel of the barrel from engagement with the barrel and breech block.

Although unsuccessful, this gun led to the 1904 model. This gun introduced the Webley V-type recoil spring. The V-spring was chosen as the best answer to the problems of making a recoil spring and had nothing to do with being a mere continuation of Webley revolver design philosophy, as some have charged. Locking in this version was by a vertically sliding bolt. Fit and finish of the M1904 was on par with the Best Quality shotguns of the day.

During development of the M1904, the cartridge utilized was changed from the standard rimmed revolver round to a modified rimmed cartridge with a narrow extraction groove, then to the final version, the .455 SL.

The 1906 model approached final form of the design. This

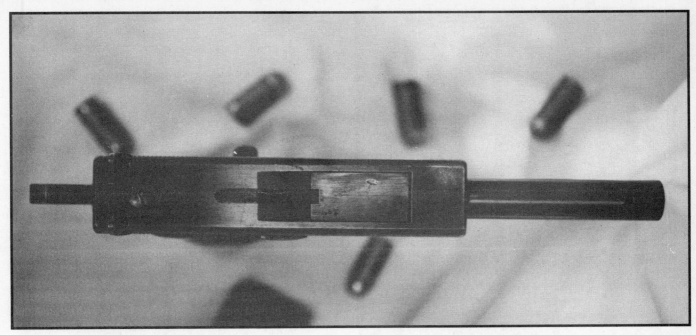

This view of the Webley shows the positive extractor with its wide engagement area. The gun is void of ornamentation.

barrel was locked with three ribs on each side.

In 1909, the design was perfected. Among the changes, the inclined grooves on the barrel were reduced to two on each side. A grip safety — or back safe, as they say in England — developed in 1908 was added. The slide release stud was positioned in the most handy place, and the hammer safety was dropped as superfluous now that there was a grip-type safe.

The new pistol withstood the most severe tests the factory could devise, and passed with top marks. It was with great pride that the Webley .455 automatic pistol was introduced publicly at the annual shareholders meeting in 1909. The first military contract came when the Royal Navy adopted it in 1912 as the "Pistol Self-Loading .455 Mark I."

In April, 1912, the Ely Brothers were contacted to produce ammunition for the Royal Navy. Ammo was ready for delivery by June, 1912 — considerably ahead of the pistols, as it turned out. Only after getting a government contract could Webley afford to tool up for mass production. There were the usual delays in bringing out a new gun, and the first delivery of 934 pistols was not made to the Navy until June, 1913. This led to the gun being referred to as the "1913 Model," despite the fact that it was adopted officially in 1912.

To add to the confusion among arms collectors, there exists a limited number of pistols made before the mass production run for the Royal Navy. These are stamped simply ".455 Automatic Pistol," and have wood grips, a plain hammer and fixed sights. Most Navy pistols have sights adjustable for windage by turning a sight screw, but some don't. A few of the Navy pistols have an extra safety on the hammer. Naval contract guns are marked "Pistol, Self-Loading .455 Mark I 1913."

Repeated testing convinced the Army the gun was accurate enough to warrant adjustable sighting up to 200 yards, but the

The rear sight of the pistol is adjustable for windage.

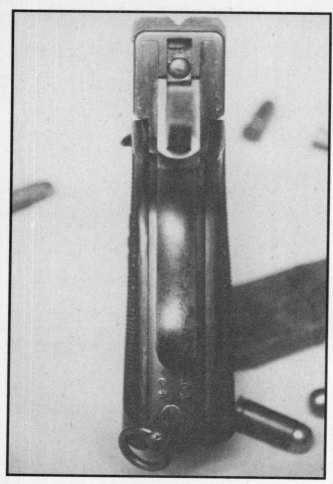

Viewed from the rear, the rear sight presents a shallow "V" which ends in a "U" notch. When the grip safety was added in 1908, the hammer safety was deleted.

To provide maximum stopping power, the .455 cartridge has a blunt shape like the .600 Nitro.

Army order did not materialize immediately, as hoped. The Army gun was finally approved on April 26, 1915, for issue to the Royal Flying Corps as "Pistol, Self-Loading, .455, Mark I, No. 2."

Shoulder stocks, each made from a flat, three-fourths-inch board, were designed to be used with the pistol held in as normal a manner as possible with the stock high under the arm, and the left hand over the stock, rather like a Lewis machine gunner.

The sights are adjustable from 50 to 200 yards in 50-yard increments. Pressing on the spring-loaded button enables the sight to be adjusted by turning the button. Releasing the button locks the sight in place at the desired setting. A hammer safety also is added to this model.

Both the British Army and Navy used the weapon in WWI extensively. It had been adopted by the Royal Navy as the official hand weapon for Royal Naval units and Royal Marines, so it was quite in the thick of things. The .455 SL cartridge was belatedly approved "For Land," meaning for Army use in 1916. In WWII, the British bought 13,510 Colt M1911A1 automatics in .455 SL caliber.

The end of WWI, with its financial austerity, brought an

end to British military interest in new automatics. The Navy had bought 5,500 pistols, and the Army's Royal Flying Corps had bought 1,500. There had been 2,500 civilian sales as well, and many of those had gone to servicemen. This is not many compared to the number of .455 revolvers at hand, so with no new funds for procurement, there were no new orders. Surviving military guns soldiered on until WWII.

Today's shooter of the .455 SL is faced with a major ammunition problem. Kynoch is out of the ammunition business. Cases have been made successfully by taking .45 Auto Rim cases and turning a semi-rim of .048-inch thickness and an extractor groove in it. The case is also shortened by .02-inch. Semi-rim diameter is .500-inch and overall length of the cartridge with 224-grain bullet should be 1.230-inch. If any longer, it won't function through the magazine reliably.

Some years ago, I obtained a spare barrel for my Webley and had the chamber relined to .45 ACP so I could shoot it. As long as cartridge length is not over 1.230 inches all is well, but standard 230-grain .45 ACP is too long and often hangs up in the gun. Since this is a heavier load than the gun was designed for, I cannot recommend this practice or take responsibility for those who would duplicate it. Still, I have had no problems

In the ready-to-fire mode, the Webley presents a totally practical profile that is maintained in its performance. The pistol fits comfortably in the shooter's hand and the grip safety well pronounced to provide positive engagement.

The double magazine catch permits the Webley to be fired as a single loader when the magazine is engaged by the top notch, while holding the magazine in reserve.

with it so long as the overall cartridge length of 1.230 inches is not exceeded.

The chances of finding a spare Webley .455 barrel today are pretty slim, and one never should alter a rare collector piece's original barrel.

There is a new hope for would-be Webley shooters, however. Westley Richards of Birmingham, England, has ordered production of this caliber beginning in January 1993. This means we should be able to shoot the proper ammo in these grand, old guns once again.

For those who want to carry their Webleys, the gun fits perfectly in the WWII soft leather Luger and P-38 German holsters. Those wishing to carry it on a daily basis will find that Roy Baker Leather Goods (P.O. Box 893, Magnolia, AR, 71753) will make one of their pancake holsters for any gun you have. They may need to borrow the gun to fit it, but Wayne Tompkins never has shied from custom work.

If you are going to carry this piece, make sure you get some of the new ammo. I have jealously guarded my supply of the last Kynoch ammo for serious shooting should I need a pistol with the ultimate in rapid-fire capability. The ACP barrel is for playing; this original .455 SL ammo and barrel are for serious use.

While I favor a M1911A1 for every day use, I am not blind to the value of the specialized pistol, be it a huge Howda pistol for point-blank defense against dangerous game, or the rapid-fire Webley, the fastest-shooting, aimed-fire, big-bore pistol ever!

THE FIRST .44 MAGNUM SINGLE-ACTION

By J. Burke

AS THE OLD Trailways bus lumbered northwest out of San Antonio, I had the rear seat all to myself. Beside me was a leather valise that had belonged to my grandfather.

Air-conditioning, supplied by Mother Nature and mixed with exhaust fumes, was coming through the open window. My single piece of luggage, with its own scent of mildew and Blackjack chewing gun, contained a spare change of clothes, my double-bladed Barlow jackknife with celluloid handles and a jar of homemade sauerkraut for my Aunt Lilly.

Most important of all, a used but like-new Ruger Blackhawk in .44 magnum caliber was rolled up in my extra pair of Levis. A meager supply of compatible ammunition was tied inside a large red and white bandana.

It was June, 1961. Barely a month before, I'd turned 18. High school was behind me forever, and a little paperback book, written by Jeff Cooper, had thoroughly ignited my interest in the big-bore handgun as something other than a defensive tool.

The little volume cost me 25¢ in the spring of '61. Packed with concise, savvy advice based on Cooper's already extensive experience, it was a primer on the then-fledgling sport of handgunning beyond the conventional target range.

Cooper's early opinions ring as true today as they did more than 30 years ago. Although the collector's value attached to a copy of his *Handguns Afield* now approaches the cost of a .44 magnum Ruger Blackhawk in 1961, it's still worth the price!

Before Wall Street cratered in 1929, the legendary Elmer Keith had abandoned the .45 Long Colt in his search for the optimum combination of power and accuracy in a handgun cartridge. During the 1930s, he determined a .44 Special load of 18.5 grains of #2400 Hercules powder, behind a properly designed bullet weighing 230 to 250 grains, to be an excellent performer.

Ruger's Big-Bore Flattop Blackhawk Continues To Excel!

Ruger's current .44 magnum single-actions continue a tradition of first-rate performance and quality.

According to Roy Jinks, S&W's historian and author of the excellent *History Of Smith & Wesson*, the early 1950s found Keith urging Smith & Wesson to develop a handgun capable of handling his heavy .44 caliber loads.

Keith's dream finally came to fruition with Remington's development of the .44 magnum cartridge in 1954, and S&W's classic Model 29 double-action revolver in 1955. At that time, work on the .44 magnum project was only rumor among the rest of the firearms industry.

Early in 1956, Bill Ruger made a routine call on the Remington factory at Bridgeport, Connecticut, a short drive from the growing headquarters of Sturm, Ruger & Company in Southport. As he was about to leave, a senior Remington sales executive handed Ruger a package, saying, "Here's something you'll be interested in."

Inside that package was a box of experimental .44 magnum ammunition. Returning to the Old Red Barn which then housed the Ruger factory, Bill Ruger and his staff worked virtually around the clock to develop a handgun for the new cartridge.

In record time, the Ruger .44 magnum Blackhawk single-action revolver was designed, tested and put into production. According to Ruger factory records, the first regular produc-

tion gun was shipped in December, 1956.

As the bus passed the familiar road sign which read, *Bandera, 5 Miles*, I knew my journey would be over soon. I stuck my hand into the valise, reassuring myself for the 20th time that the powerful, sleek revolver was still there!

Amassing the princely sum of $116 needed to acquire the newer, more fashionable Super Blackhawk, introduced in 1959, had been beyond my bankroll and patience level. But, graduation gifts put me within striking distance of the barely used Ruger .44 magnum single-action on display at the old gunshop near San Antonio's Bexar County Courthouse.

The shop owner had made a statement common in the early days of the .44 magnum: "It was too much gun for the gent. He brought it back." Apparently, the original owner didn't realize the handsome Ruger would digest .44 Special cartridges just as easily as the awesome new magnums.

I exchanged $65 cash for the powerful Ruger. The deal included 18 .44 magnum cartridges, most of a box of .44 Specials that pre-dated WWII and several round of .44 Russian ammunition...something I'd never seen before.

As the bus began to slow down at the edge of town, I was still daydreaming about the latest addition to my little mismatched collection of firearms.

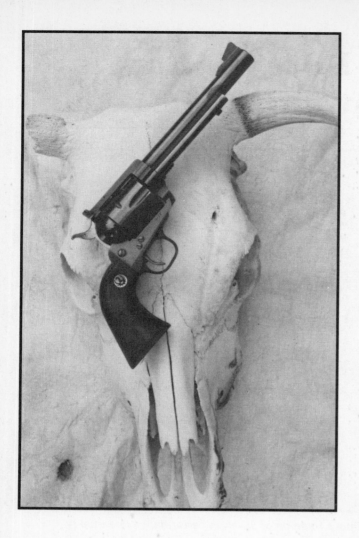

In more recent times, collectors have dubbed the original Ruger single-actions in .357 and .44 magnum "flattops," after their predecessors, target versions of the Colt Single Action Army and Bisley models. On all four of these specialized handguns, the top of the cylinder frame is flat, with some form of adjustable rear sight installed.

But the .44 magnum flattop Ruger was not the same gun as the .357 version. The .44 magnum Blackhawk, the newer of the two, was equipped with a beefed-up cylinder frame and strengthened cylinder to accommodate this most powerful of handgun cartridges.

The grip frame, however, was the same on both Ruger flattops, giving them the same feel as Colt's Single Action Army revolver. In fact, it was the same grip Samuel Colt designed for his 1851 Navy percussion revolver, which figured prominently in the War Between the States.

Although the first Ruger .44 magnum flattops sported hard rubber grips, my gun — in the 3,000 serial number range — had grip panels of varnished, figured walnut. Barrel length was 6 1/2 inches, and aluminum-alloy grip frame construction gave the handgun exceptionally good balance.

Small quantities of 7-1/2-and 10-inch barreled flattops were produced as well. Today, those specimens which can be authenticated bring premium collector prices beyond the already stout value of the more common 6-1/2-inch version.

The .44 caliber Ruger was identical in operation to my Colt single-actions. Everyone I knew had enough sense to realize only five of the six chambers could be loaded safely with live cartridges. The sixth chamber, the one in line with the hammer and barrel, always was kept empty. No exceptions!

The cylinder chambers of the first Ruger .44 magnum were counterbored, allowing cartridges to rest flush with the rear of the cylinder. The loading gate had a decidedly purple cast. The one-piece aluminum grip frame, replacing the two-part trigger guard and back strap of Colt SAs, was anodized to match the blue steel parts as closely as possible.

It appeared the rear micro sight on my .44 flattop never had been disturbed by man or screwdriver since leaving Connecticut. My new acquisition sported a thin, traditional SA trigger

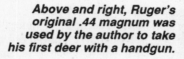

Above and right, Ruger's original .44 magnum was used by the author to take his first deer with a handgun.

and a gracefully curved hammer. It was a wondrous sight to behold!

Like most ranch and farm folk, my Aunt Lily seldom had occasion to pay for food cooked by others. But she took the start of my traditional summer visit as an excuse to treat us both to a chicken-fried steak, with all the trimmings, at the cafe next to the only bank in town.

Impatient to try my newly acquired Ruger, getting served and finishing the meal seemed to take forever. But at last, my favorite aunt and I were traversing the eight miles to our final destination in her old Dodge sedan.

In her early 50s, Aunt Lily never had bothered with a driver's license. Car insurance? Well, that was something for city folk. As we pulled off the Farm-to-Market blacktop and onto the dusty caliche road, I began to see the familiar oak and mesquite trees which never seemed to change. The old rock house looked the same; the flower and vegetable garden never looked better.

There was no need to inform my aunt I had a handgun with me. She would have been surprised if that weren't the case. It was a time and place when a boy's interest in firearms was considered an important part of growing-up.

A quick change of clothes, a drink straight from the pump off the back porch, and I was on my way. I didn't have a holster for my new handgun. I just shoved it into a well-worn .45 SAA cartridge belt I'd acquired in a trade.

As I passed through the gate to the pear orchard, I recalled one of Jeff Cooper's comments that had hit me pretty hard: The new .44 magnum was beyond the capabilities of nine out of 10 pistol shooters.

Of course, I had ignored Mr. Cooper's advice completely to borrow a .44 magnum and gain considerable experience with it before deciding to purchase one. I just knew that comment wasn't directed at me! Besides, I'd had access to a S&W Triple Lock in .44 Special and used it to practice on tin cans as often as I could acquire ammunition.

Placing an old paint can below the rim of a little hill to avoid a ricochet, I backed off 10 paces or so and loaded my prize Ruger with five .44 magnum cartridges. As the two-hand handgun stance was still considered the mark of a greenhorn in 1961, I simply cocked the hammer back, took aim and let one fly!

My first shot burst the tightly sealed paint can, spewing the contents far and wide in a colorful mist I only partially witnessed. Not fully heeding another of Mr. Cooper's warnings, in my excitement I had failed to maintain more than a casual hold on the powerful Blackhawk.

The big gun flipped sharply in my hand, smacking my knuckles and tearing at the hide between thumb and trigger finger. But the satisfying effect on the paint can far outweighed any physical discomfort.

More careful with succeeding shots, I expended half my meager supply of .44 magnum ammo before calling a halt to my first shooting session with the big Ruger. My ears were ringing. It also was not yet considered manly to wear ear protection, except on a target range.

As I made my way back to the house for the evening meal, I was quite pleased with myself, as well as the big-bore Blackhawk. I had accomplished a handgunning feat known only to a small percentage of shooters in those days.

The flattop Ruger .44 was an interim step in the development of the modern, big-bore magnum single-action. It had the feel of a Colt SA and got Ruger into the marketplace in record time, but it was not to be the ultimate solution.

At 20 yards, author's original Ruger .44 Blackhawk easily holds it own against modern counterparts.

The Blackhawk flattop .44 magnum (top), that was manufactured by Ruger in 1957, retains much of the appearance and feel of Colt's original single-action Army revolver.

Fewer than 30,000 Ruger flattop .44 magnums were produced between 1956 and 1962. Soon after the .44 Blackhawk's introduction, Elmer Keith began urging Ruger to make changes for a more powerful magnum revolver.

Keith wanted a larger and longer grip. Also, more space behind the trigger guard to make the .44 magnum less punishing while shooting full-power loads.

He suggested a wide, deeply serrated hammer spur to facilitate cocking, plus a broad, grooved trigger for improved control. Keith preferred a 7-1/2-inch barrel on a hunting handgun, and a non-fluted cylinder would provide added strength for a handgun slated to handle a consistent diet of .44 magnum cartridges.

And finally, the long-range shooting often required while handgun hunting necessitates substantial elevation of the rear sight. And since the rigors of hunting expose a firearm's sights to potential damage, Ruger was further urged to reinforce the Blackhawk's frame around the rear sight to protect it when raised sharply above its mortise.

In 1959, only three years after the introduction of Ruger's original .44 magnum flattop, Sturm, Ruger & Company began producing and shipping their improved .44 magnum, the Super Blackhawk. This second Ruger .44 magnum included all of the changes listed above, as well as a rakish Dragoon-style trigger guard.

The Super Blackhawk was so well suited for its intended purpose that no external changes have been made to this firearm in 33 years of continuous production. Internally, the 1973 adaptation of Ruger's New Model transfer bar system made it a totally different revolver, but that's another story.

In 1987, William B. Ruger, founder and chairman of the board of Sturm, Ruger & Company, instructed his staff to create a special .44 magnum single-action revolver to honor the contributions of gun writer Skeeter Skelton to the field of handgunning.

Skelton's death in January, 1988, saddened an entire industry as well as his legion of loyal fans, myself near the top of the list. In spite of events, Bill Ruger instructed that the special flattop be completed.

The unique Skeeter Skelton Special is serial numbered "SSS 001." It is a blued flattop with original Micro rear sight. The lockwork is of the New Model type.

Gold inlay and delicate engraving enhance all major component parts of this tribute to a champion of the original Ruger .44 magnum flattop — and single-actions in general. The ivory stocks are scrimshawed with a likeness of Skelton on one side and a rendering of his Deaf Smith County, Texas, sheriff's badge and the other. Grip medallions feature Skeeter's famous Turkey Track brand. A French-fitted display case completes this most valuable of all Ruger flattops.

Bill Ruger presented the Skeeter Skelton Special to Skeeter's wife, Sally. Also in attendance was their son, Bart, an accomplished firearms writer in his own right.

My most recently acquired Ruger .44 magnum single-action is crafted from stainless steel and equipped with a 5-1/2-inch barrel. As with all currently-manufactured Ruger New Model Blackhawks, this revolver sports the same cylinder frame as the New Model Super Blackhawk.

Listed as Model Number KS45N, this gun — at least to me — is a New Model Blackhawk with Super Blackhawk hammer and non-standard barrel length. Whatever you choose to call it, it's a first-class belt gun and a good bet as a future Ruger collectible.

This gun was produced originally as a limited-edition item in blue steel. As the story goes, the business decision was made by Ruger to use the existing .44 magnum Super

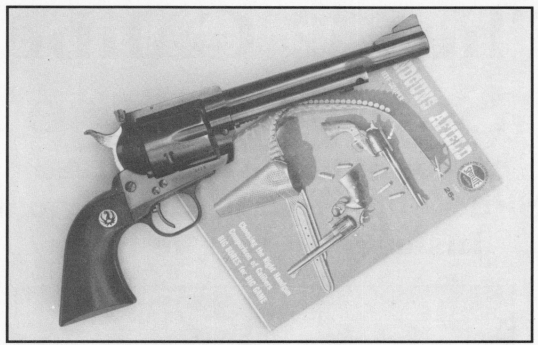

Jeff Copper's advice introduced the author to extended use of big-bore handguns for sporting use. Below, the old and new Ruger .44 magnums are near mirror images.

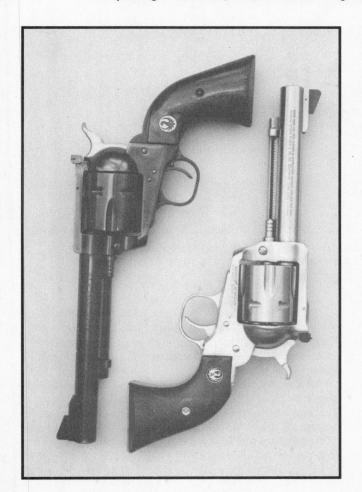

Blackhawk rollmark rather than investing in a New Model .44 magnum Blackhawk die, a designation never before utilized.

After picking up the stainless Ruger, I decided to see how my first .44 magnum stacked up against my latest. Thirty-five years separate the production of these two wheelguns.

Since Remington had developed the original .44 magnum cartridge, I used their 240-grain semi-jacketed flat-point for my testing. The results soon proved that whoever says Americans can't produce reasonably priced, top-quality products forgot to inform Bill Ruger and his employees!

At 35 years of age, and after a considerable amount of shooting, that original Ruger .44 magnum flattop delivered 1-1/4-inch groups at 20 yards. My New Model stainless "Super" Blackhawk produced 1-1/2-inch groups at the same distance...right out of the factory carton. All shooting was conducted from a benchrest.

Is Ruger's original flattop .44 magnum a better-designed, better-quality handgun than the Rugers being produced today? No. It is not. Bill Ruger's personal policy of never considering a firearm design final continues to pay-off for today's shooters.

It's true that during recent target shooting sessions, my old .44 magnum flattop — produced in 1957 — performed slightly better than my Ruger .44 magnum SA of current manufacture. But then, there are several possible explanations.

It might have been the flattop's longer barrel and sighting radius. Perhaps it was my long-term experience with the original Colt-style grip frame. Or maybe...just maybe...I subconsciously gave an edge to an old friend who's never let me down in more than 30 years.

I suspect I'll have a similar attachment to my newest Ruger .44 magnum long before the year 2022 rolls around!

The .32 Caliber Schwarzlose

This 1909 Pistol Had A Slide That Slammed Forward Instead Of To The Rear

By *Jim Dickson*

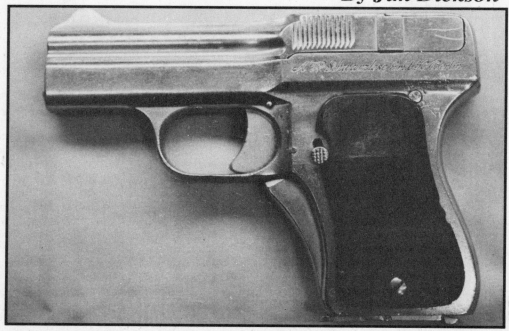

This Schwarzlose was confiscated by the Germans when they invaded Norway during World War II. After the war, it was rescued from destruction by a U.S. Army officer.

THE SCHWARZLOSE M1909 pistol is one of the most fascinating firearms ever made to function. When the gun fires, the slide goes forward instead of to the rear — for no apparent reason.

One gets the distinct impression that the gun never heard of Newton's Third Law: "For every action there is an equal and opposite reaction." In short, this gun seems to defy basic laws of physics. It is impossibly different, yet it works.

It was invented by a man who made a career of doing things the impossible way. The nemesis of all who say, "You can't do it that way," Andreas Wilhelm Schwarzlose was a brilliant contemporary of Maxim, Tesla and Edison.

Born on July 31, 1867, in Wust, Altmark, Northern Germany, Schwarzlose left the family farm to join an Austro-Hungarian artillery regiment. While in service, he attended ordnance training school in Suhl, one of the best in the world in the 1890s.

After leaving the service, he invented a characteristically unique automatic pistol that fired standard revolver ammo. The rounds were held vertically in a non-detachable magazine beneath the barrel, the bullet noses pointing toward the ground when the pistol was held in the firing position. It worked, but only one or two exist today.

While working as an armorer in Suhl, Schwarzlose built his

second design with the cartridges in an integral magazine in the grip. This eventually would develop into the Schwarzlose Military Pistol. During the final development stage of the design, he moved from the Prussian gunmaking center to Charlottenburg outside of Berlin where he produced his M1901 Military Pistol. Most of these were bought by Russia for use in the Russo-Japanese War of 1904.

In 1902, the inventor patented his famous machine gun which Steyr began producing in Austria. The adoption of this weapon by Austria ensured his reputation and success. This was the first machine gun to have a simple, uncomplicated design. It is totally unique. It fires a full-powered rifle cartridge with retarded blow-back, instead of positive locking. The final form, the M1907/12, fires without even needing lubricated ammo to prevent case separation. Any gun designer — then or now — will tell you this can't be done with full-power cartridges and blow-back. The Schwarzlose did — and still does. It is fully as reliable as the the Browning machine guns and immensely more simple, as well as easier and cheaper to make.

From its sprocket-wheel belt feed — with only two working parts — to the oversize spring that serves as buffer, bolt return and firing pin spring, the gun displays innovative genius. Disassembled in only a few seconds, it ranks as one of the all-time great water-cooled machine guns.

By 1912, Schwarzlose had 58 firearms patents in Germany alone. He was truly one of the most significant designers of firearms.

In 1907, he began work on the blow-forward pistol. The M1896 Mauser military pistol had only a bolt to keep the reciprocating slide mechanism on the gun and out of your face when firing. The consequences of metal fatigue or other parts failure were especially horrifying to shooters of that era who already were unnerved by parts bouncing back and forth in the new-fangeled autoloaders. This fear and distrust proved early selling points for both the Borchart and the Luger pistols with their safe, upward-breaking toggles.

Schwarzlose attacked the problem head-on. If shooters didn't want the slide coming back at them, he would make it go forward. If the slide should ever leave the gun, it would imperil the target instead of the shooter. The pistol remained in production until 1911 and was marketed in the U.S. by the Warner Arms Company.

As always with Schwarzlose designs, the Model 1909 was simple and innovative. The only safety is the grip type, which is plenty. This safety is hard enough to overcome to be considered childproof, but light enough that one won't notice it with the hard, adrenaline-fired grip that goes with emergency use. For target practice, the safety can be disengaged by

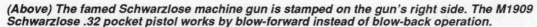

(Above) The famed Schwarzlose machine gun is stamped on the gun's right side. The M1909 Schwarzlose .32 pocket pistol works by blow-forward instead of blow-back operation.

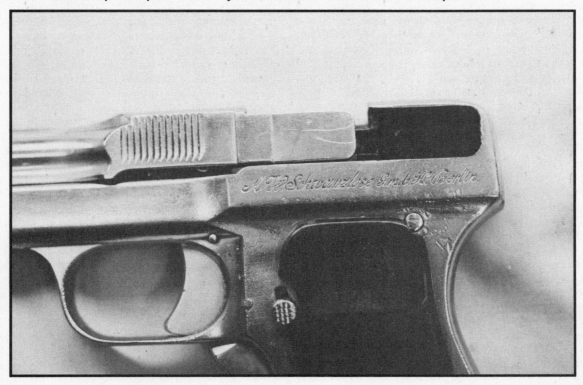

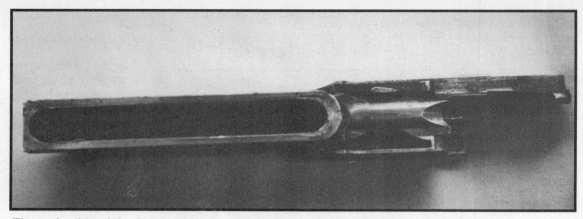

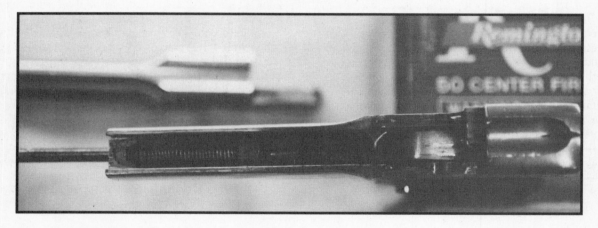

The underside of the Schwarzlose barrel (above) shows the milled-out undercarriage. Below, the top view of the receiver, with the magazine, shows the captive recoil spring.

pushing in the grip safety, then locking it in by pushing up the grip safety button on the right side of the frame.

This is an excellent system, seen only on this unique pistol and worth copying for pocket pistols today. Some guns also were made without grip safeties. Like the revolvers of its day, the firing pin and hammer all are one-piece. This massive firing pin is not a part one needed to worry about breaking.

The blow-forward operation works efficiently and simply. In simplest terms, the barrel can't go to the rear, so the bullet's friction drags it forward — but there is more to it than that.

When the gun is fired, the bullet acts as a friction plug, going down the barrel and dragging the barrel with it. The barrel is designed to be free to move forward in relationship to the frame. There also is retardation present, because the cartridge case has expanded, gripping the chamber and trying to prevent it going forward. The barrel, the cartridge case and the bullet constitute a movable cylinder with two movable pistons at each end that are operated by friction and expanding gas. For the gas to expand, it must force the two pistons apart, then the friction generated by the bullet drives the barrel forward, stripping it off the cartridge case which cannot move rearward because of the stationary breech.

The operating power here is enormous. On a simple blow-back, power is generated only as long as the case is in the barrel, but with blow-forward operation, power is generated as long as the bullet is in the barrel.

At the time this pistol was introduced, it was customary for gunmakers to offer custom-tailored ammo for their guns. The gun gained a lot of reliability that way. The Schwarzlose .32 was loaded with a truncated-cone bullet, a fulminate-of-mercury primer, a booster stick of cordite coated with fulminate of mercury, and an uncoated, single-base powder.

This ammunition provided higher pressure before the barrel started moving forward, then pressure dropped quickly, giving a high-low pressure effect similar to today's 40mm grenade cartridge. This is not a load to try to duplicate. It was considered unsafe in its own day, and contemporary writers remarked on the extra recoil when Schwarzlose ammo was used in other .32 pistols.

The powder's graphite retardant was not used as a coating, but was mixed with the powder's other components. That is the reason for the booster stick. Graphite retardant doesn't stick to nitro-cellulose, unless a solvent is used on the nitro-cellulose to make it sticky for coating. The technology of the day wasn't sufficient to do that reliably.

What would it take to make the gun 100 percent reliable? For that we must delve deeply into its design. The barrel's mass is insufficient for the retardation required, yet if one increases the mass, spring pressure must be increased drastically. The mechanism no longer can start its cycle unless a tapered-bore barrel is used. This raises the pressure so high that the cartridge case must have extremely thick walls of steel with a brass obturator at the front. The now high-tech cartridges would be high in price and have multi-part assemblies. The use of a lightweight, high-velocity projectile would be called for, along with a lightweight slide. This would not be popular ammo!

The Schwarzlose's modular design helps prevent the loss of parts when field-stripped (above) for cleaning. Left, after firing, the Schwarzlose barrel moves back, over the waiting cartridge to chamber the next round.

No standard pistol cartridge is appropriate to a blow-forward system, and any cartridge larger than .32 kicks too hard. When the barrel moves forward, it creates more recoil than would a standing breech, whereas a blow-back system absorbs recoil and spreads the remainder over a longer period for less felt recoil. The blow-forward gun shoves the barrel weight onto the hand on top of the recoil and the time lapse between cartridge recoil and barrel movement creates most unusual felt recoil.

Schwarzlose made a .45 version of this gun, intending to submit it to the U.S. Army. However, recoil was brutal, and the barrel had to be increased in size and weight to the point of impracticality. The finished gun proved too large and too ungainly to operate, plus having too much recoil to be shot fast enough for combat. The design was abandoned without being submitted.

The difficulties of making blow-forward operation workable with conventional pistol cartridges resulted in the hammer spring having to be made as weak as possible, because its cocking drags on the barrel going forward. To gain the mechanical leverage to get around the problem would require a 50 percent larger pistol. Pocket pistols are supposed to be small.

Workmanship on the Schwarzlose guns was good. Largely hand-made from milled forgings, 99 percent of the production time was spent in getting guns almost finished. The extra one percent was gladly spent to finish the job right. Assurancy was on a par with the rest of the .32 pocket pistols of the day. There is no room for complaint here.

Schwarzlose went at things in strange fashion, but almost anything he developed worked. He was a brilliant original inventor. In the blow-forward pistol design, he set out to make a solid, standing-breech automatic pocket pistol that would be as reliable as its competition, and allay the fears of those who anticipated the slide coming off the gun and ramming through their faces. In this, he was successful.

WHAT'S SO SPECIAL?

By *Terry Murbach*

This Smith & Wesson M60-3 has a three-inch barrel and sports grips from Michaels of Oregon.

LIKE MOST young kids who had been bitten by the gun bug, I read gun catalogs incessantly in my teens and before. All those gun names — Single Action Army, Blackhawk, Single-Six and *the* .357 magnum, captured my imagination, and to this day, I still like names on guns instead of a number, or even worse, a series of numbers. The cartridges for these old time guns also fired my imagination — .45 Colt, .357 magnum, .32 Long, .38 Special and .44 Special. These latter two begged the question, what is so special about these two cartridges that deserved such a specific designation?

I also was a bit of a cynic as a kid and the magnum bug had bitten deeply. They could not be that "special," as both were subloads for subsequent magnum six-guns — or so I rational-ized at the time when I bought .357 magnum and .44 magnum revolvers.

I had owned a Colt .357 magnum six-inch Trooper for a couple of years when, in one of those roundabout trades handgun people seem to love, I ended up with 10 boxes of Remington-Peters .38 Special 148-grain wadcutter Targetmaster loads as boot. For the life of me, I can't remember anymore what I traded or what else I got.

Shortly thereafter, I traded a Beretta single-barrel trap gun for a new Smith & Wesson M19 four-inch .357 magnum. Off to the range we went, the six-inch Colt Trooper, the new M19, and a couple hundred .38 wadcutters. It was the only ammu-nition I had on hand. Boy, oh boy! Did I get my eyes opened wide and consume a large portion of humility pie that day.

This Gunsmith Takes Us Down The Nostalgic Trail For His .38 And .44s!

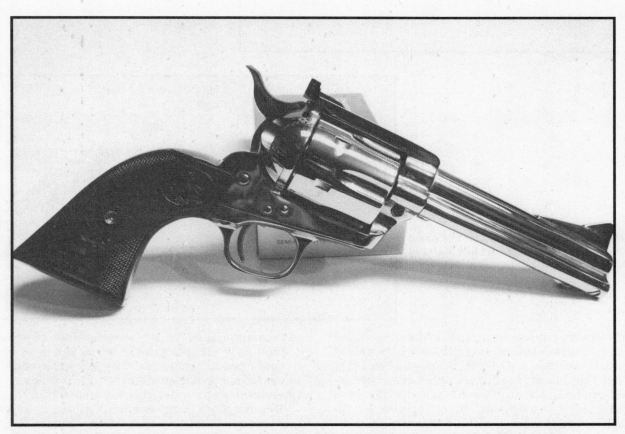

The Colt New Frontier in .44 Special traces its heritage back to the black powder Colt Model 1873.

Those R-P .38 WCs shot great in that M19, and horror of horrors, they shot better than the best .357 handload I ever had assembled for use in that accurate Trooper. What was really humiliating was that my .357 lead bullet loads had shot miserably in this Trooper; it was definitely a jacketed-bullet six-gun—or so I thought. A couple of hours on the range gave me a new-found appreciation and lit a .38 Special fire under my butt that has not ceased to this day.

I have tested dozens of different wadcutter bullets over dozens of different powder charges, always striving to find that single load that would shoot one-hole groups from my steadily growing stable of .38 Special and .357 magnum revolvers. Thousands upon thousands of my .38 WC handloads have flown downrange in the years since; the M19 has fired

some 20,000 .38s and entertained me mightily in the process. They never pummeled my eardrums, beat up my hands from recoil or required weird combinations of components to achieve outstanding results.

The .38 Special is indeed so special with its sweet shooting disposition that it alone can teach you how to shoot a medium-bore centerfire revolver and handload cartridges ranging in power from powder puff to near-.357 magnum performance. Think about that for a moment. Yes indeed, in the proper .38 Special six-gun, those .38 Special handloads known as the .38/44 trod heavily upon the .357s heels and, in some cases, beat the magnum.

In my salad days, I thought it pretty silly to buy a .38 Special six-gun when most all of the same guns were available

This Smith & Wesson M624 .44 Special has a four-inch barrel and fine wood grips.

This Smith & Wesson Model 624 has a six-inch barrel. The Model 624 features an adjustable micrometer click rear sight.

in .357 magnum. I no longer subscribe to that short-sighted viewpoint. I currently have one two-inch J-frame .38 (a M640 Centennial), two three-inch J-frame .38s (target-sighted M36 and M60 Trail Masterpieces), a six-inch K-frame (the supremely neat K38), and a 6 1/2-inch N-frame .38 Special (a 1953 issue .38/44 Outdoorsman). Every single one is a delightful gun to shoot and each one fits a different niche in the .38 Special scheme.

For instance, my M36-1 three-inch target-sighted Trail Masterpiece is an ideal centerfire kitgun with some real punch; the M36-6 and M60-4 are underlugged-barrel versions of my original M36-1; my M14 K38 is a superb handling target revolver that also qualifies as a superb let's-go-plinkin' six-gun, and the Outdoorsman .38/44 shoots all .38 Special loads from wadcutter to the .38/44 1300 fps loads straight as a moonbeam. The .38/44 Outdoorsman, with its old-fashioned stag stocks, is my link to an earlier age when this revolver and its ability to handle hellfire-breathing .38 handloads led directly to all this magnum sixgun business that holds handgunners' rapt attention still. I believe that it is important to remember in this age of the magnums that shooting is one of the supremely fun things that free people can do, and you do not have to shoot a roaring, thumping magnum sixgun to have fun shooting.

One other .38 Special handgun has permanent residence status here at the Murbach homestead, and it is not a revolver. This handgun is a Smith & Wesson Master autoloading target pistol.

These S&W M52 pistols are among the best target pistols ever developed here in America. They were factory-tested for 50-yard, 10-ring accuracy, and they will deliver the goods with a gorgeous trigger pull and a set of finely adjustable target sights.

My personal M52 is supremely picky about its diet, and I have just had a ball testing myriad .38 WC handloads in this pistol. Truth be told, I have had one hell of a challenge trying to consistently beat the accuracy of the factory .38 wadcutter ammunition — and that is a challenge I find totally irresistible. This M52 .38 Master shoots its best groups with full-charge wadcutter handloads, not midrange loads. Here again, we see one of the .38 Special's most salient features. Its range of adaptability in handloading darn near encompasses the power range from .22 LR muzzle energies to the power dished up by the .357 magnum.

The 9mm Parabellum and .38 Super levels of power can quite easily be duplicated by both the factory .38 Special +P or +P+ cartridges or easily assembled equivalent handloads. While the .38 Special may be old and have an enfeebled reputation as a defense cartridge, it is still a delightful round for all-day plinking, use in the field for small-game hunting or with which to pursue your goal of shooting that elusive one-hole group.

When that most special of Smith & Wesson revolvers, the

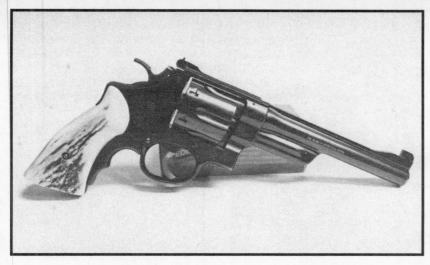

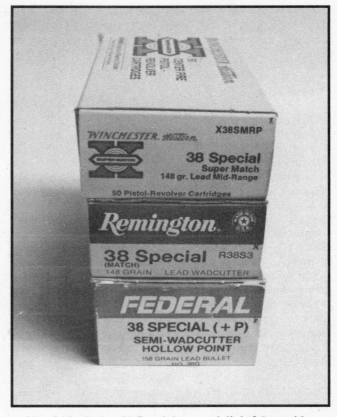

Left, the Smith & Wesson Outdoorsman
.38/44 Model 23 was introduced in 1930.
Below, author selects .38 Special ammo
from Winchester, Remington and Federal.

N-frame Triple Lock, was introduced in 1908, it also introduced that most special of revolver cartridges, the .44 Special. The new cartridge was a lengthened .44 Russian and used 26 grains of black powder, an increase of three grains over the .44 Russian's load.

Sales of the Triple Lock .44 Special were anything but stellar, and it was superseded in 1915 by the .44 Hand Ejector, Second Model, which stayed in S&W's line until 1940. The .44 Hand Ejector, Third Model was introduced in 1926. It was identical to the Second Model but had the heavy barrel lug protecting the ejector rod. The S&W .44 Special Hand Ejector, Fourth Model of 1950, was sold until 1966, when it was dropped for lack of sales.

From its inception in 1908 until 1966, S&W manufactured 28,968 of these .44 Special models, hardly a drop in the bucket of their total handgun production over that 58-year period. Just about the time the .44 Special 1950 Target could have started selling well, the .44 magnum was introduced in 1956 and pretty well put the kibosh on .44 Special sales.

Fortunately, by that period of time, a short cigar chewing cowboy from Idaho had published a book called *Sixguns*. I was in the sixth grade when I first read Elmer Keith's seminal book, and it lit a fire in my gut for a .44 Special like you would not believe.

Back in those days of 1956, our library would let you renew a book forever — or until somebody else asked for it. I can remember having it out for one entire nine-month session of school. It taught me things at least as important as anything our teacher, Miss Anderson, ever dreamed of.

About four years later, my dad gave me my first-ever handgun, a Colt 4 1/2-inch Huntsman .22 pistol, and I sort of figured a .22 was halfway to a .44 Special. By 1966, a few more guns had signed on in my outfit, and I was in the process of getting married. My old man asked me what I wanted for a wedding present. One Smith & Wesson Model 24 .44 Special 6 1/2-inch revolver would be fine, if you please.

I had a half dozen guns, a motorcycle, and 40 bucks cash to my name on the day we tied the knot, and I thought I had made a reasonable request. Such was not to be, however, and my first experiences with loading and shooting .44 Special cartridges took place using .44 magnum sixguns I had managed to acquire between three kids, mortgage payments and a car or two.

Yes, indeed, the .44 Special was a delightful cartridge to load and shoot. One of the longest and best shots I ever made in the squirrel woods saw a 255-grain Lyman #429421 bullet riding 8.0 grains of Unique. Launched from a 4 3/4-inch Ruger Super Blackhawk, it picked off a big fox squirrel from the very top of the biggest oak tree in that section of woods. It killed him deader than canned ham, and did not harm an ounce of his succulent meat.

In late January, 1983, the March issue of *Shooting Times* landed in my mailbox, and I let out a warwhoop that brought everybody running. On the cover was a S&W 6 1/2-inch M24 and the prophetic words: S&W BRINGS BACK THE MODEL 24 .44 SPECIAL.

I was in the car and out to Cleland's Gun Shop in Swanton,

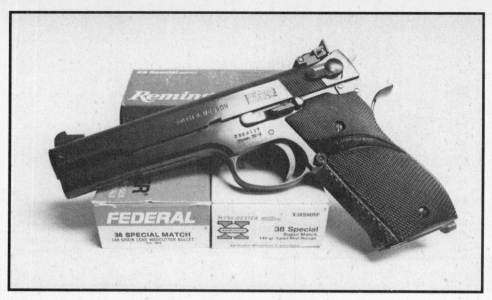

The author's Smith & Wesson Model 52 .38 Master will hold 10-ring accuracy at 50 yards.

Ohio, so fast it made my head swim. I was first on their newly started M24 list, and in August, 1983, I finally acquired my first M24 6 1/2-inch .44 Special.

Our first trip to the range that warm August day was one I have never forgotten. Shooting the same handload I mentioned earlier, that M24 would shoot consistently under 1-1/2 inches and usually four of five shots would cut each other. More than a few five-shot groups were one ragged hole. Velocities ran 875 fps, a bit lower than the 950-975 I had predicted.

But there was a problem, and it was a big one. The gun could not be sighted in, because the barrel was not straight up and down with the frame. Boy, was I ever disappointed by this turn of events. I packed it all up with a letter of explanation and shipped it back to S&W. As it turned out, this barrel had cracked the frame and S&W had to replace the gun instead of re-frame it, as no spare frames were available. One of the old-timers at S&W in those days was Fran Longtin, and he put an action job on the replacement M24 that made my mouth water every time I cocked the gun. Smooth simply is not descriptive enough.

Back to the range we went with a big batch of different handloads to test. Literally nothing I tested that day would shoot a decent group in this new M24. More loads were assembled, and when the 255-grain #429421 bullets went over 1100 fps, they started grouping beautifully. They also introduced raucous levels of recoil into the equation, and that was not what I wanted out of the slender-barreled, slick-handling six-gun. As I see it, if you want a big thump on both ends, use a .44 magnum. The .44 Special's very reason for being in this age of the magnum is shooting big 250-grain .44 bullets at or around 950 fps, with the added ability of putting them exactly where you want them from a relatively light-weight, fast-handling gun.

To make a long story short, I finally isolated one load for the cantankerous gun that fit my guidelines perfectly. This load was precisely 15.0 grains of 2400; 14.5 or 15.5 grains were nowhere near as good. I have stuck with this load over the ensuing eight years, and it still shoots well in other .44 Special guns that have joined our ranks here on the North Coast. The Cimarron 5 1/2-inch .44 Special puts it dead on with its old-fashioned sights, though I must admit this gun seems to prefer a 240-grain SWC over 7.5 grains or 8.0 grains of Unique.

Both of my favorite .44 Special loads also have given yeoman service when I quickly adapted them as the favorite diet for the lightweight Smith & Wesson M629 .44 magnum four-inch Mountain Revolver. With full bore .44 magnum loads, this diminutive six-gun is an unholy terror. With the .44 Special handloads, it is an easily handled, adequately powerful revolver that is the single most accurate .44 Special revolver I have ever shot.

I am not quite sure why we have had to return to those days when a fellow decided he could not live without a new double-action .44 Special in the rack he found none were to be had. S&W dropped the blue M24 in 1984 to "protect its collector value" (please give me a break), and introduced the stainless Model 624 in four- and six-inch lengths.

These latter two are among the neatest six-guns ever produced by Smith & Wesson. As you have aready surmised, they have been discounted as well.

I have seen numerous M624s for sale at gun shows over the past couple years, and most were priced well under the typical N-frame six-gun. While I am sure the vast majority of .44 Special ammunition is consumed in .44 magnum revolvers, the opportunity to acquire a genuine .44 Special-chambered M624 at prices approaching a fire sale is a state of affairs guaranteed not to last too much longer.

After all these years, I find it utterly amazing there are .44 Special six-guns out there wanting a kind owner to give them a good home, regular exercise and an occasional bath in Hoppe's #9. This is a sad state of affairs, my friends.

It may well have been happenstance that two of our finest non-magnum revolver cartridges were named Special. Perhaps the name was chosen by some long-forgotten sales promoter doing his job at making them a marketing success. However the name came about, the .38 Special and .44 Special revolver cartridges stand alone as remarkably capable and user-friendly; a remarkable harbinger of things to come. We are enjoying today a variety of different and more powerful cartridges. They are a reality because of a pathway lit brightly by those two Specials, the .38 and .44.

THE HANDGUNNER'S CATALOG

Table of Contents

GUNDEX®

A listing of all the guns in the catalog, by name and model, alphabetically and numerically.

A

Accu-Tek Model AT-9 Auto Pistol, 260
Accu-Tek Model AT-25SS Auto Pistol, 260
Accu-Tek Model AT-25SSB Auto Pistol, 260
Accu-Tek Model AT-32SS Auto Pistol, 260
Accu-Tek Model AT-32SSB Auto Pistol, 260
Accu-Tek Model AT-40 Auto Pistol, 260
Accu-Tek Model AT-40B Auto Pistol, 260
Accu-Tek Model AT-380SS Auto Pistol, 260
Accu-Tek Model HC-380SS Auto Pistol, 260
American Arms Buckhorn Single Action Revolver, 293
American Arms Model CX-22 DA Pistol, 260
American Arms Model P-98 Auto Pistol, 260
American Arms Model PK22 DA Pistol, 260
American Arms Model PX-22 Auto Pistol, 261
American Arms Regulator Single Actions, 293
American Arms Spectre DA Auto, 261
American Derringer 125th Anniv. Derringer, 304
American Derringer Alaskan Survival Derringer, 304
American Derringer COP 357 Derringer, 305
American Derringer DA 38 Model, 305
American Derringer Lady Derringer, 305
American Derringer Mini COP Derringer, 305
American Derringer Model 1 Derringer, 304
American Derringer Model 3 Derringer, 305
American Derringer Model 4 Derringer, 304
American Derringer Model 6 Derringer, 305
American Derringer Model 7 Derringer, 305
American Derringer Model 10 Derringer, 305
American Derringer Semmerling LM-4, 305
American Derringer Texas Comm. Derringer, 305
AMT 45 ACP Hardballer Long Slide Pistol, 262
AMT 45 ACP Hardballer Pistol, 262
AMT Automag II Auto Pistol, 261
AMT Automag III Auto Pistol, 261
AMT Automag IV Auto Pistol, 261
AMT Backup Auto Pistol, 261
AMT Backup Double Action Only Auto, 261
AMT Government Model Auto Pistol, 262
AMT On Duty DA Auto Pistol, 261

Anschutz Exemplar Bolt-Action Pistol, 305
Army 1851 Percussion Revolver, 311
Army 1860 Percussion Revolver, 311
Astra A-70 Auto Pistol, 262
Astra A-75 Decocker Auto Pistol, 262
Astra A-100 Auto Pistol, 262
Auto-Ordnance 40 S&W 1911A1 Auto Pistol, 262
Auto-Ordnance 1911A1 Auto Pistol, 262
Auto-Ordnance ZG-51 Pit Bull Auto, 262

B

Baby Dragoon 1848 Percussion Revolver, 311
Baby Dragoon 1849 Pocket Percussion Revovler, 311
Baby Dragoon Wells Fargo Percussion Revolver, 311
Baby Eagle Auto Pistol, 262
Benelli MP90S Match Pistol, 298
Beretta Model 21 Auto Pistol, 263
Beretta Model 21 EL Auto Pistol, 263
Beretta Model 80 Series Auto Pistols, 263
Beretta Model 84F Auto Pistol, 263
Beretta Model 85F Auto Pistol, 263
Beretta Model 86 Auto Pistol, 263
Beretta Model 87 Auto Pistol, 263
Beretta Model 87 Long Barrel Pistol, 263
Beretta Model 89 Sport Auto Pistol, 263
Beretta Model 89 Target Pistol, 298
Beretta Model 92D Auto Pistol, 263
Beretta Model 92F Stainless Pistol, 263
Beretta Model 92F-EL Stainless Pistol, 263
Beretta Model 92F/92FS/96 Centurion Pistols, 263
Beretta Model 92FC Auto Pistol, 263
Beretta Model 92FS Auto Pistol, 263
Beretta Model 950 BS Auto Pistol, 263
Beretta Model 96 Auto Pistol, 263
Bersa Model 23 Auto Pistol, 264
Bersa Model 83 Auto Pistol, 264
Bersa Model 85 Auto Pistol, 264
Bersa Model 86 Auto Pistol, 264
Bersa Thunder 9 Auto Pistol, 264
BF Single Shot Pistol, 298

BF Ultimate Silhouette Pistol, 298
Black Watch Scotch Pistol, 309
Browning BDA-380 DA Auto Pistol, 264
Browning BDM DA Auto Pistol, 264
Browning Buck Mark 22 Pistol, 265
Browning Buck Mark Field 5.5 Pistol, 298
Browning Buck Mark Plus Pistol, 265
Browning Buck Mark Silhouette Pistol, 298
Browning Buck Mark Target 5.5 Gold Pistol, 298
Browning Buck Mark Target 5.5 Pistol, 298
Browning Buck Mark Unlimited Match Pistol, 298
Browning Buck Mark Varmint Pistol, 265
Browning Hi-Power 40 S&W Pistol, 265
Browning Hi-Power Auto Pistol, 264
Browning Hi-Power Capitan Pistol, 264
Browning Hi-Power HP-Practical Pistol, 265
Browning Hi-Power Mark III Pistol, 264
Browning Micro Buck Mark Pistol, 265
Browning Micro Buck Mark Plus Pistol, 265
Bryco Model 38 Pistols, 265
Bryco Model 48 Pistols, 265

C

Cabela's Paterson Revolver, 311
Calico Model 110 Auto Pistol, 265
Calico Model M-950 Auto Pistol, 266
Century Gun Distributor Model 100 Revolver, 293
Century Model P9R Auto Pistol, 266
Charles Moore Flintlock Pistol, 310
Charleville Flintlock Pistol, 309
Charter Bulldog Pug Revolver, 285
Charter Off Duty Revolver, 285
Charter Police Undercover Revolver, 285
Cimarron 1873 Frontier Six Shooter Revolver, 293
Cimarron 1873 Peacemaker Repro Revolver, 293
Cimarron Artillery Model Single Action, 294
Cimarron Peacekeeper Single Action, 293
Cimarron Single Action Army Revolver, 293
Cimarron U.S. Cavalry Model Single Action, 294
Claridge Hi-Tec Model L Pistol, 266

Includes models suitable for several forms of competition and other sporting purposes.

ACCU-TEK MODEL AT-9 AUTO PISTOL **Caliber:** 9mm Para., 7-shot magazine. **Barrel:** 3.2". **Weight:** 28 oz. **Length:** 6.25" overall. **Stocks:** Black checkered nylon. **Sights:** Blade front, rear adjustable for windage; three-dot system. **Features:** Stainless steel construction. Double action only. Firing pin block with no external safeties. Lifetime warranty. Introduced 1992. Made in U.S. by Accu-Tek.
Price: Satin stainless $270.00
Price: Black finish over stainless $275.00

Accu-Tek AT-40 Auto Pistol Same as the Model AT-9 except chambered for 40 S&W. Introduced 1992.
Price: Stainless $270.00
Price: Black finish over stainless (AT-40B) $275.00

ACCU-TEK MODEL HC-380SS AUTO PISTOL **Caliber:** 380 ACP, 13-shot magazine. **Barrel:** 2.75". **Weight:** 28 oz. **Length:** 6" overall. **Stocks:** Checkered black composition. **Sights:** Blade front, rear adjustable for windage. **Features:** External hammer; manual thumb safety with firing pin and trigger disconnect; bottom magazine release. Stainless finish. Introduced 1993. Made in U.S. by Accu-Tek.
Price: $230.00

ACCU-TEK MODEL AT-380SS AUTO PISTOL **Caliber:** 380 ACP, 5-shot magazine. **Barrel:** 2.75". **Weight:** 20 oz. **Length:** 5.6" overall. **Stocks:** Grooved black composition. **Sights:** Blade front, rear adjustable for windage. **Features:** Stainless steel frame and slide. External hammer; manual thumb safety; firing pin block, trigger disconnect. Lifetime warranty. Introduced 1992. Made in U.S. by Accu-Tek.
Price: Satin stainless $182.00
Price: Black finish over stainless (AT-380SSB) $187.00

Accu-Tek Model AT-32SS Auto Pistol Same as the AT-380SS except chambered for 32 ACP. Introduced 1990.
Price: Satin stainless $176.00
Price: Black finish over stainless (AT-32SSB) $181.00

Accu-Tek Model AT-25SS Auto Pistol Similar to the AT-380SS except chambered for 25 ACP with 7-shot magazine. Also available with aluminum frame and slide with 11-oz. weight. Introduced 1991.
Price: Satin stainless $158.00
Price: Black finish over stainless (AT-25SSB) $163.00

AMERICAN ARMS MODEL CX-22 DA AUTO PISTOL **Caliber:** 22 LR, 8-shot magazine. **Barrel:** 3⅓". **Weight:** 22 oz. **Length:** 6½" overall. **Stocks:** Checkered black polymer. **Sights:** Blade front, rear adjustable for windage. **Features:** Double action with manual hammer-block safety, firing pin safety. Alloy frame. Has external appearance of Walther PPK. Blue/black finish. Introduced 1990. Made in U.S. by American Arms, Inc.
Price: $198.00

AMERICAN ARMS MODEL PK22 DA AUTO PISTOL **Caliber:** 22 LR, 8-shot magazine. **Barrel:** 3.3". **Weight:** 22 oz. **Length:** 6.3" overall. **Stocks:** Checkered plastic. **Sights:** Fixed. **Features:** Double action. Polished blue finish. Slide-mounted safety. Made in the U.S. by American Arms, Inc.
Price: $198.00

AMERICAN ARMS MODEL P-98 AUTO PISTOL **Caliber:** 22 LR, 8-shot magazine. **Barrel:** 5". **Weight:** 25 oz. **Length:** 8⅛" overall. **Stocks:** Grooved black polymer. **Sights:** Blade front, rear adjustable for windage. **Features:** Double action with hammer-block safety, magazine disconnect safety. Alloy frame. Has external appearance of the Walther P-38 pistol. Introduced 1989. Made in U.S. by American Arms, Inc.
Price: $213.00

Accu-Tek AT-9

Accu-Tek HC-380SS

Accu-Tek AT-380SS

American Arms PK22

American Arms Spectre

AMERICAN ARMS SPECTRE DA PISTOL **Caliber:** 9mm Para., 30-shot; 45 ACP, 30-shot magazine. **Barrel:** 6". **Weight:** 4 lbs., 8 oz. **Length:** 13.75". **Stocks:** Black nylon. **Sights:** Post front adjustable for windage and elevation, fixed U-notch rear. **Features:** Triple action blowback fires from closed bolt; ambidextrous safety and decocking levers; matte black finish; magazine loading tool. For standard velocity ammunition only. From American Arms, Inc.
Price: 9mm **$429.00**
Price: 45 ACP **$457.00**

American Arms PX-22

AMERICAN ARMS MODEL PX-22 AUTO PISTOL **Caliber:** 22 LR, 7-shot magazine. **Barrel:** 2.85". **Weight:** 15 oz. **Length:** 5.39" overall. **Stocks:** Black checkered plastic. **Sights:** Fixed. **Features:** Double action; 7-shot magazine. Polished blue finish. Introduced 1989. Made in U.S. From American Arms, Inc.
Price: **$193.00**

AMT AUTOMAG II AUTO PISTOL **Caliber:** 22 WMR, 9-shot magazine (7-shot with 3⅜" barrel). **Barrel:** 3⅜", 4½", 6". **Weight:** About 23 oz. **Length:** 9⅜" overall. **Stocks:** Grooved carbon fiber. **Sights:** Blade front, adjustable rear. **Features:** Made of stainless steel. Gas-assisted action. Exposed hammer. Slide flats have brushed finish, rest is sandblast. Squared trigger guard. Introduced 1986. From AMT.
Price: **$375.95**

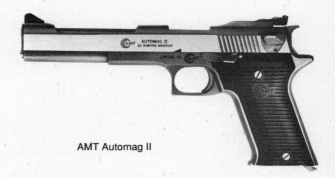

AMT Automag II

AMT AUTOMAG III PISTOL **Caliber:** 30 Carbine, 9mm Win. Mag., 8-shot magazine. **Barrel:** 6⅜". **Weight:** 43 oz. **Length:** 10½" overall. **Stocks:** Carbon fiber. **Sights:** Blade front, adjustable rear. **Features:** Stainless steel construction. Hammer-drop safety. Slide flats have brushed finish, rest is sandblasted. Introduced 1989. From AMT.
Price: **$465.95**

AMT AUTOMAG IV PISTOL **Caliber:** 10mm Magnum, 45 Winchester Magnum, 6-shot magazine. **Barrel:** 6.5" (45), 8⅝" (10mm only). **Weight:** 46 oz. **Length:** 10.5" overall with 6.5" barrel. **Stocks:** Carbon fiber. **Sights:** Blade front, adjustable rear. **Features:** Made of stainless steel with brushed finish. Introduced 1990. Made in U.S. by AMT.
Price: **$679.99**

AMT Backup DAO

AMT BACKUP AUTO PISTOL **Caliber:** 380 ACP, 5-shot magazine. **Barrel:** 2½". **Weight:** 18 oz. **Length:** 5" overall. **Stocks:** Carbon fiber. **Sights:** Fixed, open, recessed. **Features:** Concealed hammer, blowback operation; manual and grip safeties. All stainless steel construction. Smallest domestically-produced pistol in 380. From AMT.
Price: **$295.99**

AMT Backup Double Action Only Pistol Similar to the standard Backup except has double-action-only mechanism, enlarged trigger guard, slide is rounded ar rear. Has 6-shot magazine. Introduced 1992. From AMT.
Price: **$295.99**

> Consult our Directory pages for the location of firms mentioned.

AMT On Duty

AMT ON DUTY DA PISTOL **Caliber:** 9mm Para., 15-shot; 40 S&W, 11-shot; 45 ACP, 9-shot magazine. **Barrel:** 4½". **Weight:** 32 oz. **Length:** 7¾" overall. **Stocks:** Smooth carbon fiber. **Sights:** Blade front, rear adjustable for windage; three-dot system. **Features:** Choice of DA with decocker or double action only. Inertia firing pin, trigger disconnector safety. Aluminum frame with steel recoil shoulder, stainless steel slide and barrel. Introduced 1991. Made in the U.S. by AMT.
Price: 9mm, 40 S&W **$469.99**
Price: 45 ACP **$529.99**

AMT 45 ACP HARDBALLER **Caliber:** 45 ACP. **Barrel:** 5". **Weight:** 39 oz. **Length:** 8½" overall. **Stocks:** Wrap-around rubber. **Sights:** Adjustable. **Features:** Extended combat safety, serrated matte slide rib, loaded chamber indicator, long grip safety, beveled magazine well, adjustable target trigger. All stainless steel. From AMT.
Price: **$529.99**
Price: Government model (as above except no rib, fixed sights) **$475.95**

AMT 45 ACP HARDBALLER LONG SLIDE **Caliber:** 45 ACP. **Barrel:** 7". **Length:** 10½" overall. **Stocks:** Wrap-around rubber. **Sights:** Fully adjustable rear sight. **Features:** Slide and barrel are 2" longer than the standard 45, giving less recoil, added velocity, longer sight radius. Has extended combat safety, serrated matte rib, loaded chamber indicator, wide adjustable trigger. From AMT.
Price: **$575.95**

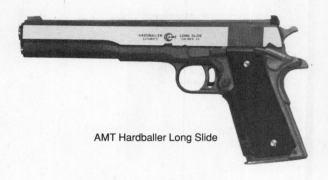

AMT Hardballer Long Slide

ASTRA A-70 AUTO PISTOL **Caliber:** 9mm Para., 8-shot; 40 S&W, 7-shot magazine. **Barrel:** 3.5". **Weight:** 29.3 oz. **Length:** 6.5" overall. **Stocks:** Checkered black plastic. **Sights:** Blade front, rear adjustable for windage. **Features:** All steel frame and slide. Checkered grip straps and trigger guard. Nickel or blue finish. Introduced 1992. Imported from Spain by European American Armory.
Price: Blue, 9mm Para. **$495.00**
Price: Blue, 40 S&W **$495.00**
Price: Nickel, 9mm Para. **$540.00**
Price: Nickel, 40 S&W **$540.00**

Astra A-75 Decocker Auto Pistol Same as the A-70 except has decocker system, different trigger, contoured pebble-grain grips. Introduced 1993. Imported from Spain by European American Armory.
Price: Blue, 9mm or 40 S&W **$575.00**
Price: Nickel, 9mm or 40 S&W **$620.00**
Price: Blue, 45 ACP **$595.00**
Price: Nickel, 45 ACP **$640.00**

Astra A-75

ASTRA A-100 AUTO PISTOL **Caliber:** 9mm Para., 17-shot; 40 S&W, 13-shot; 45 ACP, 9-shot magazine. **Barrel:** 3.9". **Weight:** 29 oz. **Length:** 7.1" overall. **Stocks:** Checkered black plastic. **Sights:** Blade front, interchangeable rear blades for elevation, screw adjustable for windage. **Features:** Selective double action. Decocking lever permits lowering hammer onto locked firing pin. Automatic firing pin block. Side button magazine release. Introduced 1993. Imported from Spain by European American Armory.
Price: Blue, 9mm, 40 S&W, 45 ACP **$625.00**
Price: As above, nickel **$660.00**
Price: Blue with night sights **$750.00**
Price: Nickel with night sights **$785.00**

AUTO-ORDNANCE 1911A1 AUTOMATIC PISTOL **Caliber:** 9mm Para., 38 Super, 9-shot; 10mm, 45 ACP, 7-shot magazine. **Barrel:** 5". **Weight:** 39 oz. **Length:** 8½" overall. **Stocks:** Checkered plastic with medallion. **Sights:** Blade front, rear adjustable for windage. **Features:** Same specs as 1911A1 military guns—parts interchangeable. Frame and slide blued; each radius has non-glare finish. Made in U.S. by Auto-Ordnance Corp.
Price: 45 cal. **$388.95**
Price: 9mm, 38 Super **$415.00**
Price: 10mm (has three-dot combat sights, rubber wrap-around grips) . . **$420.95**
Price: 45 ACP General Model (Commander style) **$427.95**
Price: Duo Tone (nickel frame, blue slide, three-dot sight system, textured black wrap-around grips) **$575.00**

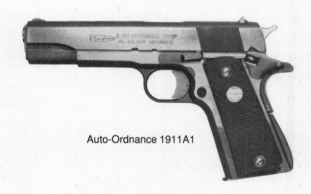

Auto-Ordnance 1911A1

Auto-Ordnance ZG-51 Pit Bull Auto Same as the 1911A1 except has 3½"barrel, weighs 36 oz. and has an over-all length of 7¼". Available in 45 ACP only; 7-shot magazine. Introduced 1989.
Price: **$420.95**

Auto-Ordnance 40 S&W 1911A1 Similar to the standard 1911A1 except has 4½" barrel giving overall length of 7¾", and weighs 37 oz. Has three-dot combat sight system, black rubber wrap-around grips, 8-shot magazine. Introduced 1991.
Price: **$427.95**

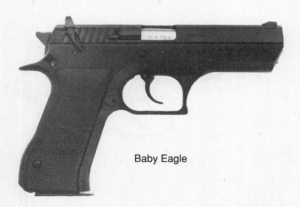

Baby Eagle

BABY EAGLE AUTO PISTOL **Caliber:** 9mm Para., 40 S&W, 41 A.E. **Barrel:** 4.37". **Weight:** 35 oz. **Length:** 8.14" overall. **Stocks:** High-impact black polymer. **Sights:** Combat. **Features:** Double-action mechanism; polygonal rifling; ambidextrous safety. Introduced 1992. Imported by Magnum Research.
Price: 9mm Para., 40 S&W, 41 A.E. **$569.00**
Price: Conversion kit, 9mm Para. to 41 A.E. **$239.00**

BERETTA MODEL 80 SERIES DA PISTOLS **Caliber:** 380 ACP, 13-shot magazine (8-shot for M85F); 22 LR, 7-shot (M87), 22 LR, 8-shot (M89). **Barrel:** 3.82". **Weight:** About 23 oz. (M84/85); 20.8 oz. (M87). **Length:** 6.8" overall. **Stocks:** Glossy black plastic (wood optional at extra cost). **Sights:** Fixed front, drift-adjustable rear. **Features:** Double action, quick takedown, convenient magazine release. Introduced 1977. Imported from Italy by Beretta U.S.A.

Price: Model 84F (380 ACP) **$525.00**
Price: Model 84F wood grips **$555.00**
Price: Model 84F nickel finish **$600.00**
Price: Model 85F nickel finish, 8-shot **$550.00**
Price: Model 85F plastic grips, 8-shot **$485.00**
Price: Model 85F wood grips, 8-shot **$510.00**
Price: Model 87, 22 LR, 7-shot magazine, wood grips **$490.00**
Price: Model 87 Long Barrel, 22 LR, single action **$510.00**
Price: Model 89 Sport Wood, single action, 22 LR **$735.00**

Beretta Model 84F

Beretta Model 86 Similar to the 380-caliber Model 85 except has tip-up barrel for first-round loading. Barrel length is 4.33", overall length of 7.33". Has 8-shot magazine, walnut or plastic grips. Introduced 1989.
Price: **$510.00**

BERETTA MODEL 92FS PISTOL **Caliber:** 9mm Para., 15-shot magazine. **Barrel:** 4.9". **Weight:** 34 oz. **Length:** 8.5" overall. **Stocks:** Checkered black plastic; wood optional at extra cost. **Sights:** Blade front, rear adjustable for windage. **Features:** Double action. Extractor acts as chamber loaded indicator, squared trigger guard, grooved front- and backstraps, inertia firing pin. Matte finish. Introduced 1977. Made in U.S. and imported from Italy by Beretta U.S.A.
Price: With plastic grips **$625.00**
Price: With wood grips **$645.00**

Beretta Model 92FS

Beretta Model 92FC Pistol Similar to the Beretta Model 92FS except has cut down frame, 4.3" barrel, 7.8" overall length, 13-shot magazine, weighs 31.5 oz. Introduced 1989.
Price: With plastic grips **$625.00**
Price: With wood grips **$645.00**
Price: For Trijicon sights, add **$65.00**

Beretta Model 92F Stainless Pistol Same as the Model 92FS except has stainless steel barrel and slide, and frame of aluminum-zirconium alloy. Has three-dot sight system. Introduced 1992.
Price: **$755.00**
Price: Model 92F-EL Stainless (gold trim, engraved barrel, slide, frame, gold-finished safety-levers, trigger, magazine release, grip screws) **$1,240.00**
Price: For Trijicon sights, add **$65.00**

Beretta Centurion

Beretta Model 96 Auto Pistol Same as the Model 92F except chambered for 40 S&W. Ambidextrous triple safety mechanism with passive firing pin catch, slide safety/decocking lever, trigger bar disconnect. Has 10-shot magazine. Available with Trijicon or three-dot sights. Introduced 1992.
Price: Model 96F, plastic grips **$640.00**
Price: Model 96D, double action only, three-dot sights **$605.00**
Price: For Trijicon sights, add **$65.00**

Beretta Model 92D Pistol Same as the Model 92FS except double action only and has bobbed hammer, no external safety. Introduced 1992.
Price: With plastic grips, three-dot sights **$585.00**
Price: As above with Trijicon sights **$650.00**

Beretta Models 92FS/96 Centurion Pistols Same as the Model 92FS and 96 except uses slide and barrel (4.3") of the Compact version. Trijicon or three-dot sight systems. Plastic or wood grips. Available in 9mm or 40 S&W. Introduced 1992.
Price: Model 92FS Centurion, three-dot sights, plastic grips **$625.00**
Price: Model 92FS Centurion, wood grips **$645.00**
Price: Model 96 Centurion, three-dot sights, plastic grips **$640.00**
Price: For Trijicon sights, add **$65.00**

Beretta 950 BS

BERETTA MODEL 950 BS AUTO PISTOL **Caliber:** 25 ACP, 8-shot. **Barrel:** 2.5". **Weight:** 9.9 oz. **Length:** 4.5" overall. **Stocks:** Checkered black plastic or walnut. **Sights:** Fixed. **Features:** Single action, thumb safety; tip-up barrel for direct loading/unloading, cleaning. From Beretta U.S.A.
Price: Blue, 25 . . . . **$180.00**
Price: Nickel, 25 . . . . **$210.00**
Price: Engraved **$260.00**
Price: Matte blue **$150.00**

Beretta Model 21 Pistol Similar to the Model 950 BS. Chambered for 22 LR and 25 ACP. Both double action. 2.5" barrel, 4.9" overall length. 7-round magazine on 22 cal.; 8-round magazine; available in nickel or blue finish. Both have walnut grips. Introduced in 1985.
Price: 22-cal. **$235.00**
Price: 22-cal., nickel finish **$260.00**
Price: 25-cal. **$235.00**
Price: 25-cal., nickel finish **$260.00**
Price: EL model, 22 or 25 . . . . **$285.00**
Price: Matte blue, plastic grips, 22 or 25 . . . . **$185.00**

BERSA MODEL 23 AUTO PISTOL **Caliber:** 22 LR, 10-shot magazine. **Barrel:** 3.5". **Weight:** 24.5 oz. **Length:** 6.6" overall. **Stocks:** Walnut with stippled panels. **Sights:** Blade front, notch rear adjustable for windage; three-dot system. **Features:** Double action; firing pin and magazine safeties. Available in blue or nickel. Introduced 1989. Distributed by Eagle Imports, Inc.
Price: Blue **$281.95**
Price: Nickel **$314.95**

Bersa Model 85

BERSA MODEL 83, 85 AUTO PISTOLS **Caliber:** 380 ACP, 7-shot (M83), 13-shot magazine (M85). **Barrel:** 3.5". **Weight:** 25.75 oz. **Length:** 6.6" overall. **Stocks:** Walnut with stippled panels. **Sights:** Blade front, notch rear adjustable for windage; three-dot system. **Features:** Double action; firing pin and magazine safeties. Available in blue or nickel. Introduced 1989. Distributed by Eagle Imports, Inc.
Price: Model 85, blue **$331.95**
Price: Model 85, nickel **$391.95**
Price: Model 83 (as above, except 7-shot magazine), blue **$281.95**
Price: Model 83, nickel **$314.95**

BERSA MODEL 86 AUTO PISTOL **Caliber:** 380 ACP, 13-shot magazine. **Barrel:** 3.5". **Weight:** 22 oz. **Length:** 6.6" overall. **Stocks:** Wraparound textured rubber. **Sights:** Blade front, rear adjustable for windage; three-dot system. **Features:** Double action; firing pin and magazine safeties; combat-style trigger guard. Matte blue or satin nickel. Introduced 1992. Distributed by Eagle Imports, Inc.
Price: Matte blue **$366.95**
Price: Satin nickel **$399.95**

Bersa Thunder 9

BERSA THUNDER 9 AUTO PISTOL **Caliber:** 9mm Para., 15-shot magazine. **Barrel:** 4". **Weight:** 30 oz. **Length:** 7⅜" overall. **Stocks:** Checkered black polymer. **Sights:** Blade front, rear adjustable for windage and elevation; three-dot system. **Features:** Double action. Ambidextrous safety, decocking levers and slide release; internal automatic firing pin safety; reversible extended magazine release; adjustable trigger stop; alloy frame. Link-free locked breech design. Matte blue finish. Introduced 1993. Imported from Argentina by Eagle Imports, Inc.
Price: Blue only **$414.95**

BROWNING BDA-380 DA AUTO PISTOL **Caliber:** 380 ACP, 13-shot magazine. **Barrel:** 3¹³/₁₆". **Weight:** 23 oz. **Length:** 6¾" overall. **Stocks:** Smooth walnut with inset Browning medallion. **Sights:** Blade front, rear drift-adjustable for windage. **Features:** Combination safety and de-cocking lever will automatically lower a cocked hammer to half-cock and can be operated by right- or left-hand shooters. Inertia firing pin. Introduced 1978. Imported from Italy by Browning.
Price: Blue **$592.95**
Price: Nickel **$624.95**

Browning BDA-380

BROWNING BDM DA AUTO PISTOL **Caliber:** 9mm Para., 15-shot magazine. **Barrel:** 4.73" **Weight:** 31 oz. **Length:** 7.85" overall. **Stocks:** Moulded black composition; checkered, with thumbrest on both sides. **Sights:** Low profile removable blade front, rear screw adjustable for windage. **Features:** Mode selector allows switching from DA pistol to "revolver" mode via a switch on the slide. Decocking lever/safety on the frame. Two redundant, passive, internal safety systems. All steel frame; matte black finish. Introduced 1991. Made in the U.S. From Browning.
Price: **$559.95**

BROWNING HI-POWER 9mm AUTOMATIC PISTOL **Caliber:** 9mm Para., 13-shot magazine. **Barrel:** 4²¹/₃₂". **Weight:** 32 oz. **Length:** 7¾" overall. **Stocks:** Walnut, hand checkered, or black Polyamide. **Sights:** ⅛" blade front; rear screw-adjustable for windage and elevation. Also available with fixed rear (drift-adjustable for windage). **Features:** External hammer with half-cock and thumb safeties. A blow on the hammer cannot discharge a cartridge; cannot be fired with magazine removed. Fixed rear sight model available. Ambidextrous safety available only with matte finish, moulded grips. Imported from Belgium by Browning.
Price: Fixed sight model, walnut grips **$524.95**
Price: 9mm with rear sight adj. for w. and e., walnut grips . . . **$571.95**
Price: Mark III, standard matte black finish, fixed sight, moulded grips, ambidextrous safety **$493.95**
Price: Silver chrome, adjustable sight, Pachmayr grips **$581.95**

Browning BDM

Browning Capitan Hi-Power Pistol Similar to the standard Hi-Power except has adjustable tangent rear sight authentic to the early-production model. Also has Commander-style hammer. Checkered walnut grips, polished blue finish. Reintroduced 1993. Imported from Belgium by Browning.
Price: **$619.95**

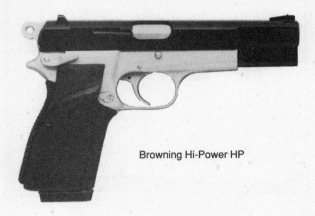

Browning Hi-Power HP

Browning Micro Buck Mark

Browning Buck Mark Varmint

BRYCO MODEL 38 AUTO PISTOLS   Caliber: 22 LR, 32 ACP, 380 ACP, 6-shot magazine. **Barrel:** 2.8". **Weight:** 15 oz. **Length:** 5.3" overall. **Stocks:** Polished resin-impregnated wood. **Sights:** Fixed. **Features:** Safety locks sear and slide. Choice of satin nickel, bright chrome or black Teflon finishes. Introduced 1988. From Jennings Firearms.
Price: 22 LR, 32 ACP, about **$109.95**
Price: 380 ACP, about **$129.95**

BRYCO MODEL 48 AUTO PISTOLS   Caliber: 22 LR, 32 ACP, 380 ACP, 6-shot magazine. **Barrel:** 4". **Weight:** 19 oz. **Length:** 6.7" overall. **Stocks:** Polished resin-impregnated wood. **Sights:** Fixed. **Features:** Safety locks sear and slide. Choice of satin nickel, bright chrome or black Teflon finishes. Announced 1988. From Jennings Firearms.
Price: 22 LR, 32 ACP, about **$139.00**
Price: 380 ACP, about **$139.00**

CALICO MODEL 110 AUTO PISTOL   Caliber: 22 LR, 100-shot magazine. **Barrel:** 6". **Weight:** 3.7 lbs. (loaded). **Length:** 17.9" overall. **Stocks:** Moulded composition. **Sights:** Adjustable post front, notch rea . **Features:** Aluminum alloy frame; flash suppressor; pistol grip compartment; ambidextrous safety. Uses same helical-feed magazine as M-100 Carbine. Introduced 1986. Made in U.S. From Calico.
Price: **$301.90**

Browning Hi-Power HP-Practical Pistol   Similar to the standard Hi-Power except has silver-chromed frame with blued slide, wrap-around Pachmayr rubber grips, round-style serrated hammer and removable front sight, fixed rear (drift-adjustable for windage). Introduced 1991.
Price: **$565.95**
Price: With fully adjustable rear sight **$612.95**

Browning 40 S&W Hi-Power Pistol   Similar to the standard Hi-Power except chambered for 40 S&W, 10-shot magazine, weighs 35 oz., and has 4¾" barrel. Comes with matte blue finish, low profile front sight blade, drift-adjustable rear sight, ambidextrous safety, moulded polyamide grips with thumb rest. Introduced 1993. Imported from Belgium by Browning.
Price: **$612.95**

BROWNING BUCK MARK 22 PISTOL   Caliber: 22 LR, 10-shot magazine. **Barrel:** 5½". **Weight:** 32 oz. **Length:** 9½" overall. **Stocks:** Black moulded composite with skip-line checkering. **Sights:** Ramp front, Browning Pro Target rear adjustable for windage and elevation. **Features:** All steel, matte blue finish or nickel, gold-colored trigger. Buck Mark Plus has laminated wood grips. Made in U.S. Introduced 1985. From Browning.
Price: Buck Mark, blue **$234.95**
Price: Buck Mark, nickel finish with contoured rubber stocks **$274.95**
Price: Buck Mark Plus **$284.95**

Browning Micro Buck Mark   Same as the standard Buck Mark and Buck Mark Plus except has 4" barrel. Available in blue or nickel. Has 16-click Pro Target rear sight. Introduced 1992.
Price: Blue **$234.95**
Price: Nickel **$274.95**
Price: Micro Buck Mark Plus **$284.95**

Browning Buck Mark Varmint   Same as the Buck Mark except has 9⅞" heavy barrel with .900" diameter and full-length scope base (no open sights); walnut grips with optional forend, or finger-groove walnut. Overall length is 14", weight is 48 oz. Introduced 1987.
Price: **$354.95**

Bryco Model 48

Calico M-110

CALICO MODEL M-950 AUTO PISTOL **Caliber:** 9mm Para., 50- or 100-shot magazine. **Barrel:** 7.5". **Weight:** 2.25 lbs. (empty). **Length:** 14" overall (50-shot magazine). **Stocks:** Glass-filled polymer. **Sights:** Post front adjustable for windage and elevation, fixed notch rear. **Features:** Helical feed 50- or 100-shot magazine. Ambidextrous safety, static cocking handle. Retarded blowback action. Glass-filled polymer grip. Introduced 1989. From Calico.
Price: $572.90

CENTURY MODEL P9R PISTOL **Caliber:** 9mm Para., 15-shot magazine. **Barrel:** 4.6". **Weight:** 35 oz. **Length:** 8" overall. **Stocks:** Checkered walnut. **Sights:** Blade front, rear drift adjustable for windage. **Features:** Double action with hammer-drop safety. Polished blue finish. Comes with spare magazine. Imported from Hungary by Century International Arms.
Price: About $263.00
Price: Chrome finish, about $375.00

CLARIDGE HI-TEC MODEL S, L, T PISTOLS **Caliber:** 9mm Para., 18-shot magazine. **Barrel:** 5" (S model); 7.5" (L model); 9.5" (T model). **Weight:** 3 lbs., 2 oz. (L model). **Length:** 15.1" overall (L model). **Stocks:** Moulded composition. **Sights:** Adjustable post front in ring, open rear adjustable for windage. **Features:** Aluminum or stainless frame. Telescoping bolt; floating firing pin. Safety locks the firing pin. Also available in 40 S&W and 45 ACP. Made in U.S. by Claridge Hi-Tec, Inc.
Price: Model S (5") $419.50
Price: Model L (7.5") $466.50
Price: Model T (target, 9.5") $466.50
Price: Model ZL-9 (7.5" with laser sight) $776.50
Price: Model ZT-9 (9.5" with laser sight) $776.50

> Consult our Directory pages for the location of firms mentioned.

COLT ALL AMERICAN MODEL 2000 DA AUTO **Caliber:** 9mm Para., 15-shot magazine. **Barrel:** 4.5". **Weight:** 29 oz. (polymer frame); 33 oz. (aluminum frame). **Length:** 7.5" overall. **Stocks:** Checkered polymer. **Sights:** Ramped blade front, rear drift-adjustable for windage. Three dot system. **Features:** Double-action only. Moulded polymer or aluminum frame, blued steel slide. Internal striker block safety. Introduced 1991. Made in U.S. by Colt's Mfg. Co., Inc.
Price: Polymer frame $575.00
Price: Aluminum frame . . . . NA
Price: 3¾" barrel and bushing kit . . . . NA

COLT COMBAT COMMANDER AUTO PISTOL **Caliber:** 38 Super, 9-shot; 45 ACP, 8-shot. **Barrel:** 4¼". **Weight:** 36 oz. **Length:** 7¾" overall. **Stocks:** Rubber combat. **Sights:** Fixed, glare-proofed blade front, square notch rear; three-dot system. **Features:** Long trigger; arched housing; grip and thumb safeties.
Price: 45, blue $694.95
Price: 45, stainless $749.95
Price: 38 Super, stainless $749.95

Colt Lightweight Commander MK IV/Series 80 Same as Commander except high strength aluminum alloy frame, rubber combat grips, weight 27½ oz. 45 ACP only.
Price: Blue $694.95

COLT DOUBLE EAGLE MKII/SERIES 90 DA PISTOL **Caliber:** 45 ACP, 8-shot magazine. **Barrel:** 4½", 5". **Weight:** 39 ozs. **Length:** 8½" overall. **Stocks:** Black checkered Xenoy thermoplastic. **Sights:** Blade front, rear adjustable for windage. High profile three-dot system. Colt Accro adjustable sight optional. **Features:** Made of stainless steel with matte finish. Checkered and curved extended trigger guard, wide steel trigger; decocking lever on left side; traditional magazine release; grooved frontstrap; bevelled magazine well; extended grip guard; rounded, serrated combat-style hammer. Announced 1989.
Price: $695.95
Price: Combat Comm., 45, 4½" bbl. $695.95

Colt Double Eagle Officer's ACP Similar to the regular Double Eagle except 45 ACP only, 3½" barrel, 34 oz., 7¼" overall length. Has 5¼" sight radius. Also offered in Lightweight version weighing 25 oz. Introduced 1991.
Price: Standard or Lightweight $695.95

Calico M-950

Claridge Hi-Tec ZL-9

Colt All American 2000

Colt Double Eagle MkII

COLT OFFICER'S ACP MK IV/SERIES 80 **Caliber:** 45 ACP, 6-shot magazine. **Barrel:** 3½". **Weight:** 34 oz. (steel frame); 24 oz. (alloy frame). **Length:** 7¼" overall. **Stocks:** Rubber combat. **Sights:** Ramp blade front with white dot, square notch rear with two white dots. **Features:** Trigger safety lock (thumb safety), grip safety, firing pin safety; long trigger; flat mainspring housing. Also available with lightweight alloy frame and in stainless steel. Introduced 1985.
Price: Blue $694.95
Price: L.W., blue finish $694.95
Price: Stainless $739.95
Price: Bright stainless $814.95

COLT GOVERNMENT MODEL MK IV/SERIES 80 **Caliber:** 38 Super, 9-shot; 45 ACP, 8-shot magazine. **Barrel:** 5". **Weight:** 38 oz. **Length:** 8½" overall. **Stocks:** Rubber combat. **Sights:** Ramp front, fixed square notch rear; three-dot system. **Features:** Grip and thumb safeties and internal firing pin safety, long trigger.
Price: 45 ACP, blue **$693.95**
Price: 45 ACP, stainless **$738.95**
Price: 45 ACP, bright stainless **$813.95**
Price: 38 Super, blue **$704.95**
Price: 38 Super, stainless **$727.95**
Price: 38 Super, bright stainless **$819.95**

Colt 10mm Delta Elite Similar to the Government Model except chambered for 10mm auto cartridge. Has three-dot high profile front and rear combat sights, rubber combat stocks with Delta medallion, internal firing pin safety, and new recoil spring/buffer system. Introduced 1987.
Price: Blue **$765.95**

Colt Combat Elite MK IV/Series 80 Similar to the Government Model except has stainless frame with ordnance steel slide and internal parts. High profile front, rear sights with three-dot system, extended grip safety, beveled magazine well, rubber combat stocks. Introduced 1986.
Price: 45 ACP, STS/B **$841.95**
Price: 38 Super, STS/B **$852.95**

COLT MODEL 1991 A1 AUTO PISTOL **Caliber:** 45 ACP, 7-shot magazine. **Barrel:** 5". **Weight:** 38 oz. **Length:** 8.5" overall. **Stocks:** Checkered black composition. **Sights:** Ramped blade front, fixed square notch rear, high profile. **Features:** Parkerized finish. Continuation of serial number range used on original G.I. 1911-A1 guns. Comes with one magazine and moulded carrying case. Introduced 1991.
Price: **$499.95**

Colt Model 1991 A1 Commander Auto Pistol Similar to the Model 1991 A1 except has 4¼" barrel. Parkerized finish. 7-shot magazine. Comes in moulded case. Introduced 1993.
Price: **$499.95**

Colt Model 1991 A1 Compact Auto Pistol Similar to the Model 1991 A1 except has 3½" barrel. Overall length is 7", and gun is ⅜" shorter in height. Comes with one 6-shot magazine, moulded case. Introduced 1993.
Price: **$499.95**

COLT GOVERNMENT MODEL 380 **Caliber:** 380 ACP, 7-shot magazine. **Barrel:** 3¼". **Weight:** 21¾ oz. **Length:** 6" overall. **Stocks:** Checkered composition. **Sights:** Ramp front, square notch rear, fixed. **Features:** Scaled-down version of the 1911A1 Colt G.M. Has thumb and internal firing pin safeties. Introduced 1983.
Price: Blue **$432.95**
Price: Nickel **$483.95**
Price: Stainless **$463.95**
Price: Pocketlite 380, blue **$432.95**

Colt Mustang Plus II Similar to the 380 Government Model except has the shorter barrel and slide of the Mustang. Introduced 1988.
Price: Blue **$432.95**
Price: Stainless **$463.95**

Colt Mustang 380, Mustang Pocketlite Similar to the standard 380 Government Model. Mustang has steel frame (18.5 oz.), Pocketlite has aluminum alloy (12.5 oz.). Both are ½" shorter than 380 G.M., have 2¾" barrel. Introduced 1987.
Price: Mustang 380, blue **$432.95**
Price: As above, nickel **$483.95**
Price: As above, stainless **$463.95**
Price: Mustang Pocketlite, blue **$432.95**
Price: Mustang Pocketlite STS/N **$463.95**

Coonan Compact 357 Magnum Cadet Pistol Similar to the 357 Magnum full-size gun except has 3.9" barrel, shorter frame, 6-shot magazine. Weight is 39 oz., overall length 7.8". Linkless bull barrel, full-length recoil spring guide rod, extended slide latch. Introduced 1993. Made in U.S. by Coonan Arms, Inc.
Price: **$841.00**

Colt Government Model

Colt 1991A1 Compact

Colt Government Pocketlite

Coonan Compact 357

COONAN 357 MAGNUM PISTOL **Caliber:** 357 Mag., 7-shot magazine. **Barrel:** 5". **Weight:** 42 oz. **Length:** 8.3" overall. **Stocks:** Smooth walnut. **Sights:** Interchangeable ramp front, rear adjustable for windage. **Features:** Stainless and alloy steel construction. Unique barrel hood improves accuracy and reliability. Linkless barrel. Many parts interchange with Colt autos. Has grip, hammer, half-cock safeties, extended slide latch. Made in U.S. by Coonan Arms, Inc.
Price: 5" barrel **$720.00**
Price: 6" barrel **$755.00**
Price: With 6" compensated barrel **$999.00**

CZ 75 AUTO PISTOL. Caliber: 9mm Para., 15-shot magazine. **Barrel:** 4.7". **Weight:** 34.3 oz. **Length:** 8.1" overall. **Stocks:** High impact checkered plastic. **Sights:** Square post front, rear adjustable for windage; three-dot system. **Features:** Single action/double action design; choice of black polymer, matte or high-polish blue finishes. All-steel frame. Imported from the Czech Republic by Action Arms, Ltd.
Price: Black polymer finish **$485.00**
Price: Matte blue **$505.00**
Price: High-polish blue **$519.00**

CZ 75 Compact Auto Pistol Similar to the CZ 75 except has 13-shot magazine, 3.9" barrel and weighs 32 oz. Has removable front sight, non-glare ribbed slide top. Trigger guard is squared and serrated; combat hammer. Introduced 1993. Imported from the Czech Republic by Action Arms, Ltd.
Price: Black polymer finish **$519.00**
Price: Matte blue **$545.00**
Price: High-polish blue **$565.00**

CZ 75 Compact

CZ83

CZ 85 Auto Pistol Same gun as the CZ 75 except has ambidextrous slide release and safety-levers; non-glare, ribbed slide top; squared, serrated trigger guard; trigger stop to prevent overtravel. Introduced 1986. Imported from the Czech Republic by Action Arms, Ltd.
Price: Black polymer finish **$515.00**
Price: Matte blue **$529.00**
Price: High-polish blue **$559.00**

CZ 85 Combat Auto Pistol Same as the CZ 85 except has walnut grips, round combat hammer, fully adjustable rear sight, extended magazine release. Trigger parts coated with friction-free beryllium copper. Introduced 1992. Imported from the Czech Republic by Action Arms, Ltd.
Price: Black polymer finish **$625.00**

CZ 83 DOUBLE-ACTION PISTOL. Caliber: 380 ACP, 12-shot magazine. **Barrel:** 3.8". **Weight:** 26.2 oz. **Length:** 6.8" overall. **Stocks:** High impact checkered plastic. **Sights:** Removable square post front, rear adjustable for windage; three-dot system. **Features:** Single action/double action; ambidextrous magazine release and safety. Blue finish; non-glare ribbed slide top. Imported from the Czech Republic by Action Arms Ltd.
Price: **$389.00**

Daewoo DP51

DAEWOO DP51 AUTO PISTOL. Caliber: 9mm Para., 13-shot magazine. **Barrel:** 4.1". **Weight:** 28.2 oz. **Length:** 7.48" overall. **Stocks:** Checkered composition. **Sights:** Blade front, square notch rear drift adjustable for windage. **Features:** Patented tri-action mechanism. Ambidextrous manual safety and magazine catch, half-cock and firing pin block. Alloy frame, squared trigger guard. Matte black finish. Introduced 1991. Imported from Korea by Firstshot.
Price: **$369.50**

DAVIS P-32 AUTO PISTOL. Caliber: 32 ACP, 6-shot magazine. **Barrel:** 2.8". **Weight:** 22 oz. **Length:** 5.4" overall. **Stocks:** Laminated wood. **Sights:** Fixed. **Features:** Choice of black Teflon or chrome finish. Announced 1986. Made in U.S. by Davis Industries.
Price: **$87.50**

DAVIS P-380 AUTO PISTOL. Caliber: 380 ACP, 5-shot magazine. **Barrel:** 2.8". **Weight:** 22 oz. **Length:** 5.4" overall. **Stocks:** Black composition. **Sights:** Fixed. **Features:** Choice of chrome or black Teflon finish. Introduced 1991. Made in U.S. by Davis Industries.
Price: **$98.00**

Desert Eagle Magnum

DESERT EAGLE MAGNUM PISTOL. Caliber: 357 Mag., 9-shot; 41 Mag., 44 Mag., 8-shot; 50 Magnum, 7-shot. **Barrel:** 6", 10", 14" interchangeable. **Weight:** 357 Mag.—62 oz.; 41 Mag., 44 Mag.—69 oz.; 50 Mag.—72 oz. **Length:** 10¼" overall (6" bbl.). **Stocks:** Wraparound plastic. **Sights:** Blade on ramp front, combat-style rear. Adjustable available. **Features:** Rotating three-lug bolt; ambidextrous safety; combat-style trigger guard; adjustable trigger optional. Military epoxy finish. Satin, bright nickel, hard chrome, polished and blued finishes available. Imported from Israel by Magnum Research, Inc.
Price: 357, 6" bbl., standard pistol **$789.00**
Price: As above, stainless steel frame **$839.00**
Price: 41 Mag., 6", standard pistol **$799.00**
Price: 41 Mag., stainless steel frame **$849.00**
Price: 44 Mag., 6", standard pistol **$899.00**
Price: As above, stainless steel frame **$949.00**
Price: 50 Magnum, 6" bbl., standard pistol **$1,249.00**

Desert Industries Double Deuce

E.A.A. Witness Sport

E.A.A. WITNESS DA AUTO PISTOL Caliber: 9mm Para., 16-shot magazine; 10mm Auto, 10-shot magazine; 38 Super, 40 S&W, 12-shot magazine; 45 ACP, 10-shot magazine. **Barrel:** 4.72". **Weight:** 35.33 oz. **Length:** 8.10" over-all. **Stocks:** Checkered rubber. **Sights:** Undercut blade front, open rear adjustable for windage. **Features:** Double-action trigger system; squared-off trigger guard; frame-mounted safety. Introduced 1991. Imported from Italy by European American Armory.
Price: 9mm, blue **$550.00**
Price: 9mm, satin chrome **$595.00**
Price: 9mm, blue slide, chrome frame **$595.00**
Price: 9mm Compact, blue, 13-shot **$550.00**
Price: As above, blue slide, chrome frame, or all-chrome . . **$595.00**
Price: 40 S&W or 41 A.E., blue **$595.00**
Price: As above, blue slide, chrome frame, or all-chrome . . **$650.00**
Price: 40 S&W or 41 A.E. Compact, 8-shot, blue **$595.00**
Price: As above, blue slide, chrome frame, or all-chrome . . **$650.00**
Price: 45 ACP, blue **$695.00**
Price: As above, blue slide, chrome frame, or all-chrome . . **$750.00**
Price: 45 ACP Compact, 8-shot, blue **$695.00**
Price: As above, blue slide, chrome frame, or all-chrome . . **$750.00**
Price: 9mm/40 S&W Combo, blue, compact or full size **$825.00**
Price: As above, blue/chrome, compact or full size **$875.00**
Price: 9mm/40 S&W/41 A.E. Tri Caliber, blue, compact or full size . . . **$995.00**
Price: As above, blue/chrome **$1,050.00**
Price: 9mm or 40 S&W Carry Comp, blue **$775.00**
Price: As above, blue/chrome **$825.00**
Price: As above, 45 ACP **$1,010.00**

ERMA SPORTING PISTOL MODEL ESP 85A Caliber: 22 LR, 8-shot; 32 S&W Long, 5-shot. **Barrel:** 6". **Weight:** 39.9 oz. **Length:** 10" overall. **Stocks:** Checkered walnut with thumbrest. Adjustable target stocks optional. **Sights:** Interchangeable blade front, micro. rear adjustable for windage and elevation. **Features:** Interchangeable caliber conversion kit available; adjustable trigger, trigger stop. Imported from Germany by Precision Sales Int'l. Introduced 1988.
Price: 22 LR **$1,228.00**
Price: 32 S&W Long **$1,284.00**
Price: 22 LR, chrome **$1,449.00**
Price: 22 LR conversion unit **$689.00**
Price: 32 S&W conversion unit **$746.00**

ERMA KGP68 AUTO PISTOL Caliber: 32 ACP, 6-shot, 380 ACP, 5-shot. **Barrel:** 4". **Weight:** 22½ oz. **Length:** 7⅜" overall. **Stocks:** Checkered plastic. **Sights:** Fixed. **Features:** Toggle action similar to original "Luger" pistol. Action stays open after last shot. Has magazine and sear disconnect safety systems. Imported from Germany by Mandall Shooting Supplies.
Price: **$499.95**

DESERT INDUSTRIES DOUBLE DEUCE, TWO BIT SPECIAL PISTOLS Caliber: 22 LR, 6-shot; 25 ACP, 5-shot. **Barrel:** 2½". **Weight:** 15 oz. **Length:** 5½" overall. **Stocks:** Rosewood. **Sights:** Special order. **Features:** Double action; stainless steel construction with matte finish; ambidextrous slide-mounted safety. From Desert Industries, Inc.
Price: 22 . . . . **$399.95**
Price: 25 (Two-Bit Special) **$399.95**

DESERT INDUSTRIES WAR EAGLE PISTOL Caliber: 9mm Para., 14-shot magazine; 10mm, 13-shot; 40 S&W, 14-shot; 45 ACP, 12-shot. **Barrel:** 4". **Weight:** 35.5 oz. **Length:** 7.5" overall. **Stocks:** Rosewood. **Sights:** Fixed. **Features:** Double action; matte-finished stainless steel; slide mounted ambidextrous safety. Announced 1986. From Desert Industries, Inc.
Price: **$795.00**

E.A.A. EUROPEAN MODEL AUTO PISTOLS Caliber: 32 ACP or 380 ACP, 7-shot magazine. **Barrel:** 3.88". **Weight:** 26 oz. **Length:** 7⅜" overall. **Stocks:** European hardwood. **Sights:** Fixed blade front, rear drift-adjustable for windage. **Features:** Chrome or blue finish; magazine, thumb and firing pin safeties; external hammer; safety-lever takedown. Imported from Italy by European American Armory.
Price: Blue **$225.00**
Price: Blue/chrome **$249.00**
Price: Chrome **$249.00**
Price: Blue/gold **$260.00**
Price: Ladies Model **$299.00**

E.A.A. European 380/DA Pistol Similar to the standard European except in 380 ACP only, with double-action trigger mechanism. Available in blue, chrome or blue/chrome finish. Introduced 1992. From European American Armory.
Price: Blue **$275.00**
Price: Chrome **$299.00**
Price: Blue/chrome **$299.00**
Price: Blue/gold **$310.00**
Price: Ladies Model **$365.00**

Erma ESP 85A

FEG B9R

FEG B9R AUTO PISTOL Caliber: 380 ACP, 15-shot magazine. **Barrel:** 4". **Weight:** 25 oz. **Length:** 7" overall. **Stocks:** Hand-checkered walnut. **Sights:** Blade front, drift-adjustable rear. **Features:** Hammer-drop safety; grooved backstrap; squared trigger guard. Comes with spare magazine. Introduced 1993. Imported from Hungary by Century International Arms.
Price: About **$312.00**

FALCON AUTO PISTOL **Caliber:** 10mm, 40 S&W, 10-shot magazine, 45 ACP, 8-shot magazine. **Barrel:** 5". **Weight:** 37.5 oz. **Length:** 8.5" overall. **Stocks:** Black Du Pont Zytel with stipple finish. **Sights:** Post front, rear adjustable for windage and elevation; Tri-Square system. **Features:** Double-action with passive firing pin lock, decocking lever, ambidextrous thumb safety levers; reversible magazine release; beveled magazine well; stainless steel magazine. Black slide, stainless frame. Announced 1990. Made in U.S. by Falcon Industries.
Price: 10mm, 40 S&W, 45 ACP **$795.00**

FEG FP9 AUTO PISTOL **Caliber:** 9mm Para., 14-shot magazine. **Barrel:** 5". **Weight:** 35 oz. **Length:** 7.8" overall. **Stocks:** Checkered walnut. **Sights:** Blade front, windage-adjustable rear. **Features:** Full-length ventilated rib. Polished blue finish. Comes with extra magazine. Introduced 1993. Imported from Hungary by Century International Arms.
Price: About **$269.00**

FEG PMK-380

FEG P9R AUTO PISTOL **Caliber:** 9mm Para., 15-shot magazine. **Barrel:** 4.6". **Weight:** 35 oz. **Length:** 7.9" overall. **Stocks:** Checkered walnut. **Sights:** Blade front, rear adjustable for windage. **Features:** Double-action mechanism; slide-mounted safety. All-Steel construction with polished blue finish. Comes with extra magazine. Introduced 1993. Imported from Hungary by Century International Arms.
Price: About **$262.00**

Glock 19

Glock 21

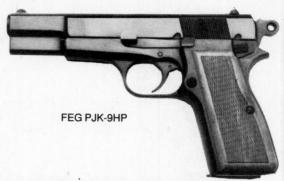

FEG PJK-9HP

FEG PJK-9HP AUTO PISTOL **Caliber:** 9mm Para., 13-shot magazine. **Barrel:** 4.75". **Weight:** 32 oz. **Length:** 8" overall. **Stocks:** Hand-checkered walnut. **Sights:** Blade front, rear adjustable for windage. **Features:** Single action; polished blue or hard chrome finish; rounded combat-style serrated hammer. Comes with two magazines and cleaning rod. Imported from Hungary by K.B.I., Inc.
Price: Blue **$329.00**
Price: Hard chrome **$435.00**

FEG PMK-380 AUTO PISTOL **Caliber:** 380 ACP, 7-shot magazine. **Barrel:** 4". **Weight:** 21 oz. **Length:** 7" overall. **Stocks:** Checkered black nylon with thumbrest. **Sights:** Blade front, rear adjustable for windage. **Features:** Double action; anodized aluminum frame, polished blue slide. Comes with two magazines, cleaning rod. Introduced 1992. Imported from Hungary by K.B.I., Inc.
Price: **$249.00**

FEG SMC-380 AUTO PISTOL **Caliber:** 380 ACP, 6-shot magazine. **Barrel:** 3.5". **Weight:** 18.5 oz. **Length:** 6.1" overall. **Stocks:** Checkered composition with thumbrest. **Sights:** Blade front, rear adjustable for windage. **Features:** Patterned after the PPK pistol. Alloy frame, steel slide; double action. Blue finish. Comes with two magazines, cleaning rod. Imported from Hungary by K.B.I.
Price: **$299.00**

GLOCK 17 AUTO PISTOL **Caliber:** 9mm Para., 17-shot magazine. **Barrel:** 4.49". **Weight:** 21.9 oz. (without magazine). **Length:** 7.28" overall. **Stocks:** Black polymer. **Sights:** Dot on front blade, white outline rear adjustable for windage. **Features:** Polymer frame, steel slide; double-action trigger with "Safe Action" system; mechanical firing pin safety, drop safety; simple takedown without tools; locked breech, recoil operated action. Adopted by Austrian armed forces 1983. NATO approved 1984. Imported from Austria by Glock, Inc.
Price: With extra magazine, magazine loader, cleaning kit **$579.95**
Price: Model 17L (6" barrel) **$768.25**

Glock 19 Auto Pistol Similar to the Glock 17 except has a 4" barrel, giving an overall length of 6.85" and weight of 20.99 oz. Magazine capacity is 15 rounds. Fixed or adjustable rear sight. Introduced 1988.
Price: **$579.95**

Glock 20 10mm Auto Pistol Similar to the Glock Model 17 except chambered for 10mm Automatic cartridge. Barrel length is 4.60", overall length is 7.59", and weight is 26.3 oz. (without magazine). Magazine capacity is 15 rounds. Fixed or adjustable rear sight. Comes with an extra magazine, magazine loader, cleaning rod and brush. Introduced 1990. Imported from Austria by Glock, Inc.
Price: **$638.49**

Glock 21 Auto Pistol Similar to the Glock 17 except chambered for 45 ACP, 13-shot magazine. Overall length is 7.59", weight is 25.2 oz. (without magazine). Fixed or adjustable rear sight. Introduced 1991.
Price: **$638.49**

Glock 22 Auto Pistol Similar to the Glock 17 except chambered for 40 S&W, 15-shot magazine. Overall length is 7.28", weight is 22.3 oz. (without magazine). Fixed or adjustable rear sight. Introduced 1990.
Price: **$579.95**

Glock 23 Auto Pistol Similar to the Glock 19 except chambered for 40 S&W, 13-shot magazine. Overall length is 6.85", weight is 20.6 oz. (without magazine). Fixed or adjustable rear sight. Introduced 1990.
Price: **$579.95**

Grendel P-12

HAMMERLI MODEL 212 AUTO PISTOL **Caliber:** 22 LR, 8-shot magazine. **Barrel:** 4.9". **Weight:** 31 oz. **Stocks:** Checkered walnut. **Sights:** Blade front, rear adjustable for windage only. **Features:** Polished blue finish. Imported from Switzerland by Mandall Shooting Supplies and Hammerli Pistols USA.
Price: About **$1,395.00**

HASKELL JS-45 CALIBER PISTOL **Caliber:** 45 ACP, 7-shot magazine. **Barrel:** 4.5". **Weight:** 44 oz. **Length:** 7.95" overall. **Stocks:** Checkered acetal resin. **Sights:** Fixed; low profile. **Features:** Internal drop-safe mechanism; all aluminum frame. Introduced 1991. From MKS Supply, Inc.
Price: Matte black **$149.95**
Price: Brushed nickel **$159.95**

Heckler & Koch P7M10

Heckler & Koch USP

GRENDEL P-12 AUTO PISTOL **Caliber:** 380 ACP, 11-shot magazine. **Barrel:** 3". **Weight:** 13 oz. **Length:** 5.3" overall. **Stocks:** Checkered DuPont ST-800 polymer. **Sights:** Fixed. **Features:** Double action only with inertia safety hammer system. All steel frame; grip forms magazine well and trigger guard. Introduced 1992. Made in U.S. by Grendel, Inc.
Price: Blue **$175.00**
Price: Electroless nickel **$195.00**

GRENDEL P-30 AUTO PISTOL **Caliber:** 22 WMR, 30-shot magazine. **Barrel:** 5", 8". **Weight:** 21 oz. (5" barrel). **Length:** 8.5" overall (5" barrel). **Stocks:** Checkered Zytel. **Sights:** Blade front, fixed rear. **Features:** Blowback action with fluted chamber; ambidextrous safety, reversible magazine catch. Scope mount available. Introduced 1990.
Price: With 5" barrel **$225.00**
Price: With removable muzzlebrake (Model P-30M) **$235.00**
Price: With 8" barrel (Model P-30L) **$280.00**

GRENDEL P-31 AUTO PISTOL **Caliber:** 22 WMR, 30-shot magazine. **Barrel:** 11". **Weight:** 48 oz. **Length:** 17.5" overall. **Stocks:** Checkered black Zytel grip and forend. **Sights:** Blade front adjustable for windage and elevation, fixed rear. **Features:** Blowback action with fluted chamber. Ambidextrous safety. Matte black finish. Muzzlebrake. Scope mount optional. Introduced 1991. Made in the U.S. by Grendel, Inc.
Price: **$345.00**

Hammerli Model 212

HECKLER & KOCH P7M8 AUTO PISTOL **Caliber:** 9mm Para., 8-shot magazine. **Barrel:** 4.13". **Weight:** 29 oz. **Length:** 6.73" overall. **Stocks:** Stippled black plastic. **Sights:** Blade front, adjustable rear; three dot system. **Features:** Unique "squeeze cocker" in frontstrap cocks the action. Gas-retarded action. Squared combat-type trigger guard. Blue finish. Compact size. Imported from Germany by Heckler & Koch, Inc.
Price: P7M8, blued **$1,059.00**
Price: P7M8, nickel **$1,059.00**
Price: P7M13 (13-shot capacity, ambidextrous magazine release, forged steel frame), blued **$1,284.00**
Price: P7M13, nickel **$1,284.00**

Heckler & Koch P7M10 Auto Pistol Similar to the P7M8 except chambered for 40 S&W with 10-shot magazine. Weighs 43 oz., overall length is 6.9". Introduced 1992. Imported from Germany by Heckler & Koch, Inc.
Price: Blue **$1,314.00**
Price: Nickel **$1,314.00**

Heckler & Koch P7K3 Auto Pistol Similar to the P7M8 and P7M13 except chambered for 22 LR or 380 ACP, 8-shot magazine. Uses an oil-filled buffer to decrease recoil. Introduced 1988.
Price: **$1,059.00**
Price: 22 LR conversion unit **$524.00**
Price: 32 ACP conversion unit **$228.00**

HECKLER & KOCH USP AUTO PISTOL **Caliber:** 9mm Para., 16-shot magazine, 40 S&W, 13-shot magazine. **Barrel:** 4.13". **Weight:** 28 oz. (USP40). **Length:** 6.9" overall. **Stocks:** Non-slip stippled black polymer. **Sights:** Blade front, rear adjustable for windage. **Features:** New HK design with polymer frame, modified Browning action with recoil reduction system, single control lever. Special "hostile environment" finish on all metal parts. Available in SA/DA, DAO, left- and right-hand versions. Introduced 1993. Imported from Germany by Heckler & Koch, Inc.
Price: Right-hand **$624.00**
Price: Left-hand **$644.00**

Heckler & Koch SP89

HI-POINT FIREARMS MODEL C-9MM PISTOL
Caliber: 9mm Para., 8-shot magazine. **Barrel:** 3.5". **Weight:** 35 oz. **Length:** 6.7" overall. **Stocks:** Textured acetal plastic. **Sights:** Combat-style fixed three-dot system; low profile. **Features:** Single-action design; frame-mounted magazine release. Scratch-resistant matte finish. Introduced 1993. From MKS Supply, Inc.
Price: **$129.95**

HUNGARIAN T-58 AUTO PISTOL
Caliber: 7.62mm and 9mm Para., 8-shot magazine. **Barrel:** 4.5". **Weight:** 31 oz. **Length:** 7.68" overall. **Stocks:** Grooved composition. **Sights:** Blade front, rear adjustable for windage. **Features:** Comes with both barrels and magazines. Thumb safety locks hammer. Blue finish. Imported by Century International Arms.
Price: About **$187.00**

IBERIA FIREARMS JS-40 S&W AUTO
Caliber: 40 S&W, 8-shot magazine. **Barrel:** 4.5". **Weight:** 44 oz. **Length:** 7.95" overall. **Stocks:** Checkered acetal resin. **Sights:** Fixed; low profile. **Features:** Internal drop-safe mechansim; all aluminum frame. Introduced 1991. From MKS Supply, Inc.
Price: Matte black **$149.95**
Price: Brushed nickel **$159.95**

INTRATEC CATEGORY 9 AUTO PISTOL
Caliber: 9mm Para., 8-shot magazine. **Barrel:** 3". **Weight:** 21 oz. **Length:** 5.5" overall. **Stocks:** Textured black polymer. **Sights:** Fixed channel. **Features:** Black polymer frame. Announced 1993. Made in U.S. by Intratec.
Price: About **$200.00**

INTRATEC PROTEC-22, 25 AUTO PISTOLS
Caliber: 22 LR, 10-shot; 25 ACP, 8-shot magazine. **Barrel:** 2½". **Weight:** 14 oz. **Length:** 5" overall. **Stocks:** Wraparound composition in gray, black or driftwood color. **Sights:** Fixed. **Features:** Double-action only trigger mechanism. Choice of black, satin or TEC-KOTE finish. Announced 1991. Made in U.S. by Intratec.
Price: 22 or 25, black finish **$99.95**
Price: 22 or 25, satin or TEC-KOTE finish **$104.95**

INTRATEC TEC-DC9 AUTO PISTOL
Caliber: 9mm Para., 32-shot magazine. **Barrel:** 5". **Weight:** 50 oz. **Length:** 12½" overall. **Stock:** Moulded composition. **Sights:** Fixed. **Features:** Semi-auto, fires from closed bolt; firing pin block safety; matte blue finish. Made in U.S. by Intratec.
Price: **$260.00**
Price: TEC-DC9S (as above, except stainless) **$353.00**
Price: TEC-DC9K (finished with TEC-KOTE) **$290.00**

Intratec TEC-DC9M Auto Pistol
Similar to the TEC-DC9 except smaller. Has 3" barrel, weighs 44 oz.; 20-shot magazine. Made in U.S. by Intratec.
Price: **$239.00**
Price: TEC-DC9MS (as above, stainless) **$330.00**
Price: TEC-DC9MK (finished with TEC-KOTE) **$270.00**

INTRATEC TEC-22T AUTO PISTOL
Caliber: 22 LR, 30-shot magazine. **Barrel:** 4". **Weight:** 30 oz. **Length:** 11³⁄₁₆" overall. **Stocks:** Moulded composition. **Sights:** Protected post front, front and rear adjustable for windage and elevation. **Features:** Ambidextrous cocking knobs and safety. Matte black finish. Accepts any 10/22-type magazine. Introduced 1988. Made in U.S. by Intratec.
Price: **$157.00**
Price: TEC-22TK (as above, TEC-KOTE finish) **$178.95**

HECKLER & KOCH SP89 AUTO PISTOL
Caliber: 9mm Para., 15- or 30-shot magazine. **Barrel:** 4.5". **Weight:** 4.4 lbs. **Length:** 12.8" overall. **Stocks:** Black high-impact plastic. **Sights:** Post front, diopter rear adjustable for windage and elevation. **Features:** Semi-auto pistol inspired by the HK94. Has special flash-hider forend. Introduced 1989. Imported from Germany by Heckler & Koch, Inc.
Price: **$1,324.00**

HELWAN "BRIGADIER" AUTO PISTOL
Caliber: 9mm Para., 8-shot magazine. **Barrel:** 4.5". **Weight:** 32 oz. **Length:** 8" overall. **Stocks:** Grooved plastic. **Sights:** Blade front, rear adjustable for windage. **Features:** Polished blue finish. Single-action design. Cross-bolt safety. Imported by Interarms.
Price: **$262.00**

HERITAGE MODEL HA25 AUTO PISTOL
Caliber: 25 ACP, 6-shot magazine. **Barrel:** 2½". **Weight:** 12 oz. **Length:** 4⅝" overall. **Stocks:** Smooth walnut. **Sights:** Fixed. **Features:** Exposed hammer, manual safety; open-top slide. Polished blue or chrome finish. Introduced 1993. Made in U.S. by Heritage Mfg., Inc.
Price: . . . . **$69.95 to $89.95**

Hi-Point C-9MM

Hungarian T-58

Intratec TEC-DC9

Jennings J-25

JENNINGS J-22, J-25 AUTO PISTOLS **Caliber:** 22 LR, 25 ACP, 6-shot magazine. **Barrel:** 2½". **Weight:** 13 oz. (J-22). **Length:** 4¹⁵⁄₁₆" overall (J-22). **Stocks:** Walnut on chrome or nickel models; grooved black Cycolac or resin-impregnated wood on Teflon model. **Sights:** Fixed. **Features:** Choice of bright chrome, satin nickel or black Teflon finish. Introduced 1981. From Jennings Firearms.
Price: J-22, about $75.00
Price: J-25, about $89.95

Iver Johnson Compact

IVER JOHNSON COMPACT 25 ACP **Caliber:** 25 ACP. **Barrel:** 2". **Weight:** 9.3 oz. **Stocks:** Checkered composition. **Sights:** Fixed. **Features:** Ordnance steel construction with bright blue slide, matte blue frame, color case-hardened trigger. Comes in jewelry-type presentation box. Introduced 1991. From Iver Johnson.
Price: $199.95

IVER JOHNSON ENFORCER AUTO **Caliber:** 30 M-1 Carbine, 15- or 30-shot magazine, or 9mm Para. **Barrel:** 10½". **Weight:** 4 lbs. **Length:** 18½" overall. **Stocks:** American walnut with metal handguard. **Sights:** Gold bead ramp front. Peep rear. **Features:** Accepts 15- or 30-shot magazines. From Iver Johnson.
Price: 30 M-1 . . . . $416.50
Price: 9mm Para. $448.95

KAREEN MK II AUTO PISTOL **Caliber:** 9mm Para., 13-shot magazine. **Barrel:** 4.75". **Weight:** 32 oz. **Length:** 8" overall. **Stocks:** Textured composition. **Sights:** Blade front, rear adjustable for windage. **Features:** Single-action mechanism; external hammer safety; magazine safety; combat trigger guard. Blue finish standard, optional two-tone or matte black. Optional Meprolight sights, improved rubberized grips. Comes with two magazines. Imported from Israel by J.O. Arms & Ammunition. Introduced 1969.
Price: . . . . $389.00 to $525.00

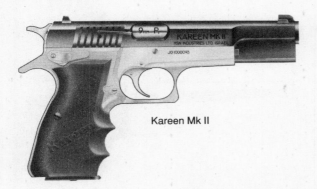

Kareen Mk II

KIMEL AP9 AUTO PISTOL **Caliber:** 9mm Para., 20-shot magazine. **Barrel:** 5". **Weight:** 3.5 lbs. **Length:** 11.8" overall. **Stocks:** Checkered plastic. **Sights:** Adjustable post front in ring, fixed open rear. **Features:** Matte blue/black or nickel finish. Lever safety blocks trigger and sear. Fires from closed bolt. Introduced 1988. Made in U.S. Available from Kimel Industries.
Price: Matte blue/black $264.00
Price: Nickel finish $274.00
Price: Mini AP9 (3" barrel) $258.00
Price: Nickel finish $268.00
Price: Target AP9 (12" bbl., grooved forend), blue $279.00

Kimel AP9

L.A.R. GRIZZLY WIN MAG MK I PISTOL **Caliber:** 357 Mag., 357/45, 10mm, 44 Mag., 45 Win. Mag., 45 ACP, 7-shot magazine. **Barrel:** 5.4", 6.5". **Weight:** 51 oz. **Length:** 10½" overall. **Stocks:** Checkered rubber, non-slip combat-type. **Sights:** Ramped blade front, fully adjustable rear. **Features:** Uses basic Browning/Colt 1911A1 design; interchangeable calibers; beveled magazine well; combat-type flat, checkered rubber mainspring housing; lowered and back-chamfered ejection port; polished feed ramp; throated barrel; solid barrel bushings. Available in satin hard chrome, matte blue, Parkerized finishes. Introduced 1983. From L.A.R. Mfg., Inc.
Price: 45 Win. Mag. $920.00
Price: 357 Mag. $933.00
Price: Conversion units (357 Mag.) $228.00
Price: As above, 45 ACP, 10mm, 45 Win. Mag., 357/45 Win. Mag. . . . $214.00

L.A.R. Grizzly Win Mag 8" & 10" Similar to the standard Grizzly Win Mag except has lengthened slide and either 8" or 10" barrel. Available in 45 Win. Mag., 45 ACP, 357/45 Grizzly Win. Mag., 10mm or 357 Magnum. Introduced 1987.
Price: 8", 45 ACP, 45 Win. Mag., 357/45 Grizzly Win. Mag. $1,313.00
Price: As above, 10" $1,375.00
Price: 8", 357 Magnum $1,337.50
Price: As above, 10" $1,400.00

L.A.R. Grizzly Win Mag

L.A.R. Grizzly 44 Mag MK IV Similar to the Win. Mag. Mk I except chambered for 44 Magnum, has beavertail grip safety. Matte blue finish only. Has 5.4" or 6.5" barrel. Introduced 1991. From L.A.R. Mfg., Inc.
Price: $933.00

L.A.R. Grizzly 50 Mark V Pistol Similar to the Grizzly Win Mag Mark I except chambered for 50 Action Express with 6-shot magazine. Weight, empty, is 56 oz., overall length 10⅝". Choice of 5.4" or 6.5" barrel. Has same features as Mark I, IV pistols. Introduced 1993. From L.A.R. Mfg., Inc.
Price: $1,060.00

Laseraim Arms Series I

LLAMA COMPACT FRAME AUTO PISTOL **Caliber:** 9mm Para., 9-shot, 40 S&W, 8-shot, 45 ACP, 7-shot. **Barrel:** 4¼" (40 S&W), 4⁵⁄₁₆" (9mm, 45). **Weight:** 37 oz. **Stocks:** Smooth walnut. **Sights:** Blade front, rear adjustable for windage. **Features:** Scaled-down version of the Large Frame gun. Locked breech mechanism; manual and grip safeties. Introduced 1985. Imported from Spain by SGS Importers Int'l., Inc.
Price: Model XI-B (9mm Para.), blue **$314.95**
Price: As above, nickel **$363.95**
Price: Model XII-B (40 S&W), blue **$324.95**
Price: As above, nickel **$363.95**
Price: Model IX-B (45 ACP), blue **$324.95**
Price: As above, nickel **$363.95**

LLAMA XV, III-A SMALL FRAME AUTO PISTOLS **Caliber:** 22 LR, 380. **Barrel:** 3¹¹⁄₁₆". **Weight:** 23 oz. **Length:** 6½" overall. **Stocks:** Checkered plastic, thumbrest. **Sights:** Fixed front, adjustable notch rear. **Features:** Ventilated rib, manual and grip safeties. Imported from Spain by SGS Importers Int'l., Inc.
Price: Blue **$281.95**
Price: Satin Chrome **$314.95**

LLAMA LARGE FRAME AUTO PISTOL **Caliber:** 38 Super, 40 S&W, 45 ACP. **Barrel:** 5" (38 Super, 45 ACP), 5⅛" (40 S&W). **Weight:** 40 oz. **Length:** 8½" overall. **Stocks:** Checkered walnut. **Sights:** Fixed. **Features:** Grip and manual safeties, ventilated rib. Imported from Spain by SGS Importers Int'l., Inc.
Price: Model VIII (38 Super), blue **$324.95**
Price: As above, nickel **$363.95**
Price: Model XII-A (40 S&W), blue **$324.95**
Price: As above, nickel **$363.95**
Price: Model IX-A (45 ACP), blue **$324.95**
Price: As above, nickel **$363.95**

LLAMA M-82 DA AUTO PISTOL **Caliber:** 9mm Para., 40 S&W, 15-shot magazine. **Barrel:** 4¼". **Weight:** 39 oz. **Length:** 8" overall. **Stocks:** Matte black polymer. **Sights:** Blade front, rear drift adjustable for windage. High visibility three-dot system. **Features:** Double-action mechanism; ambidextrous safety. Introduced 1987. Imported from Spain by SGS Importers Int'l., Inc.
Price: **$584.95**

LORCIN L-22 AUTO PISTOL **Caliber:** 22 LR, 9-shot magazine. **Barrel:** 2.5". **Weight:** 16 oz. **Length:** 5.25" overall. **Stocks:** Black combat, or pink or pearl. **Sights:** Fixed three-dot system. **Features:** Available in chrome or black Teflon finish. Introduced 1989. From Lorcin Engineering.
Price: About **$79.95**

LORCIN L-25, LT-25 AUTO PISTOLS **Caliber:** 25 ACP, 7-shot magazine. **Barrel:** 2.4". **Weight:** 14.5 oz. **Length:** 4.8" overall. **Stocks:** Smooth composition. **Sights:** Fixed. **Features:** Available in choice of finishes: chrome, black Teflon or camouflage. Introduced 1989. From Lorcin Engineering.
Price: **$79.95**

LORCIN L-32, L-380 AUTO PISTOLS **Caliber:** 32 ACP, 380 ACP, 7-shot magazine. **Barrel:** 3.5". **Weight:** 27 oz. **Length:** 6.6" overall. **Stocks:** Grooved composition. **Sights:** Fixed. **Features:** Black Teflon or chrome finish with black grips. Introduced 1992. From Lorcin Engineering.
Price: 32 ACP **$85.00**
Price: 380 ACP **$95.00**

LASERAIM ARMS SERIES I AUTO PISTOL **Caliber:** 10mm Auto, 40 S&W, 8-shot, 45 ACP, 7-shot magazine. **Barrel:** 5.5", with compensator. **Weight:** 52 oz. **Length:** 10.5" overall. **Stocks:** Pebble-grained black composite. **Sights:** Blade front, fully adjustable rear. **Features:** Single action; barrel compensator; stainless steel construction; ambidextrous safety-levers; extended slide release; matte black Teflon finish; integral mount for laser sight. Introduced 1993. Made in U.S. by Emerging Technologies, Inc.
Price: Standard **$599.00**
Price: Compact (3⅞" barrel, 40 S&W, 45 ACP only) **$599.00**

Laseraim Arms Series II Auto Pistol Similar to the Series I except without compensator, has matte stainless finish. Standard Series II has 5" barrel, weighs 46 oz., Compact has 3⅜" barrel, weighs 43 oz. Blade front sight, rear adjustable for windage. Introduced 1993. Made in U.S. by Emerging Technologies, Inc.
Price: Standard or Compact **$529.00**

Llama Small Frame

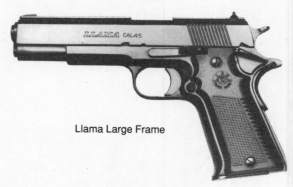

Llama Large Frame

Llama M-82

Lorcin 25 ACP

Mitchell American Eagle

MITCHELL ARMS AMERICAN EAGLE AUTO **Caliber:** 9mm Para., 7-shot magazine. **Barrel:** 4". **Weight:** 29.6 oz. **Length:** 9.6" overall. **Stocks:** Checkered walnut. **Sights:** Blade front, fixed rear. **Features:** Recreation of the American Eagle Parabellum pistol in stainless steel. Chamber loaded indicator. Made in U.S. From Mitchell Arms, Inc.
Price: **$695.00**

MITCHELL ARMS TROPHY II AUTO PISTOL **Caliber:** 22 LR, 10-shot magazine. **Barrel:** 5.5" bull, 7.25" fluted. **Weight:** 44.5 oz. (5.5" barrel). **Length:** 9.75" overall (5.5" barrel). **Stocks:** Checkered walnut with thumbrest. **Sights:** Undercut ramp front, click-adjustable frame-mounted rear. **Features:** Grip duplicates feel of military 45; positive action magazine latch; front- and backstraps stippled. Trigger adjustable for pull, over-travel; gold-filled roll marks, gold-plated trigger, safety, magazine release; push-button barrel takedown. Available in stainless steel. Announced 1992. From Mitchell Arms, Inc.
Price: Stainless steel **$479.00**

MITCHELL ARMS SHARPSHOOTER AUTO PISTOL **Caliber:** 22 LR, 10-shot magazine. **Barrel:** 5.5" bull. **Weight:** 42 oz. **Length:** 10.25" overall. **Stocks:** Checkered walnut with thumbrest. **Sights:** Ramp front, slide-mounted square notch rear adjustable for windage and elevation. **Features:** Military grip. Slide lock; smooth gripstraps; push-button takedown. Announced 1992. From Mitchell Arms, Inc.
Price: Stainless steel **$364.00**

Mountain Eagle

NAVY ARMS TT-OLYMPIA PISTOL **Caliber:** 22 LR. **Barrel:** 4.6". **Weight:** 28 oz. **Length:** 8" overall. **Stocks:** Checkered hardwood. **Sights:** Blade front, rear adjsutable for windage. **Features:** Reproduction of the Walther Olympia pistol. Polished blue finish. Introduced 1992. Imported by Navy Arms.
Price: **$300.00**

NORINCO MODEL 59 MAKAROV DA PISTOL **Caliber:** 9x18mm, 380 ACP, 8-shot magazine. **Barrel:** 3.5". **Weight:** 21 oz. **Length:** 6.3" overall. **Stocks:** Checkered plastic. **Sights:** Blade front, adjustable rear. **Features:** Blue finish. Double action. Introduced 1990. Imported from China by China Sports, Inc.
Price: . . . . **NA**

NORINCO MODEL 77B AUTO PISTOL **Caliber:** 9mm Para., 8-shot magazine. **Barrel:** 5". **Weight:** 34 oz. **Length:** 7.5" overall. **Stocks:** Checkered wood. **Sights:** Blade front, adjustable rear. **Features:** Uses trigger guard cocking, gas-retarded recoil action. Front of trigger guard can be used to cock the action with the trigger finger. Introduced 1989. Imported from China by China Sports, Inc.
Price: . . . . **NA**

MAUSER MODEL 80 SA AUTO PISTOL **Caliber:** 9mm Para., 13-shot magazine. **Barrel:** 4.67". **Weight:** 31.7 oz. **Length:** 8" overall. **Stocks:** Checkered beechwood. **Sights:** Blade front, rear adjustable for windage. **Features:** Uses basic Hi-Power design. Polished blue finish. Introduced 1992. Imported from Germany by Precision Imports, Inc.
Price: **$372.00**

Mauser Model 90 DA Auto Pistols Similar to the Mauser Model 80 except has double-action trigger system. Has 14-shot magazine, weighs 35.2 oz. Introduced 1992. Imported from Germany by Precision Imports, Inc.
Price: Model 90 DA **$399.00**
Price: Model 90 DA Compact (4.13" bbl., 7.4" overall, 33.5 oz.) **$425.00**

Mitchell Trophy II

Mitchell Arms Citation II Auto Pistol Same as the Trophy II except has nickel-plated trigger, safety and magazine release, and has silver-filled roll marks. Available in stainless steel. Announced 1992. From Mitchell Arms, Inc.
Price: Stainless steel **$454.00**

MITCHELL ARMS SPORT-KING AUTO PISTOL **Caliber:** 22 LR, 10-shot magazine. **Barrel:** 4.5", 6.75". **Weight:** 39 oz. (4.5" barrel). **Length:** 9" overall (4.5" barrel). **Stocks:** Checkered black plastic. **Sights:** Blade front, rear adjustable for windage. **Features:** Military grip; standard trigger; push-button barrel takedown. All stainless steel. Announced 1992. From Mitchell Arms, Inc.
Price: **$299.00**

MOUNTAIN EAGLE AUTO PISTOL **Caliber:** 22 LR, 15-shot magazine. **Barrel:** 6.5". **Weight:** 21 oz. **Length:** 10.6" overall. **Stocks:** One-piece impact-resistant polymer in "conventional contour"; checkered panels. **Sights:** Serrated ramp front with interchangeable blades, rear adjustable for windage and elevation; interchangeable blades. **Features:** Injection moulded grip frame, alloy receiver; hybrid composite barrel replicates shape of the Desert Eagle pistol. Flat, smooth trigger. Introduced 1992. From Magnum Research.
Price: **$239.00**

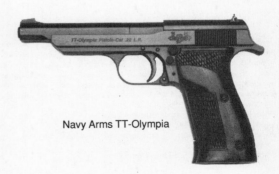

Navy Arms TT-Olympia

NORINCO M93 SPORTSMAN AUTO PISTOL **Caliber:** 22 LR, 10-shot magazine. **Barrel:** 4.6". **Weight:** 26 oz. **Length:** 8.6" overall. **Stocks:** Checkered composition. **Sights:** Blade front, rear adjustable for windage. **Features:** All steel construction with blue finish. Introduced 1992. Imported from China by Interarms.
Price: **$238.00**

Para-Ordnance P12.45

PARA-ORDNANCE P14.45 AUTO PISTOL **Caliber:** 45 ACP, 13-shot magazine. **Barrel:** 5". **Weight:** 28 oz. (alloy frame). **Length:** 8.5" overall. **Stocks:** Textured composition. **Sights:** Blade front, rear adjustable for windage. High visibility three-dot system. **Features:** Available with alloy, steel or stainless steel frame with black finish (silver or stainless gun). Steel and stainless steel frame guns weigh 38 oz. (P14.45), 35 oz. (P13.45), 33 oz. (P12.45). Grooved match trigger, rounded combat-style hammer. Double column, high-capacity magazine gives 14-shot total capacity (P14.45). Beveled magazine well. Manual thumb, grip and firing pin lock safeties. Solid barrel bushing. Introduced 1990. Made in Canada by Para-Ordnance.
Price: P14.45 . . . . **$716.25**
Price: P12.45 (11-shot magazine, 3½" bbl., 24 oz., alloy) **$650.00**
Price: P14.45E steel frame **$716.25**
Price: P12.45E steel frame **$708.75**

PHOENIX ARMS HP22, HP25 AUTO PISTOLS **Caliber:** 22 LR, 11-shot (HP22), 25 ACP, 10-shot (HP25). **Barrel:** 2⁷⁄₁₆". **Weight:** 20 oz. **Length:** 5½" overall. **Stocks:** Checkered composition. **Sights:** Blade front, adjustable rear. **Features:** Single action, exposed hammer; manual hold-open; button magazine release. Available in bright chrome, satin nickel, polished blue finish. Introduced 1993. Made in U.S. by Phoenix Arms.
Price: **$99.95**

PHOENIX ARMS MODEL RAVEN AUTO PISTOL **Caliber:** 25 ACP, 6-shot magazine. **Barrel:** 2⁷⁄₁₆". **Weight:** 15 oz. **Length:** 4¾" overall. **Stocks:** Smooth walnut, ivory-colored or black slotted plastic. **Sights:** Ramped front, fixed rear. **Features:** Available in blue, nickel or chrome finish. Made in U.S. Available from Phoenix Arms.
Price: **$69.95**

ROCKY MOUNTAIN ARMS 1911A1-LH PISTOL **Caliber:** 40 S&W, 45 ACP, 7-shot magazine. **Barrel:** 5¼". **Weight:** 37 0z. **Length:** 8¹³⁄₁₆" overall. **Stocks:** Checkered walnut. **Sights:** Red insert Patridge front, white outline rear click adjustable for windage and elevation. **Features:** Fully left-handed pistol. Slide, frame, barrel made from stainless steel; working parts coated with Teflon-S. Single-stage trigger with 3½ lb. pull. Introduced 1993. Made in U.S. by Rocky Mountain Arms, Inc.
Price: **$1,395.00**

RUGER P89 AUTOMATIC PISTOL **Caliber:** 9mm Para., 15-shot magazine. **Barrel:** **Weight:** 32 oz. **Length:** 7.84" overall. **Stocks:** Grooved black Xenoy composition. **Sights:** Square post front, square notch rear adjustable for windage, both with white dot inserts. **Features:** Double action with ambidextrous slide-mounted safety-levers. Slide is 4140 chrome moly steel or 400-series stainless steel, frame is a lightweight aluminum alloy. Ambidextrous magazine release. Blue or stainless steel. Introduced 1986; stainless introduced 1990.
Price: P89, blue, with extra magazine and magazine
loading tool, plastic case **$410.00**
Price: KP89, stainless, with extra magazine and magazine loading tool,
plastic case **$452.00**
Price: KP89X Convertible 30 Luger/9mm Para. **$497.00**

Ruger P89 Double-Action Only Automatic Pistol Same as the KP89 except operates only in the double-action mode. Has a bobbed, spurless hammer, gripping grooves on each side of the rear of the slide; no external safety or decocking lever. An internal safety prevents forward movement of the firing pin unless the trigger is pulled. Available in 9mm Para., stainless steel only. Introduced 1991.
Price: With lockable case, extra magazine, magazine loading tool **$452.00**

NORINCO M1911A1 AUTO PISTOL **Caliber:** 45 ACP, 7-shot magazine. **Barrel:** 5". **Weight:** 39 oz. **Length:** 8.5" overall. **Stocks:** Checkered wood. **Sights:** Blade front, rear adjustable for windage. **Features:** Matte blue finish. Comes with two magazines. Imported from China by China Sports, Inc.
Price: . . . . **NA**

NORINCO NP-15 TOKAREV AUTO PISTOL **Caliber:** 7.62x25mm, 8-shot magazine. **Barrel:** 4.5". **Weight:** 29 oz. **Length:** 7.7" overall. **Stocks:** Grooved black plastic. **Sights:** Fixed. **Features:** Matte blue finish. Imported from China by China Sports, Inc.
Price: . . . . **NA**

OLYMPIC ARMS OA-93 AR PISTOL **Caliber:** 223, 20- or 30-shot, 7.62x39mm, 5- or 30-shot magazine. **Barrel:** 6", 9", 14"; 4140 steel or 416 stainless. **Weight:** 4 lbs., 15 0z. **Length:** 15.75" overall (6" barrel). **Stocks:** A2 stowaway pistol grip. **Sights:** Cut-off carrying handle with scope rail attached. **Features:** AR-15 receiver with special bolt carrier; short slotted aluminum handguard; button-cut 4140 chrome moly or broach-cut stainless barrel, Vortex flash suppressor. Introduced 1993. Made in U.S. by Olympic Arms, Inc.
Price: **$952.00**

Phoenix Arms Model Raven

PSP-25 AUTO PISTOL **Caliber:** 25 ACP, 6-shot magazine. **Barrel:** 2⅛". **Weight:** 9.5 oz. **Length:** 4⅛" overall. **Stocks:** Checkered black plastic. **Sights:** Fixed. **Features:** All steel construction with polished finish. Introduced 1990. Made in the U.S. under F.N. license; distributed by K.B.I., Inc.
Price: Blue **$249.00**
Price: Hard chrome **$329.99**

ROCKY MOUNTAIN ARMS PATRIOT PISTOL **Caliber:** 223, 5-, 20-, 30-shot magazine. **Barrel:** 7", with Max Dynamic muzzle brake. **Weight:** 6.5 lbs. **Length:** 21" overall. **Stocks:** Black composition. **Sights:** None furnished. **Features:** Uses AR-type receiver with flat top for optical sight mount with Weaver-style bases. Finished in DuPont Teflon-S matte black or NATO green. Comes with black nylon case, one magazine. Introduced 1993. From Rocky Mountain Arms, Inc.
Price: **$1,095.00**

Ruger KP89D

Ruger P89D Decocker Automatic Pistol Similar to the standard P89 except has ambidextrous decocking levers in place of the regular slide-mounted safety. The decocking levers move the firing pin inside the slide where the hammer can not reach it, while simultaneously blocking the firing pin from forward movement—allows shooter to decock a cocked pistol without manipulating the trigger. Conventional thumb decocking procedures are therefore unnecessary. Blue or stainless steel. Introduced 1990.
Price: P89D, blue with extra magazine and loader, plastic case **$410.00**
Price: KP89D, stainless, with extra magazine, plastic case **$452.00**

Ruger P93 Compact Automatic Pistol Similar to the P89 except has 3.9" barrel, 7.3" overall length, and weighs 31 oz. The forward third of the slide is tapered and polished to the muzzle. Front of the slide is crowned with a convex curve. Slide has seven finger grooves. Trigger guard bow is higher for better grip. Square post front sight, square notch rear drift adjustable for windage, both with white dot inserts. Slide is 400-series stainless steel, black-finished alloy frame. Available as decocker-only or double action-only. Introduced 1993.
Price: KP93DAO (double action only), KP93 (decocker) **$452.00**

RUGER P90 AUTOMATIC PISTOL **Caliber:** 45 ACP, 7-shot magazine. **Barrel:** 4.50". **Weight:** 33.5 oz. **Length:** 7.87" overall. **Stocks:** Grooved black Xenoy composition. **Sights:** Square post front, square notch rear adjustable for windage, both with white dot inserts. **Features:** Double action with ambidextrous slide-mounted safety-levers which move the firing pin inside the slide where the hammer can not reach it, while simultaneously blocking the firing pin from forward movement. Stainless steel only. Introduced 1991.
Price: KP90 with lockable case, extra magazine **$488.65**

Ruger P90 Decocker Automatic Pistol Similar to the P90 except has a manual decocking system. The ambidextrous decocking levers move the firing pin inside the slide where the hammer can not reach it, while simultaneously blocking the firing pin from forward movement—allows shooter to decock a cocked pistol without manipulating the trigger. Available only in stainless steel. Overall length 7.87", weight 34 oz. Introduced 1991.
Price: P90D with lockable case, extra magazine, and magazine loading tool **$488.65**

RUGER P91 DECOCKER AUTOMATIC PISTOL **Caliber:** 40 S&W, 11-shot magazine. **Barrel:** 4.50". **Weight:** 33 oz. **Length:** 7.87" overall. **Stocks:** Grooved black Xenoy composition. **Sights:** Square post front, square notch rear adjustable for windage, both with white dot inserts. **Features:** Ambidextrous slide-mounted decocking levers move the firing pin inside the slide where the hammer can not reach it while simultaneously blocking the firing pin from forward movement. Allows shooter to decock a cocked pistol without manipulating the trigger. Conventional thumb decocking procedures are therefore unnecessary. Stainless steel only. Introduced 1991.
Price: KP91D with lockable case, extra magazine, and magazine loading tool **$488.65**

Ruger KP90C

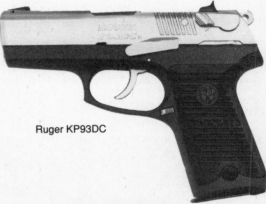

Ruger KP93DC

Ruger P91 Double-Action-Only Automatic Pistol Same as the KP91D except operates only in the double-action mode. Has a bobbed, spurless hammer, gripping grooves on each side at the rear of the slide, no external safety or decocking levers. An internal safety prevents forward movement of the firing pin unless the trigger is pulled. Available in 40 S&W, stainless steel only. Introduced 1992.
Price: KP91DAO with lockable case, extra magazine, and magazine loading tool **$488.65**

Consult our Directory pages for the location of firms mentioned.

Ruger 22/45 Mark II

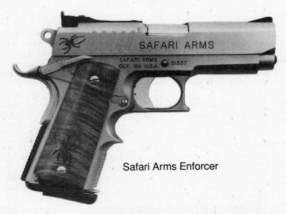

Safari Arms Enforcer

Safari Arms Enforcer Carrycomp II Pistol Similar to the Enforcer except has Wil Schueman-designed hybrid compensator system. Introduced 1993. Made in U.S. by Safari Arms, Inc.
Price: **$1,010.00**

RUGER MARK II STANDARD AUTO PISTOL **Caliber:** 22 LR, 10-shot magazine. **Barrel:** 4¾" or 6". **Weight:** 36 oz. (4¾" bbl.). **Length:** 8⁵⁄₁₆" (4¾" bbl.). **Stocks:** Checkered plastic. **Sights:** Fixed, wide blade front, square notch rear adjustable for windage. **Features:** Updated design of the original Standard Auto. Has new bolt hold-open latch. 10-shot magazine, magazine catch, safety, trigger and new receiver contours. Introduced 1982.
Price: Blued (MK 4, MK 6) **$252.00**
Price: In stainless steel (KMK 4, KMK 6) **$330.25**

Ruger 22/45 Mark II Pistol Similar to the other 22 Mark II autos except has grip frame of Zytel that matches the angle and magazine latch of the Model 1911 45 ACP pistol. Available in 4¾" standard, 5¼" tapered and 5½" bull barrel. Introduced 1992.
Price: KP4 (4¾" barrel) **$280.00**
Price: KP514 (5¼" barrel) **$330.00**
Price: KP512 (5½" bull barrel) **$330.00**

SAFARI ARMS ENFORCER PISTOL **Caliber:** 45 ACP, 6-shot magazine. **Barrel:** 3.8". **Weight:** 36 oz. **Length:** 7.5" overall. **Stocks:** Smooth walnut with etched black widow spider logo. **Sights:** Ramped blade front, rear adjustable for windage and elevation. **Features:** Extended safety, extended slide release; Commander-style hammer; beavertail grip safety; throated, ported, tuned, with cone-shaped barrel, no bushing. Parkerized matte black or satin stainless steel. From Safari Arms, Inc.
Price: **$690.00**

SAFARI ARMS CREST SERIES PISTOLS **Caliber:** 9mm Para., 38 Super, 45 ACP, 7-shot magazine (standard), 6-shot (4-Star). **Barrel:** 5" (standard), 4.5" (4-Star); 416 stainless steel. **Weight:** 39 oz. (standard), 35.7 oz. (4-Star). **Length:** 8.5" overall (standard). **Stocks:** Checkered walnut. **Sights:** Ramped blade front, fully adjustable rear. **Features:** Right- or left-hand models available. Long aluminum trigger, long recoil spring guide, extended safety and slide stop. Stainless steel. Introduced 1993. Made in U.S. by Safari Arms, Inc.
Price: Right-hand, standard **$740.00**
Price: Left-hand, standard **$880.00**
Price: Right-hand, 4-Star **$770.00**
Price: Left-hand, 4-Star **$910.00**

SEECAMP LWS 32 STAINLESS DA AUTO **Caliber:** 32 ACP Win. Silvertip, 6-shot magazine. **Barrel:** 2", integral with frame. **Weight:** 10.5 oz. **Length:** 4⅛" overall. **Stocks:** Glass-filled nylon. **Sights:** Smooth, no-snag, contoured slide and barrel top. **Features:** Aircraft quality 17-4 PH stainless steel. Inertia-operated firing pin. Hammer fired double-action only. Hammer automatically follows slide down to safety rest position after each shot—no manual safety needed. Magazine safety disconnector. Polished stainless. Introduced 1985. From L.W. Seecamp.
Price: **$375.00**

SIG SAUER P220 "AMERICAN" AUTO PISTOL **Caliber:** 9mm, 38 Super, 45 ACP, (9-shot in 9mm and 38 Super, 7 in 45). **Barrel:** 4⅜". **Weight:** 28¼ oz. (9mm). **Length:** 7¾" overall. **Stocks:** Checkered black plastic. **Sights:** Blade front, drift adjustable rear for windage. **Features:** Double action. De-cocking lever permits lowering hammer onto locked firing pin. Squared combat-type trigger guard. Slide stays open after last shot. Imported from Germany by SIGARMS, Inc.
Price: "American," blue (side-button magazine release, 45 ACP only) . . **$780.00**
Price: 45 ACP, blue, Siglite night sights **$880.00**
Price: K-Kote finish **$850.00**
Price: K-Kote, Siglite night sights **$950.00**

SIG Sauer P228

SIG Sauer P228 DA Auto Pistol Similar to the P226 except has 3.86" barrel, with 7.08" overall length and 3.35" height. Chambered for 9mm Para. only, 13-shot magazine. Weight is 29.1 oz. with empty magazine. Introduced 1989. Imported from Germany by SIGARMS, Inc.
Price: Blue **$805.00**
Price: Blue, with Siglite night sights **$905.00**
Price: Blue, double-action only **$805.00**
Price: Blue, double-action only, Siglite night sights **$905.00**
Price: K-Kote finish **$875.00**
Price: K-Kote, Siglite night sights **$975.00**
Price: K-Kote, double-action only **$875.00**
Price: K-Kote, double-action only, Siglite night sights **$975.00**

SIG Sauer P229 DA Auto Pistol Similar to the P228 except chambered for 40 S&W with 12-shot magazine. Has 3.86" barrel, 7.08" overall length and 3.35" height. Weight is 30.5 oz. Introduced 1991. Imported from Germany by SIGARMS, Inc.
Price: Blue **$875.00**
Price: Blue, double-action only **$875.00**

SIG SAUER P230 DA AUTO PISTOL **Caliber:** 32 ACP, 8-shot; 380 ACP, 7-shot. **Barrel:** 3¾". **Weight:** 16 oz. **Length:** 6½" overall. **Stocks:** Checkered black plastic. **Sights:** Blade front, rear adjustable for windage. **Features:** Double action. Same basic action design as P220. Blowback operation, stationary barrel. Introduced 1977. Imported from Germany by SIGARMS, Inc.
Price: Blue **$510.00**
Price: In stainless steel (P230 SL) **$595.00**

SAFARI ARMS G.I. SAFARI PISTOL **Caliber:** 45 ACP, 7-shot magazine. **Barrel:** 5". **Weight:** 39.9 oz. **Length:** 8.5" overall. **Stocks:** Checkered walnut. **Sights:** Blade front, fixed rear. **Features:** Beavertail grip safety, extended safety and slide release, Commander-style hammer. Barrel is chrome-lined 4140 steel; National Match 416 stainless optional. Parkerized matte black finish. Introduced 1991. Made in U.S. by Safari Arms, Inc.
Price: **$430.00**

SIG P-210-2 AUTO PISTOL **Caliber:** 7.65mm or 9mm Para., 8-shot magazine. **Barrel:** 4¾". **Weight:** 31¾ oz. (9mm). **Length:** 8½" overall. **Stocks:** Checkered black composition. **Sights:** Blade front, rear adjustable for windage. **Features:** Lanyard loop; matte finish. Conversion unit for 22 LR available. Imported from Switzerland by Mandall Shooting Supplies.
Price: P-210-2 Service Pistol **$3,000.00**

SIG P-210-6 AUTO PISTOL **Caliber:** 9mm Para., 8-shot magazine. **Barrel:** 4¾". **Weight:** 36.2 oz. **Length:** 8½" overall. **Stocks:** Checkered black plastic; walnut optional. **Sights:** Blade front, micro. adjustable rear for windage and elevation. **Features:** Adjustable trigger stop; target trigger; ribbed frontstrap; sandblasted finish. Conversion unit for 22 LR consists of barrel, recoil spring, slide and magazine. Imported from Switzerland by Mandall Shooting Supplies.
Price: P-210-6 . . . . **$3,200.00**
Price: P-210-5 Target **$3,500.00**

SIG Sauer P220 "American"

SIG Sauer P230

SIG SAUER P225 DA AUTO PISTOL **Caliber:** 9mm Para., 8-shot magazine. **Barrel:** 3.8". **Weight:** 26 oz. **Length:** 7³⁄₃₂" overall. **Stocks:** Checkered black plastic. **Sights:** Blade front, rear adjustable for windage. Optional Siglite night sights. **Features:** Double action. De-cocking lever permits lowering hammer onto locked firing pin. Square combat-type trigger guard. Shortened, lightened version of P220. Imported from Germany by SIGARMS, Inc.
Price: **$775.00**
Price: With Siglite night sights **$875.00**
Price: K-Kote finish **$845.00**
Price: K-Kote with Siglite night sights **$945.00**

SIG Sauer P226 DA Auto Pistol Similar to the P220 pistol except has 15-shot magazine, 4.4" barrel, and weighs 26½ oz. 9mm only. Imported from Germany by SIGARMS, Inc.
Price: Blue **$805.00**
Price: With Siglite night sights **$905.00**
Price: Blue, double-action only **$805.00**
Price: Blue, double-action only, Siglite night sights **$905.00**
Price: K-Kote finish **$875.00**
Price: K-Kote, Siglite night sights **$975.00**
Price: K-Kote, double-action only **$875.00**
Price: K-Kote, double-action only, Siglite night sights **$975.00**

SMITH & WESSON MODEL .356 TSW LIMITED PISTOL **Caliber:** 356 TSW, 15-shot magazine. **Barrel:** 5". **Weight:** 44 oz. **Length:** 8.5" overall. **Stocks:** Checkered black composition. **Sights:** Blade front drift adjustable for windage, fully adjustable Bo-Mar rear. **Features:** Single action trigger. Stainless steel frame and slide, hand-fitted titanium-coated stainless steel bushing, match grade barrel. Extended magazine well and oversize release; magazine pads; extended safety. Checkered front strap. Introduced 1993. Available from Lew Horton Dist.
Price: About $1,300.00

Smith & Wesson Model .356 TSW Compact Pistol Similar to the .356 TSW Limited except has 3½" barrel, 12-shot magazine, Novak LoMount combat sights. Overall length 7", weight 37 oz. Introduced 1993. Available from Lew Horton Dist.
Price: . . . . **NA**

Smith & Wesson .356 TSW

SMITH & WESSON MODEL 422, 622 AUTO **Caliber:** 22 LR, 10-shot magazine. **Barrel:** 4½", 6". **Weight:** 22 oz. (4½" bbl.). **Length:** 7½" overall (4½" bbl.). **Stocks:** Checkered plastic (Field), checkered walnut (Target). **Sights:** Field—serrated ramp front, fixed rear; Target—Patridge front, adjustable rear. **Features:** Aluminum frame, steel slide, brushed blue finish; internal hammer. Introduced 1987. Model 2206 introduced 1990.
Price: Blue, 4½", 6", fixed sight $225.00
Price: As above, adjustable sight $278.00
Price: Stainless (Model 622), 4½", 6", fixed sight $272.00
Price: As above, adjustable sight $324.00

Smith & Wesson Model 2214 Sportsman Auto Similar to the Model 422 except has 3" barrel, 8-shot magazine; dovetail Patridge front sight with white dot, fixed rear with two white dots; matte blue finish, black composition grips with checkered panels. Overall length 6⅛", weight 18 oz. Introduced 1990.
Price: $258.00

Smith & Wesson Model 2214

Smith & Wesson Model 2206 Auto Similar to the Model 422/622 except made entirely of stainless steel with non-reflective finish. Weight is 35 oz. with 4½" barrel, 39 oz. with 6" barrel. Other specs are the same. Introduced 1990.
Price: With fixed sight $314.00
Price: With adjustable sight $370.00

SMITH & WESSON MODEL 915 DA AUTO PISTOL **Caliber:** 9mm Para., 15-shot magazine. **Barrel:** 4". **Weight:** 28.5 oz. **Length:** 7.5" overall. **Stocks:** One-piece Xenoy, wraparound with straight backstrap. **Sights:** Post front with white dot, fixed rear. **Features:** Alloy frame, blue carbon steel slide. Slide-mounted decocking lever. Introduced 1992.
Price: $467.00

Smith & Wesson Model 915

SMITH & WESSON MODEL 3913/3914 DOUBLE ACTIONS **Caliber:** 9mm Para., 8-shot magazine. **Barrel:** 3½". **Weight:** 26 oz. **Length:** 6¹³⁄₁₆" overall. **Stocks:** One-piece Delrin wraparound, textured surface. **Sights:** Post front with white dot, Novak LoMount Carry with two dots, adjustable for windage. **Features:** Aluminum alloy frame, stainless slide (M3913) or blue steel slide (M3914). Bobbed hammer with no half-cock notch; smooth .304" trigger with rounded edges. Straight backstrap. Extra magazine included. Introduced 1989.
Price: Model 3913 . . . . $597.00
Price: Model 3914 . . . . $539.00

Smith & Wesson Model 3953DA Pistol Same as the Models 3913/3914 except double-action only. Model 3953 has stainless slide with alloy frame. Overall length 7"; weight 25.5 oz. Extra magazine included. Introduced 1990.
Price: $597.00

Smith & Wesson Model 3913-NL Pistol Same as the 3913/3914 LadySmith autos except without the LadySmith logo and it has a slightly modified frame design. Right-hand safety only. Has stainless slide on alloy frame; extra magazine included. Introduced 1990.
Price: $597.00

Smith & Wesson Model 3913 LadySmith Auto Similar to the standard Model 3913/3914 except has frame that is upswept at the front, rounded trigger guard. Comes in frosted stainless steel with matching gray grips. Grips are ergonomically correct for a woman's hand. Novak LoMount Carry rear sight adjustable for windage, smooth edges for snag resistance. Extra magazine included. Introduced 1990.
Price: $615.00

Smith & Wesson 3913 LadySmith

SMITH & WESSON MODEL 4006 DA AUTO **Caliber:** 40 S&W, 11-shot magazine. **Barrel:** 4". **Weight:** 36 oz. **Length:** 7½" overall. **Stocks:** Xenoy wraparound with checkered panels. **Sights:** Replaceable post front with white dot, Novak LoMount Carry fixed rear with two white dots, or micro. click adjustable rear with two white dots. **Features:** Stainless steel construction with non-reflective finish. Straight back-strap. Extra magazine included. Introduced 1990.
Price: With adjustable sights **$743.00**
Price: With fixed sight **$715.00**
Price: With fixed night sights **$820.00**

Smith & Wesson Model 4046 DA Pistol Similar to the Model 4006 except is double-action only. Has a semi-bobbed hammer, smooth trigger, 4" barrel; Novak LoMount Carry rear sight, post front with white dot. Overall length is 7½", weight 39 oz. Extra magazine included. Introduced 1991.
Price: **$715.00**
Price: With fixed night sights **$820.00**

SMITH & WESSON MODEL 4013/4014, 4053 AUTOS **Caliber:** 40 S&W, 7-shot magazine. **Barrel:** 3½". **Weight:** 26 oz. **Length:** 7" overall. **Stocks:** One-piece Xenoy wraparound with straight backstrap. **Sights:** Post front with white dot, fixed Novak LoMount Carry rear with two white dots. **Features:** Models 4013/4014 are traditional double action; Model 4053 is double-action only; Models 4013, 4053 have stainless slide on alloy frame; 4014 has blued steel slide. Introduced 1991.
Price: Models 4013, 4053 . . . . **$693.00**
Price: Model 4014 . . . . **$635.00**

SMITH & WESSON MODEL 4026 DA AUTO **Caliber:** 40 S&W, 11-shot magazine. **Barrel:** 4". **Weight:** 39 oz. **Length:** 7.5" overall. **Stocks:** Xenoy one-piece wraparound. **Sights:** Post front with white dot, Novak LoMount Carry rear with two white dots. **Features:** Stainless steel. Has spring-loaded, frame-mounted decocking lever, magazine disconnector safety and firing pin safety. Matte finish. Bobbed hammer, smooth trigger. Introduced 1992.
Price: **$731.00**

SMITH & WESSON MODEL 4500 SERIES AUTOS **Caliber:** 45 ACP, 8-shot magazine (M4506, 4566/4586). **Barrel:** 5" (M4506). **Weight:** 41 oz. (4506). **Length:** 7⅛" overall (4516). **Stocks:** Delrin one-piece wraparound, arched or straight backstrap on M4506, straight only on M4516. **Sights:** Post front with white dot, adjustable or fixed Novak LoMount Carry on M4506. **Features:** M4506 has serrated hammer spur. Extra magazine included. Contact Smith & Wesson for complete data. Introduced 1989.
Price: Model 4506, fixed sight **$742.00**
Price: Model 4506, adjustable sight **$773.00**
Price: Model 4566 (stainless, 4¼", traditional DA, ambidextrous
  safety) **$742.00**
Price: Model 4586 (stainless, 4¼", DA only) **$742.00**

Smith & Wesson Model 1006 Double-Action Auto Similar to the Model 4506 except chambered for 10mm auto with 9-shot magazine. Available with either Novak LoMount Carry fixed rear sight with two white dots or adjustable micrometer-click rear with two white dots. All stainless steel construction; one-piece Delrin stocks with straight backstrap; curved backstrap available as option. Has 5" barrel, 8½" overall length, weighs 38 oz. with fixed sight. Rounded trigger guard with knurling. Extra magazine included. Introduced 1990.
Price: With fixed sight **$769.00**
Price: With adjustable sight **$796.00**

SMITH & WESSON MODEL 5900 SERIES AUTO PISTOLS **Caliber:** 9mm Para., 15-shot magazine. **Barrel:** 4". **Weight:** 28½ to 37½ oz. (fixed sight); 29 to 38 oz. (adj. sight). **Length:** 7½" overall. **Stocks:** Xenoy wraparound with curved backstrap. **Sights:** Post front with white dot, fixed or fully adjustable with two white dots. **Features:** All stainless, stainless and alloy or carbon steel and alloy construction. Smooth .304" trigger, .260" serrated hammer. Extra magazine included. Introduced 1989.
Price: Model 5903 (stainless, alloy frame, traditional DA, adjustable sight,
  ambidextrous safety) **$693.00**
Price: As above, fixed sight **$662.00**
Price: Model 5904 (blue, alloy frame, traditional DA, adjustable sight,
  ambidextrous safety) **$645.00**
Price: As above, fixed sight **$616.00**
Price: Model 5906 (stainless, traditional DA, adjustable sight,
  ambidextrous safety) **$711.00**
Price: As above, fixed sight **$679.00**
Price: With fixed night sights **$784.00**
Price: Model 5946 (as above, stainless frame and slide) **$679.00**

Smith & Wesson Model 4006

Smith & Wesson Model 4506

Smith & Wesson Model 1006

Smith & Wesson Model 5946

Smith & Wesson Model 1076 Auto Same as the Model 1006 except has frame-mounted decocking lever, fixed sight only; traditional double-action mechanism. Extra magazine included. Introduced 1990.
Price: **$778.00**

Smith & Wesson Model 6904/6906 Double-Action Autos Similar to the Models 5904/5906 except with 3½" barrel, 12-shot magazine (20-shot available), fixed rear sight, .260" bobbed hammer. Extra magazine included. Introduced 1989.
Price: Model 6904, blue $590.00
Price: Model 6906, stainless $650.00
Price: Model 6946 (stainless, DA only, fixed sights) $650.00
Price: With fixed night sights $756.00

Smith & Wesson Model 6904

SPHINX AT-380M AUTO PISTOL **Caliber:** 380 ACP, 10-shot magazine. **Barrel:** 3.27". **Weight:** 25 oz. **Length:** 6.03" overall. **Stocks:** Checkered plastic. **Sights:** Fixed. **Features:** Double-action-only mechanism, Chamber loaded indicator; ambidextrous magazine release and slide latch. Blued slide, bright Palladium frame, or bright Palladium overall. Introduced 1993. Imported from Switzerland by Sile Distributors, Inc.
Price: Two-tone $571.95
Price: Palladium finish $629.95

SPHINX AT-2000S DOUBLE-ACTION PISTOL **Caliber:** 9mm Para., 9x21mm, 15-shot, 40 S&W, 11-shot magazine. **Barrel:** 4.53". **Weight:** 36.3 oz. **Length:** 8.03" overall. **Stocks:** Checkered neoprene. **Sights:** Fixed, three-dot system. **Features:** Double-action changeable to double-action-only. Stainless frame, blued slide. Ambidextrous safety, magazine release, slide latch. Introduced 1993. Imported from Switzerland by Sile Distributors, Inc.
Price: 9mm, two-tone $902.95
Price: 9mm, Palladium finish $989.95
Price: 40 S&W, two-tone $911.95
Price: 40 S&W, Palladium finish $998.95

Sphinx AT-380M

Sphinx AT-2000H Auto Pistol Similar to the AT-2000P except has shorter slide with 3.54" barrel, shorter frame, 10-shot magazine, with 7" overall length. Weight is 32.2 oz. Stainless frame with blued slide, or overall bright Palladium finish. Introduced 1993. Imported from Switzerland by Sile Distributors, Inc.
Price: 9mm, two-tone $858.95
Price: 9mm, Palladium finish $945.95
Price: 40 S&W, two-tone $867.95
Price: 40 S&W, Palladium $954.95

Sphinx AT-2000P, AT-2000PS Auto Pistols Same as the AT-2000S except AT-2000P has shortened frame (13-shot magazine), 3.74" barrel, 7.25" overall length, and weighs 34 oz. Model AT-2000PS has full-size frame. Both have stainless frame with blued slide or bright Palladium finish. Introduced 1993. Imported from Switzerland by Sile Distributors, Inc.
Price: 9mm, two-tone $858.95
Price: 9mm, Palladium finish $945.95
Price: 40 S&W, two-tone $867.95
Price: 40 S&W, Palladium finish $954.95

Sphinx AT-2000S

SPORTARMS TOKAREV MODEL 213 **Caliber:** 9mm Para., 8-shot magazine. **Barrel:** 4.5". **Weight:** 31 oz. **Length:** 7.6" overall. **Stocks:** Grooved plastic. **Sights:** Fixed. **Features:** Blue finish, hard chrome optional. 9mm version of the famous Russian Tokarev pistol. Made in China by Norinco. Imported by Sportarms of Florida. Introduced 1988.
Price: Blue, about $150.00
Price: Hard chrome, about $179.00

SPRINGFIELD INC. 1911A1 AUTO PISTOL **Caliber:** 9mm Para., 9-shot; 38 Super, 10-shot; 45 ACP, 8-shot. **Barrel:** 5". **Weight:** 35.06 oz. **Length:** 8.59" overall. **Stocks:** Checkered walnut. **Sights:** Fixed low-profile combat-style. **Features:** Beveled magazine well. All forged parts, including frame, barrel, slide. All new production. Introduced 1990. From Springfield Inc.
Price: Basic, 45 ACP, Parkerized $449.00
Price: Standard, 45 ACP, blued $489.00
Price: Basic, 45 ACP, stainless $532.00

Springfield Inc. 1911A1

Springfield Inc. 1911A1 Custom Carry Gun Similar to the standard 1911A1 except has fixed three-dot low profile sights, Videki speed trigger, match barrel and bushing; extended thumb safety, beavertail grip safety; beveled, polished magazine well, polished feed ramp and throated barrel; match Commander hammer and sear, tuned extractor; lowered and flared ejection port; Shok Buff, full-length spring guide rod; walnut grips. Comes with two magazines with slam pads, plastic carrying case. Available in 45 ACP only. Introduced 1992. From Springfield Inc.
Price: . . . . P.O.R.

Springfield Inc. 1911A1 Factory Comp

Springfield Inc. Product Improved 1911A1 Defender Pistol Similar to the 1911A1 Champion except has tapered cone dual-port compensator system, rubberized grips. Has reverse recoil plug, full-length recoil spring guide, serrated frontstrap, extended thumb safety, Commander-style hammer with modified grip safety to match and a Videki speed trigger. Bi-Tone finish. Introduced 1991.
Price: 45 ACP **$959.00**

Springfield Inc. 1911A1 Compact Pistol Similar to the Champion model except has a shortened slide with 4.025" barrel, 7.75" overall length. Magazine capacity is 7 shots. Has Commander hammer, checkered walnut grips. Available in 45 ACP only. Introduced 1989.
Price: Blued **$509.00**
Price: Bi-Tone (blue slide, stainless frame) **$829.00**
Price: Stainless **$558.00**

STAR FIRESTAR AUTO PISTOL Caliber: 9mm Para., 7-shot; 40 S&W, 6-shot. **Barrel:** 3.39". **Weight:** 30.35 oz. **Length:** 6.5" overall. **Stocks:** Checkered rubber. **Sights:** Blade front, fully adjustable rear; three-dot system. **Features:** Low-profile, combat-style sights; ambidextrous safety. Available in blue or weather-resistant Starvel finish. Introduced 1990. Imported from Spain by Interarms.
Price: Blue, 9mm **$460.00**
Price: Starvel finish 9mm **$492.00**
Price: Blue, 40 S&W **$488.00**
Price: Starvel finish, 40 S&W **$517.00**

Star Firestar M45 Auto Pistol Similar to the standard Firestar except chambered for 45 ACP with 6-shot magazine. Has 3.6" barrel, weighs 35 oz., 6.85" overall length. Reverse-taper Acculine barrel. Introduced 1992. Imported from Spain by Interarms.
Price: Blue **$525.00**
Price: Starvel finish **$553.00**

STAR MODEL 31P & 31PK DOUBLE-ACTION PISTOLS Caliber: 9mm Para., 15-shot magazine. **Barrel:** 3.86". **Weight:** 30 oz. **Length:** 7.6" overall. **Stocks:** Checkered black plastic. **Sights:** Square blade front, square notch rear click-adjustable for windage and elevation. **Features:** Double or single action; grooved front- and backstraps and trigger guard face; ambidextrous safety cams firing pin forward; removable backstrap houses the firing mechanism. Model 31P has steel frame; Model PK is alloy. Introduced 1984. Imported from Spain by Interarms.
Price: Model 31P, 40 S&W, blue, steel frame **$643.00**
Price: Model 31P, 40 S&W, Starvel finish, steel frame **$675.00**
Price: Model 31P, 9mm, blue, steel frame, ... **$580.00**
Price: Model 31P, 9mm, Starvel finish, steel frame **$612.00**
Price: Model 31PK, 9mm only, blue, alloy frame **$580.00**

STAR MEGASTAR 45 ACP AUTO PISTOL Caliber: 10mm, 45 ACP, 12-shot magazine. **Barrel:** 4.6". **Weight:** 47.6 oz. **Length:** 8.44" overall. **Stocks:** Checkered composition. **Sights:** Blade front, adjustable rear. **Features:** Double-action mechanism; steel frame and slide; reverse-taper Acculine barrel. Introduced 1992. Imported from Spain by Interarms.
Price: Blue, 10mm **$693.00**
Price: Starvel finish, 10mm **$725.00**
Price: Blue, 45 ACP **$693.00**
Price: Starvel finish, 45 ACP **$725.00**

Springfield Inc. 1911A1 High Capacity Pistol Similar to the Standard 1911A1 except available in 45 ACP and 9x21mm with 10-shot magazine (45 ACP), 16-shot magazine (9x21mm). Has Commander-style hammer, walnut grips, ambidextrous thumb safety, beveled magazine well, plastic carrying case. Blue finish only. Introduced 1993. From Springfield, Inc.
Price: 45 ACP **$799.00**
Price: 9x21mm **$879.00**
Price: 45 ACP Factory Comp **$999.00**

Springfield Inc. 1911A1 Factory Comp Similar to the standard 1911A1 except comes with bushing-type dual-port compensator, adjustable rear sight, extended thumb safety, Videki speed trigger, and beveled magazine well. Checkered walnut grips standard. Available in 38 Super or 45 ACP, blue only. Introduced 1992.
Price: 38 Super **$899.00**
Price: 45 ACP **$869.00**

Springfield Inc. 1911A1 Champion Pistol Similar to the standard 1911A1 except slide and barrel are ½" shorter. Has low-profile three-dot sight system. Comes with Commander hammer and walnut stocks. Available in 45 ACP only; blue or stainless. Introduced 1989.
Price: Blue **$513.00**
Price: Stainless **$558.00**
Price: Blue, comp **$829.00**

STALLARD JS-9MM AUTO PISTOL Caliber: 9mm Para., 8-shot magazine. **Barrel:** 4.5". **Weight:** 41 oz. **Length:** 7.72" overall. **Stocks:** Textured acetal plastic. **Sights:** Fixed, low profile. **Features:** Single-action design. Scratch-resistant, non-glare blue finish. Introduced 1990. From MKS Supply, Inc.
Price: Matte black **$139.95**
Price: Brushed nickel **$149.95**

Star Firestar

Consult our Directory pages for the location of firms mentioned.

Star Model 31P

STEYR SSP SEMI-AUTOMATIC PISTOL **Caliber:** 9mm Para., 15- or 30-shot magazine. **Barrel:** 5.9". **Weight:** 42 oz. **Length:** 12.75" overall. **Stocks:** Grooved synthetic. **Sights:** Post front adjustable for elevation, open rear adjustable for windage. **Features:** Delayed blowback, rotating barrel operating system. Synthetic upper and lower receivers. Drop and cross-bolt safeties. Rail mount for optics. Introduced 1993. Imported from Austria by GSI, Inc.
Price: **$895.00**

Sundance BOA

Steyr SSP

TAURUS MODEL PT 22/PT 25 AUTO PISTOLS **Caliber:** 22 LR, 9-shot (PT 22); 25 ACP, 8-shot (PT 25). **Barrel:** 2.75". **Weight:** 12.3 oz. **Length:** 5.25" overall. **Stocks:** Smooth Brazilian hardwood. **Sights:** Blade front, fixed rear. **Features:** Double action. Tip-up barrel for loading, cleaning. Blue only. Introduced 1992. Made in U.S. by Taurus International.
Price: 22 LR or 25 ACP **$182.00**

TAURUS MODEL PT58 AUTO PISTOL **Caliber:** 380 ACP, 12-shot magazine. **Barrel:** 4.01". **Weight:** 30 oz. **Length:** 7.2" overall. **Stocks:** Brazilian hardwood. **Sights:** Integral blade on slide front, notch rear adjustable for windage. Three-dot system. **Features:** Double action with exposed hammer; inertia firing pin. Introduced 1988. Imported by Taurus International.
Price: Blue **$423.00**
Price: Satin nickel **$454.00**
Price: Stainless steel **$481.00**

TAURUS MODEL PT 92AF AUTO PISTOL **Caliber:** 9mm Para., 15-shot magazine. **Barrel:** 4.92". **Weight:** 34 oz. **Length:** 8.54" overall. **Stocks:** Brazilian hardwood. **Sights:** Fixed notch rear. Three-dot sight system. **Features:** Double action, exposed hammer, chamber loaded indicator. Inertia firing pin. Imported by Taurus International.
Price: Blue **$473.00**
Price: Blue, Deluxe Shooter's Pak (extra magazine, case) **$501.00**
Price: Nickel **$511.00**
Price: Nickel, Deluxe Shooter's Pak (extra magazine, case) **$539.00**
Price: Stainless steel **$538.00**
Price: Stainless, Deluxe Shooter's Pak (extra magazine, case) **$564.00**

Taurus PT 92AFC Compact Pistol Similar to the PT-92 except has 4.25" barrel, 13-shot magazine, weighs 31 oz. and is 7.5" overall. Available in stainless steel, blue or satin nickel. Introduced 1991. Imported by Taurus International.
Price: Blue **$473.00**
Price: Blue, Deluxe Shooter's Pak (extra magazine, case) **$501.00**
Price: Nickel **$511.00**
Price: Nickel, Deluxe Shooter's Pak (extra magazine, case) **$539.00**
Price: Stainless steel **$538.00**
Price: Stainless, Deluxe Shooter's Pak (extra magazine and case) **$564.00**

Taurus PT 99AF Auto Pistol Similar to the PT-92 except has fully adjustable rear sight, smooth Brazilian walnut stocks and is available in stainless steel, polished blue or satin nickel. Introduced 1983.
Price: Blue **$512.00**
Price: Blue, Deluxe Shooter's Pak (extra magazine, case) **$540.00**
Price: Nickel **$554.00**
Price: Nickel, Deluxe Shooter's Pak (extra magazine, case) **$583.00**
Price: Stainless steel **$582.00**
Price: Stainless, Deluxe Shooter's Pak (extra magazine, case) **$609.00**

TAURUS PT 100 AUTO PISTOL **Caliber:** 40 S&W, 11-shot magazine. **Barrel:** 5". **Weight:** 34 oz. **Stocks:** Smooth Brazilian hardwood. **Sights:** Fixed front, drift-adjustable rear. Three-dot combat. **Features:** Double action, exposed hammer. Ambidextrous hammer-drop safety; inertia firing pin; chamber loaded indicator. Introduced 1991. Imported by Taurus International.
Price: Blue **$482.00**
Price: Blue, Deluxe Shooter's Pak (extra magazine, case) **$510.00**
Price: Nickel **$521.00**
Price: Nickel, Deluxe Shooter's Pak (extra magazine, case) **$548.00**
Price: Stainless **$547.00**
Price: Stainless, Deluxe Shooter's Pak (extra magazine, case) **$575.00**

SUNDANCE BOA AUTO PISTOL **Caliber:** 25 ACP, 7-shot magazine. **Barrel:** 2½". **Weight:** 16 oz. **Length:** 4⅞". **Stocks:** Grooved ABS or smooth simulated pearl; optional pink. **Sights:** Fixed. **Features:** Patented grip safety, manual rotary safety; button magazine release; lifetime warranty. Bright chrome or black Teflon finish. Introduced 1991. Made in the U.S. by Sundance Industries, Inc.
Price: **$95.00**

SUNDANCE MODEL A-25 AUTO PISTOL **Caliber:** 25 ACP, 7-shot magazine. **Barrel:** 2.5". **Weight:** 16 oz. **Length:** 4⅞" overall. **Stocks:** Grooved black ABS or simulated smooth pearl; optional pink. **Sights:** Fixed. **Features:** Manual rotary safety; button magazine release. Bright chrome or black Teflon finish. Introduced 1989. Made in U.S. by Sundance Industries, Inc.
Price: **$79.95**

Taurus PT 92C

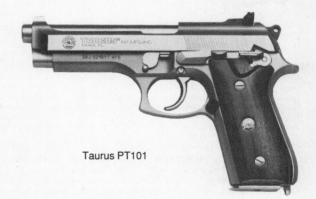
Taurus PT101

Taurus PT 101 Auto Pistol Same as the PT 100 except has micro-click rear sight adjustable for windage and elevation, three-dot combat-style. Introduced 1991.
Price: Blue **$522.00**
Price: Blue, Deluxe Shooter's Pak (extra magazine, case) **$549.00**
Price: Nickel **$564.00**
Price: Nickel, Deluxe Shooter's Pak (extra magazine, case) **$592.00**
Price: Stainless **$592.00**
Price: Stainless, Deluxe Shooter's Pak (extra magazine, case) **$623.00**

TAURUS MODEL PT-908 AUTO PISTOL **Caliber:** 9mm Para., 8-shot magazine. **Barrel:** 3.8". **Weight:** 30 oz. **Length:** 7.05" overall. **Stocks:** Checkered black composition. **Sights:** Drift-adjustable front and rear; three-dot combat. **Features:** Double action, exposed hammer; manual ambidextrous hammer-drop; inertia firing pin; chamber loaded indicator. Introduced 1993. Imported by Taurus International.
Price: Blue **$473.00**
Price: Nickel **$511.00**
Price: Stainless steel **$538.00**

Taurus PT-908

WALTHER PP AUTO PISTOL **Caliber:** 22 LR, 15-shot; 32 ACP, 380 ACP, 7-shot magazine. **Barrel:** 3.86". **Weight:** 23½ oz. **Length:** 6.7" overall. **Stocks:** Checkered plastic. **Sights:** Fixed, white markings. **Features:** Double action; manual safety blocks firing pin and drops hammer; chamber loaded indicator on 32 and 380; extra finger rest magazine provided. Imported from Germany by Interarms.
Price: 22 LR **$948.00**
Price: 32 . . . . **$1,448.00**
Price: 380 . . . . **$1,492.00**
Price: Engraved models . . . . **On Request**

Walther PPK/S American Auto Pistol Similar to Walther PP except made entirely in the United States. Has 3.27" barrel with 6.1" length overall. Introduced 1980.
Price: 380 ACP only **$627.00**
Price: As above, stainless **$627.00**

Walther PPK/S American

Walther PPK American Auto Pistol Similar to Walther PPK/S except weighs 21 oz., has 6-shot capacity. Made in the U.S. Introduced 1986.
Price: Stainless, 380 ACP only **$627.00**
Price: Blue, 380 ACP only **$627.00**

Walther P88 Compact

Walther P-38

WALTHER P-88 AUTO PISTOL **Caliber:** 9mm Para., 15-shot magazine. **Barrel:** 4". **Weight:** 31½ oz. **Length:** 7⅜" overall. **Stocks:** Checkered black composition. **Sights:** Blade front, rear adjustable for windage and elevation. **Features:** Double action with ambidextrous decocking lever and magazine release; alloy frame; loaded chamber indicator; matte finish. Imported from Germany by Interarms.
Price: **$1,200.00**
Price: P-88 Compact (14-shot) **$1,200.00**

WALTHER P-38 AUTO PISTOL **Caliber:** 9mm Para., 8-shot. **Barrel:** 4¹⁵⁄₁₆". **Weight:** 28 oz. **Length:** 8½" overall. **Stocks:** Checkered plastic. **Sights:** Fixed. **Features:** Double action; safety blocks firing pin and drops hammer. Matte finish standard, polished blue, engraving and/or plating available. Imported from Germany by Interarms.
Price: **$1,000.00**
Price: Engraved models . . . . **On Request**

Walther TPH

Walther P-5 Auto Pistol Latest Walther design that uses the basic P-38 double-action mechanism. Caliber 9mm Para., barrel length 3½"; weight 28 oz., overall length 7".
Price: **$1,257.00**
Price: P-5 Compact **$1,257.00**

WALTHER MODEL TPH AUTO PISTOL **Caliber:** 22 LR, 25 ACP, 6-shot magazine. **Barrel:** 2¼". **Weight:** 14 oz. **Length:** 5⅜" overall. **Stocks:** Checkered black composition. **Sights:** Blade front, rear drift-adjustable for windage. **Features:** Made of stainless steel. Scaled-down version of the Walther PP/PPK series. Made in U.S. Introduced 1987. From Interarms.
Price: Blue or stainless steel, 22 or 25 . . . . **$473.00**

Wildey Auto

WILDEY AUTOMATIC PISTOL **Caliber:** 10mm Wildey Mag., 11mm Wildey Mag., 30 Wildey Mag., 357 Peterbuilt, 45 Win. Mag., 475 Wildey Mag., 7-shot magazine. **Barrel:** 5", 6", 7", 8", 10", 12", 14" (45 Win. Mag.); 8", 10", 12", 14" (all other cals.). Interchangeable. **Weight:** 64 oz. (5" barrel). **Length:** 11" overall (7" barrel). **Stocks:** Hardwood. **Sights:** Ramp front (interchangeable blades optional), fully adjustable rear. Scope base available. **Features:** Gas-operated action. Made of stainless steel. Has three-lug rotary bolt. Double or single action. Polished and matte finish. Made in U.S. by Wildey, Inc.
Price: . . . . **$1,175.00 to $1,495.00**

WILKINSON "LINDA" AUTO PISTOL **Caliber:** 9mm Para., 31-shot magazine. **Barrel:** 8⁵⁄₁₆". **Weight:** 4 lbs., 13 oz. **Length:** 12¼" overall. **Stocks:** Checkered black plastic pistol grip, maple forend. **Sights:** Protected blade front, aperture rear. **Features:** Fires from closed bolt. Semi-auto only. Straight blowback action. Cross-bolt safety. Removable barrel. From Wilkinson Arms.
Price: **$412.00**

WILKINSON "SHERRY" AUTO PISTOL **Caliber:** 22 LR, 8-shot magazine. **Barrel:** 2⅛". **Weight:** 9¼ oz. **Length:** 4⅜" overall. **Stocks:** Checkered black plastic. **Sights:** Fixed, groove. **Features:** Cross-bolt safety locks the sear into the hammer. Available in all blue finish or blue slide and trigger with gold frame. Introduced 1985.
Price: **$169.95**

Wilkinson "Sherry"

HANDGUNS—DOUBLE ACTION REVOLVERS, SERVICE & SPORT

Includes models suitable for hunting and competitive courses for fire, both police and international.

CHARTER BULLDOG PUG REVOLVER **Caliber:** 44 Spec., 5-shot. **Barrel:** 2½". **Weight:** 19½ oz. **Length:** 7" overall. **Stocks:** Checkered walnut Bulldog. **Sights:** Ramp-style front, fixed rear. **Features:** Blue or stainless steel construction. Fully shrouded barrel. Reintroduced 1993. Made in U.S. by Charco, Inc.
Price: Blue **$278.75**
Price: Stainless steel **$334.33**

CHARTER OFF DUTY REVOLVER **Caliber:** 22 LR, 6-shot, 38 Spec., 5-shot. **Barrel:** 2". **Weight:** 17 oz. (38 Spec.). **Length:** 6¼" overall. **Stocks:** Checkered walnut. **Sights:** Ramp-style front, fixed rear. **Features:** Available in blue, stainless or electroless nickel. Fully shrouded barrel. Introduced 1993. Made in U.S. by Charco, Inc.
Price: Blue, 22 or 38 Spec. **$208.83**
Price: Stainless steel, 22 or 38 Spec. **$267.83**
Price: Electroless nickel, 22 or 38 Spec. **$243.00**

COLT ANACONDA REVOLVER **Caliber:** 44 Rem. Magnum, 45 Colt, 6-shot. **Barrel:** 4", 6", 8". **Weight:** 53 oz. (6" barrel). **Length:** 11⅝" overall. **Stocks:** Combat-style black neoprene with finger grooves. **Sights:** Red insert front, adjustable white outline rear. **Features:** Stainless steel; full-length ejector rod housing; ventilated barrel rib; offset bolt notches in cylinder; wide spur hammer. Introduced 1990.
Price: **$584.95**
Price: 45 Colt, 6" barrel only **$584.95**

COLT DETECTIVE SPECIAL REVOLVER **Caliber:** 38 Special, 6-shot. **Barrel:** 2". **Weight:** 22 oz. **Length:** 6⅝" overall. **Stocks:** Black composition. **Sights:** Fixed. Ramp front, square notch rear. **Features:** Glare-proof sights, grooved trigger, shrouded ejector rod. Colt blue finish. Reintroduced 1993.
Price: **$383.95**

COLT KING COBRA REVOLVER **Caliber:** 357 Magnum, 6-shot. **Barrel:** 4", 6". **Weight:** 42 oz. (4" bbl.). **Length:** 9" overall (4" bbl.). **Stocks:** Checkered rubber. **Sights:** Red insert ramp front, adjustable white outline rear. **Features:** Full-length contoured ejector rod housing, barrel rib. Introduced 1986.
Price: Stainless **$434.95**

CHARTER POLICE UNDERCOVER REVOLVER **Caliber:** 32 H&R Mag., 38 Spec., 6-shot. **Barrel:** 2½". **Weight:** 16 oz. (38 Spec.). **Length:** 6¼" overall. **Stocks:** Checkered walnut. **Sights:** Ramp-style front, fixed rear. **Features:** Blue or stainless steel. Fully shrouded barrel. Reintroduced 1993. Made in U.S. by Charco, Inc.
Price: Blue **$250.00**
Price: Stainless **$275.88**

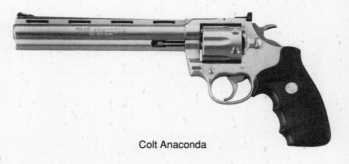

Colt Anaconda

Colt Detective Special

COLT PYTHON REVOLVER **Caliber:** 357 Magnum (handles all 38 Spec.), 6-shot. **Barrel:** 4", 6" or 8", with ventilated rib. **Weight:** 38 oz. (4" bbl.). **Length:** 9¼" (4" bbl.). **Stocks:** Rubber wraparound. **Sights:** ⅛" ramp front, adjustable notch rear. **Features:** Ventilated rib; grooved, crisp trigger; swing-out cylinder; target hammer.
Price: Royal blue, 4", 6", 8" **$791.95**
Price: Stainless, 4", 6", 8" **$882.95**
Price: Bright stainless, 4", 6", 8" **$912.95**

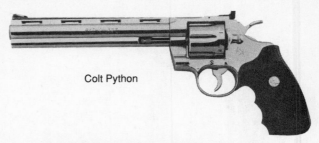

Colt Python

E.A.A. Standard Grade

ERMA ER-777 SPORTING REVOLVER **Caliber:** 22 LR, 32 S&W, 357 Mag., 6-shot. **Barrel:** 4", 5½". **Weight:** 43.3 oz. **Length:** 9½" overall (4" barrel). **Stocks:** Stippled walnut service-type. **Sights:** Interchangeable blade front, micro-adjustable rear for windage and elevation. **Features:** Polished blue finish. Adjustable trigger. Imported from Germany by Precision Sales Int'l. Introduced 1988.
Price: **$1,200.00**
Price: ER-772 (22 LR), ER-773 (32 S&W) **$1,265.00**

HARRINGTON & RICHARDSON SPORTSMAN 999 REVOLVER **Caliber:** 22 Short, Long, Long Rifle, 9-shot. **Barrel:** 4", 6". **Weight:** 30 oz. (4" barrel). **Length:** 8.5" overall. **Stocks:** Walnut-finished hardwood. **Sights:** Blade front adjustable for elevation, rear adjustable for windage. **Features:** Top-break loading; polished blue finish; automatic shell ejection. Reintroduced 1992. From H&R 1871, Inc.
Price: **$279.95**

HERITAGE SENTRY DOUBLE-ACTION REVOLVERS **Caliber:** 38 Spec., 6-shot. **Barrel:** 2", 4". **Weight:** 23 oz. (2" barrel). **Length:** 6¼" overall (2" barrel). **Stocks:** Magnum-style round butt; checkered plastic. **Sights:** Ramp front, fixed rear. **Features:** Pull-pin-type ejection; serrated hammer and trigger. Polished blue or chrome finish. Introduced 1993. Made in U.S. by Heritage Mfg., Inc.
Price: . . . . **$104.95 to $129.95**

KORTH REVOLVER **Caliber:** 22 LR, 22 Mag., 32 H&R Mag., 32 S&W Long, 357 Mag., 9mm Parabellum. **Barrel:** 3", 4", 6". **Weight:** 33 to 38 oz. **Length:** 8" to 11" overall. **Stocks:** Checkered walnut, sport or combat. **Sights:** Blade front, rear adjustable for windage and elevation. **Features:** Four interchangeable cylinders available. Major parts machined from hammer-forged steel; cylinder gap of .002". High polish blue finish. Presentation models have gold trim. Imported from Germany by Mandall Shooting Supplies.
Price: With two cylinders **$3,300.00**

LLAMA COMANCHE REVOLVER **Caliber:** 22 LR, 357 Mag. **Barrel:** 4", 6". **Weight:** 28 oz. **Length:** 9¼" (4" bbl.). **Stocks:** Checkered walnut. **Sights:** Fixed blade front, rear adjustable for windage and elevation. **Features:** Ventilated rib, wide spur hammer. Satin chrome finish available. Imported from Spain by SGS Importers International., Inc.
Price: Blue finish **$274.95**

Llama Super Comanche Revolver Similar to the Comanche except: large frame, 44-Mag. with 6", 8½" barrel, 6-shot cylinder; smooth, extra wide trigger; wide spur hammer; over-size walnut, target-style grips. Weight is 3 lbs., 2 oz. Blue finish only.
Price: 44 Mag. **$366.95**

E.A.A. STANDARD GRADE REVOLVERS **Caliber:** 22 LR, 22 LR/22 WMR, 8-shot; 32 H&R Mag., 7-shot; 38 Special, 6-shot. **Barrel:** 4", 6" (22 rimfire); 2" (32 H&R Mag.); 2", 4" (38 Special). **Weight:** 38 oz. (22 rimfire, 4"). **Length:** 8.8" overall (4" bbl.). **Stocks:** Hardwood with finger grooves. **Sights:** Blade front, fixed or adjustable on rimfires; fixed only on 32, 38. **Features:** Swing-out cylinder; hammer block safety; blue finish. Introduced 1991. Imported from Germany by European American Armory.
Price: 22 LR 4", 32 H&R 2", 38 Special 2" **$250.00**
Price: 38 Special, 4" **$275.00**
Price: 22 LR, 6" **$295.00**
Price: 22 LR/22 WMR combo, 4" **$350.00**
Price: As above, 6" **$375.00**

E.A.A. Tactical Grade Revolvers Similar to the Standard Grade revolvers except in 38 Special only, 2" or 4" barrel, fixed sights. Compensator on 4", bobbed hammer (DA only) on 2" model. Introduced 1991. Imported from Germany by European American Armory.
Price: 2", bobbed hammer **$275.00**
Price: 4", compensator **$350.00**

Erma ER-777

Harrington & Richardson Sportsman 999

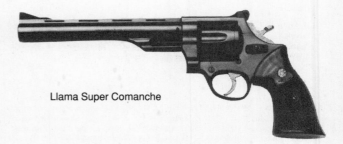

Llama Super Comanche

NEW ENGLAND FIREARMS STANDARD REVOLVERS Caliber: 22 LR, 9-shot; 32 H&R Mag., 5-shot. **Barrel:** 2½", 4". **Weight:** 26 oz. (22 LR, 2½"). **Length:** 8½" overall (4" bbl.). **Stocks:** Walnut-finished American hardwood with NEF medallion. **Sights:** Fixed. **Features:** Choice of blue or nickel finish. Introduced 1988. From New England Firearms Co.
Price: 22 LR, 32 H&R Mag., blue $119.95
Price: 22 LR, 2½", 4", nickel, 32 H&R Mag. 2½" nickel $129.95

NEW ENGLAND FIREARMS LADY ULTRA REVOLVER Caliber: 32 H&R Mag., 5-shot. **Barrel:** 3". **Weight:** 31 oz. **Length:** 7.25" overall. **Stocks:** Walnut-finished hardwood with NEF medallion. **Sights:** Blade front, fully adjustable rear. **Features:** Swing-out cylinder; polished blue finish. Comes with lockable storage case. Introduced 1992. From New England Firearms Co.
Price: $149.95

New England Lady Ultra

NEW ENGLAND FIREARMS ULTRA REVOLVER Caliber: 22 LR, 9-shot; 22 WMR, 6-shot. **Barrel:** 4", 6". **Weight:** 36 oz. **Length:** 10⅝" overall (6" barrel). **Stocks:** Walnut-finished hardwood with NEF medallion. **Sights:** Blade front, fully adjustable rear. **Features:** Blue finish. Bull-style barrel with recessed muzzle, high "Lustre" blue/black finish. Introduced 1989. From New England Firearms.
Price: $149.95
Price: Ultra Mag 22 WMR $149.95

ROSSI MODEL 68 REVOLVER Caliber: 38 Spec. **Barrel:** 2", 3". **Weight:** 22 oz. **Stocks:** Checkered wood. **Sights:** Ramp front, low profile adjustable rear. **Features:** All-steel frame, thumb latch operated swing-out cylinder. Introduced 1978. Imported from Brazil by Interarms.
Price: 38, blue, 3" $227.00
Price: M68/2 (2" barrel), wood or rubber grips $238.00
Price: 3", nickel $232.00

Rossi 971 Comp

Rossi Model 971 Comp Gun Same as the Model 971 stainless except has 3¼" barrel with integral compensator. Overall length is 9", weight 32 oz. Has red insert front sight, fully adjustable rear. Checkered, contoured rubber grips. Introduced 1993. Imported from Brazil by Interarms.
Price: $320.00

RUGER GP-100 REVOLVERS Caliber: 38 Special, 357 Magnum, 6-shot. **Barrel:** 3", 3" heavy, 4", 4" heavy, 6", 6" heavy. **Weight:** 3" barrel—35 oz., 3" heavy barrel—36 oz., 4" barrel—37 oz., 4" heavy barrel—38 oz. **Sights:** Fixed; adjustable on 4" heavy, 6", 6" heavy barrels. **Stocks:** Ruger Santoprene Cushioned Grip with Goncalo Alves inserts. **Features:** Uses action and frame incorporating improvements and features of both the Security-Six and Redhawk revolvers. Full length and short ejector shroud. Satin blue and stainless steel. Introduced 1988.
Price: GP-141 (357, 4" heavy, adj. sights, blue) $413.50
Price: GP-160 (357, 6", adj. sights, blue) $413.50
Price: GP-161 (357, 6" heavy, adj. sights, blue) $413.50
Price: GPF-330 (357, 3"), GPF-830 (38 Spec.) $397.00
Price: GPF-331 (357, 3" heavy), GPF-831 (38 Spec.) $397.00
Price: GPF-340 (357, 4"), GPF-840 (38 Spec.) $397.00
Price: GPF-341 (357, 4" heavy), GPF-841 (38 Spec.) $397.00
Price: KGP-141 (357, 4" heavy, adj. sights, stainless) $446.50
Price: KGP-160 (357, 6", adj. sights, stainless) $446.50
Price: KGP-161 (357, 6" heavy, adj. sights, stainless) $446.50
Price: KGPF-330 (357, 3", stainless), KGPF-830 (38 Spec.) $430.00
Price: KGPF-331 (357, 3" heavy, stainless), KGPF-831 (38 Spec.) . . . $430.00
Price: KGPF-340 (357, 4", stainless), KGPF-840 (38 Spec.) $430.00
Price: KGPF-341 (357, 4" heavy, stainless), KGPF-841 (38 Spec.) . . . $430.00

ROSSI MODEL 88 STAINLESS REVOLVER Caliber: 32 S&W, 38 Spec., 5-shot. **Barrel:** 2", 3". **Weight:** 22 oz. **Length:** 7.5" overall. **Stocks:** Checkered wood, service-style. **Sights:** Ramp front, square notch rear drift adjustable for windage. **Features:** All metal parts except springs are of 440 stainless steel; matte finish; small frame for concealability. Introduced 1983. Imported from Brazil by Interarms.
Price: 3" barrel $262.00
Price: M88/2 (2" barrel), wood or rubber grips $275.00

ROSSI MODEL 720 REVOLVER Caliber: 44 Special, 5-shot. **Barrel:** 3". **Weight:** 27.5 oz. **Length:** 8" overall. **Stocks:** Checkered rubber, combat style. **Sights:** Red insert front on ramp, fully adjustable rear. **Features:** All stainless steel construction; solid barrel rib; full ejector rod shroud. Introduced 1992. Imported from Brazil by Interarms.
Price: $332.00

ROSSI MODEL 851 REVOLVER Caliber: 38 Special, 6-shot. **Barrel:** 3" or 4". **Weight:** 27.5 oz. (3" bbl.). **Length:** 8" overall (3" bbl.). **Stocks:** Checkered Brazilian hardwood. **Sights:** Blade front with red insert, rear adjustable for windage. **Features:** Medium-size frame; stainless steel construction; ventilated barrel rib. Introduced 1991. Imported from Brazil by Interarms.
Price: $280.00

> Consult our Directory pages for the location of firms mentioned.

ROSSI MODEL 971 REVOLVER Caliber: 357 Mag., 6-shot. **Barrel:** 2½", 4", 6", heavy. **Weight:** 36 oz. **Length:** 9" overall. **Stocks:** Checkered Brazilian hardwood. Stainless models have checkered, contoured rubber. **Sights:** Blade front, fully adjustable rear. **Features:** Full-length ejector rod shroud; matted sight rib; target-type trigger, wide checkered hammer spur. Introduced 1988. Imported from Brazil by Interarms.
Price: 4", stainless $315.00
Price: 6", stainless $315.00
Price: 4", blue $280.00
Price: 2½", stainless $320.00

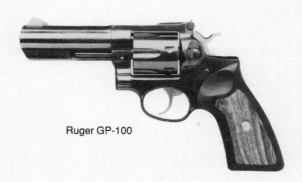
Ruger GP-100

Ruger SP101 DAO

Ruger SP101 Double-Action-Only Revolver Similar to the standard SP101 except is double action only with no single-action sear notch. Has spurless hammer for snag-free handling, floating firing pin and Ruger's patented transfer bar safety system. Available with 2½" barrel in 38 Special +P and 357 Magnum only. Weight is 25½ oz., overall length 7.06". Natural brushed satin stainless steel. Introduced 1993.
Price: KSP821L (38 Spec.), KSP321XL (357 Mag.) **$408.00**

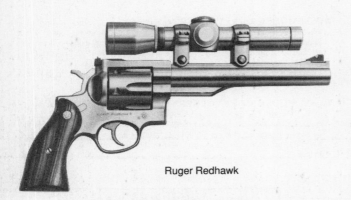

Ruger Redhawk

SMITH & WESSON MODEL 10 M&P REVOLVER **Caliber:** 38 Special, 6-shot. **Barrel:** 2", 4". **Weight:** 30½ oz. **Length:** 9¼" overall. **Stocks:** Checkered walnut, Service. Round or square butt. **Sights:** Fixed, ramp front, square notch rear.
Price: Blue **$361.00**

Smith & Wesson Model 10 38 M&P Heavy Barrel Same as regular M&P except: 4" heavy ribbed bbl. with ramp front sight, square rear, square butt, wgt. 33½ oz.
Price: Blue **$361.00**

SMITH & WESSON MODEL 13 H.B. M&P **Caliber:** 357 and 38 Special, 6-shot. **Barrel:** 3" or 4". **Weight:** 34 oz. **Length:** 9⁵⁄₁₆" overall (4" bbl.). **Stocks:** Checkered walnut, Service. **Sights:** ⅛" serrated ramp front, fixed square notch rear. **Features:** Heavy barrel, K-frame, square butt (4"), round butt (3").
Price: Blue **$367.00**
Price: Model 65, as above in stainless steel **$402.00**

SMITH & WESSON MODEL 14 FULL LUG REVOLVER **Caliber:** 38 Special, 6-shot. **Barrel:** 6", full lug. **Weight:** 47 oz. **Length:** 11⅛" overall. **Stocks:** Combat-style Morado with square butt. **Sights:** Pinned Patridge front, adjustable micrometer click rear. **Features:** Has .500" target hammer, .312" smooth combat trigger. Polished blue finish. Reintroduced 1991. Limited production.
Price: **$442.00**

SMITH & WESSON MODEL 17 K-22 FULL LUG **Caliber:** 22 LR, 6-shot. **Barrel:** 4", 6". **Weight:** 39 oz. (6" bbl.). **Length:** 11⅛" overall. **Stocks:** Square butt Goncalo Alves, combat-style. **Sights:** Patridge front with 6", serrated on 4", S&W micro-click rear adjustable for windage and elevation. **Features:** Grooved tang, polished blue finish, full lug barrel. Introduced 1990.
Price: 4" **$410.00**
Price: 6" **$449.00**

RUGER SP101 REVOLVERS **Caliber:** 22 LR, 32 H&R Mag., 6-shot, 9mm Para., 38 Special +P, 357 Mag., 5-shot. **Barrel:** 2¼", 3¹⁄₁₆", 4". **Weight:** 2¼"—25 oz.; 3¹⁄₁₆"—27 oz. **Sights:** Adjustable on 22, 32, fixed on others. **Stocks:** Ruger Santoprene Cushioned Grip with Xenoy inserts. **Features:** Incorporates improvements and features found in the GP-100 revolvers into a compact, small frame, double-action revolver. Full-length ejector shroud. Stainless steel only. Introduced 1988.
Price: KSP-821 (2½", 38 Spec.) **$408.00**
Price: KSP-831 (3¹⁄₁₆", 38 Spec.) **$408.00**
Price: KSP-221 (2¼", 22 LR) **$408.00**
Price: KSP-240 (4", 22 LR) **$408.00**
Price: KSP-241 (4" heavy bbl., 22 LR) **$408.00**
Price: KSP-3231 (3¹⁄₁₆", 32 H&R) **$408.00**
Price: KSP-921 (2¼", 9mm Para.) **$408.00**
Price: KSP-931 (3¹⁄₁₆", 9mm Para.) **$408.00**
Price: KSP-321 (2¼", 357 Mag.) **$408.00**
Price: KSP-331 (3¹⁄₁₆", 357 Mag.) **$408.00**
Price: KSP-821L (2½", 38 Spec., double action only) **$408.00**
Price: KSP-32LXL (2½", 357 Mag., double action only) **$408.00**

RUGER REDHAWK **Caliber:** 44 Rem. Mag., 6-shot. **Barrel:** 5½", 7½". **Weight:** About 54 oz. (7½" bbl.). **Length:** 13" overall (7½" barrel). **Stocks:** Square butt Goncalo Alves. **Sights:** Interchangeable Patridge-type front, rear adjustable for windage and elevation. **Features:** Stainless steel, brushed satin finish, or blued ordnance steel. Has a 9½" sight radius. Introduced 1979.
Price: Blued, 44 Mag., 5½", 7½" **$458.50**
Price: Blued, 44 Mag., 7½", with scope mount, rings **$496.50**
Price: Stainless, 44 Mag., 5½", 7½" **$516.75**
Price: Stainless, 44 Mag., 7½", with scope mount, rings **$557.25**

Ruger Super Redhawk Revolver Similar to the standard Redhawk except has a heavy extended frame with the Ruger Integral Scope Mounting System on the wide topstrap. The wide hammer spur has been lowered for better scope clearance. Incorporates the mechanical design features and improvements of the GP-100. Choice of 7½" or 9½" barrel, both with ramp front sight base with Redhawk-style Interchangeable Insert sight blades, adjustable rear sight. Comes with Ruger "Cushioned Grip" panels of Santoprene with Goncalo Alves wood panels. Satin polished stainless steel, 44 Magnum only. Introduced 1987.
Price: KSRH-7 (7½"), KSRH-9 (9½") **$589.00**

Smith & Wesson Model 65

Smith & Wesson Model 15

SMITH & WESSON MODEL 15 COMBAT MASTERPIECE **Caliber:** 38 Special, 6-shot. **Barrel:** 4". **Weight:** 32 oz. **Length:** 9⁵⁄₁₆" (4" bbl.). **Stocks:** Checkered walnut. Grooved tangs. **Sights:** Front, Baughman Quick Draw on ramp, micro-click rear, adjustable for windage and elevation.
Price: Blued **$391.00**

Smith & Wesson Model 617 Full Lug Revolver Similar to the Model 17 Full Lug except made of stainless steel. Has semi-target .375" hammer, .312" smooth combat trigger on 4"; 6", 8⅜" available with either .312" smooth combat trigger or .400" serrated trigger and .500" target hammer. Introduced 1990.
Price: 4" **$432.00**
Price: 6", semi-target hammer, combat trigger **$432.00**
Price: 6", target hammer, target trigger **$466.00**
Price: 8⅜" **$476.00**

Smith & Wesson Model 19

Smith & Wesson Model 648 K-22 Masterpiece MRF Similar to the Model 17 except made of stainless steel and chambered for 22 WMR cartridge. Available with 6" full-lug barrel only, combat-style square butt grips, combat trigger and semi-target hammer. Introduced 1991.
Price: **$437.00**

SMITH & WESSON MODEL 19 COMBAT MAGNUM Caliber: 357 Magnum and 38 Special, 6-shot. Barrel: 2½", 4", 6". Weight: 36 oz. Length: 9⁹⁄₁₆" (4" bbl.). Stocks: Checkered hardwood, target. Grooved tangs. Sights: Serrated ramp front 2½" or 4" bbl., red ramp on 4", 6" bbl., micro-click rear adjustable for windage and elevation.
Price: S&W Bright Blue, adj. sights . . . . **$388.00** to **$420.00**

Smith & Wesson Model 27

SMITH & WESSON MODEL 27 357 MAGNUM REVOLVER
Caliber: 357 Magnum and 38 Special, 6-shot. Barrel: 6". Weight: 45½ oz. Length: 11⁵⁄₁₆" overall. Stocks: Checkered walnut, Magna. Grooved tangs and trigger. Sights: Serrated ramp front, micro-click rear, adjustable for windage and elevation.
Price: **$462.00**

SMITH & WESSON MODEL 29 44 MAGNUM REVOLVER Caliber: 44 Magnum, 6-shot. Barrel: 6", 8⅜". Weight: 47 oz. (6" bbl.). Length: 11⅜" overall (6" bbl.). Stocks: Oversize target-type, checkered hardwood. Tangs and target trigger grooved, checkered target hammer. Sights: ⅛" red ramp front, micro-click rear, adjustable for windage and elevation.
Price: S&W Bright Blue, 6", 8⅜" **$526.00**
Price: Model 629 (stainless steel), 4", 6" **$557.00**
Price: Model 629, 8⅜" barrel **$575.00**

Smith & Wesson Model 629

Smith & Wesson Model 29, 629 Classic Revolvers Similar to the standard Model 29 and 629 except has full-lug 5", 6½" or 8⅜" barrel; chamfered front of cylinder; interchangable red ramp front sight with adjustable white outline rear; Hogue square butt Santoprene grips with S&W monogram; the frame is drilled and tapped for scope mounting. Factory accurizing and endurance packages. Overall length with 5" barrel is 10½"; weight is 51 oz. Introduced 1990.
Price: Model 29 Classic, 5", 6½" **$567.00**
Price: As above, 8⅜" **$578.00**
Price: Model 629 Classic (stainless), 5", 6½" **$598.00**
Price: As above, 8⅜" **$617.00**

Smith & Wesson Model 629 Classic DX Revolver Similar to the Classic Hunters except offered only with 6½" or 8⅜" full-lug barrel; comes with five front sights: 50-yard red ramp; 50-yard black Patridge; 100-yard black Patridge with gold bead; 50-yard black ramp; and 50-yard black Patridge with white dot. Comes with combat-type grips with Carnuba wax finish and Hogue combat-style square butt conversion grip. Introduced 1991.
Price: Model 629 Classic DX, 6½" **$786.00**
Price: As above, 8⅜" **$811.00**

Smith & Wesson Model 629 Classic DX

SMITH & WESSON MODEL 36, 37 CHIEFS SPECIAL & AIR-WEIGHT Caliber: 38 Special, 5-shot. Barrel: 2", 3". Weight: 19½ oz. (2" bbl.); 13½ oz. (Airweight). Length: 6½" (2" bbl. and round butt). Stocks: Checkered walnut, round or square butt. Sights: Fixed, serrated ramp front, square notch rear.
Price: Blue, standard Model 36, 2" **$366.00**
Price: As above, 3" **$378.00**
Price: Blue, Airweight Model 37, 2" only **$394.00**
Price: As above, nickel, 2" only **$410.00**

Smith & Wesson Model 36LS, 60LS LadySmith Similar to the standard Model 36. Available with 2" barrel. Comes with smooth, contoured rosewood grips with the S&W monogram. Has a speedloader cutout. Comes in a fitted carry/storage case. Introduced 1989.
Price: Model 36LS **$398.00**
Price: Model 60LS (as above except in stainless) **$450.00**

Smith & Wesson Model 36LS LadySmith

Smith & Wesson Model 60 3" Full Lug Revolver Similar to the Model 60 Chief's Special except has 3" full-lug barrel, adjustable micrometer click black blade rear sight; rubber Uncle Mike's Custom Grade combat grips. Overall length 7½"; weight 24½ oz. Introduced 1991.
Price: **$443.00**

Smith & Wesson Model 60 Chiefs Special Stainless Same as Model 36 except all stainless construction, 2" bbl. and round butt only.
Price: Stainless steel **$417.00**

SMITH & WESSON MODEL 38 BODYGUARD Caliber: 38 Special, 5-shot. Barrel: 2". Weight: 14½ oz. Length: 6⁵⁄₁₆" overall. Stocks: Checkered walnut. Sights: Fixed serrated ramp front, square notch rear. Features: Alloy frame; internal hammer.
Price: Blue **$418.00**
Price: Nickel **$433.00**

Smith & Wesson Model 49, 649 Bodyguard Revolvers Same as Model 38 except steel construction, weight 20½ oz.
Price: Blued, Model 49 . . . . **$389.00**
Price: Stainless, Model 649 . . . . **$441.00**

SMITH & WESSON MODEL 57, 657 41 MAGNUM REVOLVERS Caliber: 41 Magnum, 6-shot. Barrel: 6". Weight: 48 oz. Length: 11⅜" overall. Stocks: Oversize target-type checkered Goncalo Alves. Sights: ⅛" red ramp front, micro-click rear adjustable for windage and elevation.
Price: S&W Bright Blue, 6" **$466.00**
Price: Stainless, Model 657, 6" **$497.00**

SMITH & WESSON MODEL 63 22/32 KIT GUN Caliber: 22 LR, 6-shot. Barrel: 2", 4". Weight: 24 oz. (4" bbl.). Length: 8⅜" (4" bbl. and round butt). Stocks: Checkered walnut, round or square butt. Sights: Front, serrated ramp, micro-click rear, adjustable for windage and elevation. Features: Stainless steel construction.
Price: 4" **$435.00**
Price: 2" round butt **$435.00**

SMITH & WESSON MODEL 64 STAINLESS M&P Caliber: 38 Special, 6-shot. Barrel: 2", 3", 4". Weight: 34 oz. Length: 9⁵⁄₁₆" overall. Stocks: Checkered walnut, Service style. Sights: Fixed, ⅛" serrated ramp front, square notch rear. Features: Satin finished stainless steel, square butt.
Price: **$402.00**

SMITH & WESSON MODEL 65LS LADYSMITH Caliber: 357 Magnum, 6-shot. Barrel: 3". Weight: 31 oz. Length: 7.94" overall. Stocks: Rosewood, round butt. Sights: Serrated ramp front, fixed notch rear. Features: Stainless steel with frosted finish. Smooth combat trigger, service hammer, shrouded ejector rod. Comes with soft case. Introduced 1992.
Price: **$450.00**

SMITH & WESSON MODEL 66 STAINLESS COMBAT MAGNUM Caliber: 357 Magnum and 38 Special, 6-shot. Barrel: 2½", 4", 6". Weight: 36 oz. Length: 9⁹⁄₁₆" overall. Stocks: Checkered Goncalo Alves target. Sights: Ramp front, micro-click rear adjustable for windage and elevation. Features: Satin finish stainless steel.
Price: . . . . **$437.00 to $447.00**

SMITH & WESSON MODEL 586, 686 DISTINGUISHED COMBAT MAGNUMS Caliber: 357 Magnum. Barrel: 4", 6", full shroud. Weight: 46 oz. (6"), 41 oz. (4"). Stocks: Goncalo Alves target-type with speed loader cutaway. Sights: Baughman red ramp front, four-position click-adjustable front, S&W micrometer click rear (or fixed). Features: Uses new L-frame, but takes all K-frame grips. Full-length ejector rod shroud. Smooth combat-type trigger, semi-target style hammer. Trigger stop on 6" models. Also available in stainless as Model 686. Introduced 1981.
Price: Model 586, blue, 4", from **$439.00**
Price: Model 686, stainless, from **$467.00**
Price: Model 686, 6", adjustable front sight **$499.00**
Price: Model 686, 8⅜" **$489.00**
Price: Model 686, 2½" **$457.00**

Smith & Wesson Model 60 3"

Smith & Wesson Model 49

Smith & Wesson Model 65LS

Smith & Wesson Model 625-2

SMITH & WESSON MODEL 625-2 REVOLVER Caliber: 45 ACP, 6-shot. Barrel: 5". Weight: 46 oz. Length: 11.375" overall. Stocks: Pachmayr SK/GR Gripper rubber. Sights: Patridge front on ramp, S&W micrometer click rear adjustable for windage and elevation. Features: Stainless steel construction with .400" semi-target hammer, .312" smooth combat trigger; full lug barrel. Introduced 1989.
Price: **$562.00**

SMITH & WESSON MODEL 640, 940 CENTENNIAL Caliber: 38 Special, 9mm Para., 5-shot. Barrel: 2", 3". Weight: 20 oz. Length: 6⁵⁄₁₆" overall. Stocks: Round butt hardwood (M640), Santoprene (M940). Sights: Serrated ramp front, fixed notch rear. Features: Stainless steel version of the original Model 40 but without the grip safety. Fully concealed hammer, snag-proof smooth edges. Model 640 introduced 1990; Model 940 introduced 1991.
Price: Model 640 (38 Special) **$441.00**
Price: Model 940 (9mm Para., rubber grips) **$446.00**

Smith & Wesson Model 442 Centennial Airweight Similar to the Model 640 Centennial except has alloy frame giving weight of 15.8 oz. Chambered for 38 Special, 2" carbon steel barrel; carbon steel cylinder; concealed hammer; Uncle Mike's Custom Grade Santoprene grips. Fixed square notch rear sight, serrated ramp front. Introduced 1993.
Price: Blue **$418.00**
Price: Nickel **$433.00**

SMITH & WESSON MODEL 651 REVOLVER **Caliber:** 22 WMR, 6-shot cylinder. **Barrel:** 4". **Weight:** 24½ oz. **Length:** 8¹¹/₁₆" overall. **Stocks:** Checkered service Morado; square butt. **Sights:** Red ramp front, adjustable micrometer click rear. **Features:** Stainless steel construction with semi-target hammer, smooth combat trigger. Reintroduced 1991. Limited production.
Price: **$428.00**

SPORTARMS MODEL HS38S REVOLVER **Caliber:** 38 Special, 6-shot. **Barrel:** 3", 4". **Weight:** 31.3 oz. **Length:** 8" overall (3" barrel). **Stocks:** Checkered hardwood; round butt on 3" model, target-style on 4". **Sights:** Blade front, adjustable rear. **Features:** Polished blue finish; ventilated rib on 4" barrel. Made in Germany by Herbert Schmidt; Imported by Sportarms of Florida.
Price: About **$150.00**

TAURUS MODEL 66 REVOLVER **Caliber:** 357 Magnum, 6-shot. **Barrel:** 2.5", 4", 6". **Weight:** 35 oz.(4" barrel). **Stocks:** Checkered Brazilian hardwood. **Sights:** Serrated ramp front, micro-click rear adjustable for windage and elevation. Red ramp front with white outline rear on stainlees models only. **Features:** Wide target-type hammer spur, floating firing pin, heavy barrel with shrouded ejector rod. Introduced 1978. Imported by Taurus International.
Price: Blue, 2.5" **$292.00**
Price: Blue, 4", 6" **$290.00**
Price: Blue, 4", 6" compensated **$299.00**
Price: Stainless, 2.5" **$371.00**
Price: Stainless, 4", 6" **$368.00**
Price: Stainless, 4", 6" compensated **$375.00**

Taurus Model 65 Revolver Same as the Model 66 except has fixed rear sight and ramp front. Available with 2.5" or 4" barrel only, round butt grip. Imported by Taurus International.
Price: Blue, 2.5" **$266.00**
Price: Blue, 4" **$264.00**
Price: Stainless, 2.5", 4" **$338.00**

TAURUS MODEL 80 STANDARD REVOLVER **Caliber:** 38 Spec., 6-shot. **Barrel:** 3" or 4". **Weight:** 30 oz. (4" bbl.). **Length:** 9¼" overall (4" bbl.). **Stocks:** Checkered Brazilian hardwood. **Sights:** Serrated ramp front, square notch rear. **Features:** Imported by Taurus International.
Price: Blue **$229.00**
Price: Stainless **$282.00**

TAURUS MODEL 82 HEAVY BARREL REVOLVER **Caliber:** 38 Spec., 6-shot. **Barrel:** 3" or 4", heavy. **Weight:** 34 oz. (4" bbl.). **Length:** 9¼" overall (4" bbl.). **Stocks:** Checkered Brazilian hardwood. **Sights:** Serrated ramp front, square notch rear. **Features:** Imported by Taurus International.
Price: Blue **$229.00**
Price: Stainless **$282.00**

TAURUS MODEL 83 REVOLVER **Caliber:** 38 Spec., 6-shot. **Barrel:** 4" only, heavy. **Weight:** 34 oz. **Stocks:** Oversize checkered Brazilian hardwood. **Sights:** Ramp front, micro-click rear adjustable for windage and elevation. **Features:** Blue or nickel finish. Introduced 1977. Imported by Taurus International.
Price: Blue **$241.00**
Price: Stainless **$292.00**

TAURUS MODEL 85 REVOLVER **Caliber:** 38 Spec., 5-shot. **Barrel:** 2", 3". **Weight:** 21 oz. **Stocks:** Checkered Brazilian hardwood. **Sights:** Ramp front, square notch rear. **Features:** Blue, satin nickel finish or stainless steel. Introduced 1980. Imported by Taurus International.
Price: Blue, 2", 3" **$251.00**
Price: Stainless steel **$315.00**

Taurus Model 85CH Revolver Same as the Model 85 except has 2" barrel only and concealed hammer. Smooth Brazilian hardwood stocks. Introduced 1991. Imported by Taurus International.
Price: Blue **$251.00**
Price: Stainless **$315.00**

Smith & Wesson Model 651

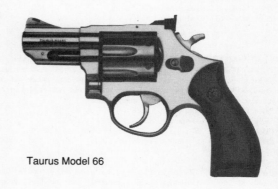

Taurus Model 66

Taurus Model 82

Taurus Model 85CH

TAURUS MODEL 86 REVOLVER **Caliber:** 38 Spec., 6-shot. **Barrel:** 6" only. **Weight:** 34 oz. **Length:** 11¼" overall. **Stocks:** Oversize target-type, checkered Brazilian hardwood. **Sights:** Patridge front, micro-click rear adjustable for windage and elevation. **Features:** Blue finish with non-reflective finish on barrel. Imported by Taurus International.
Price: **$326.00**

TAURUS MODEL 94 REVOLVER **Caliber:** 22 LR, 9-shot cylinder. **Barrel:** 3", 4". **Weight:** 25 oz. **Stocks:** Checkered Brazilian hardwood. **Sights:** Serrated ramp front, click-adjustable rear for windage and elevation. **Features:** Floating firing pin, color case-hardened hammer and trigger. Introduced 1989. Imported by Taurus International.
Price: Blue **$264.00**
Price: Stainless **$314.00**

TAURUS MODEL 96 REVOLVER **Caliber:** 22 LR, 6-shot. **Barrel:** 6". **Weight:** 34 oz. **Length:** NA. **Stocks:** Checkered Brazilian hardwood. **Sights:** Patridge-type front, micrometer click rear adjustable for windage and elevation. **Features:** Heavy solid barrel rib; target hammer; adjustable target trigger. Blue only. Imported by Taurus International.
Price: $326.00

TAURUS MODEL 441/431 REVOLVERS **Caliber:** 44 Special, 5-shot. **Barrel:** 3", 4", 6". **Weight:** 40.4 oz. (6" barrel). **Length:** NA. **Stocks:** Checkered Brazilian hardwood. **Sights:** Serrated ramp front, micrometer click rear adjustable for windage and elevation. **Features:** Heavy barrel with solid rib and full-length ejector shroud. Introduced 1992. Imported by Taurus International.
Price: Blue, 3", 4", 6" $307.00
Price: Stainless, 3", 4", 6" $386.00
Price: Model 431 (fixed sights), blue $281.00
Price: Model 431 (fixed sights), stainless $351.00

TAURUS MODEL 669 REVOLVER **Caliber:** 357 Mag., 6-shot. **Barrel:** 4", 6". **Weight:** 37 oz., (4" bbl.). **Stocks:** Checkered Brazilian hardwood. **Sights:** Serrated ramp front, micro-click rear adjustable for windage and elevation. **Features:** Wide target-type hammer, floating firing pin, full-length barrel shroud. Introduced 1988. Imported by Taurus International.
Price: Blue, 4", 6" $301.00
Price: Blue, 4", 6" compensated $308.00
Price: Stainless, 4", 6" $379.00
Price: Stainless, 4", 6" compensated $386.00

Taurus Model 689 Revolver Same as the Model 669 except has full-length ventilated barrel rib. Available in blue or stainless steel. Introduced 1990. From Taurus International.
Price: Blue, 4" or 6" $313.00
Price: Stainless, 4" or 6" $392.00

TAURUS MODEL 761 REVOLVER **Caliber:** 32 H&R Magnum, 6-shot. **Barrel:** 6", heavy, solid rib. **Weight:** 34 oz. **Stocks:** Checkered Brazilian hardwood. **Sights:** Patridge-type front, micro-click rear adjustable for windage and elevation. **Features:** Target hammer, adjustable target trigger. Blue only. Introduced 1991. Imported by Taurus International.
Price: $326.00

Taurus Model 741 Revolver Same as the Model 761 except with 3" or 4" heavy barrel only, serrated ramp front sight, micro click rear adjustable for windage and elevation. Introduced 1991. Imported by Taurus International.
Price: Blue, 3", 4" $254.00
Price: Stainless, 3", 4" $342.00

TAURUS MODEL 941 REVOLVER **Caliber:** 22 WMR, 8-shot. **Barrel:** 3", 4". **Weight:** 27.5 oz. (4" barrel). **Length:** NA. **Stocks:** Checkered Brazilian hardwood. **Sights:** Serrated ramp front, rear adjustable for windage and elevation. **Features:** Solid rib heavy barrel with full-length ejector rod shroud. Blue or stainless steel. Introduced 1992. Imported by Taurus International.
Price: Blue $290.00
Price: Stainless $346.00

THUNDER FIVE REVOLVER **Caliber:** 45 Colt/410 shotshell, 2" and 3"; 5-shot cylinder. **Barrel:** 2". **Weight:** 48 oz. **Length:** 9" overall. **Stocks:** Pachmayr checkered rubber. **Sights:** Fixed. **Features:** Double action with ambidextrous hammer-block safety; squared trigger guard; internal draw bar safety. Made of chrome moly steel, with matte blue finish. Announced 1991. From Tapco, Inc.
Price: $379.00

WESSON FIREARMS MODEL 8 & MODEL 14 **Caliber:** 38 Special (Model 8-2); 357 (14-2), both 6-shot. **Barrel:** 2½", 4", 6", 8"; interchangeable. **Weight:** 30 oz. (2½"). **Length:** 9¼" overall (4" bbl.). **Stocks:** Checkered, interchangeable. **Sights:** ⅛" serrated front, fixed rear. **Features:** Interchangeable barrels and grips; smooth, wide trigger; wide hammer spur with short double-action travel. Available in stainless or Brite blue. Contact Wesson Firearms for complete price list.
Price: Model 8-2, 2½", blue $267.00
Price: As above except in stainless $311.00
Price: Model 714-2 Pistol Pac, stainless $522.00

Taurus Model 761

Taurus Model 741

Taurus Model 941

Wesson Model 32M

Wesson Firearms Model 9-2, 15-2 & 32M Revolvers Same as Models 8-2 and 14-2 except they have adjustable sight. Model 9-2 chambered for 38 Special, Model 15-2 for 357 Magnum. Model 32M is chambered for 32 H&R Mag. Same specs and prices as for 15-2 guns. Available in blue or stainless. Contact Wesson Firearms for complete price list.
Price: Model 9-2 or 15-2, 2½", blue $338.00
Price: As above except in stainless $366.00

Wesson Firearms Model 15 Gold Series Similar to the Model 15 except has smoother action to reduce DA pull to 8-10 lbs.; comes with either 6" or 8" vent heavy slotted barrel shroud with bright blue barrel. Shroud is stamped "Gold Series" with the Wesson signature engraved and gold filled. Hammer and trigger are polished bright; rosewood grips. New sights with orange dot Patridge front, white triangle on rear blade. Introduced 1989.
Price: 6" . . . . NA
Price: 8" . . . . NA

WESSON FIREARMS MODEL 22 REVOLVER **Caliber:** 22 LR, 22 WMR, 6-shot. **Barrel:** 2½", 4", 6", 8"; interchangeable. **Weight:** 36 oz. (2½"), 44 oz. (6"). **Length:** 9¼" overall (4" barrel). **Stocks:** Checkered; undercover, service or over-size target. **Sights:** ⅛" serrated, interchangeable front, white outline rear adjustable for windage and elevation. **Features:** Built on the same frame as the Wesson 357; smooth, wide trigger with over-travel adjustment, wide spur hammer, with short double-action travel. Available in Brite blue or stainless steel. Contact Wesson Firearms for complete price list.
Price: 2½" bbl., blue **$349.00**
Price: As above, stainless **$391.00**
Price: With 4", vent. rib, blue **$357.00**
Price: As above, stainless **$399.00**
Price: Stainless Pistol Pac, 22 LR, blue **$637.00**

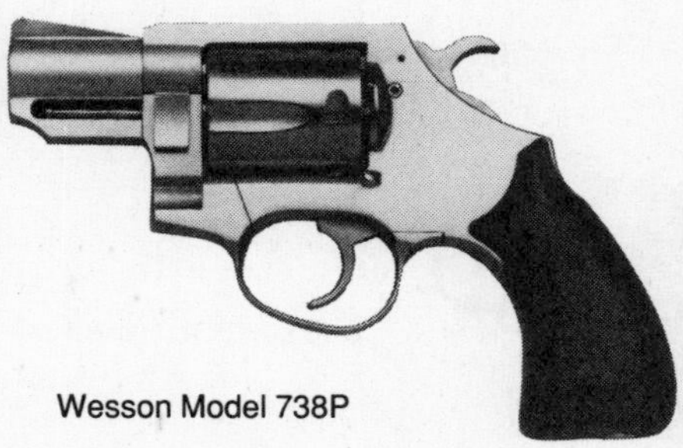
Wesson Model 738P

WESSON FIREARMS MODEL 41V, 44V, 45V REVOLVERS **Caliber:** 41 Mag., 44 Mag., 45 Colt, 6-shot. **Barrel:** 4", 6", 8", 10"; interchangeable. **Weight:** 48 oz. (4"). **Length:** 12" overall (6" bbl.). **Stocks:** Smooth. **Sights:** ⅛" serrated front, white outline rear adjustable for windage and elevation. **Features:** Available in blue or stainless steel. Smooth, wide trigger with adjustable over-travel; wide hammer spur. Available in Pistol Pac set also. Contact Wesson Firearms for complete price list.
Price: 41 Mag., 4", vent **$433.55**
Price: As above except in stainless **$508.30**
Price: 44 Mag., 4", blue **$433.55**
Price: As above except in stainless **$508.30**
Price: 45 Colt, 4", vent **$433.55**
Price: As above except in stainless **$508.30**

WESSON FIREARMS MODEL 738P REVOLVER **Caliber:** 38 Special +P, 5-shot. **Barrel:** 2". **Weight:** 24.6 oz. **Length:** 6.5" overall. **Stocks:** Pauferro wood or rubber. **Sights:** Blade front, fixed notch rear. **Features:** Designed for +P ammunition. Stainless steel construction. Introduced 1992. Made in U.S. by Wesson Firearms Co., Inc.
Price: **$285.00**

HANDGUNS—SINGLE-ACTION REVOLVERS

Both classic six-shooters and modern adaptations for hunting and sport.

AMERICAN ARMS REGULATOR SINGLE ACTIONS **Caliber:** 357 Mag. 44-40, 45 Colt. **Barrel:** 4¾", 5½", 7½". **Weight:** 32 oz. (4¾" barrel) **Length:** 8⅙" overall (4¾" barrel). **Stocks:** Smooth walnut. **Sights:** Blade front, groove rear. **Features:** Blued barrel and cylinder, brass trigger guard and backstrap. Introduced 1992. Imported from Italy by American Arms, Inc.
Price: Regulator, single cylinder **$305.00**
Price: Regulator, dual cylinder (44-40/44 Spec. or 45 Colt/45 ACP) **$349.00**

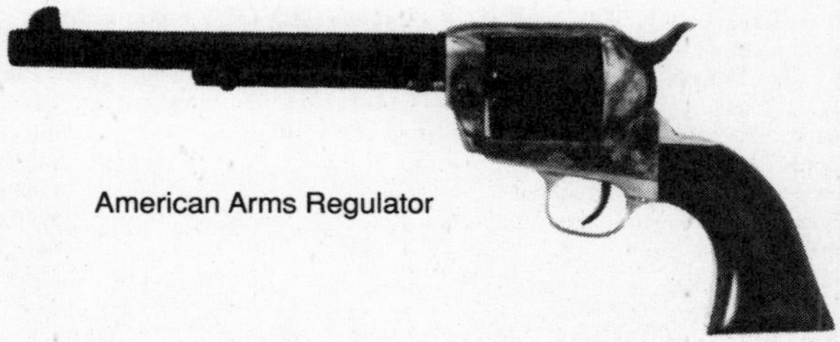
American Arms Regulator

American Arms Buckhorn Single Action Similar to the Regulator single action except chambered for 44 Magnum. Available with 4¾", 6" or 7½" barrel. Overall length 11¾", weight is 44 oz. with 6" barrel. Introduced 1993. Imported from Italy by American Arms, Inc.
Price: **$320.00**

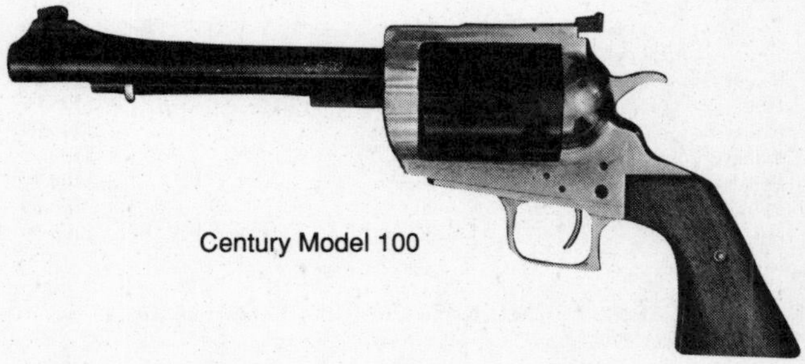
Century Model 100

CENTURY GUN DIST. MODEL 100 SINGLE ACTION **Caliber:** 30-30, 375 Win., 444 Marlin, 45-70, 50-70. **Barrel:** 6½" (standard), 8", 10", 12". **Weight:** 6 lbs. (loaded). **Length:** 15" overall (8" bbl.). **Stocks:** Smooth walnut. **Sights:** Ramp front, Millett adjustable square notch rear. **Features:** Highly polished high tensile strength manganese bronze frame, blue cylinder and barrel; coil spring trigger mechanism. Calibers other than 45-70 start at $1,500.00. Contact maker for full price information. Introduced 1975. Made in U.S. From Century Gun Dist., Inc.
Price: 6½" barrel, 45-70 . . . . **$1,250.00**

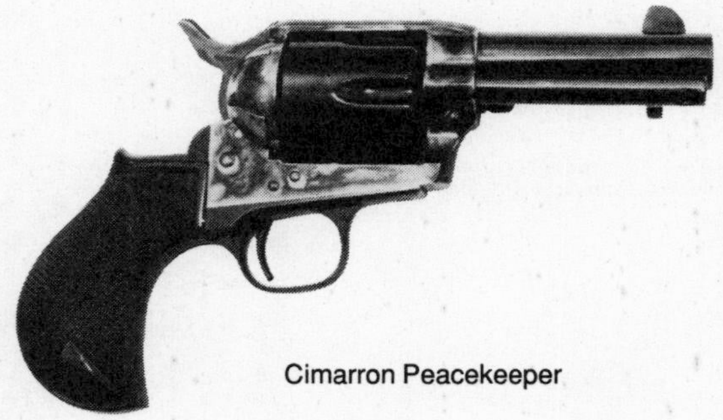
Cimarron Peacekeeper

CIMARRON PEACEKEEPER REVOLVER **Caliber:** 357 Mag., 44 WCF, 44 Spec., 45 Colt, 6-shot. **Barrel:** 3½", 4¾", with ejector. **Weight:** 38 oz. (3$E1/2" barrel). **Length:** NA. **Stocks:** Hand-checkered walnut. **Sights:** Blade front, notch rear. **Features:** Thunderer grip; color case-hardened frame with balance blued, or nickel finish. Introduced 1993. Imported by Cimarron Arms.
Price: Color case-hardened **$459.00**
Price: Nickeled **$559.00**

CIMARRON 1873 PEACEMAKER REPRO **Caliber:** 22 LR, 22 WMR, 38 WCF, 357 Mag., 44 WCF, 44 Spec., 45 Colt. **Barrel:** 4¾", 5½", 7½". **Weight:** 39 oz. **Length:** 10" overall (4" barrel). **Stocks:** Walnut. **Sights:** Blade front, fixed or adjustable rear. **Features:** Uses "old model" blackpowder frame with "Bullseye" ejector or New Model frame. Imported by Cimarron Arms.
Price: Peacemaker, 4¾" barrel **$429.00**
Price: Frontier Six Shooter, 5½" barrel **$429.00**
Price: Single Action Army, 7½" barrel **$429.00**

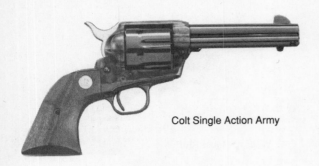

Colt Single Action Army

CIMARRON U.S. CAVALRY MODEL SINGLE ACTION **Caliber:** 45 Colt. **Barrel:** 7½". **Weight:** 42 oz. **Length:** 13½" overall. **Stocks:** Walnut. **Sights:** Fixed. **Features:** Has "A.P. Casey" markings; "U.S." plus patent dates on frame, serial number on backstrap, trigger guard, frame and cylinder, "APC" cartouche on left grip; color case-hardened frame and hammer, rest charcoal blue. Exact copy of the original. Imported by Cimarron Arms.
Price: **$459.00**

Cimarron Artillery Model Single Action Similar to the U.S. Cavalry model except has 5½" barrel, weighs 39 oz., and is 11½" overall. U.S. markings and cartouche, case-hardened frame and hammer; 45 Colt only.
Price: **$459.00**

COLT SINGLE ACTION ARMY REVOLVER **Caliber:** 44-40, 45 Colt, 6-shot. **Barrel:** 4¾", 5½", 7½". **Weight:** 40 oz. (4¾" barrel). **Length:** 10¼" overall (4¾" barrel). **Stocks:** American walnut. **Sights:** Blade front, notch rear. **Features:** Available in full nickel finish with nickel grip medallions, or Royal Blue with color case-hardened frame, gold grip medallions. Reintroduced 1992.
Price: **$1,273.95**

Dakota New Model Single-Action Revolvers Similar to the standard Dakota except has color case-hardened forged steel frame, black nickel backstrap and trigger guard. Calibers 357 Mag., 44-40, 45 Colt only.
Price: **$490.00**
Price: Nickel **$636.00**

DAKOTA 1875 OUTLAW REVOLVER **Caliber:** 357, 44-40, 45 Colt. **Barrel:** 7½". **Weight:** 46 oz. **Length:** 13½" overall. **Stocks:** Smooth walnut. **Sights:** Blade front, fixed groove rear. **Features:** Authentic copy of 1875 Remington with firing pin in hammer; color case-hardened frame, blue cylinder, barrel, steel backstrap and brass trigger guard. Also available in nickel, factory engraved. Imported by E.M.F.
Price: All calibers **$465.00**
Price: Nickel **$550.00**
Price: Engraved **$600.00**
Price: Engraved Nickel **$710.00**

Dakota 1890 Police Revolver Similar to the 1875 Outlaw except has 5½" barrel, weighs 40 oz., with 12½" overall length. Has lanyard ring in butt. No web under barrel. Calibers 357, 44-40, 45 Colt. Imported by E.M.F.
Price: All calibers **$470.00**
Price: Nickel **$560.00**
Price: Engraved **$620.00**
Price: Engraved nickel **$725.00**

DAKOTA HARTFORD SINGLE-ACTION REVOLVERS **Caliber:** 22 LR, 357 Mag., 32-20, 38-40, 44-40, 44 Spec., 45 Colt. **Barrel:** 4¾", 5½", 7½". **Weight:** 45 oz. **Length:** 13" overall (7½" barrel). **Stocks:** Smooth walnut. **Sights:** Blade front, fixed rear. **Features:** Identical to the origianl Colts with inspector cartouche on left grip, original patent dates and U.S. markings. All major parts serial numbered using original Colt-style lettering, numbering. Bullseye ejector head and color case-hardening on frame and hammer. Introduced 1990. From E.M.F.
Price: **$600.00**
Price: Cavalry or Artillery **$655.00**
Price: Nickel plated **$760.00**
Price: Cattlebrand engraved nickel **$1,150.00**
Price: Scroll engraved **$840.00**
Price: Scroll engraved nickel **$1,000.00**

E.A.A. BIG BORE BOUNTY HUNTER SA REVOLVERS **Caliber:** 357 Mag., 41 Mag., 44-40, 44 Mag., 45 Colt, 6-shot. **Barrel:** 4⅝", 5½", 7½". **Weight:** 2.5 lbs. **Length:** 11" overall (5" barrel). **Stocks:** Smooth walnut. **Sights:** Blade front, grooved topstrap rear. **Features:** Transfer bar safety; three position hammer; hammer forged barrel. Introduced 1992. Imported by European American Armory.
Price: Blue **$425.00**
Price: Color case-hardened frame **$440.00**
Price: Blue with gold-plated grip frame **$440.00**
Price: Chrome-plated **$475.00**

E.A.A. BOUNTY HUNTER REVOLVER **Caliber:** 22 LR, 22 WMR, 6-shot cylinder. **Barrel:** 4¾", 6", 9". **Weight:** 32 oz. **Length:** 10" overall (4¾" barrel). **Stocks:** European hardwood. **Sights:** Blade front, rear adjustable for windage. **Features:** Available in blue or blue/gold finish. Introduced 1991. From European American Armory Corp.
Price: 4¾", blue **$115.00**
Price: 4¾", blue, 22 LR/22 WMR combo . . . **$135.00**
Price: 4¾", blue/gold, 22 LR/22 WMR combo . **$145.00**
Price: 6", blue, 22 LR/22 WMR combo **$140.00**
Price: 6", blue/gold, 22 LR/22 WMR combo . **$150.00**
Price: 9", blue, 22 LR/22 WMR combo **$155.00**
Price: 9", blue/gold, 22 LR/22 WMR combo . **$165.00**

E.A.A. Big Bore Bounty Hunter

FREEDOM ARMS PREMIER 454 CASULL **Caliber:** 44 Mag., 45 Colt/45 ACP (optional cylinder), 454 Casull, 5-shot. **Barrel:** 3", 4¾", 6", 7½", 10". **Weight:** 50 oz. **Length:** 14" overall (7½" bbl.). **Stocks:** Impregnated hardwood. **Sights:** Blade front, notch or adjustable rear. **Features:** All stainless steel construction; sliding bar safety system. Hunter Pak includes 7½" gun, sling and studs, aluminum carrying case with tool and cleaning kit. Lifetime warranty. Made in U.S.A.
Price: Field Grade (matte finish, Pachmayr grips), adjustable sights, 4¾", 6", 7½", 10" **$1,115.00**
Price: Field Grade, fixed sights, 4¾" only . . . **$1,035.00**
Price: Field Grade, 44 Rem. Mag., adjustable sights, all lengths . . . **$1,115.00**
Price: Premier Grade (brush finish, impregnated hardwood grips) adjustable sights, 4¾", 6", 7½", 10" . . . **$1,385.00**
Price: Premier Grade, fixed sights, 7½" only . . . **$1,298.00**
Price: Premier Grade, 44 Rem. Mag., adjustable sights, all lengths . . . **$1,385.00**
Price: Premier Grade Hunter Pak, black micarta grips, no front sight base **$1,611.10**
Price: Premier Grade Hunter Pak, adjustable sight, black micarta grips . . . **$1,711.35**
Price: Field Grade Hunter Pak, Pachmayr grips, 2x Leupold scope, Leupold rings and base, no front sight base **$1,332.85**
Price: Field Grade Hunter Pak, Pachmayr grips, low-profile adjustable sight . . . **$1,408.85**
Price: Fitted 45 ACP or 45 Colt cylinder, add . . . **$213.00**

Freedom 454 Field Grade

Heritage Rough Rider

MITCHELL SINGLE-ACTION ARMY REVOLVERS **Caliber:** 357 Mag., 44 Mag., 45 ACP, 45 Colt, 6-shot. **Barrel:** 4¾", 5½", 7½". **Weight:** NA. **Length:** NA. **Stocks:** One-piece walnut. **Sights:** Serrated ramp front, fixed or adjustable rear. **Features:** Color case-hardened frame, brass or steel backstrap/trigger guard; hammer-block safety. Bright nickel-plated model and dual cylinder models available. Contact importer for complete price list. Imported by Mitchell Arms, Inc.
Price: Cowboy, 4¾", Army 5½", Cavalry 7½", blue, 357,
45 Colt, 45 ACP **$399.00**
Price: As above, nickel **$439.00**
Price: 45 Colt/45 ACP dual cyl., blue **$549.00**
Price: As above, nickel **$588.00**
Price: Bat Masterson model, 45 Colt, 4¾", nickel **$439.00**

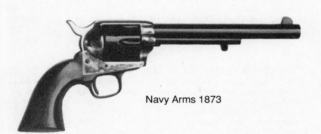

Navy Arms 1873

Consult our Directory pages for the location of firms mentioned.

North American Mini

North American Mini-Master

Freedom Arms Casull Model 353 Revolver Similar to the Premier 454 Casull except chambered for 357 Magnum with 5-shot cylinder; 4¾", 6", 7½" or 9" barrel. Weighs 59 oz. with 7½" barrel. Standard model has adjustable sights, matte finish, Pachmayr grips, 7½" or 9" barrel; Silhouette has 9" barrel, Patridge front sight, Iron Sight Gun Works Silhouette adjustable rear, Pachmayr grips, trigger over-travel adjustment screw. All stainless steel. Introduced 1992.
Price: Field Grade **$1,115.00**
Price: Premier Grade (brushed finish, impregnated hardwood grips, Premier Grade sights) **$1,385.00**
Price: Silhouette **$1,213.80**

HERITAGE ROUGH RIDER REVOLVER **Caliber:** 22 LR, 22 LR/22 WMR combo, 6-shot. **Barrel:** 3", 4¾", 6½", 9". **Weight:** 31 to 38 oz. **Length:** NA **Stocks:** Smooth walnut. **Sights:** Blade front, fixed rear. **Features:** Hammer block safety. High polish blue finish, gold-tone screws, polished hammer. Introduced 1993. Made in U.S. by Heritage Mfg., Inc.
Price: . . . . **$104.95 to $139.95**

Mitchell Single Action

NAVY ARMS 1873 SINGLE-ACTION REVOLVER **Caliber:** 44-40, 45 Colt, 6-shot cylinder. **Barrel:** 3", 4¾", 5½", 7½". **Weight:** 36 oz. **Length:** 10¾" overall (5½" barrel). **Stocks:** Smooth walnut. **Sights:** Blade front, groove in topstrap rear. **Features:** Blue with color case-hardened frame, or nickel. Introduced 1991. Imported by Navy Arms.
Price: Blue **$370.00**
Price: Nickel **$435.00**
Price: 1873 U.S. Cavalry Model (7½", 45 Colt, arsenal markings) **$455.00**
Price: 1895 U.S. Artillery Model (as above, 5½" barrel) **$455.00**

NORTH AMERICAN MINI-REVOLVERS **Caliber:** 22 LR, 22 WMR, 5-shot. **Barrel:** 1⅛", 1⅝". **Weight:** 4 to 6.6 oz. **Length:** 3⅝" to 6⅛" overall. **Stocks:** Laminated wood. **Sights:** Blade front, notch fixed rear. **Features:** All stainless steel construction. Polished satin and matte finish. Engraved models available. From North American Arms.
Price: 22 LR, 1⅛" bbl. **$164.50**
Price: 22 LR, 1⅝" bbl. **$164.50**
Price: 22 WMR, 1⅝" bbl. **$184.50**
Price: 22 WMR, 1⅛" or 1⅝" bbl. with extra 22 LR cylinder **$219.50**

NORTH AMERICAN MINI-MASTER **Caliber:** 22 LR, 22 WMR, 5-shot cylinder. **Barrel:** 4". **Weight:** 10.7 oz. **Length:** 7.75" overall. **Stocks:** Checkered hard black rubber. **Sights:** Blade front, white outline rear adjustable for elevation, or fixed. **Features:** Heavy vent barrel; full-size grips. Non-fluted cylinder. Introduced 1989.
Price: Adjustable sight, 22 WMR or 22 LR **$267.50**
Price: As above with extra WMR/LR cylinder **$302.50**
Price: Fixed sight, 22 WMR or 22 LR **$257.50**
Price: As above with extra WMR/LR cylinder **$292.50**

North American Black Widow Revolver Similar to the Mini-Master except has 2" Heavy Vent barrel. Built on the 22 WMR frame. Non-fluted cylinder, black rubber grips. Available with either Millett Low Profile fixed sights or Millett sight adjustable for elevation only. Overall length 5⅞", weight 8.8 oz. From North American Arms.
Price: Adjustable sight, 22 LR or 22 WMR **$235.50**
Price: As above with extra WMR/LR cylinder **$270.50**
Price: Fixed sight, 22 LR or 22 WMR **$225.50**
Price: As above with extra WMR/LR cylinder **$260.50**

PHELPS HERITAGE I, EAGLE I, GRIZZLY REVOLVERS **Caliber:** 444 Marlin, 45-70, 50-70, 6-shot. **Barrel:** 8", 12", 16" (45-70). **Weight:** 5½ lbs. **Length:** 19½" overall (12" bbl.). **Stocks:** Smooth walnut. **Sights:** Ramp front, adjustable rear. **Features:** Single action; polished blue finish; safety bar. From Phelps Mfg. Co.
Price: 8", 45-70 or 444 Marlin, about **$1,085.00**
Price: 12", 45-70 or 444 Marlin, about **$1,165.00**
Price: 8", 50-70, about **$1,550.00**

Ruger Blackhawk

Ruger Bisley

Ruger New Super Bearcat

Ruger SSM Single-Six

Ruger Super Blackhawk Hunter

Ruger Vaquero

RUGER BLACKHAWK REVOLVER **Caliber:** 30 Carbine, 357 Mag./38 Spec., 41 Mag., 45 Colt, 6-shot. **Barrel:** 4⅝" or 6½", either caliber; 7½" (30 Carbine, 45 Colt only). **Weight:** 42 oz. (6½" bbl.). **Length:** 12¼" overall (6½" bbl.). **Stocks:** American walnut. **Sights:** ⅛" ramp front, micro-click rear adjustable for windage and elevation. **Features:** Ruger interlock mechanism, independent firing pin, hardened chrome moly steel frame, music wire springs throughout.
Price: Blue, 30 Carbine (7½" bbl.), BN31 . . . . **$328.00**
Price: Blue, 357 Mag. (4⅝", 6½"), BN34, BN36 . . . . **$328.00**
Price: Blue, 357/9mm Convertible (4⅝", 6½"), BN34X, BN36X . . **$343.50**
Price: Blue, 41 Mag., 45 Colt (4⅝", 6½"), BN41, BN42, BN45 . . . . **$328.00**
Price: Stainless, 357 Mag. (4⅝", 6½"), KBN34, KBN36 . . . . **$404.00**

Ruger Bisley Single-Action Revolver Similar to standard Blackhawk except the hammer is lower with a smoothly curved, deeply checkered wide spur. The trigger is strongly curved with a wide smooth surface. Longer grip frame has a hand-filling shape. Adjustable rear sight, ramp-style front. Has an unfluted cylinder and roll engraving, adjustable sights. Chambered for 357, 41, 44 Mags. and 45 Colt; 7½" barrel; overall length of 13". Introduced 1985.
Price: **$391.00**

RUGER SUPER BLACKHAWK **Caliber:** 44 Magnum, 6-shot. Also fires 44 Spec. **Barrel:** 5½", 7½", 10½". **Weight:** 48 oz. (7½" bbl.), 51 oz. (10½" bbl.). **Length:** 13⅜" overall (7½" bbl.). **Stocks:** American walnut. **Sights:** ⅛" ramp front, micro-click rear adjustable for windage and elevation. **Features:** Ruger interlock mechanism, non-fluted cylinder, steel grip and cylinder frame, square back trigger guard, wide serrated trigger and wide spur hammer.
Price: Blue (S45N, S47N, S411N) **$378.50**
Price: Stainless (KS45N, KS47N, KS411N) **$413.75**
Price: Stainless KS47NH Hunter with scope rings, 7½" **$479.50**

RUGER NEW SUPER BEARCAT SINGLE ACTION **Caliber:** 22 LR/22 WMR, 6-shot. **Barrel:** 4". **Weight:** 23 oz. **Length:** 8⅞" overall. **Stocks:** Smooth rosewood with Ruger medallion. **Sights:** Blade front, fixed notch rear. **Features:** Reintroduction of the Ruger Super Bearcat with slightly lengthened frame, Ruger patented transfer bar safety system. Comes with two cylinders. Available in blue or stainless steel. Introduced 1993. From Sturm, Ruger & Co.
Price: SBC4, blue **$298.00**
Price: KSBC4, stainless **$325.00**

RUGER SUPER SINGLE-SIX CONVERTIBLE **Caliber:** 22 LR, 6-shot; 22 WMR in extra cylinder. **Barrel:** 4⅝", 5½", 6½", or 9½" (6-groove). **Weight:** 34½ oz. (6½" bbl.). **Length:** 11¹³⁄₁₆" overall (6½" bbl.). **Stocks:** Smooth American walnut. **Sights:** Improved Patridge front on ramp, fully adjustable rear protected by integral frame ribs. **Features:** Ruger interlock mechanism, transfer bar ignition, gate-controlled loading, hardened chrome moly steel frame, wide trigger, music wire springs throughout, independent firing pin.
Price: 4⅝", 5½", 6½", 9½" barrel **$281.00**
Price: 5½", 6½" bbl. only, stainless steel **$354.00**

Ruger SSM Single-Six Revolver Similar to the Super Single-Six revolver except chambered for 32 H&R Magnum (also handles 32 S&W and 32 S&W Long). Weight is about 34 oz. with 6½" barrel. Barrel lengths: 4⅝", 5½", 6½", 9½". Introduced 1985.
Price: **$281.00**

Ruger Bisley Small Frame Revolver Similar to the Single-Six except frame is styled after the classic Bisley "flat-top." Most mechanical parts are unchanged. Hammer is lower and smoothly curved with a deeply checkered spur. Trigger is strongly curved with a wide smooth surface. Longer grip frame designed with a hand-filling shape, and the trigger guard is a large oval. Adjustable dovetail rear sight; front sight base accepts interchangeable square blades of various heights and styles. Has an unfluted cylinder and roll engraving. Weight about 41 oz. Chambered for 22 LR and 32 H&R Mag., 6½" barrel only. Introduced 1985.
Price: **$328.75**

RUGER VAQUERO SINGLE-ACTION REVOLVER **Caliber:** 44-40, 44 Magnum, 45 Colt, 6-shot. **Barrel:** 4⅝", 5½", 7½". **Weight:** 41 oz. **Length:** 13⅜" overall (7½" barrel). **Stocks:** Smooth rosewood with Ruger medallion. **Sights:** Blade front, fixed notch rear. **Features:** Uses Ruger's patented transfer bar safety system and loading gate interlock with classic styling. Blued model has color case-hardened finish on the frame, the rest polished and blued. Stainless model is polished. Introduced 1993. From Sturm, Ruger & Co.
Price: BNV44 (4⅝"), BNV445 (5½"), BNV45 (7½"), blue **$394.00**
Price: KBNV44 (4⅝"), KBNV455 (5½"), KBNV45 (7½"), stainless . . **$394.00**

SPORTARMS MODEL HS21S SINGLE ACTION **Caliber:** 22 LR or 22 LR/22 WMR combo, 6-shot. **Barrel:** 5½". **Weight:** 33.5 oz. **Length:** 11" overall. **Stocks:** Smooth hardwood. **Sights:** Blade front, rear drift adjustable for windage. **Features:** Available in blue with imitation stag or wood stocks. Made in Germany by Herbert Schmidt; Imported by Sportarms of Florida.
Price: 22 LR, blue, "stag" grips, about **$100.00**
Price: 22 LR/22 WMR combo, blue, wood stocks, about **$120.00**

TEXAS LONGHORN ARMS GROVER'S IMPROVED NO. FIVE **Caliber:** 44 Magnum, 6-shot. **Barrel:** 5½". **Weight:** 44 oz. **Length:** NA. **Stocks:** Fancy AAA walnut. **Sights:** Square blade front on ramp, fully adjustable rear. **Features:** Music wire coil spring action with double locking bolt; polished blue finish. Handmade in limited 1,200-gun production. Grip contour, straps, oversized base pin, lever latch and lockwork identical copies of Elmer Keith design. Lifetime warranty to original owner. Introduced 1988.
Price: **$985.00**

Texas Longhorn Grovers No. Five

TEXAS LONGHORN ARMS RIGHT-HAND SINGLE ACTION **Caliber:** All centerfire pistol calibers. **Barrel:** 4¾". **Weight:** NA. **Length:** NA. **Stocks:** One-piece fancy walnut, or any fancy AAA wood. **Sights:** Blade front, grooved topstrap rear. **Features:** Loading gate and ejector housing on left side of gun. Cylinder rotates to the left. All steel construction; color case-hardened frame; high polish blue; music wire coil springs. Lifetime guarantee to original owner. Introduced 1984. From Texas Longhorn Arms.
Price: South Texas Army Limited Edition—handmade, only 1,000 to be produced; "One of One Thousand" engraved on barrel **$1,500.00**

Texas Longhorn Arms Texas Border Special Similar to the South Texas Army Limited Edition except has 3½" barrel, bird's-head style grip. Same special features. Introduced 1984.
Price: **$1,500.00**

Texas Longhorn Border Special

Texas Longhorn Arms Sesquicentennial Model Revolver Similar to the South Texas Army Model except has ¾-coverage Nimschke-style engraving, antique golden nickel plate finish, one-piece elephant ivory grips. Comes with handmade solid walnut presentation case, factory letter to owner. Limited edition of 150 units. Introduced 1986.
Price: **$2,500.00**

Texas Longhorn Arms Cased Set Set contains one each of the Texas Longhorn Right-Hand Single Actions, all in the same caliber, same serial numbers (100, 200, 300, 400, 500, 600, 700, 800, 900). Ten sets to be made (#1000 donated to NRA museum). Comes in hand-tooled leather case. All other specs same as Limited Edition guns. Introduced 1984.
Price: **$5,750.00**
Price: With ¾-coverage "C-style" engraving **$7,650.00**

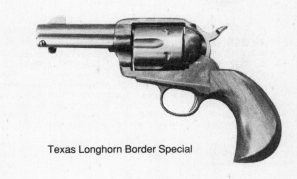

Uberti Cattleman

Texas Longhorn Arms West Texas Flat Top Target Similar to the South Texas Army Limited Edition except choice of barrel length from 7½" through 15"; flat-top style frame; ⅛" contoured ramp front sight, old model steel microclick rear adjustable for windage and elevation. Same special features. Introduced 1984.
Price: **$1,500.00**

Uberti 1875 Army

UBERTI 1873 CATTLEMAN SINGLE ACTIONS **Caliber:** 38 Spec., 357 Mag., 44 Spec., 44-40, 45 Colt/45 ACP, 6-shot. **Barrel:** 4¾", 5½", 7½"; 44-40, 45 Colt also with 3". **Weight:** 38 oz. (5½" bbl.). **Length:** 10¾" overall (5½" bbl.). **Stocks:** One-piece smooth walnut. **Sights:** Blade front, groove rear; fully adjustable rear available. **Features:** Steel or brass backstrap, trigger guard; color case-hardened frame, blued barrel, cylinder. Imported from Italy by Uberti USA.
Price: Steel backstrap, trigger guard, fixed sights **$410.00**
Price: Brass backstrap, trigger guard, fixed sights **$365.00**

Uberti 1873 Buckhorn Single Action A slightly larger version of the Cattleman revolver. Available in 44 Magnum or 44 Magnum/44-40 convertible, otherwise has same specs.
Price: Steel backstrap, trigger guard, fixed sights **$410.00**
Price: Convertible (two cylinders) **$460.00**

UBERTI 1875 SA ARMY OUTLAW REVOLVER **Caliber:** 357 Mag., 44-40, 45 Colt, 6-shot. **Barrel:** 7½". **Weight:** 44 oz. **Length:** 13¾" overall. **Stocks:** Smooth walnut. **Sights:** Blade front, notch rear. **Features:** Replica of the 1875 Remington S.A. Army revolver. Brass trigger guard, color case-hardened frame, rest blued. Imported by Uberti USA.
Price: **$405.00**
Price: 45 Colt/45 ACP convertible **$450.00**

UBERTI 1890 ARMY OUTLAW REVOLVER **Caliber:** 357 Mag., 44-40, 45 Colt, 6-shot. **Barrel:** 5½". **Weight:** 37 oz. **Length:** 12½" overall. **Stocks:** American walnut. **Sights:** Blade front, groove rear. **Features:** Replica of the 1890 Remington single action. Brass trigger guard, rest is blued. Imported by Uberti USA.
Price: **$410.00**
Price: 45 Colt/45 ACP convertible **$415.00**

Models specifically designed for classic competitive shooting sports.

Benelli MP90S

BF SINGLE SHOT PISTOL **Caliber:** 22 LR, 357 Mag., 44 Mag., 7-30 Waters, 30-30 Win., 375 Win., 45-70; custom chamberings from 17 Rem. through 45-cal. **Barrel:** 10", 10.75", 12", 15+". **Weight:** 52 oz. **Length:** NA. **Stocks:** Custom Herrett finger-groove grip and forend. **Sights:** Undercut Patridge front, 1/2-MOA match-quality fully adjustable RPM Iron Sight rear; barrel or receiver mounting. Drilled and tapped for scope mounting. **Features:** Rigid barrel/receiver; falling block action with short lock time; automatic ejection; air-gauged match barrels by Wilson or Douglas; matte black oxide finish standard, electroless nickel optional. Barrel has 11-degree recessed target crown. Introduced 1988. Made in U.S. by E.A. Brown Mfg.

Price: 10", no sights $499.95
Price: 10", RPM sights $564.95
Price: 10.75", no sights $529.95
Price: 10.75", RPM sights $594.95
Price: 12", no sights $562.95
Price: 12", RPM sights $627.95
Price: 15", no sights $592.95
Price: 15", RPM sights $658.95
Price: 10.75" Ultimate Silhouette (heavy barrel, special forend, RPM rear sight with hooded front, gold-plated trigger) $687.95

BERETTA MODEL 89 TARGET PISTOL **Caliber:** 22 LR, 8-shot magazine. **Barrel:** 6" **Weight:** 41 oz. **Length:** 9.5" overall. **Stocks:** Target-type walnut with thumbrest. **Sights:** Interchangeable blade front, fully adjustable rear. **Features:** Single-action target pistol. Matte blue finish. Imported from Italy by Beretta U.S.A.
Price: $735.00

> Consult our Directory pages for the location of firms mentioned.

Browning Buck Mark Target 5.5 Same as the Buck Mark Silhouette except has a 5½" barrel with .900" diameter. Has hooded sights mounted on a scope base that accepts an optical or reflex sight. Rear sight is a Browning fully adjustable Pro Target, front sight is an adjustable post that customizes to different widths, and can be adjusted for height. Contoured walnut grips with thumbrest, or finger-groove walnut. Matte blue finish. Overall length is 9⅝", weight is 35½ oz. Has 10-shot magazine. Introduced 1990. From Browning.
Price: $374.95
Price: Target 5.5 Gold (as above with gold anodized frame and top rib) $399.95

Browning Buck Mark Field 5.5 Same as the Target 5.5 except has hoodless ramp-style front sight and low profile rear sight. Matte blue finish, contoured or finger-groove walnut stocks. Introduced 1991.
Price: $374.95

Browning Buck Mark Unlimited Match Same as the Buck Mark Silhouette except has 14" heavy barrel. Conforms to IHMSA 15" maximum sight radius rule. Introduced 1991.
Price: $469.95

BENELLI MP90S MATCH PISTOL **Caliber:** 22 Short, 22 LR, 32 S&W wadcutter, 5-shot magazine. **Barrel:** 4.33". **Weight:** 38.8 oz. **Length:** 11.81" overall. **Stocks:** Stippled walnut match type with fully adjustable palm shelf; anatomically shaped. **Sights:** Match type. Blade front, click-adjustable rear for windage and elevation. **Features:** Fully adjustable trigger for pull and position, and is removable. Special internal weight box on sub-frame below barrel. Comes with loading tool, cleaning rods. Introduced 1993. Imported from Italy by European American Armory.
Price: $1,895.00

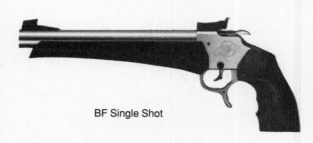

BF Single Shot

Beretta Model 89

BROWNING BUCK MARK SILHOUETTE **Caliber:** 22 LR, 10-shot magazine. **Barrel:** 9⅞". **Weight:** 53 oz. **Length:** 14" overall. **Stocks:** Smooth walnut stocks and forend, or finger-groove walnut. **Sights:** Post-type hooded front adjustable for blade width and height; Pro Target rear fully adjustable for windage and elevation. **Features:** Heavy barrel with .900" diameter; 12½" sight radius. Special sighting plane forms scope base. Introduced 1987. Made in U.S. From Browning.
Price: $394.95

Browning Buck Mark Target 5.5

COLT GOLD CUP NATIONAL MATCH MK IV/SERIES 80 **Caliber:** 45 ACP, 8-shot magazine. **Barrel:** 5", with new design bushing. **Weight:** 39 oz. **Length:** 8½". **Stocks:** Rubber combat with silver-plated medallion. **Sights:** Patridge-style front, Colt-Elliason rear adjustable for windage and elevation, sight radius 6¾". **Features:** Arched or flat housing; wide, grooved trigger with adjustable stop; ribbed-top slide, hand fitted, with improved ejection port.

Price: Blue **$885.95**
Price: Stainless **$948.95**
Price: Bright stainless **$1,018.95**
Price: Delta Gold Cup (10mm, stainless) **$975.95**

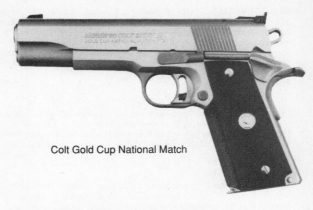

Colt Gold Cup National Match

COMPETITOR SINGLE SHOT PISTOL **Caliber:** 22 LR through 50 Action Express, including belted magnums. **Barrel:** 14" standard; 10.5" silhouette; 16" optional. **Weight:** About 59 oz. (14" bbl.). **Length:** 15.12" overall. **Stocks:** Ambidextrous; synthetic (standard) or laminated or natural wood. **Sights:** Ramp front, adjustable rear. **Features:** Rotary canon-type action cocks on opening; cammed ejector; interchangeable barrels, ejectors. Adjustable single stage trigger, sliding thumb safety and trigger safety. Matte blue finish. Introduced 1988. From Competitor Corp., Inc.

Price: 14", standard calibers, synthetic grip **$364.90**
Price: Extra barrels, from **$132.95**

E.A.A. EUROPEAN EA22T TARGET AUTO **Caliber:** 22 LR, 12-shot. **Barrel:** 6". **Weight:** 40 oz. **Length:** 9.10" overall. **Stocks:** Checkered walnut, with thumbrest. **Sights:** Blade on ramp front, rear adjustable for windage and elevation. **Features:** Blue finish. Finger-rest magazine. Imported by European American Armory Corp.

Price: **$399.00**

E.A.A. European EA22T

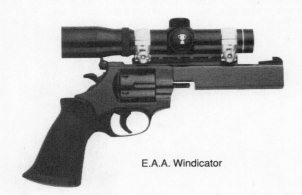

E.A.A. Windicator

E.A.A. WINDICATOR TARGET GRADE REVOLVERS **Caliber:** 22 LR, 8-shot, 38 Special, 357 Mag., 6-shot. **Barrel:** 6". **Weight:** 50.2 oz. **Length:** 11.8" overall. **Stocks:** Walnut, competition style. **Sights:** Blade front with three interchangeable blades, fully adjustable rear. **Features:** Adjustable trigger with trigger stop and trigger shoe; frame drilled and tapped for scope mount; target hammer. Comes with barrel weights, plastic carrying box. Introduced 1991. Imported from Germany by European American Armory.

Price: **$499.00**

E.A.A. Witness Gold Team

E.A.A. WITNESS GOLD TEAM AUTO **Caliber:** 9mm Para., 9x21, 10mm Auto, 38 Super, 40 S&W, 45 ACP. **Barrel:** 5.1". **Weight:** 41.6 oz. **Length:** 9.6" overall. **Stocks:** Checkered walnut, competition style. **Sights:** Square post front, fully adjustable rear. **Features:** Triple-chamber compensator; competition SA trigger; extended safety and magazine release; competition hammer; beveled magazine well; beavertail grip. Hand-fitted major components. Hard chrome finish. Match-grade barrel. From E.A.A. Custom Shop. Introduced 1992. From European American Armory.

Price: **$2,195.00**

E.A.A. Witness Silver Team Auto Similar to the Wittness Gold Team except has double-chamber compensator, paddle magazine release, checkered walnut grips, double-dip blue finish. Comes with Super Sight or drilled and tapped for scope mount. Built for the intermediate competition shooter. Introduced 1992. From European American Armory Custom Shop.

Price: 9mm Para., 9x21, 10mm Auto, 38 Super, 40 S&W, 45 ACP . . . **$1,195.00**

Erma ER Match

ERMA ESP 85A COMPETITION PISTOL **Caliber:** 22 LR, 8-shot; 32 S&W, 5-shot magazine. **Barrel:** 6". **Weight:** 39 oz. **Length:** 10" overall. **Stocks:** Match-type of stippled walnut; adjustable. **Sights:** Interchangeable blade front, micrometer adjustable rear with interchangeable leaf. **Features:** Five-way adjustable trigger; exposed hammer and separate firing pin block allow unlimited dry firing practice. Blue or matte chrome; right- or left-hand. Introduced 1988. Imported from Germany by Precision Sales International.

Price: 22 LR **$1,345.00**
Price: 22 LR, left-hand **$1,375.00**
Price: 22 LR, matte chrome **$1,568.00**
Price: 32 S&W **$1,400.00**

ERMA ER MATCH REVOLVERS **Caliber:** 22 LR, 32 S&W Long, 6-shot. **Barrel:** 6". **Weight:** 47.3 oz. **Length:** 11.2" overall. **Stocks:** Stippled walnut, adjustable match-type. **Sights:** Blade front, micrometer rear adjustable for windage and elevation. **Features:** Polished blue finish. Introduced 1989. Imported from Germany by Precision Sales International.

Price: 22 LR or 32 S&W Long **$1,345.00**

FAS 602 MATCH PISTOL **Caliber:** 22 LR, 5-shot. **Barrel:** 5.6". **Weight:** 37 oz. **Length:** 11" overall. **Stocks:** Walnut wraparound; sizes small, medium or large, or adjustable. **Sights:** Match. Blade front, open notch rear fully adjustable for windage and elevation. Sight radius is 8.66". **Features:** Line of sight is only $1\frac{1}{32}$" above centerline of bore; magazine is inserted from top; adjustable and removable trigger mechanism; single lever takedown. Full 5-year warranty. Imported from Italy by Nygord Precision Products.
Price: **$995.00**

FAS 601 Match Pistol Similar to Model 602 except has different match stocks with adjustable palm shelf, 22 Short only for rapid fire shooting; weighs 40 oz., 5.6" bbl.; has gas ports through top of barrel and slide to reduce recoil; slightly different trigger and sear mechanisms. Imported from Italy by Nygord Precision Products.
Price: **$1,095.00**

FAS 603 Match Pistol Similar to the FAS 602 except chambered for 32 S&W with 5-shot magazine; 5.3" barrel; 8.66" sight radius; overall length 11.0"; weighs 42.3 oz. Imported from Italy by Nygord Precision Products.
Price: **$1,050.00**

FREEDOM ARMS CASULL MODEL 252 SILHOUETTE **Caliber:** 22 LR, 5-shot cylinder. **Barrel:** 9.95". **Weight:** 63 oz. **Length:** NA **Stocks:** Black micarta, western style. **Sights:** $\frac{1}{8}$" Patridge front, Iron Sight Gun Works silhouette rear, click adjustable for windage and elevation. **Features:** Stainless steel. Built on the 454 Casull frame. Two-point firing pin, lightened hammer for fast lock time. Trigger pull is 3 to 5 lbs. with pre-set overtravel screw. Introduced 1991. From Freedom Arms.
Price: Silhouette Class **$1,295.00**
Price: Extra fitted 22 WMR cylinder **$213.00**

GAUCHER GP SILHOUETTE PISTOL **Caliber:** 22 LR, single shot. **Barrel:** 10". **Weight:** 42.3 oz. **Length:** 15.5" overall. **Stocks:** Stained hardwood. **Sights:** Hooded post on ramp front, open rear adjustable for windage and elevation. **Features:** Matte chrome barrel, blued bolt and sights. Other barrel lengths available on special order. Introduced 1991. Imported by Mandall Shooting Supplies.
Price: **$323.00**

HAMMERLI MODEL 160/162 FREE PISTOLS **Caliber:** 22 LR, single shot. **Barrel:** 11.30". **Weight:** 46.94 oz. **Length:** 17.52" overall. **Stocks:** Walnut; full match style with adjustable palm shelf. Stippled surfaces. **Sights:** Changeable blade front, open, fully adjustable match rear. **Features:** Model 160 has mechanical set trigger; Model 162 has electronic trigger; both fully adjustable with provisions for dry firing. Introduced 1993. Imported from Switzerland by Hammerli Pistols USA.
Price: Model 160, about **$1,910.00**
Price: Model 162, about **$2,095.00**

Hammerli 280

Freedom Arms Casull 252 Varmint

Freedom Arms Casull Model 252 Varmint Similar to the Silhouette Class revolver except has 7.5" barrel, weighs 59 oz., has black and green laminated hardwood grips, and comes with brass bead front sight, express shallow V rear sight with windage and elevation adjustments. Introduced 1991. From Freedom Arms.
Price: Varmint Class **$1,248.00**
Price: Extra fitted 22 WMR cylinder **$213.00**

GLOCK 17L COMPETITION AUTO **Caliber:** 9mm Para., 17-shot magazine. **Barrel:** 6.02". **Weight:** 23.3 oz. **Length:** 8.85" overall. **Stocks:** Black polymer. **Sights:** Blade front with white dot, fixed or adjustable rear. **Features:** Polymer frame, steel slide; double-action trigger with "Safe Action" system; mechanical firing pin safety, drop safety; simple takedown without tools; locked breech, recoil operated action. Introduced 1989. Imported from Austria by Glock, Inc.
Price: **$768.25**

Hammerli 208s

HAMMERLI MODEL 208s PISTOL **Caliber:** 22 LR, 8-shot magazine. **Barrel:** 5.9". **Weight:** 37.5 oz. **Length:** 10" overall. **Stocks:** Walnut, target-type with thumbrest. **Sights:** Blade front, open fully adjustable rear. **Features:** Adjustable trigger, including length; interchangeable rear sight elements. Imported from Switzerland by Hammerli Pistols USA, Mandall Shooting Supplies.
Price: About **$1,695.00**

HAMMERLI MODEL 280 TARGET PISTOL **Caliber:** 22 LR, 6-shot; 32 S&W Long WC, 5-shot. **Barrel:** 4.5". **Weight:** 39.1 oz. (32). **Length:** 11.8" overall. **Stocks:** Walnut match-type with stippling, adjustable palm shelf. **Sights:** Match sights, micrometer adjustable; interchangeable elements. **Features:** Has carbon-reinforced synthetic frame and bolt/barrel housing. Trigger is adjustable for pull weight, take-up weight, let-off, and length, and is interchangeable. Interchangeable metal or carbon fiber counterweights. Sight radius of 8.8". Comes with barrel weights, spare magazine, loading tool, cleaning rods. Introduced 1990. Imported from Switzerland by Hammerli Pistols USA and Mandall Shooting Supplies.
Price: 22-cal., about **$1,465.00**
Price: 32-cal., about **$1,650.00**

McMILLAN SIGNATURE JR. LONG RANGE PISTOL **Caliber:** Any suitable caliber. **Barrel:** To customer specs. **Weight:** 5 lbs. **Stock:** McMillan fiberglass. **Sights:** None furnished; comes with scope rings. **Features:** Right- or left-hand McMillan benchrest action of titanium or stainless steel; single shot or repeater. Comes with bipod. Introduced 1992. Made in U.S. by McMillan Gunworks, Inc.
Price: **$2,370.00**

Ram-Line Exactor Target

Remington XP-100 Silhouette

Ruger Government Target

Ruger Mark II Government Target Model Same gun as the Mark II Target Model except has 6⅞" barrel, higher sights and is roll marked "Government Target Model" on the right side of the receiver below the rear sight. Identical in all aspects to the military model used for training U.S. armed forces except for markings. Comes with factory test target. Introduced 1987.
Price: Blued (MK-678G) $356.50
Price: Stainless (KMK-678G) $427.29

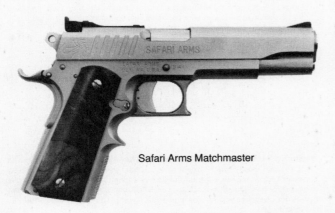

Safari Arms Matchmaster

McMILLAN WOLVERINE AUTO PISTOL Caliber: 9mm Para., 10mm Auto, 38 Wadcutter, 38 Super, 45 Italian, 45 ACP. Barrel: 6". Weight: 45 oz. Length: 9.5" overall. Stocks: Pachmayr rubber. Sights: Blade front, fully adjustable rear; low profile. Features: Integral compensator; round burr-style hammer; extended grip safety; checkered backstrap; skeletonized aluminum match trigger. Many finish options. Announced 1992. Made in U.S. by McMillan Gunworks, Inc.
Price: Combat or Competition Match $1,500.00

MITCHELL ARMS OLYMPIC I.S.U. AUTO PISTOL Caliber: 22 Short, 10-shot magazine. Barrel: 6.75" round tapered, with stabilizer. Weight: 40 oz. Length: 11.25" overall. Stocks: Checkered walnut with thumbrest. Sights: Undercut ramp front, frame-mounted click adjustable square notch rear. Features: Integral stabilizer with two removable weights. Trigger adjustable for pull and over-travel; blue finish; stippled front and backstraps; push-button barrel takedown. Announced 1992. From Mitchell Arms.
Price: $599.00

RAM-LINE EXACTOR TARGET PISTOL Caliber: 22 LR, 15-shot magazine. Barrel: 8.0". Weight: 23 oz. Length: 12.3" overall. Stocks: One-piece injection moulded in conventional contour; checkered side panels, ridged front and backstraps. Sights: Ramp front with interchangeable .125" blade, rear adjustable for windage and elevation. Features: Injection moulded grip frame, alloy receiver; hybrid composite barrel. Constant force sear spring gives 2.5-lb. trigger pull. Adapt-A-Barrel allows mounting weights, flashlight. Drilled and tapped receiver for scope mounting. Jewelled bolt. Comes with carrying case, test target. Introduced 1990. Made in U.S. by Ram-Line, Inc.
Price: $279.97

REMINGTON XP-100 SILHOUETTE PISTOL Caliber: 7mm BR Rem., single shot. Barrel: 10½". Weight: 3⅞ lbs. Length: 17¼" overall. Stock: American walnut. Sights: Blade front, fully adjustable square notch rear. Features: Mid-handle grip with scalloped contours for left- or right-handed shooters; match=type trigger; two-postion thumb safety. Matte blue finish.
Price: $613.00

RUGER MARK II TARGET MODEL AUTO PISTOL Caliber: 22 LR, 10-shot magazine. Barrel: 5¼", 6⅞". Weight: 42 oz. Length: 11⅛" overall. Stocks: Checkered hard plastic. Sights: .125" blade front, micro-click rear, adjustable for windage and elevation. Sight radius 9⅜". Features: Introduced 1982.
Price: Blued (MK-514, MK-678) $310.50
Price: Stainless (KMK-514, KMK-678) $389.00

Ruger Mark II Bull Barrel Same gun as the Target Model except has 5½" or 10" heavy barrel (10" meets all IHMSA regulations). Weight with 5½" barrel is 42 oz., with 10" barrel, 52 oz.
Price: Blued (MK-512) $310.50
Price: Blued (MK-10) $294.50
Price: Stainless (KMK-10) $373.00
Price: Stainless (KMK-512) $389.00

Ruger Stainless Government Competition Model 22 Pistol Similar to the Mark II Government Target Model stainless pistol except has 6⅞" slab-sided barrel; the receiver top is drilled and tapped for a Ruger scope base adaptor of blued, chromemoly steel; comes with Ruger 1" stainless scope rings with integral bases for mounting a variety of optical sights; has checkered laminated grip panels with right-hand thumbrest. Has blued open sights with 9¼" radius. Overall length is 11⅛", weight 44 oz. Introduced 1991.
Price: KMK-678GC $441.00

SAFARI ARMS MATCHMASTER PISTOL Caliber: 45 ACP, 7-shot magazine. Barrel: 5"; National Match, stainless steel. Weight: 38 oz. Length: 8.5" overall. Stocks: Smooth walnut with etched scorpion logo. Sights: Ramped blade front, rear adjustable for windage and elevation. Features: Beavertail grip safety, extended safety, extended slide release, Commander-style hammer; throated, ported, tuned. Finishes: Parkerized matte black, or satin stainless steel. Available from Safari Arms, Inc.
Price: $670.00

Safari Arms Matchmaster Carrycomp I Pistol Similar to the Matchmaster except has Wil Schueman-designed hybrid compensator system. Introduced 1993. Made in U.S. by Safari Arms, Inc.
Price: $1,010.00

SMITH & WESSON MODEL 41 TARGET **Caliber:** 22 LR, 10-shot clip. **Barrel:** 5½", 7". **Weight:** 44 oz. **Length:** 9" overall. **Stocks:** Checkered walnut with modified thumbrest, usable with either hand. **Sights:** ⅛" Patridge on ramp base; S&W micro-click rear adjustable for windage and elevation. **Features:** ⅜" wide, grooved trigger; adjustable trigger stop.
Price: S&W Bright Blue, satin matted top area **$753.00**

SMITH & WESSON MODEL 52 38 MASTER AUTO **Caliber:** 38 Special (for mid-range W.C. with flush-seated bullet only), 5-shot magazine. **Barrel:** 5". **Weight:** 40 oz. with empty magazine. **Length:** 8⅝" overall. **Stocks:** Checkered walnut. **Sights:** ⅛" Patridge front, S&W micro-click rear adjustable for windage and elevation. **Features:** Top sighting surfaces matte finished. Locked breech, moving barrel system; checked for 10-ring groups at 50 yards. Coin-adjustable sight screws. Dry-firing permissible if manual safety on.
Price: S&W Bright Blue **$908.00**

SPHINX AT-2000C COMPETITOR PISTOL **Caliber:** 9mm Para., 9x21mm, 15-shot, 40 S&W, 11-shot. **Barrel:** 5.31". **Weight:** 40.56 oz. **Length:** 9.84" overall. **Stocks:** Checkered neoprene. **Sights:** Fully adjustable Bo-Mar or Tasco Pro-Point dot sight in Sphinx mount. **Features:** Extended magazine release. Competition slide with dual-port compensated barrel. Two-tone finish only. Introduced 1993. Imported from Switzerland by Sile Distributors, Inc.
Price: With Bo-Mar sights (AT-2000CS) **$1,902.00**
Price: With Tasco Pro-Point and mount **$2,189.00**

Sphinx AT-2000GM Grand Master Pistol Similar to the AT-2000C except has single-action-only trigger mechanism, squared trigger guard, extended beavertail grip, safety and magazine release; notched competition slide for easier cocking. Two-tone finish only. Has dual-port compensated barrel. Available with fully adjustable Bo-Mar sights or Tasco Pro-Point and Sphinx mount. Introduced 1993. Imported from Switzerland by Sile Distributors, Inc.
Price: With Bo-Mar sights (AT-2000GMS) **$2,893.00**
Price: With Tasco Pro-Point and mount (AT-2000GM) **$2,971.00**

SPRINGFIELD INC. 1911A1 BULLSEYE WADCUTTER PISTOL **Caliber:** 45 ACP. **Barrel:** 5". **Weight:** 45 oz. **Length:** 8.59" overall (5" barrel). **Stocks:** Checkered walnut. **Sights:** Bo-Mar rib with undercut blade front, fully adjustable rear. **Features:** Built for wadcutter loads only. Has full-length recoil spring guide rod, fitted Videki speed trigger with 3.5-lb. pull; match Commander hammer and sear; beavertail grip safety; lowered and flared ejection port; tuned extractor; fitted slide to frame; Shok Buff; beveled and polished magazine well; checkered front strap and steel mainspring housing (flat housing standard); polished and throated National Match barrel and bushing. Comes with two magazines with slam pads, plastic carrying case, test target. Introduced 1992. From Springfield Inc.
Price: . . . . **P.O.R.**

Springfield Inc. Entry Level Wadcutter Pistol Similar to the 1911A1 Bullseye Wadcutter Pistol except has low-mounted Bo-Mar adjustable rear sight, undercut blade front; match throated barrel and bushing; polished feed ramp; lowered and flared ejection port; fitted Videki speed trigger with tuned 3.5-lb. pull; fitted slide to frame; Shok Buff; Pachmayr mainspring housing; Pachmayr grips. Comes with two magazines with slam pads, plastic carrying case, test target. Introduced 1992. From Springfield Inc.
Price: 45 ACP, blue, 5" only . . . . **P.O.R.**

Springfield Inc. Trophy Master Expert Pistol Similar to the 1911A1 Trophy Master Competition Pistol except has triple-chamber tapered cone compensator on match barrel with dovetailed front sight; lowered and flared ejection port; fully tuned for reliability. Comes with two magazines, plastic carrying case. Introduced 1992. From Springfield Inc.
Price: 45 ACP, Duotone finish . . . . **P.O.R.**

Springfield Inc. Trophy Master Competition Pistol Similar to the 1911A1 Entry Level Wadcutter Pistol except has brazed, serrated improved ramp front sight; extended ambidextrous thumb safety; match Commander hammer and sear; serrated rear slide; Pachmay flat mainspring housing; extended magazine release; beavertail grip safety; full-length recoil spring guide; Pachmayr wrap-around grips. Comes with two magazines with slam pads, plastic carrying case. Introduced 1992. From Springfield Inc.
Price: 45 ACP, blue . . . . **P.O.R.**

Smith & Wesson Model 52

Sphinx AT-2000C Competitor

Sphinx AT-2000GM Grand Master

Springfield Inc. 1911A1 N.M. Hardball Pistol Similar to the 1911A1 Entry Level Wadcutter Pistol except has Bo-Mar adjustable rear sight with undercut front blade; fitted match Videki trigger with 4-lb. pull; fitted slide to frame; throated National Match barrel and bushing, polished feed ramp; Shok Buff; tuned extractor; Herrett walnut grips. Comes with one magazine, plastic carrying case, test target. Introduced 1992. From Springfield Inc.
Price: 45 ACP, blue . . . . **P.O.R.**

> Consult our Directory pages for the location of firms mentioned.

Springfield Inc. Trophy Master Distinguished Pistol Has all the features of the 1911A1 Trophy Master Expert except is full-house pistol with Bo-Mar low-mounted adjustable rear sight; full-length recoil spring guide rod and recoil spring retainer; beveled and polished magazine well; Pachmayr grips. Duotone finish. Comes with five magazines with slam pads, plastic carrying case. From Springfield Inc.
Price: 45 ACP . . . . **P.O.R.**
Price: Trophy Master Distinguished Limited . . . . **P.O.R.**

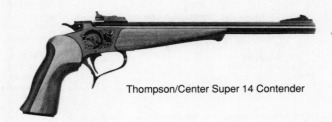

Thompson/Center Super 14 Contender

Unique D.E.S. 69U

UNIQUE MODEL 2000-U MATCH PISTOL   Caliber: 22 Short, 5-shot magazine. **Barrel:** 5.9". **Weight:** 43 oz. **Length:** 11.3" overall. **Stocks:** Anatomically shaped, adjustable, stippled French walnut. **Sights:** Blade front, fully adjustable rear; 9.7" sight radius. **Features:** Light alloy frame, steel slide and shock absorber; five barrel vents reduce recoil, three of which can be blocked; trigger adjustable for position and pull weight. Comes with 340-gram weight housing, 160-gram available. Introduced 1984. Imported from France by Nygord Precision Products.
Price: Right-hand, about **$1,350.00**
Price: Left-hand, about **$1,400.00**

WALTHER GSP MATCH PISTOL   Caliber: 22 LR, 32 S&W wadcutter (GSP-C), 5-shot. **Barrel:** 5¾". **Weight:** 44.8 oz. (22 LR), 49.4 oz. (32). **Length:** 11.8" overall. **Stocks:** Walnut, special hand-fitting design. **Sights:** Fixed front, rear adjustable for windage and elevation. **Features:** Available with either 2.2 lb. (1000 gm) or 3 lb. (1360 gm) trigger. Spare mag., bbl. weight, tools supplied in Match Pistol Kit. Imported from Germany by Interarms.
Price: GSP, with case **$1,843.00**
Price: GSP-C, with case **$2,545.00**
Price: 22 LR conversion unit for GSP-C (no trigger unit) **$1,053.00**
Price: 22 Short conversion unit for GSP-C (with trigger unit) **$1,495.00**
Price: 32 S&W conversion unit for GSP-C (no trigger unit) **$1,400.00**

WESSON FIREARMS MODEL 40 SILHOUETTE   Caliber: 357 Maximum, 6-shot. **Barrel:** 4", 6", 8", 10". **Weight:** 64 oz. (8" bbl.). **Length:** 14.3" overall (8" bbl.). **Stocks:** Smooth walnut, target-style. **Sights:** ⅛" serrated front, fully adjustable rear. **Features:** Meets criteria for IHMSA competition with 8" slotted barrel. Blue or stainless steel. Made in U.S. by Wesson Firearms Co., Inc.
Price: Blue, 4" **$488.00**
Price: Blue, 6" **$508.00**
Price: Blue, 8" **$550.94**
Price: Blue, 10" **$579.20**
Price: Stainless, 4" **$550.00**
Price: Stainless, 6" **$569.00**
Price: Stainless, 8" slotted **$571.57**
Price: Stainless, 10" **$651.16**

Wesson Firearms Model 445 Supermag Revolver   Similar size and weight as the Model 40 revolvers. Chambered for the 445 Supermag cartridge, a longer version of the 44 Magnum. Barrel lengths of 4", 6", 8", 10". Contact maker for complete price list. Introduced 1989. From Wesson Firearms Co., Inc.
Price: 4", vent heavy, blue **$539.00**
Price: As above, stainless **$615.00**
Price: 8", vent heavy, blue **$594.00**
Price: As above, stainless **$662.00**
Price: 10", vent heavy, blue **$615.00**
Price: As above, stainless **$683.00**
Price: 8", vent slotted, blue **$575.00**
Price: As above, stainless **$632.00**
Price: 10", vent slotted, blue **$597.00**
Price: As above, stainless **$657.00**

THOMPSON/CENTER SUPER 14 CONTENDER   Caliber: 22 LR, 222 Rem., 223 Rem., 7mm TCU, 7-30 Waters, 30-30 Win., 35 Rem., 357 Rem. Maximum, 44 Mag., 10mm Auto, 445 Super Mag., single shot. **Barrel:** 14". **Weight:** 45 oz. **Length:** 17¼" overall. **Stocks:** T/C "Competitor Grip" (walnut and rubber). **Sights:** Fully adjustable target-type. **Features:** Break-open action with auto safety. Interchangeable barrels for both rimfire and centerfire calibers. Introduced 1978.
Price: **$425.00**
Price: Extra barrels, blued **$200.00**

Thompson/Center Super 16 Contender   Same as the T/C Super 14 Contender except has 16¼" barrel. Rear sight can be mounted at mid-barrel position (10¾" radius) or moved to the rear (using scope mount position) for 14¾" radius. Overall length is 20¼". Comes with T/C Competitor Grip of walnut and rubber. Available in 22 LR, 22 WMR, 223 Rem., 7-30 Waters, 30-30 Win., 35 Rem., 44 Mag., 45-70 Gov't. Also available with 16" vent rib barrel with internal choke, caliber 45 Colt/410 shotshell.
Price: **$430.00**
Price: 45-70 Gov't **$435.00**
Price: Extra 16" barrels (blued) **$205.00**
Price: As above, 45-70 . . . . **$210.00**
Price: Super 16 Vent Rib (45-410) **$460.00**
Price: Extra vent rib barrel **$235.00**

UNIQUE D.E.S. 32U RAPID FIRE MATCH   Caliber: 32 S&W Long wadcutter. **Barrel:** 5.9". **Weight:** 40.2 oz. **Stocks:** Anatomically shaped, adjustable stippled French walnut. **Sights:** Blade front, micrometer click rear. **Features:** Trigger adjustable for weight and position; dry firing mechanism; slide stop catch. Optional sleeve weights. Introduced 1990. Imported from France by Nygord Precision Products.
Price: Right-hand, about **$1,295.00**
Price: Left-hand, about **$1,345.00**

UNIQUE D.E.S. 69U TARGET PISTOL   Caliber: 22 LR, 5-shot magazine. **Barrel:** 5.91". **Weight:** 35.3 oz. **Length:** 10.5" overall. **Stocks:** French walnut target-style with thumbrest and adjustable shelf; hand-checkered panels. **Sights:** Ramp front, micro. adj. rear mounted on frame; 8.66" sight radius. **Features:** Meets U.I.T. standards. Comes with 260-gram barrel weight; 100, 150, 350-gram weights available. Fully adjustable match trigger; dry-firing safety device. Imported from France by Nygord Precision Products.
Price: Right-hand, about **$1,195.00**
Price: Left-hand, about **$1,245.00**

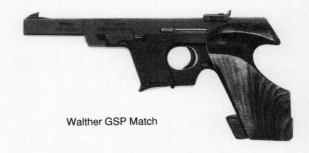

Walther GSP Match

Walther OSP Rapid-Fire Pistol   Similar to Model GSP except 22 Short only, stock has adjustable free-style hand rest.
Price: **$2,275.00**

Wesson Firearms Model 40

WESSON FIREARMS MODEL 322/7322 TARGET REVOLVER
Caliber: 32-20, 6-shot. **Barrel:** 2.5", 4", 6", 8", standard, vent, vent heavy.
Weight: 43 oz. (6" VH). **Length:** 11.25" overall. **Stocks:** Checkered walnut.
Sights: Red ramp interchangeable front, fully adjustable rear. **Features:** Brigh blue
or stainless. Introduced 1991. From Wesson Firearms Co., Inc.

Price: 6", blue $355.00
Price: 6", stainless $384.00
Price: 8", vent, blue $404.55
Price: 8", stainless $434.71
Price: 6", vent heavy, blue $412.20
Price: 6", vent heavy, stainless $441.32
Price: 8", vent heavy, blue $422.94
Price: 8", vent heavy, stainless $459.72

WICHITA INTERNATIONAL PISTOL **Caliber:** 22 LR, 22 WMR, 32 H&R
Mag., 357 Super Mag., 357 Mag., 7R, 7mm Super Mag., 7-30 Waters, 30-30 Win.,
single shot. **Barrel:** 10", 10½", 14". **Weight:** 3 lbs. 2 oz. (with 10", 10½" barrels).
Stocks: Walnut grip and forend. **Sights:** Patridge front, adjustable rear. Wichita
Multi-Range sight system optional. **Features:** Made of stainless steel. Break-open
action. Grip dimensions same as Colt 45 Auto. Drilled and tapped for furnished
see-thru rings. Extra barrels are factory fitted. Introduced 1983. Available from
Wichita Arms.

Price: International 10" $550.00
Price: International 14" $585.00
Price: Extra barrels, 10" $325.00
Price: Extra barrels, 14" $355.00

WICHITA SILHOUETTE PISTOL **Caliber:** 308 Win. F.L., 7mm IHMSA,
7mm-308. **Barrel:** 14¹⁵⁄₁₆". **Weight:** 4½ lbs. **Length:** 21⅜" overall. **Stock:**
American walnut with oil finish. Glass bedded. **Sights:** Wichita Multi-Range sight
system. **Features:** Comes with left-hand action with right-hand grip. Round
receiver and barrel. Fluted bolt, flat bolt handle. Wichita adjustable trigger. Introduced
1979. From Wichita Arms.

Price: Center grip stock $1,150.00
Price: As above except with Rear Position Stock and target-type Lightpull
  trigger $1,150.00

WESSON FIREARMS MODEL 22 SILHOUETTE REVOLVER
Caliber: 22 LR, 6-shot. **Barrel:** 10", regular vent or vent heavy. **Weight:** 53 oz.
Stocks: Combat style. **Sights:** Patridge-style front, .080" narrow notch rear. **Features:** Single action only. Available in blue or stainless. Introduced 1989. From
Wesson Firearms Co., Inc.

Price: Blue, regular vent $459.72
Price: Blue, vent heavy $478.10
Price: Stainless, regular vent $488.84
Price: Stainless, vent heavy $516.40

WICHITA CLASSIC SILHOUETTE PISTOL **Caliber:** All standard
calibers with maximum overall length of 2.800". **Barrel:** 11¼". **Weight:** 3 lbs.,
15 oz. **Stocks:** AAA American walnut with oil finish, checkered grip. **Sights:**
Hooded post front, open adjustable rear. **Features:** Three locking lug bolt, three gas
ports; completely adjustable Wichita trigger. Introduced 1981. From Wichita Arms.
Price: $2,950.00

Wichita International

Wichita Silhouette

Specially adapted single-shot and multi-barrel arms.

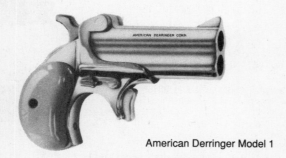

American Derringer Model 1

American Derringer Model 4 Similar to the Model 1 except has 4.1" barrel,
overall length of 6", and weighs 16½ oz.; chambered for 3" 410-bore shotshells or
45 or 44 Magnum Colt. Can be had with 45-70 upper barrel and 3" 410-bore or 45
Colt bottom barrel. Made of stainless steel. Manual hammer block safety. Introduced
1985.
Price: 3" 410/45 Colt (either barrel) $352.00
Price: 3" 410/45 Colt or 45-70 (Alaskan Survival model) $387.50
Price: 44 Magnum with oversize grips $422.00

AMERICAN DERRINGER MODEL 1 **Caliber:** 22 LR, 22 WMR, 30 Luger,
30-30 Win., 32 ACP, 380 ACP, 38 Spec., 9mm Para., 357 Mag., 357 Maximum,
10mm, 40 S&W, 41 Mag., 38-40, 44-40 Win., 44 Spec., 44 Mag., 45 Colt, 45 ACP,
410-bore (2½"). **Barrel:** 3". **Weight:** 15½ oz. (38 Spec.). **Length:** 4.82" overall. **Stocks:** Rosewood, Zebra wood. **Sights:** Blade front. **Features:** Made of
stainless steel with high-polish or satin finish. Two-shot capacity. Manual hammer
block safety. Introduced 1980. Available in almost any pistol caliber. Contact the
factory for complete list of available calibers and prices. From American Derringer
Corp.
Price: 22 LR or WMR . . . . $212.50 to $225.00
Price: 38 Spec. $219.00
Price: 357 Maximum $265.00
Price: 357 Mag. $250.00
Price: 9mm, 380, ... $215.00
Price: 10mm, 40 S&W $250.00
Price: 44 Spec., ... $320.00
Price: 44-40 Win., 45 Colt, 45 Auto Rim $320.00
Price: 30-30, 41, 44 Mags., 45 Win. Mag. $375.00
Price: 45-70, single shot $312.00
Price: 45 Colt, 410, 2½" $320.00
Price: 45 ACP, 10mm Auto $250.00
Price: 125th Anniversary model (brass frame, stainless bbl.. 44-40, 45 Colt, 38
  Spec.) $320.00
Price: Alaskan Survival model (45-70 upper, 410-45 Colt lower) $387.50

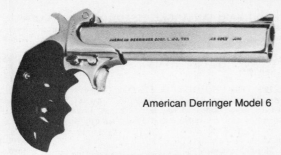

American Derringer Model 6

American Derringer Model 7 Ultra Lightweight Similar to Model 1 except made of high strength aircraft aluminum. Weighs 7½ oz., 4.82" o.a.l., rosewood stocks. Available in 22 LR, 32 H&R Mag., 380 ACP, 38 Spec., 44 Spec. Introduced 1986.
Price: 22 LR **$200.00**
Price: 38 Spec. **$202.50**
Price: 380 ACP **$199.95**
Price: 32 H&R Mag. **$202.50**
Price: 44 Spec. **$500.00**

American Derringer Model 10 Lightweight Similar to the Model 1 except frame is of aluminum, giving weight of 10 oz. Available in 45 Colt or 45 ACP only. Matte gray finish. Introduced 1989.
Price: 45 Colt **$320.00**
Price: 45 ACP **$250.00**
Price: Model 11 (38 Spec., aluminum bbls., wgt. 11 oz.) **$205.00**

American Derringer Semmerling

AMERICAN DERRINGER COP 357 DERRINGER **Caliber:** 38 Spec. or 357 Mag., 4-shot. **Barrel:** 3.14". **Weight:** 16 oz. **Length:** 5.53" overall. **Stocks:** Rosewood. **Sights:** Fixed. **Features:** Double-action only. Four shots. Made of stainless steel. Introduced 1990. Made in U.S. by American Derringer Corp.
Price: **$375.00**

ANSCHUTZ EXEMPLAR BOLT-ACTION PISTOL **Caliber:** 22 LR, 5-shot; 22 Hornet, 5-shot. **Barrel:** 10", 14". **Weight:** 3½ lbs. **Length:** 17" overall. **Stock:** European walnut with stippled grip and forend. **Sights:** Hooded front on ramp, open notch rear adjustable for windage and elevation. **Features:** Uses Match 64 action with left-hand bolt; Anschutz #5091 two-stage trigger set at 9.85 oz. Receiver grooved for scope mounting; open sights easily removed. Introduced 1987. Imported from Germany by Precision Sales International.
Price: 22 LR **$499.50**
Price: 22 LR, left-hand **$499.50**
Price: 22 LR, 14" barrel **$522.00**
Price: 22 Hornet (no sights, 10" bbl.) **$822.00**

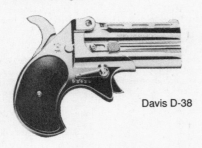

Davis D-38

American Derringer Model 6 Similar to the Model 1 except has 6" barrels chambered for 3" 410 shotshells or 45 Colt, rosewood stocks, 8.2" o.a.l. and weighs 21 oz. Shoots either round for each barrel. Manual hammer block safety. Introduced 1986.
Price: High polish or satin finish **$387.50**
Price: Gray matte finish **$362.50**

AMERICAN DERRINGER MODEL 3 **Caliber:** 38 Special. **Barrel:** 2.5". **Weight:** 8.5 oz. **Length:** 4.9" overall. **Stocks:** Rosewood. **Sights:** Blade front. **Features:** Made of stainless steel. Single shot with manual hammer block safety. Introduced 1985. From American Derringer Corp.
Price: **$120.00**

American Derringer Lady Derringer Same as the Model 1 except has tuned action, is fitted with scrimshawed synthetic ivory grips; chambered for 32 H&R Mag. and 38 Spec.; 22 LR, 22 WMR, 380 ACP, 357 Mag., 9mm Para., 45 ACP, 45 Colt/410 shotshell available at extra cost. Deluxe Grade is highly polished; Deluxe Engraved is engraved in a pattern similar to that used on 1880s derringers. All come in a French fitted jewelry box. Introduced 1991.
Price: Deluxe Grade **$235.00**
Price: Deluxe Engraved Grade **$750.00**

American Derringer Texas Commemorative A Model 1 Derringer with solid brass frame, stainless steel barrel and rosewood grips. Available in 38 Speical, 44-40 Win., or 45 Colt. Introduced 1987.
Price: 38 Spec. **$215.00**
Price: 44-40 or 45 Colt **$320.00**

AMERICAN DERRINGER SEMMERLING LM-4 **Caliber:** 9mm Para., 7-shot magazine; 45 ACP, 5-shot magazine. **Barrel:** 3.625". **Weight:** 24 oz. **Length:** 5.2" overall. **Stocks:** Checkered plastic on blued guns, rosewood on stainless guns. **Sights:** Open, fixed. **Features:** Manually-operated repeater. Height is 3.7", width is 1". Comes with manual, leather carrying case, spare stock screws, wrench. From American Derringer Corp.
Price: Blued **$1,750.00**
Price: Stainless steel **$1,875.00**

AMERICAN DERRINGER DA 38 MODEL **Caliber:** 9mm Para., 38 Spec., 357 Mag., 40 S&W. **Barrel:** 3". **Weight:** 14.5 oz. **Length:** 4.8" overall. **Stocks:** Rosewood, walnut or other hardwoods. **Sights:** Fixed. **Features:** Double-action only; two-shots. Manual safety. Made of satin-finished stainless steel and aluminum. Introduced 1989. From American Derringer Corp.
Price: 38 Spec. **$250.00**
Price: 9mm Para. **$275.00**
Price: 357 Mag., 40 S&W **$300.00**

American Derringer Mini COP Derringer Similar to the COP 357 except chambered for 22 WMR. Barrel length of 2.85", overall length of 4.95", weight is 16 oz. Double action with automatic hammer-block safety. Made of stainless steel. Grips of rosewood, walnut or other hardwoods. Introduced 1990. Made in U.S. by American Derringer Corp.
Price: **$312.50**

Anschutz Exemplar

DAVIS D-38 DERRINGER **Caliber:** 38 Special. **Barrel:** 2.75". **Weight:** 11.5 oz. **Length:** 4.65" overall. **Stocks:** Textured black synthetic. **Sights:** Blade front, fixed notch rear. **Features:** Alloy frame, stee-lined barrels, steel breech block. Plunger-type safety with integral hammer block. Chrome or black Teflon finish. Introduced 1992. Made in U.S. by Davis Industries.
Price: **$89.90**

DAVIS DERRINGERS **Caliber:** 22 LR, 22 WMR, 25 ACP, 32 ACP. **Barrel:** 2.4". **Weight:** 9.5 oz. **Length:** 4" overall. **Stocks:** Laminated wood. **Sights:** Blade front, fixed notch rear. **Features:** Choice of black Teflon or chrome finish; spur trigger. Introduced 1986. Made in U.S. by Davis Industries.
Price: **$64.90**

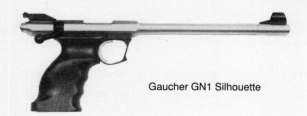

Gaucher GN1 Silhouette

HIGH STANDARD DERRINGER **Caliber:** 22 LR, 22 WMR, 2-shot. **Barrel:** 3.5". **Weight:** 11 oz. **Length:** 5.12" overall. **Stocks:** Black composition. **Sights:** Fixed. **Features:** Double action, dual extraction. Hammer-block safety. Blue finish. Introduced 1990. Made in U.S. by American Derringer Corp.
Price: **$169.50**

HJS FRONTIER FOUR DERRINGER **Caliber:** 22 LR. **Barrel:** 2".
Weight: 5½ oz. **Length:** 3¹⁵⁄₁₆" overall. **Stocks:** Black plastic. **Sights:** None.
Features: Four barrels fire with rotating firing pin. Stainless steel construction. Introduced 1993. Made in U.S. by HJS Arms, Inc.
Price: **$160.00**

HJS LONE STAR DERRINGER **Caliber:** 380 ACP, 38 S&W. **Barrel:** 2".
Weight: 6 oz. **Length:** 3¹⁵⁄₁₆" overall. **Stocks:** Black plastic. **Sights:** Groove.
Features: Stainless steel Construction. Beryllium copper firing pin. Button-rifled barrel. Introduced 1993. Made in U.S. by HJS Arms, Inc.
Price: **$180.00**

Magnum Research Lone Eagle

MAGNUM RESEARCH LONE EAGLE SINGLE SHOT PISTOL
Caliber: 22 Hornet, 223, 22-250, 243, 7mm BR, 7mm-08, 30-30, 308, 30-06, 357 Max., 35 Rem., 358 Win., 44 Mag., 444 Marlin. **Barrel:** 14", interchangable.
Weight: 4lbs., 3 oz. to 4 lbs., 7 oz. **Length:** 15" overall. **Stocks:** Composition, with thumbrest. **Sights:** None furnished; drilled and tapped for scope mounting and open sights. Open sights optional. **Features:** Cannon-type rotating breech with spring-activated ejector. Ordnance steel with matte blue finish. Cross-bolt safety. External cocking lever on left side of gun. Introduced 1991. Available from Magnum Research, Inc.
Price: Complete pistol **$344.00**
Price: Barreled action only **$254.00**
Price: Scope base **$14.00**
Price: Adjustable open sights **$35.00**

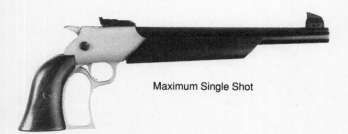

Maximum Single Shot

FEATHER GUARDIAN ANGEL PISTOL **Caliber:** 22 LR/22 WMR.
Barrel: 2". **Weight:** 12 oz. **Length:** 5" overall. **Stocks:** Black composition.
Sights: Fixed. **Features:** Uses a pre-loaded two-shot drop-in "magazine." Stainless steel construction; matte finish. From Feather Industries. Introduced 1988.
Price: **$119.95**

GAUCHER GN1 SILHOUETTE PISTOL **Caliber:** 22 LR, single shot.
Barrel: 10". **Weight:** 2.4 lbs. **Length:** 15.5" overall. **Stock:** European hardwood. **Sights:** Blade front, open adjustable rear. **Features:** Bolt action, adjustable trigger. Introduced 1990. Imported from France by Mandall Shooting Supplies.
Price: About **$319.95**
Price: Model GP Silhouette **$380.00**

High Standard Derringer

HJS Frontier Four

ITHACA X-CALIBER SINGLE SHOT **Caliber:** 22 LR, 44 Mag. **Barrel:** 10", 15". **Weight:** 3¼ lbs. **Length:** 15" overall (10" barrel). **Stocks:** Goncalo Alves grip and forend on Model 20; American walnut on Model 30. **Sights:** Blade on ramp front; Model 20 has adjustable, removable target-type rear. Drilled and tapped for scope mounting. **Features:** Dual firing pin for RF/CF use. Polished blue finish.
Price: 22 LR, 10", 44 Mag., 10" or 15" **$270.00**
Price: 22 LR/44 Mag. combo, 10" and 15" **$365.00**
Price: As above, both 10" barrels **$365.00**

MANDALL/CABANAS PISTOL **Caliber:** 177, pellet or round ball; single shot. **Barrel:** 9". **Weight:** 51 oz. **Length:** 19" overall. **Stock:** Smooth wood with thumbrest. **Sights:** Blade front on ramp, open adjustable rear. **Features:** Fires round ball or pellets with 22 blank cartridge. Automatic safety; muzzlebrake. Imported from Mexico by Mandall Shooting Supplies.
Price: **$139.95**

MAXIMUM SINGLE SHOT PISTOL **Caliber:** 22 LR, 22 Hornet, 22 BR, 223 Rem., 22-250, 6mm BR, 6mm-223, 243, 250 Savage, 6.5mm-35, 7mm TCU, 7mm BR, 7mm-35, 7mm INT-R, 7mm-08, 7mm Rocket, 7mm Super Mag., 30 Herrett, 30 Carbine, 308 Win., 7.62 x 39, 32-20, 357 Mag., 357 Maximum, 358 Win., 44 Mag. **Barrel:** 8¾", 10½", 14". **Weight:** 61 oz. (10½" bbl.); 78 oz. (14" bbl.). **Length:** 15", 18½" overall (with 10½" and 14" bbl., respectively). **Stocks:** Smooth walnut stocks and forend. **Sights:** Ramp front, fully adjustable open rear. **Features:** Falling block action; drilled and tapped for M.O.A. scope mounts; integral grip frame/receiver; adjustable trigger; Douglas barrel (interchangeable). Introduced 1983. Made in U.S. by M.O.A. Corp.
Price: Stainless receiver, blue barrel **$622.00**
Price: Stainless receiver, stainless barrel **$677.00**
Price: Extra blued barrel **$164.00**
Price: Extra stainless barrel **$222.00**
Price: Scope mount **$52.00**

New Advantage Derringer

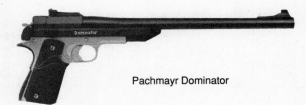

Pachmayr Dominator

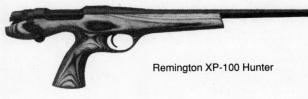

Remington XP-100 Hunter

Remington XP-100R KS

NEW ADVANTAGE ARMS DERRINGER **Caliber:** 22 LR, 22 WMR, 4-shot. **Barrel:** 2½". **Weight:** 15 oz. **Length:** 4½" overall. **Stocks:** Smooth walnut. **Sights:** Fixed. **Features:** Double-action mechanism, four barrels, revolving firing pin. Rebounding hammer. Blue or stainless. Reintroduced 1989. From New Advantage Arms Corp.
Price: 22 LR, 22 WMR, blue, about **$199.00**
Price: As above, stainless, about **$229.00**

PACHMAYR DOMINATOR PISTOL **Caliber:** 22 Hornet, 223, 7mm-06, 308, 35 Rem., 44 Mag., single shot. **Barrel:** 10½" (44 Mag.), 14" all other calibers. **Weight:** 4 lbs. (14" barrel). **Length:** 16" overall (14" barrel). **Stocks:** Pachmayr Signature system. **Sights:** Optional sights or drilled and tapped for scope mounting. **Features:** Bolt-action pistol on 1911A1 frame. Comes as complete gun. Introduced 1988. From Pachmayr.
Price: Either barrel **$524.50**

REMINGTON XP-100 HUNTER PISTOL **Caliber:** 223 Rem., 7mm BR Rem., 7mm-08 Rem., 35 Rem., single shot. **Barrel:** 14½". **Weight:** 4½ lbs. **Length:** 21¼" overall. **Stocks:** Laminated wood with contoured grip. **Sights:** None furnished. Drilled and tapped for scope mounting. **Features:** Mid-handle grip design with scalloped contours for right- or left-handed shooters; two-position safety. Matte blue finish. Introduced 1993.
Price: **$532.00**

Remington XP-100 Custom HB Long Range Pistol Similar to the XP-100 "Hunter" except chambered for 223 Rem., 22-250, 7mm-08 Rem., 35 Rem., 250 Savage, 6mm BR, 7mm BR, 308. Offered with standard 14½" barrel with adjustable rear leaf and front bead sights, or with heavy 15½" barrel without sights. Custom Shop 14½" barrel, Custom Shop English walnut stock in right- or left-hand configuration. Action tuned in Custom Shop. Weight is under 4½ lbs. (heavy barrel, 5½ lbs.). Introduced 1986.
Price: Right- or left-hand **$945.00**

Remington XP-100R KS Repeater Pistol Similar to the Custom Long Range Pistol except chambered for 223 Rem., 22-250, 7mm-08 Rem., 250 Savage, 308, 350 Rem. Mag., and 35 Rem., and has a blind magazine holding 5 rounds (7mm-08 and 35), or 6 (223 Rem.). Comes with a rear-handle, synthetic stock of Du Pont Kevlar to eliminate the transfer bar between the forward trigger and rear trigger assembly. Fitted with front and rear sling swivel studs. Has standard-weight 14½" barrel with adjustable leaf rear sight, bead front. The receiver is drilled and tapped for scope mounts. Weight is about 4½ lbs. Introduced 1990. From Remington Custom Shop.
Price: **$840.00**

RPM XL SINGLE SHOT PISTOL **Caliber:** 22 LR, 22 WMR, 225 Win., 25 Rocket, 6.5 Rocket, 32 H&R Mag., 357 Max., 357 Mag., 30-30 Win., 30 Herrett, 357 Herrett, 41 Mag., 44 Mag., 454 Casull, 375 Win., 7mm UR, 7mm Merrill, 30 Merrill, 7mm Rocket, 270 Ren, 270 Rocket, 270 Max., 45-70. **Barrel:** 8" slab, 10¾", 12", 14" bull; .450" wide rib, matted to prevent glare. **Weight:** About 60 oz. **Length:** 12¼" overall (10¾" bbl.). **Stocks:** Smooth Goncalo with thumb and heel rest. **Sights:** Front .100" blade, Millett rear adjustable for windage and elevation. Hooded front with interchangeable post optional. **Features:** Blue finish, hard chrome optional. Barrel is drilled and tapped for scope mounting. Cocking indicator visible from rear of gun. Has spring-loaded barrel lock, positive hammer block thumb safety. Trigger adjustable for weight of pull and over-travel. For complete price list contact RPM.
Price: Regular ¾" frame, right-hand action **$807.50**
Price: As above, left-hand action **$832.50**
Price: Wide ⅞" frame, right-hand action **$857.50**
Price: Extra barrel, 8", 10¾" **$287.50**
Price: Extra barrel, 12", 14" **$357.50**

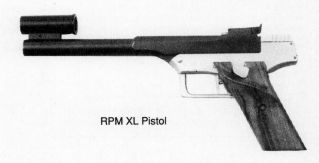

RPM XL Pistol

Texas Arms Defender

TEXAS ARMS DEFENDER DERRINGER **Caliber:** 9mm Para., 38 Spec., 357 Mag., 40 S&W, 44 Mag., 45 ACP, 45 Colt/410. **Barrel:** 3", 3.5". **Weight:** 21 oz. **Length:** 5" overall. **Stocks:** Smooth wood. **Sights:** Blade front, fixed rear. **Features:** Interchangeable barrels; retracting firing pins; rebounding hammer; cross-bolt safety; removable trigger guard; automatic extractor. Matte finish stainless steel. Introduced 1993. Made in U.S. by Texas Arms.
Price: **$310.00**
Price: Extra barrel sets **$100.00**

TEXAS LONGHORN "THE JEZEBEL" PISTOL **Caliber:** 22 Short, Long, Long Rifle, single shot. **Barrel:** 6". **Weight:** 15 oz. **Length:** 8" overall. **Stocks:** One-piece fancy walnut grip (right- or left-hand), walnut forend. **Sights:** Bead front, fixed rear. **Features:** Handmade gun. Top-break action; all stainless steel; automatic hammer block safety; music wire coil springs. Barrel is half-round, half-octagon. Announced 1986. From Texas Longhorn Arms.
Price: About **$250.00**

T/C Contender

Thompson/Center Contender Hunter Package Package contains the Contender pistol in 223, 7-30 Waters, 30-30, 375 Win., 357 Rem. Maximum, 35 Rem., 44 Mag. or 45-70 with 12" or 14" barrel with T/C's Muzzle Tamer, a 2.5x Recoil Proof Long Eye Relief scope with lighted reticle, q.d. sling swivels with a nylon carrying sling. Comes with a suede leather case with foam padding and fleece lining. Introduced 1990. From Thompson/Center Arms.
Price: 12" barrel **$695.00**
Price: 14" barrel **$705.00**

T/C Stainless Super 14

UBERTI ROLLING BLOCK TARGET PISTOL **Caliber:** 22 LR, 22 WMR, 22 Hornet, 357 Mag., single shot. **Barrel:** 9⅞", half-round, half-octagon. **Weight:** 44 oz. **Length:** 14" overall. **Stocks:** Walnut grip and forend. **Sights:** Blade front, fully adjustable rear. **Features:** Replica of the 1871 rolling block target pistol. Brass trigger guard, color case-hardened frame, blue barrel. Imported by Uberti USA.
Price: **$380.00**

Consult our Directory pages for the location of firms mentioned.

ULTRA LIGHT ARMS MODEL 20 REB HUNTER'S PISTOL **Caliber:** 22-250 thru 308 Win. standard. Most silhouette calibers and others on request. 5-shot magazine. **Barrel:** 14", Douglas No. 3. **Weight:** 4 lbs. **Stock:** Composite Kevlar, graphite reinforced. Du Pont Imron paint in green, brown, black and camo. **Sights:** None furnished. Scope mount included. **Features:** Timney adjustable trigger; two-position, three-function safety; benchrest quality action; matte or bright stock and metal finish; right- or left-hand action. Shipped in hard case. Introduced 1987. From Ultra Light Arms.
Price: **$1,600.00**

WICHITA MASTER PISTOL **Caliber:** 6mm BR, 7mm BR, 243, 7mm-08, 22-250, 308, 3 or 5-shot magazine. **Barrel:** 13", 14.875". **Weight:** 4.5 lbs. (13" barrel). **Length:** NA. **Stock:** American walnut with oil finish; glass bedded. **Sights:** Hooded post front, open adjustable rear. **Features:** Comes with left-hand action with right-hand grip. round receiver and barrel. Wichita adjustable trigger. Introduced 1991. From Wichita Arms.
Price: **$1,500.00**

THOMPSON/CENTER CONTENDER **Caliber:** 7mm TCU, 30-30 Win., 22 LR, 22 WMR, 22 Hornet, 223 Rem., 270 Ren, 7-30 Waters, 32-20 Win., 357 Mag., 357 Rem. Max., 44 Mag., 10mm Auto, 445 Super Mag., 45/410, single shot. **Barrel:** 10", tapered octagon, bull barrel and vent. rib. **Weight:** 43 oz. (10" bbl.). **Length:** 13¼" (10" bbl.). **Stocks:** T/C "Competitor Grip." Right or left hand. **Sights:** Under-cut blade ramp front, rear adjustable for windage and elevation. **Features:** Break-open action with automatic safety. Single-action only. Interchangeable bbls., both caliber (rim & centerfire), and length. Drilled and tapped for scope. Engraved frame. See T/C catalog for exact barrel/caliber availability.
Price: Blued (rimfire cals.) **$415.00**
Price: Blued (centerfire cals.) **$415.00**
Price: Extra bbls. (standard octagon) **$190.00**
Price: 45/410, internal choke bbl. **$210.00**

Thompson/Center Stainless Contender Same as the standard Contender except made of stainless steel with blued sights, black Rynite forend and ambidextrous finger-groove grip with a built-in rubber recoil cushion that has a sealed-in air pocket. Receiver has a different cougar etching. Available with 10" bull barrel in 22 LR, 22 LR Match, 22 Hornet, 223 Rem., 30-30 Win., 357 Mag., 44 Mag., 45 Colt/410. Introduced 1993.
Price: **$445.00**
Price: 45 Colt/410 . . . . **$465.00**

Thompson/Center Stainless Super 14, Super 16 Contender Same as the standard Super 14 and Super 16 except they are made of stainless steel with blued sights. Both models have black Rynite forend and finger-groove, ambidextrous grip with a built-in rubber recoil cushion that has a sealed-in air pocket. Receiver has a different cougar etching. Available in 22 LR, 22 LR Match, 22 Hornet, 223 Rem., 30-30 Win., 35 Rem. (Super 14), 45-70 (Super 16 only), 45 Colt/410. Introduced 1993.
Price: 14" bull barrel **$455.00**
Price: 16¼" bull barrel **$460.00**
Price: 45 Colt/410, 14" **$475.00**
Price: 45 Colt/410, 16" **$480.00**

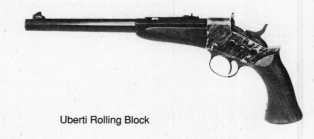

Uberti Rolling Block

Ultra Light Model 20

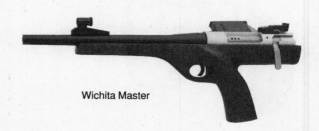

Wichita Master

Dixie Charleville

CVA Hawken

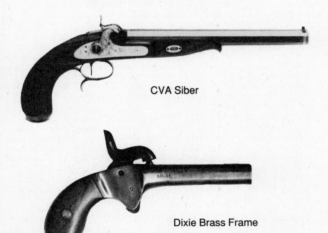

CVA Siber

Dixie Brass Frame

DIXIE PENNSYLVANIA PISTOL Caliber: 44 (.430" round ball). Barrel: 10" (⅞" octagon). Weight: 2½ lbs. Stock: Walnut-stained hardwood. Sights: Blade front, open rear drift-adjustable for windage; brass. Features: Available in flint only. Brass trigger guard, thimbles, nosecap, wedgeplates; high-luster blue barrel. Imported from Italy by Dixie Gun Works.
Price: Finished $149.95
Price: Kit $119.95

Dixie Tornado

FRENCH-STYLE DUELING PISTOL Caliber: 44. Barrel: 10". Weight: 35 oz. Length: 15¾" overall. Stock: Carved walnut. Sights: Fixed. Features: Comes with velvet-lined case and accessories. Imported by Mandall Shooting Supplies.
Price: $295.00

BLACK WATCH SCOTCH PISTOL Caliber: 577 (.500" round ball). Barrel: 7", smoothbore. Weight: 1½ lbs. Length: 12" overall. Stock: Brass. Sights: None. Features: Faithful reproduction of this military flintlock. From Dixie Gun Works, E.M.F.
Price: . . . . $175.00 to $310.00

CHARLEVILLE FLINTLOCK PISTOL Caliber: 69 (.680" round ball). Barrel: 7½". Weight: 48 oz. Length: 13½" overall. Stock: Walnut. Sights: None. Features: Brass frame, polished steel barrel, iron belt hook, brass buttcap and backstrap. Replica of original 1777 pistol. Imported by Dixie Gun Works, E.M.F.
Price: . . . . $195.00 to $325.00

CVA HAWKEN PISTOL Caliber: 50. Barrel: 9¾"; ¹⁵⁄₁₆" flats. Weight: 50 oz. Length: 16½" overall. Stock: Select hardwood. Sights: Beaded blade front, fully adjustable open rear. Features: Color case-hardened lock, polished brass wedge plate, nose cap, ramrod thimbles, trigger guard, grip cap. Hooked breech. Imported by CVA.
Price: $176.95
Price: Kit $109.95

CVA SIBER PISTOL Caliber: 45. Barrel: 10½". Weight: 34 oz. Length: 15½" overall. Stock: High-grade French walnut, checkered grip. Sights: Barleycorn front, micro-adjustable rear. Features: Reproduction of pistol made by Swiss watchmaker Jean Siber in the 1800s. Precision lock and set-trigger give fast lock time. Has engraved, polished steel barrel, trigger guard. Imported by CVA.
Price: $439.95

CVA VEST POCKET DERRINGER Caliber: 44. Barrel: 2½", brass. Weight: 7 oz. Stock: Two-piece walnut. Features: All brass frame with brass ramrod. A muzzle-loading version of the Colt No. 3 derringer. Imported by CVA.
Price: Finished $69.95

DIXIE BRASS FRAME DERRINGER Caliber: 41. Barrel: 2½". Weight: 7 oz. Length: 5½" overall. Stock: Walnut. Features: Brass frame, color case-hardened hammer and trigger. Shoots .395" round ball. Engraved model available. From Dixie Gun Works.
Price: Plain model $69.95
Price: Engraved model $95.50

DIXIE LINCOLN DERRINGER Caliber: 41. Barrel: 2", 8 lands, 8 grooves. Weight: 7 oz. Length: 5½" overall. Stock: Walnut finish, checkered. Sights: Fixed. Features: Authentic copy of the "Lincoln Derringer." Shoots .400" patched ball. German silver furniture includes trigger guard with pineapple finial, wedge plates, nose, wrist, side and teardrop inlays. All furniture, lockplate, hammer, and breech plug engraved. Imported from Italy by Dixie Gun Works.
Price: With wooden case $285.95
Price: Kit (not engraved) $89.95

DIXIE SCREW BARREL PISTOL Caliber: .445". Barrel: 2½". Weight: 8 oz. Length: 6½" overall. Stock: Walnut. Features: Trigger folds down when hammer is cocked. Close copy of the originals once made in Belgium. Uses No. 11 percussion caps. From Dixie Gun Works.
Price: $89.00
Price: Kit $74.95

DIXIE TORNADO TARGET PISTOL Caliber: 44 (.430" round ball). Barrel: 10", octagonal, 1:22 twist. Stocks: Walnut, target-style. Left unfinished for custom fitting. Walnut forend. Sights: Blade on ramp front, micro-type open rear adjustable for windage and elevation. Features: Grip frame style of 1860 Colt revolver. Improved model of the Tingle and B.W. Southgate pistol. Trigger adjustable for pull. Frame, barrel, hammer and sights in the white, brass trigger guard. Comes with solid brass, walnut-handled cleaning rod with jag and nylon muzzle protector. Introduced 1983. From Dixie Gun Works.
Price: $215.50

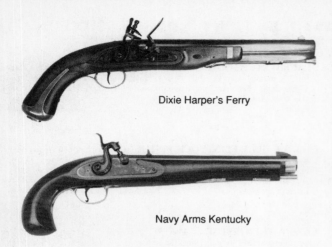

Dixie Harper's Ferry

Navy Arms Kentucky

KENTUCKY PERCUSSION PISTOL Similar to flint version but percussion lock. Imported by The Armoury, E.M.F., Navy Arms, CVA (50-cal.).
Price: . . . . **$141.95 to $250.00**
Price: Brass barrel (E.M.F.) **$275.00**
Price: Steel barrel (Armoury) **$179.00**
Price: Single cased set (Navy Arms) **$300.00**
Price: Double cased set (Navy Arms) **$515.00**

Lyman Plains Pistol

CHARLES MOORE FLINTLOCK PISTOL Caliber: 45. Barrel: 10", octagonal. Weight: 36 oz. Length: 15" overall. Stock: Checkered hardwood. Sights: Blade front, fixed notch rear. Features: German silver trigger guard, rest blued. Imported from Italy by E.M.F.
Price: **$400.00**

Pedersoli Mang

PEDERSOLI MANG TARGET PISTOL Caliber: 38. Barrel: 10.5", octagonal; 1:15" twist, Weight: 2.5 lbs. Length: 17.25" overall. Stock: Walnut with fluted grip. Sights: Blade front, open rear adjustable for windage. Features: Browned barrel, polished breech plug, rest color case-hardened. Imported from Italy by Dixie Gun Works.
Price: **$595.00**

Dixie Queen Anne

HARPER'S FERRY 1806 PISTOL Caliber: 58 (.570" round ball). Barrel: 10". Weight: 40 oz. Length: 16" overall. Stock: Walnut. Sights: Fixed. Features: Case-hardened lock, brass-mounted browned barrel. Replica of the first U.S. Gov't.-made flintlock pistol. Imported by Navy Arms, Dixie Gun Works, E.M.F.
Price: . . . . **$249.95 to $405.00**
Price: Kit (Dixie) **$184.95**

HAWKEN PERCUSSION PISTOL Caliber: 54. Barrel: 9", octagonal. Weight: 40 oz. Length: 14" overall. Stock: Checkered walnut. Sights: Blade front, fixed notch rear. Features: German silver trigger guard, blued barrel. Imported from Italy by E.M.F.
Price: **$370.00**

KENTUCKY FLINTLOCK PISTOL Caliber: 44, 45. Barrel: 10⅛". Weight: 32 oz. Length: 15½" overall. Stock: Walnut. Sights: Fixed. Features: Specifications, including caliber, weight and length may vary with importer. Case-hardened lock, blued barrel; available also as brass barrel flint Model 1821. Imported by Navy Arms (44 only), The Armoury, E.M.F.
Price: . . . . **$145.00 to $207.00**
Price: Brass barrel (E.M.F.) **$265.00**
Price: In kit form, from . . . . **$90.00 to $112.00**
Price: Single cased set (Navy Arms) **$300.00**
Price: Double cased set (Navy Arms) **$515.00**

Consult our Directory pages for the location of firms mentioned.

LE PAGE PERCUSSION DUELING PISTOL Caliber: 45. Barrel: 10", rifled. Weight: 40 oz. Length: 16" overall. Stock: Walnut, fluted butt. Sights: Blade front, notch rear. Features: Double-set triggers. Blued barrel; trigger guard and buttcap are polished silver. Imported by Dixie Gun Works, E.M.F.
Price: . . . . **$259.95 to $400.00**

LYMAN PLAINS PISTOL Caliber: 50 or 54. Barrel: 8", 1:30 twist, both calibers. Weight: 50 oz. Length: 15" overall. Stock: Walnut half-stock. Sights: Blade front, square notch rear adjustable for windage. Features: Polished brass trigger guard and ramrod tip, color case-hardened coil spring lock, spring-loaded trigger, stainless steel nipple, blackened iron furniture. Hooked patent breech, detachable belt hook. Introduced 1981. From Lyman Products.
Price: Finished **$219.95**
Price: Kit **$179.95**

MOORE & PATRICK FLINT DUELING PISTOL Caliber: 45. Barrel: 10", rifled. Weight: 32 oz. Length: 14½" overall. Stock: European walnut, checkered. Sights: Fixed. Features: Engraved, silvered lockplate, blue barrel. German silver furniture. Imported from Italy by Dixie Gun Works.
Price: **$335.00**

NAVY ARMS LE PAGE DUELING PISTOL Caliber: 44. Barrel: 9", octagon, rifled. Weight: 34 oz. Length: 15" overall. Stock: European walnut. Sights: Adjustable rear. Features: Single-set trigger. Polished metal finish. From Navy Arms.
Price: Percussion **$475.00**
Price: Single cased set, percussion **$685.00**
Price: Double cased set, percussion **$1,290.00**
Price: Flintlock, rifled **$550.00**
Price: Flintlock, smoothbore (45-cal.) **$550.00**
Price: Flintlock, single cased set **$760.00**
Price: Flintlock, double cased set **$1,430.00**

W. PARKER FLINTLOCK PISTOL Caliber: 45. Barrel: 11", rifled. Weight: 40 oz. Length: 16½" overall. Stock: Walnut. Sights: Blade front, notch rear. Features: Browned barrel, silver-plated trigger guard, finger rest, polished and engraved lock. Double-set triggers. Imported by Dixie Gun Works.
Price: **$310.00**

QUEEN ANNE FLINTLOCK PISTOL Caliber: 50 (.490" round ball). Barrel: 7½", smoothbore. Stock: Walnut. Sights: None. Features: Browned steel barrel, fluted brass trigger guard, brass mask on butt. Lockplate left in the white. Made by Pedersoli in Italy. Introduced 1983. Imported by Dixie Gun Works.
Price: **$189.95**
Price: Kit **$138.50**

BLACKPOWDER SINGLE SHOT PISTOLS—FLINT & PERCUSSION

THOMPSON/CENTER SCOUT PISTOL **Caliber:** 45, 50 and 54. **Barrel:** 12", interchangeable. **Weight:** 4 lbs., 6 oz. **Length:** NA. **Stocks:** American black walnut stocks and forend. **Sights:** Blade on ramp front, fully adjustable Patridge rear. **Features:** Patented in-line ignition system with special vented breech plug. Patented trigger mechanism consists of only two moving parts. Interchangeable barrels. Wide grooved hammer. Brass trigger guard assembly. Introduced 1990. From Thompson/Center.
Price: 45-, 50- or 54-cal. **$315.00**
Price: Extra barrel, 45-, 50- or 54-cal. **$140.00**

TRADITIONS BUCKSKINNER PISTOL **Caliber:** 50. **Barrel:** 10" octagonal, $^{15}/_{16}$" flats. **Weight:** 40 oz. **Length:** 15" overall. **Stocks:** Stained beech or laminated wood. **Sights:** Blade front, rear adjustable for windage. **Features:** Percussion ignition. Blackened furniture. Imported by Traditions, Inc.
Price: Beech stocks **$157.00**
Price: Laminated stocks **$182.00**

Traditions Pioneer

TRADITIONS WILLIAM PARKER PISTOL **Caliber:** 45 and 50. **Barrel:** $10^{3}/_{8}$", $^{15}/_{16}$" flats; polished steel. **Weight:** 40 oz. **Length:** $17^{1}/_{2}$" overall. **Stock:** Walnut with checkered grip. **Sights:** Brass blade front, fixed rear. **Features:** Replica dueling pistol with 1:18" twist, hooked breech. Brass wedge plate, trigger guard, cap guard; separate ramrod. Double-set triggers. Polished steel barrel, lock. Imported by Traditions, Inc.
Price: **$265.00**

Thompson/Center Scout

TRADITIONS PHILADELPHIA DERRINGER **Caliber:** 45. **Barrel:** $3^{1}/_{4}$" octagonal, $^{7}/_{8}$" flats. **Weight:** 16 oz. **Length:** $7^{1}/_{8}$" overall. **Stock:** Stained beech. **Sights:** Blade front. **Features:** Color case-hardened percussion lock has coil mainspring. Brass furniture, engraved wedge plate. Imported by Traditions, Inc.
Price: **$109.00**
Price: Kit **$82.00**

TRADITIONS PIONEER PISTOL **Caliber:** 45. **Barrel:** $9^{5}/_{8}$", $^{13}/_{16}$" flats. **Weight:** 36 oz. **Length:** 15" overall. **Stock:** Beech. **Sights:** Blade front, fixed rear. **Features:** V-type mainspring; 1:18" twist. Single trigger. German silver furniture, blackened hardware. From Traditions, Inc.
Price: **$169.00**
Price: Kit **$119.00**

TRADITIONS TRAPPER PISTOL **Caliber:** 50. **Barrel:** $9^{3}/_{4}$", $^{7}/_{8}$" flats. **Weight:** $2^{3}/_{4}$ lbs. **Length:** 16" overall. **Stock:** Beech. **Sights:** Blade front, adjustable rear. **Features:** Double-set triggers; brass buttcap, trigger guard, wedge plate, forend tip, thimble. From Traditions, Inc.
Price: **$170.00**
Price: Kit **$130.00**

TRADITIONS VEST POCKET DERRINGER **Caliber:** 31. **Barrel:** $2^{1}/_{2}$", round. **Weight:** 16 oz. **Length:** 5" overall. **Stocks:** White composite. **Sights:** Post front. **Features:** Polished brass barrel and frame, blued trigger and screws. Imported by Traditions, Inc.
Price: **$75.00**

BLACKPOWDER REVOLVERS

Army 1851

ARMY 1851 PERCUSSION REVOLVER **Caliber:** 44, 6-shot. **Barrel:** $7^{1}/_{2}$". **Weight:** 45 oz. **Length:** 13" overall. **Stocks:** Walnut finish. **Sights:** Fixed. **Features:** 44-caliber version of the 1851 Navy. Imported by The Armoury, Armsport.
Price: **$129.00**

American Arms 1860

ARMY 1860 PERCUSSION REVOLVER **Caliber:** 44, 6-shot. **Barrel:** 8". **Weight:** 40 oz. **Length:** $13^{5}/_{8}$" overall. **Stocks:** Walnut. **Sights:** Fixed. **Features:** Engraved Navy scene on cylinder; brass trigger guard; case-hardened frame, loading lever and hammer. Some importers supply pistol cut for detachable shoulder stock, have accessory stock available. Imported by American Arms, Cabela's, E.M.F., Navy Arms, The Armoury, Cimarron, Dixie Gun Works (half-fluted cylinder, not roll engraved), Euroarms of America (brass or steel model), Armsport, Mitchell, Traditions, Inc. (brass or steel), Uberti USA.
Price: About . . . . **$92.95 to $300.00**
Price: Single cased set (Navy Arms) **$265.00**
Price: Double cased set (Navy Arms) **$430.00**
Price: 1861 Navy: Same as Army except 36-cal., $7^{1}/_{2}$" bbl., wgt. 41 oz., cut for shoulder stock; round cylinder (fluted avail.), from E.M.F., CVA (brass frame, 44-cal.), Cabela's, Mitchell . . . . **$99.95 to $249.00**
Price: Steel frame kit (E.M.F., Mitchell, Navy, Euroarms) . . . **$125.00 to $187.00**
Price: Colt Army Police, fluted cyl., $5^{1}/_{2}$", 36-cal. (Cabela's) . . . **$96.95**

BABY DRAGOON 1848, 1849 POCKET, WELLS FARGO **Caliber:** 31. **Barrel:** 3", 4", 5", 6"; seven-groove, RH twist. **Weight:** About 21 oz. **Stock:** Varnished walnut. **Sights:** Brass pin front, hammer notch rear. **Features:** No loading lever on Baby Dragoon or Wells Fargo models. Unfluted cylinder with stagecoach holdup scene; cupped cylinder pin; no grease grooves; one safety pin on cylinder and slot in hammer face; straight (flat) mainspring. From Armsport, Dixie Gun Works, Uberti USA, Cabela's.
Price: 6" barrel, with loading lever (Dixie Gun Works) **$185.00**
Price: 4" (Uberti USA) **$295.00**

CABELA'S PATERSON REVOLVER **Caliber:** 36, 5-shot cylinder. **Barrel:** $7^{1}/_{2}$". **Weight:** 24 oz. **Length:** $11^{1}/_{2}$" overall. **Stocks:** One-piece walnut. **Sights:** Fixed. **Features:** Recreation of the 1836 gun. Color case-hardened frame, steel backstrap; roll-engraved cylinder scene. Imported by Cabela's.
Price: **$199.95**

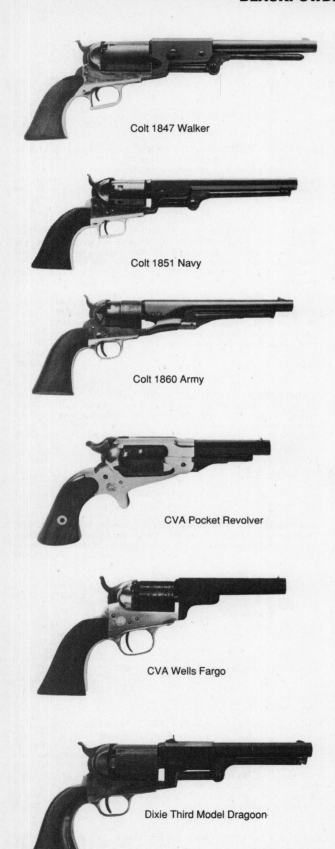

Colt 1847 Walker

Colt 1851 Navy

Colt 1860 Army

CVA Pocket Revolver

CVA Wells Fargo

Dixie Third Model Dragoon

COLT 1847 WALKER PERCUSSION REVOLVER **Caliber:** 44. **Barrel:** 9", 7 groove, right-hand twist. **Weight:** 73 oz. **Stocks:** One-piece walnut. **Sights:** German silver front sight, hammer notch rear. **Features:** Made in U.S. Faithful reproduction of the original gun, including markings. Color case-hardened frame, hammer, loading lever and plunger. Blue steel backstrap, brass square-back trigger guard. Blue barrel, cylinder, trigger and wedge. From Colt Blackpowder Arms Co.
Price: **$395.00**

COLT 1849 POCKET DRAGOON REVOLVER **Caliber:** 31. **Barrel:** 4". **Weight:** 24 oz. **Length:** 9½" overall. **Stocks:** One-piece walnut. **Sights:** Fixed. Brass pin front, hammer notch rear. **Features:** Color case-hardened frame. No loading lever. Unfluted cylinder with engraved scene. Exact reproduction of original. From Colt Blackpowder Arms Co.
Price: **$360.00**

COLT 1851 NAVY PERCUSSION REVOLVER **Caliber:** 36. **Barrel:** 7½", octagonal, 7 groove left-hand twist. **Weight:** 40½ oz. **Stocks:** One-piece oiled American walnut. **Sights:** Brass pin front, hammer notch rear. **Features:** Faithful reproduction of the original gun. Color case-hardened frame, loading lever, plunger, hammer and latch. Blue cylinder, trigger, barrel, screws, wedge. Silver-plated brass backstrap and square-back trigger guard. From Colt Blackpowder Arms Co.
Price: **$395.00**

COLT 1860 ARMY PERCUSSION REVOLVER **Caliber:** 44. **Barrel:** 8", 7 groove, left-hand twist. **Weight:** 42 oz. **Stocks:** One-piece walnut. **Sights:** German silver front sight, hammer notch rear. **Features:** Steel backstrap cut for shoulder stock; brass trigger guard. Cylinder has Navy scene. Color case-hardened frame, hammer, loading lever. Reproduction of original gun with all original markings. From Colt Blackpowder Arms Co.
Price: **$395.00**

CVA POCKET REVOLVER **Caliber:** 31. **Barrel:** 4", octagonal. **Weight:** 15½ oz. **Length:** 7½" overall. **Stocks:** Two-piece walnut. **Sights:** Post front, grooved topstrap rear. **Features:** Spur trigger, brass frame with blued barrel and cylinder. Introduced 1984. Imported by CVA.
Price: Finished **$129.95**

CVA WELLS FARGO MODEL **Caliber:** 31. **Barrel:** 4", octagonal. **Weight:** 28 oz. (with extra cylinder). **Length:** 9" overall. **Stocks:** Walnut. **Sights:** Post front, hammer notch rear. **Features:** Brass frame and backstrap; blue finish. Comes with extra cylinder. Imported by CVA.
Price: Brass frame, finished **$129.95**

DIXIE THIRD MODEL DRAGOON **Caliber:** 44 (.454" round ball). **Barrel:** 7⅜". **Weight:** 4 lbs., 2½ oz. **Stocks:** One-piece walnut. **Sights:** Brass pin front, hammer notch rear, or adjustable folding leaf rear. **Features:** Cylinder engraved with Indian fight scene. This is the only Dragoon replica with folding leaf sight. Brass backstrap and trigger guard; color case-hardened steel frame, blue-black barrel. Imported by Dixie Gun Works.
Price: **$149.95**

CVA Third Model Dragoon Similar to the Dixie Third Dragoon except has 7½" barrel, weighs 4 lbs., 6 oz., blade front sight. Overall length of 14". 44-caliber, 6-shot.
Price: **$279.95**

DIXIE WYATT EARP REVOLVER **Caliber:** 44. **Barrel:** 12" octagon. **Weight:** 46 oz. **Length:** 18" overall. **Stocks:** Two-piece walnut. **Sights:** Fixed. **Features:** Highly polished brass frame, backstrap and trigger guard; blued barrel and cylinder; case-hardened hammer, trigger and loading lever. Navy-size shoulder stock ($45) will fit with minor fitting. From Dixie Gun Works.
Price: **$130.00**

GRISWOLD & GUNNISON PERCUSSION REVOLVER **Caliber:** 36 or 44, 6-shot. **Barrel:** 7½". **Weight:** 44 oz. (36-cal.). **Length:** 13" overall. **Stocks:** Walnut. **Sights:** Fixed. **Features:** Replica of famous Confederate pistol. Brass frame, backstrap and trigger guard; case-hardened loading lever; rebated cylinder (44-cal. only). Rounded Dragoon-type barrel. Imported by Navy Arms (as Reb Model 1860), E.M.F.
Price: About **$229.00**
Price: Single cased set (Navy Arms) **$205.00**
Price: Double cased set (Navy Arms) **$335.00**
Price: Reb 1860 (Navy Arms) **$110.00**
Price: As above, kit **$90.00**

BLACKPOWDER REVOLVERS

LE MAT CAVALRY MODEL REVOLVER **Caliber:** 44/65. **Barrel:** 6¾" (revolver); 4⅞" (single shot). **Weight:** 3 lbs., 7 oz. **Stocks:** Hand-checkered walnut. **Sights:** Post front, hammer notch rear. **Features:** Exact reproduction with all-steel construction; 44-cal. 9-shot cylinder, 65-cal. single barrel; color case-hardened hammer with selector; spur trigger guard; ring at butt; lever-type barrel release. From Navy Arms.
Price: Cavalry model (lanyard ring, spur trigger guard) $595.00
Price: Army model (round trigger guard, pin-type barrel release) $595.00
Price: Naval-style (thumb selector on hammer) $595.00

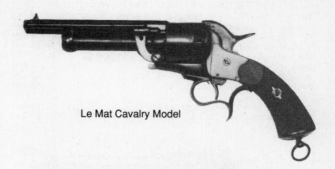

Le Mat Cavalry Model

Uberti 1851 Squareback

Uberti 1861 Navy Percussion Revolver Similar to 1851 Navy except has round 7½" barrel, rounded trigger guard, German silver blade front sight, "creeping" loading lever. Available with fluted or round cylinder. Imported by Uberti USA.
Price: Steel backstrap, trigger guard, cut for stock $300.00

CVA Colt Sheriff's Model Similar to the Uberti 1861 Navy except has 5½" barrel, brass or steel frame, semi-fluted cylinder. In 36-caliber only.
Price: Brass frame, finished $157.95
Price: As above, brass frame, 44-cal. $139.95
Price: As above, kit $129.95
Price: Brass frame (Armsport) $155.00
Price: Steel frame (Armsport) $193.00

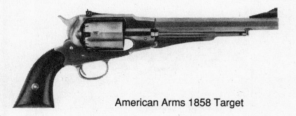

American Arms 1858 Target

Consult our Directory pages for the location of firms mentioned.

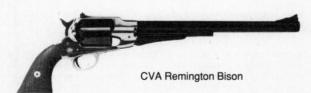

CVA Remington Bison

POCKET POLICE 1862 PERCUSSION REVOLVER **Caliber:** 36, 5-shot. **Barrel:** 4½", 5½", 6½", 7½". **Weight:** 26 oz. **Length:** 12" overall (6½" bbl.). **Stocks:** Walnut. **Sights:** Fixed. **Features:** Round tapered barrel; half-fluted and rebated cylinder; case-hardened frame, loading lever and hammer; silver or brass trigger guard and backstrap. Imported by CVA (7½" only), Navy Arms (5½" only), Uberti USA (5½" only, 6½" only).
Price: About . . . . $143.95 to $310.00
Price: Single cased set with accessories (Navy Arms) $360.00

NAVY MODEL 1851 PERCUSSION REVOLVER **Caliber:** 36, 44, 6-shot. **Barrel:** 7½". **Weight:** 44 oz. **Length:** 13" overall. **Stocks:** Walnut finish. **Sights:** Post front, hammer notch rear. **Features:** Brass backstrap and trigger guard; some have 1st Model squareback trigger guard, engraved cylinder with navy battle scene; case-hardened frame, hammer, loading lever. Imported by American Arms, The Armoury, Cabela's, Mitchell, Navy Arms, E.M.F., Dixie Gun Works, Euroarms of America, Armsport, CVA (36-cal. only), Traditions, Inc., Uberti USA.
Price: Brass frame . . . . $125.00 to $280.00
Price: Steel frame . . . . $130.00 to $285.00
Price: Kit form . . . . $110.00 to $123.95
Price: Engraved model (Dixie Gun Works) $139.95
Price: Single cased set, steel frame (Navy Arms) $245.00
Price: Double cased set, steel frame (Navy Arms) $405.00
Price: Confederate Navy (Cabela's) $69.95

NAVY ARMS DELUXE 1858 REMINGTON-STYLE REVOLVER **Caliber:** 44. **Barrel:** 8". **Weight:** 2 lbs., 13 oz. **Stocks:** Smooth walnut. **Sights:** Dovetailed blade front. **Features:** First exact reproduction—correct in size and weight to the original, with progressive rifling; highly polished with blue finish, silver-plated trigger guard. From Navy Arms.
Price: Deluxe model $365.00

NEW MODEL 1858 ARMY PERCUSSION REVOLVER **Caliber:** 36 or 44, 6-shot. **Barrel:** 6½" or 8". **Weight:** 40 oz. **Length:** 13½" overall. **Stocks:** Walnut. **Sights:** Blade front, groove-in-frame rear. **Features:** Replica of Remington Model 1858. Also available from some importers as Army Model Belt Revolver in 36-cal., a shortened and lightened version of the 44. Target Model (Uberti USA, Navy Arms) has fully adjustable target rear sight, target front, 36 or 44. Imported by American Arms, Cabela's, CVA (as 1858 Army), Dixie Gun Works, Navy Arms, The Armoury, E.M.F., Euroarms of America (engraved, stainless and plain), Armsport, Mitchell, Traditions, Inc., Uberti USA.
Price: Steel frame, about . . . . $99.95 to $280.00
Price: Steel frame kit (Euroarms, Navy Arms) . . . . . . $115.95 to $150.00
Price: Single cased set (Navy Arms) $255.00
Price: Double cased set (Navy Arms) $420.00
Price: Stainless steel Model 1858 (American Arms, Euroarms, Uberti USA, Cabela's, Navy Arms, Armsport, Traditions) . . . . $169.95 to $380.00
Price: Target Model, adjustable rear sight (Cabela's, Euroarms, Uberti USA, Navy Arms, E.M.F.) . . . . $95.95 to $399.00
Price: Brass frame (CVA, Cabela's, Traditions, Navy Arms) . . $79.95 to $212.95
Price: As above, kit (CVA, Dixie Gun Works, Navy Arms) . $145.00 to $188.95
Price: Remington "Texas" (Mitchell) $199.00
Price: Buffalo model, 44-cal. (Cabela's) $109.95
Price: Lawman model, 44-cal. (Cabela's) $159.95
Price: Police model, 36-cal. (Cabela's) $99.95
Price: Old Silver model, 44-cal. (Cabela's) $199.95

CVA 1858 Target Revolver Similar to the New Model 1858 Army revolver except has ramp-mounted blade front sight on 8" barrel, adjustable rear sight, overall blue finish. Imported by CVA.
Price: $239.95

CVA Bison Revolver Similar to the CVA 1858 Target except has 10¼" octagonal barrel, 44-caliber, brass frame.
Price: Finished $247.95
Price: From Armsport $222.00

ROGERS & SPENCER PERCUSSION REVOLVER **Caliber:** 44. **Barrel:** 7½". **Weight:** 47 oz. **Length:** 13¾" overall. **Stocks:** Walnut. **Sights:** Cone front, integral groove in frame for rear. **Features:** Accurate reproduction of a Civil War design. Solid frame; extra large nipple cut-out on rear of cylinder; loading lever and cylinder easily removed for cleaning. From Euroarms of America (standard blue, engraved, burnished, target models), Navy Arms.
Price: . . . . $160.00 to $240.00
Price: Nickel-plated $215.00
Price: Engraved (Euroarms) $286.00
Price: Kit version $95.00
Price: Target version (Euroarms, Navy Arms) $260.00
Price: Burnished London Gray (Euroarms, Navy Arms) $260.00

Euroarms Rogers & Spencer

Ruger Old Army

RUGER OLD ARMY PERCUSSION REVOLVER **Caliber:** 45, 6-shot. Uses .457" dia. lead bullets. **Barrel:** 7½" (6-groove, 16" twist). **Weight:** 46 oz. **Length:** 13¾" overall. **Stocks:** Smooth walnut. **Sights:** Ramp front, rear adjustable for windage and elevation. **Features:** Stainless steel; standard size nipples, chrome-moly steel cylinder and frame, same lockwork as in original Super Blackhawk. Also available in stainless steel. Made in USA. From Sturm, Ruger & Co.
Price: Stainless steel (Model KBP-7) $428.00
Price: Blued steel (Model BP-7) $378.50

TEXAS PATERSON 1836 REVOLVER **Caliber:** 36 (.376" round ball). **Barrel:** 7½". **Weight:** 42 oz. **Stocks:** One-piece walnut. **Sights:** Fixed. **Features:** Copy of Sam Colt's first commercially-made revolving pistol. Has no loading lever but comes with loading tool. From Dixie Gun Works, Navy Arms, Uberti USA.
Price: About . . . . $335.00 to $395.00
Price: With loading lever (Uberti USA) $450.00
Price: Engraved (Navy Arms) $465.00

Texas Paterson

SPILLER & BURR REVOLVER **Caliber:** 36 (.375" round ball). **Barrel:** 7", octagon. **Weight:** 2½ lbs. **Length:** 12½" overall. **Stocks:** Two-piece walnut. **Sights:** Fixed. **Features:** Reproduction of the C.S.A. revolver. Brass frame and trigger guard. Also available as a kit. From Dixie Gun Works, Mitchell, Navy Arms.
Price: . . . . $89.95 to $199.00
Price: Kit form $95.00
Price: Single cased set (Navy Arms) $230.00
Price: Double cased set (Navy Arms) $370.00

UBERTI 1862 POCKET NAVY PERCUSSION REVOLVER **Caliber:** 36, 5-shot. **Barrel:** 5½", 6½", octagonal, 7-groove, LH twist. **Weight:** 27 oz. (5½" barrel). **Length:** 10½" overall (5½" bbl.). **Stocks:** One-piece varnished walnut. **Sights:** Brass pin front, hammer notch rear. **Features:** Rebated cylinder, hinged loading lever, brass or silver-plated backstrap and trigger guard, color-cased frame, hammer, loading lever, plunger and latch, rest blued. Has original-type markings. From Uberti USA.
Price: With brass backstrap, trigger guard $310.00

UBERTI 1st MODEL DRAGOON **Caliber:** 44. **Barrel:** 7½", part round, part octagon. **Weight:** 64 oz. **Stocks:** One-piece walnut. **Sights:** German silver blade front, hammer notch rear. **Features:** First model has oval bolt cuts in cylinder, square-back flared trigger guard, V-type mainspring, short trigger. Ranger and Indian scene roll-engraved on cylinder. Color case-hardened frame, loading lever, plunger and hammer; blue barrel, cylinder, trigger and wedge. Available with old-time charcoal blue or standard blue-black finish. Polished brass backstrap and trigger guard. From Uberti USA.
Price: $325.00

Uberti 2nd Model Dragoon Revolver Similar to the 1st Model except distinguished by rectangular bolt cuts in the cylinder.
Price: $325.00

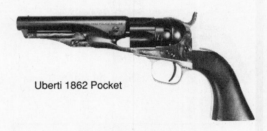
Uberti 1862 Pocket

Uberti 3rd Model Dragoon Revolver Similar to the 2nd Model except for oval trigger guard, long trigger, modifications to the loading lever and latch. Imported by Uberti USA.
Price: Military model (frame cut for shoulder stock, steel backstrap) . . . $330.00
Price: Civilian (brass backstrap, trigger guard) $325.00

SHERIFF MODEL 1851 PERCUSSION REVOLVER **Caliber:** 36, 44, 6-shot. **Barrel:** 5". **Weight:** 40 oz. **Length:** 10½" overall. **Stocks:** Walnut. **Sights:** Fixed. **Features:** Brass backstrap and trigger guard; engraved navy scene; case-hardened frame, hammer, loading lever. Imported by E.M.F.
Price: Steel frame $172.00
Price: Brass frame $140.00

WALKER 1847 PERCUSSION REVOLVER **Caliber:** 44, 6-shot. **Barrel:** 9". **Weight:** 84 oz. **Length:** 15½" overall. **Stocks:** Walnut. **Sights:** Fixed. **Features:** Case-hardened frame, loading lever and hammer; iron backstrap; brass trigger guard; engraved cylinder. Imported by American Arms, Cabela's, CVA, Navy Arms, Dixie Gun Works, Uberti USA, E.M.F., Cimarron, Traditions, Inc.
Price: About . . . . $225.00 to $360.00
Price: Single cased set (Navy Arms) $385.00

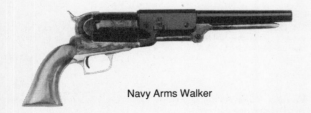
Navy Arms Walker

PERIODICAL PUBLICATIONS

Action Pursuit Games Magazine (M)
CFW Enterprises, Inc., 4201 W. Vanowen Pl., Burbank, CA 91505. $2.95 single copy U.S., $3.50 Canada. Editor: Randy Kamiya, 818-845-2656. World's leading magazine of paintball sports.

Airgun World
10 Sheet St., Windsor, Berks., SL4 1BG, England. £19.20 (£26.00 overseas) for 12 issues. Monthly magazine catering exclusively to the airgun enthusiast.

Alaska Magazine
Alaska Publishing Properties Inc., 808 E St., Suite 200, Anchorage, AK 99501. $26.00 yr. Hunting, Fishing and Life on the Last Frontier articles of Alaska and western Canada. Outdoors Editor, Ken Marsh.

American Airgunner (Q)
P.O. Box 1459, Abilene, TX 79604-1459. $15 yr. Anything and everything about airguns.

American Firearms Industry
Nat'l. Assn. of Federally Licensed Firearms Dealers, 2455 E. Sunrise Blvd., Ft. Lauderdale, FL 33304. $25.00 yr. For firearms retailers, distributors and manufacturers.

American Handgunner*
591 Camino de la Reina, Suite 200, San Diego, CA 92108. $16.75 yr. Articles for handgun enthusiasts, competitors, police and hunters.

American Hunter (M)
National Rifle Assn., 1600 Rhode Island Ave., NW, Washington, DC 20036. Publications Div., 470 Spring Park Pl., Suite 1000, Herndon, VA 22070. $25.00 yr. Wide scope of hunting articles.

American Survival Guide
McMullen and Yee Publishing, Inc., 774 S. Placentia Ave., Placentia, CA 92670-6846. 12 issues $26.95/714-572-2255; FAX: 714-572-1864.

American West*
American West Management Corp., 7000 E. Tanque Verde Rd., Suite #30, Tucson, AZ 85715. $15.00 yr.

Arms Collecting (Q)
Museum Restoration Service, P.O. Drawer 390, Bloomfield, Ont., Canada K0K 1G0 and P.O. Box 70, Alexandria Bay, NY 13607. $15.00 yr.; $41.50 3 yrs.; $75.00 5 yrs.

Australian Shooters' Journal
Sporting Shooter's Assn. of Australia, P.O. Box 2066, Kent Town SA 5071, Australia. $40.00 yr. locally; $50.00 yr. overseas surface mail only. Hunting and shooting articles.

The Backwoodsman Magazine
P.O. Box 627, Westcliffe, CO 81252. $14.00 for 6 issues per yr.; $26.00 for 2 yrs.; sample copy $2.50. Subjects include muzzle-loading, woodslore, primitive survival, trapping, homesteading, blackpowder cartridge guns, 19th century how-to.

Black Powder Times
P.O. Box 842, Mount Vernon, WA 98273. $15.00 yr.; add $2 per year for Canada, $5 per year other foreign. Tabloid newspaper for blackpowder activities; test reports.

The Caller (Q) (M)
National Wild Turkey Federation, P.O. Box 530, Edgefield, SC 29824. Tabloid newspaper for members; 4 issues per yr.

The Cast Bullet*(M)
Official journal of The Cast Bullet Assn. Director of Membership, 4103 Foxcraft Dr., Traverse City, MI 49684. Annual membership dues $14, includes 6 issues.

Combat Handguns*
Harris Publications, Inc., 1115 Broadway, New York, NY 10010. Single copy $2.95 U.S.A.; $3.25 Canada.

The Derringer Peanut (M)
The National Association of Derringer Collectors, P.O. Box 160671, San Antonio, TX 78280-2871. A newsletter dedicated to developing the best derringer information. Write for details.

Deutsches Waffen Journal
Journal-Verlag Schwend GmbH, Postfach 100340, D7170 Schwäbisch Hall, Germany/0791-404-500; FAX:0791-404-505. DM97.10 yr. (interior); DM114.60 (abroad), postage included. Antique and modern arms and equipment. German text.

The Engraver (M) (Q)
P.O. Box 4365, Estes Park, CO 80517. Mike Dubber, editor. The journal of firearms engraving.

The Field
6 Sheet Street, Windsor, Berkshire, SL4 1BG, England. £35.00 sterling U.S. (approx. $70.00) yr. Hunting and shooting articles, and all country sports.

Field & Stream
Times Mirror Magazines, Two Park Ave., New York, NY 10016. $11.94 yr. Articles on hunting and fishing.

FIRE
Euro-Editions, Boulevard Du Triomphe 132, B1160 Brussels, Belgium. Belg. Franc 1500 for 6 issues. Arms, shooting, ammunition. French text.

Fur-Fish-Game
A.R. Harding Pub. Co., 2878 E. Main St., Columbus, OH 43209. $15.95 yr. "Gun Rack" column by Don Zutz.

Gray's Sporting Journal
Gray's Sporting Journal, Inc., P.O. Box 1207, Augusta, GA 30903. $34.95 per yr. for 6 consecutive issues. Hunting and fishing journals.

Gun List
700 E. State St., Iola, WI 54990. $24.95 yr. (26 issues); $46.50 2 yrs. (52 issues). Indexed market publication for firearms collectors and active shooters; guns, supplies and services.

The Gun Report
World Wide Gun Report, Inc., Box 38, Aledo, IL 61231-0038. $29.95 yr. For the antique and collectable gun dealer and collector.

Gunmaker (M)†
ACGG, P.O. Box 812, Burlington, IA 52601-0812. The journal of custom gunmaking.

The Gunrunner
Div. of Kexco Publ. Co. Ltd., Box 565G, Lethbridge, Alb., Canada T1J 3Z4. $23.00 yr. Monthly newspaper, listing everything from antiques to artillery.

Gun Show Calendar (Q)
700 E. State St., Iola, WI 54990. $12.95 yr. (4 issues). Gun shows listed chronologically by date, and alphabetically by state.

Gun Tests
11 Commerce Blvd., Palm Coast, FL 32142. The consumer resource for the serious shooter. Write for information.

Gun Week†
Second Amendment Foundation, P.O. Box 488, Station C, Buffalo, NY 14209. $32.00 yr. U.S. and possessions; $40.00 yr. other countries. Tabloid paper on guns, hunting, shooting and collecting.

Gun World
Gallant/Charger Publications, Inc., 34249 Camino Capistrano, Capistrano Beach, CA 92624. $20.00 yr. For the hunting, reloading and shooting enthusiast.

Guns & Ammo
Petersen Publishing Co., 6420 Wilshire Blvd., Los Angeles, CA 90048. $21.94 yr. Guns, shooting, and technical articles.

Guns
Guns Magazine, P.O. Box 85201, San Diego, CA 92138. $19.95 yr. In-depth articles on a wide range of guns, shooting equipment and related accessories for gun collectors, hunters and shooters.

Guns Review
Ravenhill Publishing Co. Ltd., Box 35, Standard House, Bonhill St., London EC 2A 4DA, England. £20.00 sterling (approx. U.S. $38 USA & Canada) yr. For collectors and shooters.

Handgunning (Q)
PJS Publications, News Plaza, P.O. Box 1790, Peoria, IL 61656. Cover price $3.95; subscriptions $19.95 for 6 issues. Various recreational uses of handguns; hunting, silhouette, practical pistol and target shooting.

Handloader*
Wolfe Publishing Co., 6471 Airpark Dr., Prescott, AZ 86301. $19.00 yr. The journal of ammunition reloading.

HUNT Magazine*
TimberLine-B, Inc., P.O. Box 58069, Renton, WA 98058. $19.97 yr.; Canadian and foreign countries add U.S. $12 for postage. Geared to the serious hunter, with action hunting articles.

Hunting Horizons
Wolfe Publishing Co., 6471 Airpark Dr., Prescott, AZ 86301. $34.00 yr. Dedicated to the finest pursuit of the hunt.

The Insider Gun News
The Gunpress Publishing Co., 1347 Webster St. NE, Washington, DC 20017. Editor, John D. Aquilino. $50.00 yr. (12 issues). Newsletter by former NRA communications director.

INSIGHTS*
NRA, 1600 Rhode Island Ave., NW, Washington, DC 20036. Editor, John E. Robbins. $10.00 yr., which includes NRA junior membership; $10.00 for adult subscriptions (12 issues). Plenty of details for the young hunter and target shooter; emphasizes gun safety, marksmanship training, hunting skills.

International Shooting Sport*/UIT Journal
International Shooting Union (UIT), Bavariaring 21, D-8000 Munich 2, Fed. Rep. of Germany. Europe: (Deutsche Mark) DM44.00 yr.; outside Europe: DM50.00 yr. (air mail postage included.) For international sport shooting.

Internationales Waffen-Magazin
Habegger-Verlag Zürich, Postfach 9230 CH-8036 Zürich, Switzerland. SF 91.00 (approx. U.S. $61.00) surface mail for 10 issues. Modern and antique arms. German text; English summary of contents.

The Journal of the Arms & Armour Society (M)
E.J.B. Greenwood (Hon. Sec.), Field House, Upper Dicker, Hailsham, East Sussex, BN27 3PY, England. $20.00 yr. Articles for the historian and collector.

Journal of the Historical Breechloading Smallarms Assn.
Published annually. Imperial War Museum, Lambeth Road, London SE1 6HZ, England. $13.00 yr. Articles for the collector plus mailings of lecture transcripts, short articles on specific arms, reprints, newsletters, etc.; a surcharge is made for airmail.

Law and Order
Law and Order Magazine, 1000 Skokie Blvd., Wilmette, IL 60091. $20.00 yr. Articles for law enforcement professionals.

Machine Gun News
Lane Publishing, P.O. Box 759, Dept. GD, Hot Springs, AR 71902/501-623-4951. $29.95 yr.; $3.50 sample copy. The magazine for full-auto enthusiasts, full-auto news, how to solve functioning problems, machinegun shoots from around the country and free classifieds for subscribers.

Man At Arms*
P.O. Box 460, Lincoln, RI 02865. $24.00 yr., $46.00 2 yrs. plus $8.00 for foreign subscribers. The N.R.A. magazine of arms collecting-investing, with excellent articles for the collector of antique arms and militaria.

MAN/MAGNUM
S.A. Man (Pty) Ltd., P.O. Box 35204, Northway, Durban 4065, Republic of South Africa. SA Rand 78.00 for 12 issues. Africa's only publication on hunting, shooting, firearms, bushcraft, knives, etc.

Muzzle Blasts (M)
National Muzzle Loading Rifle Assn., P.O. Box 67, Friendship, IN 47021. $30.00 yr. annual membership. For the blackpowder shooter.

Muzzleloader Magazine*
Rebel Publishing Co., Inc., Dept. Gun, Route 5, Box 347-M, Texarkana, TX 75501. $14.00 U.S.; $17.00 U.S. for foreign subscribers a yr. The publication for blackpowder shooters.

National Defense (M)*
American Defense Preparedness Assn., Two Colonial Place, Suite 400, 2101 Wilson Blvd., Arlington, VA 22201-3061/703-522-1820; FAX: 703-522-1885. $35.00 yr. Articles on both military and civil defense field, including weapons, materials technology, management.

National Rifle Assn. Journal (British) (Q)
Natl. Rifle Assn. (BR.), Bisley Camp, Brookwood, Woking, Surrey, England. GU24, OPB. £15.50 Sterling including air postage.

National Wildlife*
Natl. Wildlife Fed., 1400 16th St. NW, Washington, DC 20036, $16.00 yr. (6 issues); International Wildlife, 6 issues, $16.00 yr. Both, $22.00 yr., includes all membership benefits. Write attn.: Membership Services Dept., for more information.

New Zealand GUNS*
Waitekauri Publishing, P.O. 45, Waikino 3060, New Zealand. $NZ90.00 (6 issues) yr. Covers the hunting and firearms scene in New Zealand.

PERIODICAL PUBLICATIONS

New Zealand Wildlife (Q)
New Zealand Deerstalkers Assoc., Inc., P.O. Box 6514, Wellington, N.Z. $30.00 (N.Z.). Hunting, shooting and firearms/game research articles.

North American Hunter* (M)
P.O. Box 3401, Minnetonka, MN 55343. $18.00 yr. (7 issues). Articles on all types of North American hunting.

Outdoor Life
Times Mirror Magazines, Two Park Ave., New York, NY 10016. Special 1-yr. subscription, $11.97. Extensive coverage of hunting and shooting. Shooting column by Jim Carmichel.

La Passion des Courteaux (Q)
Phenix Editions, 25 rue Mademoiselle, 75015 Paris, France. French text.

Petersen's HUNTING Magazine
Petersen Publishing Co., 8490 Sunset Blvd., Los Angeles, CA 90069. $19.94 yr.; Canada $29.34 yr.; foreign countries $29.94 yr. Hunting articles for all game; test reports.

Point Blank
Citizens Committee for the Right to Keep and Bear Arms (sent to contributors), Liberty Park, 12500 NE 10th Pl., Bellevue, WA 98005

POINTBLANK (M)
Natl. Firearms Assn., Box 4384 Stn. C, Calgary, AB T2T 5N2, Canada. Official publication of the NFA.

The Police Marksman*
6000 E. Shirley Lane, Montgomery, AL 36117. $17.95 yr. For law enforcement personnel.

Police Times (M)
Membership Records, 3801 Biscayne Blvd., Miami, FL 33137.

Popular Mechanics
Hearst Corp., 224 W. 57th St., New York, NY 10019. $15.94 yr. Firearms, camping, outdoor oriented articles.

Precision Shooting
Precision Shooting, Inc., 37 Burnham St., East Hartford, CT 06108. $25.00 yr. Journal of the International Benchrest Shooters, and target shooting in general. Also considerable coverage of varmint shooting, as well as big bore, small bore, schuetzen, lead bullet and wildcats.

Safari* (M)
Safari Magazine, 4800 W. Gates Pass Rd., Tucson, AZ 85745/602-620-1220. $30.00 (6 times). The journal of big game hunting, published by Safari Club International. Also publish *Safari Times*, a monthly newspaper, included in price of $30.00 field membership.

Second Amendment Reporter
Second Amendment Foundation, James Madison Bldg., 12500 NE 10th Pl., Bellevue, WA 98005. $15.00 yr. (non-contributors).

Shooting Industry
Publisher's Dev. Corp., 591 Camino de la Reina, Suite 200, San Diego, CA 92108. $50.00 yr. To the trade $25.00.

Shooting Sports Retailer*
SSR Publishing, Inc., P.O. Box 25, Cuba, NY 14727-0025/716-968-3858. 6 issues yr. Free to qualifying retailers, wholesalers, manufacturers, distributors; $30 annually for all other subscribers; $35 for foreign subscriptions; single copy $5.

Shooting Sports USA
National Rifle Assn. of America, 1600 Rhode Island Ave., NW, Washington, DC 20036. Annual subscriptions for NRA members are $5 for classified shooters and $10 for non-classified shooters. Non-NRA member subscriptions are $15. Covering events, techniques and personalities in competitive shooting.

The Shooting Times & Country Magazine (England)†
10 Sheet St., Windsor, Berkshire SL4 1BG, England. £65 (approx. $98.00) yr.;£79 yr. overseas (52 issues). Game shooting, wild fowling, hunting, game fishing and firearms articles. Britain's best selling field sports magazine.

Shooting Times
PJS Publications, News Plaza, P.O. Box 1790, Peoria, IL 61656. $19.98 yr. Guns, shooting, reloading; articles on every gun activity.

The Shotgun News‡
Snell Publishing Co., Box 669, Hastings, NE 68902. $20.00 yr.; all other countries $100.00 yr. Sample copy $3.00. Gun ads of all kinds.

SHOT Business
Flintlock Ridge Office Center, 11 Mile Hill Rd., Newtown, CT 06470-2359/203-426-1320; FAX: 203-426-1087. For the shooting, hunting and outdoor trade retailer.

The Sixgunner (M)
Handgun Hunters International, P.O. Box 357, MAG, Bloomingdale, OH 43910

Soldier of Fortune
Subscription Dept., P.O. Box 348, Mt. Morris, IL 61054. $24.95 yr.; $34.95 Canada; $45.95 foreign.

Sporting Goods Business
Miller Freeman, Inc., 1515 Broadway, New York, NY 10036. Trade journal.

Sporting Goods Dealer
Two Park Ave., New York, NY 10016. $100.00 yr. Sporting goods trade journal.

Sports Afield
The Hearst Corp., 250 W. 55th St., New York, NY 10019. $13.97 yr. Tom Gresham on firearms, ammunition; Grits Gresham on shooting and Thomas McIntyre on hunting.

The Squirrel Hunter
P.O. Box 368, Chireno, TX 75937. $14.00 yr. Articles about squirrel hunting.

TACARMI
Via E. De Amicis, 25; 20123 Milano, Italy. $120.00 yr. approx. Antique and modern guns. (Italian text.)

Turkey Call* (M)
Natl. Wild Turkey Federation, Inc., P.O. Box 530, Edgefield, SC 29824. $20.00 with membership (6 issues per yr.)

The U.S. Handgunner* (M)
U.S. Revolver Assn., 96 West Union St., Ashland, MA 01721. $8.00 yr. General handgun and competition articles. Bi-monthly sent to members.

U.S. Airgun Magazine
2603 Rollingbrook, Benton, AR 72015. Cover the sport from hunting, 10-meter, field target and collecting. Write for details.

The Varmint Hunter Magazine (Q)
The Varmint Hunters Assn., Box 730, Lone Grove, OK 73443/405-657-3098. $24.00 yr.

VDB-Aktuell (Q)
GFI-Verlag, Theodor-Heuss-Ring 62, 5000 Koln 1, Germany. For hunters, target shooters and outdoor people. (German text.)

Wild Sheep (M) (Q)
Foundation for North American Wild Sheep, 720 Allen Ave., Cody, WY 82414. Official journal of the foundation.

Women & Guns
P.O. Box 488, Sta. C, Buffalo, NY 14209. $24.00 yr. U.S.; (12 issues). Only magazine edited by and for women gun owners.

---

*Published bi-monthly †Published weekly ‡Published three times per month. All others are published monthly.
M=Membership requirements; write for details. Q=Published Quarterly.

HANDGUNNER'S LIBRARY

American Police Handgun Training, by Charles R. Skillen and Mason Williams, Charles C. Thomas, Springfield, IL, 1980. 216 pp., illus. $50.00.

Deals comprehensively with all phases of current handgun training procedures in America.

Askins on Pistols and Revolvers, by Col. Charles Askins, NRA Books, Wash., DC, 1980. 144 pp., illus. Paper covers. $14.95.

A book full of practical advice, shooting tips, technical analysis and stories of guns in action.

Astra Automatic Pistols, by Leonardo M. Antaris, FIRAC Publishing Co., Sterling, CO, 1989. 248 pp., illus. $45.00.

Charts, tables, serial ranges, etc. The definitive work on Astra pistols.

Beretta Automatic Pistols, by J.B. Wood, Stackpole Books, Harrisburg, PA, 1985. 192 pp., illus. $24.95.

Only English-language book devoted entirely to the Beretta line. Includes all important models.

Blacksmith Guide to Ruger Flat-top & Super Blackhawks, by H.W. Ross, Jr., Blacksmith Corp., Chino Valley, AZ, 1990. 96 pp., illus. Paper covers. $9.95.

A key source on the extensively collected Ruger Blackhawk revolvers.

*****Blue Book of Gun Values, 14th edition,** compiled by S.P. Fjestad, Investment Rarities, Inc., Minneapolis, MN, 1993. 621 pp., illus. Soft covers. $24.95.

Uses percentage grading system to determine each gun's value based on its unique condition.

Blue Steel and Gun Leather, by John Bianchi, Beinfeld Publishing, Inc., No. Hollywood, CA, 1978. 200 pp., illus. $14.95.

A complete and comprehensive review of holster uses plus an examination of available products on today's market.

The Bren Gun Saga, by Thomas B. Dugelby, Collector Grade Publications, Toronto, Canada, 1986. 300 pp., illus. $50.00.

Contains information on all models of Bren guns used by all nations.

Browning Hi-Power Pistols, Desert Publications, Cornville, AZ, 1982. 20 pp., illus. Paper covers. $9.00.

Covers all facets of the various military and civilian models of the Browning Hi-Power pistol.

Burning Powder, compiled by Major D.B. Wesson, Wolfe Publishing Company, Prescott, AZ, 1992. 110 pp. Soft cover. $10.95.

A rare booklet from 1932 for Smith & Wesson collectors.

*****Civil War Pistols,** by John D. McAulay, Andrew Mowbray Inc., Lincoln, RI, 1992. 166 pp., illus. $38.50.

A survey of the handguns used during the American Civil War.

Colt Automatic Pistols, by Donald B. Bady, Borden Publ. Co., Alhambra, CA, 1974, 368 pp., illus. $19.95.

The rev. and enlarged ed. of a key work on a fascinating subject. Complete information on every automatic marked with Colt's name.

The Colt Double Action Revolvers: A Shop Manual, Volume 1, by Jerry Kuhnhausen, VSP Publishers, McCall, ID, 1988. 224 pp., illus. Paper covers. $22.95.

Covers D, E, and I frames.

The Colt Double Action Revolvers: A Shop Manual, Volume 2, by Jerry Kuhnhausen, VSP Publishers, McCall, ID, 1988. 156 pp., illus. Paper covers. $17.95.

Covers J, V, and AA models.

Colt Firearms, by James E. Serven, Wolfe Publishing, Prescott, AZ, 1991. 400 pp., illus. $45.00.

An illustrated history of the Colt company and its firearms including the story of the Gatling gun and an outline of Colt automatic weapons.

The Colt .45 Auto Pistol, compiled from U.S. War Dept. Technical Manuals, and reprinted by Desert Publications, Cornville, AZ, 1978. 80 pp., illus. Paper covers. $9.95.

Covers every facet of this famous pistol from mechanical training, manual of arms, disassembly, repair and replacement of parts.

The Colt .45 Automatic Shop Manual, by Jerry Kuhnhausen, VSP Publishers, McCall, ID, 1987. 200 pp., illus. Paper covers. $19.95.

Covers repairing, accurizing, trigger/sear work, action tuning, springs, bushings, rebarreling, and custom .45 modification.

*****Colt 45 Service Pistol Models of 1911 and 1911A1,** by Charles W. Clawson, Charles W. Clawson, Fort Wayne, IN, 1991. 429 pp., illus. $65.00.

Complete military history, development and production 1900 through 1945 plus foreign pistols, gallery pistols, revolvers, cartridge development, and much more.

Colt Heritage, by R.L. Wilson, Simon & Schuster, 1979. 358 pp., illus. $75.00.

The official history of Colt firearms 1836 to the present.

Colt Peacemaker British Model, by Keith Cochran, Cochran Publishing Co., Rapid City, SD, 1989. 160 pp., illus. $35.00.

Covers those revolvers Colt squeezed in while completing a large order of revolvers for the U.S. Cavalry in early 1874, to those magnificent cased target revolvers used in the pistol competitions at Bisley Commons in the 1890s.

Colt Peacemaker Encyclopedia, by Keith Cochran, Keith Cochran, Rapid City, SD, 1986. 434 pp., illus. $59.95.

A must book for the Peacemaker collector.

*****Colt Peacemaker Encyclopedia, Volume 2,** by Keith Cochran, Cochran Publishing Co., SD, 1992. 416 pp., illus. $60.00.

Included in this volume are extensive notes on engraved, inscribed, historical and noted revolvers, as well as those revolvers used by outlaws, lawmen, movie and television stars.

Colt Peacemaker Yearly Variations, by Keith Cochran, Keith Cochran, Rapid City, SD, 1987. 96 pp., illus. $17.95.

A definitive, precise listing for each year the Peacemaker was manufactured from 1873-1940.

Colt Pistols 1836-1976, by R.L. Wilson in association with R.E. Hable, Jackson Arms, Dallas, TX, 1976. 380 pp., illus. $125.00.

A magnificently illustrated book in full color featuring Colt firearms from the famous Hable collection.

Colt Revolvers and the Tower of London, by Joseph G. Rosa, Royal Armouries of the Tower of London, London, England, 1988. 72 pp., illus. Soft covers. $15.00.

Details the story of Colt in London through the early cartridge period.

Colt Revolvers and the U.S. Navy 1865-1889, by C. Kenneth Moore, Dorrance and Co., Bryn Mawr, PA, 1987. 140 pp., illus. $29.95.

The Navy's use of all Colt handguns and other revolvers during this era of change.

Colt Single Action Army Revolvers and the London Agency, by C. Kenneth Moore, Andrew Mowbray Publishers, Lincoln, RI, 1990. 144 pp., illus. $35.00.

Drawing on vast documentary sources, this work chronicles the relationship between the London Agency and the Hartford home office.

The Colt U.S. General Officers' Pistols, by Horace Greeley IV, Andrew Mowbray Inc., Lincoln, RI, 1990. 199 pp., illus. $38.00.

These unique weapons, issued as a badge of rank to General Officers in the U.S. Army from WWII onward, remain highly personal artifacts of the military leaders who carried them. Includes serial numbers and dates of issue.

Colt's Dates of Manufacture 1837-1978, by R.L. Wilson, published by Maurie Albert, Coburg, Australia; N.A. distributor I.D.S.A. Books, Hamilton, OH, 1983. 61 pp. $10.00.

A pocket guide to the dates of manufacture of Colt firearms up to 1978.

*****Colt's 100th Anniversary Firearms Manual 1836-1936: A Century of Achievement,** Wolfe Publishing Co., Prescott, AZ, 1992. 100 pp., illus. Paper covers. $12.95.

Originally published by the Colt Patent Firearms Co., this booklet covers the history, manufacturing procedures and the guns of the first 100 years of the genius of Samuel Colt.

Colt's SAA Post War Models, George Garton, revised edition, Gun Room Press, Highland Park, NJ, 1987. 166 pp., illus. $29.95.

The complete facts on Colt's famous post war single action army revolver using factory records to cover types, calibers, production numbers and many variations of this popular firearm.

The Colt Whitneyville-Walker Pistol, by Lt. Col. Robert D. Whittington, Brownlee Books, Hooks, TX, 1984. 96 pp., illus. Limited edition. $20.00.

A study of the pistol and associated characters 1846-1851.

The Combat .45 Automatic, by Bill Wilson, Wilson's Gun Shop, Tampa, FL, 1988. 241 pp., illus. Soft covers. $14.95.

A guide to purchasing, modifying and using the .45 automatic.

Combat Handgunnery, 3nd Edition, The Gun Digest Book of by Chuck Karwan, DBI Books, Inc., Northbrook, IL, 1992. 256 pp., illus. Paper covers. $15.95.

This all-new edition looks at real world combat handgunnery from three different perspectives—military, police and civilian.

Combat Handgun Shooting, by James D. Mason, Charles C. Thomas Publisher, Springfield, IL, 1990. 280 pp., illus. $47.00.

The most detailed and exciting book on this sport to date.

Combat Pistols, by Terry Gander, Sterling Publishing Co., Inc., 1991. Paper covers. $9.95.

The world's finest and deadliest pistols are shown close-up, with detailed specifications, muzzle velocity, rate of fire, ammunition, etc.

HANDGUNNER'S LIBRARY

Competitive Pistol Shooting, by Laslo Antal, A&C Black, Cambs, England, 1989. 176 pp., illus. Soft covers. $24.00

Covers free pistol, air pistol, rapid fire, etc.

Competitive Shooting, by A.A. Yuryev, introduction by Gary L. Anderson, NRA Books, The National Rifle Assoc. of America, Wash., DC, 1985. 399 pp., illus. $29.95

A unique encyclopedia of competitive rifle and pistol shooting.

The Complete Book of Combat Handgunning, by Chuck Taylor, Desert Publications, Cornville, AZ, 1982. 168 pp., illus. Paper covers. $16.95

Covers virtually every aspect of combat handgunning.

Complete Book of Shooting: Rifles, Shotguns, Handguns, by Jack O'Connor, Stackpole Books, Harrisburg, PA, 1983. 392 pp., illus. $24.95

A thorough guide to each area of the sport, appealing to those with a new or ongoing interest in shooting.

*Compliments of Col. Ruger: A Study of Factory Engraved Single Action Revolvers, by John C. Dougan, Taylor Publishing Co., El Paso, TX, 1992. 238 pp., illus. $46.50

Clearly detailed black and white photographs and a precise text present an accurate istory of the Sturm, Ruger & Co. single-action revolver engraving project.

Confederate Revolvers, by William A. Gary, Taylor Publishing Co., Dallas, TX, 1987. 174 pp., illus. $45.00

Comprehensive work on the rarest of Confederate weapons.

*The Custom Government Model Pistol, by Layne Simpson, Wolfe Publishing Co., Prescott, AZ, 1992. 639 pp., illus. $24.50

This book is about one of the world's greatest firearms and the things pistolsmiths do to make it even better.

The CZ-75 Family: The Ultimate Combat Handgun, by J.M. Ramos, Paladin Press, Boulder, CO, 1990. 100 pp., illus. Soft covers. $16.00

And in-depth discussion of the early-and-late model CZ-75s, as well as the many newest additions to the Czech pistol family.

The Deringer in America, Volume 1, The Percussion Period, by R.L. Wilson and L.D. Eberhart, Andrew Mowbray Inc., Lincoln, RI, 1985. 271 pp., illus. $48.00

A long awaited book on the American percussion deringer.

*Encyclopedia of Ruger Rimfire Semi-Automatic Pistols: 1949-1992, by Chad Hiddleson, Krause Publications, Iola, WI, 1993. 250 pp., illus. $29.95

Covers all physical aspects of Ruger 22-caliber pistols including important features such as boxes, grips, muzzlebrakes, instruction manuals, serial numbers, etc.

English Pistols: The Armories of H.M. Tower of London Collection, by Howard L. Blackmore, Arms and Armour Press, London, England, 1985. 64 pp., illus. Soft covers. $14.95

All the pistols described and pictured are from this famed collection.

Experiments of a Handgunner, by Walter Roper, Wolfe Publishing Co., Prescott, AZ, 1989. 202 pp., illus. $37.00

A limited edition reprint. A listing of experiments with functioning parts of handguns, with targets, stocks, rests, handloading, etc.

Exploded Handgun Drawings, The Gun Digest Book of, edited by Harold A. Murtz, DBI Books, Inc., Northbrook, IL. 1992. 512 pp., illus. Paper covers. $19.95

Exploded or isometric drawings for 494 of the most popular handguns.

Fast and Fancy Revolver Shooting, by Ed. McGivern, Anniversary Edition, Winchester Press, Piscataway, NJ, 1984. 484 pp., illus. $18.95

A fascinating volume, packed with handgun lore and solid information by the acknowledged dean of revolver shooters.

*'51 Colt Navies, by Nathan L. Swayze, The Gun Room Press, Highland Park, NJ, 1993. 243 pp., illus. $59.95

The Model 1851 Colt Navy, its variations and markings.

Firearms Assembly 4: The NRA Guide to Pistols and Revolvers, NRA Books, Wash., DC, 1980. 253 pp., illus. Paper covers. $11.50

The takedown of 124 pistol and revolver models, domestic and foreign.

Firearms Assembly/Disassembly, Part I: Automatic Pistols, Revised Edition, The Gun Digest Book of, by J.B. Wood, DBI Books, Inc., Northbrook, IL, 1990. 480 pp., illus. Soft covers. $17.95

Covers 58 popular autoloading pistols plus nearly 200 variants of those models integrated into the text and completely cross-referenced in the index.

Firearms Assembly/Disassembly Part II: Revolvers, Revised Edition, The Gun Digest Book of, by J.B. Wood, DBI Books, Inc., Northbrook, IL, 1990. 480 pp., illus. Soft covers. $17.95

Covers 49 popular revolvers plus 130 variants. The most comprehensive and professional presentation available to either hobbyist or gunsmith.

Flayderman's Guide to Antique American Firearms...and Their Values, 5th Edition, by Norm Flayderman, DBI Books, Inc., Northbrook, IL, 1990. 624 pp., illus. Soft covers. $27.95

Updated edition of this bible of the antique gun field.

.45 ACP Super Guns, by J.M. Ramos, Paladin Press, Boulder, CO, 1991. 144 pp., illus. Paper covers. $20.00

Modified .45 automatic pistols for competition, hunting and personal defense.

The .45, The Gun Digest Book of by Dean A. Grennell, DBI Books, Inc., Northbrook, IL, 1989. 256 pp., illus. Paper covers. $15.95

Definitive work on one of America's favorite calibers.

German Military Pistols 1904-1930, by Fred A. Datig, Michael Zomber Co., Culver City, CA, 1990. 88 pp., illus. Paper covers. $14.95

Monograph #2 in the series "The Luger Pistol Its History & Development from 1893-1945."

German Military Rifles and Machine Pistols, 1871-1945, by Hans Dieter Gotz, Schiffer Publishing Co., West Chester, PA, 1990. 245 pp., illus. $35.00

This book portrays in words and pictures the development of the modern German weapons and their ammunition including the scarcely known experimental types.

German Pistols and Holsters 1934-1945, Vol. 2, by Robert Whittington, Brownlee Books, Hooks, TX, 1990. 312 pp., illus. $55.00

This volume addresses pistols only: military (Heer, Luftwaffe, Kriegsmarine & Waffen-SS), captured, commercial, police, NSDAP and government.

German 7.9mm Military Ammunition, by Daniel W. Kent, Daniel W. Kent, Ann Arbor, MI, 1991. 244 pp., illus. $35.00

The long-awaited revised edition of a classic among books devoted to ammunition.

German Pistols and Holsters, 1934-1945, Volume 4, by Lt. Col. Robert D. Whittington, 3rd, U.S.A.R., Brownlee Books, Hooks, TX, 1991. 208 pp. $30.00

Pistols and holsters issued in 412 selected armed forces, army and Waffen-SS units including information on personnel, other weapons and transportation.

Good Friends, Good Guns, Good Whiskey: The Selected Works of Skeeter Skelton, by Skeeter Skelton, PJS Publications, Peoria, IL, 1989. 347 pp. $21.95

A guidebook to the world of Skeeter Skelton.

The Government Models: The Development of the Colt Model of 1911, by William H.D. Goddard, Andrew Mowbray, Inc., Publishers, Lincoln, RI, 1988. 223 pp., illus. $58.50

An authoritative source on the world's most popular military sidearm.

Guide to Ruger Single Action Revolvers Production Dates, 1953-73, by John C. Dougan, Blacksmith Corp., Chino Valley, AZ, 1991. 22 pp., illus. Paper covers. $9.95

A unique pocket-sized handbook providing production information for the popular Ruger single-action revolvers manufactured during the first 20 years.

Gun Collector's Digest, 5th Edition, edited by Joseph J. Schroeder, DBI Books, Inc., Northbrook, IL, 1989. 224 pp., illus. Paper covers. $15.95

The latest edition of this sought-after series.

Gun Digest, 1994, 48th Edition, edited by Ken Warner, DBI Books, Inc., Northbrook, IL, 1993. 544 pp., illus. Paper Covers. $21.95

All-new edition of the world's best selling gun book; the only one to make the USA Today list of best-selling sports books.

Gun Owner's Book of Care, Repair & Improvement, by Roy Dunlap, Outdoor Life-Harper & Row, NY, 1977. 336 pp., illus. $12.95

A basic guide to repair and maintenance of guns, written for the average firearms owner.

The Gunfighter, Man or Myth? by Joseph G. Rosa, Oklahoma Press, Norman, OK, 1969. 229 pp., illus. (including weapons). Paper covers. $12.95

A well-documented work on gunfights and gunfighters of the West and elsewhere. Great treat for all gunfighter buffs.

Gunproof Your Children/Handgun Primer, by Massad Ayoob, Police Bookshelf, Concord, NH, 1989. Paper covers. $4.95

Two books in one. The first, keeping children safe from unauthorized guns in their hands; the second, a compact introduction to handgun safety.

Guns Illustrated, 1994, 26th Edition, edited by Harold A. Murtz, DBI Books, Inc., Northbrook, IL, 1993. 320 pp., illus. Paper covers. $18.95

Truly the Journal of Gun Buffs, this all-new edition consists of articles of interest to every shooter as well as a complete catalog of all U.S. and imported firearms with latest specs and prices.

Guns of the Elite, by George Markham, Arms and Armour Press, Poole, England, 1987. 184 pp., illus. $24.95

Special Forces firearms, 1940 to the present.

Guns of the Empire, by George Markham, Arms & Armour Press, London, England, 1991. 160 pp., illus. $29.95

The firearms that carved out the worldwide British Empire come together in a riveting display of handguns, rifles, and automatics.

Guns of the First World War, Rifle, Handguns and Ammunition from the Text Book of Small Arms, 1909, edited by John Walter, Presidio Press, Novato, CA, 1991. $30.00

Details of the Austro-Hung. Mann., French Lebels, German Mausers, U.S. Springfields, etc.

Guns of the Reich, by George Markham, Arms & Armour Press, London, England, 1989. 175 pp., illus. $24.95

The pistols, rifles, submachine guns, machineguns and support weapons of the German armed forces, 1939-1945.

Guns of the Wild West, by George Markham, Arms & Armour Press, London, England, 1991. 160 pp., illus. $19.95

The handguns, longarms and shotguns of the Gold Rush, the American Civil War, and the Armed Forces.

Hallock's .45 Auto Handbook, by Ken Hallock, The Mihan Co., Oklahoma City, OK, 1981. 178 pp., illus. Paper covers. $11.95

For gunsmiths, dealers, collectors and serious hobbyists.

The Handgun, by Geoffrey Boothroyd, David and Charles, North Pomfret, VT, 1989. 566 pp., illus. $60.00

Every chapter deals with an important period in handgun history from the 14th century to the present.

Handgun Digest, 2nd Edition, by Dean A. Grennell, DBI Books, Inc., Northbrook, IL, 1991. 256 pp., illus. Paper covers. $16.95.

Full coverage of all aspects of handguns and handgunning from a highly readable, knowledgeable author.

Handgun Reloading, The Gun Digest Book of, by Dean A. Grennell and Wiley M. Clapp, DBI Books, Inc., Northbrook, IL, 1987. 256 pp., illus. Paper covers. $15.95.

Detailed discussions of all aspects of reloading for handguns, from basic to complex. New loading data.

*Handguns '94, 6th Edition, edited by Jack Lewis, DBI Books, Inc., Northbrook, IL, 1993. 320 pp., illus. Paper covers. $18.95

What's new in handguns for 1994 plus informative and interesting articles on all aspects of handguns.

Handguns of the World, by Edward C. Ezell, Marboro Book, Corp., Rockleigh, NJ, 1991. 704 pp., illus. $16.95.

A comprehensive international guide to military revolvers and self-loaders.

"Hell, I Was There!," by Elmer Keith, Petersen Publishing Co., Los Angeles, CA, 1979. 308 pp., illus. $24.95.

Adventures of a Montana cowboy who gained world fame as a big game hunter.

High Standard: A Collector's Guide to the Hamden & Hartford Target Pistols, by Tom Dance, Andrew Mowbray, Inc., Lincoln, RI, 1991. 192 pp., illus. Paper covers. $24.00.

From Citation to Supermatic, all of the production models and specials made from 1951 to 1984 are covered according to model number or series.

*Hi-Standard Autoloading Pistols 1951-1984, by James V. Spacek, Jr., James V. Spacek, Jr., Berlin, CT, 1993. 60 pp., illus. Paper covers. $10.00.

Information on takedown styles, serial numbers, production numbers, model charts and magazine references. Includes a price guide.

High Standard Automatic Pistols 1932-1950, by Charles E. Petty, The Gunroom Press, Highland Park, NJ, 1989. 124 pp., illus. $19.95.

A definitive source of information for the collector of High Standard arms.

Historic Pistols: The American Martial Flintlock 1760-1845, by Samuel E. Smith and Edwin W. Bitter, The Gun Room Press, Highland Park, NJ, 1986. 353 pp., illus. $45.00.

Covers over 70 makers and 163 models of American martial arms.

Historical Hartford Hardware, by William W. Dalrymple, Colt Collector Press, Rapid City, SD, 1976. 42 pp., illus. Paper covers. $5.50.

Historically associated Colt revolvers.

The History of Smith and Wesson, by Roy G. Jinks, Willowbrook Enterprises, Springfield, MA, 1988. 290 pp., illus. $23.95.

Revised 10th Anniversary edition of the definite book on S&W firearms.

*How to Become a Master Handgunner: The Mechanics of X-Count Shooting, by Charles Stephens, Paladin Press, Boulder, CO, 1993. 64 pp., illus. Paper covers. $10.00.

Offers a simple formula for success to the handgunner who strives to master the technique of shooting accurately.

Hunting for Handgunners, by Larry Kelly and J.D. Jones, DBI Books, Inc., Northbrook, IL, 1990. 256 pp., illus. Paper covers. $15.95.

Covers the entire spectrum of hunting with handguns in an amusing, easy-flowing manner that combines entertainment with solid information.

Instinct Combat Shooting, by Chuck Klein, Chuck Klein, The Goose Creek, IN, 1989. 49 pp., illus. Paper covers. $10.95.

Defensive handgunning for police.

Iver Johnson's Arms & Cycle Works Handguns, 1871-1964, by W.E. "Bill" Goforth, Blacksmith Corp., Chino Valley, AZ, 1991. 160 pp., illus. Paper covers. $14.95.

Covers all of the famous Iver Johnson handguns from the early solid-frame pistols and revolvers to optional accessories, special orders and patents.

James Reid and His Catskill Knuckledusters, by Taylor Brown, Andrew Mowbray Publishers, Lincoln, RI, 1990. 288 pp., illus. $24.95.

A detailed history of James Reid, his factory in the picturesque Catskill Mountains, and the pistols which he manufactured there.

Japanese Handguns, by Frederick E. Leithe, Borden Publishing Co., Alhambra, CA, 1985. 160 pp., illus. $19.95.

This book is an identification guide to all models and variations of Japanese handguns.

Kentucky Rifles and Pistols 1756-1850, compiled by members of the Kentucky Rifle Association, Wash., DC, Golden Age Arms Co., Delaware, OH, 1976. 275 pp., illus. $45.00.

Profusely illustrated with more than 300 examples of rifles and pistols never before published.

Know Your Broomhandle Mausers, by R.J. Berger, Blacksmith Corp., Southport, CT, 1985. 96 pp., illus. Paper covers. $9.95.

An interesting story on the big Mauser pistol and its variations.

Know Your Czechoslovakian Pistols, by R.J. Berger, Blacksmith Corp., Chino Valley, AZ, 1989. 96 pp., illus. Soft covers. $9.95.

A comprehensive reference which presents the fascinating story of Czech pistols.

Know Your 45 Auto Pistols—Models 1911 & A1, by E.J. Hoffschmidt, Blacksmith Corp., Southport, CT, 1974. 58 pp., illus. Paper covers. $9.95.

A concise history of the gun with a wide variety of types and copies.

Know Your Walther P.38 Pistols, by E.J. Hoffschmidt, Blacksmith Corp., Southport, CT, 1974. 77 pp., illus. Paper covers. $9.95.

Covers the Walther models Armee, M.P., H.P., P.38—history and variations.

Know Your Walther PP & PPK Pistols, by E.J. Hoffschmidt, Blacksmith Corp., Southport, CT, 1975. 87 pp., illus. Paper covers. $9.95.

A concise history of the guns with a guide to the variety and types.

The Krieghoff Parabellum, by Randall Gibson, Midland, TX, 1988. 279 pp., illus. $40.00.

A comprehensive text pertaining to the Lugers manufactured by H. Krieghoff Waffenfabrik.

The Law Enforcement Book of Weapons, Ammunition and Training Procedures, Handguns, Rifles and Shotguns, by Mason Williams, Charles C. Thomas, Publisher, Springfield, IL, 1977. 496 pp., illus. $135.00.

Data on firearms, firearm training, and ballistics.

*Luger Holsters and Accessories of the 20th Century, by Eugene J. Bender, Eugene J. Bender, Margate, FL, 1993. 640 pp., illus. $65.00.

A major new book for collectors, dealers, and historians, with over 1,000 photographs.

Luger: The Multi-National Pistol, by Charles Kenyon, Jr., Richard Ellis Publications, Moline, IL, 1991. 192 pp. $69.95 (hardcover); $150.00 (leather bound).

A fresh approach to this most historical handgun.

Luger Variations, by Harry E. Jones, Harry E. Jones, Torrance, CA, 1975. 328 pp., 160 full page illus., many in color. $45.00.

A rev. ed. of the book known as "The Luger Collector's Bible."

Lugers at Random, by Charles Kenyon, Jr., Handgun Press, Glenview, IL, 1990. 420 pp., illus. $39.95.

A new printing of this classic and sought-after work on the Luger pistol. A boon to the Luger collector/shooter.

*The Luger Pistol Its History & Development From 1893 to 1947; Monograph IV: The Swiss Variations 1897-1947, by Fred A. Datig, Fred A. Datig, Los Angeles, CA, 1992. 88 pp., illus. Paper covers. $14.95.

A definitive work on the Swiss variations of this most collectible pistol.

Luger: The Multi-National Pistol, by Charles Kenyon, Jr., Richard Ellis Publications, Moline, IL, 1991. 192 pp., illus. $69.95 (hardcover); $150.00 (leather bound).

A fresh approach to this historical handgun. A must for the serious collector.

The Luger Book, by John Walter, Sterling Publishing Co., New York, NY, 1991. 287 pp., illus. $19.95.

The encyclopedia of the Borchardt and Borchardt-Luger handgun 1885-1985.

Lyman Pistol & Revolver Handbook, edited by C. Kenneth Ramage, Lyman Publications, Middlefield, CT, 1978. 280 pp., illus. Paper covers. $14.95.

An extensive reference of load and trajectory data for the handgun.

Manual of Pistol and Revolver Cartridges, Volume 2, Centerfire U.S. and British Calibers, by Hans A. Erlmeier and Jakob H. Brandt, Journal-Verlag, Wiesbaden, Germany, 1981. 270 pp., illus. $34.95.

Catalog system allows cartridges to be traced by caliber or alphabetically.

Mauser Rifles and Pistols, by Walter H.B. Smith, Wolfe Publishing Co., Prescott, AZ, 1990. 234 pp., illus. $30.00.

A handbook covering Mauser history and the amrs Mauser manufactured.

The Mauser Self-Loading Pistol, by Belford & Dunlap, Borden Publ. Co., Alhambra, CA. Over 200 pp., 300 illus., large format. $24.95.

The long-awaited book on the "Broom Handles," covering their inception in 1894 to the end of production. Complete and in detail: pocket pistols, Chinese and Spanish copies, etc.

Metallic Silhouette Shooting, 2nd Edition, The Gun Digest Book of, by Elgin Gates, DBI Books, Inc., Northbrook, IL, 1988. 256 pp., illus. Paper covers. $15.95.

All about the rapidly growing sport. With a history and rules of the International Handgun Metallic Silhouette Association.

Military Pistols of Japan, by Fred L. Honeycutt, Jr., Julin Books, Palm Beach Gardens, FL, 1991. 168 pp., illus. $34.00.

Covers every aspect of military pistol production in Japan through WWII.

Military Small Arms of the 20th Century, 6th Edition, by Ian V. Hogg, DBI Books, Inc., Northbrook, IL, 1991. 352 pp., illus. Paper covers. $19.95.

Fully revised and updated edition of the standard reference in its field.

Modern American Pistols and Revolvers, by A.C. Gould, Wolfe Publishing Co., Prescott, AZ, 1988. 222 pp., illus. $37.00.

A limited edition reprint. An account of the development of those arms as well as the manner of shooting them.

*Modern Gun Values, The Gun Digest Book of 9th Edition, by Jack Lewis, DBI Books, Inc., Northbrook, IL. 560 pp., illus. Paper covers. $20.95.

Updated and expanded edition of the book that has become the standard for valuing modern firearms.

*Modern Guns Identification & Values, 9th Edition, by Russell & Steve Quertermous, Collector Books, Paducah, KY, 1992. 480 pp., illus. Paper covers, $12.95.

Over 2,250 models of rifles, handguns and shotguns from 1900 to the present are described and priced in excellent and very good condition with suggested retail prices for those models still in production.

*The Modern Technique of the Pistol, by Gregory Boyce Morrison, Gunsite Press, Paulden, AZ, 1991. 153 pp., illus. $45.00.

The theory of effective defensive use of modern handguns.

The Navy Luger, by Joachim Gortz and John Walter, Handgun Press, Glenview, IL, 1988. 128 pp., illus. $24.95.

The 9mm Pistole 1904 and the Imperial German Navy. A concise illustrated history.

The New Handbook of Handgunning, by Paul B. Weston, Charles C. Thomas, Publisher, Springfield, IL, 1980. 102 pp., illus. $35.00.

A step-by-step, how-to manual of handgun shooting.

*9mm Handguns, 2nd Edition, The Gun Digest Book of,** edited by Steve Comus, DBI Books, Inc., Northbrook, IL, 1993. 256 pp., illus. Paper covers. $17.95.

Covers the 9mmP cartridge and the guns that have been made for it in greater depth than any other work available. (October '93)

*9mm Parabellus; The History & Developement of the World's 9mm Pistols & Ammunition,** by Klaus-Peter Konig and Martin Hugo, Schiffer Publishing Ltd., Atglen, PA, 1993. 304 pp., illus. $39.95.

Detailed history of 9mm weapons from Belguim, Italy, Germany, Israel, France, USA, Czechoslovakia, Hungary, Poland, Brazil, Finland and Spain.

No Second Place Winner, by Wm. H. Jordan, publ. by the author, Shreveport, LA (Box 4072), 1962. 114 pp., illus. $15.95.

Guns and gear of the peace officer, ably discussed by a U.S. Border Patrolman for over 30 years, and a first-class shooter with handgun, rifle, etc.

NRA Firearms Fact Book, by the editors of NRA, National Rifle Association, Wash., DC, 1991. 330 pp., illus. Paper covers. $10.95.

The second, revised edition of the classic *NRA Firearms and Ammunition Fact Book.* Covers gun collecting, firearms safety, ballistics and general references.

The P-08 Parabellum Luger Automatic Pistol, edited by J. David McFarland, Desert Publications, Cornville, AZ, 1982. 20 pp., illus. Paper covers. $8.00.

Covers every facet of the Luger, plus a listing of all known Luger models.

The P.38 Pistol, Volume 3, by Warren H. Buxton, Ucross Books, Los Alamos, NM, 1991. 270 pp., illus. $54.50.

The postwar distribution of the P.38 pistol.

*P-38 Automatic Pistol,** by Gene Gangarosa, Jr., Stoeger Publishing Co., S. Hackensack, NJ, 1993. 272 pp., illus. Paper covers. $16.95

This book traces the origins and development of the P-38, including the momentous political forces of the World War II era that caused its near demise and, later, its rebirth.

Paterson Colt Pistol Variations, by R.L. Wilson and R. Phillips, Jackson Arms Co., Dallas, TX, 1979. 250 pp., illus. $35.00.

A book about the different models and barrel lengths in the Paterson Colt story.

*Pin Shooting: A Complete Guide,** by Mitchell A. Ota, Wolfe Publishing Co., Prescott, AZ, 1992. 145 pp., illus. Paper covers. $14.95.

Traces the sport from its humble origins to today's thoroughly enjoyable social event, including the mammoth eight-day Second Chance Pin Shoot in Michigan.

Pistol & Revolver Guide, 3rd Ed., by George C. Nonte, Stoeger Publ. Co., So. Hackensack, NJ, 1975. 224 pp., illus. Paper covers. $11.95.

The standard reference work on military and sporting handguns.

The Pistol Book, by John Walter, 2nd edition, 1991. Sterling Publishing Co., Inc., 1991. 176 pp., illus. $29.95.

Beretta, Colt, Mauser—plus a wealth of information and specs on other worldwide manufacturers of pistols and ammunition.

Pistol Guide, by George C. Nonte, Jr., Stoeger Publishing Co., So. Hackensack, NJ, 1991. 280 pp., illus. Paper covers. $13.95.

Covers handling and marksmanship, care and maintenance, pistol ammunition, how to buy a used gun, military pistols, air pistols and repairs.

Pistols of the World, 3rd Edition, by Ian Hogg and John Weeks, DBI Books, Inc., Northbrook, IL, 1992. 320 pp., illus. Paper covers. $19.95.

A totally revised edtion of one of the leading studies of small arms.

Pistolsmithing, The Gun Digest Book of, by Jack Mitchell, DBI Books, Inc., Northbrook, IL, 1980, 288 pp., illus. Paper covers. $14.95.

An expert's guide to the operation of each of the handgun actions with all the major functions of pistolsmithing explained.

Pistolsmithing, by George C. Nonte, Jr., Stackpole Books, Harrisburg, PA, 1974. 560 pp., illus. $29.95.

A single source reference to handgun maintenance, repair, and modification at home, unequaled in value.

The Pitman Notes on U.S. Martial Small Arms and Ammunition, 1776-1933, Volume 2, Revolvers and Automatic Pistols, by Brig. Gen. John Pitman, Thomas Publications, Gettysburg, PA, 1990. 192 pp., illus. $29.95.

A most important primary source of information on United States military small arms and ammunition.

Police Handgun Manual, by Bill Clede, Stackpole Books, Inc., Harrisburg, PA, 1985. 128 pp., illus. $18.95.

How to get street-smart survival habits.

Practical Handgun Ballistics, by Mason Williams, Charles C. Thomas, Publisher, Springfield, IL, 1980. 215 pp., illus. $55.00.

Factual information on the practical aspects of ammunition performance in revolvers and pistols.

Powerhouse Pistols—The Colt 1911 and Browning Hi-Power Source

book, by Duncan Long, Paladin Press, Boulder, CO, 1989. 152 pp., illus. Soft covers. $19.95.

The author discusses internal mechanisms, outward design, test-firing results, maintenance and accessories.

Report of Board on Tests of Revolvers and Automatic Pistols. From the Annual Report of the Chief of Ordnance, 1907. Reprinted by J.C. Tillinghast, Marlow, NH, 1969. 34 pp., 7 plates, paper covers. $9.95.

A comparison of handguns, including Luger, Savage, Colt, Webley-Fosbery and other makes.

Revolver Guide, by George C. Nonte, Jr., Stoeger Publishing Co., So. Hackensack, NJ, 1991. 288 pp., illus. Paper covers. $10.95.

A detailed and practical encyclopedia of the revolver, the most common handgun to be found.

Revolvers of the British Services 1854-1954, by W.H.J. Chamberlain and A.W.F. Taylerson, Museum Restoration Service, Ottawa, Canada, 1989. 80 pp., illus. $27.50.

Covers the types issued among many of the United Kingdom's naval, land or air services.

Ruger, edited by Joseph Roberts, Jr., the National Rifle Association of America, Washington, D.C., 1991. 109 pp. illus. Paper covers. $14.95.

The story of Bill Ruger's indelible imprint in the history of sporting firearms.

Ruger Double Action Revolvers, Vol. 1, Shop Manual, by Jerry Kuhnhausen, VSP Publishers, McCall, ID, 1989. 176 pp., illus. Soft covers. $18.95.

Covers the Ruger Six series of revolvers: Security-Six, Service-Six, and Speed-Six. Includes step-by-step function checks, disassembly, inspection, repairs, rebuilding, reassembly, and custom work.

Ruger Rimfire Handguns 1949-1982, by J.C. Munnell, G.D.G.S. Inc., McKeesport, PA, 1982. 189 pp., illus. Paper covers. $13.50.

Updated edition with additional material on the semi-automatic pistols and the New Model revolvers.

*The Ruger P-85 Family of Handguns,** by Duncan Long, Desert Publications, El Dorado, AZ, 1993. 128 pp., illus. Paper covers. $14.95.

A full-fledged documentary on a remarkable series of Sturm Ruger handguns. The P-85 emerged as the "Volksgun" of the '90s, offering great reliability with affordability.

The Ruger .22 Automatic Pistol, Standard/Mark I/Mark II Series, by Duncan Long, Paladin Press, Boulder, CO, 1989. 168 pp., illus. Paper covers. $12.00.

The definitive book about the pistol that has served more than 1 million owners so well.

The S&W Revolver: A Shop Manual, by Jerry Kuhnhausen, VSP Publishers, McCall, ID, 1987. 152 pp., illus. Paper covers. $17.95.

Covers accurizing, trigger jobs, action tuning, rebarreling, barrel setback, forcing cone angles, polishing and rebluing.

*Sam Colt's Own Record 1847,** by John Parsons, Wolfe Publishing Co., Prescott, AZ, 1992. 167 pp., illus. $24.50.

Chronologically presented, the correspondence published here completes the account of the manufacture, in 1847, of the Walker Model Colt revolver.

The Semiautomatic Pistols in Police Service and Self Defense, by Massad Ayoob, Police Bookshelf, Concord, NH, 1990. 25 pp., illus. Soft covers. $9.95.

First quantitative, documented look at actual police experience with 9mm and 45 police service automatics.

*The Sharpshooter—How to Stand and Shoot Handgun Metallic Silhouettes,** by Charles Stephens, Yucca Tree Press, Las Cruces, NM, 1993. 86 pp., illus. Paper covers. $7.95.

A narration of some of the author's early experiences in silhouette shooting, plus how-to information.

Shoot a Handgun, by Dave Arnold, PVA Books, Canyon County, CA, 1983. 144 pp., illus. Paper covers. $11.95.

A complete manual of simplified handgun instruction.

Shoot to Win, by John Shaw, Blacksmith Corp., Southport, CT, 1985. 160 pp., illus. Paper covers. $11.95.

The lessons taught here are of interest and value to all handgun shooters.

Shooting, by Edward A. Matunas, Stackpole Books, Harrisburg, PA, 1986. 416 pp., illus. $31.95.

How to become an expert marksman with rifle, shotgun, handgun, muzzle loader and bow.

*Shooting,** by J.H. FitzGerald, Wolfe Publishing Co., Prescott, AZ, 1993. 421 pp., illus. $29.00

Exhaustive coverage of handguns and their use for target shooting, defense, trick shooting, and in police work by an noted firearms expert.

Sierra Handgun Manual, 3rd Edition, edited by Kenneth Ramage, Sierra Bullets, Santa Fe Springs, CA, 1990. 704 pp., illus. 3-ring binder. $19.95.

New listings for XP-100 and Contender pistols and TCU cartridges...part of a new single shot section. Covers the latest loads for 10mm Auto, 455 Super Mag, and Accurate powders.

Simeon North: First Official Pistol Maker of the United States, by S. North and R. North, The Gun Room Press, Highland Park, NJ, 1972. 207 pp., illus. $9.95.

Reprint of the rare first edition.

Sixgun Cartridges and Loads, by Elmer Keith, reprint edition by The Gun Room Press, Highland Park, NJ, 1984. 151 pp., illus. $24.95.

A manual covering the selection, use and loading of the most suitable and popular revolver cartridges.

Sixguns, by Elmer Keith, Wolfe Publishing Company, Prescott, AZ, 1992. 336 pp. Hardcover. $34.95.

The history, selection, repair, care, loading, and use of this historic frontiersman's friend—the one-hand firearm.

Skeeter Skelton on Handguns, by Skeeter Skelton, PJS Publications, Peoria, IL, 1980. 122 pp., illus. Soft covers. $5.00.

A treasury of facts, fiction and fables.

Small Arms of the World, 12th Edition, fully updated and revised, by Edward C. Ezell, Marboro Book Corp., New York, NY, 1990. 894 pp., illus. $16.95.

An encyclopedia of global weapons with over 3,500 entries.

Small Arms Today, 2nd Edition, by Edward C. Ezell, Stackpole Books, Harrisburg, PA, 1988. 479 pp., illus. Paper covers. $19.95.

Latest reports on the world's weapons and ammunition.

Southern Derringers of the Mississippi Valley, by Turner Kirkland, Pioneer Press, Tenn., 1971. 80 pp., illus., paper covers. $5.00.

A guide for the collector, and a much-needed study.

Soviet Russian Postwar Military Pistols and Cartridges, by Fred A. Datig, Handgun Press, Glenview, IL, 1988. 152 pp., illus. $29.95.

Thoroughly researched, this definitive sourcebook covers the development and adoption of the Makarov, Stechkin and the new PSM pistols. Also included in this source book is coverage on Russian clandestine weapons and pistol cartridges.

The SPIW: Deadliest Weapon that Never Was, by R. Blake Stevens, and Edward C. Ezell, Collector Grade Publications, Inc., Toronto, Canada, 1985. 138 pp., illus. $29.95.

The complete saga of the fantastic flechette-firing Special Purpose Individual Weapon.

Steindler's New Firearms Dictionary, by R.A. Steindler, Stackpole Books, Inc., Harrisburg, PA, 1985. 320 pp., illus. $24.95.

Completely revised and updated edition of this standard work.

*Stevens Pistols & Pocket Rifles, by K.L. Cope, Museum Restoration Service, Alexandria Bay, NY, 1992. 114 pp., illus. $24.50.

This is the story of the guns and the man who designed them and the company which he founded to make them.

The Street Smart Gun Book, by John Farnam, Police Bookshelf, Concord, NH, 1986. 45 pp., illus. Paper covers. $11.95.

Weapon selection, defensive shooting techniques, and gunfight-winning tactics from one of the world's leading authorities.

Stress Fire, Vol. 1: Stress Fighting for Police, by Massad Ayoob, Police Bookshelf, Concord, NH, 1984. 149 pp., illus. Paper covers. $9.95.

Gunfighting for police, advanced tactics and techniques.

Successful Handgun Hunting, by Phil W. Johnson. The Shooting Sports Press, Minneapolis, MN, 1988. 216 pp., illus. $19.95.

The definitive work on the most exciting sport in America.

Successful Pistol Shooting, by Frank and Paul Leatherdale, The Crowood Press, Ramsbury, England, 1988. 144 pp., illus. $34.95.

Easy-to-follow instructions to help you achieve better results and gain more enjoyment from both leisure and competitive shooting.

*Survival Guns, by Mel Tappan, Desert Publications, El Dorado, AZ, 1993. 456 pp., illus. Paper covers. $21.95.

Discusses in a frank and forthright manner which handguns, rifles and shotguns to buy for personal defense and securing food, and the ones to avoid.

Survival Gunsmithing, by J.B. Wood, Desert Publications, Cornville, AZ, 1986. 92 pp., illus. Paper covers. $9.95.

A guide to repair and maintenance of many of the most popular rifles, shotguns and handguns.

Textbook of Automatic Pistols, by R.K. Wilson, Wolfe Publishing Co., Prescott, AZ, 1990. 349 pp., illus. $54.00.

Reprint of the 1943 classic being a treatise on the history, development and functioning of modern military self-loading pistols.

Textbook of Pistols & Revolvers, by Julian Hatcher, Wolfe Publishing Co., Prescott, AZ, 1988. 533 pp., illus. $65.00.

A limited edition reprint. Hatcher wrote this shooters' bible in 1935 and it remains a classic full of invaluable information.

U.S. Marine Corp Rifle and Pistol Marksmanship, 1935, reprinting of a government publication, Lancer Militaria, Mt. Ida, AR, 1991. 99 pp., illus. Paper covers. $11.95.

The old corps method of precision shooting.

U.S. Naval Handguns, 1808-1911, by Fredrick R. Winter, Andrew Mowbray Publishers, Lincoln, RI, 1990. 128 pp., illus. $26.00.

The story of U.S. Naval Handguns spans an entire century—included are sections on each of the important naval handguns within the period.

Vietnam Weapons Handbook, by David Rosser-Owen, Patrick Stephens, Wellingborough, England, 1986. 136 pp., illus. Paper covers. $9.95.

Covers every weapon used by both sides.

Walther Models PP and PPK, 1929-1945, by James L. Rankin, assisted by Gary Green, James L. Rankin, Coral Gables, FL, 1974. 142 pp., illus. $35.00.

Complete coverage on the subject as to finish, proofmarks and Nazi Party inscriptions.

Walther P-38 Pistol, by Maj. George Nonte, Desert Publications, Cornville, AZ, 1982. 100 pp., illus. Paper covers. $9.95.

Complete volume on one of the most famous handguns to come out of WWII. All models covered.

Walther Volume II, Engraved, Presentation and Standard Models, by James L. Rankin, J.L. Rankin, Coral Gables, FL, 1977. 112 pp., illus. $35.00.

The new Walther book on embellished versions and standard models. Has 88 photographs, including many color plates.

Walther, Volume III, 1908-1980, by James L. Rankin, Coral Gables, FL, 1981. 226 pp., illus. $35.00.

Covers all models of Walther handguns from 1908 to date, includes holsters, grips and magazines.

Warsaw Pact Weapons Handbook, by Jacques F. Baud, Paladin Press, Boulder, CO, 1989. 168 pp., illus. Soft covers. $20.00.

The most complete handbook on weapons found behind the Iron Curtain.

Weapons of the Waffen-SS, by Bruce Quarrie, Sterling Publishing Co., Inc., 1991. 168 pp., illus. $24.95.

An in-depth look at the weapons that made Hitler's Waffen-SS the fearsome fighting machine it was.

Webley Revolvers, by Gordon Bruce and Christien Reinhart, Stocker-Schmid, Zurich, Switzerland, 1988. 256 pp., illus. $69.50.

A revised edition of Dowell's "Webley Story."

*Webley & Scott Automatic Pistols, by Gordon Bruch, Stocker-Schmid Publishing Co., Dietikon, Switzerland, 1992. 256 pp., illus. $69.50.

The fundamental representation of the history and development of all Webley & Scott automatic pistols.

World War 2 Small Arms, by John Weeks, Chartwell Books, Inc., Secaucus, NJ, 1989. 144 pp., illus. $10.95.

Assesses the weapons of each of the major combatant nations, their production, history, design and features.

World's Deadliest Rimfire Battleguns, by J.M. Ramos, Paladin Press, Boulder, CO, 1990. 184 pp., illus. Paper covers. $14.00.

This heavily illustrated book shows international rimfire assault weapon innovations from World War II to the present.

ARMS ASSOCIATIONS

UNITED STATES

ALABAMA

Alabama Gun Collectors Assn.
Secretary, P.O. Box 6080, Tuscaloosa, AL 35405

ALASKA

Alaska Gun Collectors Assn., Inc.
Gereth Stillman, Pres., 1554 Myrtle, Eagle River, AK 99577

ARIZONA

Arizona Arms Assn.
Don DeBusk, President, 4837 Bryce Ave., Glendale, AZ 85301

CALIFORNIA

Greater Calif. Arms & Collectors Assn.
Donald L. Bullock, 8291 Carburton St., Long Beach, CA 90808-3302
Los Angeles Gun Ctg. Collectors Assn.
F.H. Ruffra, 20810 Amie Ave., Apt. #9, Torrance, CA 90503

COLORADO

Colorado Gun Collectors Assn.
L.E.(Bud) Greenwald, 2553 S. Quitman St., Denver, CO 80219/303-935-3850

CONNECTICUT

Ye Connecticut Gun Guild, Inc.
Dick Fraser, P.O. Box 425, Windsor, CT 06095

FLORIDA

Tampa Bay Arms Collectors' Assn.
John Tuvell, 2461-67th Ave., S., St., Petersburg, FL 33712
Unified Sportsmen of Florida
P.O. Box 6565, Tallahassee, FL 32314

GEORGIA

Georgia Arms Collectors Assn., Inc.
Michael Kindberg, President, P.O. Box 277, Alpharetta, GA 30239-0277

ILLINOIS

Illinois Gun Collectors Assn.
T.J. Curl, Jr., P.O. Box 971, Kankakee, IL 60901
Mississippi Valley Gun & Cartridge Coll. Assn.
Bob Filbert, P.O. Box 61, Port Byron, IL 61275/309-523-2593
Sauk Trail Gun Collectors
Gordell M. Matson, P.O. Box 1113, Milan, IL 61264
Wabash Valley Gun Collectors Assn., Inc.
Jerry D. Holycross, RR #6, Box 341, Danville, IL 61832

INDIANA

Indiana Sportsmen's Council-Legislative
Maurice Latimer, P.O. Box 93, Bloomington, IN 47402
Indiana State Rifle & Pistol Assn.
Thos. Glancy, P.O. Box 552, Chesterton, IN 46304
Southern Indiana Gun Collectors Assn., Inc.
Sheila McClary, 309 W. Monroe St., Boonville, IN 47601/812-897-3742

IOWA

Beaver Creek Plainsmen Inc.
Steve Murphy, Secy., P.O. Box 298, Bondurant, IA 50035
Central States Gun Collectors Assn.
Avery Giles, 1104 S. 1st Ave., Marshtown, IA 50158

KANSAS

Kansas Cartridge Collectors Assn.
Bob Linder, Box 84, Plainville, KS 67663

KENTUCKY

Kentuckiana Arms Collectors Assn.
Ralph Handy, President, Box 1776, Louisville, KY 40201
Kentucky Gun Collectors Assn., Inc.
Ruth Johnson, Box 64, Owensboro, KY 42302/502-729-4197

LOUISIANA

Washitaw River Renegades
Sandra Rushing, P.O. Box 256, Main St., Grayson, LA 71435

MARYLAND

Baltimore Antique Arms Assn.
Stanley I. Kellert, 8340 Dubbs Dr., Severn, MD 21144

MASSACHUSETTS

Bay Colony Weapons Collectors, Inc.
John Brandt, Box 111, Hingham, MA 02043
Massachusetts Arms Collectors
John J. Callan, Jr., 1887 Main St., Leicester, MA 01524-1943/508-892-3837

MISSISSIPPI

Mississippi Gun Collectors Assn.
Jack E. Swinney, P.O. Box 16323, Hattiesburg, MS 39402

MISSOURI

Mineral Belt Gun Collectors Assn.
D.F. Saunders, 1110 Cleveland Ave., Monett, MO 65708
Missouri Valley Arms Collectors Assn., Inc.
L.P Brammer II, Membership Secy., P.O. Box 33033, Kansas City, MO 64114

MONTANA

Montana Arms Collectors Assn.
Lewis E. Yearout, 308 Riverview Dr. East, Great Falls, MT 59404
The Winchester Arms Collectors Assn.
Richard Berg, P.O. Box 6754, Great Falls, MT 59406

NEW HAMPSHIRE

New Hampshire Arms Collectors, Inc.
Frank H. Galeucia, Rt. 28, Box 44, Windham, NH 03087

NEW JERSEY

Jersey Shore Antique Arms Collectors
Joe Sisia, P.O. Box 100, Bayville, NJ 08721
New Jersey Arms Collectors Club, Inc.
Angus Laidlaw, President, 230 Valley Rd., Montclair, NJ 07042/201-746-0939

NEW YORK

Empire State Arms Collectors Assn.
P.O. Box 2328, Rochester, NY 14623
Iroquois Arms Collectors Assn.
Bonnie Robinson, Show Secy., P.O. Box 142, Ransomville, NY 14131/716-791-4096
Mid-State Arms Coll. & Shooters Club
Jack Ackerman, 24 S. Mountain Terr., Binghamton, NY 13903

NORTH CAROLINA

North Carolina Gun Collectors Assn.
Jerry Ledford, 3231-7th St. Dr. NE, Hickory, NC 28601

OHIO

Ohio Gun Collectors Assn.
P.O. Box 24170, Cincinnati, OH 45224-0170
The Stark Gun Collectors, Inc.
William I. Gann, 5666 Waynesburg Dr., Waynesburg, OH 44688

OKLAHOMA

Indian Territory Gun Collector's Assn.
P.O. Box 4491, Tulsa, OK 74159

OREGON

Oregon Arms Collectors Assn., Inc.
Phil Bailey, P.O. Box 13000-A, Portland, OR 97213
Oregon Cartridge Collectors Assn.
Gale Stockton, 52 N.W. 2nd, Gresham, OR 97030

PENNSYLVANIA

Presque Isle Gun Collectors Assn.
James Welch, 156 E. 37 St., Erie, PA 16504

SOUTH CAROLINA

Belton Gun Club, Inc.
J.K. Phillips, 195 Phillips Dr., Belton, SC 29627
South Carolina Shooting Assn.
P.O. Box 12658, Columbia, SC 29211-2658
Membership Div.: William Strozier, Secretary, P.O. Box 70, Johns Island, SC 29457-0070

SOUTH DAKOTA

Dakota Territory Gun Coll. Assn., Inc.
Curt Carter, Castlewood, SD 57223

TENNESSEE

Smoky Mountain Gun Coll. Assn., Inc.
Hugh W. Yabro, President, P.O. Box 23225, Knoxville, TN 37933
Tennessee Gun Collectors Assn., Inc.
M.H. Parks, 3556 Pleasant Valley Rd., Nashville, TN 37204

TEXAS

Houston Gun Collectors Assn., Inc.
P.O. Box 741429, Houston, TX 77274-1429
Texas Cartridge Collectors Assn., Inc.
James C. Sartor, Sec./Tres., 5606 Duxbury St., Houston, TX 77035
Texas Gun Collectors Assn.
13201 Wells Fargo Trail, Austin, TX 78737

WASHINGTON

Washington Arms Collectors, Inc.
J. Dennis Cook, P.O. Box 7335, Tacoma, WA 98407

WISCONSIN

Great Lakes Arms Collectors Assn., Inc.
Edward C. Warnke, 2913 Woodridge Lane, Waukesha, WI 53188
Wisconsin Gun Collectors Assn., Inc.
Lulita Zellmer, P.O. Box 181, Sussex, WI 53089

WYOMING

Wyoming Weapons Collectors
P.O. Box 284, Laramie, WY 82070/307-745-4652 or 745-9530

ARMS ASSOCIATIONS

NATIONAL ORGANIZATIONS

American Custom Gunmakers Guild
Jan Billeb, Exec. Director, P.O. Box 812, Burlington, IA 52601-0812/319-752-6114

American Defense Preparedness Assn.
Two Colonial Place, 2101 Wilson Blvd., Suite 400, Arlington, VA 22201-3061

American Pistolsmiths Guild
Hamilton S. Bowen, President, P.O. Box 67, Louisville, TN 37777

American Police Pistol & Rifle Assn.
3801 Biscayne Blvd., Miami, FL 33137

American Society of Arms Collectors
George E. Weatherly, P.O. Box 2567, Waxahachie, TX 75165

Association of Firearm and Toolmark Examiners
Eugenia A. Bell, Secy., 7857 Esterel Dr., LaJolla, CA 92037; Membership Secy., Andrew B. Hart, 80 Mountain View Ave., Rensselaer, NY 12144

Boone & Crockett Club
241 South Fraley Blvd., P.O. Box 547, Dumfries, VA 22026

Browning Collectors Assn.
Bobbie Hamit, P.O. Box 526, Aurora, NE 68818/402-694-6602

The Cast Bullet Assn., Inc.
Ralland J. Fortier, Membership Director, 4103 Foxcraft Dr., Traverse City, MI 49684

Citizens Committee for the Right to Keep and Bear Arms
Natl. Hq., Liberty Park, 12500 NE Tenth Pl., Bellevue, WA 98005

Colt Collectors Assn.
3200 Westminster, Dallas, TX 75205

Fifty Caliber Shooters Assn.
11469 Olive St. Rd., Suite 50, St. Louis, MO 63141

Firearms Coalition
Box 6537, Silver Spring, MD 20906/301-871-3006

Firearms Engravers Guild of America
Robert Evans, Secy., 332 Vine St., Oregon City, OR 97045

Foundation for North American Wild Sheep
720 Allen Ave., Cody, WY 82414

Golden Eagle Collectors Assn.
Chris Showler, 11144 Slate Creek Rd., Grass Valley, CA 95945

Gun Owners of America
8001 Forbes Place, Suite 102, Springfield, VA 22151/703-321-8585

Handgun Hunters International
J.D. Jones, Director, P.O. Box 357 MAG, Bloomingdale, OH 43910

Harrington & Richardson Gun Coll. Assn.
George L. Cardet, 525 NW 27th Ave., Suite 201, Miami, FL 33125

Hopkins & Allen Arms & Memorabilia Society (HAAMS)
1309 Pamela Circle, Delphos, OH 45833

International Cartridge Coll. Assn., Inc.
Charles Spano, P.O. Box 5297, Ormond Beach, FL 32174-5297

IHMSA (Intl. Handgun Metallic Silhouette Assn.)
Frank Scotto, 127 Winthrop Terr., Meriden, CT 06450

IPPA (International Paintball Players Assn.)
P.O. Box 90974, Los Angeles, CA 90009/310-322-3107

Jews for the Preservation of Firearms Ownership (JPFO)
2872 S. Wentworth Ave., Milwaukee, WI 53207/414-769-0760

Miniature Arms Collectors/Makers Society, Ltd.
Donald A. Beck, Secretary, 3329 Palm St., Granite City, IL 62040/618-877-5284

National Association of Buckskinners
Tim Pray, 1981 E. 94th Ave., Thornton, CO 80229

The National Association of Derringer Collectors
P.O. Box 160671, San Antonio, TX 78280

National Assn. of Federally Licensed Firearms Dealers
Andrew Molchan, 2455 E. Sunrise, Ft. Lauderdale, FL 33304

National Association to Keep and Bear Arms
P.O. Box 78336, Seattle, WA 98178

National Automatic Pistol Collectors Assn.
Tom Knox, P.O. Box 15738, Tower Grove Station, St. Louis, MO 63163

National Firearms Assn.
P.O. Box 160038, Austin, TX 78716

National Reloading Manufacturers Assn.
One Centerpointe Dr., Suite 300, Lake Oswego, OR 97035

National Rifle Assn. of America
1600 Rhode Island Ave., NW, Washington, DC 20036

National Shooting Sports Foundation, Inc.
Robert T. Delfay, President, Flintlock Ridge Office Center, 11 Mile Hill Rd., Newtown, CT 06470-2359/203-426-1320; FAX: 203-426-1087

National Wild Turkey Federation, Inc.
P.O. Box 530, Edgefield, SC 29824

North American Hunting Club
P.O. Box 3401, Minnetonka, MN 55343

North-South Skirmish Assn., Inc.
Stevan F. Meserve, Exec. Secretary, 204 W. Holly Ave., Sterling, VA 22170-4006

Remington Society of America
Leon W. Wier Jr., President, 22526 Leyte Dr., Torrance, CA 90505

Rocky Mountain Elk Foundation
P.O. Box 8249, Missoula, MT 59807-8249

Ruger Collector's Assn., Inc.
P.O. Box 1441, Yazoo City, MS 39194

Safari Club International
Philip DeLone, Admin. Dir., 4800 W. Gates Pass Rd., Tucson, AZ 85745/602-620-1220

Second Amendment Foundation
James Madison Building, 12500 NE 10th Pl., Bellevue, WA 98005

Smith & Wesson Collectors Assn.
George Linne, 2711 Miami St., St. Louis, MO 63118

Sporting Arms & Ammunition Manufacturers Institute (SAAMI)
Flintlock Ridge Office Center, 11 Mile Hill Rd., Newtown, CT 06470-2359/203-426-1320; FAX: 203-426-1087

The Thompson/Center Assn.
Joe Wright, President, Box 792, Northboro, MA 01532/508-393-3834

USPSA/IPSC
Dave Stanford, P.O. Box 811, Sedro Woolley, WA 98284/206-855-2245

U.S. Revolver Assn.
Chick Shuter, 96 West Union St., Ashland, MA 01721

The Varmint Hunters Assn., Inc.
Box 730, Lone Grove, OK 73443/405-657-3098

The Wildcatters
P.O. Box 170, Greenville, WI 54942

Winchester Arms Collectors Assn.
Richard Berg, Executive Secy., P.O. Box 6754, Great Falls, MT 59406

The Women's Shooting Sports Foundation (WSSF)
Glynne Moseley, 1505 Highway 6 South, Suite 103, Houston, TX 77077

AUSTRALIA

Sporting Shooters Assn. of Australia, Inc.
P.O. Box 2066, Kent Town, SA 5071, Australia

CANADA

ALBERTA

Canadian Historical Arms Society
P.O. Box 901, Edmonton, Alb., Canada T5J 2L8

National Firearms Assn.
Natl. Hq: P.O. Box 1779, Edmonton, Alb., Canada T5J 2P1

ONTARIO

Tri-County Antique Arms Fair
P.O. Box 122, RR #1, North Lancaster Ont., Canada K0C 1Z0

EUROPE

ENGLAND

Arms and Armour Society
E.J.B. Greenwood, Field House, Upper Dicker, Hailsham, East Sussex, BN27 3PY, England

Historical Breechloading Smallarms Assn.
D.J. Penn M.A., Imperial War Museum, Lambeth Rd., London SE 1 6HZ, England. Journal and newsletter are $12 a yr., plus surcharge for airmail.

National Rifle Assn.
(Great Britain) Bisley Camp, Brookwood, Woking Surrey GU24 OPB, England/0483.797777

FRANCE

Syndicat National de l'Arquebuserie du Commerce de l'Arme Historique
B.P. No. 3, 78110 Le Vesinet, France

GERMANY

Deutscher Schützenbund
Lahnstrasse 120, W-6200 Wiesbaden-Klarenthal, Germany

NEW ZEALAND

New Zealand Deerstalkers Assn.
Michael Watt, P.O. Box 6514, Wellington, New Zealand

SOUTH AFRICA

Historical Firearms Soc. of South Africa
P.O. Box 145, 7725 Newlands, Republic of South Africa

SAGA (S.A. Gunowners' Assn.)
P.O. Box 35204, Northway 4065, Republic of South Africa

DIRECTORY OF THE HANDGUN TRADE

AMMUNITION, COMMERCIAL

Action Arms Ltd., P.O. Box 9573, Philadelphia, PA 19124/215-744-0100; FAX: 215-533-2188

Black Hills Ammunition, P.O. Box 3090, Rapid City, SD 57709/605-348-5150; FAX: 605-348-9827

Blammo Ammo, P.O. Box 1677, Seneca, SC 29679/803-882-1768

Blount, Inc., Sporting Equipment Div., 2299 Snake River Ave., P.O. Box 856, Lewiston, ID 83501/800-627-3640, 208-746-2351

California Magnum, 20746 Dearborn St., Chatsworth, CA 91313/818-341-7302; FAX: 818-341-7304

CBC, Avenida Industrial, 3330, Santo Andre-SP-BRAZIL 09080/11-449-5600 (U.S. importer—MAGTECH Recreational Products, Inc.)

Century International Arms, Inc., 48 Lower Newton St., St. Albans, VT 05478/802-527-1252; FAX: 802-527-0470

ChinaSports, Inc., 2010 S. Lynx Place, Ontario, CA 91761/714-923-1411; FAX: 714-923-0775

Denver Bullets, Inc., 1811 W. 13th Ave., Denver, CO 80204/303-893-3146

Dynamit Nobel-RWS, Inc., 81 Ruckman Rd., Closter, NJ 07624/201-767-1995

Eley Ltd., P.O. Box 705, Witton, Birmingham, B6 7UT, ENGLAND/21-356-8899; FAX: 21-331-4173

Elite Ammunition, P.O. Box 3251, Oakbrook, IL 60522/708-366-9006

Enguix Import-Export, Alpujarras 58, Alzira, Valencia, SPAIN 46600/(96) 241 43 95; FAX: (96) 241 43 95

Federal Cartridge Co., 900 Ehlen Dr., Anoka, MN 55303/612-422-2840

Fiocchi of America, Inc., Rt. 2, P.O. Box 90-8, Ozark, MO 65721/417-725-4118; FAX: 417-725-1039

FN Herstal, Voie de Liege 33, Herstal 4040, BELGIUM/(32)41.40.82.83; FAX: (32)40.86.79

Garrett Cartridges, Inc., P.O. Box 178, Chehalis, WA 98532/206-736-0702

GDL Enterprises, 409 Le Gardeur, Slidell, LA 70460/504-649-0693

Glaser Safety Slug, Inc., P.O. Box 8223, Foster City, CA 94404/415-345-7677; FAX: 415-345-8217

"Gramps" Antique Cartridges, Box 341, Washago, Ont. L0K 2B0 CANADA/705-689-5348

Hansen & Co. (See Hansen Cartridge Co.)

Hirtenberger Aktiengesellschaft, Leobersdorferstrasse 31, A-2552 Hirtenberg, AUSTRIA

Hornady Mfg. Co., P.O. Box 1848, Grand Island, NE 68801/800-338-3220, 308-382-1390

ICI-America, P.O. Box 751, Wilmington, DE 19897/302-575-3000

IMI, P.O. Box 1044, Ramat Hasharon 47100, ISRAEL/972-3-5485222 (U.S. importer—Magnum Research, Inc.)

J.D. Jones, 721 Woodvue Lane, Wintersville, OH 43952/614-264-0176

Kent Cartridge Mfg. Co. Ltd., Unit 16, Branbridges Industrial Estate, East Peckham, Tonbridge, Kent, TN12 5HF ENGLAND/622-872255; FAX: 622-873645

Lethal Force Institute (See Police Bookshelf)

M&D Munitions Ltd., 127 Verdi St., Farmingdale, NY 11735/516-752-1038; FAX: 516-752-1905

Maionchi-L.M.I., Via Di Coselli-Zona Industriale Di Guamo, Lucca, ITALY 55060/011 39-583 94291

MAGTECH Recreational Products, Inc., 5030 Paradise Rd., Suite C211, Las Vegas, NV 89119/702-795-7191, 800-460-7191; FAX: 702-795-2769

Men-Metallwerk Elisenhuette, GmbH, P.O. Box 1263, W-5408 Nassau, GERMANY/2604-7819

Midway Arms, Inc., P.O. Box 1483, Columbia, MO 65205/314-445-6363; FAX: 314-446-1018

New England Ammunition Co., 1771 Post Rd. East, Suite 223, Westport, CT 06880/203-254-8048

Neutralizer Police Munitions, 5029 Middle Rd., Horseheads, NY 14845-9568/607-739-8362; FAX: 607-594-3900

Old Western Scrounger, Inc., 12924 Hwy. A-l2, Montague, CA 96064/916-459-5445

Omark, Div. of Blount, Inc., 2299 Snake River Ave., P.O. Box 856, Lewiston, ID 83501/800-627-3640, 208-746-2351

Paragon Sales & Services, Inc., P.O. Box 2022, Joliet, IL 60434/815-725-9212; FAX: 815-725-8974

PMC/Eldorado Cartridge Corp., P.O. Box 62508, 12801 U.S. Hwy. 95 S., Boulder City, NV 89006-2508/702-294-0025; FAX: 702-294-0121

Precision Prods. of Wash., Inc., N. 311 Walnut Rd., Spokane, WA 99206/509-928-0604

Pro Load Ammunition, Inc., 5180 E. Seltice Way, Post Falls, ID 83854/208-773-9444; FAX: 208-773-9441

Remington Arms Co., Inc., 1007 Market St., Wilmington, DE 19898/302-773-5291

RWS (See U.S. importer—Dynamit Nobel-RWS, Inc.)

Safari Gun Co., 6410 Brandon Ave., Springfield, VA 22150/703-569-1097

Sherwood Intl. Export Corp., 18714 Parthenia St., Northridge, CA 91324/818-349-7600

Speer Products, Div. of Blount, Inc., P.O. Box 856, Lewiston, ID 83501/208-746-2351

Star Reloading Co., Inc., 5520 Rock Hampton Ct., Indianapolis, IN 46268/317-872-5840

3-D Ammunition & Bullets, 112 W. Plum St., P.O. Box J, Doniphan, NE 68832/402-845-2285; FAX: 402-845-6546

United States Ammunition Co. (See USAC)

USAC, 4500-15th St. East, Tacoma, WA 98424/206-922-7589

Winchester Div., Olin Corp., 427 N. Shamrock, E. Alton, IL 62024/618-258-3566; FAX: 618-258-3180

Zero Ammunition Co., Inc., 1601 22nd St. SE, P.O. Box 1188, Cullman, AL 35055-1188/800-545-9376; FAX: 205-739-4683

AMMUNITION, CUSTOM

AFSCO Ammunition, 731 W. Third St., P.O. Box L, Owen, WI 54460/715-229-2516

Ballistica Maximus North, 107 College Park Plaza, Johnstown, PA 15904/814-266-8380

Ballistica Maximus South, 3242 Mary St., Suite S-318, Miami, FL 33133/305-446-5549

Cartridges Unlimited, 190 Bull's Bridge Rd., South Kent, CT 06785/203-927-3053

Country Armourer, The, P.O. Box 308, Ashby, MA 01431/508-386-7789

Custom Hunting Ammo & Arms, 2900 Fisk Rd., Howell, MI 48843/517-546-9498

Custom Tackle and Ammo, P.O. Box 1886, Farmington, NM 87499/505-632-3539

DKT, Inc., 14623 Vera Drive, Union, MI 49130-9744/616-641-7120; FAX: 616-641-2015

E.A.A. Corp., 4480 E. 11th Ave., Hialeah, FL 33013/305-688-4442; FAX: 305-688-5656

Elite Ammunition, P.O. Box 3251, Oakbrook, IL 60522/708-366-9006

Elk River, Inc., 1225 Paonia St., Colorado Springs, CO 80915/719-574-4407

Elko Arms, Dr. L. Kortz, 28 rue Ecole Moderne, B-7060 Soignies, BELGIUM/(32)67-33-29-34

Ellis Sport Shop, E.W., RD 1, Route 9N, P.O. Box 315, Corinth, NY 12822/518-654-6444

Epps "Orillia" Ltd., Ellwood, RR 3, Hwy. 11 North, Orillia, Ont. L3V 6H3, CANADA/705-689-5333

Freedom Arms, Inc., P.O. Box 1776, Freedom, WY 83120/307-883-2468; FAX: 307-883-2005

Gammog, Gregory B. Gally, 16009 Kenny Rd., Laurel, MD 20707/301-725-3838

GDL Enterprises, 409 Le Gardeur, Slidell, LA 70460/504-649-0693

"Gramps" Antique Cartridges, Box 341, Washago, Ont. L0K 2B0 CANADA/705-689-5348

Hardin Specialty Dist., P.O. Box 338, Radcliff, KY 40159-0338/502-351-6649

Hindman, Ace, 1880 1/2 Upper Turtle Creek Rd., Kerrville, TX 78028/512-257-4290

Hirtenberger Aktiengesellschaft, Leobersdorferstrasse 31, A-2552 Hirtenberg, AUSTRIA

Jensen's Custom Ammunition, 5146 E. Pima, Tucson, AZ 85712/602-325-3346; FAX: 602-322-5704

Jett & Co., Inc., RR 3, Box 167-B, Litchfield, IL 62056/217-324-3779

Kaswer Custom, Inc., 13 Surrey Drive, Brookfield, CT 06804/203-775-0564; FAX: 203-775-6872

Keeler, R.H., 817 "N" St., Port Angeles, WA 98362/206-457-4702

Kent Cartridge Mfg. Co. Ltd., Unit 16, Branbridges Industrial Estate, East Peckham, Tonbridge, Kent, TN12 5HF ENGLAND/622-872255; FAX: 622-873645

Lindsley Arms Ctg. Co., P.O. Box 757, 20 College Hill Rd., Henniker, NH 03242/603-428-3127

Linebaugh Custom Sixguns & Rifle Works, P.O. Box 1263, Cody, WY 82414/307-587-8010

Lomont Precision Bullets, 4236 W. 700 South, Poneto, IN 46781/219-694-6792; FAX: 219-694-6797

MagSafe Ammo Co., Box 5692, 2725 Friendly Grove Rd NE, Olympia, WA 98506/206-357-6383

M&D Munitions Ltd., 127 Verdi St., Farmingdale, NY 11735/516-752-1038; FAX: 516-752-1905

Monte Kristo Pistol Grip Co., P.O. Box 85, Whiskeytown, CA 96095/916-623-4019

Mountain South, P.O. Box 381, Barnwell, SC 29812/FAX: 803-259-3227

Newman Gunshop, Rt. 1, Box 90F, Agency, IA 52530/515-937-5775

Old Western Scrounger, Inc., 12924 Hwy. A-l2, Montague, CA 96064/916-459-5445

Old World Gunsmithing, 2901 SE 122nd St., Portland, OR 97236/503-760-7681

Personal Protection Systems, RD 5, Box 5027-A, Moscow, PA 18444/717-842-1766

Precision Delta Corp., P.O. Box 128, Ruleville, MS 38771/601-756-2810; FAX: 601-756-2590

Precision Munitions, Inc., P.O. Box 326, Jasper, IN 47547

Sanders Custom Gun Service, 2358 Tyler Ln., Louisville, KY 40205/502-454-3338

Spence, George W., 115 Locust St., Steele, MO 63877/314-695-4916

SSK Industries, 721 Woodvue Lane, Wintersville, OH 43952/614-264-0176; FAX: 614-264-2257

State Arms Gun Co., 815 S. Division St., Waunakee, WI 53597/608-849-5800

3-D Ammunition & Bullets, 112 W. Plum St., P.O. Box J, Doniphan, NE 68832/402-845-2285; FAX: 402-845-6546

3-Ten Corp., P.O. Box 269, Feeding Hills, MA 01030/413-789-2086

AMMUNITION, FOREIGN

Action Ammo Ltd. (See Action Arms Ltd.)

Action Arms Ltd., P.O. Box 9573, Philadelphia, PA 19124/215-744-0100; FAX: 215-533-2188

AFSCO Ammunition, 731 W. Third St., P.O. Box L, Owen, WI 54460/715-229-2516

Cartridges Unlimited, 190 Bull's Bridge Rd., South Kent, CT 06785/203-927-3053

CBC, Avenida Industrial, 3330, Santo Andre-SP-BRAZIL 09080/11-449-5600 (U.S. importer—MAGTECH Recreational Products, Inc.)

Century International Arms, Ltd., 48 Lower Newton St., St. Albans, VT 05478/802-527-1252; FAX: 802-524-5631

Champion's Choice, Inc., 223 Space Park South, Nashville, TN 37211/615-834-6666; FAX: 615-831-2753

Dynamit Nobel-RWS, Inc., 81 Ruckman Rd., Closter, NJ 07624/201-767-1995

Fiocchi of America, Inc., Rt. 2, P.O. Box 90-8, Ozark, MO 65721/417-725-4118; FAX: 417-725-1039

FN Herstal, Voie de Liege 33, Herstal 4040, BELGIUM/(32)41.40.82.83; FAX: (32)40.86.79

"Gramps" Antique Cartridges, Box 341, Washago, Ont. L0K 2B0 CANADA/705-689-5348

Hansen & Co. (See Hansen Cartridge Co.)

Hansen Cartridge Co., 244 Old Post Rd., Southport, CT 06490/203-259-6222

Hirtenberger Aktiengesellschaft, Leobersdorferstrasse 31, A-2552 Hirtenberg, AUSTRIA

Kassnar (See U.S. importer—K.B.I., Inc.)

MAGTECH Recreational Products, Inc., 5030 Paradise Rd., Suite C211, Las Vegas, NV 89119/702-795-7191, 800-460-7191; FAX: 702-795-2769

Maionchi-L.M.I., Via Di Coselli-Zona Industriale Di Guamo, Lucca, ITALY 55060/011 39-583 94291

Merkuria Ltd., Argentinska 38, 17005 Praha 7, CZECH REPUBLIC/422-875117; FAX: 422-809152

New England Arms Co., Box 278, Lawrence Lane, Kittery Point, ME 03905/207-439-0593; FAX: 207-439-6726

Old Western Scrounger, Inc., 12924 Hwy. A-l2, Montague, CA 96064/916-459-5445

Paragon Sales & Services, Inc., P.O. Box 2022, Joliet, IL 60434/815-725-9212; FAX: 815-725-8974

PMC/Eldorado Cartridge Corp., P.O. Box 62508, 12801 U.S. Hwy. 95 S., Boulder City, NV 89006-2508/702-294-0025; FAX: 702-294-0121

Precision Delta Corp., P.O. Box 128, Ruleville, MS 38771/601-756-2810; FAX: 601-756-2590

R.E.T. Enterprises, 2608 S. Chestnut, Broken Arrow, OK 74012/918-251-GUNS; FAX: 918-251-0587

RWS (See U.S. importer—Dynamit Nobel-RWS, Inc.)

Safari Gun Co., 6410 Brandon Ave., Springfield, VA 22150/703-569-1097

Samco Global Arms, Inc., 6995 NW 43rd St., Miami, FL 33166/305-593-9782

AMMUNITION COMPONENTS—BULLETS, POWDER, PRIMERS

Accuracy Unlimited, 16036 N. 49 Ave., Glendale, AZ 85306/602-978-9089

Accurate Arms Co., Inc., Rt. 1, Box 167, McEwen, TN 37101/615-729-4207; FAX 615-729-4217

Allred Bullet Co., 932 Evergreen Drive, Logan, UT 84321/801-752-6983

American Bullets, 2190 C. Coffee Rd., Lithonia, GA 30058/404-482-4253

Armfield Custom Bullets, 4775 Caroline Drive, San Diego, CA 92115/619-582-7188

Ballard Built, P.O. Box 1443, Kingsville, TX 78364/512-592-0853

Bertram Bullet Co., P.O. Box 313, Seymour, Victoria 3660, AUSTRALIA/61-57-922912; FAX: 61-47-991650

Black Hills Shooters Supply, P.O. Box 4220, Rapid City, SD 57709/605-348-4477; FAX: 605-348-5037

Black Mountain Bullets, Rt. 7, P.O. Box 297, Warrenton, VA 22186/703-347-1199

Blount, Inc., Sporting Equipment Div., 2299 Snake River Ave., P.O. Box 856, Lewiston, ID 83501/800-627-3640, 208-746-2351

Blue Mountain Bullets, HCR 77, P.O. Box 231, John Day, OR 97845/503-820-4594

Bruno Shooters Supply, 106 N. Wyoming St., Hazleton, PA 18201/717-455-2211; FAX: 717-455-2211

Bull-X, Inc., 520 N. Main St., Farmer City, IL 61842/309-928-2574, 800-248-3845 orders only

Buzztail Brass, 5306 Bryant Ave., Klamath Falls, OR 97603/503-884-1072

Competitor Corp., Inc., P.O. Box 244, 293 Townsend Rd., West Groton, MA 01472/508-448-3521; FAX: 603-673-4540

Cor-Bon, Inc., 4828 Michigan Ave., P.O. Box 10126, Detroit, MI 48210/313-894-2373

Denver Bullets, Inc., 1811 W. 13th Ave., Denver, CO 80204/303-893-3146

DKT, Inc., 14623 Vera Drive, Union, MI 49130-9744/616-641-7120; FAX: 616-641-2015

DuPont (See IMR Powder Co.)

E.A.A. Corp., 4480 E. 11th Ave., Hialeah, FL 33013/305-688-4442; FAX: 305-688-5656

Enguix Import-Export, Alpujarras 58, Alzira, Valencia, SPAIN 46600//(96) 241 43 95; FAX: (96) 241 43 95

Federal Cartridge Co., 900 Ehlen Dr., Anoka, MN 55303/612-422-2840

Fiocchi of America, Inc., Rt. 2, P.O. Box 90-8, Ozark, MO 65721/417-725-4118; FAX: 417-725-1039

Fitz Pistol Grip Co., P.O. Box 610, Douglas City, CA 96024/916-623-4019

Fowler Bullets, 4003 Linwood Rd., Gastonia, NC 28052/704-867-3259

Freedom Arms, Inc., P.O. Box 1776, Freedom, WY 83120/307-883-2468; FAX: 307-883-2005

GOEX, Inc., 1002 Springbrook Ave., Moosic, PA 18507/717-457-6724; FAX: 717-457-1130

Green Bay Bullets, 1860 Burns Ave., Green Bay, WI 54313/414-494-5166

Hansen & Co. (See Hansen Cartridge Co.)

Hansen Cartridge Co., 244 Old Post Rd., Southport, CT 06490/203-789-7337

Hercules, Inc., Hercules Plaza, 1313 N Market St., Wilmington, DE 19894/302-594-5000

Hirtenberger Aktiengesellschaft, Leobersdorferstrasse 31, A-2552 Hirtenberg, AUSTRIA

Hodgdon Powder Co., Inc., P.O. Box 2932, Shawnee Mission, KS 66201/913-362-9455; FAX: 913-362-1307

Hornady Mfg. Co., P.O. Box 1848, Grand Island, NE 68801/800-338-3220, 308-382-1390

IMI, P.O. Box 1044, Ramat Hasharon 47100, ISREAL/972-3-5485222 (U.S. importer—Magnum Research

IMR Powder Co., Box 247E, Xplo Complex, RTS, Plattsburgh, NY 12901/518-561-9530; FAX: 518-563-0044

Israel Military Industries Ltd. (See IMI)

Jensen Bullets, 86 North, 400 West, Blackfoot, ID 83221/208-785-5590

Jensen's Custom Ammunition, 5146 E. Pima, Tucson, AZ 85712/602-325-3346; FAX: 602-322-5704

Kaswer Custom, Inc., 13 Surrey Drive, Brookfield, CT 06804/203-775-0564; FAX: 203-775-6872

Kent Cartridge Mfg. Co. Ltd., Unit 16, Branbridges Industrial Estate, East Peckham, Tonbridge, Kent, TN12 5HF ENGLAND/622-872255; FAX: 622-873645

Kodiak Custom Bullets, 8261 Henry Circle, Anchorage, AK 99507/907-349-2282

Lane Bullets, Inc., 1011 S. 10th St., Kansas City, KS 66105/913-621-6113, 800-444-7468

Lindsley Arms Ctg. Co., P.O. Box 757, 20 College Hill Rd., Henniker, NH 03242/603-428-3127

Lomont Precision Bullets, 4236 W. 700 South, Poneto, IN 46781/219-694-6792; FAX: 219-694-6797

Maionchi-L.M.I., Via Di Coselli-Zona Industriale Di Guamo, Lucca, ITALY 55060/011 39-583 94291

Master Class Bullets, 4110 Alder St., Eugene, OR 97405/503-687-1263

McMurdo, Lynn (See Specialty Gunsmithing)

M&D Munitions Ltd., 127 Verdi St., Farmingdale, NY 11735/516-752-1038; FAX: 516-752-1905

Montana Precision Swaging, P.O. Box 4746, Butte, MT 59702/406-782-7502

Mushroom Express Bullet Co., 601 W. 6th St., Greenfield, IN 46140/317-462-6332

Naval Ordnance Works, Rt. 2, Box 919, Sheperdstown, WV 25443/304-876-0998

Necromancer Industries, Inc., 14 Communications Way, West Newton, PA 15089/412-872-8722

Norma (See U.S. importer—Paul Co., The)

Northern Precision Custom Swaged Bullets, 337 S. James St., Carthage, NY 13619/315-493-3456

Nosler, Inc., P.O. Box 671, Bend, OR 97709/800-285-3701, 503-382-3921; FAX: 503-388-4667

Old Western Scrounger, Inc., 12924 Hwy. A-I2, Montague, CA 96064/916-459-5445

Omark, Div. of Blount, Inc., 2299 Snake River Ave., P.O. Box 856, Lewiston, ID 83501/800-627-3640, 208-746-2351

Pace Marketing, Inc., 9474 NW 48th St., Sunrise, FL 33351-5137/305-741-4361; FAX: 305-741-2901

Patriot Manufacturing, P.O. Box 50065, Lighthouse Point, FL 33074/305-783-4849

Paul Co., The, Rt. 1, Box 177A, Wellsville, KS 66092/913-883-4444

Pomeroy, Robert, RR1, Box 50, E. Corinth, ME 04427/207-285-7721

Pony Express Reloaders, 608 E. Co. Rd. D, Suite 3, St. Paul, MN 55117/612-483-9406

Precision Components and Guns, Rt. 55, P.O. Box 337, Pawling, NY 12564/914-855-3040

Precision Delta Corp., P.O. Box 128, Ruleville, MS 38771/601-756-2810; FAX: 601-756-2590

Precision Munitions, Inc., P.O. Box 326, Jasper, IN 47547

Precision Reloading, Inc., P.O. Box 122, Stafford Springs, CT 06076/203-684-7979; FAX: 203-684-6788

Remington Arms Co., Inc., 1007 Market St., Wilmington, DE 19898/302-773-5291

Renner Co./Radical Concepts, R.J., P.O. Box 10731, Canoga Park, CA 91309/818-700-8131

R.I.S. Co., Inc., 718 Timberlake Circle, Richardson, TX 75080/214-235-0933

Rolston Jr., Fred, 210 E. Cummins, Tecumseh, MI 49286/517-423-6002

Rossi S.A. Metalurgica E Municoes, Amadeo, Rua Amadeo Rossi, 143, Sao Leopoldo, RS, BRAZIL 93 030/0512-92-5566 (U.S. importer—Interarms)

Rubright Bullets, 1008 S. Quince Rd., Walnutport, PA 18088/215-767-1339

Scot Powder Co. of Ohio, Inc., 430 Powder Plant Rd., McArthur, OH 45651/614-596-2706; FAX: 614-596-4050

Shappy Bullets, 76 Milldale Ave., Plantsville, CT 06479/203-621-3704

Southern Ammunition Co., Inc., Rt. 1, Box 6B, Latta, SC 29565/803-752-7751; FAX: 803-752-2022

Specialty Gunsmithing, Lynn McMurdo, P.O. Box 404, Afton, WY 83110/307-886-5535

Speer Products, Div. of Blount, P.O. Box, Lewiston, ID 83501/208-746-2351

Stevi Machine, Inc., 4004 Hwy. 93 North, Stevensville, MT 59870/406-777-5401

Swift Bullet Co., P.O. Box 27, 201 Main St., Quinter, KS 67752/913-754-3959; FAX: 913-754-2359

T.F.C. S.p.A., Via G. Marconi 118, B, Villa Carcina, Brescia 25069, ITALY/030-881271; FAX: 030-881826

3-D Ammunition & Bullets, 112 W. Plum St., P.O. Box J, Doniphan, NE 68832/402-845-2285; FAX: 402-845-6546

Thompson Precision, 110 Mary St., P.O. Box 251, Warren, IL 61087/815-745-3625

TMI Products, 930 S. Plumer Ave., Tucson, AZ 85719/602-792-1075; FAX: 602-792-0093

Trophy Bonded Bullets, Inc., 900 S. Loop W., Suite 190, Houston, TX 77054/713-645-4499; FAX: 713-741-6393

True Flight Bullet Co., 5581 Roosevelt St., Whitehall, PA 18052/800-875-3625; FAX: 215-262-7806

United States Ammunition Co. (See USAC)

USAC, 4500-15th St. East, Tacoma, WA 98424/206-922-7589

Vihtavuori Oy, SF-41330 Vihtavuori, FINLAND/358-41-779-211; FAX: 358-41-771643

Warren Muzzleloading Co., Inc., Hwy. 21 North, Ozone, AR 72854/501-292-3268

Watson Trophy Match Bullets, 2404 Wade Hampton Blvd., Greenville, SC 29615/803-244-7948

Whitestone Lumber Corp., 148-02 14th Ave., Whitestone, NY 11357/718-746-4400; FAX: 718-767-1748

Widener's Reloading & Shooting Supply, Inc., P.O. Box 3009 CRS, Johnson City, TN 37602/615-282-6786; FAX: 615-282-6651

Winchester Div., Olin Corp., 427 N. Shamrock, E. Alton, IL 62024/618-258-3566; FAX: 618-258-3180

Woodland Bullets, 638 Woodland Dr., Manheim, PA 17545/717-665-4332

Wyoming Casting Co., 305 Commerce Dr. 10D, P.O. Box 1492, Gillette, WY 82717/307-687-7779, 800-821-2167

Zero Ammunition Co., Inc., 1601 22nd St. SE, P.O. Box 1188, Cullman, AL 35055-1188/800-545-9376; FAX: 205-739-4683

BULLET AND CASE LUBRICANTS

Armite Laboratories, 1845 Randolph St., Los Angeles, CA 90001/213-587-7768; FAX: 213-587-5075

Blackhawk East, P.O. Box 2274, Loves Park, IL 61131

Blackhawk Mountain, P.O. Box 210, Conifer, CO 80433

Blackhawk West, P.O. Box 285, Hiawatha, KS 66434

Blackinton & Co., Inc., V.H., 221 John L. Dietsch, Attleboro Falls, MA 02763-3000/508-699-4436; FAX: 508-695-5349

Blount, Inc., Sporting Equipment Div., 2299 Snake River Ave., P.O. Box 856, Lewiston, ID 83501/800-627-3640, 208-746-2351

Bullet Swaging Supply, Inc., P.O. Box 1056, 303 McMillan Rd, West Monroe, LA 71291/318-387-7257; FAX: 318-387-7779

Camp-Cap Products, P.O. Box 173, Chesterfield, MO 63006/314-532-4340

Campbell, Dick, 20,000 Silver Ranch Rd., Conifer, CO 80433/303-697-0150

CF Ventures, 509 Harvey Dr., Bloomington, IN 47403-1715

Cooper-Woodward, P.O. Box 1788, East Helena, MT 59635/406-475-3321

Corbin, Inc., 600 Industrial Circle, P.O. Box 2659, White City, OR 97503/503-826-5211; FAX: 503-826-8669

Corkys Gun Clinic, 111 North 11th Ave., Greeley, CO 80631/303-330-0516

Dillon Precision Products, Inc., 7442 E. Butherus Dr., Scottsdale, AZ 85260/602-948-8009

Fitz Pistol Grip Co., P.O. Box 610, Douglas City, CA 96024/916-623-4019

Gamba S.p.A., Renato, Via Artigiani, 93, 25063 Gardone V.T. (Brescia), ITALY

Gozon Corp., P.O. Box 6278, Fulsom, CA 95763/916-983-1807; FAX: 916-983-9500

Guardsman Products, 411 N. Darling, Fremont, MI 49412/616-924-3950

Hollywood Engineering, 10642 Arminta St., Sun Valley, CA 91352/818-842-8376

Hornady Mfg. Co., P.O. Box 1848, Grand Island, NE 68801/800-338-3220, 308-382-1390

Huntington Die Specialties, 601 Oro Dam Blvd., Oroville, CA 95965/916-534-1210; FAX: 916-534-1212

INTEC International, P.O. Box 5828, Sparks, NV 89432-5828

Javelina Products, P.O. Box 337, San Bernardino, CA 92402/714-882-5847; FAX: 714-434-6937

Lane Bullets, Inc., 1011 S. 10th St., Kansas City, KS 66105/913-621-6113, 800-444-7468

LBT, HCR 62, Box 145, Moyie Springs, ID 83845/208-267-3588

Lee Precision, Inc., 4275 Hwy. U, Hartford, WI 53027/414-673-3075

Lighthouse Mfg. Co., Inc., 443 Ashwood Place, Boca Raton, FL 33431/407-394-6011

Lithi Bee Bullet Lube, 2161 Henry St., Muskegon, MI 49441/616-755-4707

Magma Engineering Co., P.O. Box 161, Queen Creek, AZ 85242/602-987-9008; FAX: 602-987-0148

Micro-Lube, Rt. 2, P.O. Box 201, Deming, NM 88030/505-546-9116

Monte Kristo Pistol Grip Co., P.O. Box 85, Whiskeytown, CA 96095/916-623-4019

M&N Bullet Lube, P.O. Box 495, 151 NE Jefferson St., Madras, OR 97741/503-255-3750

Ox-Yoke Originals, Inc., 34 Main St., Milo, ME 04463/800-231-8313; FAX: 207-943-2416

Ravell Ltd., 289 Diputacion St., 08009, Barcelona SPAIN

RCBS, Div. of Blount, Inc., 605 Oro Dam Blvd., Oroville, CA 95965/800-533-5000, 916-533-5191

Reardon Products, P.O. Box 126, Morrison, IL 61270/815-772-3155

Redding Reloading, Inc., 1089 Starr, Courtland, NY 13045/607-753-3331; FAX: 607-756-8445

DIRECTORY OF THE HANDGUN TRADE

SAECO (See Redding Reloading, Inc.)
Shay's Gunsmithing, 931 Marvin Ave., Lebanon, PA 17042
Shooters Accessory Supply (See Corbin, Inc.)
Slipshot MTS Group, P.O. Box 5, Postal Station D, Etobicoke, Ont., CANADA M9A 4X1/FAX: 416-762-0962
Small Custom Mould & Bullet Co., Box 17211, Tucson, AZ 85731
Tamarack Prods.,Inc., P.O. Box 625, Wauconda, IL 60084/708-526-9333
Thompson Bullet Lube Co., P.O. Box 472343, Garland, TX 75047/214-271-8063; FAX: 214-840-6743
Thompson/Center Arms, Farmington Rd., P.O. Box 5002, Rochester, NH 03867/603-332-2394
Watson Trophy Match Bullets, 2404 Wade Hampton Blvd., Greenville, SC 29615/803-244-7948
White Systems, Inc., P.O. Box 190, Roosevelt, UT 84066/801-722-3085; FAX: 801-722-3085
Young Country Arms, P.O. Box 3615, Simi Valley, CA 93093

BULLET SWAGE DIES AND TOOLS

Advance Car Mover Co., Rowell Div., P.O. Box 1, 240 N. Depot St., Juneau, WI 53039/414-386-4464
Adventure 16, Inc., 4620 Alvarado Canyon Rd., San Diego, CA 92120/619-283-6314
Blount, Inc., Sporting Equipment Div., 2299 Snake River Ave., P.O. Box 856, Lewiston, ID 83501/800-627-3640, 208-746-2351
Bruno Shooters Supply, 106 N. Wyoming St., Hazleton, PA 18201/717-455-2211; FAX: 717-455-2211
Brynin, Milton, P.O. Box 383, Yonkers, NY 10710/914-779-4333
Bullet Swaging Supply, Inc., P.O. Box 1056, 303 McMillan Rd., West Monroe, LA 71291/318-387-7257; FAX: 318-387-7779
The BulletMakers Workshop, RFD 1 Box 1755, Brooks, ME 04921
C-H Tool & Die Corp. (See 4-D Custom Die Co.)
Corbin, Inc., 600 Industrial Circle, P.O. Box 2659, White City, OR 97503/503-826-5211; FAX: 503-826-8669
Fitz Pistol Grip Co., P.O. Box 610, Douglas City, CA 96024/916-623-4019
Hollywood Engineering, 10642 Arminta St., Sun Valley, CA 91352/818-842-8376
Lachaussee, S.A., 29 Rue Kerstenne, Ans, B-4430 BELGIUM/041-63 88 77
MoLoc Bullets, P.O. Box 2810, Turlock, CA 95381/209-632-1644
Monte Kristo Pistol Grip Co., P.O. Box 85, Whiskeytown, CA 96095/916-623-4019
NECO, 1316-67th St., Emeryville, CA 94608/510-450-0420
Necromancer Industries, Inc., 14 Communications Way, West Newton, PA 15089/412-872-8722
Rorschach Precision Products, P.O. Box 151613, Irving, TX 75015/214-790-3487
Speer Products, Div. of Blount, Inc., P.O. Box 856, Lewiston, ID 83501/208-746-2351
Sport Flite Manufacturing Co., P.O. Box 1082, Bloomfield Hills, MI 48303/313-647-3747

CHRONOGRAPHS AND PRESSURE TOOLS

Canons Delcour, Rue J.B. Cools, B-4040 Herstal, BELGIUM/32.(0)41.40.13.40; FAX: 32(0)412.40.22.88
Chronotech, 1655 Siamet Rd. Unit 6, Mississauga, Ont. L4W 1Z4 CANADA/416-625-5200; FAX: 416-625-5190
Competition Electronics, Inc., 3469 Precision Dr., Rockford, IL 61109/815-874-8001; FAX: 815-874-8181
Custom Chronograph, Inc., 5305 Reese Hill Rd., Sumas, WA 98295/206-988-7801
D&H Precision Tooling, 7522 Barnard Mill Rd., Ringwood, IL 60072/815-653-4011
Dedicated Systems, 105-B Cochrane Circle, Morgan Hill, CA 95037/408-779-2808; FAX: 408-779-2673
Lachaussee, S.A., 29 Rue Kerstenne, Ans, B-4430 BELGIUM/041-63 88 77
Oehler Research, Inc., P.O. Box 9135, Austin, TX 78766/512-327-6900
P.A.C.T., Inc., P.O. Box 531525, Grand Prairie, TX 75053/214-641-0049
Shooting Chrony, Inc., P.O. Box 101 LP, Niagara Falls, NY 14304/416-276-6292; FAX: 416-276-6295
Stratco, Inc., 200 E. Center St., Kalispell, MT 59901/406-755-4034; FAX: 406-257-4753
Tepeco, P.O. Box 342, Friendswood, TX 77546/713-482-2702

CLEANING AND REFINISHING SUPPLIES

Acculube II, Inc., 22261 68th Ave. S., Kent, WA 98032-1914/206-395-7171
Accupro Gun Care, 15512-109 Ave., Surrey, BC U3R 7E8, CANADA/604-583-7807
Accuracy Products, S.A., 14 rue de Lawsanne, Brussels, 1060 BELGIUM/32-2-539-34-42; FAX: 32-2-539-39-60
ADCO International, 1 Wyman St., Woburn, MA 01801-2341/617-935-1799; FAX: 617-932-4807
American Gas & Chemical Co., Ltd., 220 Pegasus Ave., Northvale, NJ 07647/201-767-7300
Armoloy Co. of Ft. Worth, 204 E. Daggett St., Fort Worth, TX 76104/817-332-5604; FAX: 817-335-6517
Belltown, Ltd., 11 Camps Rd., Kent, CT 06757/203-354-5750
Beretta, Dr. Franco, via Rossa, 4, Concesio (BC), Italy I-25062/030-2751955; FAX: 030-218-0414
Big 45 Frontier Gun Shop, 515 Cliff Ave., Valley Springs, SD 57068/605-757-6248; FAX: 605-757-6248
Bill's Gun Repair, 1007 Burlington St., Mendota, IL 61342/815-539-5786
Birchwood Laboratories, Inc., 7900 Fuller Rd., Eden Prairie, MN 55344/612-937-7933; FAX: 612-937-7979
Blount, Inc., Sporting Equipment Div., 2299 Snake River Ave., P.O. Box 856, Lewiston, ID 83501/800-627-3640, 208-746-2351
Break-Free, P.O. Box 25020, Santa Ana, CA 92799/714-953-1900
Bridgers Best, P.O. Box 1410, Berthoud, CO 80513
Brobst, Jim, 299 Poplar St., Hamburg, PA 19526/215-562-2103
Browning Arms Co. (Gen. Offices), 1 Browning Place, Morgan, UT 84050/801-876-2711; FAX: 801-876-3331
Bruno Shooters Supply, 106 N. Wyoming St., Hazleton, PA 18201/717-455-2211; FAX: 717-455-2211
Chopie Mfg., Inc., 700 Copeland Ave., LaCrosse, WI 54603/608-784-0926
Clenzoil Corp., P.O. Box 80226, Canton, OH 44708/216-833-9758
Corbin, Inc., 600 Industrial Circle, P.O. Box 2659, White City, OR 97503/503-826-5211; FAX: 503-826-8669
Crane & Crane Ltd., 105 N. Edison Way 6, Reno, NV 89502-2355/702-856-1516; FAX: 702-856-1616

Creedmoor Sports, Inc., P.O. Box 1040, Oceanside, CA 92051/619-757-5529
Crouse's Country Cover, P.O. Box 160, Storrs, CT 06268/203-423-0702
Jones Custom Products, Neil, RD 1, Box 483A, Saegertown, PA 16443/814-763-2769; FAX: 814-763-4228
Decker Shooting Products, 1729 Laguna Ave., Schofield, WI 54476/715-359-5873
Dewey Mfg. Co., Inc., J., P.O. Box 2014, Southbury, CT 06488/203-598-7912; FAX: 203-598-3119
Dri-Slide, Inc., 411 N. Darling, Fremont, MI 49412/616-924-3950
Du-Lite Corp., 171 River Rd., Middletown, CT 06457/203-347-2505
Dutchman's Firearms, Inc., The, 4143 Taylor Blvd., Louisville, KY 40215/502-366-0555
Dykstra, Doug, 411 N. Darling, Fremont, MI 49412/616-924-3950
Eezox, Inc., P.O. Box 772, Waterford, CT 06385-0772/203-447-8282; FAX: 203-447-3484
Faith Associates, Inc., 1139 S. Greenville Hwy., Hendersonville, NC 28792/704-692-1916; FAX: 704-697-6827
Flitz International Ltd., 821 Mohr Ave., Waterford, WI 53185/414-534-5898; FAX: 414-534-2991
Flouramics, Inc., 103 Pleasant Ave., Upper Saddle River, NJ 07458/201-825-8110
Forster Products, 82 E. Lanark Ave., Lanark, IL 61046/815-493-6360; FAX: 815-493-2371
Forty Five Ranch Enterprises, Box 1080, Miami, OK 74355-1080/918-542-5875
Frontier Products Co., 164 E. Longview Ave., Columbus, OH 43202/614-262-9357
G96 Products Co., Inc., 237 River St., Paterson, NJ 07524/201-684-4050; FAX: 201-684-3848
Golden Age Arms Co., 115 E. High St., Ashley, OH 43003/614-747-2488
Gozon Corp., P.O. Box 6278, Fulsom, CA 95763/916-983-1807; FAX: 916-983-9500
Graves Co., 1800 Andrews Av., Pompano Beach, FL 33069/800-327-9103; FAX: 305-960-0301
Guardsman Products, 411 N. Darling, Fremont, MI 49412/616-924-3950
Gun Works, The, 236 Main St., Springfield, OR 97477/503-741-4118
Half Moon Rifle Shop, 490 Halfmoon Rd., Columbia Falls, MT 59912/406-892-4409
Heatbath Corp., P.O. Box 2978, Springfield, MA 01101/413-543-3381
Hoppe's Div., Penguin Industries, Inc., Airport Industrial Mall, Coatesville, PA 19320/251-384-6000
INTEC International, Inc., P.O. Box 5828, Sparks, NV 89432-5828
Iosso Products, 1485 Lively Blvd., Elk Grove Villiage, IL 60007/708-437-8400
Jantz Supply, P.O. Box 584-GD, Davis, OK 73030/405-369-2316; FAX: 405-369-3082
J-B Bore Cleaner, 299 Poplar St., Hamburg, PA 19526/215-562-2103
Johnson Gunsmithing, Inc., Neal G., 111 Marvin Dr., Hampton, VA 23666/804-838-8091; FAX: 804-838-8157
Johnston Bros., 1889 Rt. 9, Unit 22, Toms River, NJ 08755/800-257-2595; FAX: 800-257-2534
Jonad Corp., 2091 Lakeland Ave., Lakewood, OH 44107/216-226-3161
Kleen-Bore, Inc., 20 Ladd Ave., Northampton, MA 01060/413-586-7240; FAX: 413-586-0236
Kopp, Terry, 1301 Franklin, Lexington, MO 64067/816-259-2636
Lee Supplies, Mark, 9901 France Ct., Lakeville, MN 55444/612-461-2114
LEM Gun Specialties, P.O. Box 87031, College Park, GA 30337
LPS Laboratories, Inc., 4647 Hugh Howell Rd., P.O. Box 3050, Tucker, GA 30084/404-934-7800
LT Industries, Inc., 20504 Hillgrove Ave., Maple Heights, OH 44137/216-587-5005
Marble Arms Corp., 420 Industrial Park, P.O. Box 111, Gladstone, MI 49837/906-428-3710; FAX: 906-428-3711
Micro Sight Co., 242 Harbor Blvd., Belmont, CA 94002/415-591-0769; FAX: 415-591-7531
Mountain View Sports, Inc., Box 188, Troy, NH 03465/603-357-9690; FAX: 603-357-9691
Munger, Robert D. (See Rusteprufe Laboratories)
Muscle Products Corp. (See MPC)
Nesci Enterprises, Inc., P.O. Box 119, Summit St., East Hampton, CT 06424/203-267-2588
Northern Precision Custom Swaged Bullets, 337 S. James St., Carthage, NY 13619/315-493-3456
Old World Oil Products, 3827 Queen Ave. N., Minneapolis, MN 55412/612-522-5037
Omark, Div. of Blount, Inc., 2299 Snake River Ave., P.O. Box 856, Lewiston, ID 83501/800-627-3640, 208-746-2351
Outers Laboratories, Div. of Blount, Inc., Route 2, Onalaska, WI 54650/608-781-5800
Ox-Yoke Originals, Inc., 34 Main St., Milo, ME 04463/800-231-8313; FAX: 207-943-2416
Parker Gun Finishes, 9337 Smokey Row Rd., Strawberry Plains, TN 37871/615-933-3286
Pendleton Royal, 4/7 Highgate St., Birmingham, ENGLAND B12 0X5/44 21 440 3060; FAX: 44 21 446 4165
Pflumm Gun Mfg. Co., 6139 Melrose Ln., Shawnee, KS 66203/800-888-4867
P&M Sales and Service, 5724 Gainsborough Pl., Oak Forest, IL 60452/708-687-7149
Precision Sports, 3736 Kellogg Rd., P.O. Box 5588, Cortland, NY 13045-5588/607-756-2851, 800-847-6787; FAX: 607-753-8835
Prolix®, 15578 Mojave Dr. Unit D, Victorville, CA 92392/800-248-LUBE, 619-243-3129; FAX: 619-241-0148
Pro-Shot Products, Inc., P.O. Box 763, Taylorville, IL 62568/217-824-9133; FAX: 217-824-8861
Radiator Specialty Co., 1900 Wilkinson Blvd., P.O. Box 34689, Charlotte, NC 28234/800-438-6947; FAX: 800-421-9525
Ravell Ltd., 289 Diputacion St., 08009, Barcelona SPAIN
R&S Industries Corp., 8255 Brentwood Industrial Dr., St. Louis, MO 63144/314-781-5400
Rice, Keith (See White Rock Tool & Die)
Richards Classic Oil Finish, John, Rt. 2, Box 325, Bedford, KY 40006/502-255-7222
Rickard, Pete, RD 1, Box 292, Cobleskill, NY 12043/800-282-5663; FAX: 518-234-2454
RIG Products, 87 Coney Island Dr., Sparks, NV 89431-1990/702-331-5666; FAX: 702-331-5669
Robar Co.'s, Inc., The, 21438 N. 7th Ave., Suite B, Phoenix, AZ 85027/602-581-2648; FAX: 602-582-0059
Rusteprufe Laboratories, Robert D. Munger, 1319 Jefferson Ave., Sparta, WI 54656/608-269-4144
Rusty Duck Premium Gun Care Products, 7785 Founion Dr., Florence, KY 41042/606-342-5553
San Angelo Sports Products, Inc., 909 W. 14th St., San Angelo, TX 76903/915-655-7126; FAX: 915-653-6720
Scott, Inc., Tyler, 313 Rugby Ave., Terrace Park, OH 45174/513-831-7603
Shooter's Choice, 16770 Hilltop Park Place, Chagrin Falls, OH 44022/216-543-8808; FAX: 216-543-8811
Shootin' Accessories, Ltd., P.O. Box 6810, Auburn, CA 95604/916-889-2220
Slipshot MTS Group, P.O. Box 5, Postal Station D, Etobicoke, Ont., CANADA M9A 4X1/FAX: 416-762-0962
Speer Products, Div. of Blount, Inc., P.O. Box 856, Lewiston, ID 83501/208-746-2351
Sports Support Systems, Inc., 28416 Pacheco, Mission Viejo, CA 92692/714-367-0343

Stoney Point Products, Inc., 124 Stoney Point Rd., Courtland, MN 56021/507-354-3360; FAX: 507-354-7236

Svon Corp., 280 Eliot St., Ashland, MA 01721/508-881-8852

TDP Industries, Inc., 603 Airport Blvd., Doylestown, PA 18901/215-345-8687

TETRA Gun Lubricants, 1812 Margaret Ave., Annapolis, MD 21401/410-268-6451; FAX: 410-268-8377

Texas Platers Supply, 2453 W. Five Mile Parkway, Dallas, TX 75233/214-330-7168

T.F.C. S.p.A., Via G. Marconi 118, B, Villa Carcina, Brescia 25069, ITALY/030-881271; FAX: 030-881826

Treso, Inc., P.O. Box 4640, Pagosa Springs, CO 81157/303-731-2295

United States Products Co., 518 Melwood Ave., Pittsburgh, PA 15213/412-621-2130

Valor Corp., 5555 NW 36th Ave., Miami, FL 33142/305-633-0127

Van Gorden & Son, Inc., C.S., 1815 Main St., Bloomer, WI 54724/715-568-2612

Verdemont Fieldsports, P.O. Box 9337, San Bernardino, CA 92427/714-880-8255; FAX: 714-880-8255

Watson Trophy Match Bullets, 2404 Wade Hampton Blvd., Greenville, SC 29615/803-244-7948

WD-40 Co., P.O. Box 80607, San Diego, CA 92138/619-275-1400; FAX: 619-275-5823

White Rock Tool & Die, 6400 N. Brighton Ave., Kansas City, MO 64119/816-454-0478

Williams Shootin' Iron Service, The Lynx-Line, 8857 Bennett Hill Rd., Central Lake, MI 49622/616-544-6615

Young Country Arms, P.O. Box 3615, Simi Valley, CA 93093

Z-Coat Industrial Coatings, Inc., 3375 U.S. Hwy. 98 S. No. A, Lakeland, FL 33803-8365/813-665-1734

GUNS AND GUN PARTS, U.S. AND FOREIGN

Armscorp USA, Inc., 4424 John Ave., Baltimore, MD 21227/301-247-6200

Behlert Precision, P.O. Box 288, 7067 Easton Rd., Pipersville, PA 18947/215-766-8681; FAX: 215-766-8681

Bob's Gun Shop, P.O. Box 200, Royal, AR 71968/501-767-1970

Caspian Arms, 14 North Main St., Hardwick, VT 05843/802-472-6454

Century International Arms, Inc., 48 Lower Newton St., St. Albans, VT 05478/802-527-1252; FAX: 802-527-0470

Clark Custom Guns, Inc., P.O. Box 530, 11462 Keatchie Rd., Keithville, LA 71047/318-925-0836; FAX: 318-925-9425

First Distributors, Jack, Inc., 44633 Sierra Hwy., Lancaster, CA 93534/805-945-6981; FAX: 805-942-0844

Gun Parts Corp., The, Williams Lane, West Hurley, NY 12491/914-679-2417; FAX: 914-679-5849

J.O. Arms & Ammunition Co., 5709 Hartsdale, Houston, TX 77036/713-789-0745; FAX: 713-789-7513

Kopp, Terry, 1301 Franklin, Lexington, MO 64067/816-259-2636

Lock's Philadelphia Gun Exchange, 6700 Rowland Ave., Philadelphia, PA 19149/215-332-6225; FAX: 215-332-4800

Mac's .45 Shop, P.O. Box 2028, Seal Beach, CA 90740/310-438-5046

Markell, Inc., 422 Larkfield Center 235, Santa Rosa, CA 95403/707-573-0792; FAX: 707-573-9867

McCormick Corp., Chip, 1825 Fortview Rd., Ste. 115, Austin, TX 78704/512-462-0004; FAX: 512-462-0009

Nu-Line Guns, Inc., 1053 Caulks Hill Rd., Harvester, MO 63303/314-441-4500; FAX: 314-447-5018

Old Western Scrounger, Inc., 12924 Hwy. A-l2, Montague, CA 96064/916-459-5445

Olympic Arms, Inc., 624 Old Pacific Hwy. SE, Olympia, WA 98503/206-456-3471; FAX: 206-491-3447

Ram-Line, Inc., 10601 W. 48th Ave., Wheat Ridge, CO 80033/303-467-0300; FAX: 303-467-9833

Retting, Inc., Martin B., 11029 Washington, Culver City, CA 90232/213-837-2412

Ruvel & Co., Inc., 4128-30 W. Belmont Ave., Chicago, IL 60641/312-286-9494

Safari Arms/SGW (See Olympic Arms, Inc.)

Sarco, Inc., 323 Union St., Stirling, NJ 07980/908-647-3800

Sherwood Intl. Export Corp., 18714 Parthenia St., Northridge, CA 91324/818-349-7600

Springfield, Inc., 25144 Ridge Rd., Colona, IL 61241/309-441-6002; FAX: 309-441-6003

Taurus, S.A., Forjas, Avenida Do Forte 511, Porto Alegre, BRAZIL 91360/55 512-40 22 44

Triple-K Mfg. Co., Inc., 2222 Commercial St., San Diego, CA 92113/619-232-2066; FAX: 619-232-7675

Weisz Antique Gun Parts, P.O. Box 311, Arlington, VA 22210/703-243-9161

W.C. Wolff Co., P.O. Box I, Newtown Square, PA 19073/215-359-9600

GUNS, FOREIGN—IMPORTERS (Manufacturers)

Action Arms Ltd., P.O. Box 9573, Philadelphia, PA 19124/215-744-0100; FAX: 215-533-2188 (BRNO; CZ)

American Arms, Inc., 715 E. Armour Rd., N. Kansas City, MO 64116/816-474-3161; FAX: 816-474-1225 (blackpowder arms)

Armoury, The, Rt. 202, Box 2340, New Preston, CT 06777/203-868-0001 (blackpowder)

Armsport, Inc., 3950 NW 49th St., Miami, FL 33142/305-635-7850; FAX: 305-633-2877 (Armsport, Inc.; blackpowder arms)

Beretta U.S.A. Corp., 17601 Beretta Drive, Accokeek, MD 20607/301-283-2191 (Beretta Firearms, Pietro)

Browning Arms Co., (Gen. Offices), 1 Browning Place, Morgan, UT 84050/801-876-2711; FAX: 801-876-3331 (Browning Arms Co.)

Cabela's, 812-13th Ave., Sidney, NE 69160/308-254-5505; FAX: 308-254-7809 (Pedersoli Davide & C.; blackpowder arms)

Century International Arms, Inc., 48 Lower Newton St., St. Albans, VT 05478/802-527-1252; FAX: 802-527-0470 (BRNO; FEG; Norinco)

ChinaSports, Inc., 2010 S. Lynx Place, Ontario, CA 91761/714-923-1411; FAX: 714-923-0775 (Norinco)

Cimarron Arms, 1106 Wisterwood G, Houston, TX 77043/713-468-2007; FAX: 713-461-8320 (Uberti, Aldo; blackpowder arms)

CVA, 5988 Peachtree Corners East, Norcross, GA 30071/404-449-4687; FAX: 404-242-8546 (blackpowder arms)

Dixie Gun Works, Hwy. 51 South, Union City, TN 38261/901-885-0700, order 800-238-6785; FAX: 901-885-0440 (Pedersoli Davide & C.; blackpowder arms)

E.A.A. Corp., 4480 E. 11th Ave., Hialeah, FL 33013/305-688-4442; FAX: 305-688-5656 (Astra-Unceta Y Cia, S.A.; Benelli Armi S.p.A.; Tanfoglio S.r.l., Fratelli/Witness; Weihrauch KG, Hermann)

Eagle Imports, Inc., 1907 Highway 35, Ocean, NJ 07712/908-531-8375; FAX: 908-531-1520 (Bersa S.A.)

EMF Co., Inc., 1900 E. Warner Ave. Suite 1-D, Santa Ana, CA 92705/714-261-6611; FAX: 714-956-0133 (Dakota; blackpowder arms)

Firstshot, Inc., 4101 Far Green Rd., Harrisburg, PA 17110/717-238-2575 (Daewoo Precision Industries Ltd.)

Glock, Inc., 6000 Highlands Parkway, Smyrna, GA 30082/404-432-1202 (Glock GmbH)

GSI, Inc., 108 Morrow Ave., P.O. Box 129, Trussville, AL 35173/205-655-8299; FAX: 205-655-7078 (Steyr-Daimler-Puch)

Hammerli USA, 19296 Oak Grove Circle, Groveland, CA 95321/209-962-5311; FAX: 209-962-5931 (Hammerli Ltd.)

Heckler & Koch, Inc., 21480 Pacific Blvd., Sterling, VA 20166/703-450-1900; FAX: 703-450-8160 (Heckler & Koch, GmbH)

Interarms, 10 Prince St., Alexandria, VA 22314/703-548-1400 (Helwan; Interarms; Norinco; Rossi, Amadeo; Star Bonifacio Echeverria S.A.; Walther GmbH, Carl)

J.O. Arms & Ammunition Co., 5709 Hartsdale, Houston, TX 77036/713-789-0745; FAX: 713-789-7513 (J.O. Arms & Ammunition Co.)

K.B.I., Inc., P.O. Box 6346, Harrisburg, PA 17112/717-540-8518; FAX: 717-540-8567 (FEG; K.B.I., Inc.)

Magnum Research, Inc., 7110 University Ave., Minneapolis, MN 55432/612-574-1868; FAX: 612-574-0109 (IMI/Desert Eagle)

Mandall Shooting Supplies, Inc., 3616 N. Scottsdale Rd., Scottsdale, AZ 85252/602-945-2553; FAX: 602-949-0734 (Erma Werke GmbH; Gaucher Armes S.A.; Korth; SIG; blackpowder arms)

Marent, Rudolf, 9711 Tiltree St., Houston, TX 77075/713-946-7028 (Hammerli Ltd.)

McMillan Gunworks, Inc., 302 W. Melinda Lane, Phoenix, AZ 85027/602-582-9627; FAX: 602-582-5178 (Peters Stahl GmbH)

Mitchell Arms, Inc., 3400 W. MacArthur Blvd., Ste. 1, Santa Ana, CA 92704/714-957-5711; FAX: 714-957-5732 (Mitchell Arms, Inc.; blackpowder arms)

Navy Arms Co., 689 Bergen Blvd., Ridgefield, NJ 07657/201-945-2500; FAX: 201-945-6859 (Navy Arms Co; Uberti, Aldo; blackpowder arms)

Nygord Precision Products, P.O. Box 8394, La Crescenta, CA 91224/818-352-3027; FAX: 818-352-3027 (FAS; Morini; Unique/M.A.P.F.; Vostok)

Para-Ordnance Mfg., Inc., 3411 McNicoll Ave., Unit 14, Scarborough, Ont. M1V 2V6, CANADA/416-297-7855; FAX: 416-297-1289 (Para-Ordnance Mfg., Inc.)

Precision Imports, Inc., 5040 Space Center Dr., San Antonio, TX 78218/512-666-3033; FAX: 512-666-2723 (Mauser-Werke)

PSI, Inc., P.O. Box 1776, Westfield, MA 01086/413-562-5055; FAX: 413-562-5056 (Anschutz GmbH; Erma Werke GmbH)

Safari Arms/SGW, 624 Old Pacific Hwy. SE, Olympia, WA 98503/206-456-3471; FAX: 206-491-3447 (Peters Stahl GmbH)

SGS Importers International, Inc., 1907 Hwy. 35, Ocean, NJ 07712/908-531-9424; FAX: 908-531-1520 (Llama Gabilondo Y Cia)

Sigarms, Inc., Industrial Drive, Exeter, NH 03833/603-772-2302; FAX: 603-772-9082 (SIG-Sauer)

Sile Distributors, 7 Centre Market Pl., New York, NY 10013/212-925-4389; FAX: 212-925-3149 (Solothurn)

Sportarms of Florida, 5555 NW 36 Ave., Miami, FL 33142/305-635-2411; FAX: 305-634-4536 (Norinco; Schmidt, Herbert; Tokarev)

Springfield, Inc., 25144 Ridge Rd., Colona, IL 61241/309-441-6002; FAX: 309-441-6003 (Springfield, Inc.)

Taurus Firearms, Inc., 16175 NW 49th Ave., Miami, FL 33014/305-624-1115; FAX: 305-623-7506 (Taurus International Firearms)

Uberti USA, Inc., 362 Limerock Rd., P.O. Box 469, Lakeville, CT 06039/203-435-8068; FAX: 203-435-8146 (Uberti, Aldo; blackpowder arms)

GUNS, FOREIGN—MANUFACTURERS (Importers)

Anschutz GmbH, Postfach 1128, D-7900 Ulm, Donau, GERMANY (PSI, Inc.)

Armsport, Inc., 3950 NW 49th St., Miami, FL 33142/305-635-7850; FAX: 305-633-2877 (Armsport, Inc.)

Astra-Unceta Y Cia, S.A., Apartado 3, 48300 Guernica, Espagne, SPAIN (E.A.A. Corp.)

Benelli Armi S.p.A., Via della Stazione, 61029 Urbino, ITALY (E.A.A. Corp.)

Beretta Firearms, Pietro, 25063 Gardone V.T., ITALY (Beretta U.S.A. Corp.)

Bersa S.A., Gonzales Castillo 312, 1704 Ramos Mejia, ARGENTINA (Eagle Imports, Inc.)

BRNO, (See U.S. importers—Action Arms Ltd.; Bohemia Arms Co.; Century International Arms, Inc.)

Browning Arms Co., 1 Browning Place, Morgan, UT 84050/801-876-2711; FAX: 801-876-3331 (Browning Arms Co.)

CVA, 5988 Peachtree Corners East, Norcross, GA 30071/404-449-4687; FAX: 404-242-8546 (blackpowder arms)

CZ, (See U.S. importer—Action Arms Ltd.)

Daewoo Precision Industries Ltd., 34-3 Yeoeuido-Dong, Yeongdeungpo-GU, 15th Fl., Seoul, KOREA (Firstshot, Inc.)

Dakota, (See U.S. importer—EMF Co., Inc.)

Erma Werke GmbH, Johan Ziegler St., 13/15/FeldiglSt., D-8060 Dachau, GERMANY (Mandall Shooting Supplies, Inc.; PSI, Inc.)

FAS, Via E. Fermi, 8, 20019 Settimo Milanese, Milano, ITALY (Nygord Precision Products)

FEG, Budapest, Soroksariut 158, H-1095 HUNGARY (Century International Arms, Inc.; K.B.I., Inc.)

FN Herstal, Voie de Liege 33, Herstal 4040, BELGIUM/(32)41.40.82.83; FAX: (32)40.86.79

Gaucher Armes S.A., 46, rue Desjoyaux, 42000 Saint-Etienne, FRANCE/77 33 38 92 (Mandall Shooting Supplies, Inc.)

Glock GmbH, P.O. Box 50, A-2232 Deutsch Wagram, AUSTRIA (Glock, Inc.)

Hammerli Ltd., Seonerstrasse 37, CH-5600 Lenzburg, SWITZERLAND/064-50 11 44; FAX: 064-51 38 27 (Hammerli USA; Marent, Rudolph)

Heckler & Koch, GmbH, Postfach 1329, D-7238 Oberndorf, Neckar, GERMANY (Heckler & Koch, Inc.)

Helwan, (See U.S. importer—Interarms)

IMI/Desert Eagle, P.O. Box 1044, Ramat Hasharon 47100, ISRAEL/972-3-5485222 (Magnum Research, Inc.)

Interarms, 10 Prince St., Alexandria, VA 22314/703-548-1400 (Interarms)

J.O. Arms & Ammunition Co., 5709 Hartsdale, Houston, TX 77036/713-789-0745; FAX: 713-789-7513 (J.O. Arms & Ammunition Co.)

K.B.I., Inc., P.O. Box 6346, Harrisburg, PA 17112/717-540-8518; FAX: 717-540-8567 (K.B.I., Inc.)

Korth, Robert-Bosch-Str. 4, P.O. Box 1320, 2418 Ratzeburg, GERMANY/0451-4991497;

FAX: 0451-4993230 (Mandall Shooting Supplies, Inc.)

Llama Gabilondo Y Cia, Apartado 290, E-01080, Victoria, SPAIN (SGS Importers International, Inc.)

Mauser-Werke, P.O. Box 1349, 7238 Oberndorf, Neckar, GERMANY (Precision Imports, Inc.)

Mitchell Arms, Inc., 3400 W. MacArthur Blvd., Ste. 1, Santa Ana, CA 92704/714-957-5711; FAX: 714-957-5732 (Mitchell Arms, Inc.)

Morini, (See U.S. importer—Nygord Precision Products)

Navy Arms Co., 689 Bergen Blvd., Ridgefield, NJ 07657/201-945-2500; FAX: 201-945-6859 (Navy Arms Co.)

Norinco, 7A, Yun Tan N Beijing, CHINA (Century International Arms, Inc.; ChinaSports, Inc.; Interarms; Midwest Sport Distributors; Sportarms of Florida)

Para-Ordnance Mfg., Inc., 3411 McNicoll Ave., Unit 14, Scarborough, Ont. M1V 2V6, CANADA/416-297-7855; FAX: 416-297-1289 (Para-Ordnance Mfg., Inc.)

Pardini Armi Commerciale Srl, Via Italica 154, 55043 Lido Di Camaiore Lu, ITALY/584-90121; FAX: 584-90122 (MCS, Inc.)

Peters Stahl GmbH, Stettiner Str. 42, D-4790 Paderborn, GERMANY/05251-750025-27; FAX: 05251-75611 (McMillan Gunworks, Inc.; Safari Arms/SGW)

Rossi, Amadeo, Rua Amadeo Rossi, 143, Sao Leopoldo, RS, BRAZIL 93 030/0512-92-5566 (Interarms)

Schmidt, Herbert, (See U.S. importer—Sportarms of Florida)

SIG, CH-8212 Neuhausen, SWITZERLAND (Mandall Shooting Supplies, Inc.)

SIG-Sauer, (See U.S. importer—Sigarms, Inc.)

Solothurn, (See U.S. importer—Sile Distributors)

Springfield, Inc., 25144 Ridge Rd., Colona, IL 61241/309-441-6002; FAX: 309-441-6003 (Springfield, Inc.)

Star Bonifacio Echeverria S.A., Torrekva 3, Eibar, SPAIN 20600/43-117340; FAX: 43-111524 (Interarms)

Steyr-Daimler-Puch, Schonauerstrasse 5, A-4400 Steyr AUSTRIA (GSI, Inc.)

Tanfoglio S.r.l., Fratelli/Witness, via Valtrompia 39, 41, 25068 Gardone V.T., Brescia, ITALY/30-8910361; FAX: 30-8910183 (E.A.A. Corp.)

Taurus International Firearms, (See U.S. importer—Taurus Firearms, Inc.)

Tokarev, (See U.S. importer—Sportarms of Florida)

Uberti, Aldo, Casella Postale 43, I-25063 Gardone V.T., ITALY (Cimarron Arms; Navy Arms Co.; Uberti USA, Inc.)

Unique/M.A.P.F., 10, Les Allees, 64700 Hendaye, FRANCE 64700/33-59 20 71 93 (Nygord Precision Products)

Vostok, (See U.S. importer—Nygord Precision Products)

Walther GmbH, Carl, B.P. 4325, D-89033 Ulm, GERMANY (Interarms)

Weihrauch KG, Hermann, Industriestrasse 11, 8744 Mellrichstadt, GERMANY/09776-497-498 (Beeman Precision Airguns, Inc.; E.A.A. Corp.)

GUNS, U.S.-MADE

Accu-Tek, 4525 Carter Ct., Chino, CA 91710/714-627-2404; FAX: 714-627-7817

AMAC, Iver Johnson, 2202 Redmond Rd., Jacksonville, AR 72076/501-982-1633; FAX: 501-982-8075

American Arms, Inc., 715 E. Armour Rd., N. Kansas City, MO 64116/816-474-3161; FAX: 816-474-1225

American Derringer Corp., P.O. Box 8983, Waco, TX 76714/800-642-7817, 817-799-9111; FAX: 817-799-7935

AMT, 6226 Santos Diaz St., Irwindale, CA 91702/818-334-6629; FAX: 818-969-5247

Auto-Ordnance Corp., Williams Lane, West Hurley, NY 12491/914-679-7225; FAX: 914-679-2698

Beretta Firearms, Pietro, 25063 Gardone V.T., ITALY (U.S. importer—Beretta U.S.A. Corp.)

Brown Co., E. Arthur, 3404 Pawnee Dr., Alexandria, MN 56308/612-762-8847

Browning Arms Co. (Parts & Service), 3005 Arnold Tenbrook Rd., Arnold, MO 63010-9406/314-287-6800; FAX: 314-287-9751

Bryco Arms (See U.S. distributor—Jennings Firearms, Inc.)

Calico Light Weapon Systems, 405 E. 19th St., Bakersfield, CA 93305/805-323-1327; FAX: 805-323-7844

Century Gun Dist., Inc., 1467 Jason Rd., Greenfield, IN 46140/317-462-4524

CHARCO, 26 Beaver St., Ansonia, CT 06401/203-377-8080

Charter Arms (See CHARCO)

Claridge Hi-Tec, Inc., 19350 Business Center Dr., Northridge, CA 91324/818-700-9093; FAX: 818-700-0026

Colt Blackpowder Arms Co., 5 Centre Market Place, New York, NY 10013/212-925-4881; FAX: 212-966-4986

Colt's Mfg. Co., Inc., P.O. Box 1868, Hartford, CT 06144-1868/203-236-6311; FAX: 203-244-1449

Competitor Corp., Inc., P.O. Box 244, 293 Townsend Rd., West Groton, MA 01472/508-448-3521; FAX: 603-673-4540

Coonan Arms, Inc., 830 Hampden Ave., St. Paul, MN 55114/612-646-0902; FAX: 612-646-0902

CVA, 5988 Peachtree Corners East, Norcross, GA 30071/404-449-4687; FAX: 404-242-8546

Davis Industries, 11186 Venture Dr., Mira Loma, CA 91752/909-360-5598

Desert Industries, Inc., 3245 E. Patrick Ln., Suite H, Las Vegas, NV 89120/702-597-1066; FAX: 702-434-9495

Falcon Industries, Inc., P.O. Box 1310, Huntington Beach, CA 92647-1310/714-847-4700; 714-847-4141

Feather Industries, Inc., 2300 Central Ave. K, Boulder, CO 80301/303-442-7021; FAX: 303-447-0944

Freedom Arms, Inc., P.O. Box 1776, Freedom, WY 83120/307-883-2468; FAX: 307-883-2005

Grendel, Inc., P.O. Box 560909, Rockledge, FL 32953/800-274-7427, 407-636-1211; FAX: 407-633-6710

H&R 1871, Inc., 60 Industrial Rowe, Gardner, MA 01440/508-632-9393; FAX: 508-632-2300

HJS Arms, Inc., P.O. Box 3711, Brownsville, TX 78523-3711/800-453-2767, 210-542-2767

Intratec, 12405 SW 130th St., Miami, FL 33186/305-232-1821; FAX: 305-253-7207

Ithaca Aquisition Corp., Ithaca Gun Co., 891 Route 34B, King Ferry, NY 13081/315-364-7171; FAX: 315-364-5134

Jennings Firearms, Inc., 17692 Cowan, Irvine, CA 92714/714-252-7621; FAX: 714-252-7626

Johnson, Iver (See AMAC)

Kimel Industries, 3800 Old Monroe Rd., P.O. Box 335, Matthews, NC 28105/800-438-9288

L.A.R. Manufacturing, Inc., 4133 W. Farm Rd., West Jordan, UT 84088/801-255-7106; FAX: 801-569-1972

Laseraim Arms, Sub. of Emerging Technologies, Inc., P.O. Box 3548, Little Rock, AR 72203/501-375-2227; FAX: 501-372-1445

Lorcin Engineering Co., Inc., 10427 San Sevaine Way, Ste. A, Mira Loma, CA 91752/714-360-1406; FAX: 714-360-0623

McMillan Gunworks, Inc., 302 W. Melinda Lane, Phoenix, AZ 85027/602-582-9627; FAX: 602-582-5178

Mitchell Arms, Inc., 3400 W. MacArthur Blvd., Ste. 1, Santa Ana, CA 92704/714-957-5711; FAX: 714-957-5732

M.O.A. Corp., 2451 Old Camden Pike, Eaton, OH 45320/513-456-3669

New Advantage Arms Corp., 2843 N. Alvernon Way, Tucson, AZ 85712/602-881-7444; FAX: 602-323-0949

New England Firearms, 60 Industrial Rowe, Gardner, MA 01440/508-632-9393; FAX: 508-632-2300

North American Arms, 1800 North 300 West, Spanish Fork, UT 84660/800-821-5783, 801-897-7401; FAX: 801-798-9418

Phelps Mfg. Co., Box 2266, Evansville, IN 47714/812-476-8791

Phoenix Arms Co. Ltd. (See Hy-Score Arms Co. Ltd.)

Ram-Line, Inc., 10601 W. 48th Ave., Wheat Ridge, CO 80033/303-467-0300; FAX: 303-467-9833

Remington Arms Co., Inc., 1007 Market St., Wilmington, DE 19898/302-773-5291

Rocky Mountain Arms, Inc., 600 S. Sunset, Unit C, Longmont, CO 80501/303-768-8522; FAX: 303-678-8766

RPM, 15481 N. Twin Lakes Dr., Tucson, AZ 85737/602-825-1233; FAX: 602-825-3333

Safari Arms/SGW (See Olympic Arms, Inc.)

Seecamp Co., Inc., L.W., P.O. Box 255, New Haven, CT 06502/203-877-3429

Smith & Wesson, 2100 Roosevelt Ave., Springfield, MA 01102/413-781-8300

SSK Industries, 721 Woodvue Lane, Wintersville, OH 43952/614-264-0176; FAX: 614-264-2257

Sturm, Ruger & Co., Inc., Lacey Place, Southport, CT 06490/203-259-7843

Sundance Industries, Inc., 25163 W. Avenue Stanford, Valencia, CA 91355/805-257-4807

Texas Arms, P.O. Box 154906, Waco, TX 76715/817-776-5294

Texas Longhorn Arms, Inc., 5959 W. Loop South, Suite 424, Bellaire, TX 77401/713-660-6323; FAX: 713-660-0493

Thompson/Center Arms, Farmington Rd., P.O. Box 5002, Rochester, NH 03867/603-332-2394

Ultra Light Arms, Inc., P.O. Box 1270, 214 Price St., Granville, WV 26534/304-599-5687

Wesson Firearms Co., Inc., Maple Tree Industrial Center, Rt. 20, Wilbraham Rd., Palmer, MA 01069/413-267-4081; FAX: 413-267-3601

Wichita Arms, Inc., 923 E. Gilbert, P.O. Box 11371, Wichita, KS 67211/316-265-0661; FAX: 316-265-0760

Wildey, Inc., P.O. Box 475, Brookfield, CT 06804/203-355-9000; FAX: 203-354-7759

Wilkinson Arms, 26884 Pearl Rd., Parma, ID 83660/208-722-6771

GUNSMITH SCHOOLS

Brooker, Dennis, Rt. 1, Box 12A, Derby, IA 50068/515-533-2103

Colorado School of Trades, 1575 Hoyt St., Lakewood, CO 80215/800-234-4594; FAX: 303-233-4723

Cylinder & Slide, Inc., William R. Laughridge, 245 E. 4th St., Fremont, NE 68025/402-721-4277; FAX: 402-721-0263

Lassen Community College, Gunsmithing Dept., P.O. Box 3000, Hwy. 139, Susanville, CA 96130/916-257-6181 ext. 109; FAX: 916-257-8964

Modern Gun Repair School, 2538 N. 8th St., P.O. Box 5338, Dept. GJY94, Phoenix, AZ 85010/602-990-8346

Montgomery Community College, P.O. Box 787, Troy, NC 27371/919-572-3691

Murray State College, 100 Faculty Dr., Tishomingo, OK 73460/405-371-2371

North American Correspondence Schools, The Gun Pro School, Oak & Pawney St., Scranton, PA 18515/717-342-7701

Nowlin Custom Barrels Mfg., Rt. 1, Box 308, Claremore, OK 74017/918-342-0689; FAX: 918-342-0624

Pennsylvania Gunsmith School, 812 Ohio River Blvd., Avalon, Pittsburgh, PA 15202/412-766-1812

Piedmont Community College, P.O. Box 1197, Roxboro, NC 27573/919-599-1181

Pine Technical College, 1100 4th St., Pine City, MN 55063/800-521-7463; FAX: 612-629-6766

Professional Gunsmiths of America, Inc., 1301 Franklin, P.O. Box 224E, Lexington, MO 64067/816-259-2636

Ravell Ltd., 289 Diputacion St., 08009, Barcelona SPAIN

Southeastern Community College, 1015 S. Gear Ave., West Burlington, IA 52655/319-752-2731

Trinidad State Junior College, Gunsmithing Dept., 600 Prospect St., Trinidad, CO 81082/719-846-5631; FAX: 719-846-5667

Yavapai College, 1100 E. Sheldon St., Prescott, AZ 86301/602-776-2359; FAX: 602-776-2193

GUNSMITH SUPPLIES, TOOLS, SERVICES

Ackley Rifle Barrels, P.O. (See Bellm Contenders)

Aldis Gunsmithing & Shooting Supply, 502 S. Montezuma St., Prescott, AZ 86303/602-445-6723; FAX: 602-445-6763

Alley Supply Co., P.O. Box 848, Gardnerville, NV 89410/702-782-3800

American Pistolsmiths Guild, P.O. Box 67, Louisville, TN 37777/615-984-3583

Atlantic Mills, Inc., 1325 Washington Ave., Asbury Park, NJ 07712/201-774-4882

Bald Eagle Precision Machine Co., 101 Allison St., Lock Haven, PA 17745/717-748-6772; FAX: 717-748-4443

Bellm Contenders, P.O. Ackley Rifle Barrels, P.O. Box 459, Cleveland, UT 84518/801-653-2530

Bengtson Arms Co., L., 6345-B E. Akron St., Mesa, AZ 85205/602-981-6375

Biesen, Al, 5021 Rosewood, Spokane, WA 99208/509-328-9340

Biesen, Roger, 5021 W. Rosewood, Spokane, WA 99208/509-328-9340

Blue Ridge Machinery & Tools, Inc., P.O. Box 536-GD, Hurricane, WV 25526/304-562-3538; FAX: 304-562-5311

Brownells, Inc., 200 S. Front St., Montezuma, IA 50171/515-623-5401; FAX: 515-623-3896

Browning Arms Co. (Gen. Offices), 1 Browning Place, Morgan, UT 84050/801-876-2711; FAX: 801-876-3331

Brown Products, Ed, Inc., Rt. 2, Box 2922, Perry, MO 63462/314-565-3261; FAX: 565-2791

B-Square Co., P.O. Box 11281, 2708 St. Louis Ave., Ft. Worth, TX 76110/817-923-0964, 800-433-2909; FAX: 817-926-7012

Buckhorn Gun Works, Rt. 6, Box 2230, Rapid City, SD 57702/605-787-6289

Buehler Scope Mounts, 17 Orinda Way, Orinda, CA 94563/510-254-3201; FAX: 510-254-9720

Can Am Enterprises, Box 27, Fruitland, Ont. LOR ILO, CANADA/416-643-4357

C-H Tool & Die Corp. (See 4-D Custom Die Co.)

Chapman Manufacturing Co., The, 471 New Haven Rd., P.O. Box 250, Durham, CT 06422/203-349-9228; FAX: 203-349-0084

Choate Machine & Tool Co., Inc., P.O. Box 218, Bald Knob, AR 72010/501-724-6193, 800-972-6390; FAX: 501-724-5873

Clymer Manufacturing Co., Inc., 1645 W. Hamlin Rd., Rochester Hills, MI 48309/313-853-5555; FAX: 313-853-1530

Colonial Arms, Inc., P.O. Box 636, Selma, AL 36702-0636/205-872-9455; FAX: 205-872-9540

Conetrol Scope Mounts, 10225 Hwy. 123 S., Seguin, TX 78155/210-379-3030, 800-CONETROL

Crouse's Country Cover, P.O. Box 160, Storrs, CT 06268/203-423-0702

Cumberland Arms, Rt. I, Box 1150 Shafer Rd., Blantons Chapel, Manchester, TN 37355

Custom Checkering Service, Kathy Forster, 2124 SE Yamhill St., Portland, OR 97214/503-236-5874

Custom Gun Products, 5021 W. Rosewood, Spokane, WA 99208/509-328-9340

D&D Gunsmiths, Ltd., 363 E. Elmwood, Troy, MI 48083/313-583-1512

Dan's Whetstone Co., Inc., 109 Remington Terrace, Hot Springs, AR 71913/501-767-1616; FAX: 501-767-9598

Davidson Products, 2020 Huntington Dr., Las Cruces, NM 88001/505-522-5612

Dayton Traister, P.O. Box 593, Oak Harbor, WA 98277

Decker Shooting Products, 1729 Laguna Ave., Schofield, WI 54476/715-359-5873

Dem-Bart Checkering Tools, Inc., 6807 Hwy. 2, Bickford Ave., Snohomish, WA 98290/206-568-7356; FAX: 206-568-3134

Dremel Mfg. Co., 4915-21st St., Racine, WI 53406

Duffy, Charles E., Williams Lane, West Hurley, NY 12491/914-679-2997

Du-Lite Corp., 171 River Rd., Middletown, CT 06457/203-347-2505

Dutchman's Firearms, Inc., The, 4143 Taylor Blvd., Louisville, KY 40215/502-366-0555

E.A.A. Corp., 4480 E. 11th Ave., Hialeah, FL 33013/305-688-4442; FAX: 305-688-5656

Echols & Co., D'Arcy, 164 W. 580 S., Providence, UT 84332/801-753-2367

Edmund Scientific Co., 101 E. Gloucester Pike, Barrington, NJ 08033/609-543-6250

Ed's Gun House, Rt. 1, Box 62, Minnesota City, MN 55959/507-689-2925

Eilan S.A.L., Paseo San Andres N8, Eibar, SPAIN 20600/(34)43118916; FAX: (34)43 114038

Faith Associates, Inc., 1139 S. Greenville Hwy., Hendersonville, NC 28792/704-692-1916; FAX: 704-697-6827

First Distributors, Jack, Inc., 44633 Sierra Hwy., Lancaster, CA 93534/805-945-6981; FAX: 805-942-0844

Fisher, Jerry A., 535 Crane Mt. Rd., Big Fork, MT 59911/406-837-1024

Flashette Co., 4725 S. Kolin Ave., Chicago, IL 60632/312-927-1302

Flitz International Ltd., 821 Mohr Ave., Waterford, WI 53185/414-534-5898; FAX: 414-534-2991

Forgreens Tool Mfg., Inc., P.O. Box 990, Robert Lee, TX 76945/915-453-2800

Forster, Kathy (See Custom Checkering Service)

Forster Products, 82 E. Lanark Ave., Lanark, IL 61046/815-493-6360; FAX: 815-493-2371

Frazier Brothers Enterprises, 1118 N. Main St., Franklin, IN 46131/317-736-4000; FAX: 317-736-4000

Garrett Accur-Lt. D.F.S. Co., P.O. Box 8675, 1413B East Olive Ct., Ft. Collins, CO 80524/303-224-3067

Global Industries, 1501 E. Chapman Ave., 306, Fullerton, CA 92631/714-879-8922

Grace Metal Products, Inc., P.O. Box 67, Elk Rapids, MI 49629/616-264-8133

Graybill's Gun Shop, 1035 Ironville Pike, Columbia, PA 17512/717-684-6220

GRS Corp., Glendo, P.O. Box 1153, 900 Overlander St., Emporia, KS 66801/316-343-1084

Gunline Tools, P.O. Box 478, Placentia, CA 92670/714-528-5252; FAX: 714-572-4128

Guns, 81 E. Streetsboro St., Hudson, OH 44236/216-650-4563

Gun-Tec, P.O. Box 8125, W. Palm Beach, FL 33407

Gutridge, Inc., 2143 Gettler St., Dyer, IN 46311/219-865-8617

Half Moon Rifle Shop, 490 Halfmoon Rd., Columbia Falls, MT 59912/406-892-4409

Henriksen Tool Co., Inc., 8515 Wagner Creek Rd., Talent, OR 97540/503-535-2309

Huey Gun Cases, Marvin, P.O. Box 22456, Kansas City, MO 64113/816-444-1637

Iosso Products, 1485 Lively Blvd., Elk Grove Villiage, IL 60007/708-437-8400

Ivanoff, Thomas G. (See Tom's Gun Repair)

Jantz Supply, P.O. Box 584-GD, Davis, OK 73030/405-369-2316; FAX: 405-369-3082

JGS Precision Tool Mfg., 1141 S. Summer Rd., Coos Bay, OR 97420/503-267-4331; FAX: 503-267-5996

K-D, Inc., 665 W. 300 South, Price, UT 84501/801-653-2530

Kasenit Co., Inc., 13 Park Ave., Highland Mills, NY 10930/914-928-9595; FAX: 914-928-7292

Kleinendorst, K.W., RR 1, Box 1500, Hop Bottom, PA 18824/717-289-4687; FAX: 717-289-4687

Kopp, Terry, 1301 Franklin, Lexington, MO 64067/816-259-2636

LaRocca Gun Works, Inc., 51 Union Place, Worcester, MA 01608/508-754-2887; FAX: 508-754-2887

Lea Mfg. Co., 237 E. Aurora St., Waterbury, CT 06720/203-753-5116

Lee Supplies, Mark, 9901 France Ct., Lakeville, MN 55044/612-461-2114

Lortone, Inc., 2856 NW Market St., Seattle, WA 98107/206-789-3100

Marsh, Mike, Croft Cottage, Main St., Elton, Derbyshire DE4 2BY, ENGLAND/0629 650 669

MCRW Associates, R.R. 1 Box 1425, Sweet Valley, PA 18656

MCS, Inc., 34 Delmar Dr., Brookfield, CT 06804/203-775-1013; FAX: 203-775-9462

MDS, Inc., 1640 Central Ave., St. Petersburg, FL 33712/813-894-3512

Menck, Thomas W., 5703 S. 77th St., Ralston, NE 68127-4201

Metalife Industries, Box 53 Mong Ave., Reno, PA 16343/814-436-7747; FAX: 814-676-5662

Millett Sights, 16131 Gothard St., Huntington Beach, CA 92647/714-842-5575, 714-847-5245; FAX: 714-843-5707

Milliron Custom Machine Carving, Earl, 1249 NE 166th Ave., Portland, OR 97230/503-252-3725

Miniature Machine Co. (See MMC)

MMC, 606 Grace Ave., Ft. Worth, TX 76111/817-831-0837

Morrow, Bud, 11 Hillside Lane, Sheridan, WY 82801-9729/307-674-8360

Newman Gunshop, Rt. 1, Box 90F, Agency, IA 52530/515-937-5775

NgraveR Co., The, 67 Wawecus Hill Rd., Bozrah, CT 06334/203-823-1533

Nitex, Inc., P.O. Box 1706, Uvalde, TX 78801/512-278-8843

N&J Sales, Lime Kiln Rd., Northford, CT 06472/203-484-0247

Nowlin Custom Barrels Mfg., Rt. 1, Box 308, Claremore, OK 74017/918-342-0689; FAX: 918-342-0624

Ole Frontier Gunsmith Shop, 2617 Hwy. 29 S., Cantonment, FL 32533/904-477-8074

Pace Marketing, Inc., 9474 NW 48th St., Sunrise, FL 33351-5137/305-741-4361; FAX: 305-741-2901

Palmgren Steel Products, 8383 S. Chicago Ave., Chicago, IL 60617/312-721-9675; FAX: 312-721-9739

PanaVise Products, Inc., 1485 Southern Way, Sparks, NV 89431/702-353-2900; FAX: 702-353-2929

Pease Accuracy, Bob, P.O. Box 310787, New Braunfels, TX 78131/210-625-1342

PEM's Mfg. Co., 5063 Waterloo Rd., Atwater, OH 44201/216-947-3721

Power Custom, Inc., RR 2, P.O. Box 756AB, Gravois Mills, MO 65037/314-372-5684

Precise Metalsmithing Enterprises, 146 Curtis Hill Rd., Chehalis, WA 98532/206-748-3743; FAX: 206-748-8102

Precision Arms International, Inc., Rt. 17, Box 456, Bldg. 810, Saluda, VA 23149/804-758-5233; FAX: 804-758-2690

Precision Specialties, 131 Hendom Dr., Feeding Hills, MA 01030/413-786-3365; FAX: 413-786-3365

Prolix®, 15578 Mojave Dr. Unit D, Victorville, CA 92392/800-248-LUBE, 619-243-3129; FAX: 619-241-0148

Ravell Ltd., 289 Diputacion St., 08009, Barcelona SPAIN

Reardon Products, P.O. Box 126, Morrison, IL 61270/815-772-3155

Robar Co.'s, Inc., The, 21438 N. 7th Ave., Suite B, Phoenix, AZ 85027/602-581-2648; FAX: 602-582-0059

Roto Carve, 2754 Garden Ave., Janesville, IA 50647

Scott/McDougall Custom Gunsmiths, 880 Piner Rd., Suite 50, Santa Rosa, CA 95403/707-546-2264

Shaw's Finest in Guns, 1255 N. Broadway 351, Escondido, CA 92026-2858

Sheridan USA, Inc., Austin, P.O. Box 67, Durham, CT 06422

S.K. Guns, Inc., 3041A Main Ave., Fargo, ND 58103/701-293-4867; FAX: 701-232-0001

Smith Whetstone Co., Inc., 1700 Sleepy Valley Rd., P.O. Box 5095, Hot Springs, AR 71902-5095/501-321-2244; FAX: 501-321-9232

Starrett Co., L.S., 121 Crescent St., Athol, MA 01331/617-249-3551

Stoney Point Products, Inc., 124 Stoney Point Rd., Courtland, MN 56021/507-354-3360; FAX: 507-354-7236

Stuart Products, Inc., P.O. Box 1587, Easley, SC 29641/803-859-9360

Sure Shot of LA, Inc., 103 Coachman Dr., Houma, LA 70360/504-876-6709

TDP Industries, Inc., 603 Airport Blvd., Doylestown, PA 18901/215-345-8687

Texas Platers Supply, 2453 W. Five Mile Parkway, Dallas, TX 75233/214-330-7168

Tom's Gun Repair, Thomas G. Ivanoff, 76-6 Rt. Southfork Rd., Cody, WY 82414/307-587-6949

Trulock Tool, Broad St., Whigham, GA 31797/912-762-4678

Turnbull Restoration, Doug, 6426 County Rd. 30, Holcomb, NY 14469/716-657-6338

Unick's Gunsmithing, 5005 Center Rd., Lowellville, OH 44436/216-536-8015

Walker Arms Co., Inc., 499 County Rd. 820, Selma, AL 36701/205-872-6231

Washita Mountain Whetstone Co., P.O. Box 378, Lake Hamilton, AR 71951/501-525-3914

Weaver's Gun Shop, P.O. Box 8, Dexter, MO 63841/314-568-3101

Wessinger Custom Guns & Engraving, 268 Limestone Rd., Chapin, SC 29036/803-345-5677

Westfield Engineering, 6823 Watcher St., Commerce, CA 90040/FAX: 213-928-8270

Westrom, John (See Precise Metalsmithing Enterprises)

Wilcox All-Pro Tools & Supply, RR 1, Montezuma, IA 50171/515-623-3138

Will-Burt Co., 169 S. Main, Orrville, OH 44667

Williams Gun Sight Co., 7389 Lapeer Rd., Box 329, Davison, MI 48423/313-653-2131, 800-530-9028; FAX: 313-658-2140

Williams Shootin' Iron Service, The Lynx-Line, 8857 Bennett Hill Rd., Central Lake, MI 49622/616-544-6615

Yavapai College, 1100 E. Sheldon St., Prescott, AZ 86301/602-776-2359; FAX: 602-776-2193

HANDGUN ACCESSORIES

Action Ammo Ltd. (See Action Arms Ltd.)

Action Arms Ltd., P.O. Box 9573, Philadelphia, PA 19124/215-744-0100; FAX: 215-533-2188

ADCO International, 1 Wyman St., Woburn, MA 01801-2341/617-935-1799; FAX: 617-932-4807

Adventurer's Outpost, P.O. Box 70, Cottonwood, AZ 86326/800-762-7471; FAX: 602-634-8781

Ajax Custom Grips, Inc., Div. of A. Jack Rosenberg & Sons, 9130 Viscount Row, Dallas, TX 75247/214-630-8893

All American Bullets, 889 Beatty St., Medford, OR 97501/503-770-5649

American Pistolsmiths Guild, P.O. Box 67, Louisville, TN 37777/615-984-3583

Ansen Enterprises, Inc., 1506 W. 228th St., Torrance, CA 90501-5105/213-534-1837

Auto-Ordnance Corp., Williams Lane, West Hurley, NY 12491/914-679-7225; FAX: 914-679-2698

Bar-Sto Precision Machine, 73377 Sullivan Rd., P.O. Box 1838, Twentynine Palms, CA 92277/619-367-2747; FAX: 619-367-2407

Barami Corp., 6250 E. 7 Mile Rd., Detroit, MI 48234/313-891-2536

Baumannize Custom, 4784 Sunrise Hwy., Bohemia, NY 11716/800-472-4387; FAX: 516-567-0001

Behlert Precision, P.O. Box 288, 7067 Easton Rd., Pipersville, PA 18947/215-766-8681; FAX: 215-766-8681

Bob's Tactical Indoor Shooting Range & Gun Shop, 122 Lafayette Rd., Salisbury, MA 01952/508-465-5561

Boonie Packer Products, P.O. Box 12204, Salem, OR 97309/800-477-3244; FAX: 503-581-3191

Brauer Bros. Mfg. Co., 2020 Delmar Blvd., St. Louis, MO 63103/314-231-2864; FAX: 314-249-4952

Brownells, Inc., 200 S. Front St., Montezuma, IA 50171/515-623-5401; FAX: 515-623-3896

Browning Arms Co. (Gen. Offices), 1 Browning Place, Morgan, UT 84050/801-876-2711; FAX: 801-876-3331

Brown Products, Ed, Inc., Rt. 2, Box 2922, Perry, MO 63462/314-565-3261; FAX: 565-2791

B-Square Co., P.O. Box 11281, 2708 St. Louis Ave., Ft. Worth, TX 76110/817-923-0964, 800-433-2909; FAX: 817-926-7012

Bucheimer, J.M., Jumbo Sports Products, 721 N. 20th St., St. Louis, MO 63103/314-241-1020

Centaur Systems, Inc., 1602 Foothill Rd., Kalispell, MT 59901/406-755-8609; FAX: 406-755-8609

Central Specialties Ltd., 1122 Silver Lake Road, Cary, IL 60013/708-537-3300; FAX: 708-537-3615

Champion's Choice, Inc., 223 Space Park South, Nashville, TN 37211/615-834-6666; FAX: 615-831-2753

Clark Custom Guns, Inc., P.O. Box 530, 11462 Keatchie Rd., Keithville, LA 71047/318-925-0836; FAX: 318-925-9425

Clymer Manufacturing Co., Inc., 1645 W. Hamlin Rd., Rochester Hills, MI 48309/313-853-5555; FAX: 313-853-1530

Cobra Gunskin, 133-30 32nd Ave., Flushing, NY 11354/718-762-8181; FAX: 718-762-0890

DIRECTORY OF THE HANDGUN TRADE

C3 Systems, 678 Killingly St., Johnston, RI 02919

Dade Screw Machine Products, 2319 NW 7th Ave., Miami, FL 33127/305-573-5050

Doskocil Mfg. Co., Inc., P.O. Box 1246, Arlington, TX 76004/817-467-5116

E.A.A. Corp., 4480 E. 11th Ave., Hialeah, FL 33013/305-688-4442; FAX: 305-688-5656

Eagle Imports, Inc., 1907 Highway 35, Ocean, NJ 07712/908-531-8375; FAX: 908-531-1520

Eagle International, Inc., 5195 W. 58th Ave., Suite 300, Arvada, CO 80002/303-426-8100

E&L Mfg., Inc., 39042 N. School House Rd., Cave Creek, AZ 85331/602-488-2598; FAX: 602-488-0813

EMF Co., Inc., 1900 E. Warner Ave. Suite 1-D, Santa Ana, CA 92705/714-261-6611; FAX: 714-956-0133

Faith Associates, Inc., 1139 S. Greenville Hwy., Hendersonville, NC 28792/704-692-1916; FAX: 704-697-6827

Feminine Protection, Inc., 10514 Shady Trail, Dallas, TX 75220/214-351-4500

Ferris Firearms, 1827 W. Hildebrand, San Antonio, TX 78201/210-734-0304

Fleming Firearms, 7720 E. 126 St N., Collinsville, OK 74021/918-665-3624

Frielich Police Equipment, 211 East 21st St., New York, NY 10010/212-254-3045

Glock GmbH, P.O. Box 50, A-2232 Deutsch Wagram, AUSTRIA (U.S. importer—Glock, Inc.)

Greider Precision, 431 Santa Marina Ct., Escondido, CA 92029/619-480-8892

Gremmel Enterprises, 271 Sterling Dr., Eugene, OR 97404/503-688-3319

Gun-Alert/Master Products, Inc., 1010 N. Maclay Ave., San Fernando, CA 91340/818-365-0864; FAX: 818-365-1308

Guncraft Books (See Guncraft Sports, Inc.)

Guncraft Sports, Inc., 10737 Dutchtown Rd., Knoxville, TN 37932/615-966-4501

Gunfitters, The, P.O. 426, Cambridge, WI 53523-0426/608-764-8128

Gunline Tools, P.O. Box 478, Placentia, CA 92670/714-528-5252; FAX: 714-572-4128

Gun-Ho Sports Cases, 110 E. 10th St., St. Paul, MN 55101/612-224-9491

Hebard Guns, Gil, 125-129 Public Square, Knoxville, IL 61448

Heinie Specialty Products, 323 W. Franklin St., Havana, IL 62644/309-543-4535; FAX: 309-543-2521

Hill Speed Leather, Ernie, 4507 N. 195th Ave., Litchfield Park, AZ 85340/602-853-9222; FAX: 602-853-9235

H.K.S. Products, 7841 Founion Dr., Florence, KY 41042/606-342-7841

Holster Shop, The, 720 N. Flagler Dr., Ft. Lauderdale, FL 33304/305-463-7910; FAX: 305-761-1483

Jeffredo Gunsight, P.O. Box 669, San Marcos, CA 92079/619-728-2695

Jet Comp Systems, Rt. 1, Box 112-C, Surry, VA 23883/804-357-0881

Jett & Co., Inc., RR 3, Box 167-B, Litchfield, IL 62056/217-324-3779

J.O. Arms & Ammunition Co., 5709 Hartsdale, Houston, TX 77036/713-789-0745; FAX: 713-789-7513

Johnson Gunsmithing, Inc., Neal G., 111 Marvin Dr., Hampton, VA 23666/804-838-8091; FAX: 804-838-8157

J.D. Jones, 721 Woodvue Lane, Wintersville, OH 43952/614-264-0176

Jumbo Sports Products (See Bucheimer, J.M.)

Keller Co., The, 4215 McEwen Rd., Dallas, TX 75244/214-788-4254

King's Gun Works, 1837 W. Glenoaks Blvd., Glendale, CA 91201/818-956-6010

K&K Ammo Wrist Band, R.D. 1, P.O. Box 448-CA18, Lewistown, PA 17044/717-242-2329

KLP, Inc., 215 Charles Dr., Holland, MI 49424/616-396-2575; FAX: 616-396-1287

Kopp, Terry, 1301 Franklin, Lexington, MO 64067/816-259-2636

Lakewood Products, Inc., P.O. Box 1527, 1445 Eagle St., Rhinelander, WI 54501/715-369-3445

La Prade, Rt. 5, P.O. Box 240AD, Tazewell, TN 37879

LaRocca Gun Works, Inc., 51 Union Place, Worcester, MA 01608/508-754-2887; FAX: 508-754-2887

Laseraim (Emerging Technologies, Inc.), P.O. Box 3548, Little Rock, AR 72203/501-375-2227; FAX: 501-372-1445

Lee's Red Ramps, Box 291240, Phelan, CA 92329-1240/619-868-5731

Lighthouse Mfg. Co., Inc., 443 Ashwood Place, Boca Raton, FL 33431/407-394-6011

Loch Leven Industries, P.O. Box 2751, Santa Rosa, CA 95405/707-573-8735

Lohman Mfg. Co., Inc., 4500 Doniphan Dr., P.O. Box 220, Neosho, MO 64850/417-451-4438; FAX: 417-451-2576

Mac's .45 Shop, P.O. Box 2028, Seal Beach, CA 90740/310-438-5046

Mag-na-Port International, Inc., 41302 Executive Dr., Harrison Twp., MI 48045-3448/313-469-6727; FAX: 313-469-0723

Magnolia Sports, Inc., 211 W. Main, Magnolia, AR 71753/800-530-7816; FAX: 501-234-8117

Magnum Research, Inc., 7110 University Ave., Minneapolis, MN 55432/612-574-1868; FAX: 612-574-0109

Mag-Pack Corp., P.O. Box 846, Chesterland, OH 44026

Markell, Inc., 422 Larkfield Center 235, Santa Rosa, CA 95403/707-573-0792; FAX: 707-573-9867

Masen Co., John, P.O. Box 5050, Suite 165, Lewisville, TX 75057/817-430-8732

Master Products, Inc. (See Gun-Alert/Master Products, Inc.)

McCormick Corp., Chip, 1825 Fortview Rd., Ste. 115, Austin, TX 78704/512-462-0004; FAX: 512-462-0009

MEC-Gar S.R.L., Via Madonnina 64, Gardone V.T. (BS), ITALY 25063/39-30-8911719; FAX: 39-30-8910065 (U.S. importer—MEC-Gar U.S.A., Inc.)

Menck, Thomas W., 5703 S. 77th St., Ralston, NE 68127-4201

Merit Corp., Box 9044, Schenectady, NY 12309/518-346-1420

Merkuria Ltd., Argentinska 38, 17005 Praha 7, CZECH REPUBLIC/422-875117; FAX: 422-809152

Michaels of Oregon Co., P.O. Box 13010, Portland, OR 97213/503-255-6890; FAX: 503-255-0746

MTM Molded Products Co., Inc., 3370 Obco Ct., Dayton, OH 45414/513-890-7461; FAX: 513-890-1747

Mustra's Custom Guns, Inc., Carl, 1002 Pennsylvania Ave., Palm Harbor, FL 34683/813-785-1403

N.C. Ordnance Co., P.O. Box 3254, Wilson, NC 27895/919-237-2440

Nielsen Custom Cases, P.O. Box 26297, Las Vegas, NV 89126/800-377-1341, 702-878-5611; FAX: 702-877-4433

No-Sho Mfg. Co., 10727 Glenfield Ct., Houston, TX 77096/713-723-5332

Novak's .45 Shop, Wayne, 1206 1/2 30th St., P.O. Box 4045, Parkersburg, WV 25101/304-485-9295

Owen, Harry, Sport Specialties, 100 N. Citrus Ave. 412, W. Covina, CA 91791-1614/818-968-5806

Pace Marketing, Inc., 9474 NW 48th St., Sunrise, FL 33351-5137/305-741-4361; FAX: 305-741-2901

Pachmayr Ltd., 1875 S. Mountain Ave., Monrovia, CA 91016/818-357-7771, 800-423-9704; FAX: 818-358-7251

Pardini Armi Commerciale Srl, Via Italica 154, 55043 Lido Di Camaiore Lu, ITALY/584-90121; FAX: 584-90122 (U.S. importer—MCS, Inc.)

PistolPAL Products, 2930 N. Campbell Ave., Chicago, IL 60618/800-788-7725; FAX: 312-267-8080

Power Custom, Inc., RR 2, P.O. Box 756AB, Gravois Mills, MO 65037/314-372-5684

Practical Tools, Inc., Austin Behlerts, P.O. Box 133, Pipersville, PA 18947/215-766-7301

Precision Arms International, Inc., Rt. 17, Box 456, Bldg. 810, Saluda, VA 23149/804-758-5233; FAX: 804-758-2690

Ranch Products, P.O. Box 145, Malinta, OH 43535/313-277-3118; FAX: 313-565-8536

Ravell Ltd., 289 Diputacion St., 08009, Barcelona SPAIN

Sheridan USA, Inc., Austin, P.O. Box 577, Durham, CT 06422

Sile Distributors, Inc., 7 Centre Market Pl., New York, NY 10013/212-925-4389; FAX: 212-925-3149

Slings 'N Things, Inc., 8909 Bedford Circle, Suite 11, Omaha, NE 68134/402-571-6954; FAX: 402-571-7082

Sonderman, Robert, 735 Kenton Dr., Charleston, IL 61920/217-345-5429

Southwind Sanctions, P.O. Box 445, Aledo, TX 76008/817-441-8917

Specialized Weapons, Inc. (See Tapco, Inc.)

Sport Specialties (See Owen, Harry)

SSK Industries, 721 Woodvue Lane, Wintersville, OH 43952/614-264-0176; FAX: 614-264-2257

TacTell, Inc., P.O. Box 5654, Maryville, TN 37802/615-982-7855

Tapco, Inc., P.O. Box 546, Smyrna, GA 30081/404-435-9782, 800-359-6195; FAX: 404-333-9798

Taurus, S.A., Forjas, Avenida Do Forte 511, Porto Alegre, BRAZIL 91360/55 512-40 22 44

T.F.C. S.p.A., Via G. Marconi 118, B, Villa Carcina, Brescia 25069, ITALY/030-881271; FAX: 030-881826

Thompson/Center Arms, Farmington Rd., P.O. Box 5002, Rochester, NH 03867/603-332-2394

Triple-K Mfg. Co., Inc., 2222 Commercial St., San Diego, CA 92113/619-232-2066; FAX: 619-232-7675

Tyler Mfg.-Dist., Melvin, 1326 W. Britton Rd., Oklahoma City, OK 73114/405-842-8044

Valor Corp., 5555 NW 36th Ave., Miami, FL 33142/305-633-0127

Volquartsen Custom Ltd., RR 1, Box 33A, P.O. Box 271, Carroll, IA 51401/712-792-4238; FAX: 712-792-2542

Wessinger Custom Guns & Engraving, 268 Limestone Rd., Chapin, SC 29036/803-345-5677

Western Design, 1629 Via Monserate, Fallbrook, CA 92028/619-723-9279

Whitestone Lumber Corp., 148-02 14th Ave., Whitestone, NY 11357/718-746-4400; FAX: 718-767-1748

Wilson's Gun Shop, Box 578, Rt. 3, Berryville, AR 72616/501-545-3635; FAX: 501-545-3310

Wichita Arms, Inc., 923 E. Gilbert, P.O. Box 11371, Wichita, KS 67211/316-265-0661; FAX: 316-265-0760

HANDGUN GRIPS

African Import Co., 20 Braunecker Rd., Plymouth, MA 02360/508-746-8552

Ahrends, Kim, Custom Firearms, Box 203, Clarion, IA 50525/515-532-3449

Ajax Custom Grips, Inc., Div. of A. Jack Rosenberg & Sons, 9130 Viscount Row, Dallas, TX 75247/214-630-8893

Altamont Co., 901 N. Church St., P.O. Box 309, Thomasboro, IL 61878/217-643-3125; FAX: 217-643-7973

American Gripcraft, 3230 S. Dodge 2, Tucson, AZ 85713/602-790-1222

Art Jewel Enterprises Ltd., Eagle Business Ctr., 460 Randy Rd., Carol Stream, IL 60188/708-260-0400

Barami Corp., 6250 E. 7 Mile Rd., Detroit, MI 48234/313-891-2536

Bear Hug Grips, Inc., 17230 County Rd. 338, Buena Vista, CO 81211/800-232-7710

Bell Originals, Inc., Sid, 7776 Sharkham Rd., Tully, NY 13159-9333/607-842-6431

Bob's Gun Shop, P.O. Box 200, Royal, AR 71968/501-767-1970

Boone's Custom Ivory Grips, Inc., 562 Coyote Rd., Brinnon, WA 98320/206-796-4330

CAM Enterprises, 5090 Iron Springs Rd., Box 2, Prescott, AZ 86301/602-776-9640

Champion's Choice, Inc., 223 Space Park South, Nashville, TN 37211/615-834-6666; FAX: 615-831-2753

Cobra Gunskin, 133-30 32nd Ave., Flushing, NY 11354/718-762-8181; FAX: 718-762-0890

Cole-Grip, 16135 Cohasset St., Van Nuys, CA 91406/818-782-4424

Colonial Repair, P.O. Box 372, Hyde Park, MA 02136-9998/617-469-4951

Custom Firearms (See Ahrends, Kim)

Desert Industries, Inc., 3245 E. Patrick Ln., Suite H, Las Vegas, NV 89120/702-597-1066; FAX: 702-434-9495

E.A.A. Corp., 4480 E. 11th Ave., Hialeah, FL 33013/305-688-4442; FAX: 305-688-5656

Eagle Imports, Inc., 1907 Highway 35, Ocean, NJ 07712/908-531-8375; FAX: 908-531-1520

EMF Co., Inc., 1900 E. Warner Ave. Suite 1-D, Santa Ana, CA 92705/714-261-6611; FAX: 714-956-0133

Eyears Insurance, 4926 Annhurst Rd., Columbus, OH 43228-1341

Fitz Pistol Grip Co., P.O. Box 610, Douglas City, CA 96024/916-623-4019

Forrest, Inc., Tom, P.O. Box 326, Lakeside, CA 92040/619-561-5800; FAX: 619-561-0227

Greene, M.L., 17200 W. 57th Ave., Golden, CO 80403/303-279-2383

Guns, 81 E. Streetsboro St., Hudson, OH 44236/216-650-4563

Harrison-Hurtz Enterprises, Inc., P.O. Box 268, Wymore, NE 68466/402-645-3378; FAX: 402-645-3606

Herrett's Stocks, Inc., P.O. Box 741, Twin Falls, ID 83303/208-733-1498

Hogue Grips, P.O. Box 2038, Atascadero, CA 93423/FAX: 805-466-7329

Holster Shop, The, 720 N. Flagler Dr., Ft. Lauderdale, FL 33304/305-463-7910; FAX: 305-761-1483

Johnson Gunsmithing, Inc., Neal G., 111 Marvin Dr., Hampton, VA 23666/804-838-8091; FAX: 804-838-8157

Linebaugh Custom Sixguns & Rifle Works, P.O. Box 1263, Cody, WY 82414/307-587-8010

Logan Security Products Co., 4926 Annhurst Rd., Columbus, OH 43228-1341

Mac's .45 Shop, P.O. Box 2028, Seal Beach, CA 90740/310-438-5046

Masen Co., John, P.O. Box 5050, Suite 165, Lewisville, TX 75057/817-430-8732

Monte Kristo Pistol Grip Co., P.O. Box 85, Whiskeytown, CA 96095/916-623-4019

N.C. Ordnance Co., P.O. Box 3254, Wilson, NC 27895/919-237-2440

Newell, Robert H., 55 Coyote, Los Alamos, NM 87544/505-662-7135

Old Western Scrounger, Inc., 12924 Hwy. A-12, Montague, CA 96064/916-459-5445

Pace Marketing, Inc., 9474 NW 48th St., Sunrise, FL 33351-5137/305-741-4361; FAX: 305-741-2901

Pachmayr Ltd., 1875 S. Mountain Ave., Monrovia, CA 91016/818-357-7771, 800-423-9704; FAX: 818-358-7251

Pardini Armi Commerciale Srl, Via Italica 154, 55043 Lido Di Camaiore Lu, ITALY/584-90121; FAX: 584-90122 (U.S. importer—MCS, Inc.)

Pilgrim Pewter, Inc. (See Bell Originals, Sid)

Ravell Ltd., 289 Diputacion St., 08009, Barcelona SPAIN

Renner Co./Radical Concepts, R.J., P.O. Box 10731, Canoga Park, CA 91309/818-700-8131

Rosenberg & Sons, Jack A., 12229 Cox Lane, Dallas, TX 75234/214-241-6302

Royal Arms, 5126 3rd Ave. N., Great Falls, MT 59401/406-453-1149

Roy's Custom Grips, Rt. 3, Box 174-E, Lynchburg, VA 24504/804-385-6667

Safari Gun Co., 6410 Brandon Ave., Springfield, VA 22150/703-569-1097

Safariland Ltd., Inc., 3120 E. Mission Blvd., P.O. Box 51478, Ontario, CA 91761/714-923-7300; FAX: 714-923-7400

Savana Sports, Inc., 5763 Ferrier St., Montreal, Quebec, CANADA/514-739-1753; FAX: 514-739-1755

Sheridan USA, Inc., Austin, P.O. Box 577, Durham, CT 06422

Sile Distributors, Inc., 7 Centre Market Pl., New York, NY 10013/212-925-4389; FAX: 212-925-3149

Sonderman, Robert, 735 Kenton Dr., Charleston, IL 61920/217-345-5429

Spegel, Craig, P.O. Box 108, Bay City, OR 97107/503-377-2697

Taurus, S.A., Forjas, Avenida Do Forte 511, Porto Alegre, BRAZIL 91360/55 512-40 22 44

Taurus International Firearms (See U.S. importer—Taurus Firearms, Inc.)

Tyler Mfg.-Dist., Melvin, 1326 W. Britton Rd., Oklahoma City, OK 73114/405-842-8044

Valor Corp., 5555 NW 36th Ave., Miami, FL 33142/305-633-0127

Vintage Industries, Inc., P.O. Box 872, Casselberry, FL 32718-0872/FAX: 407-699-4919; FAX: 407-699-8419

Volquartsen Custom Ltd., RR 1, Box 33A, P.O. Box 271, Carroll, IA 51401/712-792-4238; FAX: 712-792-2542

Wallace's, Star Rt.1, Box 76, Grandin, MO 63943/314-593-4773

Wayland Precision Wood Products, P.O. Box 1142, Mill Valley, CA 94942/415-381-3543

HEARING PROTECTORS

Bausch & Lomb, Inc., 42 East Ave., Rochester, NY 14603/800-828-5423

Bilsom Intl., Inc., 109 Carpenter Dr., Sterling, VA 20164/703-834-1070

Blount, Inc., Sporting Equipment Div., 2299 Snake River Ave., P.O. Box 856, Lewiston, ID 83501/800-627-3640, 208-746-2351

Champion's Choice, Inc., 223 Space Park South, Nashville, TN 37211/615-834-6666; FAX: 615-831-2753

Clark Co., Inc., David, P.O. Box 15054, Worcester, MA 01615-0054/508-756-6216; FAX: 508-753-5827

Cobra Gunskin, 133-30 32nd Ave., Flushing, NY 11354/718-762-8181; FAX: 718-762-0890

E-A-R, Inc., Div. of Cabot Safety Corp., 5457 W. 79th St., Indianapolis, IN 46268/800-327-3431; FAX: 800-488-8007

Fitz Pistol Grip Co., P.O. Box 610, Douglas City, CA 96024/916-623-4019

Flents Products Co., Inc., P.O. Box 2109, Norwalk, CT 06852/203-866-2581; FAX: 203-854-9322

Johnson Gunsmithing, Inc., Neal G., 111 Marvin Dr., Hampton, VA 23666/804-838-8091; FAX: 804-838-8157

MCRW Associates, R.R. 1 Box 1425, Sweet Valley, PA 18656

North Specialty Products, 2664-B Saturn St., Brea, CA 92621/714-524-1665

Paterson Gunsmithing, 438 Main St., Paterson, NJ 07502/201-345-4100

Peltor, Inc., 63 Commercial Way, E. Providence, RI 02914/401-438-4800; FAX: 800-EAR-FAX1

R.E.T. Enterprises, 2608 S. Chestnut, Broken Arrow, OK 74012/918-251-GUNS; FAX: 918-251-0587

Rockwood Corp., Speedwell Division, 136 Lincoln Blvd., Middlesex, NJ 08846/908-560-7171

Safari Gun Co., 6410 Brandon Ave., Springfield, VA 22150/703-569-1097

Safariland Ltd., Inc., 3120 E. Mission Blvd., P.O. Box 51478, Ontario, CA 91761/714-923-7300; FAX: 714-923-7400

Safety Direct, 56 Coney Island Dr., Sparks, NV 89431/702-354-4451

Smith & Wesson, 2100 Roosevelt Ave., Springfield, MA 01102/413-781-8300

Valor Corp., 5555 NW 36th Ave., Miami, FL 33142/305-633-0127

Willson Safety Prods. Div., P.O. Box 622, Reading, PA 19603

HOLSTERS AND LEATHER GOODS

A&B Industries, Inc., 7920-28 Hamilton Ave., Cincinnati, OH 45231/513-522-2992, 800-346-6699; FAX: 513-522-0916

Action Products, Inc., 22 N. Mulberry St., Hagerstown, MD 21740/301-797-1414

Aker Leather Products, 2248 Main St., Suite 6, Chula Vista, CA 91911/619-423-5182

Alessi Holsters, Inc., 2465 Niagara Falls Blvd., Amherst, NY 14228-3527/716-691-5615

American Sales & Mfg. Co., P.O. Box 677, Laredo, TX 78042/210-723-6893; FAX: 210-725-0672

Arratoonian, Andy (See Horseshoe Leather Products)

Artistry in Leather (See Stuart, V. Pat)

Baker's Leather Goods, Roy, P.O. Box 893, Magnolia, AR 71753/501-234-0344

Bandcor Industries, Div. of Man-Sew Corp., 6108 Sherwin Dr., Port Richey, FL 34668/813-848-0432

Barami Corp., 6250 E. 7 Mile Rd., Detroit, MI 48234/313-891-2536

Bianchi International, Inc., 100 Calle Cortez, Temecula, CA 92590/714-676-5621

Blocker's Holsters, Inc., Ted, 5360 NE 112, Portland, OR 97220/503-254-9950

Bob's Tactical Indoor Shooting Range & Gun Shop, 122 Lafayette Rd., Salisbury, MA 01952/508-465-5561

Brauer Bros. Mfg. Co., 2020 Delmar Blvd., St. Louis, MO 63103/314-231-2864; FAX: 314-249-4952

Brown, H.R. (See Silhouette Leathers)

Brownells, Inc., 200 S. Front St., Montezuma, IA 50171/515-623-5401; FAX: 515-623-3896

Browning Arms Co. (Gen. Offices), 1 Browning Place, Morgan, UT 84050/801-876-2711; FAX: 801-876-3331

Bucheimer, J.M., Jumbo Sports Products, 721 N. 20th St., St. Louis, MO 63103/314-241-1020

Carvajal Belts & Holsters, 422 Chestnut, San Antonio, TX 78202/210-222-1634

Cathey Enterprises, Inc., P.O. Box 2202, Brownwood, TX 76804/915-643-2553; FAX: 915-643-3653

Chace Leather Products, 507 Alden St., Fall River, MA 02722/508-678-7556; FAX: 508-675-9666

Clements' Custom Leathercraft, Chas, 1741 Dallas St., Aurora, CO 80010-2018/303-364-0403

Cobra Gunskin, 133-30 32nd Ave., Flushing, NY 11354/718-762-8181; FAX: 718-762-0890

Cobra Sport s.r.l., Via Caduti Nei Lager No. 1, 56020 San Romano, Montopoli v/Arno (Pi), ITALY/0039-571-450490; FAX: 0039-571-450492

Colonial Repair, P.O. Box 372, Hyde Park, MA 02136-9998/617-469-4951

Crawford Co., Inc., R.M., P.O. Box 277, Everett, PA 15537/814-652-6536; FAX: 814-652-9526

Creedmoor Sports, Inc., P.O. Box 1040, Oceanside, CA 92051/619-757-5529

Dakota Corp., P.O. Box 543, Rutland, VT 05702/800-451-4167; FAX: 802-773-3919

Davis Leather Co., G. Wm., 3990 Valley Blvd., Unit D, Walnut, CA 91789/714-598-5620

Delhi Gun House, 1374 Kashmere Gate, Delhi, INDIA 110 006/(011)237375 239116; FAX: 91-11-2917344

DeSantis Holster & Leather Goods, P.O. Box 2039, New Hyde Park, NY 11040-0701/516-354-8000; FAX: 516-354-7501

Easy Pull Outlaw Products, 316 1st St. East, Polson, MT 59860/406-883-6822

Ekol Leather Care, P.O. Box 2652, West Lafayette, IN 47906/317-463-2250; FAX: 317-463-7004

El Paso Saddlery Co., P.O. Box 27194, El Paso, TX 79926/915-544-2233; FAX: 915-544-2535

EMF Co., Inc., 1900 E. Warner Ave. Suite 1-D, Santa Ana, CA 92705/714-261-6611; FAX: 714-956-0133

Epps "Orillia" Ltd., Ellwood, RR 3, Hwy. 11 North, Orillia, Ont. L3V 6H3, CANADA/705-689-5333

Eutaw Co., Inc., The, P.O. Box 608, U.S. Hwy. 176 West, Holly Hill, SC 29059/803-496-3341

Faust, Inc., T.G., 544 Minor St., Reading, PA 19602/215-375-8549; FAX: 215-375-4488

Fobus International Ltd., Kfar Hess, ISRAEL 40692/FAX: 972-52-911716

Galati International, P.O. Box 326, Catawissa, MO 63015/314-257-4837; FAX: 314-257-2268

GALCO International Ltd., 2019 W. Quail Ave., Phoenix, AZ 85027/602-258-8295; FAX: 602-582-6854

Glock GmbH, P.O. Box 50, A-2232 Deutsch Wagram, AUSTRIA (U.S. importer—Glock, Inc.)

GML Products, Inc., 394 Laredo Dr., Birmingham, AL 35226/205-979-4867

Gould & Goodrich, P.O. Box 1479, Lillington, NC 27546/919-893-2071; FAX: 919-893-4742

Gunfitters, The, P.O. 426, Cambridge, WI 53523-0426/608-764-8128

Gun Leather Limited, 116 Lipscomb, Ft. Worth, TX 76104/817-334-0225; 800-247-0609

Gusty Winds Corp., 2950 Bear St., Suite 120, Costa Mesa, CA 92626/714-536-3587

Gutmann Cutlery Co., Inc., 120 S. Columbus Ave., Mt. Vernon, NY 10553/914-699-4044

Gun Works, The, 236 Main St., Springfield, OR 97477/503-741-4118

Hafner Creations, Inc., Rt. 1, P.O. Box 248A, Lake City, FL 32055/904-755-6481

Hebard Guns, Gil, 125-129 Public Square, Knoxville, IL 61448

Henigson & Associates, Steve, 2049 Kerwood Ave., Los Angeles, CA 90025/213-305-8288

High North Products, Inc., P.O. Box 2, Antigo, WI 54409

Hill Speed Leather, Ernie, 4507 N. 195th Ave., Litchfield Park, AZ 85340/602-853-9222; FAX: 602-853-9235

Holster Outpost, 950 Harry St., El Cajon, CA 92020/619-588-1222

Holster Shop, The, 720 N. Flagler Dr., Ft. Lauderdale, FL 33304/305-463-7910; FAX: 305-761-1483

Horseshoe Leather Products, Andy Arratoonian, The Cottage Sharow, Ripon HG4 5BP ENGLAND/0765-605858

Hoyt Holster Co., Inc., P.O. Box 69, Coupeville, WA 98239-0069/206-678-6640; FAX: 206-678-6549

Hume, Don, P.O. Box 351, Miami, OK 74355/918-542-6604

Hunter Co., Inc., 3300 W. 71st Ave., Westminster, CO 80030/303-427-4626

J.O. Arms & Ammunition Co., 5709 Hartsdale, Houston, TX 77036/713-789-0745; FAX: 713-789-7513

John's Custom Leather, 523 S. Liberty St., Blairsville, PA 15717/412-459-6802

Jumbo Sports Products (See Bucheimer, J.M.)

Kane Products, Inc., 5572 Brecksville Rd., Cleveland, OH 44131/216-524-9962

Kirkpatrick Leather Co., 1910 San Bernardo, Laredo, TX 78040/512-723-6631; FAX: 512-725-0672

KLP, Inc., 215 Charles Dr., Holland, MI 49424/616-396-2575; FAX: 616-396-1287

Kolpin Mfg., Inc., P.O. Box 107, 205 Depot St., Fox Lake, WI 53933/414-928-3118; FAX: 414-928-3687

L.A.R. Manufacturing, Inc., 4133 W. Farm Rd., West Jordan, UT 84088/801-255-7106; FAX: 801-569-1972

Law Concealment Systems, Inc., P.O. Box 3952, Wilmington, NC 28406/919-791-6656, 800-373-0116 orders

Lawrence Leather Co., P.O. Box 1479, Lillington, NC 27546/919-893-2071; FAX: 919-893-4742

Leather Arsenal, 27549 Middleton Rd., Middleton, ID 83644/208-585-6212

Lethal Force Institute (See Police Bookshelf)

Lone Star Gunleather, 1301 Brushy Bend Dr., Round Rock, TX 78681/512-255-1805

Magnolia Sports, Inc., 211 W. Main, Magnolia, AR 71753/800-530-7816; FAX: 501-234-8117

Markell, Inc., 422 Larkfield Center 235, Santa Rosa, CA 95403/707-573-0792; FAX: 707-573-9867

MCRW Associates, R.R. 1 Box 1425, Sweet Valley, PA 18656

Michaels of Oregon Co., P.O. Box 13010, Portland, OR 97213/503-255-6890; FAX: 503-255-0746

Mixson Leathercraft, Inc., 7435 W. 19th Ct., Hialeah, FL 33014/305-821-5190; FAX: 305-558-9318

Nelson Combat Leather, Bruce, P.O. Box 8691 CRB, Tucson, AZ 85738/602-825-9047

Nielsen Custom Cases, P.O. Box 26297, Las Vegas, NV 89126/800-377-1341, 702-878-5611; FAX: 702-877-4433

Noble Co., Jim, 1305 Columbia St., Vancouver, WA 98660/206-695-1309

No-Sho Mfg. Co., 10727 Glenfield Ct., Houston, TX 77096/713-723-5332

Null Holsters Ltd., K.L., Hill City Station, Resaca, GA 30735/404-625-5643; FAX: 404-625-9392

October Country, P.O. Box 969, Dept. GD, Hayden Lake, ID 83835/208-772-2068

Ojala Holsters, Arvo, P.O. Box 98, N. Hollywood, CA 91603/503-669-1404

Oklahoma Leather Products, Inc., 500 26th NW, Miami, OK 74354/918-542-6651

Old West Reproductions, Inc., 446 Florence S. Loop, Florence, MT 59833/406-273-2615

Pace Marketing, Inc., 9474 NW 48th St., Sunrise, FL 33351-5137/305-741-4361; FAX: 305-741-2901

Pathfinder Sports Leather, 2920 E. Chambers St., Phoenix, AZ 85040/602-276-0016

Police Bookshelf, P.O. Box 122, Concord, NH 03301/603-224-6814; FAX: 603-226-3554

Proline Handgun Leather, P.O. Box 112154, Tacoma, WA 98411/206-564-6652

PW Gunleather, P.O. Box 450432, Atlanta, GA 30345/404-822-1640; FAX: 404-822-1704

Red Head, Inc., P.O. Box 7100, Springfield, MO 65801/417-864-5430

Red River Frontier Outfitters, P.O. Box 241, Dept. GD, Tujunga, CA 91043/818-821-3167

Renegade, P.O. Box 31546, Phoenix, AZ 85046/602-482-6777

Ringler Custom Leather Co., P.O. Box 206, Cody, WY 82414/307-645-3255
Rybka Custom Leather Equipment, Thad, 32 Havilah Hill, Odenville, AL 35120
Safari Gun Co., 6410 Brandon Ave., Springfield, VA 22150/703-569-1097
Safariland Ltd., Inc., 3120 E. Mission Blvd., P.O. Box 51478, Ontario, CA 91761/714-923-7300; FAX: 714-923-7400
Safety Speed Holster, Inc., 910 S. Vail Ave., Montebello, CA 90640/213-723-4140; FAX: 213-726-6973
Savana Sports, Inc., 5763 Ferrier St., Montreal, Quebec, CANADA/514-739-1753; FAX: 514-739-1755
Schulz Industries, 16247 Minnesota Ave., Paramount, CA 90723/213-439-5903
Schumakers Gun Shop, William, 512 Prouty Corner Lp. A, Colville, WA 99114/509-684-4848
Sheridan USA, Inc., Austin, P.O. Box 577, Durham, CT 06422
Shoemaker & Sons, Inc., Tex, 714 W. Cienega Ave., San Dimas, CA 91750/714-592-2071; FAX: 714-592-2378
Shurkatch Corp., P.O. Box 850, Richfield Springs, NY 13439/315-858-1470; FAX: 315-858-2969
Sile Distributors, Inc., 7 Centre Market Pl., New York, NY 10013/212-925-4389; FAX: 212-925-3149
Silhouette Leathers, P.O. Box 1161, Gunnison, CO 81230/303-641-6639
Smith Saddlery, Jesse W., N. 1325 Division, Spokane, WA 99202/509-325-0622
Southwind Sanctions, P.O. Box 445, Aledo, TX 76008/817-441-8917
Sparks, Milt, 605 E. 44th St. No. 2, Boise, ID 83714-4800
Stalker, Inc., P.O. Box 21, Fishermans Wharf Rd., Malakoff, TX 75148/903-489-1010
Strong Holster Co., 105 Maplewood Ave., Gloucester, MA 01930/508-281-3300; FAX: 508-281-6321
Stuart, V. Pat, Rt. 1, Box 242-B, P.O. Box 232, Weyers Cave, VA 24486/703-234-0816
Tabler Marketing, 2554 Lincoln Blvd. 555, Marina Del Rey, CA 90291-5082/818-366-7485; FAX: 818-831-3441
Texas Longhorn Arms, Inc., 5959 W. Loop South, Suite 424, Bellaire, TX 77401/713-660-6323; FAX: 713-660-0493
Torel, Inc., 1053 N. South St., P.O. Box 592, Yoakum, TX 77995/512-293-2341; FAX: 512-293-3413
Triple-K Mfg. Co., Inc., 2222 Commercial St., San Diego, CA 92113/619-232-2066; FAX: 619-232-7675
Tyler Mfg.-Dist., Melvin, 1326 W. Britton Rd., Oklahoma City, OK 73114/405-842-8044
Uberti USA, Inc., 362 Limerock Rd., P.O. Box 469, Lakeville, CT 06039/203-435-8068; FAX: 203-435-8146
Valor Corp., 5555 NW 36th Ave., Miami, FL 33142/305-633-0127
Venus Industries, P.O. Box 246, Sialkot-1, PAKISTAN/FAX: 92 432 85579
Viking Leathercraft, Inc., 1579A Jayken Way, Chula Vista, CA 91911/800-262-6666; FAX: 619-429-8268
Walt's Custom Leather, Walt Whinnery, 1947 Meadow Creek Dr., Louisville, KY 40218/502-458-4361
Whinnery, Walt (See Walt's Custom Leather)
Wild Bill's Originals, P.O. Box 13037, Burton, WA 98013/206-463-5738
Whitestone Lumber Corp., 148-02 14th Ave., Whitestone, NY 11357/718-746-4400; FAX: 718-767-1748
Winchester Sutler, Inc., The, 270 Shadow Brook Lane, Winchester, VA 22603/703-888-3595

LABELS, BOXES, CARTRIDGE HOLDERS

Accuracy Products, S.A., 14 rue de Lawsanne, Brussels, 1060 BELGIUM/32-2-539-34-42; FAX: 32-2-539-39-60
Anderson Manufacturing Co., Inc., P.O. Box 2640, 2741 N. Crosby Rd., Oak Harbor, WA 98277/206-675-7300; FAX: 206-675-3939
Arkfeld Mfg. & Dist. Co., Inc., P.O. Box 54, Norfolk, NE 68702-0054/402-371-9430; 800-533-0676
Cabinet Mtn. Outfitter, P.O. Box 766, Plains, MT 59859/406-826-3970
Del Rey Products, P.O. Box 91561, Los Angeles, CA 90009/213-823-0494
Fitz Pistol Grip Co., P.O. Box 610, Douglas City, CA 96024/916-623-4019
Flambeau Products Corp., P.O. Box 97, Middlefield, OH 44062/216-632-1631; FAX: 216-632-1581
Huey Gun Cases, Marvin, P.O. Box 22456, Kansas City, MO 64113/816-444-1637
J&J Products Co., 9240 Whitmore, El Monte, CA 91731/818-571-5228; FAX: 818-571-8704
KLP, Inc., 215 Charles Dr., Holland, MI 49424/616-396-2575; FAX: 616-396-1287
Kolpin Mfg., Inc., P.O. Box 107, 205 Depot St., Fox Lake, WI 53933/414-928-3118; FAX: 414-928-3687
Lakewood Products, Inc., P.O. Box 1527, 1445 Eagle St., Rhinelander, WI 54501/715-369-3445
Monte Kristo Pistol Grip Co., P.O. Box 85, Whiskeytown, CA 96095/916-623-4019
Peterson Instant Targets, Inc. (See Lyman Products Corp.)
Ravell Ltd., 289 Diputacion St., 08009, Barcelona SPAIN
Scharch Mfg., Inc., 10325 Co. Rd. 120, Unit C, Salida, CO 81201/719-539-7242
Stalwart Corp., P.O. Box 357, Pocatello, ID 83204/208-232-7899

LOAD TESTING AND PRODUCT TESTING,
  (Chronographing, Ballistic Studies)

ADC, Inc., 32654 Coal Creek Rd., Scappoose, OR 97056-2601/503-543-5088
Ballistic Research, 1108 W. May Ave., McHenry, IL 60050/815-385-0037
Bustani Appraisers, Leo, P.O. Box 8125, W. Palm Beach, FL 33407/305-622-2710
Clerke Co., J.A., P.O. Box 627, Pearblossom, CA 93553-0627/805-945-0713
Corbin Applied Technology, P.O. Box 2171, White City, OR 97503/503-826-5211
D&H Precision Tooling, 7522 Barnard Mill Rd., Ringwood, IL 60072/815-653-4011
Farr Studio, Inc., 1231 Robinhood Rd., Greeneville, TN 37743/615-638-8825
Jensen Bullets, 86 North, 400 West, Blackfoot, ID 83221/208-785-5590
J.D. Jones, 721 Woodvue Lane, Wintersville, OH 43952/614-264-0176
Jurras, L.E., P.O. Box 680, Washington, IN 47501/812-254-7698
Lachaussee, S.A., 29 Rue Kerstenne, Ans, B-4430 BELGIUM/041-63 88 77
Lomont Precision Bullets, 4236 W. 700 South, Poneto, IN 46781/219-694-6792; FAX: 219-694-6797
Maionchi-L.M.I., Via Di Coselli-Zona Industriale Di Guamo, Lucca, ITALY 55060/011 39-583 94291
McMurdo, Lynn (See Specialty Gunsmithing)
Neutralizer Police Munitions, 5029 Middle Rd., Horseheads, NY 14845-9568/607-739-8362; FAX: 607-594-3900

Pejsa Ballistics, 2120 Kenwood Pkwy., Minneapolis, MN 55405/612-374-3337; FAX: 612-374-3337
Rupert's Gun Shop, 2202 Dick Rd., Suite B, Fenwick, MI 48834/517-248-3252
Russell's Rifle Shop, Rt. 5, P.O. Box 92, Georgetown, TX 78626/512-778-5338
Schumakers Gun Shop, William, 512 Prouty Corner Lp. A, Colville, WA 99114/509-684-4848
SSK Industries, 721 Woodvue Lane, Wintersville, OH 43952/614-264-0176; FAX: 614-264-2257
Star Custom Bullets, P.O. Box 608, 468 Main St., Ferndale, CA 95536/707-786-4040; FAX: 707-786-9117
White Laboratory, Inc., H.P., 3114 Scarboro Rd., Street, MD 21154/410-838-6550; FAX: 410-838-2802
Wildcatters, The, P.O. Box 170, Greenville, WI 54942

MUZZLE-LOADING GUNS, BARRELS AND EQUIPMENT

Accuracy Unlimited, 7479 S. DePew St., Littleton, CO 80123
Adkins, Luther, 1292 E. McKay Rd., Shelbyville, IN 46176-9353/317-392-3795
All American Bullets, 889 Beatty St., Medford, OR 97501/503-770-5649
Anderson Manufacturing Co., Inc., P.O. Box 2640, 2741 N. Crosby Rd., Oak Harbor, WA 98277/206-675-7300; FAX: 206-675-3939
Armi San Paolo, via Europa 172-A, I-25062 Concesio, (BS) ITALY/030-2751725
Armoury, Inc., The, Rt. 202, Box 2340, New Preston, CT 06777/203-868-0001
Armsport, Inc., 3950 NW 49th St., Miami, FL 33142/305-635-7850; FAX: 305-633-2877
Barton, Michael D. (See Tiger-Hunt)
Beauchamp & Son, Inc., 160 Rossiter Rd., Richmond, MA 01254
Beaver Lodge (See Fellowes, Ted)
Bentley, John, 128-D Watson Dr., Turtle Creek, PA 15145
Blackhawk East, P.O. Box 2274, Loves Park, IL 61131
Blackhawk Mountain, P.O. Box 210, Conifer, CO 80433
Blackhawk West, P.O. Box 285, Hiawatha, KS 66434
Blount, Inc., Sporting Equipment Div., 2299 Snake River Ave., P.O. Box 856, Lewiston, ID 83501/800-627-3640, 208-746-2351
Bridgers Best, P.O. Box 1410, Berthoud, CO 80513
Buckskin Machine Works, A. Hunkeler, 3235 S. 358th St., Auburn, WA 98001/206-927-5412
Buffalo Bullet Co., Inc., 12637 Los Nietos Rd. Unit A, Santa Fe Springs, CA 90670/310-944-0322; FAX: 310-944-5054
Burgess & Son Gunsmiths, R.W., P.O. Box 3364, Warner Robins, GA 31099/912-328-7487
Butler Creek Corp., 290 Arden Dr., Belgrade, MT 59714/406-388-1356; FAX: 406-388-7204
Cape Outfitters, Rt. 2, Box 437C, Cape Girardeau, MO 63701/314-335-4103; FAX: 314-335-1555
Camas Hot Springs Mfg., P.O. Box 639, Hot Springs, MT 59845/406-741-3756
Chopie Mfg., Inc., 700 Copeland Ave., LaCrosse, WI 54603/608-784-0926
CONKKO, P.O. Box 40, Broomall, PA 19008/215-356-0711
Cousin Bob's Mountain Products, 7119 Ohio River Blvd., Ben Avon, PA 15202/412-766-5114; FAX: 412-766-5114
Cumberland Arms, Rt. I, Box 1150 Shafer Rd., Blantons Chapel, Manchester, TN 37355
Cumberland Knife & Gun Works, 5661 Bragg Blvd., Fayetteville, NC 28303/919-867-0009
CVA, 5988 Peachtree Corners East, Norcross, GA 30071/404-449-4687; FAX: 404-242-8546
Dangler, Homer L., Box 254, Addison, MI 49220/517-547-6745
Dan's Whetstone Co., Inc., 109 Remington Terrace, Hot Springs, AR 71913/501-767-1616; FAX: 501-767-9598
Day & Sons, Inc., Leonard, P.O. Box 122, Flagg Hill Rd., Heath, MA 01346/413-337-8369
Dayton Traister, P.O. Box 593, Oak Harbor, WA 98277
Denver Arms, Ltd., P.O. Box 4640, Pagosa Springs, CO 81157/303-731-2295
DGS, Inc., Dale A. Storey, 1117 E. 12th, Casper, WY 82601/307-237-2414
Dixon Muzzleloading Shop, Inc., RD 1, Box 175, Kempton, PA 19529/215-756-6271
Ed's Gun House, Rt. 1, Box 62, Minnesota City, MN 55959/507-689-2925
EMF Co., Inc., 1900 E. Warner Ave. Suite 1-D, Santa Ana, CA 92705/714-261-6611; FAX: 714-956-0133
Eutaw Co., Inc., The, P.O. Box 608, U.S. Hwy. 176 West, Holly Hill, SC 29059/803-496-3341
Fautheree, Andy, P.O. Box 4607, Pagosa Springs, CO 81157/303-731-5003
Fellowes, Ted, Beaver Lodge, 9245 16th Ave. SW, Seattle, WA 98106/206-763-1698
Fish, Marshall F., Rt. 22 N., P.O. Box 2439, Westport, NY 12993/518-962-4897
Flintlock Muzzle Loading Gun Shop, The, 1238 "G" S. Beach Blvd., Anaheim, CA 92804/714-821-6655
Flintlocks, Etc. (See Beauchamp & Son, Inc.)
Forster Products, 82 E. Lanark Ave., Lanark, IL 61046/815-493-6360; FAX: 815-493-2371
Frontier, 2910 San Bernardo, Laredo, TX 78040/512-723-5409
Getz Barrel Co., P.O. Box 88, Beavertown, PA 17813/717-658-7263
Golden Age Arms Co., 115 E. High St., Ashley, OH 43003/614-747-2488
Green Bay Bullets, 1860 Burns Ave., Green Bay, WI 54313/414-494-5166
Gun Works, The, 236 Main St., Springfield, OR 97477/503-741-4118
Hege Jagd-u. Sporthandels, GmbH, P.O. Box 101461, W-7770 Ueberlingen a.Bodensee, GERMANY
Hodgdon Powder Co., Inc., P.O. Box 2932, Shawnee Mission, KS 66201/913-362-9455; FAX: 913-362-1307
Hornady Mfg. Co., P.O. Box 1848, Grand Island, NE 68801/800-338-3220, 308-382-1390
Hunkeler, A. (See Buckskin Machine Works)
Jamison's Forge Works, 4527 Rd. 6.5 NE, Moses Lake, WA 98837/509-762-2659
K&M Industries, Inc., Box 66, 510 S. Main, Troy, ID 83871/208-835-2281; FAX: 208-835-5211
Kolpin Mfg., Inc., P.O. Box 107, 205 Depot St., Fox Lake, WI 53933/414-928-3118; FAX: 414-928-3687
Kwik-Site Co., 5555 Treadwell, Wayne, MI 48184/313-326-1500; FAX: 313-326-4120
Lite Tek International, 133-30 32nd Ave., Flushing, NY 11354/718-463-0650; FAX: 718-762-0890
Log Cabin Sport Shop, 8010 Lafayette Rd., Lodi, OH 44254/216-948-1082
Lyman Products Corp., Rt. 147 West St., Middlefield, CT 06455
McCann's Muzzle-Gun Works, 14 Walton Dr., New Hope, PA 18938/215-862-9180
Mitchell Arms, Inc., 3400 W. MacArthur Blvd., Ste. 1, Santa Ana, CA 92704/714-957-5711; FAX: 714-957-5732
MMP, Rt. 6, Box 384, Harrison, AR 72601/501-741-5019; FAX: 501-741-3104
Mountain State Muzzleloading Supplies, Box 154-1, Rt. 2, Williamstown, WV 26187/304-375-7842; FAX: 304-375-3737
Muzzleload Magnum Products (See MMP)
Muzzleloaders Etcetera, Inc., 9901 Lyndale Ave. S., Bloomington, MN 55420/612-884-1161

DIRECTORY OF THE HANDGUN TRADE

Mt. Alto Outdoor Products, Rt. 735, Howardsville, VA 24562
Mushroom Express Bullet Co., 601 W. 6th St., Greenfield, IN 46140/317-462-6332
Muzzleloaders Etcetera, Inc., 9901 Lyndale Ave. S., Bloomington, MN 55420/612-884-1161
Neumann GmbH, Untere Ringstr. 17, 8506 Langenzenn, GERMANY/09101-8258
Newman Gunshop, Rt. 1, Box 90F, Agency, IA 52530/515-937-5775
October Country, P.O. Box 969, Dept. GD, Hayden Lake, ID 83835/208-772-2068
Oklahoma Leather Products, Inc., 500 26th NW, Miami, OK 74354/918-542-6651
Olde Pennsylvania, P.O. Box 912, New Kensington, PA 15068/412-337-1552
Ox-Yoke Originals, Inc., 34 Main St., Milo, ME 04463/800-231-8313; FAX: 207-943-2416
Parker Gun Finishes, 9337 Smokey Row Rd., Strawberry Plains, TN 37871/615-933-3286
Patchbox & Museum of the Great Divide, The, 600 Farm Rd., Kalispell, MT 59901/406-756-8851
Pedersoli Davide & C., Via Artigiani 53, Gardone V.T. (BS) ITALY 25063/030-8912402; FAX: 030-8911019 (U.S. importers—Beauchamp & Son, Inc.; Cabela's; Dixie Gun Works, EMF Co., Inc.; Navy Arms Co.; Trail Guns Armory, Inc.)
Peterson Gun Shop, Inc., A.W., 4255 W. Old U.S. 441, Mt. Dora, FL 32757-3299/904-383-4258
Peterson Instant Targets, Inc. (See Lyman Products Corp.)
Robinson Firearms Mfg. Ltd., RR2, Suite 51, Comp. 24, Winfield, B.C. CANADA V0H 2C0/604-766-5353
R.V.I., P.O. Box Q-1, 1300 Boblett St., Blaine, WA 98230/206-595-2933
Scott, Inc., Tyler, 313 Rugby Ave., Terrace Park, OH 45174/513-831-7603
Selsi Co., Inc., 40 Veterans Blvd., Carlstadt, NJ 07072-0497/201-935-5851
Safari Gun Co., 6410 Brandon Ave., Springfield, VA 22150/703-569-1097
S&B Industries, 11238 McKinley Rd., Montrose, MI 48457/313-639-5491
Shooter's Choice, 16770 Hilltop Park Place, Chagrin Falls, OH 44022/216-543-8808; FAX: 216-543-8811
Sile Distributors, Inc., 7 Centre Market Pl., New York, NY 10013/212-925-4389; FAX: 212-925-3149
Siler Locks, 7 Acton Woods Rd., Candler, NC 28715/704-667-9991
Single Shot, Inc. (See Montana Armory, Inc.)
Southern Bloomer Mfg. Co., P.O. Box 1621, Bristol, TN 37620/615-878-6660
SPG Lubricants, Box 761-H, Livingston, MT 59047
Storey, Dale A. (See DGS, Inc.)
Sturm, Ruger & Co., Inc., Lacey Place, Southport, CT 06490/203-259-7843
Taylor's & Co., Inc., 299 Broad Ave., Winchester, VA 22602/703-722-2017; FAX: 703-722-2018
TDP Industries, Inc., 603 Airport Blvd., Doylestown, PA 18901/215-345-8687
Tennessee Valley Mfg., P.O. Box 1175, Corinth, MS 38834/601-286-5014
TETRA Gun Lubricants, 1812 Margaret Ave., Annapolis, MD 21401/410-268-6451; FAX: 410-268-8377
Thompson/Center Arms, Farmington Rd., P.O. Box 5002, Rochester, NH 03867/603-332-2394
Thunder Mountain Arms, P.O. Box 593, Oak Harbor, WA 98277/206-679-4657; FAX: 206-675-1114
Tiger-Hunt, Michael D. Barton, Box 379, Beaverdale, PA 15921/814-472-5161
Track of the Wolf, Inc., P.O. Box 6, Osseo, MN 55369-0006/612-424-2500; FAX: 612-424-9860
Traditions, P.O. Box 235, Deep River, CT 06417/203-526-9555; FAX: 203-526-4564
Trail Guns Armory, Inc., 1422 E. Main St., League City, TX 77573/713-332-5833; FAX: 713-332-5833
Uberti USA, Inc., 362 Limerock Rd., P.O. Box 469, Lakeville, CT 06039/203-435-8068; FAX: 203-435-8146
Upper Missouri Trading Co., 304 Harold St., Crofton, NE 68730/402-388-4844
Warren Muzzleloading Co., Inc., Hwy. 21 North, Ozone, AR 72854/501-292-3268
Wescombe, P.O. Box 488, Glencoe, CA 95232/209-293-7010
Winchester Sutler, Inc., The, 270 Shadow Brook Lane, Winchester, VA 22603/703-888-3595
Young Country Arms, P.O. Box 3615, Simi Valley, CA 93093
Ziegel Engineering, 2108 Lomina Ave., Long Beach, CA 90815/310-596-9481; FAX: 310-598-4734

PISTOLSMITHS

Accuracy Gun Shop, 3651 University Ave., San Diego, CA 92104/619-282-8500
Accuracy Unlimited, 16036 N. 49 Ave., Glendale, AZ 85306/602-978-9089
Accurate Plating & Weaponry, Inc., 1937 Calumet St., Clearwater, FL 34625/813-449-9112
Ahlman Guns, Rt. 1, Box 20, Morristown, MN 55052/507-685-4243; FAX: 507-685-4247
Aldis Gunsmithing & Shooting Supply, 502 S. Montezuma St., Prescott, AZ 86303/602-445-6723; FAX: 602-445-6763
Alpha Precision, Inc., 2765-B Preston Rd. NE, Good Hope, GA 30641/404-267-6163
American Pistolsmiths Guild, P.O. Box 67, Louisville, TN 37777/615-984-3583
Amodei, Jim (See D.O.C. Specialists, Inc.)
Armament Gunsmithing Co., Inc., 525 Rt. 22, Hillside, NJ 07205/908-686-0960
Bain & Davis, Inc., 307 E. Valley Blvd., San Gabriel, CA 91776-3522/818-573-4241, 213-283-7449
Baity's Custom Gunworks, 414 2nd St., N. Wilkesboro, NC 28659/919-667-8785
Banks, Ed, 2762 Hwy. 41 N., Ft. Valley, GA 31030/912-987-4665
Bar-Sto Precision Machine, 73377 Sullivan Rd., P.O. Box 1838, Twentynine Palms, CA 92277/619-367-2747; FAX: 619-367-2407
Barta's Gunsmithing, 10231 US Hwy. 10, Cato, WI 54206/414-732-4472
Bengtson Arms Co., L., 6345-B E. Akron St., Mesa, AZ 85205/602-981-6375
Border Guns & Leather, P.O. Box 1423, 110 E. Spruce St., Deming, NM 88031
Bowen Classic Arms Corp., P.O. Box 67, Louisville, TN 37777/615-984-3583
Brian, C.T., 1101 Indiana Ct., Decatur, IL 62521/217-429-2290
Briley Mfg., Inc., 1230 Lumpkin, Houston, TX 77043/B713-932-6995; FAX: 713-932-1043
Broken Gun Ranch, RR2, Box 92, Spearville, KS 67876/316-385-2587
Brown Products, Ed, Inc., Rt. 2, Box 2922, Perry, MO 63462/314-565-3261; FAX: 565-2791
Campbell, Dick, 20,000 Silver Ranch Rd., Conifer, CO 80433/303-697-0150
Cannon's Guns, Box 1036, Polson, MT 59860/406-883-3583
Caraville Manufacturing, P.O. Box 4545, Thousand Oaks, CA 91359/805-499-1234
Carter's Gun Shop, 225 G St., Penrose, CO 81240/719-372-6240
Chesire & Perez Dist., 425 W. Allen Ave., San Dimas, CA 91773-1485
Chuck's Gun Shop, P.O. Box 597, Waldo, FL 32694/904-468-2264
Clark Custom Guns, Inc., P.O. Box 530, 11462 Keatchie Rd., Keithville, LA 71047/318-925-0836; FAX: 318-925-9425
Colonial Repair, P.O. Box 372, Hyde Park, MA 02136-9998/617-469-4951

Corkys Gun Clinic, 111 North 11th Ave., Greeley, CO 80631/303-330-0516
Curtis Custom Shop, RR1, Box 193A, Wallingford, KY 41093/703-659-4265
Custom Gunsmiths, 4303 Friar Lane, Colorado Springs, CO 80907/719-599-3366
Cylinder & Slide, Inc., William R. Laughridge, 245 E. 4th St., Fremont, NE 68025/402-721-4277; FAX: 402-721-0263
Davis Service Center, Bill, 10173 Croydon Way 9, Sacramento, CA 95827/916-369-6789
D&D Gunsmiths, Ltd., 363 E. Elmwood, Troy, MI 48083/313-583-1512
D&L Sports, P.O. Box 651, Gillette, WY 82717/307-686-4008
D.O.C. Specialists, Inc., Doc & Bud Ulrich, Jim Amodei, 2209 S. Central Ave., Cicero, IL 60650/708-652-3606; FAX: 708-652-2516
Duncan's Gun Works, Inc., 1619 Grand Ave., San Marcos, CA 92069/619-727-0515
E.A.A. Corp., 4480 E. 11th Ave., Hialeah, FL 33013/305-688-4442; FAX: 305-688-5656
EMF Co., Inc., 1900 E. Warner Ave. Suite 1-D, Santa Ana, CA 92705/714-261-6611; FAX: 714-956-0133
Ferris Firearms, 1827 W. Hildebrand, San Antonio, TX 78201/210-734-0304
First Distributors, Jack, Inc., 44633 Sierra Hwy., Lancaster, CA 93534/805-945-6981; FAX: 805-942-0844
Fisher Custom Firearms, 2199 S. Kittredge Way, Aurora, CO 80013/303-755-3710
Francesca Stabilizer's, Inc., 3115 Old Ranch Rd., San Antonio, TX 78217/512-826-2584
Frielich Police Equipment, 211 East 21st St., New York, NY 10010/212-254-3045
Frontier Arms Co., Inc., 401 W. Rio Santa Cruz, Green Valley, AZ 85614-3932
Garthwaite, Jim, Rt. 2, Box 310, Watsontown, PA 17777/717-538-1566
Greider Precision, 431 Santa Marina Ct., Escondido, CA 92029/619-480-8892
Guncraft Books (See Guncraft Sports, Inc.)
Guncraft Sports, Inc., 10737 Dutchtown Rd., Knoxville, TN 37932/615-966-4545
Gunsite Gunsmithy, P.O. Box 451, Paulden, AZ 86334/602-636-4565; FAX: 602-636-1236
Gunsmithing Ltd., 57 Unquowa Rd., Fairfield, CT 06430/203-254-0436
Gutridge, Inc., 2143 Gettler St., Dyer, IN 46311/219-865-8617
Hamilton, Keith, P.O. Box 871, Gridley, CA 95948/916-846-2316
Hank's Gun Shop, Box 370, 50 West 100 South, Monroe, UT 84754/801-527-4456
Hanson's Gun Center, Dick, 233 Everett Dr., Colorado Springs, CO 80911
Hardison, Charles, P.O. Box 356, 200 W. Baseline Rd., Lafayette, CO 80026 0356/303-666-5171
Hebard Guns, Gil, 125-129 Public Square, Knoxville, IL 61448
Heinie Specialty Products, 323 W. Franklin St., Havana, IL 62644/309-543-4535; FAX: 309-543-2521
High Bridge Arms, Inc., 3185 Mission St., San Francisco, CA 94110/415-282-8358
Highline Machine Co., 654 Lela Place, Grand Junction, CO 81504/303-434-4971
Hindman, Ace, 1880 1/2 Upper Turtle Creek Rd., Kerrville, TX 78028/512-257-4290
Hoag, James W., 8523 Canoga Ave., Suite C, Canoga Park, CA 91304/818-998-1510
Irwin, Campbell H., 140 Hartland Blvd., East Hartland, CT 06027/203-653-3901
Ivanoff, Thomas G. (See Tom's Gun Repair)
Ken's Gun Specialties, Rt. 1, Box 147, Lakeview, AR 72642/501-431-5606
Jarvis Gunsmithing, Inc., 1123 Cherry Orchard Lane, Hamilton, MT 59840/406-961-4392
Johnston, James (See North Fork Custom Gunsmithing)
J.D. Jones, 721 Woodvue Lane, Wintersville, OH 43952/614-264-0176
Jungkind, Reeves C., 5001 Buckskin Pass, Austin, TX 78745/512-442-1094
Kilham & Co., Main St., P.O. Box 37, Lyme, NH 03768/603-795-4112
Kimball, Gary, 1526 N. Circle Dr., Colorado Springs, CO 80909/719-634-1274
Kopec Enterprises, John (See Peacemaker Specialists)
Kopp Publishing Co., Div. of Koppco Industries, 1301 Franklin, Lexington, MO 64067/816-259-2636
Kopp, Terry, 1301 Franklin, Lexington, MO 64067/816-259-2636
La Clinique du .45, 1432 Rougemont, Chambly, Quebec, J3L 2L8 CANADA/514-658-1144
LaFrance Specialties, P.O. Box 178211, San Diego, CA 92117/619-293-3373
LaRocca Gun Works, Inc., 51 Union Place, Worcester, MA 01608/508-754-2887; FAX: 508-754-2887
Laughridge, William R. (See Cylinder & Slide, Inc.)
Lawson, John G. (See Sight Shop, The)
Lee's Red Ramps, Box 291240, Phelan, CA 92329-1240/619-868-5731
Linebaugh Custom Sixguns & Rifle Works, P.O. Box 1263, Cody, WY 82414/307-587-8010
Lock's Philadelphia Gun Exchange, 6700 Rowland Ave., Philadelphia, PA 19149/215-332-6225; FAX: 215-332-4800
Long, George F., 1500 Rogue River Hwy., Ste. F, Grants Pass, OR 97527/503-476-7552
Mac's .45 Shop, P.O. Box 2028, Seal Beach, CA 90740/310-438-5046
Mahony, Philip Bruce, 67 White Hollow Rd., Lime Rock, CT 06039-2418/203-435-9341
Martz, John V., 8060 Lakeview Lane, Lincoln, CA 95648/916-645-2250
Marvel, Alan, 3922 Madonna Rd., Jarrettsville, MD 21084/301-557-6545
McMillan Gunworks, Inc., 302 W. Melinda Lane, Phoenix, AZ 85027/602-582-9627; FAX: 602-582-5178
MCS, Inc., 34 Delmar Dr., Brookfield, CT 06804/203-775-1013; FAX: 203-775-9462
Mid-America Recreation, Inc., 1328 5th Ave., Moline, IL 52807/309-764-5089; FAX: 309-764-2722
Miller Custom, 210 E. Julia, Clinton, IL 61727/217-935-9362
Mitchell's Accuracy Shop, 68 Greenridge Dr., Stafford, VA 22554/703-659-0165
MJK Gunsmithing, Inc., 417 N. Huber St., E. Wenatchee, WA 98802/509-884-7683
Moran, Jerry, P.O. Box 357, Mt. Morris, MI 45458-0357
Mountain Bear Rifle Works, Inc., 100 B Ruritan Rd., Sterling, VA 20164/703-430-0420
Mullis Guncraft, 3523 Lawyers Road E., Monroe, NC 28110/704-283-6683
Mustra's Custom Guns, Inc., Carl, 1002 Pennsylvania Ave., Palm Harbor, FL 34683/813-785-1403
Nastoff's 45 Shop, Inc., Steve, 12288 Mahoning Ave., P.O. Box 446, North Jackson, OH 44451
North Fork Custom Gunsmithing, James Johnston, 428 Del Rio Rd., Roseburg, OR 97470/503-673-4467
Novak's .45 Shop, Wayne, 1206 1/2 30th St., P.O. Box 4045, Parkersburg, WV 25101/304-485-9295
Nowlin Custom Barrels Mfg., Rt. 1, Box 308, Claremore, OK 74017/918-342-0689; FAX: 918-342-0624
Nu-Line Guns, Inc., 1053 Caulks Hill Rd., Harvester, MO 63303/314-441-4500; FAX: 314-447-5018
Nygord Precision Products, P.O. Box 8394, La Crescenta, CA 91224/818-352-3027; FAX: 818-352-3027
Oglesby & Oglesby Gunmakers, Inc., RR 5, Springfield, IL 62707/217-487-7100
Old West Reproductions, Inc., 446 Florence S. Loop, Florence, MT 59833/406-273-2615
Pace Marketing, Inc., 9474 NW 48th St., Sunrise, FL 33351-5137/305-741-4361; FAX: 305-741-2901
Pachmayr Ltd., 1875 S. Mountain Ave., Monrovia, CA 91016/818-357-7771, 800-423-9704; FAX: 818-358-7251

Pardini Armi Commerciale Srl, Via Italica 154, 55043 Lido Di Camaiore Lu, ITALY/584-90121; FAX: 584-90122 (U.S. importer—MCS, Inc.)
Paris, Frank J., 13945 Minock Dr., Redford, MI 48239/313-255-0888
Peacemaker Specialists, John Kopec Enterprises, P.O. Box 157, Whitmore, CA 96096/916-472-3438
PEM's Mfg. Co., 5063 Waterloo Rd., Atwater, OH 44201/216-947-3721
Performance Specialists, 308 Eanes School Rd., Austin, TX 78746/512-327-0119
Phillips & Bailey, Inc., 815A Yorkshire St., Houston, TX 77022/713-699-4288
Pierce Pistols, 2326 E. Hwy. 34, Newnan, GA 30263/404-253-8192
Plaxco, J. Michael, Rt. 1, P.O. Box 203, Roland, AR 72135/501-868-9787
Practical Tools, Inc., Austin Behlerts, P.O. Box 133, Pipersville, PA 18947/215-766-7301
Precision Arms International, Inc., Rt. 17, Box 456, Bldg. 810, Saluda, VA 23149/804-758-5233; FAX: 804-758-2690
Precision Specialties, 131 Hendom Dr., Feeding Hills, MA 01030/413-786-3365; FAX: 413-786-3365
Randco UK, 286 Gipsy Rd., Welling, Kent DA16 1JJ, ENGLAND/44 81 303 4118
Ravell Ltd., 289 Diputacion St., 08009, Barcelona SPAIN
Ries, Chuck, 415 Ridgecrest Dr., Grants Pass, OR 97527/503-476-5623
Riggs, Jim, 206 Azalea, Boerne, TX 78006/210-249-8567
Robar Co.'s, Inc., The, 21438 N. 7th Ave., Suite B, Phoenix, AZ 85027/602-581-2648; FAX: 602-582-0059
Rogers Gunsmithing, Bob, P.O. Box 305, 344 S. Walnut St., Franklin Grove, IL 61031/815-456-2685; FAX: 815-288-7142
Scott/McDougall Custom Gunsmiths, 880 Piner Rd., Suite 50, Santa Rosa, CA 95403/707-546-2264
Seecamp Co., Inc., L.W., P.O. Box 255, New Haven, CT 06502/203-877-3429
Shell Shack, 113 E. Main, Laurel, MT 59044/406-628-8986
Shooter Shop, The, 221 N. Main, Butte, MT 59701/406-723-3842
Singletary, Kent, 7516 W. Sells, Phoenix, AZ 85033/602-789-6004
Sipes Gun Shop, 7415 Asher Ave., Little Rock, AR 72204/501-565-8480
Sight Shop, The, John G. Lawson, 1802 E. Columbia Ave., Tacoma, WA 98404/206-474-5465
S.K. Guns, Inc., 3041A Main Ave., Fargo, ND 58103/701-293-4867; FAX: 701-232-0001
Slings & Arrows, RD 1, Box 91A, Barnet, VT 05821/802-633-3314; FAX: 802-684-1108
Spokhandguns, Inc., 1206 Fig St., Benton City, WA 99320/509-588-5255
Springfield, Inc., 25144 Ridge Rd., Colona, IL 61241/309-441-6002; FAX: 309-441-6003
SSK Industries, 721 Woodvue Lane, Wintersville, OH 43952/614-264-0176; FAX: 614-264-2257
Starnes, Ken, 32900 SW Laurelview Rd., Hillsboro, OR 97123/503-628-0705
Steger, James R., 1131 Dorsey Pl., Plainfield, NJ 07062
Strawbridge, Victor W., 6 Pineview Dr., Dover, NH 03820/603-742-0013
Stroup, Earl R., 30506 Flossmoor Way, Hayward, CA 94544/415-471-1549
Swenson's 45 Shop, A.D., P.O. Box 606, Fallbrook, CA 92028
300 Gunsmith Service, Inc., 6850 S. Yosemite Ct., Englewood, CO 80112/303-773-0300
Ten-Ring Precision, Inc., 1449 Blue Crest Lane, San Antonio, TX 78232/512-494-3063; FAX: 512-494-3066
Thompson, Randall (See Highline Machine Co.)
Thurston Sports, Inc., RD 3 Donovan Rd., Auburn, NY 13021/315-253-0966
Tom's Gun Repair, Thomas G. Ivanoff, 76-6 Rt. Southfork Rd., Cody, WY 82414/307-587-6949
T.S.W. Conversions, Inc., E. 115 Crain Rd., Paramus, NJ 07650-4017/201-265-1618
Ulrich, Doc & Bud (See D.O.C. Specialists, Inc.)
Unick's Gunsmithing, 5005 Center Rd., Lowellville, OH 44436/216-536-8015
Vic's Gun Refinishing, 6 Pineview Dr., Dover, NH 03820/603-742-0013
Volquartsen Custom Ltd., RR 1, Box 33A, P.O. Box 271, Carroll, IA 51401/712-792-4238; FAX: 712-792-2542
Wallace's, Star Rt.1, Box 76, Grandin, MO 63943/314-593-4773
Walters Industries, 6226 Park Lane, Dallas, TX 75225/214-691-6973
Wardell Precision Handguns Ltd., 48851 N. Fig Springs Rd., New River, AZ 85027/602-465-7995
Wessinger Custom Guns & Engraving, 268 Limestone Rd., Chapin, SC 29036/803-345-5677
Williamson Precision Gunsmithing, 117 W. Pipeline, Hurst, TX 76053/817-285-0064
Woods Pistolsmithing, 3840 Dahlgren Ct., Ellicott City, MD 21042/410-465-7979
Yavapai College, 1100 E. Sheldon St., Prescott, AZ 86301/602-776-2359; FAX: 602-776-2193

RELOADING TOOLS AND ACCESSORIES

Accuracy Components Co., P.O. Box 60034, Renton, WA 98058/206-255-4577
Advance Car Mover Co., Rowell Div., P.O. Box 1, 240 N. Depot St., Juneau, WI 53039/414-386-4464
Ammo Load, Inc., 1560 East Edinger, Suite G., Santa Ana, CA 92705/714-558-8858; FAX: 714-569-0319
AMT, 6226 Santos Diaz St., Irwindale, CA 91702/818-334-6629; FAX: 818-969-5247
Andela Tool & Machine, Inc., RD3, Box 246, Richfield Springs, NY 13439
Andela Tool & Machine, Inc., RD3, Box 246, Richfield Springs, NY 13439
ASI, 6226 Santos Dias St., Irwindale, CA 91706/818-334-6629
Ballisti-Cast, Inc., Box 383, Parshall, ND 58770/701-862-3324
Barlett, J., 6641 Kaiser Ave., Fontana, CA 92336-3265
Ben's Machines, 1151 S. Cedar Ridge, Duncanville, TX 75137/214-780-1807
Blount, Inc., Sporting Equipment Div., 2299 Snake River Ave., P.O. Box 856, Lewiston, ID 83501/800-627-3640, 208-746-2351
Brown Co., E. Arthur, 3404 Pawnee Dr., Alexandria, MN 56308/612-762-8847
Brynin, Milton, P.O. Box 383, Yonkers, NY 10710/914-779-4333
Buck Stix—SOS Products Co., Box 3, Neenah, WI 54956
C&D Special Products (Claybuster), 309 Sequoya Dr., Hopkinsville, KY 42240/800-922-6287, 800-284-1746
Camdex, Inc., 2330 Alger, Troy, MI 48083/313-528-2300
Carbide Die & Mfg. Co., Inc., 15615 E. Arrow Hwy., Irwindale, CA 91706/818-337-2518
C-H Tool & Die Corp. (See 4-D Custom Die Co.)
CheVron Case Master (See CheVron Bullets)
Coats, Mrs. Lester, 300 Luman Rd., Space 125, Phoenix, OR 97535/503-535-1611
Colorado Shooter's Supply, 138 S. Plum, P.O. Box 132, Fruita, CO 81521/303-858-9191
Competitor Corp., Inc., P.O. Box 244, 293 Townsend Rd., West Groton, MA 01472/508-448-3521; FAX: 603-617-8540
CONKKO, P.O. Box 40, Broomall, PA 19008/215-356-0711
Corbin, Inc., 600 Industrial Circle, P.O. Box 2659, White City, OR 97503/503-826-5211; FAX: 503-826-8669

Jones Custom Products, Neil, RD 1, Box 483A, Saegertown, PA 16443/814-763-2769; FAX: 814-763-4228
J.D. Jones, 721 Woodvue Lane, Wintersville, OH 43952/614-264-0176
D.C.C. Enterprises, 259 Wynburn Ave., Athens, GA 30601
Denver Instrument Co., 6542 Fig St., Arvada, CO 80004/800-321-1135, 303-431-7255
Destination North Software, 804 Surry Road, Wenatchee, WA 98801/509-662-6602
Dever Co., Jack, 8590 NW 90, Oklahoma City, OK 73132/405-721-6393
Dewey Mfg. Co., Inc., J., P.O. Box 2014, Southbury, CT 06488/203-598-7912; FAX: 203-598-3119
Dillon Precision Products, Inc., 7442 E. Butherus Dr., Scottsdale, AZ 85260/602-948-8009
Eagan, Donald V., P.O. Box 196, Benton, PA 17814/717-925-6134
Efemes Enterprises, P.O. Box 691, Colchester, VT 05446
Engineered Accessories, 1307 W. Wabash Ave., Effingham, IL 62401/217-347-7700; FAX: 217-347-7737
Enguix Import-Export, Alpujarras 58, Alzira, Valencia, SPAIN 46600/(96) 241 43 95; FAX: (96) 241 43 95
Fisher Enterprises, 655 Main St. 305, Edmonds, WA 98020/206-776-4365
Fitz Pistol Grip Co., P.O. Box 610, Douglas City, CA 96024/916-623-4019
Flambeau Products Corp., P.O. Box 97, Middlefield, OH 44062/216-632-1631; FAX: 216-632-1581
Forgreens Tool Mfg., Inc., P.O. Box 990, Robert Lee, TX 76945/915-453-2800
Forster Products, 82 E. Lanark Ave., Lanark, IL 61046/815-493-6360; FAX: 815-493-2371
Fremont Tool Works, 1214 Prairie, Ford, KS 67842/316-369-2338
G&C Bullet Co., Inc., 8835 Thornton Rd., Stockton, CA 95209
"Gramps" Antique Cartridges, Box 341, Washago, Ont. L0K 2B0 CANADA/705-689-5348
Graphics Direct, 18336 Gault St., Reseda, CA 91335/818-344-9002
Green, Arthur S., 485 S. Rovertson Blvd., Beverly Hills, CA 90211/310-274-1283
Hanned Line, The, P.O. Box 161565, Cupertino, CA 95016-1565/916-324-9089
HEBB Resources, P.O. Box 999, Mead, WA 99021-09996/509-466-1292
Heidenstrom Bullets, Urds GT 1 Heroya, 3900 Porsgrunn, NORWAY
Hensley & Gibbs, Box 10, Murphy, OR 97533/503-862-2341
Hindman, Ace, 1880 1/2 Upper Turtle Creek Rd., Kerrville, TX 78028/512-257-4290
Hoehn's Shooting Supply, 75 Greensburg Ct., St. Charles, MO 63304/314-441-4231
Hollywood Engineering, 10642 Arminta St., Sun Valley, CA 91352/818-842-8376
Hondo Ind., 510 S. 52nd St.,l04, Tempe, AZ 85281
Hornady Mfg. Co., P.O. Box 1848, Grand Island, NE 68801/800-338-3220, 308-382-1390
Huntington Die Specialties, 601 Oro Dam Blvd., Oroville, CA 95965/916-534-1210; FAX: 916-534-1212
INTEC International, Inc., P.O. Box 5828, Sparks, NV 89432-5828
Iosso Products, 1485 Lively Blvd., Elk Grove Villiage, IL 60007/708-437-8400
JGS Precision Tool Mfg., 1141 S. Summer Rd., Coos Bay, OR 97420/503-267-4331; FAX: 503-267-5996
Jones Custom Products, Neil, RD 1, Box 483A, Saegertown, PA 16443/814-763-2769; FAX: 814-763-4228
Kapro Mfg. Co., Inc., P.O. Box 88, Tallevast, FL 34270/813-755-0085
King & Co., P.O. Box 1242, Bloomington, IL 61701/309-473-3964
K&M Services, P.O. Box 363, 2525 Primrose Lane, York, PA 17404/717-764-1461
Lachaussee, S.A., 29 Rue Kerstenne, Ans, B-4430 BELGIUM/041-63 88 77
LeClear Industries, 1126 Donald Ave., P.O. Box 484, Royal Oak, MI 48068/313-588-1025
Lee Precision, Inc., 4275 Hwy. U, Hartford, WI 53027/414-673-3075
Liberty Metal, 2233 East 16th St., Los Angeles, CA 90021/213-581-9171
Lighthouse Mfg. Co., Inc., 443 Ashwood Place, Boca Raton, FL 33431/407-394-6011
Lortone, Inc., 2856 NW Market St., Seattle, WA 98107/206-789-3100
Loweth, Richard, 29 Hedgegrow Lane, Kirby Muxloe, Leics. LE9 9BN ENGLAND
Lyman Products Corp., Rt. 147 West St., Middlefield, CT 06455
Magma Engineering Co., P.O. Box 161, Queen Creek, AZ 85242/602-987-9008; FAX: 602-987-0148
McKillen & Heyer, Inc., 35535 Euclid Ave. Suite 11, Willoughby, OH 44094/216-942-2044
MCRW Associates, R.R. 1 Box 1425, Sweet Valley, PA 18656
MCS, Inc., 34 Delmar Dr., Brookfield, CT 06804/203-775-1013; FAX: 203-775-9462
Midway Arms, Inc., P.O. Box 1483, Columbia, MO 65205/314-445-6363; FAX: 314-446-1018
MMP, Rt. 6, Box 384, Harrison, AR 72601/501-741-5019; FAX: 501-741-3104
Monte Kristo Pistol Grip Co., P.O. Box 65, Whiskeytown, CA 96095/916-623-4019
Mountain South, P.O. Box 381, Barnwell, SC 29812/FAX: 803-259-3227
MTM Molded Products Co., Inc., 3370 Obco Ct., Dayton, OH 45414/513-890-7461; FAX: 513-890-1747
NECO, 1316-67th St., Emeryville, CA 94608/510-450-0420
Necromancer Industries, Inc., 14 Communications Way, West Newton, PA 15089/412-872-8722
Newman Gunshop, Rt. 1, Box 90F, Agency, IA 52530/515-937-5775
Niemi Engineering, W.B., Box 126 Center Road, Greensboro, VT 05841/802-533-7180 days, 802-533-7141 evenings
Old West Bullet Moulds, P.O. Box 519, Flora Vista, NM 87415
Old Western Scrounger, Inc., 12924 Hwy. A-l2, Montague, CA 96064/916-459-5445
Omark, Div. of Blount, Inc., 2299 Snake River Ave., P.O. Box 856, Lewiston, ID 83501/800-627-3640, 208-746-2351
Pend Oreille Sport Shop, 3100 Hwy. 200 East, Sandpoint, ID 83864/208-263-2412
Peterson Instant Targets, Inc. (See Lyman Products Corp.)
Plum City Ballistic Range, N2162 80th St., Plum City, WI 54761-8622/715-647-2539
Ponsness/Warren, P.O. Box 8, Rathdrum, ID 83858/208-687-2231; FAX: 208-687-2233
Precision Castings & Equipment, Inc., P.O. Box 326, Jasper, IN 47547-0135/812-634-9167
Precision Reloading, Inc., P.O. Box 122, Stafford Springs, CT 06076/203-684-7979; FAX: 203-684-6788
Quinetics Corp., P.O. Box 13237, San Antonio, TX 78213/512-684-8561; FAX: 512-684-2912
Rapine Bullet Mould Mfg. Co., P.O. Box 1119, East Greenville, PA 18041/215-679-5413
Ravell Ltd., 289 Diputacion St., 08009, Barcelona SPAIN
Raytech, Div. of Lyman Products Corp., Rt. 32 Stafford Ind. Park, Box 6, Stafford Springs, CT 06076/203-684-4273; FAX: 203-684-7938
RCBS, Div. of Blount, Inc., 605 Oro Dam Blvd., Oroville, CA 95965/800-533-5000, 916-533-5191
R.D.P. Tool Co., Inc., 49162 McCoy Ave., East Liverpool, OH 43920/216-385-5129
Redding Reloading, Inc., 1089 Starr Rd., Cortland, NY 13045/607-753-3331; FAX: 607-756-8445
Riebe Co., W.J., 3434 Tucker Rd., Boise, ID 83703
Roberts Products, 25238 SE 32nd, Issaquah, WA 98027/206-392-8172
Rooster Laboratories, P.O. Box 412514, Kansas City, MO 64141/816-474-1622; FAX: 816-474-1307

Rorschach Precision Products, P.O. Box 151613, Irving, TX 75015/214-790-3487
Rucker Ammunition Co., P.O. Box 479, Terrell, TX 75160
SAECO (See Redding Reloading, Inc.)
Safari Gun Co., 6410 Brandon Ave., Springfield, VA 22150/703-569-1097
Sandia Die & Ctg. Co., 37 Atancacio Rd. NE, Albuquerque, NM 87123/505-298-5729
Scharch Mfg., Inc., 10325 Co. Rd. 120, Unit C, Salida, CO 81201/719-539-7242
Scot Powder Co. of Ohio, Inc., 430 Powder Plant Rd., McArthur, OH 45651/614-596-2706; FAX: 614-596-4050
Shooters Accessory Supply (See Corbin, Inc.)
Sierra Bullets, 1400 W. Henry St., Sedalia, MO 65301/816-827-6300; FAX: 816-827-4999
Sierra Specialty Prod. Co., 1344 Oakhurst Ave., Los Altos, CA 94024
Silver Eagle Machining, 18007 N. 69th Ave., Glendale, AZ 85308
Simmons, Jerry, 715 Middlebury St., Goshen, IN 46526/219-533-8546
Sinclair International, Inc., 2330 Wayne Haven St., Fort Wayne, IN 46803/219-493-1858; FAX: 219-493-2530
Skip's Machine, 364 29 Road, Grand Junction, CO 81501/303-245-5417
Slipshot MTS Group, P.O. Box 5, Postal Station D, Etobicoke, Ont., CANADA M9A 4X1/FAX: 416-762-0962
Small Custom Mould & Bullet Co., Box 17211, Tucson, AZ 85731
SOS Products Co. (See Buck Stix—SOS Products Co.)
Speer Products, Div. of Blount, Inc., P.O. Box 856, Lewiston, ID 83501/208-746-2351
Sportsman Supply Co., 714 East Eastwood, P.O. Box 650, Marshall, MO 65340/816-886-9393
Stalwart Corp., P.O. Box 357, Pocatello, ID 83204/208-232-7899
Star Machine Works, 418 10th Ave., San Diego, CA 92101/619-232-3216
Stoney Point Products, Inc., 124 Stoney Point Rd., Courtland, MN 56021/507-354-3360; FAX: 507-354-7236
Taracorp Industries, Inc., 16th & Cleveland Blvd., Granite City, IL 62040/618-451-4400
TETRA Gun Lubricants, 1812 Margaret Ave., Annapolis, MD 21401/410-268-6451; FAX: 410-268-8377
Thompson Bullet Lube Co., P.O. Box 472343, Garland, TX 75047/214-271-8063; FAX: 214-840-6743
Timber Heirloom Products, 618 Roslyn Ave. SW, Canton, OH 44710/216-453-7707; FAX: 216-478-4723
Trammco, 839 Gold Run Rd., Boulder, CO 80302
Tru-Square Metal Prods., Inc., 640 First St. SW, P.O. Box 585, Auburn, WA 98001/206-833-2310
Varner's Service, 102 Shaffer Rd., Antwerp, OH 45813/419-258-8631
Vega Tool Co., 1840 Commerce St. Unit H, Boulder, CO 80301/303-443-4750
VibraShine, Inc., Rt. 1, P.O. Box 64, Mt. Olive, MS 39119/601-733-5614; FAX: 601-733-2226
Vibra-Tek Co., 1844 Arroya Rd., Colorado Springs, CO 80906/719-634-8611; FAX: 719-634-6886
Webster Scale Mfg. Co., P.O. Box 188, Sebring, FL 33870/813-385-6362
Welsh, Bud, 80 New Road, E. Amherst, NY 14051/716-688-6344
Westfield Engineering, 6823 Watcher St., Commerce, CA 90040/FAX: 213-928-8270
Whitestone Lumber Corp., 148-02 14th Ave., Whitestone, NY 11357/718-746-4400; FAX: 718-767-1748
Whitetail Design & Engineering Ltd., 9421 E. Mannsiding Rd., Clare, MI 48617/517-386-3932
Widener's Reloading & Shooting Supply, Inc., P.O. Box 3009 CRS, Johnson City, TN 37602/615-282-6786; FAX: 615-282-6651
William's Gun Shop, Ben, 1151 S. Cedar Ridge, Duncanville, TX 75137/214-780-1807
Wilson, Inc., L.E., Box 324, 404 Pioneer Ave., Cashmere, WA 98815/509-782-1328
Young Country Arms, P.O. Box 3615, Simi Valley, CA 93093

SCOPES, MOUNTS, ACCESSORIES, OPTICAL EQUIPMENT

Action Ammo Ltd. (See Action Arms Ltd.)
Action Arms Ltd., P.O. Box 9573, Philadelphia, PA 19124/215-744-0100; FAX: 215-533-2188
ADCO International, 1 Wyman St., Woburn, MA 01801-2341/617-935-1799; FAX: 617-932-4807
Aimpoint, Inc., 580 Herndon Parkway, Suite 500, Herndon, VA 22070/703-471-6828; FAX: 703-689-0575
Aimtech Mount Systems, 101 Inwood Acres, Thomasville, GA 31792/912-226-4313; FAX: 912-227-0222
Alley Supply Co., P.O. Box 848, Gardnerville, NV 89410/702-782-3800
Anderson Manufacturing Co., Inc., P.O. Box 2640, 2741 N. Crosby Rd., Oak Harbor, WA 98277/206-675-7300; FAX: 206-675-3939
Applied Laser Systems, 2160 NW Vine St., Grants Pass, OR 97526/503-479-0484; FAX: 503-476-5105
Bausch & Lomb, Inc., 42 East Ave., Rochester, NY 14603/800-828-5423
Bellm Contenders, P.O. Ackley Rifle Barrels, P.O. Box 459, Cleveland, UT 84518/801-653-2530
Blount, Inc., Sporting Equipment Div., 2299 Snake River Ave., P.O. Box 856, Lewiston, ID 83501/800-627-3640, 208-746-2351
Brownells, Inc., 200 S. Front St., Montezuma, IA 50171/515-623-5401; FAX: 515-623-3896
Brunton U.S.A., 620 E. Monroe Ave., Riverton, WY 82501/307-856-6559; FAX: 307-856-1840
B-Square Co., P.O. Box 11281, 2708 St. Louis Ave., Ft. Worth, TX 76110/817-923-0964, 800-433-2909; FAX: 817-926-7012
Buehler Scope Mounts, 17 Orinda Way, Orinda, CA 94563/510-254-3201; FAX: 510-254-9720
Burris Co., Inc., P.O. Box 1747, Greeley, CO 80631/303-356-1670; FAX: 303-356-8702
Bushnell, Bausch & Lomb Sports Optics Div., 9200 Cody, Overland Park, KS 66214/913-888-0220
Butler Creek Corp., 290 Arden Dr., Belgrade, MT 59714/406-388-1356; FAX: 406-388-7204
California Grip, 1323 Miami Ave., Clovis, CA 93612/209-299-1316
Celestron International, P.O. Box 3578, Torrance, CA 90503
Clark Custom Guns, Inc., P.O. Box 530, 11462 Keatchie Rd., Keithville, LA 71047/318-925-0836; FAX: 318-925-9425
Conetrol Scope Mounts, 10225 Hwy. 123 S., Seguin, TX 78155/210-379-3030, 800-CONETROL
D&H Prods. Co., Inc., 465 Denny Rd., Valencia, PA 16059/412-898-2840
E.A.A. Corp., 4480 E. 11th Ave., Hialeah, FL 33013/305-688-4442; FAX: 305-688-5656
Ednar, Inc., 2-4-8 Kayabacho, Nihonbashi, Chuo-ku, Tokyo, JAPAN/81(Japan)-3-3667-1651
Eggleston, Jere D., 400 Saluda Ave., Columbia, SC 29205/803-799-3402

Farr Studio, Inc., 1231 Robinhood Rd., Greeneville, TN 37743/615-638-8825
Fujinon, Inc., 10 High Point Dr., Wayne, NJ 07470/201-633-5600
Global Industries, 1501 E. Chapman Ave., 306, Fullerton, CA 92631/714-879-8922
G.U., Inc., 4325 S. 120th St., Omaha, NE 68137/402-330-4492
Hakko Co. Ltd., 5F Daini-Tsunemi Bldg., 1-13-12, Narimasu, Itabashiku Tokyo 175, JAPAN/(03)5997-7870-2
Hermann Leather Co., H.J., Rt. 1, P.O. Box 525, Skiatook, OK 74070/918-396-1226
Hertel & Reuss, Werk für Optik und Feinmechanik GmbH, Quellhofstrabe 67, 3500 Kassel, GERMANY/0561-83006; FAX: 0561-893308
Holden Co., J.B., P.O. Box 700320, 975 Arthur, Plymouth, MI 48170/313-455-4850; FAX: 313-455-4212
Imatronic, Inc., 1275 Paramount Pkwy., P.O. Box 520, Batavia, IL 60510/708-406-1920; FAX: 708-879-6749
Jason Empire, Inc., 9200 Cody, Overland Park, KS 66214-3259/913-888-0220; FAX: 913-888-0222
Jeffredo Gunsight, P.O. Box 669, San Marcos, CA 92079/619-728-2695
Kowa Optimed, Inc., 20001 S. Vermont Ave., Torrance, CA 90502/310-327-1913; FAX: 310-327-4177
L&S Technologies, Inc. (See Aimtech Mount Systems)
Laseraim (Emerging Technologies, Inc.), P.O. Box 3548, Little Rock, AR 72203/501-375-2227; FAX: 501-372-1445
Laser Devices, Inc., 2 Harris Ct. A-4, Monterey, CA 93940/408-373-0701; FAX: 408-373-0903
Leupold, P.O. Box 688, Beaverton, OR 97075/503-526-1491
Lite Tek International, 133-30 32nd Ave., Flushing, NY 11354/718-463-0650; FAX: 718-762-0890
London Guns Ltd., Box 3750, Santa Barbara, CA 93130/805-683-4141; FAX: 805-683-1712
Mac's .45 Shop, P.O. Box 2028, Seal Beach, CA 90740/310-438-5046
McKee, Arthur, 121 Eatons Neck Rd., Northport, NY 11768/516-757-8850
Military Armament Corp., P.O. Box 120, Mt. Zion Rd., Lingleville, TX 76461/817-965-3253
Millett Sights, 16131 Gothard St., Huntington Beach, CA 92647/714-842-5575, 714-847-5245; FAX: 714-843-5707
Mirador Optical Corp., 4501 Glencoe Ave., Marina Del Rey, CA 90292/310-821-5587; FAX: 310-305-0386
Muzzle-Nuzzle Co., 609 N. Virginia Ave., Roswell, NM 88201/505-624-1260
Nichols Sports Optics, P.O. Box 37669, Omaha, NE 68137/402-339-3530; FAX: 402-330-8029
Night Vision Equipment Co., Inc., P.O. Box 266, Emmaus, PA 18049/215-391-9101
Nikon, Inc., 1300 Walt Whitman Rd., Melville, NY 11747/516-547-4200
Oakshore Electronic Sights, Inc., P.O. Box 4470, Ocala, FL 32678-4470/904-629-7112; FAX: 904-629-1433
Old Western Scrounger, Inc., 12924 Hwy. A-I2, Montague, CA 96064/916-459-5445
Olympic Optical Co., P.O. Box 752377, Memphis, TN 38175-2377/901-794-3890
OMR Feinmechanik, Jagd-und Sportwaffen, GmbH, Postfach 1231, Schutzenstr. 20, D-5400 Koblenz, GERMANY/0261-31865-15351
Optolyth-USA, Inc., 18805 Melvista Lane, Hillsboro, OR 97123/503-628-0246; FAX: 503-628-0797
Orchard Park Enterprise, P.O. Box 563, Orchard Park, NY 14227/616-656-0356
Outdoor Connection, Inc., The, 201 Douglas, P.O. Box 7751, Waco, TX 76712/800-533-6076; 817-772-5575; FAX: 817-776-6076
Pace Marketing, Inc., 9474 NW 48th St., Sunrise, FL 33351-5137/305-741-4361; FAX: 305-741-2901
Pachmayr Ltd., 1875 S. Mountain Ave., Monrovia, CA 91016/818-357-7771, 800-423-9704; FAX: 818-358-7251
PECAR Herbert Schwarz, GmbH, Kreuzbergstrasse 6, Berlin 61, 1000 GERMANY/004930-785-7383; FAX: 004930-785-1934
Pentax Corp., 35 Inverness Dr. E., Englewood, CO 80112/303-799-8000
Pilkington Gun Co., P.O. Box 1296, Muskogee, OK 74402/918-683-9418
Precise Metalsmithing Enterprises, 146 Curtis Hill Rd., Chehalis, WA 98532/206-748-3743; FAX: 206-748-8102
Precision Sport Optics, 15571 Producer Lane, Unit G, Huntington Beach, CA 92649/714-891-1309; FAX: 714-892-6920
Premier Reticles, 920 Breckenridge Lane, Winchester, VA 22601-6707
Ram-Line, Inc., 10601 W. 48th Ave., Wheat Ridge, CO 80033/303-467-0300; FAX: 303-467-9833
Ranch Products, P.O. Box 145, Malinta, OH 43535/313-277-3118; FAX: 313-565-8536
Ranging, Inc., Routes 5 & 20, East Bloomfield, NY 14443/716-657-6161
Redfield, Inc., 5800 E. Jewell Ave., Denver, CO 80224/303-757-6411; FAX: 303-756-2338
Seattle Binocular & Scope Repair Co., P.O. Box 46094, Seattle, WA 98146/206-932-3733
Selsi Co., Inc., 40 Veterans Blvd., Carlstadt, NJ 07072-0497/201-935-5851
Shooters Supply, 1120 Tieton Dr., Yakima, WA 98902/509-452-1181
Simmons Outdoor Corp., 2571 Executive Ctr. Circle E, Tallahassee, FL 32301/904-878-5100; FAX: 904-878-0300
S&K Mfg. Co., P.O. Box 247, Pittsfield, PA 16340/814-563-7808; FAX: 814-563-7808
Societa Armi Bresciane Srl., Via Artigiani 93, Gardone Val Trompia, ITALY 25063/30-8911640, 30-8911648
SSK Industries, 721 Woodvue Ln., Wintersville, OH 43952/614-264-0176; FAX: 614-264-2257
Swift Instruments, Inc., 952 Dorchester Ave., Boston, MA 02125/617-436-2960; FAX: 617-436-3232
Tapco, Inc., P.O. Box 546, Smyrna, GA 30081/404-435-9782, 800-359-6195; FAX: 404-333-9798
Tasco Sales, Inc., 7600 NW 84th Ave., Miami, FL 33122/305-591-3670; FAX: 305-592-5895
Tele-Optics, 5514 W. Lawrence Ave., Chicago, IL 60630/312-283-7757
Tele-Optics, Inc., P.O. Box 176, 219 E. Higgins Rd., Gilberts, IL 60136/708-426-7444
Thompson/Center Arms, Farmington Rd., P.O. Box 5002, Rochester, NH 03867/603-332-2394
Warne Manufacturing Co., 9039 SE Jannsen Rd., Clackamas, OR 97015/503-657-5590; FAX: 503-657-5695
WASP Shooting Systems, Rt. 1, Box 147, Lakeview, AR 72642/501-431-5606
Weaver Products, Div. of Blount, Inc., P.O. Box 39, Onalaska, WI 54650/800-635-7656; FAX: 608-781-0368
Weaver Scope Repair Service, 1121 Larry Mahan Dr., Suite B, El Paso, TX 79925/915-593-1005
Wideview Scope Mount Corp., 26110 Michigan Ave., Inkster, MI 48141/313-274-1238; FAX: 313-274-2814
Williams Gun Sight Co., 7389 Lapeer Rd., Box 329, Davison, MI 48423/313-653-2131, 800-530-9028; FAX: 313-658-2140
Zeiss Optical, Inc., Carl, 1015 Commerce St., Petersburg, VA 23803/804-861-0033; FAX: 804-862-3734

SHOOTING/TRAINING SCHOOLS

Alpine's Precision Gunsmithing & Indoor Shooting Range, 2401 Government Way, Coeur d'Alene, ID 83814/208-765-3559
American Pistol Institute, P.O. Box 401, Paulden, AZ 86334/602-636-4565; FAX: 602-636-1236
American Small Arms Academy, P.O. Box 12111, Prescott, AZ 86304/602-778-5623
Auto Arms, 738 Clearview, San Antonio, TX 78228/512-434-5450
Bob's Tactical Indoor Shooting Range & Gun Shop, 122 Lafayette Rd., Salisbury, MA 01952/508-465-5561
Chapman Academy of Practical Shooting, 4350 Academy Rd., Hallsville, MO 65255/314-696-5544; FAX: 314-696-2266
Chelsea Gun Club of New York City, Inc., 237 Ovington Ave., Apt. D53, Brooklyn, NY 11209/718-836-9422, 718-833-2704
CQB Training, P.O. Box 1739, Manchester, MO 63011
Defense Training International, Inc., 749 S. Lemay, Ste. A3-337, Ft. Collins, CO 80524/303-482-2520
Executive Protection Institute, Rt. 2, Box 3645, Berryville, VA 22611/703-955-1128
Firearm Training Center, The, 9555 Blandville Rd., West Paducah, KY 42086/502-554-5886
Firearms Academy of Seattle, P.O. Box 6691, Lynnwood, WA 98036/206-827-0533
G.H. Enterprises Ltd., Bag 10, Okotoks, Alberta T0L 1T0 CANADA/403-938-6070
Guardian Group International, 21 Warren St., Suite 3E, New York, NY 10007/212-619-3838
Guncraft Books (See Guncraft Sports, Inc.)
Gunfitters, The, P.O. 426, Cambridge, WI 53523-0426/608-764-8128
InSights Training Center, Inc., 240 NW Gilman Blvd., Issaquah, WA 98027/206-391-4834
International Shootists, Inc., P.O. Box 5354, Mission Hills, CA 91345/818-891-1723
Jensen's Firearms Academy, 1280 W. Prince, Tucson, AZ 85705/602-293-8516
Lethal Force Institute (See Police Bookshelf)
McMurdo, Lynn (See Specialty Gunsmithing)
Mendez, John A., P.O. Box 1534, Radio City Station, New York, NY 10019/212-315-2580
North American Shooting Systems, P.O. Box 306, Osoyoos, B.C. V0H 1V0 CANADA
Northeast Training Institute, Inc., 1142 Rockland St., Suite 380, Reading, PA 19604/215-373-1940
North Mountain Pine Training Center (See Executive Protection Institute)
Pacific Pistolcraft, 1810 E. Columbia Ave., Tacoma, WA 98404/206-474-5465
Police Bookshelf, P.O. Box 122, Concord, NH 03301/603-224-6814; FAX: 603-226-3554
Quigley's Personal Protection Strategies, Paxton, 9903 Santa Monica Blvd., 300 Beverly Hills, CA 90212/310-281-1762
Robar Co.'s, Inc., The, 21438 N. 7th Ave., Suite B, Phoenix, AZ 85027/602-581-2648; FAX: 602-582-0059
S.A.F.E., P.O. Box 864, Post Falls, ID 83854/208-773-3624
Shooter's World, 3828 N. 28th Ave., Phoenix, AZ 85017/602-266-0170
Sipes Gun Shop, 7415 Asher Ave., Little Rock, AR 72204/501-565-8480
Slings & Arrows, RD 1, Box 91A, Barnet, VT 05821/802-633-3314; FAX: 802-684-1108
Specialty Gunsmithing, Lynn McMurdo, P.O. Box 404, Afton, WY 83110/307-886-5535
Starlight Training Center, Inc., Rt. 1, P.O. Box 88, Bronaugh, MO 64728/417-843-3555
S.W.I.F.T., 4610 Blue Diamond Rd., Las Vegas, NV 89118/702-897-1100
Tactical Training Center, 574 Miami Bluff Ct., Loveland, OH 45140/513-677-8229
Threat Management Institute, 1 St. Francis Place 2801, San Francisco, CA 94107/415-777-0303
Western Missouri Shooters Alliance, P.O. Box 11144, Kansas City, MO 64119/816-597-3950; FAX: 816-229-7350
Yavapai Firearms Academy Ltd., P.O. Box 27290, Prescott Valley, AZ 86312/602-772-8262

SIGHTS, METALLIC

Alley Supply Co., P.O. Box 848, Gardnerville, NV 89410/702-782-3800
Alpec Team, Inc., 55 Oak Ct., Danville, CA 94526/510-820-1763; FAX: 510-820-8738
Andela Tool & Machine, Inc., RD3, Box 246, Richfield Springs, NY 13439
Armurier Hiptmayer, RR 112 750, P.O. Box 136, Eastman, Quebec J0E 1P0 CANADA/514-297-2492
Bo-Mar Tool & Mfg. Co., Rt. 12, Box 405, Longview, TX 75605/903-759-4784; FAX: 903-759-9141
Bradley Gunsight Co., P.O. Box 140, Plymouth, VT 05056/203-589-0531; FAX: 203-582-6294
Carter's Gun Shop, 225 G St., Penrose, CO 81240/719-372-6240
Champion's Choice, Inc., 223 Space Park South, Nashville, TN 37211/615-834-6666; FAX: 615-831-2753
Colonial Repair, P.O. Box 372, Hyde Park, MA 02136-9998/617-469-4951
E.A.A. Corp., 4480 E. 11th Ave., Hialeah, FL 33013/305-688-4442; FAX: 305-688-5656
Engineered Accessories, 1307 W. Wabash Ave., Effingham, IL 62401/217-347-7700; FAX: 217-347-7737
Fausti & Figlie s.n.c., Stefano, Via Martini Zudipeudente, 70, Marcheno, 25060 ITALY (U.S. importer—American Arms, Inc.)
Fautheree, Andy, P.O. Box 4607, Pagosa Springs, CO 81157/303-731-5003
Francesca Stabilizer's, Inc., 3115 Old Ranch Rd., San Antonio, TX 78217/512-826-2584
Guardian Group International, 21 Warren St., Suite 3E, New York, NY 10007/212-619-3838
Gun Doctor, The, 435 East Maple, Roselle, IL 60172/708-894-0668
Heinie Specialty Products, 323 W. Franklin St., Havana, IL 62644/309-543-4535; FAX: 309-543-2521
Hesco-Meprolight, 2821 Greenville Rd., LaGrange, GA 30240/706-884-7967; FAX: 706-882-4683
Hiptmayer, Klaus, RR 112 750, P.O. Box 136, Eastman, Quebec J0E 1P0, CANADA/514-297-2492
Imatronic, Inc., 1275 Paramount Pkwy., P.O. Box 520, Batavia, IL 60510/708-406-1920; FAX: 708-879-6749
J.O. Arms & Ammunition Co., 5709 Hartsdale, Houston, TX 77036/713-789-0745; FAX: 713-789-7513
Johnson Gunsmithing, Inc., Neal G., 111 Marvin Dr., Hampton, VA 23666/804-838-8091; FAX: 804-838-8157
Kopp, Terry, 1301 Franklin, Lexington, MO 64067/816-259-2636
Lofland, James W., 2275 Larkin Rd., Boothwyn, PA 19061/215-485-0391
L.P.A. Snc, Via V. Alfieri 26, Gardone V.T. BS, ITALY 25063/(30)8911481; FAX: (30)8910951
Lyman Products Corp., Rt. 147 West St., Middlefield, CT 06455
Marble Arms Corp., 420 Industrial Park, P.O. Box 111, Gladstone, MI 49837/906-428-3710; FAX: 906-428-3711
McKee, Arthur, 121 Eatons Neck Rd., Northport, NY 11768/516-757-8850
MCS, Inc., 34 Delmar Dr., Brookfield, CT 06804/203-775-1013; FAX: 203-775-9462

Meier Works, P.O. Box 423, Tijeras, NM 87059/505-281-3783
Meprolight (See Hesco-Meprolight)
Mid-America Recreation, Inc., 1328 5th Ave., Moline, IA 52807/309-764-5089; FAX: 309-764-2722
Millett Sights, 16131 Gothard St., Huntington Beach, CA 92647/714-842-5575, 714-847-5245; FAX: 714-843-5707
Miniature Machine Co. (See MMC)
MMC, 606 Grace Ave., Ft. Worth, TX 76111/817-831-0837
Newman Gunshop, Rt. 1, Box 90F, Agency, IA 52530/515-937-5775
Novak's .45 Shop, Wayne, 1206 1/2 30th St., P.O. Box 4045, Parkersburg, WV 25101/304-485-9295
OMR Feinmechanik, Jagd-und Sportwaffen, GmbH, Postfach 1231, Schutzenstr. 20, D-5400 Koblenz, GERMANY/0261-31865-15351
Pachmayr Ltd., 1875 S. Mountain Ave., Monrovia, CA 91016/818-357-7771, 800-423-9704; FAX: 818-358-7251
PEM's Mfg. Co., 5063 Waterloo Rd., Atwater, OH 44201/216-947-3721
Ravell Ltd., 289 Diputacion St., 08009, Barcelona SPAIN
Robar Co.'s, Inc., The, 21438 N. 7th Ave., Suite B, Phoenix, AZ 85027/602-581-2648; FAX: 602-582-0059
RPM, 15481 N. Twin Lakes Dr., Tucson, AZ 85737/602-825-1233; FAX: 602-825-3333
Sheridan USA, Inc., Austin, P.O. Box 577, Durham, CT 06422
Tanfoglio S.r.l., Fratelli, via Valtrompia 39, 41, 25068 Gardone V.T., Brescia, ITALY/30-8910361; FAX: 30-8910183 (U.S. importer—E.A.A. Corp.)
T.F.C. S.p.A., Via G. Marconi 118, B, Villa Carcina, Brescia 25069, ITALY/030-881271; FAX: 030-881826
Trijicon, Inc., P.O. Box 2130, Farmington Hills, MI 48333/313-553-4960; FAX: 313-553-6129
Vintage Arms, Inc., 6003 Saddle Horse, Fairfax, VA 22030/703-968-0779
WASP Shooting Systems, Rt. 1, Box 147, Lakeview, AR 72642/501-431-5606
Wichita Arms, Inc., 923 E. Gilbert, P.O. Box 11371, Wichita, KS 67211/316-265-0661; FAX: 316-265-0760
Williams Gun Sight Co., 7389 Lapeer Rd., Box 329, Davison, MI 48423/313-653-2131, 800-530-9028; FAX: 313-658-2140

TARGETS AND BULLET TRAPS

Abbott Industries, 3368 Miller St., Philadelphia, PA 19134/215-426-3435; FAX: 215-426-1718
Action Target, Inc., P.O. Box 636, Provo, UT 84603/801-377-8033; FAX: 801-377-8096
Aldis Gunsmithing & Shooting Supply, 502 S. Montezuma St., Prescott, AZ 86303/602-445-6723; FAX: 602-445-6763
American Whitetail Target Systems, P.O. Box 41, 106 S. Church St., Tennyson, IN 47637/812-567-4527
Applied Laser Systems, 2160 NW Vine St., Grants Pass, OR 97526/503-479-0484; FAX: 503-476-5105
Armor Metal Products, P.O. Box 4609, Helena, MT 59604/406-442-5560
Aztec International Ltd., P.O. Box 1384, Clarkesville, GA 30523/404-754-8282
Birchwood Laboratories, Inc., 7900 Fuller Rd., Eden Prairie, MN 55344/612-937-7933; FAX: 612-937-7979
Blount, Inc., Sporting Equipment Div., 2299 Snake River Ave., P.O. Box 856, Lewiston, ID 83501/800-627-3640, 208-746-2351
Caswell International Corp., 1221 Marshall St. NE, Minneapolis, MN 55413/612-379-2000
Champion's Choice, Inc., 223 Space Park South, Nashville, TN 37211/615-834-6666; FAX: 615-831-2753
Cummingham Co., Eaton, Admiral Blvd. at Oak, Kansas City, MO 64106/816-842-2600
Dapkus Co., J.G., P.O. Box 293, Durham, CT 06422
Datumtech Corp., 2275 Wehrle Dr., Buffalo, NY 14221
Detroit-Armor Corp., 720 Industrial Dr. 112, Cary, IL 60013/708-639-7666
Diamond Mfg. Co., P.O. Box 174, Wyoming, PA 18644/800-233-9601
Dutchman's Firearms, Inc., The, 4143 Taylor Blvd., Louisville, KY 40215/502-366-0555
Epps "Orillia" Ltd., Ellwood, RR 3, Hwy. 11 North, Orillia, Ont. L3V 6H3, CANADA/705-689-5333
Freeman Animal Targets, 2559 W. Morris St., Plainsfield, IN 46168/317-271-5314; FAX: 317-271-9106
G.H. Enterprises Ltd., Bag 10, Okotoks, Alberta T0L 1T0 CANADA/403-938-6070
Hiti-Schuch, Atelier Wilma, A-8863 Predlitz, Pirming Y1 AUSTRIA/0353418278
Hunterjohn, P.O. Box 477, St. Louis, MO 63166/314-531-7250
Innovision Enterprises, 728 Skinner Dr., Kalamazoo, MI 49001/616-382-1681; FAX: 616-382-1830
Johnson Gunsmithing, Inc., Neal G., 111 Marvin Dr., Hampton, VA 23666/804-838-8091; FAX: 804-838-8157
Kennebec Journal, 274 Western Ave., Augusta, ME 04330/207-622-6288
Kleen-Bore, Inc., 20 Ladd Ave., Northampton, MA 01060/413-586-7240; FAX: 413-586-0236
Littler Sales Co., 20815 W. Chicago, Detroit, MI 48228/313-273-6888; FAX: 313-273-1099
Maki Industries, 26-10th St. SE, Medicine Hat, AB T1A 1P7 CANADA/403-526-7997
National Target Co., 4690 Wyaconda Rd., Rockville, MD 20852/800-827-7060, 301-770-7060; FAX: 301-770-7892
North American Shooting Systems, P.O. Box 306, Osoyoos, B.C. V0H 1V0 CANADA
Nu-Teck, 30 Industrial Park Rd., Box 37, Centerbrook, CT 06409/203-767-3573; FAX: 203-767-9137
Outers Laboratories, Div. of Blount, Inc., Route 2, Onalaska, WI 54650/608-781-5800
Ox-Yoke Originals, Inc., 34 Main St., Milo, ME 04463/800-231-8313; FAX: 207-943-2416
Red Star Target Co., 4519 Brisebois Dr. NW, Calgary AB T2L 2G3 CANADA/403-289-7939; FAX: 403-289-3275
Rockwood Corp., Speedwell Division, 136 Lincoln Blvd., Middlesex, NJ 08846/908-560-7171
Rocky Mountain Target Co., 3 Aloe Way, Leesburg, FL 34788/904-365-9598
R-Tech Corp., P.O. Box 1281, Cottage Grove, OR 97424/503-942-5126; FAX: 503-942-8624
Schaefer Shooting Sports, 2280 Grand Ave., Baldwin, NY 11510/516-379-4900; FAX: 516-379-6701
Seligman Shooting Products, Box 133, Seligman, AZ 86337/602-422-3607
Shooting Arts Ltd., Box 621399, Littleton, CO 80162/303-933-2539
Stoney Baroque Shooters Supply, John Richards, Rt. 2, Box 325, Bedford, KY 40006/502-255-7222
Thompson Target Technology, 618 Roslyn Ave., SW, Canton, OH 44710/216-453-7707; FAX: 216-478-4723
Verdemont Fieldsports, P.O. Box 9337, San Bernardino, CA 92427/714-880-8255; FAX: 714-880-8255
World of Targets, Div. of Steidle Corp., 9200 Floral Ave., Cincinnati, OH 45242/513-791-0917; FAX: 513-792-0004